The
Yan Can
Cook Book

Star of the popular TV Chinese cooking show "Yan Can" Martin Yan has
long believed that the art of Oriental cuisine is not only nutritional and
economical, but simple and easy to learn as well. Proclaiming his motto
"If Yan can, you can too" to over half a million Canadians and countless
Americans in northern states every day, Martin is one of the best known,
certainly the best loved, cooks in North America.

Born and raised in Kwongchow, China, Martin began cooking at the
age of thirteen as an apprentice in a popular Hong Kong restaurant and
by the time he was eighteen he had earned a diploma from the Overseas
Institute of Cookery. Arriving in the United States in 1969, he received a
masters degree from the University of California before returning to
Hong Kong to work for a year as special projects manager for a major
Chinese food manufacturer. While there he traveled extensively
throughout China and southeast Asia learning new techniques and studying under renowned chefs.

In addition to his daily television show, Martin maintains a hectic
schedule of personal appearances for department stores, charity benefits
and special exhibitions. His basic goal? "To make classic Chinese cooking
accessible to the broadest audience. What the heck? If this humble cook
can do it, so can you!"

MARTIN YAN

The
Yan Can
Cook Book

BROADWAY BOOKS
New York   • TORONTO • SYDNEY • AUCKLAND

BROADWAY

Published by Broadway Books

a division of Random House, Inc.

1540 Broadway, New York, New York 10036

BROADWAY BOOKS and it's logo, a letter B bisected on the diagonal, are trademarks of Broadway Books, a division of Random House, Inc.

Library of Congress Catalog Card Number: 80-2987

Reprinted June 1990
Reprinted 1991
Reprinted 1992
Reprinted 1994
Reprinted 1995
Reprinted 1997
Reprinted 1999

Typesetting by ART-U Graphics
Design by Robert Burgess Garbutt

Illustrations by Edward Lim and Chung-Kwong Cheung
Photographs by Rody Lo

Canadian Cataloguing in Publication Data
Yan, Martin.
    The Yan can cook book

Includes index.
ISBN 0-385-17903-0 (bound).—ISBN 0-385-17606-6 (pbk.)

1. Cookery, Chinese.   1. Title
TX724.5.C5Y36   641.5951   C81-094819-2

Printed in Canada on acid free paper by Transcontinental Printing

Published in Canada by Doubleday Canada Limited,
105 Bond Street, Toronto, Ontario M5B 1Y3

24   23   22

This book is dedicated to Sue, for her love, patience and understanding; to everyone who was involved in this project; to the fans of "Yan Can"; and to my students, who have given me support and inspiration. I love you all!

Contents

Loose Ends

Foreword

Whereas many North Americans consider it a special event when their spouse treats them to a dinner at a Chinese restaurant, until recently, few considered preparing that Chinese dinner in their own kitchen. Now, with simple instructions and tempting, pretested recipes, the fear of wokking is replaced by the joy of wokking, thanks to Martin Yan.

When Martin first visited me in 1971 and later enrolled in my course on cultural food patterns, it was obvious he was destined to set the world on fire—under a wok. Giving cooking courses to finance his study toward the B.S. degree in food science and his laboratory research on rice for the M.S. degree, not once did Martin deviate from his singular goal—to cook and to teach others to cook. This he is accomplishing, with style. In a few short years, Martin has established himself as a serious (yet mischievous) chef, who deftly whips up simple dishes with elegant tastes, to the delight of his TV fans and the readers of his first publication, *The Joy of Wokking.*

In *The Yan Can Cook Book*, the author even surpasses his previous effort. In addition to presenting a surprising array of appetizers, main dishes, side dishes and desserts, Martin entertains even readers with no kitchens with his description of regional Chinese gastronomy, culinary tools, interesting ingredients and amusing tid bits of information. Martin's spontaneous, light-hearted humor surfaces throughout, adding to the pleasant adventure of reading and using his book.

The Yan Can Cook Book is presented with such simplicity and clarity that you'll soon be able to work alone. However, be prepared. Once your friends learn of your new skills, you'll never wok alone!

ROSE MARIE PANGBORN
Professor of Food Science,
University of California,
Davis, California.

The Yan Can Cook Book

New Beginnings:
The Chinese
Cooking Experience

A Few Words
from the Humble Cook

A strange thing happened when the manuscript of this book was completed and delivered to my editors. My laundry wondered what happened to my sesame oil-scented T-shirts and asked if I'd lost my job. People thought my complexion was much improved after I finally got the chance to wash the soy sauce off my face. And I started to sleep better when I stopped dreaming of 500 chickens jumping over woks and chasing me with cleavers!

But then, when it was all over, I felt sad as well. There'd be no more 15-course feasts every day, and no more exciting Chinese music being performed with clanging woks and pots, sizzling stir-frying scallions and pounding typewriters. What the heck! It is all over.

We developed our own recipe for cooking up this cookbook, and I thought you'd like to know how it worked. Each dish was tested for taste (saltiness, sweetness, sourness and bitterness), appearance (color retention and contrast), cooking time (texture and doneness), and any possible improvements. We arranged our tests in three daily sessions: 9 A.M. to 12 P.M.; 2 to 4:30 P.M.; and 5 to 7 P.M. Each session included three to four people. We read the recipes in advance of preparation; the ingredients for each dish were carefully measured and arranged together; the cooking times and techniques were followed as closely as possible; then, the dishes were sampled and evaluated, and suggested improvements were made immediately. After we had tested and retested the recipes, they were passed on to home testers—mostly friends and former students—who gave their own opinions (and not always respectfully, either).

You might get the impression that this was all terribly scientific, with everyone wearing white lab coats and computers humming in the background. That might even have been what I originally had in mind. But we were still working in a kitchen, and kitchens have a mind of their own. Our kitchen was no exception. Even while we were cooking, it burned out woks, incinerated whole chickens and discovered a unique recipe for charcoaled Chinese pizza (but don't look for it here!). I don't mind recalling the accidents, as long as I don't have to make them again.

I remember one wok that caught on fire—on an *electric* range. It was a new Chinese hot pot sensation! And then, there was the case of the snow white steamed pork buns that ran out of steam and baked into burnt brown pork hockey pucks. A potholder caught fire and turned into a situation that was too hot to handle. And Irene, one of the testers, will never forget the time she got a tiny cut on her little finger, and Ed administered first aid as if it were major surgery—pressure points, elevation, ice cubes and multiple bandages. We also discovered a new slow-cooking technique—by turning on the wrong burners. And one day, when we cooked seafood, a dozen unexpected feline guests arrived for lunch. What the heck! At least, they were all very formal and wore their best fur coats.

On some good days, we tested 15-18 dishes, each of us gaining approximately 7½ pounds every 7 days. Adding it up for all of us, that's enough weight for another whole person (who shall remain nameless). At that point, I began thinking that instead of rewarding my associates with a banquet in Chinatown, I should give each of them a year's membership to Jack LaLanne's or Vic Tanny's!

Even though everyone shared and enjoyed the cooking and tasting, when it came time to do the dishes, guess who ended up with dishpan hands? One humble cook—me!!

Here's the class photo of our motley crew for the Yan Can Cook Book!

(Top Row, left to right): Edward Lim (plant scientist), Jill Morris (international relations specialist), Pam Brown (range management specialist), Margie Ogawa (home economist), Semie Doolittle (home economist), Alison Wood (dietitian), Irene Melicharek (home economist), Kristen Landsberger (nutritionist), Martin Yan (dishwasher), Susan Yan (biological scientist). (Bottom Row, left to right): Robin Wiechman (dietitian), Donna Andresen (anthropologist), Karen Loeblich (animal behaviorist), Lorelle Spees (dietitian). Not in our photo: Sung Kwak (dietician), Katy Farley (geneticist), Nancy Tennyson (home economist), Janet Huddle (Asian studies specialist), and Lean Gill (homemaker).

What makes it all worthwhile, what kept me together during all those soy-stained, sesame-perfumed months was the belief in practical food—food that you can prepare at home, after work or whenever you're hungry, and not spend weeks making. Food that's fresh and creative always excites me. But I also think that cooking should be simple, quick and spontaneous. Like other arts, cooking should incorporate contrast, harmony, vitality and imagination. Cooking should never be a chore (like washing dishes and mopping floors). It should be a pleasure that gives pleasure in both the act of cooking as well as eating.

Now I turn these recipes over to you. You will be the best judge, and your own taste can decide how each dish can become yours as much as it became mine. I hope you will find new ideas that will tempt you with new tastes and most agreeably fill your stomach. I sincerely hope this book will help you and your family to discover the enjoyment and beauty of the total Chinese food experience. So get wokking! What the heck, if Yan can, so can you!

Welcome to "Wok."

诸位朋友、读者：

　　驰名世界的中国烹调术，是中国悠久文化的一部份。向为各国食家所称道。且日渐为各国友人和知音者所精研之工艺。

　　中国菜色、香、味俱全，巧为调製，不但能增食欲，更有助家庭欢乐和彼此之友谊。

　　烹调常会误为仅家庭主妇主厨中之劳作，其实不然。倘诸君一旦兴致而亲自下厨，且调製得法时，你会首先尝到自己的劳作成果，也而体会其中之乐，更易会感到具一种享受。若继而不刻深入研究和改进，则会更感其乐无穷矣！

　　笔者自幼即对欢食兴趣甚浓。大学时能攻读此，点为食品加工等科目，並历从名以知厨学习，加之长期悉心探讨钻研，故对烹调工艺略具心得。先后亦在北美各地以此遍介绍，並有主持其电视专题节目之演出。

　　本书的编纂，乃烹调技艺之最基本资料。即将历次电视专题节目及现场表演菜单之以精选项目及笔者长期从事烹调工艺的心得和体会，加以整编而辑印成册。为此享誉全球的中国菜备受赞赏之际，谨以此书献给诸位读者、朋友和食家。並望籍此媒介将中国烹调术发扬光大，造福人类。

　　本书能顺利完成，皆得力于诸位同仁及友好鼎力协助甚多。笔者才疏学浅，错漏之处，在所难免。诚望诸位读者前辈不吝赐教、指正。至为感荷！

谭文遵
5.1.81.

True Confessions

A week in the diary of the humble writer of this humble publication who happens to be a humble and serious cook.

Deadline for manuscript: April 1, 1981.

March 5: I am eating smoke and steam from the tiny, bustling kitchen. Suddenly, I feel weak and cold like I am locked in a freezer. I can't stand the smell of the food—but it isn't particularly bad. I just can't take it any more! The afternoon recipe session is wrapping up, so we can clean up and set up for the 5-7 P.M. session. I am in panic. I think I am coming down with some kind of flu. Time is running out on me. What the heck! I will play doctor and run to the medicine cabinet and swallow any pills in sight. By 5 P.M., I feel worse and cancel the testing. I drop dead in bed with my body on fire, and feel as if I were naked on a cold winter night even though I have on two layers of thermal underwear, a bathrobe, and six blankets.

March 6: Saturday morning 9:45 A.M. I crawl out of bed to my desk and pick up my 12-pound telephone. I call and call, but no answers...until after 32 tries. "Hello, may I help you?" a lady asks. I mumble, "I need to see the doc." "How do you feel?" she asks. "There is a beat up, exhausted, and dying cook here with a temperature of 375°F. Can I make an appointment immediately?" She tells me in a very sad tone, "Dr. Mickey Mouse will not be back from vacation until March 26." My God, it is all over for this lousy cook! By the time I am able to find the only available doctor, my temperature hit 380°F. By 11:04 A.M., I am dragged to the clinic....After a gigantic injection, I am told I have "strep" and that I will have to lock myself up for the next ten days. What a shock!

March 7: Testing is cancelled!

March 8: Sunday rest.

March 9: Feeling better and testing resumes. I am sitting outside on the patio to oversee the entire operation.

March 10-12: After swallowing a whole bottle of penicillin, I am able to start washing dishes and mopping floors. I am advised not to cook or not to be close to others.

The whole week is depressing, watching everybody enjoy those delectable morsels, yet I just sit there drooling. Fortunately, it is over by March 12 and I am back to normal, eating my way through the whole day from 9 A.M. to 9:30 P.M. Hallelujah! Yan sure can!!!

NAME of RECIPE	TASTE	APPEARANCE	COOKING TIME	REMARKS
Spicy Chinese Noodles	Excellent. Sauce was perfect, not too salty. Unique	Very aesthetic. Color combination balanced	Up to 45 minutes (used microwave to cook chicken breast, it came out perfect)	I used "Udon" Japanese noodles from Lucky's produce dept. This dish was served to friends with cocktails. It worked out very well. Our friends comments ranged from superb, great, & fantastic to beautiful. Garnished with a lemon slices and scallions.
Chicken Almond Surprise	Flat on sauce— more sauce needed. Good other than that	Too Green (according to my husband) I thought carrot was perfect accent	35 minutes preparation— 7 minutes cooking time	An excellent quick dinner
Dry Garlic Flavored Spareribs	Good, maybe less salt more garlic	Retains cooked color	6 minutes cooking timing	My husband thought this was perfect; however, I thought it was too salty.
Chicken and Cauliflower Foo Young	Unique	Ham makes the perfect accent color.	6-7 minutes cooking time— 14 minutes preparation time.	My husband loved this!!
Pork and Bean Sprout Soup	Excellent	Color coordinated	Perfect	Maybe less salt → ¼ tsp. less.
Colorful Jewelers	Yummy!!	Well mixed— Colorful & true to its name	Preparation time: 15 minutes Cooking time: 4 minutes	The only downfall to this was the baby corn—I grabbed a pickled baby corn jar instead of a plain at the delli. ☺

Here's one of the charts we used for testing the recipes.

A Gastronomical Tour
—Regional Foods of China

Among the world's great cuisines, the regional cooking of China is perhaps the most difficult to classify. China is a great land with diverse weather and resources. Many parts of China are isolated. Therefore the regional styles of the cooking of China are as different as its dialects. Over the centuries, certain special dishes from one region have been adopted and adapted in other regions. Most Chinese cooks are notably inventive and flexible due to the diverse climate and the availability of ingredients. New dishes and foods were constantly being incorporated into each region. For such reasons, the best of Chinese cooking is found mostly in large cities where the art is nurtured and stimulated by the gourmets, the rich, the educated and the travelers. For simple identification, we will only discuss the four better-known culinary regions.

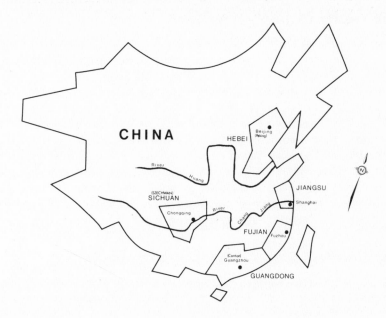

The Southern School—Canton

Canton, with its mild, tropical climate and abundant rainfall, lies on the southern tip of China. It is a rich, agricultural region with fresh food available all year round. The excellence of Cantonese cooking comes not from the taste but from the great choice and infinite combination of ingredients, characterized by a variety of textures. Very little soy sauce is used in cooking to preserve the natural color and flavor of the food. A lot of effort is put into the artful presentation of each dish with carefully selected garnishes to give a colorful and appetizing appeal. The Cantonese were the first to emigrate to North America—thus, this is also the best-known style of cooking to North Americans.

The Western School—Szechwan

Szechwan, located in the heart of China, is a relatively isolated inland area. With its hot, humid, and muggy climate, hot and spicy foods are frequently served. The generous use of red chili pepper, garlic and leeks dominate many of the area's dishes. The use of hot pepper is not intended to paralyze taste sensations but to stimulate the palate. Under such stimulation, the palate becomes more sensitive and able to appreciate a number of flavors simultaneously. Szechwan dishes are largely based on seasonings and relishes. Salted meat dishes are common. This school of cooking, along with the Hunan style, has gained increasing popularity in recent years in this country. However not all dishes from this area are overly spicy. In fact, banquet dishes are never spiced with chili pepper, for these cooks believe that good food need not be hot and spicy.

The Northern School—Peking (or Mandarin)

Peking has been the home of the Imperial courts for many centuries. It is the cultural and political center of China. Thus, anything that is the best of its kind would be presented in this great city of royal families, high officials and wealthy merchants. You will find the best food as well as the best chefs. Many fine dishes from different regions were introduced and adapted for the menus of Peking. Its cuisines mainly derive from four backgrounds: the Imperial kitchen of the capital; the local cooking of the Shantung and Hopei areas; Moslem cooking of Inner Mongolia; the dishes of the lower Yangtze region, Fukien, Kwangtung and Szechwan. Among all these regional cookings, Hopei, Moslem and Shangtung dishes play a dominant role in the representation of this school. The staple is wheat flour. Many traditional dishes, such as Peking duck, and Mu Shi Pork are served with pancakes. One of the typical cooking methods is to sizzle the ingredients with brown bean paste.

The Eastern School—Shanghai

The eastern regions of China, particularly Kangsu and Chekang, are best known for their red cooked dishes—cooking with soy sauce over slow heat. Red cooked dishes are often served along with rice dishes in everyday family meals. The extra touch of salt and sugar to enhance the flavor in a great number of dishes is quite common. Most dishes from these regions are rich. Shanghai is often considered to be the culinary center for many of these eastern provinces. Being on the coast, a great variety of fish, shellfish and meat are available. They are prepared in many different ways, served hot or cold.

Wokking for Good Health

Sometimes I jog but most of the time I wok. Good food and good health have always been closely associated, and in Chinese cooking the use of fresh and natural ingredients provides a nutritional diet. Food, as the source of vitamins, minerals and energy is a vital factor for daily existence. The Chinese diet has a good supply of carbohydrates from rice, noodles, and breads; protein from meat, eggs, soy bean curd and nuts; and vitamins and minerals from fruits and vegetables. Most Chinese prefer light desserts that are not overly sweet. They serve fresh fruits and delicate pastries to finish a meal.

The Chinese consume little saturated fat by using only a small amount of meat, complimented with lots of fresh vegetables. (You'll never see a Chinese person sit down and consume a 12-ounce steak—that is unheard of!) They use vegetable oil instead of animal fats for most home cooking. Oils increase the food flavor, creating a tantalizing taste experience.

Fiber in the Chinese diet is usually high because of the large amount of rice, fresh vegetables and fruit. These foods provide bulk that is necessary for efficient and normal muscular contraction of the intestines.

Chinese cuisine is versatile. The creative use of soy bean curd, nuts, and legumes prepared with a wide variety of seasonings and cooking methods would delight any vegetarian. Confirmed meat lovers may even develop a passion for vegetables when prepared the savory Chinese way!

Retaining vitamins such as vitamin C and thiamine, which are water soluble and heat-labile, can be tricky, but the Chinese have the problem licked! While improper cooking will destroy many vitamins, the Chinese methods of stir-frying and steaming over high temperatures for short time periods help to maintain the natural goodness and nutritional value of food.

Take up the wok for a healthy body!

Tools to Wok With

A Chinese kitchen does not require a great many utensils and only a few are needed to perform multiple functions: almost essential are a wok, a curved spatula, a wok lid and a sharp Chinese cleaver. Other important items include a set of bamboo steamers, wok stand (ring), skimmer (strainer), a heavy cutting board and chopsticks. My feeling is that it is more fun and convenient to have all these basic tools, but they are not absolutely necessary. You can use whatever is available in your kitchen.

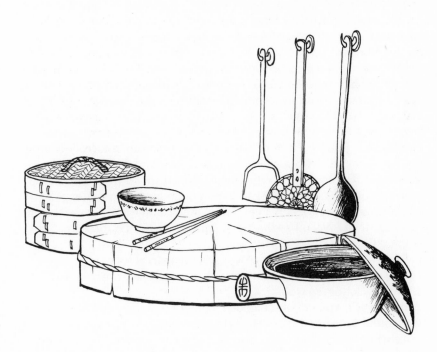

Wok Talk

The name "wok" is a romanization of the Cantonese pronunciation for "cooking vessel." The Chinese kitchen would not be complete without this all-purpose cooking pan. The wok resembles a round salad bowl with two ear-like handles or one long wooden handle.

The wok is the most versatile of all cooking pans. It can be used for stir-frying, deep-frying, stewing, braising or steaming. Its high sides and smooth slope make foods easy to stir and toss without spilling. A minimum of oil is needed to cook in a wok because of its efficient curved design and decreased surface area. The round bottom of the wok also makes it easy to clean. A wok can be used to cook a whole fish, prepare a crepe or omelet or make soup, and it is even used for cooking rice. If you were to have only one pan in your kitchen, the wok would be truly the most versatile.

It is well known that the wok works better on a gas stove than on an electric stove. While gas and electric stoves produce a similar amount of heat, the gas stove allows precise control of that heat, providing instant high heat and instant turn-off. But with a little experience you can master either system. When using the electric stove you can place the wok directly on top of the heat source or use a wok stand (ring). Always be sure to set the wok on the large burner and use the wide end of the stand facing up to allow the wok to sit closer to the heat source. To stir-fry, use the highest heat on the large burner. Let the clean wok heat for 2½-3 minutes until it is piping hot (less time for gas). Add oil and let it heat up before putting in any food. Use the same high heat throughout stir-frying.

Woks can be found in several different sizes ranging from 12"-14" in diameter up to the large 24" size used in restaurants and for barbeques. The 14" wok is ideal for home use and when preparing meals for two to eight hungry people. The wok is usually made of spun steel (rolled steel), stainless steel, teflon-coated aluminium or cast iron. Stainless steel conducts heat the slowest, which limits temperature control so food may stick and burn. Stainless steel and aluminium are also more expensive. The thick and heavy spun steel (rolled steel) is the most desirable and practical since it will retain the high temperatures which are so important to good Chinese cooking.

There are three basic types of woks on the market today:
1. the traditional round-bottomed wok with stabilizer ring
2. the flat-bottomed wok
3. the electric wok (teflon-coated aluminium or stainless steel)

The round-bottomed type was originally designed to fit the Chinese stove which burned wood, coal or hay. The round bottom sits on top of the Chinese stove without sliding or moving about. In North America when the wok is placed on a gas or electric range, a stabilizer ring helps to balance it over the heat source. The flat-bottomed wok was created specifically for use on electric stoves. Unless it has a smooth curve near the bottom, the round-bottomed wok used with a stabilizer is best. With the electric wok, the coils at the base are usually too small to achieve even heating throughout the entire pan and there is little heat control. Also, the low lids restrict its usefulness. I prefer the round-bottomed traditional wok. Its smooth surface allows easy stirring and mixing of food, and its high domed lid is perfect for roasting and steaming. Investing in a good wok makes sense since it can last a lifetime and give you years of cooking pleasure.

Do not be discouraged if you have not purchased a wok. A large frying pan can do a fair job, although you may find dinner spread all over the counter after quickly stir-frying a Chinese dish. Another drawback frying pans have is that the edges hinder a thorough mixing of ingredients. Purchase a wok if you can afford to spend a few extra dollars. You will soon find it adapts to most of your daily cooking needs.

A Well-Seasoned Wok

No Chinese cook would ever want to trade a seasoned wok for a brand new one. Iron skillets are treasured in the same way. Just like people they don't get older, they get better! Most woks on the market are made of spun (or rolled) steel which should be treated or "seasoned" before use to prevent food from sticking.

New woks are generally coated with either rust resistant industrial grease, or a gummy, shiny coating which must be removed in the seasoning process. To season a new wok:
1. Remove the protective coating by scrubbing with cleanser and scouring pads in hot water. For the hard shiny and gummy coating, sprinkle the surface with cigarette lighter fluid before scrubbing. Fill the work with water and bring it to a boil over high heat. Boil for 8-10 minutes. Clean and scrub again.
2. Dry wok over medium heat for several minutes. Spread a thin film of cooking oil (about 1 teaspoon of any vegetable oil) over entire surface. Use paper towels to rub oil into the wok until the paper towel comes away clean. For best results, repeat this step one or two times more. You can also season a new wok in the oven. Rub it with oil and put it in a preheated 350-375°F oven for 5-10 minutes. Repeat several times.
3. Wash the wok in hot water with a soft, nylon pad. Place it on a hot stove to dry. Now the wok is seasoned and ready for cooking up a storm!

After seasoning the metal may be discolored. It will continue to darken and mellow with age and use. As they say: the blacker it gets the better it cooks! Don't ever "dare" to spend five hours laboriously scrubbing away the "darkness."

One *important* reminder: Do not prepare any highly acidic food such as a sweet and sour or tomato dish in a seasoned wok, since hot, acidic food can be abrasive to the seasoning. You might end up having a tin-metal taste!

Cleaning and Maintaining a Seasoned Wok
To keep your wok in good shape, follow these humble suggestions:
1. Clean wok with a sponge, nylon pad or a bamboo brush in hot water. You may use a few drops of mild liquid soap. Rinse and pat dry.
2. Place wok on stove over medium-high heat to complete drying, then rub a tiny bit (about ¼ teaspoon) of oil in wok to prevent oxidation (rusting). Keep inside paper bag in a cool, dry area.

Those who "refuse" to follow these simple instructions to protect the wok may end up with an extraordinarily rusty wok that must be wrapped and given away to the dump as a present!

How to be Clever with a Cleaver

Any Chinese domestic engineer would feel uncomfortable without a Chinese cleaver, a fairly heavy knife with a broad, rectangular-shaped blade. An amazingly versatile tool, the Chinese cleaver is used to cut, slice, shred, chop, mince, press meat and crush garlic. Its wide, rectangular blade can be used to transfer the cut-up pieces of ingredients from the cutting board to the cooking pan. (Of course, in case of emergency, a cleaver can serve as a protective weapon!) Like any other sharp knife, the Chinese cleaver can be dangerous if not handled properly, but after practicing with it for a while, you will find it practically impossible to cut yourself in 1000 years!

First make sure that the cutting board is stationary and will not slide before cutting anything with the cleaver. (A sliding cutting board will cause you to prepare a "fingernail delicacy!") Hold the handle of the cleaver with your right hand (or left hand if you are left-handed) and slide your hand forward until your thumb reaches one side of the blade and your index finger is on the other side. Hold it tightly for better maneuvering. Now the cutting motion flows, with your left hand holding onto the food to be cut. Tuck your thumb in and then curve the four fingers of your left hand downward and inward until the first knuckle extends beyond the finger tips. The cleaver is placed so the blade is just touching the knuckle, which now serves as a cutting guide. To acquire a comfortable working position, set the cleaver at a 35-45 degree angle perpendicular and pointed away from your body. The cutting process itself is a forward and downward motion, not a sawing motion.

For safety, never swing your cleaver or lift the cutting edge higher than the level of your knuckle. Most of you might find that the cleaver is sharp and heavy enough to cut through most meats and vegetables without exerting undue force. As the cutting progresses, move all your fingers gradually backwards, leaving what still remains to be cut in place, without changing the original knuckle as a guide. This technique seems a bit awkward in the beginning. Try it slowly at first and build up your skill. With practice and perseverance, you will soon be cutting away as deftly as a professional Chinese chef.

Chopsticks

In a Chinese household chopsticks are not only used as eating utensils but also as cooking tools. They help to mix, stir, whip and pick up food during preparation. Most chopsticks are made from ivory, bamboo, wood or plastic. For cooking, bamboo or wooden ones are best as they withstand high temperatures and do not conduct heat to your hands. In dynastic times chopsticks were made from ivory because ivory discolors when it comes in contact with most poisons, and the possibility of murder by poisoning was feared in the courts. Today, chopsticks are common utensils. If you do not want to spend money on a pair, walk out with a pair the next time you dine at a Chinese restaurant. One reminder though: don't call me if you get caught!

The characters for chopsticks, *Faii Jee,* mean "quick little boys," symbolizing the quick speed and skill with which they are used. The symbol of "quick little boys" is also used when, at the time of marriage, the bride's parents present her with a set of ten red chopsticks in the hopes that she will quickly produce ten children and thus bring joy to the family.

In these times of inflation, eating with chopsticks is the only way "to make ends meet."

Playing Chopsticks
Many things are easier than trying to manipulate a pair of chopsticks for the first time. Actually it is quite easy, and all it takes to master this art is a little practice and persistence.

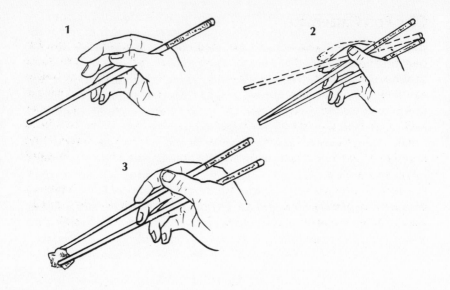

1. Place the first chopstick in between the middle and fourth fingers with the top anchored between the thumb and the index finger.
2. Hold the second chopstick as if you were holding a pencil.
3. When using the chopsticks, move only the second chopstick, keeping the other one in a stationary position. Just be sure that the tips of the two chopsticks meet so that you can pick up the food. Otherwise you might end up having to use your fingers.

Good luck with your new venture!!

Clay Pot/Casserole

Traditionally the Chinese use a covered, natural earthenware pot for casserole dishes. The interior is coated with a dark brown lead-free glaze and the exterior is frequently encased in wire mesh to protect the fragile earthenware. These pots are an inexpensive purchase in most Chinese specialty shops. They can be placed directly over gas or electric heat as well as used in the oven. Care must be taken to keep the pots from breaking: (1) Never place an empty clay pot on heat. Always have some liquid in it. (2) Never place a hot clay pot on a damp surface or in water until it has cooled.

Although clay pots are fun to use and have the appeal of authenticity, they are not essential for cooking Chinese casseroles. An aluminium, cast iron, enamel or glass casserole will work just as well as the clay pot.

Cutting Board

Since a lot of slicing, shredding, mincing and chopping are involved in the preparation of Chinese food, a good cutting board that can endure such hardship is recommended. The traditional Chinese cutting block is made from the cross section of a hardwood tree trunk and can be found in certain Chinese stores.

If you would like to make your own block, simply cut a cross section from a hardwood tree. To prepare it for use, season the block by rubbing ½ cup of oil into the entire surface. Cover the block with foil and let set for two to three days in a dry and cool place. Oil is used to saturate the wood grain, repel water and prevent cracking. After two to three days, rinse and

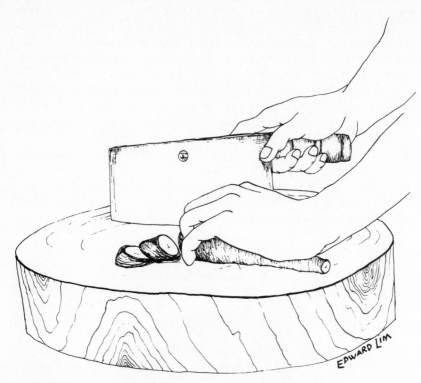

EDWARD LIM

dry the block. Now you have your own personal cutting block. A good substitute is a two-inch thick, large cutting board.

Always remember to have a steady surface that will not slide. To prevent slipping, simply place a damp cloth between the block and counter.

Exhaust

It sounds strange to mention this here, but it is a good idea to have an exhaust fan in your kitchen which can be turned on when you are wokking up a storm. Because you will be cooking several dishes and sauces at the same time, there will be a lot of heat and splashing grease. Exhaust will draw the splashing grease "out of space" and keep you "cool!"

Skimmer (Strainer)

In Chinese cooking, many dishes require that the ingredients are removed from hot oil or boiling water at some point during cooking. A good size strainer or sieve is certainly recommended. This will save you a lot of time, and you will have better control over the dish. Most Chinese strainers are made of copper wire mesh in the shape of a wide shallow ladle. Some are made of stainless steel, which I prefer for its easy cleaning.

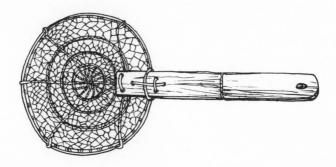

Spatula

The Chinese spatula is slightly curved to match the curvature of most woks for easy stirring and tossing of food to prevent food from burning. It usually has a long handle so you cannot burn yourself. Large kitchen spoons and spatulas may be used to replace this.

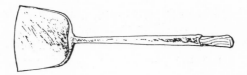

Steamer

Steaming plays an important role in Chinese cookery, both in the cooking of foods and the reheating of leftovers. Steaming foods in their natural juices preserves the original flavor and nutritional value without adding extra calories. By stacking several steamers, a number of dishes can be cooked or reheated at the same time.

There are two types of steamers on the market today—the bamboo and the aluminium. The intriguing and traditional bamboo steamers come in a variety of sizes, have no base, and will fit right inside a wok. For a fourteen-inch wok, buy a thirteen-inch bamboo steamer. The bamboo steamer allows slow dissipation of moisture through the lattice top which avoids excessive condensation of steam on the dish. The aluminium steamer is impervious to moisture, and has a tighter seal which causes more condensation. The aluminium steamer cooks faster, however the bamboo steamer is better for buns and pastries.

If you do not have a steamer you can simply set the dish to be steamed on top of a small six-ounce tin can (with both ends removed), on a cake rack, or on a pair of bamboo or wooden chopsticks placed in a cross at the bottom of the wok. Be sure the water level is at least 1" below the dish being steamed. Otherwise you may end up making soup! Also be sure to check the water level while steaming. Add ½ cup of boiling water to the wok every 3-4 minutes. If it boils dry you may find yourself in a smokey kitchen with a charcoaled steamer and a melted wok!

Wok Cover (Lid)

The wok cover is usually round, looks like a bowl and should be well fitted to trap the steam. This convex design enables the wok to build up a vapor pressure during the cooking process.

Wok Stand (Ring)

The wok stand or ring is usually designed for round-bottomed woks. It is used to set the wok right on top of the burner making it more steady. It usually has sloping sides with several holes around the sides for ventilation. For slow cooking or simmering, set your wok over the smaller opening which will lift the wok slightly. For fast cooking, you need your wok closer to the heat source, therefore, place the wok over the large opening. If you have a gas burner at home, remove the burner grid and set the ring securely over the burner before setting the wok on top.

Chop, Chop, and Other Techniques

Seeing is believing and believe me, if you have ever seen an experienced Chinese cook in action...chop, chop and before your very eyes, vegetables have been perfectly shredded in two seconds flat!! How did he do that? "It looks so easy," you say. I say, "It is!" Experience is the secret. With a little practice and a lot of patience you will master the various techniques with your cleaver such as slicing, dicing and shredding. Practice makes perfect. Many techniques such as stir-frying, deep-frying, shallow-frying, stewing, simmering, braising and smoking, have been used for centuries by the Chinese—no wonder they are so good at it!!

Clever Cleaver Techniques

There are many considerations which make cutting technique an essential part of Chinese cooking. Most of the Chinese dishes are comprised of bite-size morsels. The sizes and shapes of all the ingredients in the same dish should be similar to ensure uniformity in appearance and texture. When one ingredient is thinly shredded in a certain dish, the other ingredients should match it. It is also much easier to eat food with a pair of chopsticks when it is cut into bite-size pieces. It is a much healthier way to eat when nothing is overcooked to destroy the natural goodness of the ingredients. When the ingredients are cut into small pieces, they will be through cooking in just a few minutes when cooked over high heat.

Chopping

Most of the cleavers are used for slicing and cutting; you will damage the blade if you use it for chopping heavy bones. You will need a heavy duty cleaver to cut through pork and chicken bones. To chop, hold onto the handle firmly and use a straight up and down motion with enough force. Never wiggle or twist the cleaver from side to side. Keep the food in the center of the cutting board and make sure your free hand is out of the way. If you are not strong enough, rest the cleaver on the food to be chopped and hammer it down on the blunt edge of the cleaver. Beware not to chop your cutting board into 15 pieces!!

Crushing
Since the cleaver is the only cutting tool found in most Chinese kitchens, it is used for all kinds of action. For crushing garlic, place garlic on the cutting board close to the edge and lightly slap the blade on top of the garlic to flatten it. You can combine the garlic with salted black beans in a small bowl and crush both by using the handle of the cleaver to smash up and down until you achieve a paste.

Dicing
If any of you have tried "Almond gai ding" (diced almond chicken), you will notice everything is cut into small dices. To do so, cut the ingredients lengthwise into long strips of about ¼-½ inch wide, then cut each strip into small dices of the desired size.

Mincing
Shred ingredients into strips and dice; then rest the tip of the cleaver on the cutting board. Hold onto the handle of the cleaver with one hand and move it up and down to chop. Pivot the blade on the tip to make different angles; this will provide an even mincing action. But if you have a large amount of food to mince, just toss everything in your food processor and you will chop it all up in seconds.

Roll Cutting (or Oblique Cutting)
This is perhaps the most Chinese in origin. Slice each piece at an angle, then roll the ingredients over a quarter turn and cut again at an angle. Continue turning and cutting until you reach the final cut. Practice this technique with a carrot or zucchini. The advantage of oblique cutting is that it exposes surface area for faster cooking.

Shredding

This is perhaps the most common technique in Chinese cooking. First the ingredients are sliced at an angle of 45 degrees to the cleaver blade and then cut into thin strips.

Slanting and Parallel Slicing

This technique is used to cut thin slices from a piece of flat meat or vegetable. Place the food flat on the cutting board close to the edge. Hold the cleaver at a slant (at a small angle with the sharp edge of the blade facing down). Move the cleaver carefully back and forth to slice the food between the cutting board and fingers holding the meat. Don't rush while doing this.

Slicing

When slicing, place the piece to be cut perpendicular to the blade or at any other angle. The thickness of these slices will vary depending on the particular recipe used. Pieces cut at a slant usually have a larger surface area which allows them more exposure to heat.

Tenderizing

Most Chinese cooks and homemakers make use of the cleaver to do their tenderizing. To tenderize meat, simply turn the cleaver upide down to the blunt edge and pound the meat in crisscross patterns. For added excitement, fun and if you want to be noisy, you can even slap the meat with the blade.

Cooking Techniques

Braising

This can be considered a combined technique of stir-frying and stewing. The ingredients are first stir-fried over high heat for several minutes, then the heat is reduced to finish the cooking.

Deep-Frying

There are two things to remember when deep-frying: 1) Use enough oil so that the food is totally submerged; this will insure uniform cooking, and 2) be sure that the oil is hot enough before putting any food into it. To determine whether the oil is ready, submerge a clean bamboo chopstick into the oil. If bubbles appear around the chopstick immediately after contact with the hot oil, it is hot enough for most frying purposes. Another method is to watch for the first trace of smoke, but don't wait until the smoke fills up your kitchen. Always drop the food gently into the hot oil or slide it gently down the side of the wok into the hot oil. Cooking time varies according to the type and size of the ingredients. Turn the food around frequently during frying. As a rule of thumb, the food is usually ready when it starts to turn golden brown and float freely on the surface of the oil.

Red Cooking/Stewing

Red cooking is a form of stewing, but less water and vegetables are used. Soy sauce gives these dishes their red coloring and rich flavor. This method is used for cooking larger cuts of meat and poultry which are generally cooked with pickled, dried or salted ingredients. It is a slow method of cooking. After initially bringing the mixture to a boil the temperature is reduced and kept low.

Roasting

Roasting is a popular method in restaurant kitchens, but less common in Chinese homes where kitchens have less equipment, and an oven is uncommon. This slow method of cooking is great for larger cuts of meat and whole fowl. To cut down on cooking time and to avoid dryness you can slightly pre-cook the meat. Roasted meat is first rubbed with oil and marinated to give it color and added flavor. Then the meat is quickly seared to make the skin crisp, before being slowly roasted on hooks or on a rack. The delicious juices are collected in a pan below the meat.

Shallow-Frying

This technique is similar to stir-frying except that medium heat is used, and thus the cooking time is longer. Continuous stirring is not necessary. The food is placed evenly in the wok and turned over only a couple of times during the cooking process.

Simmering

This differs from stewing in that fewer ingredients are used in cooking and the cooking takes place in a clear broth at low heat. The objective is to achieve great tenderness and purity of food. Fresh, crisp vegetables are added at the concluding stages of cooking, and the clear cooking liquid is served as a soup with the meat and vegetables. A longer cooking time is required, and a tight lid or cover to seal in the steam is desirable.

Smoking

This is more of a flavoring technique than a cooking one. To achieve the smoked flavor, brown sugar is burned in a tightly closed pan that has been insulated with foil. The meat is placed on a rack within the pot and the strong smoke from the burning sugar flavors the food.

Stir-Frying

This technique is the predominant and best-known method in Chinese cookery. It is simply frying food over high heat with continuous tossing and stirring. A small amount of oil is added to the wok before cooking any other ingredients. If the food tends to become dry or sticky, a couple of tablespoons of soup stock or water should be added. Most of the stir-fried dishes take relatively little cooking time. Therefore, these dishes should be prepared at the last minute so they will be piping hot before serving.

When stir-frying, the sequence of adding ingredients is important to achieve the crisp texture and flavor that is essential to Chinese cooking. Ingredients requiring a longer cooking time (meats and tough vegetables) should be added to the hot oil before those requiring less cooking time. Add ingredients to the wok in descending order of delicacy. For stir-frying, cut foods need to be of uniform size and shape so that they will cook evenly. The number of ingredients should be limited so that the wok is not piled to the ceiling with vegetables and meat that cannot be stirred.

The hot oil assures quick cooking of food and helps seal in flavors.

Steaming

This unique cooking method is perhaps as Chinese as the wok itself. The food is simply cooked by steam. Most Chinese kitchens have steamers which are usually made out of bamboo and will sit directly in the wok. Several bamboo steamers can be used at the same time, one on top of another, to save fuel in the era of the energy crunch. The objective of steaming foods is to avoid direct contact between the food and the boiling water—otherwise you would be boiling everything! If you use a wok for steaming, simply place two pairs of chopsticks, tic-tac-toe style, over the water and place the plate of food on top of the chopsticks. Another way is to simply place a tin can with both ends removed in the middle of a wok or a pot. Fill the water to two-thirds of the tin can, and place the plateful of food on top of the can. Use high, medium, or medium-low heat to steam, depending on the type of food.

Ingredients
—Getting Down to Basics

Most of the food items used in this book can be obtained in your local supermarkets. A few may require a visit to a Chinese grocery store. Most of these traditional and exotic ingredients can be kept for quite a while if properly stored. If you are lucky enough to live near a Chinese specialty store, make a trip occasionally. If you happen to live in the middle of nowhere, take a train, a bus or a plane to a Chinatown and stock up for the next "30" years, or shop long distance by mail order.

For more information on ingredients, refer to the chapters at the end of this book, "Chinese Spices and Life's Ingredients, Too" and "The Chinese Connection—Mail Order."

The Basics

Bean curd (Tofu): Used widely in Chinese cooking since it goes well with most vegetables. Keep in clear water in refrigerator for up to 3-4 days. Be sure to change water every day.

Bean thread noodles: Used in soup, stir-fry dishes, and when deep fried it can be used as a garnish. Keep in dry, cool area and it will last indefinitely.

Black beans, salted: Used for flavoring. Keep in air-tight jar in a dry, cool area.

Black Mushroom, dried: Used for flavoring, color, and as a vegetable addition to a dish. Keep in an air-tight container in a dry, cool area.

Cornstarch: Used for dry coating, marinating and sauce thickening. It is used frequently and should be kept close by. "Cornstarch solution" refers to a mixture of 1 part cornstarch dissolved in 2 parts water. Be sure to stir it again just before using.

Ginger root, fresh:	Used frequently for flavoring. Buy enough to last a week or two. Keep refrigerated.
Hoisin sauce:	For barbecue meats and sauces. Keep in dry, cool area or refrigerate. Keep in air-tight jars.
Oyster-flavored sauce:	For flavoring and sauces. Keep refrigerated.
Plum sauce:	Mainly for sauces. Keep in a dry, cool area in air-tight jars.
Sesame seed oil:	For meat marinade and flavoring in cooking. Refrigerate to prolong shelf life.
Soy sauce, dark:	For flavoring or dips. Refrigerate to prolong storage.
Soy sauce, light:	For meat marinade, for flavoring or for dips. Refrigerate to prolong storage. (In this cook book, "soy sauce" generally refers to *light* soy sauce. *Dark* soy sauce will be indicated as such.)
Star anise:	Used for flavoring. Keep in air-tight container.
Szechwan peppercorn:	Used for flavoring. Keep in air-tight container.
Wonton/spring roll wrappers:	Keep refrigerated for 3-5 days or frozen for up to six months. Wrap well to prevent freezer burn.
Wine:	For meat marinade and flavoring. Chinese rice wine or dry sherry can be used.

There are many, many more Chinese ingredients, but these should get you on the right track to start "wokking."

Wokking with Oil

Chinese peanut oil, which is extracted from roasted peanuts, is the most widely used cooking oil in China. Its unusual nutty flavor adds something unique to Chinese cookery, unlike the peanut oils that are available in North America. Basically, oil is used for cooking and not for flavoring, thus most common polyunsaturated vegetable oils may be used, such as corn, soy bean, cottonseed or peanut oil. It is interesting to note that this type of oil is becoming more popular among the Chinese. Butter and olive oil are not desirable due to their strong, rich flavors and the problem of smoking at a comparative low temperature. It is important that the oil withstand high temperatures, but fire can occur if the oil is severely over-heated. Therefore, be sure not to heat oil too much over 375°F (190°C) when frying. If the oil smokes, reduce heat or remove hot oil from the stove.

During deep-frying, excessive loose moisture on foods can cause spattering, therefore blot or wipe damp foods before adding oil. After deep-frying, oil may be strained and used again, but excessive re-use can cause foaming. Discard oil if this happens. Also, excessive re-use of oil lowers the smoking point substantially, making it difficult to control cooking time. As a rule of thumb, oil that has been used for frying poultry and meat can be easily re-used for frying other foods. Oil used for frying seafood acquires a strong "fishy" flavor, and should be used again only for seafood.

If your used oil has a slight unpleasant aroma, simply heat oil over medium-high heat and toss in a few slices of ginger root—this will help to mask undesirable odors. Store used oil in the refrigerator to keep it from spoiling too quickly.

Keep in mind that it is not essential to do all of your "wokking" with Chinese peanut oil. In native China, where vegetable oil is scarce, lard and chicken fat are frequently used instead. By the way, peanut oil is fairly expensive, and who wants to spend a lot of money if you can get something cheaper to do the same job! Still, if you insist on the nutty flavor of Chinese peanut oil, it is usually sold in large quantities in Chinese groceries.

利口乃刀斧

善收人益善樂

文逸兄雅正

仲光聚

辛酉孟夏

張佩書

32

A Few Pearls of Wisdom from the Cook's Treasure Chest

Ready....Get Set....Go Stir Crazy!

If Yan can, everybody can! Over the past three years, our cooking presentations on television have proved just that. Everybody wrote to let us know about the wonderful feasts they had made for their family and friends. With practice, persistence and a little bit of luck, you will find that preparing a Chinese meal is as simple as going out for a "Big Mac."

There are a few things you should know about this book before you start to wok. Read through the entire recipe first. Each recipe should have an introduction; and if a marinade is called for, it will be listed under "Marinade." If a sauce is called for, it will be under "Sauce." Instructions for preparation are numbered and simple to understand. Oftentimes there are remarks to tell you some of the secrets. Sketches are available for your reference when instructions are difficult to put forward.

Prelude: Getting Everything Ready

1. Plan your menu and organize your time. Select a couple of dishes that can be prepared ahead of time and reheated before serving. Do not try to do more than two or three last-minute stir-fried dishes. This may prevent a nervous breakdown.
2. Wash and clean all of the ingredients. Drain and set aside.
3. Cut up all ingredients specified for the same recipe and place them on one plate so you don't have to run around and scream for help later on.
4. If a meat marinade is called for, prepare it ahead of time, and keep it refrigerated, usually 30 minutes to two hours.
5. If a sauce is called for and can be made ahead of time, prepare and keep it warm while cooking other foods.
6. Gather all of the ingredients, seasonings (such as soy sauce, salt, and sugar), and utensils needed for the menu and set aside.

7. Have the following items ready within easy reach: 1 quart of soup stock for flavoring, and to add when the food gets too dry; a small quantity of cornstarch solution (mix 1 part of cornstarch with 1 to 2 parts of water); and small saucers of chopped ginger, minced garlic and chopped green onion, since most dishes call for these.
8. Be sure that the wok is washed, dried and always ready.
9. Have a few plates or bowls nearby for cooked meat and fried foods while you are cooking the other ingredients for the same dish.
Now, you are ready for the action!

Lights....Wok....Action!

1. Have a clean, dry wok ready at all times.
2. When stir-frying dishes, always preheat the wok over high heat on a large burner for 2-3 minutes before pouring in the oil. Add ginger, garlic, or meat when a trace of smoke begins to appear. Stir-fry all dishes over high heat.
3. If a dish consists of meat and vegetables, cook them separately to retain their original flavors. If a variety of vegetables are included for the recipe, cook the thicker, more fibrous ones that require longer cooking time first, then progressively add the remaining vegetables to get uniform cooking. Use common sense. If you goof, toss everything out and try again!
4. Cooking times and temperatures should be closely oberved according to the recipe, particularly in stir-frying, deep-frying and steaming. Over-cooking will ruin the quality of the dish. Meat will be dry and tough and you will have to chew your jaws off; vegetables will become soggy, mushy, and discolored. The recipes in this book were tested on a large electric burner, therefore if a small electric burner is used, cooking time may have to be increased slightly. If using a gas burner cooking time may have to be slightly decreased. Just experiment a little!
5. During cooking, if the wok (or skillet) becomes too dry, sprinkle or add water or soup stock to avoid a new charcoal-burnt creation.
6. When thickening the liquids in a wok with cornstarch, slowly pour cornstarch solution over the boiling liquid in the center of the wok while stirring until it has thickened and is smooth. Excessive cornstarch will spoil the taste, and worst of all, you may end up with a homemade "miracle glue!"
7. When a stir-fried dish is done, remove it immediately from the stove and transfer to a platter to prevent over-cooking. Try to serve the dish as soon as possible to get the best flavor and aroma.

8. When a dish is done but cannot be served immediately, transfer to a platter and cover it with foil. Punch a few holes in the foil and keep it warm in a preheated oven (preheat at low setting for 15-20 minutes and turn heat off). Wash and dry wok to get ready for the next dish.
9. If you are simmering, stewing, braising food or making a sauce, do it in a saucepan or pot, while the wok can be used for stir-frying, deep-frying or steaming. Thus, you are able to prepare two or three things at a time.
10. When deep-frying batter foods it is very common to fry them a second time in order to achieve an extra crispy texture. To do this, deep-fry once, let food cool thoroughly, then deep-fry a second time over high-heat for 45 seconds to 1 minute. Serve immediately. This practice will produce a crispy golden brown product for almost all deep-fried batter dishes.
11. My humble recipes are intended as a reference, so be creative and enjoy your wokking experience.
12. Don't be intimidated! Don't get nervous! Don't get uptight! If some little thing goes wrong, just relax and keep calm. Don't ever push yourself too hard; otherwise you may drive yourself up the kitchen wall.

A Yan's place is in the kitchen.

Stop! Be sure you go through the previous pages carefully before you have anything to do with this humble cook's recipes.

Tantalizing Treasures: The Recipes

頭
枱

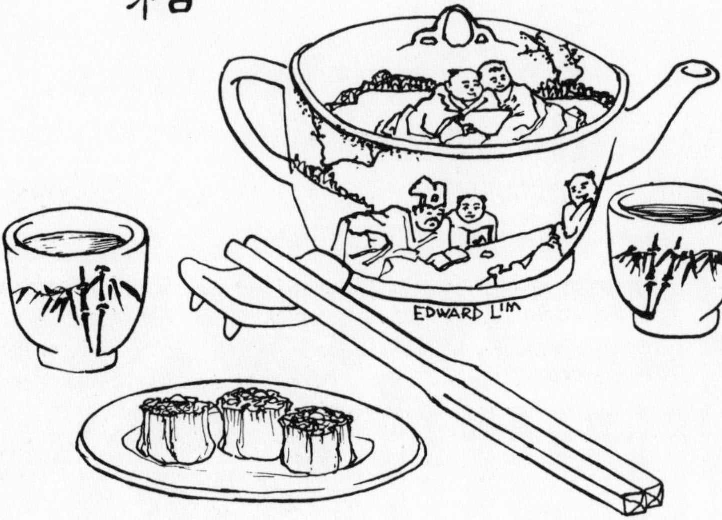

Memorable Morsels— Appetizers and Cold Dishes

There are great varieties of tempting preliminaries in Chinese cuisine. The most common appetite teasers are assorted cold meats, seafoods, and pickled vegetables, known as a "cold plate." Spring rolls, originating from the Shanghai area, are among the world's oldest hors d'oeuvres, and they remain a popular "dim sum" snack treat with tea.

Most of the ingredients are small portions of richly flavored goodies. Meats and seafoods that have been marinated, then cooked and chilled, are the Chinese counterparts of the Western cold cuts.

Most Chinese are not accustomed to eating raw vegetables, since vegetables are usually fertilized with manure which makes them unfit to be served raw. Therefore, whenever vegetables are included in the recipe, they are either parboiled or pickled to serve along with cooked meat or seafood.

These dishes are ideal as finger food, and when served in larger portions, they can be main courses. Most of the choices in this chapter will bring a new and appetizing look to your menu.

Chinese BBQ Duck Salad

If you live near a Chinese grocery store or restaurant where you can buy barbecued duck, this is your kind of dish. Simple, classy and delicious, you can make it any time and serve it to anybody. Your guests will all love you:

Dressing:
1 tablespoon (15 ml) sesame paste
2½ teaspoons (12 ml) soy sauce
2 tablespoons (30 ml) soup stock
1 teaspoon (5 ml) sugar
¼ teaspoon (1 ml) white pepper
1½ teaspoons (7 ml) sesame oil
2 tablespoons (30 ml) oil

6 ounces (168 g) barbecued duck meat
½ pound (225 g) celery, stringed and diagonally sliced
6 ounces (168 g) bean sprouts, roots removed
½ bell pepper, sliced
2 stalks green onion, shredded
2 teaspoons (10 ml) hot mustard paste
2 teaspoons (10 ml) toasted sesame seeds

1. Combine dressing mixture in a bowl. Blend well and set aside.
2. Combine vegetables and shredded duck in a serving bowl.
3. To serve, pour dressing over entire dish and toss well. Top salad with mustard and sprinkle with toasted sesame seeds. Chill until serving time. Garnish with parsley if desired.

Remarks

- For traditional Chinese style: Arrange shredded barbecued duck in a single layer on both ends of an oval-shaped platter. Cook bean sprouts in boiling water for 10 seconds, drain in a colander, and immediately rinse with cold water and drain well. Place in center of platter. Next, cook celery in boiling water for 15-20 seconds. Drain in colander and immediately rinse with cold water and drain well. Arrange on opposite sides of bean sprouts on platter.

Crispy Walnut Meatballs

Delicious morsels of meat coated with crunchy walnuts, a really special hors d'oeuvre for your next party. Sure to turn heads and disappear instantly!

1 pound (450 g) ground lean pork
1 cup (250 ml) chopped walnuts
4 cups (1 L) oil
½ cup (125 ml) catsup or sweet and
   sour sauce
1½ tablespoons (22 ml) cornstarch

Pork Marinade:
1 egg, lightly beaten
1 teaspoon (5 ml) ginger juice
½ teaspoon (2 ml) salt
½ teaspoon (2 ml) sugar
1½ teaspoons (7 ml) cornstarch
1 teaspoon (5 ml) wine

1. Marinate ground pork for 1-2 hours.
2. Mix chopped walnuts and cornstarch together. Make 28-32 one inch diameter meat balls; roll in walnut mixture until well coated. Lightly press walnuts into meat.
3. Heat oil in wok near smoking point. Reduce heat to low.
4. Carefully drop 6-8 meat balls at a time in hot oil, fry for 10-15 seconds, then turn meat balls gently to allow even cooking. Fry for about 3½ minutes or until golden brown. Remove and drain well.
5. To serve, dip into sweet and sour sauce or catsup.

Remarks

- You can serve the meat balls in a sweet and sour sauce or catsup and sprinkle extra walnuts on top.

 Fattening foods: a moment on the lips—forever on the hips.

Deep-Fried Siu Mei

This is a slightly modified version of the common steamed siu mei served at Cantonese tea lunches. In fact, this recipe is a bit better! Humble cook, huh?

Filling Mixture
½ **pound (225 g) lean ground pork**
¼ **pound (112 g) prawns, shelled, deveined and mashed**
2 dried black mushrooms, soaked and minced
2 teaspoons (10 ml) soy sauce
¼ **teaspoon (1 ml) salt**

2 teaspoons (10 ml) wine
1 teaspoon (5 ml) sesame oil
¾ **teaspoon (3 ml) sugar**
3 tablespoons (45 ml) minced green onion

19-20 wonton skins or siu mei skins
2 tablespoons (30 ml) frozen green peas
3 cups (750 ml) oil

1. Combine ingredients for filling mixture in a bowl and blend well. Let stand for 10-15 minutes.
2. Spoon 1 round tablespoon of filling mixture into center of each wonton skin. Use fingers to gather up and pleat the skin around the filling to form an open-topped pouch. Carefully squeeze the middle to give it a waist.
3. Place 2-3 green peas on top of each siu mei and arrange in an oiled pie pan. Steam over high heat for 12-15 minutes. Remove and let cool.
4. Heat 3 cups of oil in wok over high heat. Deep-fry steamed siu mei until golden brown. Serve with catsup, mustard or Worcestershire sauce.

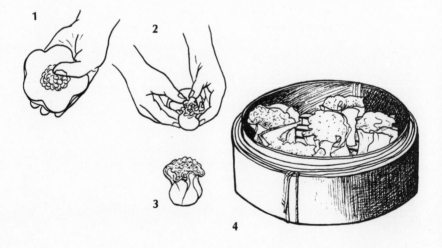

Delicious Chicken Drumsticks

Drum roll, please! This marvelous buffet dish should have nothing less. Succulent chicken will keep your mouth watering for another piece— don't be surprised if this dish gets requested often.

10 small chicken drumettes	*Braising Sauce*
2 tablespoons (30 ml) dark soy sauce	1 cup (250 ml) soup stock
4 cups (1 L) oil	¼ teaspoon (1 ml) black pepper
1½ tablespoons (22 ml) oil	1½ tablespoons (22 ml) wine
1 onion, chopped	1 whole star anise
2 slices ginger, shredded	3 tablespoons (45 ml) soy sauce
2 teaspoons (10 ml) cornstarch	1½ teaspoons (7 ml) sugar
solution	1 tablespoon (15 ml) honey

1. Dry drumettes and rub with dark soy sauce. Drain well and deep-fry in 4 cups of hot oil over medium-high heat for 3 minutes. Remove and set aside.
2. Put 1½ tablespoons oil in wok over high heat; add ginger and onion, stirring for about 30 seconds.
3. Return fried drumettes to wok; stir for one minute. Add braising sauce and mix well.
4. Reduce heat to low and braise for 12-15 minutes, stirring occasionally.
5. To serve, arrange drumettes on platter, thicken remaining juice with cornstarch and pour over drumettes.

Remarks

- When prepared as a main dish, use drumsticks.
- If prepared ahead of time, simply reheat in the oven.
- If you wish, garnish with pineapple rings and cherries.

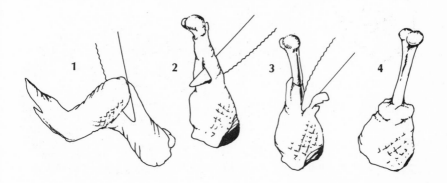

Flavorful Cabbage

This intriguing dish just might be offered to you if you visit a Shanghai restaurant. A hot but sweet cabbage makes it very appealing as an appetizer.

1⅓ pound (600 g) cabbage, cut into 2"
   squares (5 cm)
¼ cup (60 ml) oil
4 dried red chilis, halved

1 teaspoon (5 ml) salt
2 tablespoons (30 ml) sugar
3½ tablespoons (52 ml) vinegar

1. Heat oil in wok over medium-high heat. Add dried red chilis and cabbage, stirring constantly for 1-1½ minutes. Sprinkle with water if mixture is dry.
2. Add salt, stirring for 30 seconds. Mix in sugar, add vinegar and blend well. Remove from heat and let cool. Refrigerate until ready to serve.

Remarks

Red chilis turn black when cooked. Don't worry, it's not burned! It will add an interesting contrast to the dish.

 A good dish is like a successful marriage in which the parties involved are compatible and complement one another. It is a perfect harmony.

Hot and Spicy Asparagus Salad

Everybody knows that beef or chicken with fresh, tender asparagus is out of this world. The distinctive aroma and the exciting sensation of chili in this salad is absolutely unbelievable!

1½ pound (675 g) fresh asparagus
3 tablespoons (45 ml) oil
8-10 cloves garlic, cut into thin slices
    lengthwise

1 tablespoon (15 ml) Hunan chili paste
5 teaspoons (25 ml) sugar
5 teaspoons (25 ml) vinegar
2 tablespoons (30 ml) sesame oil
1 teaspoon (5 ml) salt

1. Remove stem ends and peel tough part of asparagus. Cut diagonally into 2-2½" pieces (5-5.75 cm).
2. Cook asparagus for about 2½ minutes in boiling water. Plunge in ice-cold water to stop cooking. Drain.
3. Heat oil in hot wok over medium-high heat. Add garlic slices, stirring for 30 seconds. Add the remaining ingredients and blend well. Turn off heat.
4. Stir in asparagus, toss well and transfer to a bowl. Refrigerate until ready to serve.

Papaya Salad

Picture yourself in Hawaii, enjoying the sun, surf and exotic hula dancers. Take your senses on a cruise to the beautiful islands. The variety of passionate textures and flavors in this salad will be sure to tantalize your taste buds. Aloha and come again!

1 medium-sized papaya, peeled and
    cut into ¾-inch (2 cm) cubes
8-10 canned lychees, drained
1 cup (250 ml) bean sprouts
½ bell pepper, cut into ¾" (2 cm)
    squares
1 tomato, cut into 8 wedges

Dressing
2 teaspoons (10 ml) oil
1 tablespoon (15 ml) light soy sauce
1½ tablespoons (22 ml) white vinegar
1 teaspoon (5 ml) sugar
½ teaspoon (2 ml) Chinese chili oil or
    Tabasco sauce
dash of black pepper

1. Carefully place fruits and vegetables into a salad bowl; mix well.
2. Mix dressing well and pour over salad. Serve chilled or at room temperature.

Remarks

* It is preferable to peel the tomato. Blanching tomatoes in boiling water a few seconds will loosen the skin and make them easy to peel.

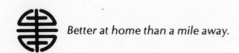

Better at home than a mile away.

Porcupine Meatballs

Right! A porcupine meat ball. You can create an uproar of excitement and be a showman when preparing these in front of your guests. Serve these porcupines to your guests with cocktails. They are sensational!

⅔ **pound (300 g) ground pork**
1 cup (250 ml) broken cellophane noodles, cut into ½" pieces (1.5 cm)
4 cups (1 L) oil

Pork Marinade
½ **teaspoon (2 ml) ginger juice**
½ **teaspoon (2 ml) salt**
1 teaspoon (5 ml) wine
½ **teaspoon (2 ml) sugar**
½ **teaspoon (2 ml) sesame oil**
1 egg yolk
1 tablespoon (15 ml) cornstarch

1. Marinate ground pork for 30 minutes. Roll into 30-32 tiny balls.
2. Roll meat balls in noodles to coat well; set aside.
3. Heat oil in hot wok over medium-high heat 325-350°F (160-180°C) and deep-fry 6-8 meat balls for about 3 minutes. Repeat with remaining meat balls. Occasionally turn meat balls in oil to ensure even cooking of noodles.

Remarks

- Rice noodles (maifun) may be used instead of cellophane noodles.
- Cut cellophane noodles in a bag or else they will fly away to your neighbor's kitchen. Use scissors to cut up the noodles or it will take you a million years to break them up!
- If oil is too hot, noodles will brown too quickly; reduce heat to keep temperature constant.

Smoked Eggs

These attractive brown colored eggs are very popular in northern China. Try them when you are tired of hard-boiled eggs! They're great hot or cold, as appetizers or snacks.

8 medium-size eggs

Smoking Mixture
½ teaspoon (2 ml) liquid smoke
2 tablespoons (30 ml) dark soy sauce
¾ teaspoon (3 ml) sugar
¼ teaspoon (1 ml) salt
½ teaspoon (2 ml) sesame oil

1. Place eggs in saucepan and cover with cold water. Bring water to a boil, reduce heat to medium and simmer eggs for about 4-5 minutes. Drain eggs and cover with cold water to cool.
2. Carefully peel eggs and set aside.
3. Combine the smoking mixture in a saucepan and heat over medium-low heat for 1½-2 minutes. Remove from heat and cool.
4. Add eggs to smoking mixture. Let stand for 1½ hours, turning frequently to coat well.

 The more you eat, the less flavor and heavier you get; the less you eat, the more flavor and the healthier you will be.

Spring Rolls

If you get spring fever, this recipe is for you! Light, crispy and just all-round delicious with lots of vegetables. It makes an ideal appetizer, as well as a delightful snack.

Filling Mixture:
1½ tablespoons (22 ml) oil
1 clove garlic, chopped
2 slices ginger, chopped
½ pound (225 g) boneless pork, chicken or barbecued pork, shredded
1½ cups (370 ml) bean sprouts
1½ cups (370 ml) thinly shredded cabbage
½ cup (125 ml) shredded bamboo shoots
½ cup (125 ml) thinly shredded carrot
4-6 dried black mushrooms, soaked and shredded (optional)
3 stalks green onion, cut into 1" (2.5 cm) pieces
1½ teaspoons (7 ml) garlic salt
¼ teaspoon (1 ml) five-spice powder (optional)
1 teaspoon (5 ml) sugar
¼ teaspoon (1 ml) white pepper

½ cup (125 ml) stock, if needed
2 tablespoons (30 ml) cornstarch solution
1 pound (450 g) spring roll wrappers
4 cups (1 L) oil

Flour Paste:
1 tablespoon (15 ml) flour
2 tablespoons (30 ml) water

1. If previously frozen, defrost wrappers inside the package at room temperature.
2. For filling mixture: Heat wok over high heat with 1½ tablespoons oil, garlic and ginger. Stir in meat and cook for approximately 2 minutes. Add remaining ingredients to wok and stir 2 minutes. Moisten with stock if needed. Add cornstarch solution and mix well.
3. Place approximately 2½ tablespoons of filling mixture in the center of each wrapper. Roll up and seal with flour paste or egg white.
4. Heat oil to near smoke point, and deep-fry over medium-high heat until golden brown and floating freely on top of oil. Serve hot, with or without plum sauce.

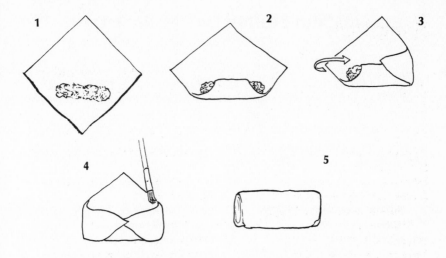

Remarks

- To avoid drying and cracking on edges of wrappers, be sure to defrost inside package. During the wrapping process, take a few out at a time and cover the rest with a damp cloth.
- You can replace bean sprouts with cabbage.
- Spring rolls can be prepared in advance and frozen. Thaw and fry to serve. Leftover spring rolls can also be refried over high heat and served again! In fact, the filling will keep better and be less watery if it is prepared in advance.
- If you leave out the meat, you have yourself a vegetarian roll.
- Spring rolls are often confused with egg rolls. Though similar, the common egg roll served in North America has different ingredients and a batter coating.

Sweet and Sour Stuffed Lychee (in Batter)

When I was young and innocent, in Kwongchow, China, we had a lychee tree in our backyard. It produced about 20 pounds of lychees a year, just enough to satisfy my tender uneducated taste buds. Since fresh, succulent lychees are unavailable in North America, we must resort to canned ones—they aren't great, but they are better than nothing! In this recipe, golden shrimps are stuffed into each lychee and then fried in a crispy batter. Wow! These are great as an appetizer or an entree.

4 ounces (112 g) small cooked
    shrimps, patted dry and diced
½ teaspoon (2 ml) salt
few drops sesame oil
1 large can (22 oz) (616 g) lychee fruits,
    drained and patted dry; reserve
    juice
cornstarch (for dry coating)
4 cups (1 L) fresh oil

Batter Mixture:
¾ cup (200 ml) flour
¼ cup (60 ml) cornstarch
½ teaspoon (2 ml) sugar
¾ cup (200 ml) flat beer (or water)
1 teaspoon (5 ml) baking powder (if
    using water increase to 1½
    teaspoons)
¾ teaspoon (3 ml) oil

Lychee Dip:
3 tablespoons (45 ml) vinegar
3 tablespoons (45 ml) sugar
3½ tablespoons (52 ml) catsup
5½ tablespoons (82 ml) lychee juice
1¾ teaspoons (8 ml) cornstarch
    solution

1. Mix shrimp with salt and sesame oil. Stuff shrimp into lychees. Dry-coat each lychee with cornstarch.
2. Combine batter mixture in a bowl. Drop the stuffed lychees into batter, coating completely. Heat oil in wok over medium-high heat. Deep-fry 2-3 at a time until golden, about 1½ minutes. Turn with chopsticks or small tongs to cook evenly. Drain.
3. Combine ingredients for lychee dip in a saucepan, and bring to a boil. Cook until thickened. Pour dip into a hollowed-out orange or bell pepper half.
4. Serve lychees and dip immediately.

Remarks

- Do not fry the lychees ahead of time as they become soggy when held.
- These can be served with or without the sauce. They are tasty either way.
- To test correct oil temperature, drop ½ teaspoon of batter into oil. It will rise to the surface immediately if the oil is hot enough.

Wino Chicken Wings

Here is a simple recipe for wings left over from deboning your own chickens. Chicken wings are also inexpensive to buy separately. Use them in this recipe and beat the rising cost of food!

3½ cups (870 ml) soup stock   1 stalk green onion
10 chicken wings   1 tablespoon (15 ml) salt
3 slices ginger   ¾ cup (200 ml) wine

1. Bring soup stock to a boil. Add wings, ginger and green onion. Bring to a second boil, reduce heat to low, cover and simmer for 15 minutes. Remove wings and drain well. Reserve stock.
2. Rub cooked wings with salt and let stand for 1-1½ hours. Shake off salt. Cut each wing at joint into 2 pieces.
3. Place wings in a bowl and cover with wine and 1 cup soup stock. Refrigerate for several hours. Serve cold.

 Every family's cooking pot has one black spot.

湯
類

Souper Duper Soups

Soup is an important, integral part of any Chinese meal: it is a delicious way to quench the thirst or clear the palate. It is usually served in a large bowl or tureen placed in the center of the dining table. Soup is commonly served throughout the dinner in everyday meals, whereas for a banquet or formal dinner, it is served at the beginning (southern China) or towards the end (northern China) of the meal.

Be it banquet or quick-boiled style, most Chinese soups are fundamentally simple. A flavorful soup depends largely on a good basic stock. Once the stock is made you can add any meat, seafood, poultry, vegetables or noodles you have on hand for a scrumptious one-dish meal. This is a great way to use your leftovers, too! The ultimate character of the soup depends on the particular blend of ingredients involved. The soup can be a very light, clear soup for everyday meals, or the hearty, rich type for banquets. The ingredients range widely from everyday, inexpensive ones, to exotic and rare ingredients, such as shark's fin or bird's nest.

A Chinese soup is usually made in four basic steps: 1) preparing the basic soup stock, 2) adding dried, salted or other preserved ingredients to give added flavor or piquancy, 3) cooking the major ingredients such as meat and vegetables in the broth, and 4) adding other seasonings and aromatic ingredients. Most Chinese people use a touch of sesame oil and white pepper to give an added zest to the soup when served.

Most of the recipes in this chapter are easy to prepare in your own kitchen.

Bean-Thread Soup with Curd

A creative way to present leftovers to your family without them suspecting a thing! It's a nutritious and delectable family-style soup, as well as economical and quick.

1 square soft bean curd, cut into 1"
    (2.5 cm) cubes
3 cups (750 ml) oil
¾ cup (200 ml) cellophane noodles
6 cups (1½ L) soup stock
1-2 slices ginger, shredded
1¼ teaspoons (6 ml) salt

4 dried black mushrooms, soaked and
    cut in half
½ cup (125 ml) carrot, cut into ¾"
    (2 cm) chunks
½ cup (125 ml) zucchini, cut into ¾"
    (2 cm) chunks
½ teaspoon (2 ml) sesame oil
pinch of white pepper

1. Drain bean curd cubes well in a colander; pat dry with paper towel. Deep-fry in 3 cups hot oil over medium-high heat until golden brown and cubes float freely on top. Remove and set aside.
2. Soak cellophane noodles for 20 minutes in warm water.
3. Bring stock to a boil, add ginger, salt, mushrooms and carrot. Cook over medium-high heat for 1-1½ minutes.
4. Add zucchini; cover and simmer for 3½ minutes.
5. Garnish with sesame oil and white pepper before serving.

 Even a smart homemaker finds it hard to cook without rice.

Everybody's Favorite Bean Curd Soup

The flavor of China is refreshingly expressed in this soup with its combination of textures, taste and color. The subtle taste of bean curd may be unfamiliar, but it is a dynamite combination with chicken and seafood; everybody will love it. I do, and you will too!

6 cups (1½ L) soup stock
1¼ teaspoons (6 ml) salt
2 slices ginger, shredded
2 ounces (56 g) cooked chicken,
    shredded
2½ tablespoons (37 ml) dried black
    mushrooms, soaked and
    shredded

1 square bean curd, ½ pound (225 g),
    shredded
2 ounces (56 g) small cooked shrimps
½ teaspoon (2 ml) sesame oil
dash of white pepper (optional)

1. Bring soup stock to a boil with salt and ginger.
2. Add cooked chicken, black mushrooms, bean curd and shrimp. Cook for 1½ minutes.
3. Spoon soup into bowl and add a few drops of sesame oil and white pepper before serving.

Hangover Chicken (Duck) Soup

This intoxicating soup is traditionally served to women during their first month after childbirth. Why? Good question and there are many answers! It's a tradition and for ladies only!

½ fryer chicken, approximately 1½ pounds (675 g) cut into 1½ " (4 cm) pieces
6 cups (1½ L) soup stock
3-4 slices ginger
½ cup (125 ml) lily buds, soaked (optional)
¼ cup (60 ml) dried wood ear, soaked (optional)

¾ teaspoon (3 ml) salt
⅔ cup (160 ml) rice wine, sake or dry sherry
dash of white pepper
⅓ cup (80 ml) rice wine, added at the last minute (optional)

1. Bring soup stock to a boil.
2. Add chicken, ginger, lily buds, wood ear, salt and wine. Let cook over medium heat for 15-17 minutes.
3. Before serving add pepper and wine to taste.

Remarks

- Chicken thighs may be substituted if you wish to spend more money on this dish.
- If desired, poach chicken in boiling water for 10 seconds to remove skum; drain and proceed with recipe.
- Adding wine will produce a better hangover!

Hearty Fish Chowder

If you are crazy about clam chowder, try this variation. It's smooth as silk and has an intriguing flavor: a Chinese version of clam chowder.

8 cups (2 L) soup stock
½ pound (225 g) fish fillet, coarsely chopped
¼ cup (60 ml) shredded bamboo shoots
4 dried black mushrooms, soaked and shredded
2 slices ginger, thinly shredded
½ pound (225 g) bean curd, shredded

2 slices cooked ham, cut into 1½" (4 cm) lengths
4½ tablespoons (67 ml) cornstarch solution
2¼ teaspoons (11 ml) salt
white pepper to taste
1-2 lightly beaten egg whites, added last
2 stalks green onion, chopped into ½" (1.5 cm) strips

1. Bring broth to a boil; add fish fillet, bamboo shoots, mushroom, ginger and bean curd. Reduce heat to medium low for 2 minutes.
2. Stir in remaining ingredients, except egg whites and green onions. When slightly thickened, remove from heat and slowly pour in beaten egg whites. Garnish with green onion and serve immediately.

 Hunger is cured by food, ignorance by study.

High Protein Cream of Corn Chowder

A cozy, warm and hearty soup, perfect for a rainy day, or a blue Monday. It's sure to brighten your spirits, with its cheerful combination of colors. Yes, China does grow corn!

6 cups (1½ L) soup stock
2 ginger slices, shredded
¼ cup (60 ml) frozen peas and carrots
10 straw mushrooms, sliced
1 square bean curd, ½ pound (225 g), cut into ½" (1.5 cm) cubes
15-ounce can cream of corn
1 peeled tomato, cut into ½" (1.5 cm) cubes

1½ teaspoons (7 ml) salt
1½ teaspoons (7 ml) wine
1 teaspoon (5 ml) sugar
pinch of white pepper
¼ teaspoon (1 ml) sesame oil
2½ tablespoons (37 ml) cornstarch solution
1 tablespoon (15 ml) chopped green onion

1. Bring soup stock and ginger to a boil. Reduce heat to medium-high.
2. Add peas and carrots, straw mushrooms and bean curd. Bring to a boil. Add remaining ingredients, except cornstarch solution and green onion. Bring to a boil.
3. Thicken with cornstarch solution and garnish with chopped green onions.

Remarks

- Seasonal fresh vegetables can be substituted for any of the vegetables listed here.
- Add another ½ tablespoon cornstarch solution if a thicker soup is desired.

 Curse not your wife in the evening, or you will have to sleep alone.

Hot and Sour Mandarin Soup

A soup with a definite bite, hot and spicy! The liberal use of vinegar and white pepper gives it a red zingy flavor. Variety is the spice of life and this recipe has just that. It is usually served in the very cold northern regions of China. There's no doubt about it—this soup will surely melt the snow on a very cold winter's day.

8 cups (2 L) soup stock
¼ pound (112 g) lean pork, shredded
2 dried black mushrooms, soaked and
    shredded
2-3 slices ginger
2-3 dried wood ears, soaked and
    shredded (optional)
½ square bean curd, ¼ pound (112 g),
    cut into ¼" x ¼" x 2" strips (0.75 x
    0.75 x 5 cm) (optional)
¼ cup (60 ml) shredded bamboo
    shoots
2 tablespoons (30 ml) mushrooms,
    sliced

1 slice cooked ham, shredded
    (optional)
½ cup (125 ml) vinegar
1 teaspoon (5 ml) white pepper
¾ teaspoon (3 ml) salt
1 teaspoon (5 ml) sesame oil
¾ teaspoon (3 ml) sugar
1 tablespoon (15 ml) dark soy sauce
1 teaspoon (5 ml) chili oil (optional)
2 eggs, lightly beaten
4 tablespoons (60 ml) cornstarch in 3
    tablespoons (43 ml) water
1 stalk green onion, shredded

1. Bring soup stock to a boil in a large pot and add shredded pork, black mushrooms, ginger and wood ears. Cook for 2-3 minutes; discard ginger.
2. Add remaining ingredients, except cornstarch, eggs and green onion. Reduce heat and simmer 2 minutes. Add cornstarch solution and cook until thickened and clear.
3. Remove from heat and slowly stir in beaten eggs. Garnish with green onion. Serve immediately.

Remarks

- If soup is to be prepared ahead of time, don't add cornstarch and eggs until serving time. Otherwise, the eggs will be overcooked and will spoil the appearance.
- The soup should be quite hot and sour. You can adjust the flavors by varying the amounts of white pepper, vinegar and chili oil.

Pork and Bean Sprout Soup

Recipes don't have to be complicated and expensive to be great. They can be simple, down to earth and still be interesting. You will surprise your guests first thing when you start your dinner with this traditional soup. This is perhaps one of the most popular soups in the Chinese household.

6 cups (1½ L) soup stock	**2 stalks green onion, shredded**
2 slices ginger	**1¼ teaspoons (6 ml) salt**
¼ pound (112 g) lean pork, cut into	**¼ teaspoon (1 ml) sesame oil**
thin 1" x 2" (2.5 cm x 5 cm) slices	**white pepper to taste**
½ pound (225 g) bean sprouts	

1. Bring soup stock to a boil. Add ginger and pork slices. Cook over medium heat for 5 minutes.
2. Add the remaining ingredients and continue to cook for 2 minutes. Serve hot.

Have you ever tried Burnt Finger Soup?

Rainbow Chowder

The crisp texture of the fresh vegetables adds an extra crunch to this gratifying chowder. The color, nutrition and taste will instantly turn any meat lover into a fish and vegetable lover.

6 cups (1½ L) soup stock
2 slices fresh ginger
4 ounces (112 g) Chinese cabbage
    (Napa), cut into 2" x ½" (5 cm x
    1.5 cm) strips
½ onion, julienned
½ cup (125 ml) carrot, julienned
2 stalks green onion, 1½-2" (4 cm x
    5 cm) strips
½ cup (125 ml) bean sprout

¼ cup (60 ml) fresh mushrooms, sliced
2-3 dried black mushrooms, soaked
    and julienned
¼ cup (60 ml) water chestnuts, sliced
    (optional)
1½ teaspoons (7 ml) sesame oil
2 teaspoons (10 ml) salt
2½ tablespoons (37 ml) cornstarch
    solution
dash of white pepper to taste

1. Bring soup stock and ginger to a boil; cook for 1½-2 minutes, then discard ginger.
2. Add cabbage, onion, and carrot to broth and cook for 2½ minutes.
3. Add remaining ingredients except cornstarch solution and cook for one minute.
4. Thicken with cornstarch to form a light chowder. Serve hot with a touch of pepper.

Sprouting Spring Soup

When you want something refreshing, extraordinary and light, try this. You'll be a better person for it! For a new twist add some sliced meat of your choice.

6 cups (1½ L) soup stock
2 slices ginger
1½ cups (370 ml) fresh bean sprouts
½ cup (123 ml) sliced water chestnuts

2 stalks green onion, cut in 1½" (4 cm) strips
1 teaspoon (5 ml) salt
1 teaspoon (5 ml) sesame oil
white pepper to taste

1. Bring soup stock and ginger to a boil and cook for 1½-2 minutes. Discard ginger.
2. Add remaining ingredients and cook over medium-high heat for 1½ minutes. Serve hot.

Remarks

- You can add 4 ounces of shredded chicken or pork and cook in broth for 2½-3 minutes if a meat soup is preferred.
- To make instant soup stock, use 1 small bouillon cube for each 2 cups of water.

Sunshine Soup with Dumplings

If you have pumpkins left over after Halloween, give this recipe a try. The color of this hearty soup mirrors the golden leaves of autumn.

6 cups (1½ L) soup stock
1 pound (450 g) pumpkin or any firm
    yellow winter squash, peeled and
    cut into 1" x 2" x ¼" (2.5 cm x 5
    cm x 0.75 cm) pieces
1 ounce (28 g) Chinese dried shrimp,
    soaked
3 stalks green onion, white part only,
    cut into 2" (5 cm) strips

1 tablespoon (15 ml) soy sauce
¾ cup (200 ml) flour
6 tablespoons (90 ml) water
¼ teaspoon (1 ml) salt
¼ teaspoon (1 ml) sugar

1. Bring soup stock to a boil. Add pumpkin, dried shrimp, green onions and soy sauce. Cover and cook over medium heat for 10-15 minutes.
2. Combine flour and water in a bowl. Add salt and sugar. Blend well to make a smooth batter.
3. Spoon 1 teaspoon portions of flour mixture into simmering pumpkin stock. Cook for 2-4 minutes or until dumplings are firm. Serve hot.

Remarks

- Dumplings may break if soup is boiling vigorously. Keep it to a slow simmer!

 The older ginger and cinnamon become, the more pungent is their flavor.

Traditional Chinese Soup Stock (Chicken)

Basic, but not forgotten—to make a good stock is to make a good soup!
Let yourself go and be creative!

1 whole chicken, approximately 2 pounds (900 g)
3 slices ginger
1½ stalks green onion
enough water to cover whole chicken
salt to taste

1. Cut chicken into several pieces. Skin and trim off fat; discard.
2. Place chicken, ginger, green onion and water into a large pot.
3. Bring to a boil, cover and simmer for about 2 hours. Salt to taste.
4. Skim off surface scum; remove chicken and seasoning. Reserve stock for soup or cooking sauces. Keep refrigerated.

Remarks

- The cooked chicken can be served with soy sauce or oyster sauce as a dip. Don't throw it away, unless you often do that with your money.
- If you do not wish to use the whole chicken, you can debone it and use just the bones for stock. In this case, you might have to use 3-4 chicken skeletons instead of one whole chicken.

Other Alternatives for Clear Broth

Chinese chefs use everything available to make broth—chicken, pork, fish bones, ham, beef, etc. Gourmet Chinese restaurants make a heavy broth using almost all of the mentioned ingredients at the same time.
   The following is another family-style homemade broth:

1 pound (450 g) pork bones
2 chicken carcasses
4 slices ginger
2 stalks green onion
water to cover
salt to taste

Prepare this the same way as the chicken broth.

Vegetarian Shark's Fin Soup

Shark's fin is one of the most expensive ingredients in a Chinese banquet; it is not an everyday item. I cannot afford it!! Fortunately, someone came up with this less expensive version of the shark's fin. I tried it once, and I cannot believe I ate the whole "fin!!"

6 cups (1½ L) soup stock
¾ teaspoon (3 ml) salt
2 slices ginger
1 teaspoon (5 ml) soy sauce
½ teaspoon (2 ml) sugar
½ teaspoon (2 ml) sesame oil
2 ounces (56 g) bean thread noodles, soaked
¼ cup (60 ml) straw mushrooms, sliced

¼ cup (125 ml) finely shredded bamboo shoots
5 dried black mushrooms, soaked and shredded
2 tablespoons (30 ml) finely shredded green onion
2 tablespoons (30 ml) cornstarch solution
dash of white pepper
6-8 sprigs of Chinese parsley

1. Bring soup stock to a boil; add salt and ginger; cook over medium heat for 1-2 minutes. Discard ginger and add soy sauce, sugar and sesame oil.
2. Drain bean thread noodles and add to stock along with remaining vegetables. Boil over medium-high heat for 2 minutes.
3. Thicken with cornstarch solution. Sprinkle with white pepper and garnish with Chinese parsley to serve.

Remarks

• Be sure to have extra soup stock on hand as bean threads soak up water.

 When the sky is clear, carry an umbrella; though your stomach is full, carry provisions.

Saucy Dips

The use of sauces is as indispensable in Chinese cooking as it is in French cuisine. The Chinese have a great variety of sauces and dips, each with its own particular flavor and purpose. Here are a few of the most popular and frequently used combinations that you can prepare ahead of time.

Basic Chicken Stock

Although there are hundreds of soups in Chinese cooking, most begin with a basic stock: meat or poultry bones, vegetables, herbs and spices cooked into a rich broth. In this humble publication, soup stock is also used instead of monosodium glutamate (MSG) to season dishes. Prepare a large quantity of stock and freeze it for future use.

6 cups (1½ L) water
2½ pounds (1025 g) chicken bones
    (legs, wings, necks, etc.)
3 stalks green onion

4-5 slices ginger
pinch of white pepper
salt to taste

Bring 6 cups of water to a boil over high heat. Add chicken bones and reduce heat to medium-low. Cover and simmer for 1½ hours. Occasionally skim foam from soup while cooking. Add ginger, green onion and remaining seasoning. Continue to simmer for 20-25 minutes. Strain and discard solid ingredients. Keep stock in refrigerator or freezer.

A Good Batter Mix

Don't believe that all Chinese dishes are deep-fried. Actually only a limited number of dishes are prepared in this fashion. For those who like crispy, golden fried food, here is a delectable batter. It is puffy, crispy and absolutely sensational.

¾ cup (200 ml) flour
¼ cup (60 ml) cornstarch
½ teaspoon (2 ml) sugar

¾ cup (200 ml) flat beer (or water)
¾ teaspoon (3 ml) baking powder
¾ teaspoon (3 ml) oil

Combine all ingredients in a large bowl. Mix well until batter is smooth and light. If water is used, increase baking powder to 1¼-1½ teaspoons. Important message! It is very common to deep-fry batter foods a second time in order to achieve an extra crispy texture. To do this, deep-fry once, let food cool thoroughly, then deep-fry a second time over high heat for 45 seconds to 1 minute. Serve immediately. This practice will produce a crispy golden brown product and should apply to all deep-fry batter dishes.

Black Bean Sauce

Salted black beans are frequently called for in Chinese recipes. Keeping black bean sauce on hand will save a lot of time when entertaining or fixing quick meals for the family. This recipe makes enough sauce to season many tasty dishes.

8 ounces salted black beans
6 medium cloves garlic, finely minced
¼ cup (60 ml) brown sugar
4½ tablespoons (67 ml) oil

Rinse salted black beans and drain well. Combine black beans and minced garlic in a bowl. Mash until blended. Mix in sugar and oil and steam over high heat for 10-12 minutes. Cool and transfer to a covered jar. This will keep several weeks in the refrigerator.

Bouillon Cubes

These are great when you are in an absolute rush. Bouillon cubes are frequently used by Chinese homemakers in place of homemade soup stock. They're especially helpful in last-minute cooking decisions as a fill-in flavor. Most Chinese cooks prefer the Swiss bouillon cubes to the American ones because of their more delicate flavor and softer texture; they're also easier to handle and less salty. If the American bouillon cube is used in stir-frying as a seasoning, dissolve 1 cube (1½ cc) of bouillon in 1-1½ cups of water, used as needed. To prepare instant stock, dissolve to adjust to your taste.

Garlic Dip

This is a popular dipping sauce for many northern-style cold meat dishes.

2 tablespoons (30 ml) finely minced garlic
¼ cup (60 ml) white vinegar

Combine garlic and vinegar in a small bowl. Let stand for several hours before serving.

Ginger Juice

Prepare enough ginger juice for several days. It keeps well in the refrigerator.

¼ cup (60 ml) finely chopped ginger

1. Place ginger in garlic press and squeeze juice into a small bowl or jar, or
2. Wrap ginger in a piece of cheese cloth or muslin and squeeze juice into a small bowl or jar. Sprinkle ginger with 1 tablespoon water and squeeze until you are totally exhausted!

Ginger Wine

Some recipes call for ginger-flavored wine for cooking. Once prepared it can be kept for several weeks in the refrigerator.

½ cup (125 ml) Shao Shing wine or dry sherry
14-16 slices ginger

Combine ginger slices and wine in an air tight bottle. Let stand for several days before using.

Ginger and Green Onion Dip

This is a popular dip for Cantonese dishes, such as steamed or parboiled fish, prawns, oysters and plain cut chicken.

2-3 stalks green onion, white part only
4-5 slices ginger
¾ teaspoon (3 ml) salt
5 tablespoons (75 ml) oil

Cut green onion and ginger into fine shreds. Toss in salt and set aside. Heat oil and pour over ginger and onion mixture. Refrigerate and use within 1-2 days.

Gourmet Soup Stock

A good stock serves as a base for great soups or a delicious dish. This expensive recipe is worth the price! You will be able to enjoy the best of dishes!

6 cups (1½ L) water
1 whole stewing hen (cleaned & trimmed)
2 ounces (56 g) Smithfield ham, cut into ½" (1.5 cm) cubes

4-5 slices ginger
3 stalks green onion
pinch of white pepper
salt to taste

Combine chicken and ham in a large pot. Cover with water and bring to a boil. Reduce heat to medium-low and simmer for 1½-2 hours. Skim foam from soup frequently. Add ginger, green onion, pepper and salt and continue to simmer for 1-1½ hours. Strain stock and discard bones and seasonings. Store in refrigerator.

Homemade Plum Sauce

A lot of my students and audiences have requested a recipe for plum sauce, which is commonly used as a dip for egg rolls and almost anything else imaginable. Here is a very simple recipe; prepare it and keep it in the refrigerator to use on anything you wish.

1 cup (250 ml) Chinese plum sauce
¾ cup (200 ml) applesauce
½ cup (125 ml) apricot preserves
½ cup (125 ml) crushed pineapple

¼ cup (60 ml) chili sauce
½ teaspoon (2 ml) garlic juice
2 teaspoons (10 ml) sugar
2 teaspoons (10 ml) vinegar

1. Discard any solid pieces from Chinese plum sauce.
2. Combine all ingredients and put in blender. Blend for 2 minutes.
3. Transfer to a sauce pan and cook over medium heat for 3-4 minutes. Let cool and put in a covered jar. Serve cool.

Remarks

- If Chinese plum sauce is not available, use ½ cup of salted plums, well-rinsed and mashed. Then increase sugar in the recipe by 1 teaspoon.

Spicy Salt Dip

This is a popular and traditional Cantonese seasoning salt. It is served as a dip with duck, chicken and squab. It is excellent as a meat marinade too.

8 tablespoons (120 ml) salt
3 teaspoons (15 ml) five-spice powder

Heat salt in a dry skillet over medium heat. Stir continuously until light brown. Turn off heat and mix in five-spice powder. Cool and transfer to a glass bottle.

Sweet and Sour Sauce (Traditional)

There are countless versions of sweet and sour sauce. Some are too sweet, others are too sour and most lack character! Here is a well-balanced recipe used by traditional Chinese chefs.

¼ cup (60 ml) vinegar
¼ cup (60 ml) sugar
6 tablespoons (90 ml) water
¾ teaspoon (3 ml) soy sauce
½ teaspoon (2 ml) finely minced
    ginger

1½ teaspoons (7 ml) finely chopped
    green onion
2½ teaspoons (12 ml) cornstarch
1 teaspoon (5 ml) oil, heated

Combine all ingredients in saucepan and bring to a boil. Cook stirring continuously until thick and smooth. Cover and keep warm.

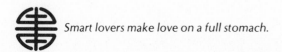 *Smart lovers make love on a full stomach.*

Sweet Bean Paste Dip

This is a popular dip served with Peking Duck, Mushi Pork and numerous other dishes. I discovered that it is absolutely terrific with rice, noodles, hot dogs and hamburgers too!

¼ cup (60 ml) sweet bean paste or hoi-
    sin sauce
3½ tablespoons (52 ml) sugar

6-8 tablespoons (90-120 ml) water
2½ tablespoons (37 ml) sesame oil

Combine sweet bean paste, sugar and water in a bowl. Heat sesame oil in a saucepan over medium-high heat for 1 minute. Add sweet bean paste mixture and cook stirring continuously until thickened. Keep in covered jar in the refrigerator.

Toasted Szechwan Pepper Salt

This is another widely used seasoning salt. It is a pungent and aromatic dip which complements many dishes.

2 tablespoons (30 ml) Szechwan peppercorns
½ cup (125 ml) salt

Stir Szechwan peppercorns in a dry skillet over medium heat for about 1-1½ minutes until fragrant. Remove and grind with a mortar and pestle or rolling pin. Heat salt in the same skillet until color turns light brown. Remove and mix with toasted peppercorns.

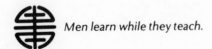 *Men learn while they teach.*

How to Marinate Different Meats

In a gourmet Chinese restaurant, it is a common practice to marinate meat before cooking. Here is a simple guide for your reference. The following is based on one pound (½ kilo) of meat. Choose whatever suits you for a particular dish. Use your own judgement and imagination. Experiment and develop your own formula for perfectly marinated meats.

Pork:

½ teaspoon (2 ml) sugar
2½ teaspoons (12 ml) light soy sauce
2 teaspoons (10 ml) cornstarch
2 teaspoons (10 ml) wine
½ teaspoon (2 ml) sesame oil
½ teaspoon (2 ml) pepper
2 tablespoons (30 ml) water (optional)
1½ teaspoons (7 ml) oil (add last)

Marinating time: 2 hours.

Beef:

¾ teaspoon (3 ml) sugar
2½ teaspoons (12 ml) light soy sauce
2½ teaspoons (12 ml) cornstarch
2 teaspoons (10 ml) wine
½ teaspoon (2 ml) sesame oil
½ teaspoon (2 ml) pepper
2 tablespoons (30 ml) water (optional)
1½ tablespoons (22 ml) oil (add last)

Marinating time: 1½-2 hours

Lamb:

¾ teaspoon (3 ml) sugar
2½ teaspoons (12 ml) light soy sauce
2½ teaspoons (12 ml) cornstarch
2 teaspoons (10 ml) wine
1 teaspoon (5 ml) ginger juice
½ teaspoon (2 ml) sesame oil
½ teaspoon (2 ml) pepper
2 tablespoons (30 ml) water (optional)
1½ tablespoons (22 ml) oil (add last)

Marinating time: 2 hours

Chicken:

½ teaspoon (2 ml) sugar
½ teaspoon (2 ml) salt
1 egg white
2 teaspoons (10 ml) cornstarch
2 teaspoons (10 ml) wine
2 teaspoons (10 ml) ginger juice
½ teaspoon (2 ml) sesame oil
½ teaspoon (2 ml) pepper
2 tablespoons (30 ml) water (optional)
1½ tablespoons (21 ml) oil (add last)

Marinating time: ½ hour

Fish:

½ teaspoon (2 ml) salt
1 teaspoon (5 ml) light soy sauce
1 egg white
2 teaspoons (10 ml) cornstarch
1 teaspoon (5 ml) ginger juice
½ teaspoon (2 ml) sesame oil
½ teaspoon (2 ml) pepper

Marinating time: ½ hour

Prawn:

½ teaspoon (2 ml) salt
1 egg white
2 teaspoons (10 ml) cornstarch
½ teaspoon (2 ml) sesame oil
½ teaspoon (2 ml) pepper

Marinating time: ½ hour

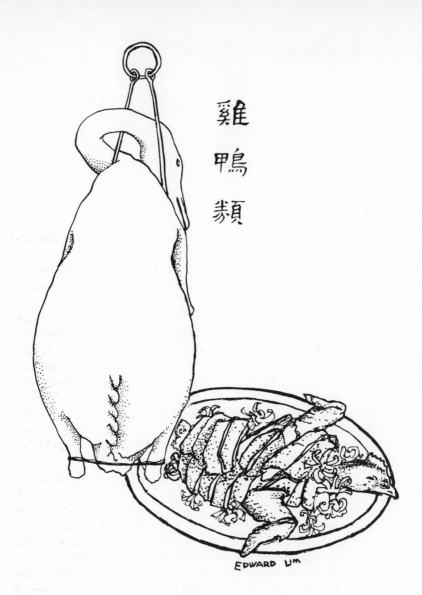

雞鴨鳥
類

EDWARD UM

Fowl Plays—Poultry

In Chinese cuisine, poultry is considered to be elegant, versatile and nutritious. Chicken is the most common meat used in Chinese cooking besides pork. It is served in a variety of dishes from very simple to simply exotic. Chicken livers and gizzards are considered delicacies, and are not discarded, but used as complementary ingredients.

When a chicken is cooked, the breast meat becomes fully cooked and dry before the dark meat is tender. So although every piece of the bird is used, the different pieces are often cooked separately. By using skill and imagination, you can prepare a meal with several chicken dishes prepared in totally different ways, each with distinctive tastes. The Chinese distinguish between the modern commercially-fed chicken which is given shots to speed up its growth and the better-flavored old-fashioned chicken which is allowed to run loose. Here is how many Chinese impress a guest—to show the guest that he is esteemed, the host will kill a chicken in his honor.

Duck is another favorite in Chinese cooking. Peking duck and roasted duck are well known to the North American public and are universally enjoyed. The Chinese mostly prepare duck by steaming, deep frying or simmering because the oven is not standard in a Chinese kitchen.

Squab and other wild fowl are also served in Chinese cuisine. Formal occasions are usually the times these are included on the menu.

Once you have experimented with these fabulous recipes using poultry, it will be hard to go back to fried chicken! They are each unique and tasty, sure to become favorites among your family and friends.

Almond Gai Ding

This is one of the most popular Cantonese dishes. "Gai" means chicken, "ding" means diced, and "Hung Yun" is almond. The whole dish should be called "Hung Yun Gai Ding." If you want to go Chinese, you might as well go all the way.

½ pound (225 g) boneless chicken breast, cut into ½" (1.5 cm) cubes

Chicken Marinade:
1 teaspoon (5 ml) soy sauce
1 teaspoon (5 ml) wine
1 teaspoon (5 ml) cornstarch

3 tablespoons (45 ml) oil
2 teaspoons (10 ml) chopped ginger
1 teaspoon (5 ml) chopped garlic
½ medium-sized carrot, cut into ½" (1.5 cm) cubes
½ cup (125 ml) soup stock

1 stalk celery, cut into ½" (1.5 cm) cubes
½ green pepper, cut into ½" (1.5 cm) cubes
½ cup (125 ml) water chestnuts, cut into ½" (1.5 cm) cubes (optional)
½ cup (125 ml) ½" (1.5 cm) cubes bamboo shoots
½ teaspoon (2 ml) salt
¾ teaspoon (3 ml) sugar
½ teaspoon (2 ml) sesame oil
1½ teaspoons (7 ml) cornstarch solution
½ cup (125 ml) toasted almonds, added at last minute

1. Marinate chicken for 30 minutes.
2. Heat 2 tablespoons oil in wok over high heat; stir in ginger and garlic and cook for 10-15 seconds. Add chicken and stir-fry until color turns white. Remove and set aside.
3. Heat wok with 1 tablespoon oil over high heat; add carrot and stir-fry 15 seconds. Add ¼ cup soup stock. Cover and cook for 1½ minutes. Add the remaining vegetables and ¼ cup soup stock, stirring for another 1½ minutes. Stir in remaining ingredients except almonds and cook until thickened.
4. Sprinkle almonds on top before serving.

Remarks

• Toasted or deep-fried unsalted almonds can be used. Other nuts may be substituted.

 If two men feed a horse, it will be thin; if two men mend a boat, it will leak.

Chicken and Cauliflower Foo Yung

Simple, elegant and delicious, this dish will remind you of one of your favorite fairy tales—*Snow White.* The color could even entice Grumpy to give it a try.

½ **medium-size cauliflower, cut into small flowerets**
2 **tablespoons (30 ml) oil**
2 **tablespoons (30 ml) chopped cooked ham**

Clear Sauce:
½ **cup (125 ml) broth**
dash sesame oil
¼ **teaspoon (1 ml) salt**
dash white pepper
1½ **teaspoons (7 ml) cornstarch solution**

Foo Yung Sauce:
4 **ounces (112 g) chicken breast, minced**
3 **egg whites**
2½ **tablespoons (37 ml) half & half**
1 **teaspoon (5 ml) cornstarch**
½ **teaspoon (2 ml) salt**
dash white pepper

1. Blanch cauliflower in boiling water for 3 minutes. Drain and set aside. Combine ingredients for clear sauce and set aside.
2. Combine ingredients for Foo Yung sauce and beat until slightly stiff.
3. Heat a non-sticking pan or wok with oil over high heat. Put in Foo Yung sauce and stir continuously for 1 minute. Add cauliflower and mix well. Stir in clear sauce, top with chopped ham and serve immediately.

Chicken in the Pot

No food is really enjoyed unless it is keenly anticipated, discussed, eaten and then commented on. Chicken in the Pot will get the positive comments and compliments from those who dare to experience its tantalizing taste.

1 small whole chicken, split in half
2 stalks green onion, cut into 3" (7.5 cm) strips
4 slices ginger
5 cups (1¼ L) soup stock
¼ cup (60 ml) wine

1¼ teaspoons (6 ml) salt
2 teaspoons (10 ml) sugar
3 tablespoons (45 ml) soy sauce
1 pound (450 g) Chinese cabbage or bok choy, cut into 1½" x 1½" (4 cm x 4 cm) pieces

1. Place chicken halves, green onion and ginger in an oven-proof casserole dish. Pour in soup stock and bring to a slow boil over medium heat. Remove from heat and remove scum. Add wine, salt, sugar and soy sauce.
2. Cover and simmer over low heat for 1-1¼ hours until tender.
3. Blanch cabbage in boiling water for about 1½ minutes. Add cabbage to casserole and continue to cook for 3-5 minutes.
4. Serve directly from the casserole.

Remarks

- When chicken is cooked, it will be so tender you can cut it with a fork.
- Use the leftover juice to pour over rice or as noodle soup base. You can also save it for stock.

 Viands have various flavors; what pleases the palate is good.

Chinese Roasted Chicken

Delight your guests with this elegant chicken entree. A dramatic presentation of sweet, golden brown skin with colorful stuffing

1 whole frying chicken, 1½ pounds
   (675 g)
1 teaspoon (5 ml) salt
1½ tablespoons (22 ml) oil
2 cloves garlic, chopped
½ cup (125 ml) frozen peas and carrots
¼ cup (60 ml) diced zucchini
3 tablespoons (45 ml) diced onion

4 water chestnuts, chopped
4 slices ginger
2 stalks green onion, chopped
¼ cup (60 ml) soaked and diced dried
   black mushrooms
2 tablespoons (30 ml) cooking wine
1½ tablespoons (22 ml) dark soy sauce
2 teaspoons (10 ml) sugar
2 teaspoons (10 ml) cornstarch

1. Sprinkle 1 teaspoon salt on surface skin and inside cavity of chicken. Let stand for 2 hours.
2. Heat oil and garlic in wok over high heat. Add all vegetables and stir-fry for 1-2 minutes. Stir in remaining ingredients and cook until thickened. Stuff inside of chicken with mixture. Secure opening with skewers.
3. Preheat oven to 350° and bake 1-1¼ hours, turning chicken occasionally for even browning.
4. To serve, remove stuffing and place in the center of a platter. Cut chicken into bite-size pieces and arrange on top of stuffing. Garnish and serve hot.

Remarks

- For a golden-brown skin, before serving, baste chicken with a mixture of 1 tablespoon (15 ml) dark soy sauce and 2 tablespoons (30 ml) honey; broil. Watch carefully to avoid burning.

Chrysanthemum Chicken

It's spring and the darkness of winter has left—especially when you serve this entree, a beautiful dish to use as a centerpiece but too good to just look at. The delicate aroma of the chrysanthemums gives a refreshing zest to this tender, juicy chicken.

2-3 large chrysanthemum flowers
⅔ pound (300 g) chicken breast, cut
    into 1" x 2" (2.5 cm x 5 cm) thin
    slices
3 tablespoons (45 ml) oil
2 slices ginger, chopped
1 tablespoon (15 ml) wine

Marinade for Chicken:
1½ tablespoons (22 ml) wine
½ teaspoon (2 ml) salt
dash of white pepper
½ teaspoon (2 ml) sugar
½ egg white, lightly beaten

1. Wash chrysanthemums in salt water and separate the petals. Let drain and set aside.
2. Marinate chicken for 10 minutes.
3. Heat wok with oil and fry ginger over high heat; add chicken and stir-fry for 2-3 minutes.
4. Add flower petals; stir for another minute.
5. Stir in 1 teaspoon wine.
6. To serve, surround chicken with flower heads and serve hot.

Remarks

- When putting chicken in hot oil, stir immediately to avoid sticking and burning of egg whites.
- Dish is supposed to be quite dry—do not expect a sauce.

 The fish sees the bait, not the hook; man sees the gain, not the danger.

Coconut Chicken Casserole

This is an adaptation of a Western dish that has established its own place in many Chinese menus. It is rich, flavorful and very easy to make. The availability of fresh coconut inspired me to share this marvelous recipe.

½ chicken, about 1¼ pound (562 g), fat trimmed

Chicken Marinade:
1 teaspoon (5 ml) salt
1½ teaspoons (7 ml) soy sauce
1½ teaspoons (7 ml) sugar
2 tablespoons (30 ml) curry powder
1 teaspoon (5 ml) wine
1 teaspoon (5 ml) flour

2½ tablespoons (37 ml) oil
2 cloves garlic, chopped
2 slices ginger, chopped
1 large onion, diced

1 medium carrot, cut into 1" (2.5 cm) cubes
1 medium-ripe tomato, cut into 1" (2.5 cm) cubes
1 medium potato, cut into 1" (2.5 cm) cubes

Coconut Sauce:
1¼ cups (310 ml) coconut milk
½ cup (125 ml) evaporated milk
dash of black pepper
2 teaspoons (10 ml) butter
¼ cup (60 ml) soup stock

1. Marinate chicken for 30 minutes.
2. Combine coconut sauce ingredients; set aside.
3. Heat 1½ tablespoons oil in wok over high heat. Add garlic, onion and ginger and stir for 1 minute. Stir in carrot and cook for 10 seconds. Add remaining tablespoon of oil and fry for another 1½ minutes, turning to brown on all sides.
4. Mix in remaining vegetables and coconut sauce; bring to a boil. Reduce heat to medium and simmer until liquid is slightly reduced, about 5-10 minutes. Transfer to a casserole dish, cover and bake for 25-30 minutes at 375°F (190°C).

Chinese clay pot for soups and casseroles.

Colorful Chicken Velvet

A rainbow full of colors and textures! This is a truly unusual chicken dish with a light and fluffy texture.

½ pound (225 g) boneless chicken
    breast
1½ teaspoons (7 ml) cornstarch
1¼ cups (310 ml) chicken broth
7 egg whites, beaten until smooth
1 tablespoon (15 ml) wine

½ teaspoon (2 ml) salt
pepper to taste
1 cup (250 ml) oil
⅓ cup (80 ml) green peas
2 dried black mushrooms, soaked and
    diced
2½ tablespoons (37 ml) chopped ham

1. Cut chicken into small cubes. Put cornstarch, 1 cup broth and chicken in a blender. Mince in blender until fine.
2. Transfer blended chicken to a bowl. Add beaten egg whites and stir until smooth; add wine, salt, and pepper; mix well.
3. Heat a non-stick pan with 1 cup oil to near smoke point. Reduce to medium-low and keep heat constant. Stir chicken mixture well and add it to the oil, ½ cup at a time. Gently stir for 1 minute. Mixture will look like a large puffy pancake. Turn over and cook for another minute.
4. When mixture is set, transfer to a strainer to drain off oil.
5. Put 2 teaspoons oil in wok; stir-fry peas and mushrooms over medium heat for 30 seconds. Gently fold in chicken mixture. Add extra broth if mixture gets too dry.
6. To serve, garnish with chopped ham and serve immediately.

Remarks

• If oil is not hot enough, increase heat when cooking chicken mixture.

Crispy Chicken Breast with Almonds

This dish has a thousand names. A crispy fried chicken topped with a delicious mixture of almond sauce, it's great for entertaining!!

8 ounces (225 g) boneless chicken breast
2 teaspoons (10 ml) wine
½ teaspoon (3 ml) salt
2 tablespoons (30 ml) cornstarch for dry coating
4 cups (1 L) oil
½ head of lettuce, shredded
1 tablespoon (15 ml) ground roasted almonds for garnishing

Almond Sauce:
2 tablespoons (30 ml) oyster-flavored sauce
1 teaspoon (5 ml) soy sauce
¼ cup (60 ml) soup stock
¾ teaspoon (4 ml) sugar
pinch of white pepper
1 teaspoon (5 ml) oil
1 tablespoon (15 ml) ground roasted almonds
¾ teaspoon (4 ml) cornstarch

Batter Mix:
¾ cup (200 ml) flour
¾ cup (200 ml) flat beer (or water)
¾ teaspoon (4 ml) baking powder (if using water increase to 1¼ teaspoons)
¼ teaspoon (2 ml) sugar
½ teaspoon (3 ml) oil
¼ cup (60 ml) cornstarch

1. Place chicken breast on cutting board; slant-cut horizontally into 2 thin slices equal in size. (Be careful when doing this.) Marinate with wine and salt for 30 minutes, then dry-coat with cornstarch; set aside.
2. Combine almond sauce ingredients except cornstarch in a sauce pan. Bring to a boil and thicken with cornstarch to a smooth consistency. Keep warm.
3. Combine batter mix in a bowl and blend well; set aside.
4. Heat oil in wok over medium-high heat until smoke begins to appear. Reduce heat to medium. Dip dry-coated chicken breasts into batter and slowly drop in hot oil. Use a chopstick or strainer to move or turn chicken while deep frying. Cook for about 2 minutes on each side or until golden brown. Drain and cut into 2" x 3" slices.
5. To serve, place shredded lettuce on a large platter. Put fried chicken on top of lettuce. Pour sauce over and sprinkle with 1 tablespoon ground almonds. Serve immediately.

Remarks
• Pour sauce over chicken right before serving to retain crispiness.

Crispy Chicken Wings with Lemon Dip

You might not be able to find the pot of gold, but with this dish, you've found a real treasure. An innovative dish—golden fried chicken with the delightful fragrance of lemon.

12 chicken wings
4 cups (1 L) oil

Chicken Marinade:
1½ tablespoons (22 ml) wine
1½ teaspoons (7 ml) ginger juice
½ teaspoon (2 ml) garlic juice
1 teaspoon (5 ml) salt
1 tablespoon (15 ml) cornstarch

Lemon Dip:
¼ cup (60 ml) soup stock
3 tablespoons (45 ml) fresh lemon juice
1 tablespoon (15 ml) vinegar
1 tablespoon (15 ml) soy sauce
1 teaspoon (5 ml) fresh lime juice
1 teaspoon (5 ml) sugar

1. Marinate chicken wings for 2 hours.
2. Mix lemon dip mixture in a bowl and set aside.
3. Heat oil in wok over high heat. Deep-fry chicken wings, 6 at a time, until golden brown—about 4-5 minutes. Reduce heat to medium if chicken is browning too quickly.
4. To serve, dip fried chicken wings in lemon sauce and serve hot.

If you don't know how to cook—wing it;

and then duck out!

Drunk Duck Fruity-Flavored Casserole

This casserole is dedicated to my fine-feathered friends and to those who enjoy eating my fine-feathered friends! The duck is cooked in a delicately balanced fruity sauce; it's out of this world with flavor.

½ duck (about 2 pounds or 900 g), cut
    in half
1 small sprig leek
¼ cup (60 ml) wine
3 slices ginger
1 teaspoon (5 ml) cornstarch

Fruit Sauce:
½ cup (125 ml) soup stock
⅔ cup (160 ml) wine
2½ tablespoons (37 ml) dark soy sauce
1 ounce (28 g) rock sugar or 2 table-
    spoons (30 ml) brown sugar
¾ orange, sliced
¼ lemon, sliced
1 piece dried tangerine (optional)

1. Trim excess fat from duck. Immerse duck in boiling water. Add leek, wine and ginger and boil for 1½ minutes. Remove duck and set aside.
2. Combine fruit sauce ingredients in a bowl; mix well.
3. Place duck in a casserole dish; add fruit sauce. Cover and bake in a preheated oven at 375°F (190°C), for 1½ hours.
4. Discard lemon and orange slices. Transfer duck to a platter. Thicken ½ cup of leftover sauce with 1 teaspoon cornstarch and pour over duck. Garnish with extra orange slices.

 Food enlivens the spirit and enthusiasm for mankind.

Five-Spice Crispy Duck

Daffy Duck finally made it into the soup pot. And surprisingly enough, he's tender when marinated in an exotic sauce. Fried to a crispy golden brown, a truly gourmet dish!

4 cups (1 L) soup stock
2½ tablespoons (37 ml) dark soy sauce
½ teaspoon (2 ml) salt
2 pieces star anise
2 slices ginger
1½ tablespoons (22 ml) brown sugar
½ duck, about 2 pounds (900 g)
1½ teaspoon (7 ml) five-spice powder

1½ tablespoons (22 ml) salted black beans
2 tablespoons (30 ml) wine
1 tablespoon (15 ml) cornstarch
1½ tablespoons (22 ml) flour
6 cups (1½ L) oil
¼ cup (60 ml) fruit chutney or plum sauce

1. Bring soup stock to a boil, add soy sauce, sugar, salt, ginger and star anise. Place duck in stock and reduce heat to low. Cover and simmer for 1½ hours until tender.
2. Remove duck and dry well.
3. Combine five-spice powder, salted black beans and wine; mash to a paste. Rub sauce mixture evenly inside and outside of duck.
4. Mix cornstarch and flour and slightly pat onto the outside of duck. Let stand dry for 30 minutes.
5. Deep-fry duck in hot oil at medium high until golden brown. Drain well and cut into bite-size pieces.
6. To serve, arrange duck and serve with fruit chutney or plum sauce.

Remarks

• Try this dish with a whole chicken in the same way.

Fried Walnut Chicken

Serving walnut chicken as an appetizer or entree for a formal dinner party is your best bet to win a new friend. The tender, juicy chicken fillet, coated with aromatic walnuts, is out of this world. Even better, serve it with a tempting sweet and sour sauce and it's absolutely heavenly.

10 ounces (280 g) boneless chicken breast
2 teaspoons (10 ml) wine
¾ teaspoon (4 ml) salt
2 egg whites, lightly beaten
¼ cup (60 ml) cornstarch
1½ cups (375 ml) chopped walnuts
4 cups (1 L) oil

Dipping sauce: (optional)
3 tablespoons (45 ml) vinegar
3 tablespoons (45 ml) sugar
¼ cup (60 ml) water
¼ teaspoon (1 ml) Tabasco sauce
2 teaspoons (10 ml) oil, heated
1½ teaspoons (7 ml) cornstarch solution

1. Cut chicken into bite-size pieces and marinate with wine and salt for 20 minutes.
2. Combine cornstarch and egg whites; blend well. Set aside.
3. Dip chicken into the white mixture, then coat with walnuts. Roll chicken around and lightly press to coat well with walnuts.
4. Heat oil in wok over medium heat and deep fry until golden brown.
5. Combine dipping sauce ingredients except cornstarch in a saucepan. Bring to a boil and thicken with cornstarch for a smooth consistency. Keep warm.
6. Serve walnut chicken with your cocktails, with or without the dipping sauce.

 Good wine reddens the face; riches excite the mind.

Fruity-Flavored Chicken

I had a dream and it came true. It is expressed in this chicken dish with its harmonious blend of citrus fruit flavors—absolutely sensational!

12 ounces (340 g) boneless chicken, cut into bite-size pieces
3 tablespoons (45 ml) oil
2 teaspoons (10 ml) cornstarch solution

Chicken Marinade:
1 tablespoon (15 ml) soy sauce
4 teaspoons (20 ml) wine
2 teaspoons (10 ml) cornstarch

Fresh Fruit Sauce:
3 tablespoons (45 ml) lemon juice
2 tablespoons (30 ml) orange juice
1 tablespoon (15 ml) lime juice
2 tablespoons (30 ml) fresh pineapple juice (optional)
2 tablespoons (30 ml) sugar
2 teaspoons (10 ml) ginger juice
¼ cup (60 ml) water
dash of salt

1. Marinate chicken for 30 minutes.
2. Combine ingredients for fruit sauce and set aside.
3. Heat wok with oil and stir-fry chicken over high heat for 1½-2 minutes.
4. Pour in fruit sauce mixture except cornstarch solution. Reduce heat to simmer. Cover and cook for 2-3 minutes.
5. Add cornstarch solution and thicken.

Remarks

- Garnish serving plate with additional slices of lemon.

Garlic-Flavored Chicken

It was once said in New York, "The only thing 50 cents will get you these days is a seat on the subway." Garlic will get you a seat in no time! Here's a power-packed dish that will remind you of your Italian mother's cooking.

1 pound (450 g) chicken, cut into 1" x
   2" x ¼" (2.5 cm x 5 cm x 0.75 cm)
   pieces
3 cloves garlic, finely chopped
1 tablespoon (15 ml) wine
1 tablespoon (15 ml) soy sauce
2 teaspoons (10 ml) garlic salt

¼ teaspoon (1 ml) sugar
2 eggs, lightly beaten
3 tablespoons (45 ml) flour
dash of five-spice powder (optional)
4 cups (1 L) oil

1. Combine chicken with garlic, wine, soy sauce, garlic salt and sugar; marinate for 2 hours.
2. Add beaten eggs and flour to chicken and mix well.
3. Heat oil in wok near smoke point. Reduce heat to medium. Deep-fry chicken for 2-3 minutes or until tender.

Stuff which end?

91

Kuei-Fei Chicken

Ever thought of eating like an empress? This dish was named after an empress who reigned about 1,300 years ago in the Dan Dynasty. She probably ate many elaborate dishes but also often enjoyed this simple, down-to-earth creation.

2 tablespoons (30 ml) oil
2-3 slices ginger
2 stalks green onion
12 chicken wings, split at joint
½ pound (225 g) bamboo shoots, cut into 1" x ½" x ½" (2.5 cm x 1.5 cm x 1.5 cm) pieces

4-6 dried black mushrooms, soaked then cut in half
2½ tablespoons (37 ml) soy sauce
1 tablespoon (15 ml) dark soy sauce
½ cup (125 ml) soup stock
1 tablespoon (15 ml) wine
2 teaspoons (10 ml) brown sugar

1. Heat oil in wok over high heat. Put in ginger and green onion and stir for 15-20 seconds. Add wings and sauté until light brown, approximately 3-4 minutes.
2. Add the remaining ingredients except cornstarch solution and simmer over low heat for 25-30 minutes. Stir in cornstarch solution and cook until thickened.

 The help one gives to others will never fail to return as a surprise.

Luscious Lemon Chicken

The taste of this dish will send you straight to heaven and you will never want to return!! A refreshing tang of lemon enhances the delicate flavor of fresh chicken, making this a memorable entree, sure to be requested by the family time after time.

½ pound (225 g) chicken or 2 breasts,
　boned
2½ tablespoons (37 ml) oil
2 tablespoons (30 ml) fresh lemon
　juice
2 tablespoons (30 ml) green onion
¼ cup (60 ml) soup stock
1 tablespoon (15 ml) wine
1½ tablespoons (37 ml) brown sugar
½ lemon, thinly sliced
1 teaspoon (5 ml) cornstarch solution

Chicken marinade:
½ teaspoon (2 ml) salt
2 teaspoons (10 ml) wine
dash black pepper
1 teaspoon (5 ml) ginger juice

1. Cut chicken into 1½" (4 cm) squares; marinate for 30 minutes.
2. Heat oil in wok over high heat and stir-fry chicken for 1½-2 minutes. Add the remaining ingredients except cornstarch and lemon. Mix well and reduce heat to medium-low. Cover and simmer for 1½ minutes. Add lemon slices and continue to cook for 1 minute.
3. Thicken with cornstarch; garnish with extra lemon slices.

Remarks

• This dish lends itself to elaborate garnishes. Be creative!! Try encircling the chicken with twists of lemon on a special platter.

Minced Chicken and Lima Beans

A delightful dish; what a dynamite combination of textures and tastes! This dish is great for a light dinner; enough to satisfy but not enough to add those extra calories.

½ pound (225 g) chicken breast, finely minced
¾ teaspoon (3 ml) salt
4 teaspoons (20 ml) wine
4 egg whites, lightly beaten
1 cup (250 ml) lima beans, frozen

2½ tablespoons (37 ml) oil
1 cup (250 ml) soup stock
1½ teaspoons (7 ml) cornstarch solution
2½ tablespoons (37 ml) cooked ham, chopped
1 tablespoon (15 ml) Chinese parsley, chopped

1. Combine minced chicken with salt and wine. Slowly mix in egg whites.
2. Blanch frozen lima beans in boiling water for 30-45 seconds. Remove and drain well.
3. Heat wok with oil over high heat. Stir-fry lima beans for 30 seconds. Pour in soup stock and cornstarch. Cook over medium-high heat until slightly thickened.
4. Put in marinated minced chicken. Stir-fry for an additional 1½-2 minutes. Remove and garnish with chopped ham and parsley; serve immediately.

Silver Sprout Chicken

In a good Cantonese restaurant, the roots and leaves of bean sprouts are snapped off leaving only the stems. The Chinese refer to these bare sprouts as "silver sprouts." Today very few Chinese restaurants in North America practice this age-old tradition. Make your table shine with this entree of silver sprouts.

½ pound (225 g) boneless chicken
   breast
2 tablespoons (30 ml) oil
2 teaspoons (10 ml) shredded ginger
2 cups (500 ml) bean sprouts
½ teaspoon (2 ml) salt

½ teaspoon (2 ml) sesame oil
dash of white pepper
1 teaspoon (5 ml) wine
3 tablespoons (45 ml) soup stock
½ teaspoon (2 ml) cornstarch solution

1. Slightly flatten chicken by pounding with the back of a knife.
2. Cook chicken in soup stock or boiling water; cover and cook for 2½-3 minutes or until tender. Hand shred chicken into 2½" (6.5 cm) pieces.
3. Heat oil in wok until hot; add ginger and stir for 10-15 seconds. Add bean sprouts and stir for 1 minute.
4. Add shredded chicken to sprouts and continue stirring for 1 minute.
5. Add remaining ingredients; thicken with cornstarch solution and serve.

Remarks

• If you like skin, don't take it off because it has a delicate flavor and a nice texture.

 He who restrains his appetite avoids debt.

Szechwan Chicken and Vegetables

A mouth-burning experience! Keep a glass of water handy! If you like adventures, you'll love this dish. This gastronomical experience would be great for a summer's night or a chilly winter's day.

3 tablespoons (45 ml) oil
1-2 dried red peppers, chopped (or 1 teaspoon (5 ml) crushed red pepper)
6 ounces (168 g) chicken breast, thinly shredded
1 stalk celery, shredded
1 small carrot, shredded
1 bell pepper, shredded

½ teaspoon (1 ml) salt
1 tablespoon (15 ml) soy sauce
¼ teaspoon (1 ml) brown sugar
¼ teaspoon (1 ml) chili oil or Tabasco sauce (optional)
¼ cup (60 ml) soup stock
½ teaspoon (2 ml) cornstarch solution

1. Heat wok over high heat with oil and dried red peppers for 10 seconds; reduce heat to medium. Stir-fry chicken for 1-1½ minutes.
2. Add celery, carrot and bell pepper and stir for 1 minute. Put in remaining ingredients and stir for another minute, until lightly thickened. Serve hot.

Remarks

• This dish should be quite dry and spicy.

 Wine should be taken in small doses, knowledge in large.

Tender Bird Over a Cloud (Mongolian Chicken)

Every cloud has a silver lining; this dish is sure to bring a sparkle of taste to your palate. It is visually attractive and marvelously delicious.

Chicken marinade:
2 teaspoons (10 ml) soy sauce
1½ teaspoons (7 ml) wine
½ teaspoon (2 ml) ginger juice
½ teaspoon (2 ml) sugar
dash of white pepper

⅔ pound (300 g) boneless chicken; cut into ¾ " x 2" (2 cm x 5 cm) slices

4 cups (1 L) oil
2 ounces (56 g) bean thread noodles
2 slices ginger, shredded
1 teaspoon (5 ml) chili sauce or Tabasco Sauce
1 teaspoon (5 ml) sesame oil
¾ cup (200 ml) soup stock
2 teaspoons (10 ml) soy sauce
3 green onions, cut into 2" (5 cm) lengths
2½ teaspoons (12 ml) cornstarch solution

1. Marinate chicken for 30 minutes.
2. Deep-fry bean thread noodles in 4 cups hot oil over medium-high heat until they puff up. Remove and drain well; place on a large serving platter.
3. Remove oil, reserving 2 tablespoons in wok. Heat reserved oil over high heat; add ginger, stirring for 10-15 seconds. Stir in chili sauce and cook for 4-10 seconds. Add chicken and continue to stir-fry for 2½ minutes.
4. Add remaining ingredients except cornstarch solution. Mix well and cook for another 1½ minutes. Thicken with cornstarch. Pour mixture over fried bean thread noodles to serve.

Remarks

- Be sure oil is very hot before adding bean thread noodles; it should be near smoke point.
- Fry a small amount of noodles at a time and remove immediately after they puff up.

牛羊肉類

EDWARD LIM

Holy Cows and Little Lambs

Traditionally in Chinese dishes, beef is not as widely consumed as chicken and pork. Water buffalo is the common source of beef in many parts of China, but these animals are used to work in the fields, and none are raised for meat; thus the meat is generally tough and not very popular. How can the aged and retired buffalo compare with the prime-cut beef that we find here?

It was also believed in China that Confucius was greatly disturbed to hear the sound of the slaughter of the farmer's best companion. He felt that the people should be kind and merciful and spare the buffalo after a life-long loyalty. Later the introduction of Buddhism reinforced the sacred status of the water buffalo.

However, contact with the outside world has caused the repertoire for beef to widen in recent years. Beef dishes are becoming more popular in Chinese homes as well as in restaurants. It is often combined with vegetables to form a delectable dish.

Lean cuts of beef are the best suited for Chinese dishes, such as flank steak, sirloin, T-bone, chuck, tenderloin, and round steak. A secret of Chinese cooking is to marinate the meat in a marinade sauce prior to cooking to seal in the juices of the meat and increase flavor. When marinated, the beef becomes more tender, so less-expensive cuts can be used to produce satisfying results.

Flank steak is often the preferred type of beef for use in Chinese dishes. Since all of the fibers run the same way, it is easy to cut across the grain to produce tender slices. This process is facilitated by cutting the slices when the meat is partially frozen.

Lamb is not widely used by the Chinese because of its strong odor. Its character is often masked by braising with plenty of powerful scallions and the addition of other pungent ingredients which disguise lamb's taste. Finely sliced mutton contributes to Mongolian hot pots and barbecues.

The following pages offer a wide variety of exciting and unusual dishes that you can try at home.

BBQ Beef Short Ribs

The tantalizing aromas of this dish will remind you of an old-fashioned Texas barbecue. Grab your ten gallon, your cowboy boots, and your favorite jeans—then sit back and enjoy this superb dish: short ribs marinated in a savory sauce and then smothered in a seductively flavored braising sauce with wild honey. Enough to make any Texan homesick!

2½ pounds (1125 g) short ribs of beef
(6-7)

Beef Marinade:
2 teaspoons (10 ml) ginger juice
1 tablespoon (15 ml) wine
1 tablespoon (15 ml) chopped green
onion
1 tablespoon (15 ml) soy sauce
½ teaspoon (2 ml) salt
1½ teaspoon (7 ml) sugar

Braising Sauce:
1½ tablespoons (22 ml) catsup
1 tablespoon (15 ml) hoisin sauce
2 tablespoons (30 ml) wild honey
2 teaspoons (10 ml) sesame oil

1. Score meat with a knife 4" x ½" deep on meat side of ribs and marinate for 2-4 hours.
2. Preheat oven at 350°F (180°C); place ribs on rack in shallow pan. Bake in oven for about 15 minutes. Turn ribs and bake another 15-20 minutes.
3. Turn oven to broil. Combine braising sauce in a bowl and brush on both sides of ribs. Broil ribs for 1½ minutes on meat side and 1 minute on the other side.

Beef with Bean Thread Noodles

Let's build protein in your diet! It's guaranteed with this recipe!! The high protein bean thread noodles are a good choice with meat or any sauce—nourishing, satisfying and a real appetite-pleaser.

Beef Marinade:
2 teaspoons (10 ml) soy sauce
1½ teaspoons (7 ml) wine
1 teaspoon (5 ml) cornstarch
½ teaspoon (2 ml) sugar

4 ounces (112 g) bean thread noodles
**½ pound (225 g) flank steak, cut into
    1" x 2" thin slices**

2½ tablespoons (37 ml) oil
1 slice ginger, shredded
2 teaspoons (10 ml) soy sauce
1½ cups (370 ml) soup stock
2 teaspoons (10 ml) oil
dash of black pepper
4 stalks green onion, shredded

1. Marinate beef for 30 minutes.
2. Soak bean thread noodles for 10-15 minutes in warm water.
3. Heat 1½ tablespoons oil in wok over high heat. Add ginger, stirring for 10 seconds. Add beef and stir-fry for 1½ minutes. Remove and set aside.
4. Drain bean thread noodles.
5. Reduce heat to medium-low. Add 1 tablespoon oil to wok and stir in bean thread noodles, stirring for 10-15 seconds. Add remaining ingredients and stir for 1 minute. Cover and simmer over low heat for 2-3 minutes.
6. Return beef to wok and mix well. Serve hot.

Remarks

- Cellophane noodles soak up a great deal of liquid. After 2 minutes of cooking, check to see if they are dry and add extra broth if necessary. This dish should not have excess sauce, however, just enough to coat the meat and noodles.

 If brothers disagree, the bystander takes advantage.

Beef with Fresh Asparagus

A great stand-by for any career person who loves to entertain—for those who don't have the time, but love instant successes. A kaleidoscope full of color—carrots, asparagus and beef—make this dish a beautiful display.

Beef Marinade:
1½ teaspoons (7 ml) soy sauce
2½ teaspoons (12 ml) wine
½ teaspoon (2 ml) sesame oil
¼ teaspoon (1 ml) ginger juice
1½ teaspoons (7 ml) cornstarch
1 teaspoon (5 ml) oil

½ pound (225 g) flank steak

½ pound (225 g) fresh asparagus
1 small carrot
3 tablespoons (45 ml) oil
2 slices ginger, shredded
1 tablespoon (15 ml) oyster sauce
½ teaspoon (2 ml) sugar
1 teaspoon (5 ml) wine
½ cup (125 ml) soup stock
1¼ teaspoons (6 ml) cornstarch solution

1. Cut beef across grain into 1½" x 2" slices. Marinate for 2 hours.
2. Break off and discard tough ends of asparagus. Cut diagonally into 1½-2" lengths. Roll-cut carrot.
3. Heat oil in wok over high heat. Add ginger, stirring for 30 seconds. Add beef to wok and stir-fry until redness disappears, about 1½-2 minutes. Remove and set aside.
4. Add asparagus and carrots to wok, stirring for 30 seconds. Stir in remaining ingredients, except cornstarch solution. Cover and cook for 2½-3 minutes.
5. Return beef, stir well and thicken. Serve hot.

Bitter Melon Beef with Black Beans

Bitter melon is one of the most common and popular fresh vegetables in southern China. It is generally available from the end of April to early September. Build up some courage to try bitter melon. You might end up wanting to grow your own. Bitter is sometimes better. It is dynamite with beef, chicken or pork.

½ pound (225 g) flank steak, cut into
   ¾" x 2" (2 cm x 5 cm) thin slices
2 medium-sized bitter melons
4 cups (1 L) water with ½ teaspoon (2
   ml) salt
2 tablespoons (30 ml) oil
1½ tablespoons (22 ml) black bean
   paste
1 tablespoon (15 ml) dark soy sauce
2 teaspoons (10 ml) sugar
¼ cup (60 ml) soup stock
½ teaspoon (2 ml) cornstarch solution

Beef Marinade:
1 teaspoon (5 ml) soy sauce
1 teaspoon (5 ml) wine
¼ teaspoon (1 ml) sesame oil
¼ teaspoon (1 ml) ginger juice
1 teaspoon (5 ml) cornstarch

1. Marinate beef for 2 hours.
2. Split bitter melon in half; discard seeds and spongy center. Cut crosswise into ¼" (0.75 cm) slices.
3. Heat oil in wok over high heat. Add beef slices stirring for 1½ minutes until redness disappears. Remove and set aside.
4. Heat wok again over high heat. Stir in black bean paste and cook for 15-20 seconds. Add parboiled melon and stir for 30 seconds. Mix in beef and remaining ingredients except cornstarch solution.
5. Thicken with cornstarch solution and serve hot.

Remarks

- Bitter melon goes well with a touch of hot chili pepper. For added spiciness, add 1-2 dried chili peppers to the black bean paste.
- For those who may not want the extra bitterness: parboil melon in 4 cups salted water for 2½ minutes. Remove and immediately plunge into cold water. Drain and set aside.

Cantonese Beef Steak

This is one of the most popular beef dishes served in Cantonese restaurants. Next time—when ordering, you can say, "Cantonese beef steak, please!" But before going to a Cantonese restaurant, try it at home. You'll find it's just as good or better than that served in the restaurant! Tender pieces of steak in a devastatingly rich sauce.

¾ pound (340 g) flank steak
2 tablespoons (30 ml) oil
¼ medium-sized onion

Beef Marinade:
4 teaspoons (20 ml) wine
1 tablespoon (15 ml) oil
4 teaspoons (20 ml) soy sauce
1½ teaspoons (7 ml) cornstarch
pinch of white pepper

Steak Sauce:
1½ tablespoons (22 ml) catsup
2¼ teaspoons (11 ml) Worcestershire sauce
½ tablespoon (7 ml) steak sauce
1 teaspoon (5 ml) sugar
¾ teaspoon (3 ml) soy sauce
2¼ teaspoons (11 ml) soup stock

1. Cut flank steak into 2" x 2" x ¼" (5 cm x 5 cm x 0.75 cm) slices and pound both sides with a mallet. Marinate for 2-4 hours.
2. Heat oil in a hot skillet or non-sticking pan over high heat. Brown beef for 1 minute on each side. Remove beef, reserving oil in skillet.
3. Combine ingredients for steak sauce in a small bowl. Add onion to skillet and sauté over high heat until light brown. Add steak sauce, stirring to blend well. Return browned beef to skillet and coat with sauce. Arrange on a platter and serve immediately.

 The great end of life is not knowledge but action.

Cantonese Steamed Beef Balls

If you have had dim sum around lunch time at a Chinese restaurant, you have probably tried this juicy and scrumptious meat ball. It is very easy to make in your own kitchen.

½ pound (225 g) lean ground beef
1 tablespoon (15 ml) wine
1 teaspoon (5 ml) ginger juice
½ teaspoon (2 ml) salt
¼ teaspoon (1 ml) sesame oil

4 teaspoons (20 ml) cornstarch
dash of black pepper
¼ cup (60 ml) soup stock or water
1 tablespoon (15 ml) mustard for dipping

1. In a large bowl, combine ground beef, wine, ginger juice, salt, sesame oil and cornstarch. Mix well.
2. Slowly stir in stock or water.
3. Make beef mixture into 14-15 roughly rounded balls. Place in a greased pie pan.
4. Steam over high heat for 15-18 minutes.

Remarks

• Serve with mustard for a flavor you will not forget.

Making meatballs with a wet spoon.

Chinese Stewed Beef Balls

The Swedish have their meat balls—the Chinese have their Stewed Beef Balls. An artistic blend of pork and beef with a whimsical flavor of ginger. Can be prepared ahead of time when entertaining.

¾ pound (340 g) ground beef
1 tablespoon (15 ml) diced pork fat
　(optional)
1 tablespoon (15 ml) water
2 teaspoons (10 ml) soy sauce
1½ teaspoons (7 ml) wine
1 egg, beaten
4 teaspoons (20 ml) cornstarch
¾ teaspoon (3 ml) ginger juice or
　grated ginger
4 cups (1 L) oil

1 pound (450 g) Chinese cabbage,
　chopped
½ teaspoon (2 ml) salt
1 tablespoon (15 ml) oyster-flavored
　sauce
1 teaspoon (5 ml) sugar
1½ tablespoons (22 ml) chopped green
　onion
½ teaspoon (2 ml) sesame oil
　(optional)
½ cup (125 ml) soup stock
2 teaspoons (10 ml) cornstarch
　solution
lettuce leaves

1. Combine ground beef, pork fat and water. Add soy sauce, wine, egg, cornstarch and ginger. Blend well. Set aside.
2. Shape beef mixture into 1½" diameter meat balls. Dust surface with extra cornstarch if desired.
3. Heat oil in wok over medium-high heat. Deep-fry meat balls, 8-10 at a time until golden brown. Drain well and set aside.
4. Remove oil from wok except 2 tablespoons. Heat remaining oil over high heat. Add cabbage, stirring for 30 seconds. Return meat balls to wok and add remaining ingredients except cornstarch solution. Reduce heat to low; cover and stew for 6-8 minutes.
5. Thicken with cornstarch and serve over lettuce leaves.

 He who sows hemp will reap hemp; he who sows beans will reap beans.

Chrysanthemum Beef

In northern Chinese cooking, the onion is referred to as a chrysanthemum. What a lovely analogy, but be careful—don't expect to get a joyous response by giving a friend a bouquet of onions! One of the simplest Chinese dishes to prepare.

Beef Marinade:
1½ teaspoons (7 ml) soy sauce
½ teaspoon (2 ml) ginger juice
2 teaspoons (10 ml) wine
1 teaspoon (5 ml) cornstarch

½ pound (225 g) flank steak

3 tablespoons (45 ml) oil
1½ medium-sized onions, sliced
¼ teaspoon (1 ml) salt
½ teaspoon (2 ml) sugar
¼ cup (60 ml) soup stock
¾ teaspoon (3 ml) cornstarch solution

1. Cut flank steak across the grain into ¾" x 2" (2 cm x 5 cm) thin slices. Marinate for 2 hours.
2. Heat 2 tablespoons oil in wok over high heat. Add beef, stirring for 1-1½ minutes. Remove and keep warm.
3. Clean wok. Add 1 tablespoon oil and heat to medium high. Add onion and stir-fry for 1½ minutes. Add remaining ingredients except cornstarch solution.
4. Return beef to wok. Stir in cornstarch solution and cook until thickened. Serve immediately.

Curry-Flavored Beef Casserole

Curry probably originated in India, yet it has been popular in southern China for the past hundred years. Many Cantonese restaurants have incorporated curry into their menus. Of course, after the creative touch of many Chinese cooks, the Chinese curry dish is quite different from the original. This is a very economical dish because beef shank is one of the cheapest cuts of meat you can buy.

1½ pounds (675 g) boneless beef
    shank
1 medium-sized onion
1 medium-sized potato
3 tablespoons (45 ml) oil
2 cloves garlic, chopped
2 red chili peppers, halved
3 tablespoons (45 ml) curry paste or
    powder

¼ teaspoon (1 ml) five-spice powder
    (optional)
1½ tablespoons (22 ml) wine
2 teaspoons (10 ml) sugar
¾ teaspoon (3 ml) salt
1 tablespoon (15 ml) soy sauce
1¼ cups (310 ml) beef stock

1. Trim excess fat from beef and cut into 1¼" (3.25 cm) cubes. Cut onion into 1" (2.5 cm) squares and potato into 1" (2.5 cm) cubes.
2. Heat 2 tablespoons oil in wok over high heat. Brown beef for 1½ minutes and remove beef. Add remaining 1 tablespoon oil to wok. Brown garlic and red pepper for 10-15 seconds. Add onion, stirring for 1 minute. Add potato chunks and stir another 30 seconds. Add curry paste and mix well.
3. Return beef to wok. Add remaining ingredients and mix well. Bring mixture to a boil and transfer to a 3-quart (2.8 L) casserole. Reduce heat to medium-low. Cover and cook for 1¼ hours. Serve garnished with Chinese parsley.

Remarks

• It's great served over rice!

Deep-Fried Stewed Lamb

This exquisite dish is designed for lamb lovers and those who have discriminating taste. Dipping the tender pieces of lamb into a savory sauce will surely get compliments.

4 cups (1 L) water
2 pounds (900 g) leg of lamb
10 cloves garlic, slightly flattened
2 slices ginger
7 stalks green onion, whole
4 cups (1 L) oil
½ medium-sized cucumber
8-12 Mandarin pancakes (see Remarks)

Dipping Sauce:
1 tablespoon (15 ml) hoisin sauce
2 teaspoons (10 ml) dark soy sauce
½ tablespoon (7 ml) Worcestershire sauce
½ tablespoon (7 ml) wine
½ teaspoon (2 ml) sugar
1 tablespoon (15 ml) hot catsup

1. Bring 4 cups water to a boil. Add lamb, garlic, ginger and 2 whole green onions. Return water to a boil, transfer to a 3-quart casserole. Cover and bake in a preheated oven at 325°F (160°C) for 1 hour and 30 minutes. Remove lamb and drain well. (Reserve broth for use in other lamb dishes.) Cut lamb into 2" x 2" x 4" pieces (5 cm x 5 cm x 10 cm).
2. Heat oil in wok over medium heat. Deep-fry lamb in hot oil for 2-3 minutes until golden brown. Cut lamb into thin slices. Arrange on a platter and keep warm.
3. Combine dipping sauce ingredients in a small bowl.
4. Cut white part of remaining green onions into 2" (5 cm) lengths. (Green parts of onion can be reserved for other dishes.) Peel cucumber, remove seeds, and cut into ½" x ½" x 2" (1.25 cm x 1.25 cm x 5 cm) pieces.
5. To serve, wrap lamb, green onions, cucumber and ½ teaspoon dipping sauce in a pancake and pick up pancake with your hands to eat.

Remarks

• Refer to the recipe for Mandarin Pancakes, page 244.

Five-Spice Beef Casserole

The combination of soy sauce, star anise, and five-spice powder will take you on a flavor adventure and bring to life rice and noodles as a main dish. A good way to enhance an economical cut of meat.

2 tablespoons (30 ml) oil
3 slices ginger
2 cloves garlic, chopped
1 onion, sliced
2½ pounds (1125 g) beef stew meat,
    cut into 1" (2.5 cm) cubes
2 tablespoons (30 ml) wine
1 whole star anise

1½ (4 cm) length cinnamon stick
½ teaspoon (2 ml) five-spice powder
3 tablespoons (45 ml) soy sauce
1½ teaspoons (7 ml) sugar
2 cups (500 ml) beef stock
few sprigs of Chinese parsley (optional
    for garnishing)

1. Heat wok over high heat with oil. Add ginger, garlic and onion. Stir-fry for 1 minute until fragrant.
2. Add beef chunks and continue to stir-fry for 2-2½ minutes over high heat until light brown.
3. Add remaining ingredients and mix well.
4. Transfer to a heat-proof casserole, cover and cook on range over medium-low heat for 2-2½ hours (or you may bake in the oven at 350°F (180°C) for the same amount of time).
5. To serve, garnish with Chinese parsley.

Remarks

- This dish can be prepared ahead of time and reheated when ready to serve. It may even taste better the second time around!

Ginger-Flavored Calf Liver and Onion

Calf liver is available in most supermarkets and meat markets. It is inexpensive and when prepared properly, the tender, juicy liver will melt in your mouth. A good choice for a family menu and an excellent source of iron. Build your blood—pump iron—eat liver!!

²/₃ **pound (300 g) calf liver**
½ **egg white, lightly beaten**
1 **teaspoon (5 ml) wine**
2 **teaspoons (10 ml) cornstarch**
½ **teaspoon (2 ml) salt**
2½ **tablespoons (37 ml) oil**
1 **large onion, sliced into ¼" (0.75 cm)**
  slices
3 **stalks green onion, cut into 2" (5 cm)**
  lengths
5 **slices ginger, shredded**
½ **teaspoon (2 ml) cornstarch solution**

Ginger Sauce:
1½ **teaspoons (7 ml) ginger juice or**
  grated ginger
1 **tablespoon (15 ml) chopped green**
  onion
1½ **tablespoons (22 ml) wine**
½ **teaspoon (2 ml) salt**
1¼ **teaspoon (6 ml) sugar**
pinch of white pepper
¼ **cup (60 ml) soup stock**

1. Trim membranes and veins off calf liver and cut liver into ¼" x 1" x 2½" (0.75 cm x 2.5 cm x 6.5 cm) pieces. Marinate with egg white, wine, cornstarch and salt for 10-15 minutes.
2. Blanch marinated liver in ample boiling water for 5-10 seconds. Remove and drain well.
3. Heat 1½ tablespoons oil in hot wok and put in blanched liver, stirring over high heat for about 30 seconds. Remove liver and set aside. Clean wok.
4. Heat 1 tablespoon oil in hot wok, put in ginger, onion, and green onion, stirring for 30 seconds. Put in ginger sauce mixture, blend well and stir for 30 seconds.
5. Return liver to wok, mix well and stir over high heat for about 1 minute. Thicken with cornstarch solution.
6. Stir in 1-2 teaspoon(s) wine if desired and serve hot.

Remarks

• You can replace calf liver with pork or beef liver.

 No medicine can cure a vulgar man.

Golden Fried Zesty Beef

The golden beauty of this dish will be sure to bring some sunshine into your life. No other beef dish compares to this one in terms of flavor and texture. One of the most exotic dishes in western China.

Beef Marinade:
1 tablespoon (15 ml) soy sauce
1 teaspoon (5 ml) sesame oil
1 teaspoon (5 ml) sugar
1 tablespoon (15 ml) wine
2 teaspoons (10 ml) cornstarch

1 pound (450 g) flank steak, cut into
    thin 2" (5 cm) strips
3 cups (750 ml) oil
1 carrot, cut in 2" (5 cm) julienne strips
1 green pepper, julienned
2 tablespoons (30 ml) vinegar
1½ teaspoons (7 ml) sugar
½-¾ teaspoon (2-3 ml) chili oil or
    Tabasco sauce

1. Marinate beef for 2 hours.
2. Heat oil in hot wok and deep-fry beef over medium-high heat for 1 minute, stirring constantly. Remove and drain. Deep-fry again for only ½ minute. Drain again. Cook a third time for ½ minute. Drain and set aside.
3. Remove frying oil except for 1 tablespoon. Heat to medium-high. Add carrot and green pepper, stirring for 1-1½ minutes. Add fried beef, vinegar, sugar and chili oil. Mix well and serve hot.

Chinese white turnip (daicon).

Hoisin-Flavored Beef Steak

Steak and hoisin are a dynamic combination of classic taste and subtle flavor. One of my favorite and most treasured recipes, this dish is simple yet elegant, and it is a perfect choice for a formal dinner.

1 pound (450 g) flank steak (or sirloin steak)
3 tablespoons (45 ml) oil
½ onion, cut in thin strips
4 ripe tomatoes, sliced

Beef Marinade:
2 teaspoons (10 ml) soy sauce
1 tablespoon (15 ml) wine
2 teaspoons (30 ml) oil
1½ tablespoons (22 ml) water
1¼ teaspoons (6 ml) cornstarch
½ **egg white** (optional)
¼ teaspoon (1 ml) baking soda (optional)

Sauce:
1½ tablespoons (22 ml) hoisin sauce
1½ tablespoons (22 ml) hot catsup
1 teaspoon (5 ml) Worcestershire Sauce

1. Trim off excess fat and membrane on beef surface. Cut into 2" x 2" x ¼" (5 cm x 5 cm x 0.75 cm) squares; marinate for 30 minutes.
2. Stir-fry onion in 1 tablespoon oil for 1 minute over high heat and set aside. Remove from pan.
3. Heat a non-stick pan with 2 tablespoons oil. Brown beef slices for 1½ minutes over medium-high heat on each side, slightly pressing down on beef for uniform browning.
4. Add sauce mixture and cooked onions and mix well. Stir for an extra 30 seconds and serve over sliced tomatoes.

Remarks

- Preparation, marinating, and cooking are equally important in order to get a tasty, tender beef dish.
- To prepare marinade, add everything except egg white, cornstarch and salt. Let stand at least 30 minutes, then add the remaining ingredients right before cooking—they help to seal in the juices and give the beef a smooth texture.
- Baking soda is strongly alkaline and helps to break up the protein fiber, but it gives a heavy alkaline taste if too much is used. For a good piece of steak, you should not add any soda. For a piece of tough steak, you might use meat tenderizer, which is actually a protein-hydrolized enzyme derived from papaya.

Hunan Stewed Oxtail

Hot and spicy! The liberal use of chili peppers is the most distinctive characteristic of Hunan-style cooking. It is close to Szechwan. And is it *hot*!

3 pounds (1350 g) oxtails, excess fat trimmed off
2½ tablespoons (30 ml) oil
1 onion, cut in 1¼" (3.25 cm) squares
½ teaspoon (2 ml) salt
1¼ teaspoons (6 ml) cornstarch solution

Stewing Sauce:
¼ cup (60 ml) dark soy sauce
⅔ cup (160 ml) wine
1½ tablespoons (22 ml) brown sugar
3-4 cloves garlic, lightly pressed
2-3 chili peppers, broken in half
1-2 star anise
½ cup (125 ml) soup stock
1 teaspoon (5 ml) sesame oil

1. Heat 2½ tablespoons oil in wok over high heat. Add oxtails and salt; cook for 1½ minutes or until browned. Add onion slices, stirring for one minute.
2. Combine ingredients for stewing sauce in a 3½-quart flame-proof casserole dish. Mix in browned oxtail and onion.
3. Bring casserole to a boil over high heat. Cover, reduce heat to medium-low and simmer for 2½ hours or cook in oven at 350°F (180°C) for 2½-3 hours.
4. Use a strainer or a slotted spoon to remove cooked oxtails and place on a serving dish.
5. Skim surface fat from stewing sauce in casserole. Thicken with cornstarch solution. Pour over oxtails and serve hot.

Hunan-Style Lamb

The strong taste of lamb combined with the zesty flavor of ginger and the tangy flavor of garlic creates a dynamic taste. Leeks with their intriguing flavor add a specialness to this dish. Serve over rice or noodles.

8 ounces (225 g) boneless leg of lamb
   or lamb chops
3 tablespoons (45 ml) oil
3 slices ginger
3-4 garlic cloves, chopped
2 dried chili peppers, halved
1 medium-sized leek, washed and cut
   into 2" (5 cm) squares

Lamb Marinade:
2 teaspoons (10 ml) soy sauce
2½ teaspoons (12 ml) wine
1½ teaspoons (7 ml) cornstarch
½ teaspoon (2 ml) ginger juice

Hunan Sauce Mixture:
2 teaspoons (10 ml) soy sauce
1 tablespoon (15 ml) dark soy sauce
¾ teaspoon (3 ml) sugar
2 teaspoons (10 ml) vinegar
1 tablespoon (15 ml) wine
⅛ teaspoon (0.5 ml) chili oil
¼ cup (60 ml) soup stock
1¼ teaspoons (6 ml) cornstarch solution

1. Slice lamb into 1" x 2" (2.5 cm x 5 cm) thin slices and marinate for 15-20 minutes.
2. Heat 2 tablespoons oil in wok over high heat. Add ginger, garlic, and chili pepper stirring for 10-15 seconds. Add lamb and stir-fry for another 1½-2 minutes until pink color disappears. Remove lamb.
3. Heat wok over high heat with remaining 1 tablespoon oil, stir in leek. Return lamb to wok and cook for 1 minute.
4. Combine Hunan sauce ingredients and pour into wok. Mix well and cook until thickened. Serve hot.

Though lamb may be good, it is difficult to cook it to suit everyone's taste.

Oriental Beef Casserole

Strong and dazzling—this dish will bring tears to your eyes. The mild taste of bean curd with the hotness of chili pepper makes this a dramatically delicious dish.

2 pounds (900 g) stew meat, cut into 1" (2.5 cm) cubes
1 large onion, cut in 1" (2.5 cm) squares
2 tablespoons (30 ml) oil
½ teaspoon (2 ml) salt
2 squares bean curd, 1 pound (450 g), cut into 1½" (4 cm) cubes
1 green pepper, cut in 1" (2.5 cm) cubes
2 stalks green onion, chopped
2 teaspoons (10 ml) cornstarch solution

Braising Sauce:
2 cloves garlic, pressed
2-3 slices ginger
1½ tablespoons (22 ml) hoisin sauce
½ teaspoon (2 ml) five-spice powder
1½ tablespoons (22 ml) soy sauce
2½ tablespoons (37 ml) wine
1 tablespoon (15 ml) brown bean sauce (optional)
1½ tablespoons (22 ml) vinegar
⅓ cup (80 ml) soup stock
1 teaspoon (5 ml) sesame oil

1. Heat 2 tablespoons oil in wok and brown beef over high heat for 1½ minutes. Stir in onion and cook for 1 minute.
2. Combine ingredients for braising sauce in a large casserole (about 3-quart size). Bring to a boil and add beef and onion. Bring to a second boil, reduce to medium-low, and cover to simmer for 1¼ hours.
3. Add bean curd and green onion and simmer for 10-15 minutes. Add green pepper and cook 2-3 minutes.
4. Thicken with cornstarch solution. For extra spiciness, add ½ teaspoon chili oil or 1 teaspoon Hunan-style garlic-flavored chili sauce.

Red-Cooked Beef Roast

Beef is a rare ingredient in China and cooking and eating a whole roast at one time is almost unheard of! Don't tell your Chinese friends until you finish the whole thing or it may break their hearts!! This beef roast is braised with garden-fresh vegetables in a scrumptious sauce.

1½ tablespoons (22 ml) oil
3½-4 pounds (1575-1800 g) beef chuck roast, with excess fat trimmed off
6 medium-sized carrots, cut into 2" (5 cm) lengths
2 cups (500 ml) peeled tomatoes, cut into wedges
1 pound (450 g) Chinese cabbage, cut into 2" (5 cm) square pieces
2½ teaspoons (10 ml) cornstarch solution

Red-Cooked Sauce:
1 tablespoon (15 ml) oil
2 medium onions, peeled and cut into 1½" (4 cm) square pieces
6 cloves garlic, pressed
¼ cup (60 ml) dark soy sauce
1 tablespoon (15 ml) soy sauce
¾ teaspoon (3 ml) sesame oil
⅔ cup (160 ml) wine
2 whole star anise
1 piece dried tangerine peel, 2" (5 cm) square
soup stock (if necessary)

1. Heat 1½ tablespoons oil in wok over high heat. Brown beef roast on all sides for 1½ minutes. Remove roast to a 4-quart casserole dish.
2. To make red-cooked sauce: heat clean wok with 1 tablespoon oil over medium-high heat. Add onions, garlic and ginger and stir for 1 minute. Add remaining sauce ingredients. If dry, add 2-3 tablespoons soup stock. Mix well.
3. Pour sauce mixture into casserole dish.
4. Bring casserole to boil, reduce heat to medium-low, cover, and cook for 1½ hours. Turn roast occasionally.
5. Add vegetables and continue to simmer for 10-15 minutes.
6. Transfer beef and vegetables to a serving dish. Thicken remaining sauce with cornstarch and pour over beef and vegetables. Serve over rice.

Remarks

- You can also bake the roast at 325°F (160°C) for 1½ hours.
- Fresh orange or tangerine peel can be used in place of dried tangerine peel.

Seafood-Flavored Beef and Snow Peas

Don't lick the chopsticks! With this recipe you'll want to savor every last drop of flavor. A simple home-style dish to serve with crisp, fresh snow peas.

Marinade:
1 teaspoon (5 ml) soy sauce
1 tablespoon (45 ml) wine
¼ teaspoon (1 ml) sesame oil
dash of white pepper
1 teaspoon (5 ml) cornstarch

½ **pound (225 g) flank steak, cut into 1" x ⅛" x 2" (2.5 cm x 0.5 cm x 5 cm) pieces**
2½ **tablespoons (37 ml) oil**
2 **slices ginger, shredded**
½ **onion, cut in wedges**
4 **ounces (112 g) snow peas, snap off ends and strings**
2 **teaspoons (10 ml) oyster-flavored sauce**
3 **tablespoons (45 ml) soup stock**

1. Marinate beef for 30 minutes.
2. Heat oil in wok over high heat. Add ginger and stir for 15 seconds. Add beef and stir-fry for 1½-2 minutes until light brown. Remove and set aside.
3. Add onion to wok and stir over medium-high heat for 30 seconds. Add snow peas, oyster-flavored sauce and soup stock. Cover and cook for 1½ minutes.
4. Return cooked beef to wok and mix well. Serve hot.

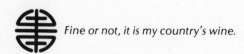
Fine or not, it is my country's wine.

Stir-Fried Lamb and Green Onions

"Mary's lamb went for a wok"…only to be greeted with some green onions. Lamb dishes in China are usually Mongolian. Very few Chinese have ever wokked a lamb, let alone tasted it! Lamb is available in most supermarkets—enjoy this delicious, mild-flavored dish often!

Lamb Marinade:
2 teaspoons (10 ml) soy sauce
1 tablespoon (15 ml) wine
2 teaspoons (10 ml) cornstarch

⅔ pound (300 g) boneless lamb, cut into 2" (5 cm) strips
3½ tablespoons (52 ml) oil
2-3 cloves garlic, pressed
8-10 stalks green onion, cut into 2" (5 cm) strips
½ teaspoon (2 ml) salt
¼ teaspoon (1 ml) chili oil
1 tablespoon (15 ml) hoisin sauce
2 tablespoons (30 ml) soup stock

1. Marinate lamb for 30 minutes.
2. Heat oil in wok over high heat. Brown garlic for 15 seconds. Add lamb and stir-fry for 2 minutes. Stir in green onions and fry for 1 minute.
3. Add remaining ingredients, mix well and serve hot.

Sweet and Sour Lamb Chops

Spring always reminds me of little lambs frolicking in fields of wild-flowers—sweet little lambs—but how about sweet and sour little lambs? This juicy and tender lamb dish is as colorful as spring with its rich and zesty sauce. Delightful and unusual!

4 thin lamb chops (about 1¼ pound or 562 g)
2½ tablespoons (37 ml) oil

Lamb Chop Marinade:
½ teaspoon (2 ml) salt
1 tablespoon (15 ml) wine
2 teaspoons (10 ml) cornstarch
½ teaspoon (2 ml) ginger juice

Sweet and Sour Sauce:
2½ tablespoons (37 ml) vinegar
2½ tablespoons (37 ml) sugar
6½ tablespoons (97 ml) catsup
1 teaspoon (5 ml) Worcestershire Sauce
3 tablespoons (45 ml) water
¼ teaspoon (1 ml) Tabasco Sauce
1 teaspoon (5 ml) cornstarch solution
2 tablespoons (30 ml) chopped Chinese pickles (optional)
3 slices pickled ginger, finely shredded (optional)

1. Pound lamb chops on both sides to tenderize.
2. Marinate chops for 30 minutes.
3. Combine ingredients for sweet and sour sauce in saucepan. Bring to a boil, reduce heat to low and keep warm.
4. Heat non-stick skillet with oil over medium heat. Place chops in hot oil and cook 3 minutes per side, or until done as desired. Occasionally press chops down while frying to ensure even cooking.
5. Remove lamb to serving platter. Pour sweet and sour sauce over chops and serve!

 No man really becomes a fool until he stops asking questions.

Szechwan Minced Beef

Another very traditional and very popular dish served in most Szechwan restaurants. Have a pitcher of water ready for this one, it's hot and spicy—sure to chase the chill away! Try it for your next dinner party.

8 ounces (225 g) sirloin beef, minced
2½ tablespoons (37 ml) oil
3 slices ginger, finely chopped
2 cloves garlic, finely chopped
1-2 dried chili peppers, crushed
4-6 water chestnuts, finely chopped
1 small carrot, finely chopped
½ bell pepper, finely chopped
½ teaspoon (2 ml) cornstarch solution
3 tablespoons (45 ml) chopped peanuts

Beef Marinade:
2 teaspoons (10 ml) wine
1 tablespoon (15 ml) soy sauce
2 teaspoons (10 ml) cornstarch
½ teaspoon (2 ml) ginger juice

Cooking Sauce:
1 tablespoon (15 ml) soy sauce
2 teaspoons (10 ml) vinegar
2 teaspoons (10 ml) wine
2 teaspoons (10 ml) sesame oil
½ teaspoon (2 ml) sugar

1. Marinate minced beef for 30 minutes.
2. Heat 1½ tablespoons oil in wok over high heat, add ginger, garlic and chili pepper, and fry for 10-15 seconds. Add beef and fry for 1 minute. Add remaining 1 tablespoon oil, water chestnuts, carrot and bell pepper; stir for 1 minute. Then pour in the cooking sauce and reduce heat to medium-low. Cook for one minute. Thicken with cornstarch solution, toss in the peanuts, and serve immediately.

Remarks

• Add only one chili pepper if you prefer food less spicy.

Tomato Beef with Bean Curd

This is exactly what the name says—beef, bean curd and tomato pepper!! What can I say, but try it! A mouth-watering, delicious combination seasoned delicately with ginger.

Beef Marinade:
1 teaspoon (5 ml) soy sauce
½ teaspoon (2 ml) ginger juice
1 teaspoon (5 ml) wine
½ teaspoon (2 ml) sesame oil
½ teaspoon (2 ml) cornstarch

4 ounces (112 g) flank steak, 1" x 2"
   (2.5 cm x 5 cm) thin slices
1 medium-ripe tomato
1 medium-sized bell pepper
8 ounces (225 g) bean curd, cut into 1"
   cubes
2½ tablespoons (27 ml) oil
2 slices ginger, shredded
1 teaspoon (5 ml) soy sauce
½ teaspoon (2 ml) sugar
¼ cup (60 ml) catsup
½ teaspoon (2 ml) Worcestershire
   Sauce
¼ cup (60 ml) soup stock
½ teaspoon (2 ml) cornstarch solution

1. Marinate beef for 30 minutes.
2. Peel tomato and cut into 6 wedges.
3. Remove seeds and cut bell pepper into 8 wedges.
4. Heat oil in hot wok over high heat. Add ginger, stirring for 10 seconds. Add beef and continue to stir over high heat for 1 minute. Remove and drain beef.
5. Add bell pepper wedges to wok, stirring for 30 seconds. Stir in remaining ingredients and mix well. Return beef to wok and reduce heat to low. Cover and simmer for 1 minute. Serve hot.

Tossed Cold Beef Platter

Ripley's Believe It Or Not would be amazed—this Moslem dish is very popular in China. A simple dish, it portrays the simplicity of the lifestyle of the Moslems.

6 cups (1½ L) soup stock	*Dressing Sauce:*
1-2 slices ginger	**2 teaspoons (10 ml) oil**
2 stalks green onion	**2 cloves garlic, finely chopped**
1½ pounds (675 g) beef rump roast	**1½ tablespoons (22 ml) soy sauce**
	4 teaspoons (20 ml) vinegar
	2 teaspoons (10 ml) sugar
	1½ teaspoons (7 ml) sesame oil
	1½ teaspoons (7 ml) chili sauce
	pinch of black pepper

1. Bring soup stock to a boil in a large pot. Add ginger, green onion and beef roast. Bring to a second boil. Reduce heat to low and simmer for 1-1¼ hours.
2. While beef is simmering, prepare dressing sauce: heat 2 teaspoons oil in wok over medium heat. Add garlic and stir for 30 seconds. Stir in remaining sauce ingredients and bring to a boil. Turn off heat and cool.
3. Remove beef and cool. Cut into 1" x 2" thin slices. Arrange on a platter.
4. To serve, pour sauce over cooked beef or use sauce as a dip.

 *Clothes and food are daily mercies.*

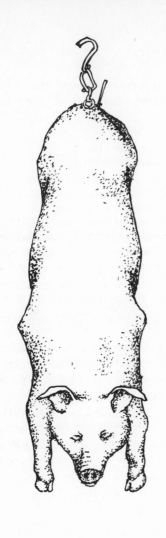

豬
肉
類

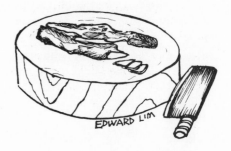

EDWARD LIM

Pork Out

Pigs are gentle creatures not to be feared, worshipped or banished—just cooked with tender loving care and enjoyed immensely at the dinner table. In China and many parts of the Orient, pork is so much more common than any other meat, that the words "meat" and "pork" are synonymous. Although in Chinese cooking all kinds of meats are used, pork is by far the most popular.

Pork has a more delicate flavor than beef, a less coarse grain, and consequently is more adaptable for the infinite variety of dishes. There are so many ways to cook pork in various regions of China that one can almost tell where a man hails from by the pork dish he orders. Shortage of fuel and livestock dictate that as little meat as possible be cooked quickly with a large quantity of fresh or pickled vegetables.

Pork is frequently cooked in relatively large pieces, sliced, shredded or ground to fry with vegetables. Partially frozen meat is firmer to handle and easier for slicing. When pork is prepared in relatively large pieces, such as red-cooked dishes, it is cooked first, then cut into smaller pieces and re-fried in combination with fresh or preserved vegetables.

You will find several interesting recipes in this chapter.

Chinese BBQ Pork (Roast Pork)

When you pass by a Chinese store or restaurant in Chinatown in New York, San Francisco, Vancouver or Toronto, you will most likely notice many red, shiny meat products: barbecued pork hanging on skewers; roast duck and chicken on specially-designed hooks. They look tempting and delicious, and each has a distinctive Chinese flavor. This dish is exotic, traditional and out of sight!

2 pounds (900 g) boneless pork shoulder, cut into 8" x 2½" x ½" (20 cm x 6.5 cm x 1.5 cm) strips

Basting Sauce:
1 tablespoon (15 ml) hoisin sauce
¼ cup (60 ml) honey

Pork Marinade:
2½ teaspoons (12 ml) sugar
¾ teaspoon (3 ml) salt
1 clove garlic, pressed
½ teaspoon (2 ml) ginger juice
2 tablespoons (30 ml) catsup
2 tablespoons (30 ml) soy sauce
2½ teaspoons (12 ml) wine
½ teaspoon (2 ml) five-spice powder
    (optional)

1. Marinate pork for 2-4 hours, or overnight if you wish.
2. Preheat oven to 375°F (190°C) and place marinated pork on a rack over a roasting pan filled with ½ cup water. Bake at 375°F (190°C) for 20 minutes. Turn over and bake another 17-20 minutes.
3. Switch oven to broil. Baste both sides of pork with basting sauce and broil for 1 minute on each side.
4. Let pork cool and cut into thin slices. Serve hot or cold. Keep in tightly-sealed containers in refrigerator or in freezer if not served right away.

Remarks

- During baking, baste with oil and remaining marinade once in a while to avoid drying out.
- Reheating at any time will not degrade the quality, but be sure to use a bit of water in the roasting pan, or wrap the pork inside foil before reheating in oven.
- Place one rack on top shelf of oven, hang pork strip with hooks onto rack, place a pan beneath rack to catch drippings (refer to illustration).
- If pork is cooked horizontally in an electric oven, place about 3" from top heating element.

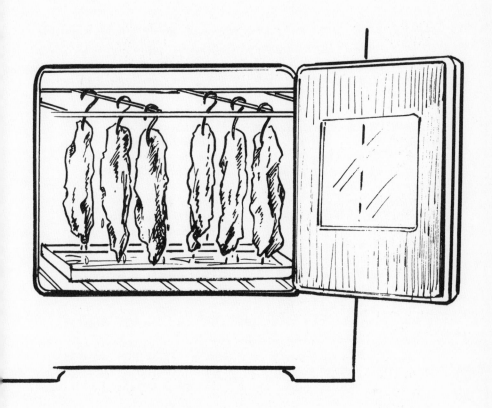

 It is impossible to satisfy one's appetite by painting pictures of cakes.

Deep-Fried Eggplant with Pork

Eggplant is one of the most popular vegetables in China. It is great in combination with any kind of meat. Because of its sponge-like property, eggplant absorbs a tremendous amount of seasoning and liquid, making it ever so succulent to bite into! It is a great complement to rice or noodles.

4 ounces (112 g) lean pork, shredded
4 cups (1 L) oil
1 large eggplant, cut into 1" x ¼" x 2"
    (2.5 cm x 0.75 cm x 2 cm) pieces
2 slices ginger, chopped
2 cloves garlic, chopped
1 tablespoon (15 ml) dried shrimp
    (optional)
2 dried black mushrooms, soaked
    and sliced
¼ cup (60 ml) broth, as needed

Pork Marinade:
1½ teaspoons (7 ml) wine
2 teaspoons (10 ml) soy sauce
½ teaspoon (2 ml) cornstarch

Braising Sauce:
½ cup (125 ml) soup stock
½ teaspoon (2 ml) sugar
½ tablespoon (7 ml) soy sauce
1 teaspoon (5 ml) dark soy sauce
1¼ teaspoons (6 ml) sesame oil

1. Marinate pork for ½-2 hours.
2. Heat oil in wok over medium-high heat and deep-fry eggplant for 2 minutes. Drain eggplant on paper towels.
3. Remove oil, reserving 1½ tablespoons. Heat remaining oil in wok over high heat. Add ginger, garlic, dried shrimp, mushroom and pork; stir for 1½-2 minutes. Add a tiny bit of broth if too dry. Return fried eggplant to wok and continue to stir for 30 seconds. Pour in braising sauce mixture.
4. Reduce to medium-low heat and simmer for 3-4 minutes or until liquid is reduced and slightly thickened.

Remarks

- Before frying the eggplant, heat the oil until it is very hot or else the eggplant will absorb too much oil. Eventually reduce to medium-high heat.
- Garnish with 1 tablespoon chopped green onion if you wish.
- If sauce appears too runny, thicken slightly with cornstarch.

Drunk Pork Plate

You may have indulged in many alcoholic drinks but how about a drunk pig? In this dish, the pork has a sensational hangover. Try it—you might end up having one yourself!

1¼ pounds (562 g) pork shoulder
4-5 cups (1-1.25 L) water
4 slices ginger
3 stalks green onion
2 cloves garlic, pressed

1 teaspoon (5 ml) salt
dash of black pepper
1 tablespoon (15 ml) soy sauce
1 cup (250 ml) wine

1. Cut pork into 5-6 large rectangular chunks.
2. Bring water to a boil; add pork, ginger, green onion, garlic, salt, pepper and soy sauce. Cover and simmer for 30-45 minutes. Drain and let cool.
3. Slice cooked pork into ½" x 1" x 2" (1.5 cm x 2.5 cm x 5 cm) pieces and pack into a shallow bowl. Fill with wine and refrigerate for 2-3 days.
4. To serve, drain pork and arrange slices on a platter. Serve with other main courses as part of a Chinese dinner.

Remarks

- Usually dry sherry (18% alcohol) is used in this recipe. If you want an instant hangover, use Chinese rice wine (40% alcohol) instead.

Typical Oriental eggplant.

Five-Spice Pork Chop—Foil Wrapped

Marinated five-spice pork fillets wrapped in foil and cooked in their own juice. The final product—juicy, tender, oil-free and exceedingly delicious!

1 pound (450 g) pork butt, cut into 2" x 2" x ¼" (5 cm x 5 cm x 0.75 cm) squares

Pork Marinade:
½ teaspoon (2 ml) garlic salt
1 teaspoon (5 ml) five-spice powder
¾ teaspoon (3 ml) sugar
2 teaspoons (10 ml) wine
1 teaspoon (5 ml) soy sauce
1 teaspoon (5 ml) ginger juice

1. Marinate pork for 2 hours.
2. Cut tin foil into 4" (10 cm) squares. Place pork in center. Fold into an envelope, tucking remaining corner in to secure.
3. Deep-fry 4 or 5 at a time, over medium-high heat for approximately 3 minutes, turning over frequently. Drain well and cool slightly before serving.

Remarks

• Try baking this dish as well in an oven at 350°F (180°C) for 17-20 minutes.

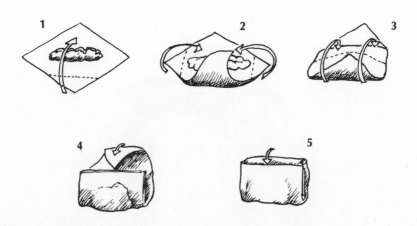

Fragrant Pork Chops

Distinctively different, like an expensive perfume, something to be enjoyed but only used for a special occasion. Indescribable taste— nothing to compare it to—out of this world.

4 pork chops, slightly pounded on
   both sides to ¼" thick
2-3 tablespoons (30-45 ml) oil

Pork Marinade:
1½ tablespoons (22 ml) wine
4 teaspoons (20 ml) soy sauce

Fragrant Sauce:
1 tablespoon (15 ml) soy sauce
1 teaspoon (5 ml) dark soy sauce
1½ teaspoons (7 ml) apple cider
   vinegar
½ teaspoon (2 ml) garlic juice
1 teaspoon (5 ml) ginger juice
½ teaspoon (2 ml) sugar
1 tablespoon (15 ml) apple sauce

1. Marinate pork chops for 2 hours or less.
2. Heat oil and sauté pork chops over medium-high heat for 2-3 minutes on each side, until golden brown. Move chops around to avoid burning.
3. Combine fragrant sauce ingredients and mix well. Pour over pork chops and cover to simmer for 2-3 extra minutes over low heat.

Fried Pork Fillet

This is no ordinary recipe—it has a seductive flavor sure to intrigue the best of gourmets. Preparation is simple, quick and delicious!

¾ **pound (340 g) lean pork, cut into 1" x 2½" x ¼" (2.5 cm x 6.5 cm x 0.75 cm) slices**
4 cups (1 L) oil

Pork Marinade:
1½ tablespoons (22 ml) wine
1 tablespoon (15 ml) soy sauce
½ teaspoon (2 ml) ginger juice
1 egg yolk, beaten

Flour Coating:
¼ cup (60 ml) flour
2 tablespoons (30 ml) cornstarch
3 tablespoons (45 ml) finely chopped onion

Serving Salt Mix:
½ teaspoon (2 ml) salt
⅛ teaspoon (0.5 ml) five-spice powder
dash of roasted Szechwan pepper powder

1. Marinate pork for 30 minutes.
2. Coat pork in flour coating and set aside.
3. Heat oil in wok over high heat to smoke point; reduce heat to medium and deep-fry 6-8 pieces of pork at a time until golden brown. Remove and drain well. Arrange pork on a platter.
4. To serve, sprinkle salt mix over pork and serve hot.

Remarks

- Roast 1½-2 teaspoons of Szechwan peppercorn and grind to a powder. Keep for future use.

Garlic Spareribs

This snappy flavored dish is best with a bottle of beer. I'll drink to that! Outstanding at a cocktail party. If you want, add additional garlic—sure to prevent colds and people from coming too close. Great as a main dish or an appetizer.

1 pound (450 g) pork spareribs, 1"
   (2.5 cm) cubes
2 eggs, lightly beaten
4 cups (1 L) oil
3-4 tablespoons (45-60 ml) flour
dash of five-spice powder (optional)

Marinade:
3 cloves garlic, finely minced
1 tablespoon (15 ml) wine
1 tablespoon (15 ml) soy sauce
¼ teaspoon (1 ml) sugar
1½ teaspoons (7 ml) garlic salt

1. Marinate ribs with garlic, wine, soy sauce, garlic salt and sugar for 2 hours.
2. Dip ribs in eggs and then dry coat with flour. Set aside.
3. Heat 4 cups oil in wok near smoke point. Reduce to medium-high heat. Deep-fry ribs in hot oil for 4-5 minutes or until golden brown. Test one if not sure. Deep fry ⅓ at a time.
4. To serve, sprinkle additional garlic salt and five-spice mixture over ribs.

Remarks

- Prepare ahead and keep warm in the oven. It can be re-fried if necessary.
- When old oil is used, the cooking time will be longer because of a lower smoke point, so be patient!

 If you are willing to eat cabbage stalks, you can accomplish a hundred affairs.

Green Onion Sauce over Pork Chops

The sauce in this recipe might surprise you—instead of a strong onion flavor, it is sweet and tangy. The pork is especially juicy, and comes out of the pan beautifully glazed.

4 pork chops
¼ cup (60 ml) cornstarch
3 tablespoons (45 ml) oil

Marinade:
1 teaspoon (5 ml) soy sauce
¾ teaspoon (3 ml) sugar
1½ teaspoons (7 ml) wine

Green Onion Sauce:
1 tablespoon (15 ml) vinegar
1 tablespoon (15 ml) sugar
2 teaspoons (10 ml) soy sauce
¼ cup (60 ml) chopped green onion
½ teaspoon (2 ml) sesame oil
⅛ teaspoon (0.5 ml) chili oil (optional)

1. Combine ingredients for green onion sauce and set aside.
2. Trim excess fat from pork chops. Pound with back of cleaver and marinate 30 minutes. Lightly coat each chop with cornstarch. Let stand 5 minutes.
3. Heat 1½ tablespoons oil in skillet or non-stick pan over medium heat. Shake off excess starch from chops, and brown in hot skillet for 2-2½ minutes on each side.
4. Pour green onion sauce over pork chops and reduce heat. Simmer for 1 minute. Serve hot.

Ground Pork with Bean Thread Noodles

This recipe stands alone; there is nothing on earth like it. The texture and taste are a real treat! And the combination of bean thread noodles, eggs and ground pork gives you protein-power!

Marinade:
2 teaspoons (10 ml) soy sauce
1 teaspoon (5 ml) wine
pinch of white pepper
1 teaspoon (5 ml) sesame oil
2 teaspoons (10 ml) cornstarch

8 ounces (225 g) lean ground pork
3½ tablespoons (52 ml) oil
2 slices ginger, shredded
6-8 dried black mushrooms, soaked and shredded
4 ounces (112 g) bean thread noodles, soaked and cut into 3½" (7 cm) lengths
1½ teaspoons (7 ml) salt
1½ teaspoons (7 ml) sugar
1-1¼ cups (250-370 ml) soup stock
4 large eggs, lightly beaten
2 tablespoons (30 ml) oil or sesame oil

1. Marinate ground pork for 15-20 minutes.
2. Heat 2 tablespoons oil in wok over high heat. Add ginger and stir for 10-15 seconds. Add ground pork; stir for 1½ minutes. Remove and set aside.
3. Heat 1½ tablespoons oil in wok over high heat. Add mushrooms and drained bean thread noodles, stirring for 30 seconds. Stir in salt, sugar, and 1 cup soup stock. Reduce heat to medium-high, cover and cook for 2 minutes. Sprinkle extra soup stock if too dry.
4. Return ground pork to wok, stirring well. Slowly pour in beaten egg, stirring constantly. Add oil if mixture sticks to pan. Serve hot.

Remarks

• Sprinkle with soup stock during cooking if the mixture appears dry.

Meat and Vegetables with Pancakes (Mushi Pork)

Like a wrapped present, the best part is inside—succulent goodies inside a steaming, flour pancake. It is both appetizing and filling. Try it, you'll love it.

3 tablespoons (45 ml) oil
2 cloves garlic, finely minced
½ pound (225 g) boneless pork, cut into thin strips
¼ cup (60 ml) dried cloud ear, soaked and shredded (optional)
½ cabbage, thinly shredded
½ small carrot, thinly shredded
1 small zucchini, thinly shredded
2 stalks green onion, 1" (2.5 cm) pieces
⅓ cup (80 ml) broth
3 eggs (beat, make into thin omelet, then shred)
¾ teaspoon (3 ml) salt
1½ tablespoons (22 ml) soy sauce

½ teaspoon (2 ml) sugar
1 teaspoon (5 ml) sesame oil
dash of white pepper
¾ teaspoon (3 ml) cornstarch solution
4-5 tablespoons (60-75 ml) hoisin sauce (for serving)
1 dozen flour pancakes, warmed

Flour Pancakes:
2 cups (500 ml) flour, sifted
¾ cup (200 ml) hot water
1 teaspoon (5 ml) sesame oil
extra oil to brush pancake
extra flour for dusting the board

1. Make pancake according to instructions below. Put aside.
2. Heat wok with oil and garlic for a few seconds over high heat. Put in pork and stir-fry for 1½ minutes. Add cloud ear, cabbage, carrot, zucchini, green onion, and broth. Stir for 2 minutes. Add shredded omelet and remaining seasonings, except hoisin sauce. Cook until thick and clear. Remove to a bowl or platter.
3. To serve, spread a thin layer of hoisin sauce over pancake and place 3 tablespoons of the meat and vegetable mixture in center. Wrap it up (and swallow the whole thing if you wish!).

Remarks

How to make the pancakes:
- Combine ingredients and knead until smooth.
- Separate into 16-20 portions and roll out into thin pancakes, 6"-7" in diameter.
- Cook two pieces at a time: brush one pancake lightly with sesame oil. Place another pancake on top and press lightly just to join.
- Brown each side in a teflon (non-stick) frying pan without oil at medium heat.
- Remove from heat and throw on counter top. It should break into the two original pancakes.

Pork with Deep-Fried Green Beans

Deep-frying a vegetable before combining it with other ingredients is a more common practice in northern than in southern Chinese cooking. Fresh green beans become more flavorful when deep-fried and go well with pork, beef and chicken.

6 ounces (168 g) lean pork
⅔ pound (300 g) fresh green beans
3 cups (750 ml) oil
3 tablespoon (45 ml) chopped Szech-
wan preserved vegetable
(optional)
¾ teaspoon (3 ml) sugar
1 teaspoon (5 ml) dark soy sauce
⅛ teaspoon (0.5 ml) chili oil (optional)
¼ cup (60 ml) soup stock
½ teaspoon (2 ml) cornstarch solution

Pork Marinade:
1 teaspoon (5 ml) soy sauce
1 teaspoon (5 ml) wine
¾ teaspoon (3 ml) cornstarch

1. Slice pork into ½" x 2" (1.5 cm x 5 cm) thin slices and marinate for 30 minutes.
2. Snap off ends of green beans and cut into 2" diagonal pieces. Dry beans and deep-fry in hot oil over high heat until beans begin to wrinkle (about 2-2½ minutes). Remove and drain well.
3. Remove oil, reserving 1 tablespoon in wok. Heat wok and oil over high heat. Add Szechwan preserved vegetable and pork, stirring for 1½ minutes. Add fried green beans and remaining ingredients. Stir-fry for 1½ minutes or until sauce is reduced but not dry.

Remarks

• For a delicious vegetarian dish simply omit the pork.

 *Disappointment is the nurse of wisdom.*

Pork Liver with Wine Sauce

Liver is inexpensive and nutritious, and it is an especially good source of iron. Don't be afraid to try it. In southern China, pork liver is commonly used in soup and other entrees. It is a delightful change from the everyday meat dishes.

⅔ **pound (300 g) pork liver**
½ **egg white, lightly beaten**
½ **teaspoon (2 ml) ginger juice**
2 **teaspoons (10 ml) cornstarch**
1½ **teaspoons (7 ml) soy sauce**
3 **tablespoons (45 ml) oil**
2 **cloves garlic, chopped**
2 **medium onions, cut in ½" (1.5 cm)**
    slices
2 **stalks green onion, cut in 2" (5 cm)**
    strips

Braising Wine Sauce:
3 **tablespoons (45 ml) wine**
1 **tablespoon (15 ml) soy sauce**
1 **teaspoon (5 ml) sugar**
¼ **teaspoon (1 ml) sesame oil**
pinch white pepper
¼ **cup (60 ml) soup stock**

1. Trim membrane and veins from pork liver and slice into ¼" x 1" x 2" (0.75 cm x 2.5 cm x 5 cm) pieces. Marinate liver for 10-15 minutes with egg white, cornstarch, ginger juice and soy sauce.
2. Drop liver into pot of boiling water. Return to a second boil. Immediately plunge liver into cold water; drain and set aside.
3. Heat 1½ tablespoons oil in wok over high heat. Add garlic and onion, stirring for 30 seconds. Add green onion and continue to stir for 30 seconds. Remove and set aside.
4. Heat 1½ tablespoons oil in wok over high heat. Add liver, stirring for 1 minute. Return onion and green onion to wok. Pour in braising sauce and mix well. Reduce heat to medium, cover and cook for 1-1½ minutes.
5. To serve, garnish with Chinese parsley.

Remarks

• This can be made with beef or calf liver, if desired.

Spiced Ground Pork

A memorable dish—taste buds never forget this exotic and traditional Szechwan entree. Salty but sweet, it keeps well in the refrigerator.

½ cup (125 ml) onion, chopped
2 teaspoons (10 ml) oil
⅔ pound (300 g) lean ground pork
½ cup (125 ml) soup stock
1 tablespoon (15 ml) sugar
2 tablespoons (30 ml) dark soy sauce

¼ cup (60 ml) chopped Chinese
    pickled cucumber or dill pickle
½ teaspoon (2 ml) ginger, mashed
¼ teaspoon (1 ml) garlic, minced
1¼ teaspoons (6 ml) cornstarch
    solution

1. Stir-fry onion in oil over high heat for 30 seconds. Add ground pork and stir an additional 1½-2 minutes.
2. Add soup stock and the rest of the ingredients except cornstarch solution. Reduce heat and simmer for 6-8 minutes, stirring occasionally. Add cornstarch solution and cook until thickened.

Remarks

* This dish can be kept in the refrigerator for several days—it's great for those moments of rushing after work. Just heat it up and POW WOW ready.

 We scheme for three meals a day, and one good sleep at night.

Spicy Szechwan Sautéed Pork

Like surprises? This surprising recipe will amaze your taste buds! A particularly hot and spicy dish, it will be a welcomed treat for your hungry family.

Pork Marinade:
1 tablespoon (15 ml) soy sauce
1 tablespoon (15 ml) wine
½ teaspoon (2 ml) sugar
¾ teaspoon (3 ml) sesame oil
1½ teaspoons (7 ml) cornstarch

6 ounces (168 g) pork tenderloin, cut into ½" (1.5 cm) cubes
2 tablespoons (30 ml) oil
3 slices ginger, shredded
1 clove garlic, chopped
½ teaspoon (2 ml) crushed dried pepper
¼ teaspoon (1 ml) toasted and crushed Szechwan pepper
1 cup (250 ml) ¾" (2 cm) cubed green pepper
1 medium-sized onion, ¾" (2 cm) cubed
2 teaspoons (10 ml) hot bean paste or chili sauce
3-4 tablespoons (45-60 ml) soup stock (More if needed)
½ teaspoon (2 ml) cornstarch solution

1. Marinate pork for 30 minutes.
2. Heat oil in hot wok over high heat with ginger, garlic, dried red pepper and Szechwan pepper, stirring for 15 seconds. Add pork cubes and stir-fry for 2½-3 minutes. Sprinkle with broth if mixture gets too dry. Add remaining ingredients except cornstarch. Stir for another 2-3 minutes. Add extra soup stock if too dry. Thicken with cornstarch and serve.

Remarks

• If possible, use Szechwan-style garlic-flavored chili sauce (available only in Chinese stores). It is superbly hot and it lasts!

Steamed Spareribs with Plum Sauce

Here is a dish that uses plum sauce, a very popular Cantonese seasoning and dipping sauce. Plum sauce gives a unique, uncompromising flavor to this dish which is just as delicious reheated for a rushed meal.

1 pound (450 g) pork spareribs, cut
    into 1-1½" (2.5 cm-4 cm) squares
2½ teaspoons (12 ml) cornstarch
1 red chili pepper, thinly sliced

Rib Sauce:
2-3 slices ginger, shredded
2½ tablespoons (37 ml) plum sauce
1 or 2 salted plums, crushed or ¼ tea-
    spoon (1 ml) salt
1½ teaspoons (7 ml) dark soy sauce
¾ teaspoon (3 ml) sugar

1. Coat spareribs with cornstarch and marinate in rib sauce.
2. Transfer ribs to a pyrex pie pan. Top with chili pepper slices. Steam over medium-high heat for 12-15 minutes. Serve hot.

Remarks

- Try to find the salted plums as they give the dish a unique flavor.
- Trim excess fat from both sides of ribs. Ask the butcher to cut spareribs across the bone into 1" to 1½" strips, so that you don't end up making firewood from your cutting board and ruining all your knives.

Stuffed Green Peppers

The savoriness of shrimp in this dish will start you thinking of the salty sea. Its tempting aromas are sure to draw guests and, baked in the shrimps' own natural juices, it makes an intriguing and succulent entree.

¼ pound (112 g) lean ground pork, dusted with cornstarch
¼ pound (112 g) fresh frozen shrimp, thawed and mashed (or cooked shrimp)
1 stalk green onion, finely chopped
2 water chestnuts, finely chopped
¾ teaspoon (3 ml) garlic salt
1 teaspoon (5 ml) wine
1 teaspoon (5 ml) cornstarch
3 medium peppers, cut into 1½" (4 cm) squares or triangles
2 tablespoons (30 ml) cooking oil

Seasoning Sauce:
½ teaspoon (2 ml) sugar
2 tablespoons (30 ml) oyster-flavored sauce
dash of white pepper
½ cup (125 ml) stock with 1½ teaspoons (7 ml) cornstarch

1. In a bowl, mix together ground pork, shrimp, green onion, water chestnuts, garlic salt, and wine.
2. Stuff peppers with 1½ teaspoons meat mixture each.
3. Heat flat frying pan with 2 tablespoons oil, fry stuffed peppers with meat side facing down for approximately 2 minutes over medium-high heat. Add seasoning sauce ingredients. Cover and simmer for 8 minutes or until thickened. Serve hot.

Remarks

- Traditionally the filling is made with fish paste.

 Blessings never come in pairs; misfortunes never come singly.

Sweet and Sour Lychee-Flavored Pork

For those who love pineapple chicken balls, you'll love this dish too! A tantalizing taste treat that's quick and simple to prepare.

10 ounces (280 g) pork tenderloin, cut
    into ½" (1.5 cm) cubes
2 tablespoons (30 ml) cornstarch for
    dry coating
4 cups (1 L) oil

Pork Marinade:
1½ teaspoons (7 ml) wine
1 tablespoon (15 ml) soy sauce
1 egg yolk, lightly beaten
1 teaspoon (5 ml) cornstarch

Sweet and Sour Sauce:
1 teaspoon (5 ml) shredded ginger
½ teaspoon (2 ml) oil
¼ cup (60 ml) vinegar
¼ cup (60 ml) water
¼ cup (60 ml) sugar
2 tablespoons (30 ml) catsup
½ cup (125 ml) lychees
1 teaspoon (5 ml) cornstarch solution

1. Marinate pork for 30 minutes. Dry-coat pork with cornstarch and set aside.
2. Heat 4 cups oil in wok over medium-high heat; deep fry pork for 3 minutes or until golden brown and floating freely on top of oil.
3. While deep frying pork, make sweet and sour sauce. Combine oil and ginger in a sauce pan over high heat. Stir in remaining sweet and sour ingredients, except lychees and cornstarch, and bring to a boil. Add lychees. Thicken with cornstarch and set aside.
4. Place pork on a platter and pour sauce on top.

Remarks

- For extra crispiness, deep-fry pork pieces again before adding sauce.
- Garnish with sesame seeds if desired.

Sweet and Sour Pork

When you think Chinese cooking, what comes to mind? Sweet and sour. This has almost become the trademark of Chinese cooking in many parts of the world. A popular traditional and appreciated dish in any season, its color, flavor and aroma make it an appetizing and appealing combination. The sauce: extraordinary!

¾ pound (340 g) boneless pork, cut
    into ¾" (2 cm) cubes
cornstarch for coating
4 cups (1 L) oil
½ tomato, cut into bite-size chunks
2½ teaspoons (12 ml) cornstarch
    solution
½ bell pepper, 1" (2.5 cm) squares
2 pineapple rings
6 lychees

Pork Marinade:
⅔ teaspoon (2.5 ml) salt
½ teaspoon (2 ml) ginger juice
1 tablespoon (15 ml) wine

Sweet and Sour Sauce:
½ teaspoon oil
1 clove garlic, minced
¼ cup (60 ml) vinegar
¼ cup (60 ml) brown sugar
3 tablespoons (45 ml) catsup (optional)
¼ cup (60 ml) water
2½ teaspoons (12 ml) cornstarch
½ teaspoon (2 ml) soy sauce
½ teaspoon (2 ml) oil
dash of Tabasco Sauce

Batter Mix:
¾ cup (200 ml) flour
¼ cup (60 ml) cornstarch
½ teaspoon (2 ml) sugar
¾ cup (200 ml) flat beer (or water)
¾ teaspoon (3 ml) baking powder (if
    using water increase to 1¼
    teaspoons)
½ teaspoon (2 ml) oil

1. Marinate pork for ½ hour.
2. Make batter mix. Coat pork with cornstarch.
3. Dip marinated pork into batter and coat evenly.
4. Heat oil in wok over high heat, near smoking; reduce to medium-high, and gently place battered pork in hot oil. Deep-fry up to 12 pieces at a time, until pieces are floating freely in oil and golden brown, approximately 2-3 minutes. Remove and drain well. Repeat with remaining pork.
5. To make sweet and sour sauce, heat garlic with ½ teaspoon oil in sauce pan. Add remaining ingredients and mix well.
6. Add tomato and bell pepper to sauce; thicken with cornstarch.
7. To serve, combine pork and sauce and mix well. Garnish with extra tomato and fruit, and serve hot.

Remarks

- Brighten up this dish with a beautiful combination of bite-size chunks of half a tomato, 2 pineapple rings and 6 lychees as garnish.

If Yan can wok out, you can pork out.

Sweet and Sour Pork Rolls

Good food. Delightful, original and appetizing. Takes time to prepare, but a truly impressive dish for a special occasion.

⅔ pound (300 g) lean pork tenderloin, cut into thin 3" x 4" (7.5 cm x 10 cm) slices
2 slices cooked ham, 3" (7.5 cm) julienne strips
2 stalks green onion, 3" (7.5 cm) lengths
4-5 dried black mushrooms, soaked and sliced
½ zucchini, 3" (7.5 cm) julienne lengths
flour paste (1½ tablespoons (22 ml) flour and 1½ tablespoons (22 ml) water)

Sweet and Sour Sauce:
3 tablespoons (45 ml) vinegar
3 tablespoons (45 ml) catsup
3 tablespoons (45 ml) sugar
5½ tablespoons (72 ml) water
1¾ teaspoons (8 ml) cornstarch solution

Pork Marinade:
2 teaspoons (10 ml) soy sauce
2 teaspoons (10 ml) wine
1 teaspoon (5 ml) sesame oil
1½ teaspoons (7 ml) cornstarch
½ teaspoon (2 ml) five-spice powder

1. Pound pork slices with flat side of cleaver to flatten.
2. Marinate slices for 30 minutes.
3. Preheat oven to 350°F (180°C).
4. On each pork slice, layer 2 to 3 slices of: ham, green onion, mushroom and zucchini. Roll up each slice and seal with flour paste. Secure with toothpicks if necessary. Trim any excess filling from ends of pork rolls.
5. Bake at 350°F (180°C) in lightly greased shallow pan for about 10-12 minutes.
6. While pork is baking, combine sweet and sour sauce ingredients, except cornstarch, in a sauce pan. Bring to a boil, thicken with cornstarch and keep warm.
7. To serve, arrange pork rolls on a platter and serve sauce over top.

Remarks

- Instead of baking, you can deep-fry pork rolls until golden, or brown pork rolls in a skillet with a small amount of oil. Serve with sauce.

Thousand-Layer Cabbage

A beautiful showpiece to enhance your table. Surprise your guests with its elegance and sophisticated taste. And it can be prepared ahead of time.

½ head medium Chinese cabbage
  (Napa)
2 tablespoons (30 ml) cornstarch

Filling:
½ pound (225 g) lean ground pork
2 tablespoons (30 ml) minced green
  onion
1 teaspoon (5 ml) finely minced ginger
½ teaspoon (2 ml) salt
1½ teaspoons (7 ml) cornstarch

Sauce:
½ teaspoon (2 ml) dark soy sauce
1½ teaspoons (7 ml) oyster-flavored
  sauce
½ teaspoon (2 ml) sugar
½ cup (125 ml) soup stock
1¾ teaspoons (8 ml) cornstarch
  solution

1. Cook cabbage leaves for 2 minutes in boiling water. Dry and sprinkle leaves with cornstarch. Reserve.
2. In a large bowl, combine filling ingredients and mix well; set aside.
3. Spread filling mixture thinly and evenly on each leaf approximately ¼" (0.75 cm) thick. Stack leaves on a plate, one on top of the other, with meat facing down.
4. Steam stuffed cabbage for 18-20 minutes over medium-high heat.
5. While steaming, prepare sauce. Combine all ingredients except cornstarch solution and bring to a boil. Thicken with cornstarch solution and keep warm.
6. To serve, transfer cooked cabbage to a platter and cut crosswise into 4 portions. Cover with sauce.

Remarks

- When preparing for a dinner party or ahead of time, keep stuffed cabbage warm and pour sauce over it just before serving.
- Garnish with 2 tablespoons chopped green onion; serve.

 When you drink from the stream, remember the spring.

Tonkatsu (Crispy Pork Cutlet)

If Yan can so can you;…this is one of my favorite Japanese dishes. It's quick, easy and delectable.

1 pound (450 g) lean pork
1 teaspoon (5 ml) garlic or onion salt
1 large egg, lightly beaten
4 teaspoons (20 ml) water
2 tablespoons (30 ml) flour

1 cup (250 ml) Japanese bread crumbs
   (Panko)
4 cups (1 L) oil
¼ cup (60 ml) Tonkatsu sauce

1. Slice pork into ¼" (0.75 cm) thick cutlets; sprinkle with garlic or onion salt.
2. Combine eggs and water. Dip each cutlet in flour then in egg mixture, and finally into bread crumbs. Let stand for a couple of minutes to allow crumbs to set.
3. Heat oil to medium high. Deep fry 2 pork cutlets at a time in hot oil for 2-2½ minutes. Turn cutlets over and cook 1-1½ minutes until golden brown. Drain well. Slice.
4. Arrange sliced cutlets on a plate; dip into Tonkatsu sauce.

Remarks

- Tonkatsu sauce is available in Japanese grocery stores, but if there are no stores in your area, you can cheat by using Worcestershire Sauce.
- Japanese bread crumbs, *Panko* in Japanese, is only available in Japanese stores. Unlike ordinary bread crumbs Panko can be found in an assortment of sizes.
- Both Tonkatsu sauce and Panko can be kept for a long period of time. If you live in the middle of nowhere take a train, a Greyhound, or a jet to shop and stock up for the next 15 years.

 All great cooks need a little compliment now and then.

Tung Por Pork Plate

This dish originated with a story that goes something like this: The famous poet, Tung Por, one day visited a temple where he smelled something extraordinarily good. "What is that wonderful aroma?" he asked. One of the priests graciously responded, "It is a pork stew that is being prepared just for you!" Prepare this dish for your favorite person—just for them!

1 pound (450 g) pork shoulder
1 pound (450 g) spinach
1½ tablespoons (22 ml) oil
1 teaspoon (5 ml) ginger, chopped
1-2 stalks green onion, chopped

3 tablespoons (45 ml) soy sauce
1 tablespoon (15 ml) dark soy sauce
¾ cup (200 ml) pork broth
¾ cup (200 ml) wine
2½ tablespoons (37 ml) packed brown sugar

1. Bring ample water (enough to cover a 1 pound pork shoulder) to a boil in a large pot. Put in pork shoulder. When water returns to a boil, remove pork and cut into 1½" x 3" x ¼" (4 cm x 7.5 cm x 0.75 cm) slices.
2. Parboil spinach in the same broth for 2 minutes; remove and set aside.
3. Heat wok with oil over high heat and stir in ginger and chopped green onion.
4. Add pork and stir for 1 minute. Add soy sauces, broth and wine. Cook over medium-high heat for about 10 minutes, until liquid is reduced to ¼ cup.
5. Add brown sugar and stir until completely melted.
6. To serve, arrange pork slices on one side of the platter and spinach on the other.

Remarks

• This dish goes well over rice and noodles.

海鮮類

EDWARD LIM

Catch of the Day —Seafood

Seafood is abundant and immensely popular on most Chinese menus. In fact, there are a great many restaurants that specialize in seafood only. These restaurants often keep fish and other sea creatures alive in gigantic vats until their appointed hour, to assure maximum freshness and taste. Sometimes you can even hand-pick your choice for a dish. Seafood can be prepared in a great many ways, for everyday meals or elaborate dinners. When seafood is properly prepared, it is superbly delicate and out of this world!

Fish

The Chinese word for fish is pronounced as "yu" and is the same word used for "remain." For this reason, it is a Chinese tradition to serve whole fish at festivities and happy occasions. A tailless, headless fish is considered incomplete and not aesthetically pleasing. The head contains many delicacies: fine cheek meat, melt-in-your-mouth lips, and a scrumptious tongue. To honor a guest, the host at a Chinese dinner will always serve fish with the head pointed in his direction. A whole fish served at dinner guarantees that the happiness felt by the guests will "remain" for a long, long time. The symbolism of fish matches the Chinese symbol for family. Fish swimming in pairs denotes marital bliss with harmony and powers of regeneration, wealth and abundance.

If you are lucky enough to have a local fish market, you will have an advantage. When buying fresh seafood of any kind, reject fish with an objectionable odor, a slimy surface or a suspicious color on the surface. Get rid of your inhibitions; poke, lift, look and sniff the fish. You may look like a beginner at first but people will come to the point of respecting your experience. Besides, by doing this little shopping ritual you will be eliminating the chances of getting a bad fish and you will be more pleased with your selection.

The Chinese use both fresh and salt-water fish. Traditionally, most chefs prefer fresh-water fish, for they can be kept alive in the vats. To tell whether a fish is fresh, look for eyes that are bright, not red or soggy, skin that is quite glossy, and a body that is firm and resilient. Fish is generally prepared with wine or ginger to disguise disagreeable fishy odors. It can be cooked whole or in fillet, either steamed or deep-fried. Prolonged cooking of any fish will not make it tender; overcooking will only toughen the meat.

In North America, fish has not found the proper place on a good menu. It is my feeling that the reason for this is the objectionable fishy taste and odor caused by prolonged storage or improper handling and preparation.

Shrimp, Prawns

These are infinitely popular among Chinese all over the world. Some hosts insist that a prawn dish be featured at every banquet because the Cantonese pronounce the Chinese character for prawn as "ha"—the element of the almost universally accepted "ha, ha" sound of laughter. Shrimps are available in several forms—fresh or frozen, with or without shell. To prepare frozen shrimps: wash under cold running water and thaw at room temperature; devein if necessary. They can be cooked in the shell or without the shell. Cook until they turn pink and curl up; they should never be overcooked. When stir-fried with other ingredients and seasonings, most Chinese believe that shrimps taste better and juicier when cooked in the shell with their own natural juices. You can fry, deep-fry, or boil them. Shrimps can be served with anything.

Lobster

The Chinese name for lobster, a specialty of the Fukien and Chekiang coastal regions, is "Dragon Shrimp." Lobsters are one of the ocean's most exotic creatures, yet they require the simplest presentation. Buy them fresh and alive whenever possible. Unfortunately, they are getting extremely expensive. One reason is that it takes about 8 years for any lobster to reach a marketable size. When cooking lobster in boiling water or by steaming, cook for 5-6 minutes. Stir-fried lobster with black bean sauce is one of my favorites. When serving lobster, be sure to have a nutcracker at hand and to suck each tiny crawler (leg), which contains its own delicate juices inside.

Squid

This tender white seafood has a delicate taste. To prepare: remove the head and tentacles (save for other dishes), then peel off the purple membrane and remove the cartilage. Rinse well under running water. Score lightly at a 45 degree angle forming small crisscross patterns. Finally cut into 1½" (4 cm) squares. Squid can be blanched, stir-fried, deep-fried, or served in soups. Whichever you choose, avoid overcooking; otherwise you may end up with a plateful of rubbery stuff!!

Oysters

Oysters are available in the shell or without the shell. They can be stored in the refrigerator for a few days and remain fresh. Serve them raw with lemon, stir-fried with ginger and onion or simply deep-fried. All of these methods of preparation will give you great plump, juicy oysters.

Clams

Clams are easy to find in most seafood sections of your local supermarket or any fish store. Be sure to pick those with tightly-closed shells. If one is open, tap it quickly, and it will close if it is still alive and well. Fresh clams in shells will keep several days refrigerated or they can be frozen. To cook clams, steam or boil them until they open. Discard any that do not open. The most popular ways to prepare clams are to steam or stir-fry them and serve with black bean sauce.

Mussels

Many people have never heard of and are not even willing to try this delicacy! They have been my favorite since I was a child. They are inexpensive and contain as much protein as steak but much less fat and calories. Buy them fresh and test them as you do clams. They can be steamed, boiled, or stir-fried. One way to prepare them is to cook them in a wine sauce until they open and just eat them right from the shell. Do not overcook.

In the oceans and lakes of the world, there is an abundance of fish and many common as well as exotic seafoods. Some day, seafood may become the inevitable daily staple of mankind. In these following pages, you will discover a whole new world of marvelous ideas with which you can enjoy a wide variety of delicate, delicious dishes.

Baked Stuffed Crab Shell

An overworked and crabby husband will be comforted with this satisfying tasty dish. The fantastic flavors of the crab, liver, mushrooms and water chestnuts make it an intriguing dish.

1 fresh or frozen uncooked crab (or cooked crab)
1 teaspoon (5 ml) finely chopped ginger
½ small onion, chopped
1 teaspoon (5 ml) oil
1 tablespoon (15 ml) green peas
1 tablespoon (15 ml) chopped cooked chicken liver (optional)
2 dried black mushrooms, soaked and shredded
1 tablespoon (15 ml) chopped water chestnuts

1½ tablespoons (22 ml) soup stock
1 egg, lightly beaten
1 teaspoon (5 ml) soy sauce
1½ teaspoons (7 ml) cornstarch
¼ teaspoon (1 ml) salt
white pepper to taste
2 teaspoons (10 ml) bread crumbs

1. If using uncooked crab, cook in boiling water for 5-6 minutes. Cool and remove meat. Set aside.
2. Stir-fry ginger and onion in oil over high heat for 30 seconds. Mix in cooked crab meat and remaining ingredients, except bread crumbs. Cook for one minute.
3. Place mixture into crab shell. Gently press to flatten. Sprinkle bread crumbs on top. Bake at 325°F (160°C) for 12-15 minutes.

Remarks

• The legs can be served separately.

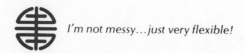 *I'm not messy…just very flexible!*

Bean Curd with Crab Meat Sauce

Feeling a little crabby? Let's change that! Bean curd with crab meat sauce is sure to make you smile. Delightful and light, it's another example of using bean curd to make a classic and popular Chinese dish. One of the most popular Cantonese dishes.

2 squares bean curd, cut into 1½" x 1" x 1½" (4 cm x 2.5 cm x 4 cm) pieces
1½ tablespoons (22 ml) oil
1 teaspoon (5 ml) ginger juice
2 teaspoons (10 ml) wine
⅓ cup (80 ml) shredded cooked crab meat

1 cup (250 ml) soup stock
¾ teaspoon (3 ml) salt
1½ tablespoons (22 ml) cornstarch solution
1 large egg white, lightly beaten
¾ teaspoon (3 ml) chopped green onion

1. Blanch bean curd in boiling water for 1 minute; drain well.
2. Heat oil in a non-stick pan over medium-high heat. Add ginger, stirring for 10-15 seconds. Stir in wine, crab meat and soup stock. Gently add bean curd and salt. Cover and cook for 2½-3 minutes.
3. Stir in cornstarch solution. Reduce heat to low and cook until thickened. Slowly pour in egg white and cook until set, stirring continuously.
4. Sprinkle chopped green onions on top and serve immediately.

Braised Fish with Brown Bean Sauce

Brown bean paste will give this an intriguing piquancy that will be foreign to your taste, but speak your language. This seasoning is traditional, exotic and used everyday in many Chinese kitchens.

1 whole fish (cleaned and scaled) or 1 pound (450 g) fillet
4 teaspoons (20 ml) brown bean sauce
2 teaspoons (10 ml) oil
2 slices ginger, shredded
1 teaspoon (5 ml) sugar

1 tablespoon (15 ml) soy sauce
¾ cup (200 ml) soup stock
1 stalk green onion, cut into 2½" (6.5 cm) strips
2 teaspoons (10 ml) cornstarch solution
1 tablespoon (15 ml) wine

1. Dry fish well. Rub brown bean sauce over fish surface.
2. Heat frying pan with oil over medium-high heat. Brown fish 1 minute on each side.
3. Add ginger, sugar, soy sauce, soup stock and green onion. Cover and reduce to low heat. Let braise in sauce for 8 minutes or until fish flakes easily.
4. Remove fish to platter, thicken braising sauce with cornstarch. Stir in 1 tablespoon wine and serve immediately.

Try some, you won't like it.

Crispy Fish with Nuts

A great dish to try. The tantilizing flavor will wake up every taste bud. The touch of nuts will drive you nuts!

1 whole small white fish, cleaned and scaled (or 1 pound (450 g) white fish fillet)
2 egg yolks (optional)
½ teaspoon (2 ml) salt
1½ tablespoons (22 ml) cornstarch
dash white pepper
4-5 cups (1 L-1¼ L) oil
¼ cup (60 ml) fried or roasted nuts, slightly chopped

Sauce:
3 tablespoons (45 ml) sugar
3½ tablespoons (52 ml) white vinegar
2½ tablespoons (37 ml) catsup
¼ cup (60 ml) water
1 teaspoon (5 ml) cornstarch solution

1. If using a whole fish, make 5-6 small diagonal incisions on each side. Coat fish or fillet with egg yolk.
2. Sprinkle evenly with salt, pepper and starch. Let stand for 30 minutes.
3. Deep-fry fish over medium-high heat until golden brown, turning occasionally. Remove and drain well.
4. While deep-frying, prepare sauce. Combine sauce ingredients in saucepan. Bring to a boil and cook until thickened. Set aside.
5. To serve, place fish on platter, cover with sauce and sprinkle with nuts.

Remarks

- If this dish is not served immediately, keep fish and sauce warm separately.
- If nuts are fried at home, use medium-low heat to deep-fry until light golden brown.

Crystal Prawns with Tri-Colored Vegetables

Just as crystal reflects many colors in the spectrum, this entree of crystal prawns reflects the beautiful bright greens, reds and oranges in the fresh vegetables used. (It is something you will only serve to the most respected and honored guest—you will probably have to get a loan to pay for the prawns!)

12-14 medium prawns, shelled and deveined
1½ teaspoon (7 ml) salt
1 egg white, lightly beaten
1 teaspoon (5 ml) cornstarch
1 small cucumber, shredded in 2" (5 cm) strips
1 medium carrot, shredded in 2" (5 cm) strips

¼ Chinese radish, shredded in 2" (5 cm) strips
¼ cup (60 ml) vinegar
5 tablespoons (75 ml) sugar
4 teaspoons (20 ml) sesame oil
3 cups (750 ml) oil

1. Sprinkle ½ teaspoon salt over shelled prawns and let stand for 2-3 minutes. Rinse under running water for 2-3 minutes. Marinate in ½ teaspoon salt, egg white, and cornstarch for 20-30 minutes.
2. In a mixing bowl, combine cucumber, carrot, radish and remaining ½ teaspoon salt. Let stand for 3-5 minutes. Squeeze out water. Add vinegar, sugar, and sesame oil. Blend well and set aside.
3. Heat oil in wok over medium-high heat. Deep fry prawns in hot oil until pink, 1½-2 minutes. Remove and drain well.
4. To serve, spread pickled vegetables on a platter, and arrange prawns on top. Serve hot or cold.

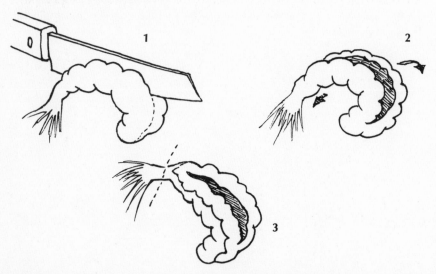

Curry-Flavor Prawns with Garlic

We were testing recipes day and night, eating up a storm. One day the kitchen was so overwhelmed with garlic aroma, that one of the recipe testers went home that night and had a dream of garlic. Katy, of Davis, California, dreamt up this wonderful recipe. I would like to share it with you. For the truly dedicated garlic lover, double the garlic!

2 tablespoons (30 ml) oil
8-10 whole garlic cloves, peeled
2 slices ginger, chopped
6 ounces (168 g) medium-sized
    prawns, shelled and deveined
8 dried black mushrooms, soaked (cut
    each in 3 wedges)

20-22 snow peas
¼ cup (60 ml) chicken stock (more if
    necessary)
¾ teaspoon (3 ml) curry powder
1½ teaspoons (7 ml) soy sauce
2 tablespoons (30 ml) wine
dash white pepper
1 teaspoon (5 ml) cornstarch solution
½ cup (125 ml) cashews

1. Heat oil in wok over medium-high heat; stir-fry garlic for one minute. Add ginger and prawns and fry one minute. Sprinkle with stock if it becomes dry; remove prawns and garlic and set aside.
2. Add mushrooms, peas and chicken stock to wok. Reduce heat to medium. Cover and cook 2½-3 minutes. Return prawns and garlic to wok; stir in remaining ingredients except cashews and cook until thickened. Toss in cashews and serve immediately.

Remarks

- Be sure to add nuts just before serving, as they get soggy very quickly.

 Man cannot be always fortunate; flowers do not last forever.

Deep-Fried Squid with Spice Salt

A popular seafood for the Chinese. If properly prepared, squid has a very tender texture and the delicate seafood flavor compliments soups, vegetables, and spicy dishes. Besides being one of the most economical dishes, squid has no bones to bite into. For a creative cook, squid can be an inspirational beginning for a unique dish.

10 medium squid, cleaned and
   eviscerated
1 egg white
¾ teaspoon (3 ml) salt
1 teaspoon (5 ml) cornstarch
3 cups (750 ml) oil

1 clove garlic, chopped
½ dried chili pepper, crushed
⅛ teaspoon (0.5 ml) five-spice powder
pinch of white pepper

1. Cut open squid. Pound with a mallet and lightly score the inside surface with a knife. Cut into 1" x 2" (2.5 cm x 5 cm) slices. Marinate with egg white, ½ teaspoon salt and cornstarch for 10-15 minutes. Drain the squid well in a strainer and add 1 teaspoon oil. Mix well.
2. Heat oil in wok over high heat. Deep-fry squid in oil for 1 minute. Remove and drain.
3. Remove oil, reserving 2 teaspoons in wok. Heat wok to high. Stir in garlic, crushed chili pepper, fried squid, five-spice powder, ¼ teaspoon salt and white pepper. Mix well and serve immediately.

Grandma Yan's Garlic Cure-All!

Hear ye, hear ye! Step right up and get a bottle of Grandma Yan's Garlic Cure-All! Do you suffer from life's annoying ailments such as athlete's foot, pimples, constipation, insomnia or the common cold? In clinical studies garlic, yes garlic, has been shown to have miraculous preventive and therapeutic powers. Some of life's more severe disorders such as hypertension, atherosclerosis, arthritis, diabetes and hypoglycemia have been treated with varying degrees of success due to a potion of garlic in some form or another. Had you begun to think anything you eat lately will probably give you cancer? In an experiment done using carcinogenic mice, the ones treated with an injection of garlic lived up to six months longer than those without the injection! Move over Laetrile.

Historically, garlic has not always been viewed so favorably. More than a half century ago many natural hygienists believed it was a poison. However, accounts from as early as 3000 B.C. have been found showing the use of garlic in treatment by the Babylonians, Chinese, Greeks, Romans, Egyptians, and Vikings. Russians used it as a treatment for grippe and whooping cough. During World War I, the British Army used garlic to control infection in wounds. Could it have been their secret weapon used to win the War?

This sounds wonderful but what about the unpleasant fragrance of this medicinal gem? What about my love life? Will I have to have relationships over the phone? Will my career as a dental hygienist be ruined? Never fear! The Japanese have developed an odorless garlic solution! It is called Kyolic and it is available in the United States in many health food stores. In Canada it is known as Leopin. So, garlic lovers of the world unite, and make garlic bread, not war!

Garlic-Flavored Prawns

If he kisses you once, he'll kiss you again! This dish is worth many kisses. An elegant dish, quick to prepare, that can be served as an appetizer or a main dish. It's also a basis for creating other dishes.

**14-16 medium-sized prawns, shelled
 and deveined**
1½ tablespoons (22 ml) oil
3 tablespoons (45 ml) chopped garlic
1 stalk green onion, chopped
1 teaspoon (5 ml) wine

Prawn Marinade:
1 teaspoon (5 ml) wine
1 teaspoon (5 ml) cornstarch
¼ teaspoon (1 ml) salt

1. Marinate prawns for 30 minutes.
2. Heat wok with 1½ tablespoons oil over high heat. Add garlic and green onion. Stir for ½ minute. Add prawns and continue stirring for another 1½ minutes. Sprinkle in 1 teaspoon wine and serve immediately.

Remarks

Dry prawns well before marinating to avoid splashing in oil.

Golden Batter Fish Rolls

Combining the delicate flavor of white fish and the crispy texture of asparagus is a gourmet's delight. It is a banquet showpiece, sure to receive praise.

⅔ pound (300 g) white fish fillet, cut into thin, 2½" x 3" (6.5 cm x 7.5 cm) strips
8-10 fresh asparagus, diagonally cut into 2-2½" (5 cm x 6.5 cm) slices
¼ cup (60 ml) flour
2 eggs, lightly beaten
3 tablespoons (45 ml) oil
4 cloves garlic, thinly sliced
2 tablespoons (30 ml) green onion, chopped

Dressing:
4 teaspoons (20 ml) wine
1 teaspoon (5 ml) dark soy sauce
1 teaspoon (5 ml) sesame oil
2 teaspoons (10 ml) oyster-flavored sauce
¼ cup (60 ml) chicken broth
½ teaspoon (2 ml) cornstarch solution

Fish Marinade:
½ teaspoon (2 ml) sugar
pinch white pepper
½ teaspoon (2 ml) salt
1 teaspoon (5 ml) cornstarch
1 teaspoon (5 ml) ginger juice

1. Marinate fish for 10-15 minutes.
2. Blanch asparagus pieces for 1½ minutes in boiling water. Plunge into cold water and drain.
3. To make batter, combine eggs and flour and mix well. Set aside.
4. Place one or two pieces of blanched asparagus on each fish fillet. Roll fillet around asparagus and secure with a toothpick. Dip each fish roll into the batter and set aside.
5. Combine all ingredients for dressing except cornstarch solution. Set aside.
6. Heat 1½ tablespoons oil over medium heat in skillet or non-stick pan. Stir in half of the garlic and green onion and cook for 10-15 seconds. Add half of the fish rolls and brown for 1½-2 minutes on each side. Remove to serving platter. Add 1½ tablespoons oil to skillet and cook remaining garlic, green onion, and fish rolls in the same manner.
7. Pour dressing mixture into the skillet and bring to a boil. Add cornstarch solution and cook until thickened.
8. Top fish rolls with dressing. Garnish with parsley and serve immediately.

Lobster Cantonese

Delight your guests with this elegant and elaborate dish which is easy to prepare. A well-known gourmet dish in most Cantonese restaurants, it's an excellent selection for a special celebration.

1-2 fresh or frozen lobster tails, approximately 1½ pounds (675 g)
3 teaspoons (15 ml) cornstarch
½ teaspoon (2 ml) salt
1½ tablespoons (22 ml) salted black beans
2 garlic cloves, minced
2½ tablespoons (37 ml) oil
½ pound (225 g) ground lean pork

¼ cup (60 ml) soup stock
½ onion, cut into bite-size pieces
1 green bell pepper, cut into bite-size pieces
2-3 slices ginger root, chopped
2 teaspoons (10 ml) cornstarch
2 egg whites with 2 tablespoons (30 ml) water

1. Cut lobster tails in half, lengthwise; wash and pat dry with towel.
2. Cut each half into 5-6 pieces. Leave the shell on, if desired. Coat lobster with cornstarch and salt. Set aside.
3. Wash black beans, drain well and combine with garlic to make a paste. Set aside.
4. Heat wok over high heat with 1½ teaspoons oil, add ground pork and stir for approximately 1½ minutes. Add soup stock if it appears too dry. Remove and set aside.
5. Clean wok. Heat remaining 2 tablespoons oil over high heat. Stir in lobster and cook for 3-3½ minutes.
6. Add ground pork and remaining ingredients except cornstarch and egg whites to lobster. Stir for 30 seconds. Stir in cornstarch; cook until thickened. Turn off heat, add egg whites and blend well. Serve immediately.

Remarks:

- Use salted black beans cautiously. The taste is strong.
- Substitute jumbo prawns for lobster if you wish, but be careful not to overcook them!

 Three nickels will get you on the subway, but garlic will get you a seat in no time.

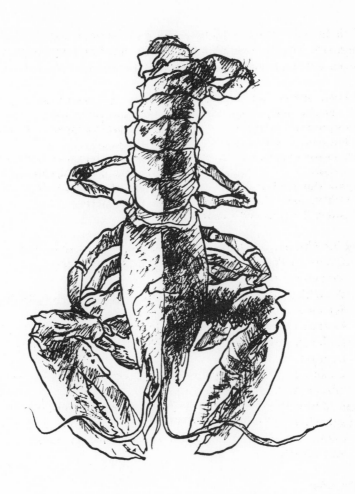

Sautéed Frog Legs

Jumpin' frog legs! Mark Twain would jump for joy over this dish. You will love it, too. The tender, juicy and delicate flavor of frog legs will remind you of chicken—a gourmet treat found frequently on the menu of fancy Chinese restaurants.

10 fresh or frozen frog legs
2 teaspoons (10 ml) wine
1½ teaspoons (7 ml) cornstarch
3 cups (750 ml) oil
2 stalks green onions, chopped
1 dried chili pepper, crushed

1½ teaspoons (7 ml) oyster-flavored sauce
½ teaspoon (2 ml) sugar
¼ teaspoon (1 ml) salt
½ teaspoon (2 ml) sesame oil
2 tablespoons (30 ml) soup stock
¼ teaspoon (1 ml) cornstarch solution

1. Cut frog legs into 1½" (4 cm) pieces. Marinate with wine and cornstarch for 15-30 minutes.
2. Heat oil over high heat. Deep-fry frog legs until golden brown. Remove and drain.
3. Remove oil, reserving 1½ tablespoons in wok. Heat oil and wok over high heat. Add green onion and chili, stirring for 10-15 seconds. Stir in frog legs and remaining ingredients. Reduce heat to medium high. Stir-fry for 1½-2 minutes and serve hot.

Remarks

• Frog legs are commonly available in specialty food shops or in the frozen food section of supermarkets.

Sesame Fish Fillet

You may have tried sesame prawns, sesame chicken or sesame pork but how about sesame fish? Tender, juicy fish fillet with an aromatic sesame seed coating are a heavenly match. Remember, this humble cook is a matchmaker!

⅔ pound (300 g) white fish fillet, cut
    into 1" x ¼" x 2½" (2.5 cm x 0.75
    cm x 6.5 cm) slices
1 egg, lightly beaten
3 tablespoons (45 ml) cornstarch
3 tablespoons (45 ml) flour
4½ tablespoons (67 ml) sesame seeds
4 cups (1 L) oil

Fish Marinade:
1 teaspoon (5 ml) ginger juice
1½ teaspoons (7 ml) wine
pinch of white pepper
½ teaspoon (2 ml) salt
½ teaspoon (2 ml) sugar

1. Marinate fish for 10-15 minutes.
2. Coat fish slices with beaten egg, then dry-coat in a mixture of cornstarch, flour and sesame seeds. Let sit for 5-10 minutes.
3. Shake off the excess coating before frying. Deep-fry fish slices, a few at a time, over medium-high heat until golden brown. Drain well and set aside.
4. Serve with catsup or make your own sweet and sour sauce dip.

 Do not covet for the mouth and belly, and so slay animals and birds with restraint.

Snow-White Foo Yung

This is a foo yung for a rich man who can spend a fortune on prawns. (The only time that I made this recipe was when I tested it!) The egg white and the light pinkish color of the prawns combine in perfect harmony. This dish bears a symbolic meaning in Chinese: "purity and chastity."

6 ounces (168 g) fresh or frozen
    prawns
7-8 egg whites, lightly beaten
3 tablespoons (45 ml) oil
1½ tablespoons (22 ml) chopped
    Virginia ham
2 tablespoons (30 ml) chopped green
    onion

Prawn Marinade:
½ teaspoon (2 ml) salt
1 teaspoon (5 ml) wine
½ teaspoon (2 ml) ginger juice
pinch of white pepper
½ teaspoon (2 ml) cornstarch

1. Shell and devein prawns; cut into thin ¼" (0.75 cm) slices and marinate for 20-30 minutes.
2. Beat egg whites until smooth. Combine prawns with egg whites and mix well.
3. Heat oil in small non-sticking pan or skillet over medium-high heat. Add half of the foo yung mixture to pan and cook for 1½ minutes on each side. Repeat with remaining half of mixture.
4. To serve, place foo yung on platter, sprinkle chopped ham in center and surround ham with chopped green onions.

Remarks

- Be sure to use a small frying pan or skillet; foo yung should not be too thin and should not be overcooked.
- To get the snow-white color, the foo yung is traditionally deep-fried. Slowly pour egg white mixture into hot oil. When it puffs up and floats, turn it over a couple of times. Drain well and place on platter.

Spicy Clams for the Great Lovers

A clam-digger's delight—venture into the world of exotic food from the sea. I love clams whether they are steamed, stir-fried or in clam chowder. In the Orient, clams, like oysters, are considered to be an aphrodisiac. This dish is dedicated to the great lovers.

12-14 medium-size clams
4 teaspoons (20 ml) oil
2 slices ginger, shredded
2 cloves garlic, chopped
1 dried red chili pepper, crushed or ½ teaspoon (2 ml) crushed red pepper

1 tablespoon (15 ml) wine
1½ teaspoons (7 ml) soy sauce
⅓ cup (80 ml) soup stock
1 stalk green onion, cut into 1½" (4 cm) pieces
1 teaspoon (5 ml) cornstarch solution

1. Scrub clam shells to remove sand. Dip clams in boiling water for 30 seconds. Remove and drain well.
2. Soak clams in salted water for 2 hours.
3. Heat oil in wok over medium-high heat. Add ginger, garlic and chili pepper, stirring for 15-20 seconds. Add clams and stir-fry over high heat for one minute. Put in remaining ingredients except cornstarch solution. Cover and cook over medium-high heat for 4-5 minutes. Remove clams, reserving sauce in wok.
4. Add cornstarch to sauce and cook until thickened. Pour over clams. Serve immediately.

Remarks

- Fresh clams may have sand dust inside; by soaking in fresh water, sand particles are expelled. Be sure to change water frequently.
- Larger clams may take a little bit longer to cook—one or two minutes extra.
- Fresh live clams should open up after cooking. Clams that do not open have passed on to the big clam bed in the sky; discard.

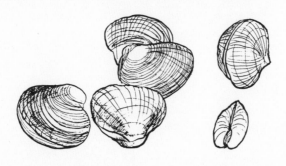

Steamed Crab with Ginger Sauce

Serving fresh crab steamed is perhaps the best way to appreciate the natural, delicate flavor and texture of crab meat. It is also the most popular way to prepare crab in most Cantonese restaurants.

6 hard-shell blue crabs
3 tablespoons (45 ml) salt

Ginger Sauce:
2 tablespoons (30 ml) soy sauce
2 tablespoons (30 ml) red wine vinegar
2 tablespoons (30 ml) sugar
2 tablespoons (30 ml) grated ginger

1. Place crabs in a large bowl. Slowly run cold tap water continuously over crabs. Add 3 tablespoons salt and let stand for 1½ hours to eliminate the sediment in crabs.
2. Rinse and drain crabs. Steam over high heat for 15-20 minutes.
3. While crab is steaming, combine ginger sauce ingredients. Mix well and set aside.
4. To serve, crack crab and remove meat. Serve with ginger sauce.

Remarks

- Leftover ginger sauce should be kept in the refrigerator for future use.
- West coast crabs are normally larger and may take a bit longer to steam.

 When you have tea and wine, you have many friends.

Steamed Fish with Black Beans

This is an exotic, hot, spicy dish, that might require some educating of your taste buds. Salted black beans are widely used in many Chinese dishes. It will be worth your while to explore this dish.

1 whole white fish (cleaned and scaled) or 1 pound (450 g) white fish fillet
½ teaspoon (2 ml) salt
2 tablespoons (30 ml) salted black beans, washed and drained (1½ tablespoons (22 ml) mashed)

1 tablespoon (15 ml) finely minced garlic
2 slices ginger, finely shredded
¼ teaspoon (1 ml) crushed red pepper
1 teaspoon (5 ml) soy sauce
2 teaspoons (10 ml) oil
1 stalk green onion, cut into 2" (5 cm) strips

1. Dry fish fillet and sprinkle with salt.
2. Combine salted black beans, ginger, chili pepper and garlic in a bowl and mash into a paste. Mix well with soy sauce and oil.
3. Rub fillet with black bean sauce mixture. Place green onion on top.
4. Steam over high heat for approximately 7-8 minutes. Serve hot.

Remarks

- Cooking time for a whole fish will be longer than for a fillet—10-11 minutes is a reasonable guess.
- The amount of black bean sauce will effect the flavor greatly. Adjust the amount to your own taste.
- To make your own black bean sauce: wash 4 ounces of fermented black beans, drain and mash with 1 teaspoon chopped garlic. Add 1 tablespoon oil and 1 tablespoon sugar. Mix well and steam over high heat for 10-12 minutes. The sauce can be kept in a jar in the refrigerator for a couple of months.

Stuffed Squid Cantonese

Tender, juicy squid stuffed with an array of exotic and tempting ingredients makes this a gourmet adventure. It is terrific!

6 squids
2½ tablespoons (37 ml) oil
1½ chopped green onions
1 teaspoon (5 ml) minced ginger
¼ cup (60 ml) finely chopped water
   chestnuts
6 dried black mushrooms, soaked and
   finely chopped
¼ cup (60 ml) finely chopped or
   grated carrot
½ teaspoon (2 ml) salt
½ teaspoon (2 ml) sugar
1 teaspoon (5 ml) wine
pinch of white pepper
1 teaspoon (5 ml) cornstarch
extra broth as needed

Dressing Sauce:
1 tablespoon (15 ml) wine
½ teaspoon (2 ml) ginger juice
1 teaspoon (5 ml) soy sauce
½ teaspoon (2 ml) sugar
½ cup (125 ml) soup stock
½ teaspoon (2 ml) sesame oil
1 teaspoon (5 ml) cornstarch solution

1. Wash squid and remove tentacles. To eviscerate, make a 1-2" (2.5-5 cm) slit at the top of each squid and remove organs.
2. Heat 2 teaspoons oil in wok over medium-high heat. Stir in green onion, ginger, water chestnuts, mushroom and carrot. Cook for 1 minute. Add salt, sugar, wine, white pepper and cornstarch. Mix well and set aside.
3. Spoon 2-3 teaspoons of vegetable mixture into each squid. Secure the open end of each squid with a toothpick. Lightly sprinkle with extra cornstarch.
4. Combine dressing sauce ingredients except cornstarch in a pan. Bring to a boil, and thicken with cornstarch solution. Keep warm.
5. In a skillet or non-stick pan, heat 1 tablespoon oil over medium-high heat. Cook 3 squids at a time for 2 minutes. Roll squid continuously and press down to allow even cooking. Add 1 tablespoon broth, cover and steam for 1 minute over medium heat. Arrange squid on a platter to serve.
6. Pour dressing sauce over squid and serve hot.

Remarks

• Tentacles can be fried and used as a garnish if desired.

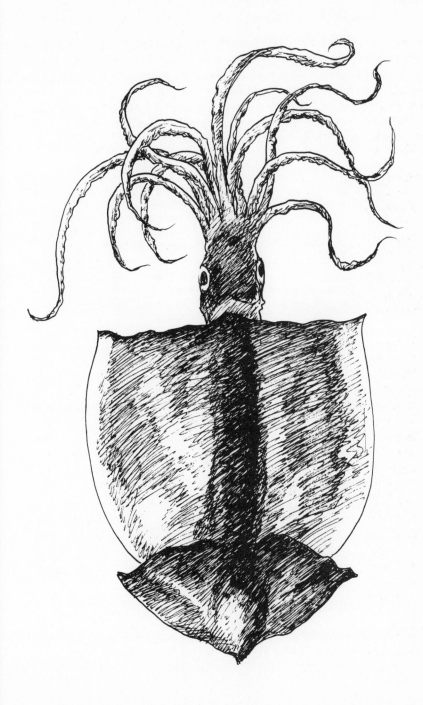

Succulent Lobster with Zesty Sauces

For those residing on the east coast, fresh lobster is comparatively inexpensive. For years, lobster has become a favorite on the Cantonese seafood menu. It can be stir-fried, boiled or steamed. One of the most requested dishes is lobster Cantonese. Steaming is the best method for retaining the original delicate flavor and texture of fresh lobster. Here is a quick but smashing recipe—steamed lobster meat dipped into different spiced sauces; a truly gastronomic experience!!

2 medium size lobster tails (1½ pounds or 675 g)
3-4 large lettuce leaves for garnishing

Dipping Sauces:
A. *Dark Soy Sauce with Garlic:*
  3 tablespoons (45 ml) dark soy sauce
  2 teaspoons (10 ml) heated oil
  1 teaspoon (5 ml) chopped garlic

B. *Szechwan Hot Sauce:*
  1 tablespoon (15 ml) sesame seed
  2 teaspoons (10 ml) sesame oil
  2 tablespoons (30 ml) soy sauce
  1 tablespoon (15 ml) red wine vinegar
  2 tablespoons (30 ml) soup stock
  1 tablespoon (15 ml) green onion, chopped
  1 teaspoon (5 ml) roasted Szechwan peppercorn, ground
  1½ teaspoons (7 ml) hot chili oil

C. *Szechwan Spiced Sauce:*
  3 tablespoons (45 ml) soy sauce
  3 tablespoons (45 ml) water
  1 tablespoon (15 ml) sesame seed paste
  2 teaspoons (10 ml) sesame oil
  1 tablespoon (15 ml) red wine vinegar
  2 teaspoons (10 ml) sugar
  1 tablespoon (15 ml) chopped green onion
  1 teaspoon (5 ml) minced garlic
  1 teaspoon (5 ml) grated ginger
  1 teaspoon (5 ml) roasted Szechwan peppercorn, ground
  2 teaspoons (10 ml) hot chili oil

1. Steam lobster over high heat for 15-18 minutes until done.
2. Split lobster in half, discard dark vein. Rinse and cut meat into ¾" (2 cm) chunks. Place lobster chunks on top of lettuce on a platter, as though the lobster is whole.
3. Combine ingredients for each sauce in separate bowls. Mix and set aside.
4. To serve, dip lobster chunks into sauce of your choice. Serve hot or cold.

Tender Scallops in Cream Sauce

If you have extra money to spend on a dish, this juicy and succulent muscle will offer you the gastronomic experience of a lifetime. Try it often to get rid of your taxable income!

⅔ pound (300 g) fresh scallops, sliced in half lengthwise
½ pound (225 g) fresh spinach
2 tablespoons (30 ml) oil
2 slices ginger, finely minced

Scallops Marinade:
1½ tablespoons (22 ml) wine
¾ tablespoon (12 ml) cornstarch

Cream Sauce:
¾ cup (200 ml) milk
½ teaspoon (2 ml) oil
3 tablespoons (45 ml) water
½ teaspoon (2 ml) salt
½ teaspoon (2 ml) sugar
1½ teaspoons (7 ml) cornstarch solution
1 tablespoon (15 ml) wine
1 beaten egg white

1. Marinate scallops for 5-10 minutes.
2. Blanch spinach in boiling water for 2 minutes, remove and drain well. Arrange on a serving platter.
3. Heat oil in wok over high heat. Stir-fry in ginger for 10 seconds. Add scallops and continue to stir-fry for 1½-2 minutes. Remove immediately.
4. Combine cream sauce ingredients over medium-high heat in a non-stick saucepan. Cook until lightly thickened, stirring continuously.
5. Add scallops to sauce and mix well.
6. To serve, pour creamy scallops over spinach. Serve hot.

Remarks

- Be careful not to overcook the delicate scallops. Overcooking will toughen the muscle.
- When cooking the cream sauce, use a non-stick pan and use a medium heat to avoid scorching.

 Don't laugh at he who is old; the same will assuredly happen to you and me.

Tomato Fish Fillet

Everybody loves tomato beef. A similar dish with fish is just as great. Tender, juicy fish fillet in a delicate tomato sauce is absolutely mouth-watering!

⅔ pound (300 g) fish fillet, cut into 1" x
   ½" x 2" (2.5 cm x 1.5 cm x 5 cm)
   pieces
½ cup (125 ml) cornstarch for dry
   coating
4 cups (1 L) oil
½ small onion, sliced
2 tomatoes, cut into wedges

Tomato Sauce:
¼ cup (60 ml) catsup
2½ tablespoons (37 ml) vinegar
2½ tablespoons (37 ml) sugar
3½ tablespoons (52 ml) water
1 teaspoon (5 ml) wine
½ teaspoon (2 ml) ginger juice
1 teaspoon (5 ml) cornstarch solution

Fish Marinade:
1 egg white, lightly beaten
1 tablespoon (15 ml) cornstarch
½ teaspoon (2 ml) salt

1. Marinate fish for 30 minutes. Dry-coat fish with cornstarch. Shake off excess.
2. Heat oil in wok over high heat and deep-fry fish until golden brown (3-4 minutes). Remove and drain well.
3. Remove all but 1½ tablespoons oil from wok and heat over medium-high. Stir in onion and cook for 15 seconds. Add tomato wedges. Add cooked fish and mix well.
4. Combine tomato sauce ingredients in saucepan and bring to a boil. Cook until thickened. Set aside.
5. To serve pour tomato sauce over fish and transfer to a platter. Arrange tomato wedges around fish. Serve hot.

 Eat well, drink well and remain healthy for a full, happy life.

Ying-Yang Fish Fillet

Ying and Yang refer to two opposite things that are in harmony. To serve two different colors and flavors of fish fillet in the same dish is not only visually exciting but appetizing as well. Using the same concept, you can create your own Ying and Yang version with any type of seafood you wish. Quite a gastronomic experience.

Ying Fish:
½ pound (225 g) white fish fillet
2 eggs, lightly beaten
½ cup (125 ml) flour
4 cups (1 L) oil

Fish Marinade:
1 tablespoon (15 ml) chopped fresh
   Chinese parsley
¾ teaspoon (3 ml) sugar
1 teaspoon (5 ml) sesame oil
2 teaspoons (10 ml) wine
½ teaspoon (2 ml) salt

Yang Fish:
½ pound (225 g) white fish fillet
2 tablespoons (30 ml) oil
2½ tablespoons (37 ml) vinegar
2 tablespoons (30 ml) brown sugar
3 tablespoons (45 ml) catsup
2 tablespoons (30 ml) water

Fish Marinade:
½ teaspoon (2 ml) salt
1 teaspoon (5 ml) wine
1 teaspoon (5 ml) sesame oil
1 egg yolk, lightly beaten

Ying Fish

1. Cut fish into 1" x ½" x 2" (2.5 cm x 1.5 cm x 5 cm) slices. Marinate for 10-15 minutes. Dip slices in egg, then flour and set aside.
2. Deep fry fish in 4 cups hot oil over high heat until golden brown, about 2 minutes. Remove, drain well and arrange on one side of a platter.

Yang Fish

1. Cut fish fillet into 1" x ½" x 2" (2.5 cm x 1.5 cm x 5 cm) slices. Marinate for 10-15 minutes.
2. Heat 2 tablespoons oil in clean wok over high heat. Add fish and stir for 2-2½ minutes. Be careful not to break fish. Add remaining ingredients and stir until thickened. Place fish on opposite side of platter as Ying fish. Use your imagination to garnish with tomato or pineapple slices if desired.

蛋
豆
腐
類

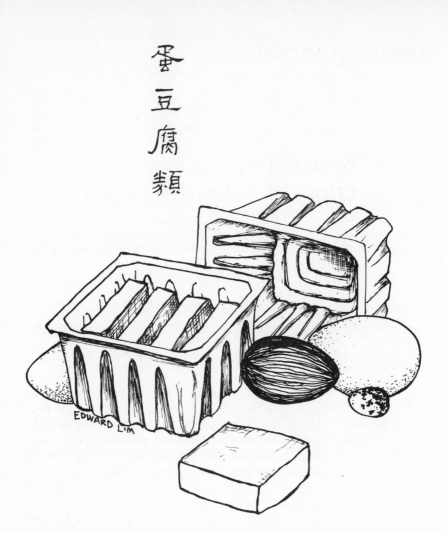

EDWARD LIM

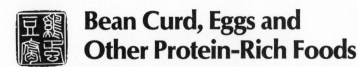

Bean Curd, Eggs and Other Protein-Rich Foods

Both eggs and soybean curd are rich in protein and are excellent supplements for the meat-poor diet.

Eggs:

Eggs represent fertility. A charming traditional custom is to offer friends and relatives hard-boiled eggs that are dyed red to show good wishes and happiness at birth announcements. When an odd number of eggs (9 or 11) is presented, a baby boy has been born—an even number of eggs (8 or 10) welcomes a baby girl. Perhaps that is why most Chinese love red-dyed hard-boiled eggs—they have resulted in over 900 million new babies! In China, eggs are sold in stores and by sidewalk vendors, individually or by the pound. One can choose any size or color. When you buy them, the owner personally checks the quality of each egg under a light bulb. (If you purchase several dozen, you may get stuck there for weeks!) The Chinese use eggs to stir-fry, deep-fry, smoke, scramble and steam. They also add them to soups and numerous other dishes.

A number of interesting egg dishes are presented in this chapter, and you may be "egged" on to try new ways of preparing this versatile food.

Soybean Curd (Tofu):

Soybean curd, or tofu, the velvety-smooth "cheese" made from soy beans, has long been an important part of the Oriental cuisine. Containing 40% protein, bean curd is the poor man's meat and the rich man's delight.

Inexpensive to buy, high in protein, low in calories and with no cholesterol, soybean curd is easy to prepare in various dishes and with its bland taste it goes well with many ingredients and flavors. For the health- and budget-conscious cook, it is the best and most natural meat substitute. For the meat eating, diet-conscious person, soybean curd, in various forms, fresh, dried, fermented, or fried, will make your favorite dishes more enjoyable without worrying about too little protein, too many calories, or too much cholesterol.

Fresh bean curd can be prepared in many different ways: stir-fried, deep-fried, steamed, red-cooked, stewed in soups or casseroles, etc. You will find several interesting dishes with bean curd as an ingredient in this chapter.

Bean Curd Nuts

You have probably never heard of this dish since it is never served in Chinese restaurants, yet the velvety smooth bean curd complimented by crispy nuts is extraordinary. It is a great choice for a rush-hour meal, and it is nutritionally sound. Just for its simplicity, you'll love it.

1½ tablespoons (22 ml) oil
1 clove garlic, chopped
2 squares bean curd, 1 pound (450 g),
    cut into ½" (1.5 cm) cubes
¼ cup (60 ml) soup stock
1 stalk green onion, chopped

1 tablespoon (15 ml) oyster-flavored
    sauce
1 tablespoon (15 ml) soy sauce
½ teaspoon (2 ml) sugar
¼ teaspoon (1 ml) garlic salt
¾ teaspoon (3 ml) cornstarch solution
¾ cup (200 ml) roasted nuts

1. Heat wok over high heat. Add oil and garlic and cook for 10 seconds. Add bean curd and stir continuously for 1½ minutes. Add soup stock and simmer for 1½ minutes.
2. Add remaining ingredients, except nuts and cornstarch solution. Stir gently for 1 minute. Thicken with cornstarch.
3. Mix in nuts and serve immediately to avoid sogginess.

Remarks

- Soybean curd is soft and fragile. Do not stir it too much. Alternatively, you can deep-fry it ahead of time. This will result in a firmer texture and a golden brown color.

 Pottery and fine porcelain must not quarrel.

Cold Bean Curd Salad

If you are a health food advocate, this dish is for you. It is light, nutritious, and can be attractively garnished. Use your creativity and your imagination!

Dressing:
¼ cup (60 ml) vinegar
2 teaspoons (10 ml) sugar
¼ teaspoon (1 ml) chili sauce
1½ tablespoons (22 ml) sesame oil
2½ tablespoons (37 ml) salad oil
1 tablespoon (15 ml) soy sauce

4 squares, 2 pounds (900 g) bean curd
1 tomato
1 pound (450 g) spinach
¼ cup (60 ml) finely chopped ham
3 tablespoons (45 ml) chopped dill
    pickle

1. Combine ingredients for dressing and set aside.
2. Mash bean curd and spread evenly in the center of a round serving plate. Slice tomato and arrange on top of bean curd.
3. Blanch spinach for 2 minutes in water. Remove and drain well. Place spinach around bean curd. Top spinach with chopped ham and pickles.
4. Pour dressing over entire dish. Refrigerate until serving time. Serve cold.

Remarks

• This salad makes a high protein appetizer as well as a main course. Serve as a dip with celery sticks and green pepper slices.

Colorful Salad

Easy to make, full of color and excitement. The combination of crisp vegetables and bean curd makes it a perfect dish to serve on a hot summer day. It is light and refreshing!

1½ squares (¾ pound or 340 g) bean curd, cut into ½" (1.5 cm) cubes
2 medium-sized carrots, peeled and cut into ½" (1.5 cm) cubes
1 medium-sized cucumber, deseeded and cut into ½" (1.5 cm) cubes

Dressing:
1½ tablespoons (22 ml) soy sauce
1 teaspoon (5 ml) sesame oil
1 tablespoon (15 ml) sesame paste (optional)
1½ teaspoons (7 ml) sugar
2 teaspoons (10 ml) vinegar
1 tablespoon (15 ml) soup stock
½ teaspoon (2 ml) Tabasco Sauce

1. Cook carrots in boiling water for 2½ minutes. Drain and set aside to cool.
2. Combine ingredients for dressing in a bowl and blend well.
3. Place carrots, bean curd and cucumber in separate bowls. Add one-third of the dressing to each bowl and mix well.
4. To serve, arrange carrots in a circle in the center of a dish. Divide portions of cucumber and bean curd in half and place alternately around the carrots, so that bean curd is opposite bean curd, and cucumber is opposite cucumber.

 *A cheerful look makes a dish a feast.*

Fried Egg Yolk Platter

Got extra egg yolks lying around? Or, if you'd like to add a little more cholesterol to your diet, try this recipe! This simple, delicious entree can be served for dinner or as a superb breakfast.

5-6 egg yolks, lightly beaten
2 tablespoons (30 ml) chopped water
    chestnuts
1 stalk green onion, chopped
¼ cup (60 ml) soup stock
¼ teaspoon (1 ml) salt

1½ teaspoons (7 ml) cornstarch
4½ teaspoons (22 ml) oil
2 tablespoons (30 ml) minced cooked
    ham (preferably Virginia ham)

1. Combine beaten egg yolks, water chestnuts, green onion, stock, salt and cornstarch. Blend to mix well.
2. Heat an 8" non-sticking pan with 1½ teaspoons oil over medium-high heat. Pour in ⅓ of the egg mixture and cook until firm. Make two more omelets with remaining egg mixture and oil.
3. Sprinkle each omelet with chopped ham and roll. Cut each omelet into 4-5 equal portions to serve.

Remarks

- Be careful not to use extremely high heat. If you overcook the egg mixture you may end up with a new dish called "Charcoal Brown Egg Yolk Platter!"

 One's acquaintances may fill the empire, but one's real friends can be but few.

Full of Beans: Making Your Own Bean Curd (Tofu)

A hill of beans—creates lots of tofu (dowfoo)! And believe me, lots of hills have been made into lots of tofu!! Tofu or soybean curd has been used for centuries in China; it's only in recent years that America has caught on to this versatile food. Vegetarians and meat eaters alike enjoy this nutritionally protein-packed food. Besides being highly nutritious, it's low in calories and very inexpensive. Bean curd can be purchased in many different forms: canned, fresh, fried and fermented.

Fresh bean curd comes both firm and soft; the difference is only water content. The first has the consistency of Monterey Jack cheese while the soft is like custard. If firm is unavailable, it can be made from soft by wrapping the squares of curd in cheesecloth and placing them under a book, brick or breadboard (2-4 pounds) for several hours or overnight.

Check out the stats on bean curd—you'll be amazed! This chart compares tofu with some animal protein sources. You can see why I call bean curd the "boneless meat."

Foods, 100 gms	Firm Bean Curd	Chicken Egg	Ground Beef	Cottage Cheese
Calories	147	180	268	95
Protein, gms	17.6	13	17.9	12.9
Carbohydrates, gms	5	0.8	0	2.6
Fats, % total	8.8	11.6	21.2	4.2
Saturated fats, %	15	33	48	52
Unsaturated fats, %	80	50	47	37
Cholesterol, mgs	0	500	63	13.7
Calcium, mgs	316	54	11	86

Time to learn to use your bean! Let's make some soybean curd! Soybean curd is made in much the same way cheese is made from milk. It

is very simple and can be done in half an hour. Once you have tasted the subtle flavor of really fresh bean curd, you may never settle for second best, the commercial....On with the show!

Commonly used solidifiers are: Epsom salt (magnesium sulfate), gypsum (calcium sulfate), magnesium chloride, calcium chloride, Nigari (a sea water extract available at health food stores), vinegar or lemon juice. The following recipe gives you the choice of several solidifiers. Experiment! Don't be frightened by the many steps involved in the preparation—it is not as bad as it may seem! Be an adventurous spirit! Go for it!

Essential Equipment
electric blender, food mill or grinder
2 large non-aluminum pots
non-aluminum colander
pressing sack (muslin, cottage gauze or nylon)
settling cloth (cheesecloth)

1½ cups (370 ml) dry soybeans
water
solidifier (2 teaspoons (10 ml) Nigari or vinegar, or 1 teaspoon (5 ml) Epsom salt or gypsum)

1. Rinse soybeans, cover with 4-6 cups cold water. Soak 4-5 hours or overnight.
2. Drain and rinse again.
3. Blend beans in small batches: 1 cup beans with 1½ cups boiling water. Blend at high speed until uniform. (NOTE: Amount of water is not critical but too little strains the blender).
4. Line colander with pressing sack and place over large pot. Pour contents of blender into sack. Rinse blender with 1 cup boiling water and pour into sack. Repeat with remaining beans.
5. Twist sack closed and press out the "soymilk." A potato masher or wine bottle can help.
6. Open sack and add 2 cups boiling water while stirring pulp. Repeat step 5.
7. Heat soymilk to boiling, stirring often to prevent scorching. Simmer 5 minutes. (NOTE: Watch carefully as milk will foam and boil over.)
8. Remove from heat.
9. Dissolve solidifier in 1 cup hot water. Use extra water for softer bean curd.
10. Slowly add ⅓ cup of solidifier solution to soymilk, stirring constantly. Allow mixture to come to rest; sprinkle ⅓ cup solidifier on top. Cover and wait 3 minutes.

11. Uncover and sprinkle in remaining ⅓ cup solidifier. Stir *gently* upper third of mixture. Cover and wait 3 minutes.
12. Uncover and stir *gently*. Curds and whey should be completely separated. Whey should be a clear pale yellow color; if cloudy, cover and wait a few more minutes or add a small amount of solidifier solution. (NOTE: Be patient before adding additional solidifier as too much will result in tough tofu.)
13. Line colander with settling cloth. Carefully ladle curds and whey into colander and let drain. Cover bean curd with cloth and gently press out whey or set a 2-4 pound weight on top and let stand 30-40 minutes. Rinse pressed curd in cool water.
14. Refrigerate under water in closed container. Change water every other day to keep fresh. Bean curd will stay fresh for about a week. (NOTE: Older bean curd can be frozen. This will completely change the texture as the water is removed. Upon thawing, by rinsing under hot water, it will be quite dry and crumbly. In this form it makes an excellent substitute for ground meat. Bean curd can be stored in the freezer for several months.)

Bean curd can be used in many ways. The recipes given in this book are just an introduction. You will find it can be eaten fresh and cold as a salad or appetizer, in soups, fried and stuffed or braised in a spicy sauce. Be a little bold. Try it!

Golden Fried Bean Curd

This preparation for bean curd is great by itself or it can be incorporated into meat dishes. Strolling past sidewalk vendors in China and Taiwan, you would find this being prepared and eaten right outside in the fresh air!

2 squares (1 pound or 450 g) bean curd
¼ teaspoon (1 ml) salt
¼ cup (60 ml) oil
2 slices ginger, finely chopped
2 tablespoons (30 ml) finely chopped green onion
1 tablespoon (15 ml) soy sauce
½ teaspoon (2 ml) sugar
½ cup (125 ml) soup stock
¾ teaspoon (3 ml) cornstarch solution

Batter:
3 medium eggs, lightly beaten
¼ cup (60 ml) flour
2 tablespoons (30 ml) water

1. Cut each square of bean curd lengthwise into halves. Sprinkle salt over entire surface. Let stand for 10-15 minutes. Pat dry with paper towel and cut into ½" x 1" x 2" (1.5 cm x 2.5 cm x 5 cm) pieces.
2. Combine batter mixture in a bowl. Blend until smooth.
3. Heat 1 tablespoon oil in a skillet or non-sticking frying pan over medium high heat. Dip bean curd into batter. Fry 6-8 pieces at a time, about 2 minutes on each side or until golden brown. Remove fried bean curd and reserve.
4. Add 1½ tablespoons oil to skillet and heat to medium high. Add ginger and green onion, stirring for 10-15 seconds. Return bean curd to skillet along with remaining ingredients except cornstarch solution. Cover and cook for 1½-2 minutes, shaking skillet frequently to prevent bean curd from sticking.
5. Thicken with cornstarch solution and serve immediately.

 Better to return and make a net, than to go down to the river and merely wish for fishes.

Honeycomb Curd

This dish will attract the bees—not because it's sweet, but because it looks like a honey-comb. Delicate, tasty, and geometrically beautiful!

3½ cups (870 ml) water
2½ squares bean curd (1½ pounds or
    675 g) cut in ½" (1.5 cm) chunks
1 tablespoon (15 ml) oil
1½ teaspoons (7 ml) chopped green
    onion
½ teaspoon (2 ml) chopped ginger
½ teaspoon (2 ml) salt
½ teaspoon (2 ml) sugar
2 teaspoons (10 ml) soy sauce
½ teaspoon (2 ml) sesame oil
3 tablespoons (45 ml) soup stock
½ teaspoon (2 ml) cornstarch solution

1. Bring water to a boil in a large pot. Add bean curd and boil over medium-high heat, cook about 15 minutes until honeycomb-like holes appear on bean curd. Add extra water if necessary. Drain and set aside.
2. Heat oil in wok over medium-high heat. Add ginger and green onion, stirring for 15 seconds.
3. Stir in bean curd and remaining ingredients and cook until thickened. Serve hot or cold.

Good cooking is not only friend, wife and lover, but playmate, hobby, craft, encounter group and psychotherapist.—William Rice

Mushroom Bean Curd with Bean Paste

Are your taste buds bored with eating the same old thing? Try this vegetarian dish; it has plenty of character! The combination of textures and flavors will dazzle your tastebuds and add spice to your life!

1½ tablespoons (22 ml) oil
1 slice ginger, chopped
1 teaspoon (5 ml) chopped garlic
1 tablespoon (15 ml) garlic-flavored
   chili paste
3-4 dried black mushrooms, soaked
   and chopped
½ cup (125 ml) ½" (1.5 cm) cubed
   bamboo shoots

1 cup (250 ml) small fresh mushrooms
2 squares bean curd (1 pound or 450
   g) cut into ¾" chunks
1¼ tablespoons (18 ml) dark soy sauce
2 teaspoons (10 ml) wine
¼ cup (60 ml) soup stock
¾ teaspoon (3 ml) cornstarch solution

1. Heat oil in wok over high heat. Add ginger and garlic and stir for 15 seconds.
2. Stir in chili paste, dried mushrooms and bamboo shoots and, cook for 10 seconds. Add fresh mushrooms and continue stirring. Stir in bean curd and mix well.
3. Add remaining ingredients except cornstarch solution. Cover and cook over medium-high heat for 3½-4 minutes. Add cornstarch and cook until thickened.

The melon seller shouts that his melons are sweet. A mellon seller never cries "bitter melon" nor a wine seller "thin wine."

Nutty Bean Curd with Sateg Sauce

Everyone will rave about this dish! The unique blend of flavors makes it exotic and pungent; the contrasting colors and textures make it an unforgettable treat!

1 square (8 ounces or 225 g) bean curd
2 cups (500 ml) oil
½ teaspoon (2 ml) salt
2 tablespoons (30 ml) sateg sauce
½ cup (125 ml) unsalted roasted
   peanuts
¼ cup (60 ml) green peas

¼ cup (60 ml) diced carrots, parboiled
¼ teaspoon (1 ml) sugar
½ teaspoon (2 ml) sesame oil
¼ cup (60 ml) shredded green onion,
   white part only
soup stock (if necessary)

1. Lightly press bean curd to remove water. Let drain in colander. Cut into ½" small cubes.
2. Heat oil to medium-high. Deep-fry bean curd cubes until light brown. Drain and set aside.
3. Remove oil, reserving 1 tablespoon in wok. Heat wok over high heat. Add salt and sateg sauce, stirring for 30 seconds. Add remaining ingredients. If too dry, add some soup stock. Stir-fry for 1½ minutes. Serve hot or cold.

Remarks

Sateg sauce is a Chinese barbecue sauce made from fish paste, garlic and chili. It is available only at Oriental markets but it will keep for a year. It may be hard to get, but it's well worth the effort. It also goes well with meats and seafood.

Savory Steamed Bean Curd Cake

Something special for the health food advocate and the diet conscious. A tiny bit of meat with lots of bean curd is an economical, low-calorie source of protein.

Chicken Marinade:
¾ teaspoon (3 ml) cornstarch
1 teaspoon (5 ml) wine
¼ teaspoon (1 ml) salt
¼ teaspoon (1 ml) sugar
dash of white pepper

4 ounces (112 g) boneless chicken
2 squares bean curd (1 pound or 450 g)
2 teaspoons (5 ml) oil
4 dried black mushrooms, soaked and cut into strips
2 tablespoons (30 ml) chopped green onion
1 teaspoon (5 ml) sesame oil
¼ teaspoon (1 ml) salt
2 teaspoons (10 ml) soy sauce
dash of white papper

1. Marinate chicken for 30 minutes.
2. Slightly mash bean curd and let drain in a sieve for 5 minutes.
3. Heat oil in wok over high heat. Add chicken and mushrooms. Stir for 1½-2 minutes or until chicken turns white. Remove and set aside.
4. In a shallow pie pan, place mashed bean curd, cooked chicken and mushroom, 1 tablespoon green onion, sesame oil and salt. Mix well and press mixture down to make a smooth surface.
5. Steam over medium-high heat for 8-10 minutes.
6. To serve, pour soy sauce and white pepper over dish. Sprinkle with remaining green onion.

Spiced Bean Curd and Eggplant

The unusual and delightful combination of bean curd and eggplant makes this a very nutritious vegetarian dish. The yellow bean paste adds a flavor you will not want to miss!

2 squares (1 pound or 450 g) bean curd
1 small eggplant, cut into ¾" (2 cm) cubes
2 tablespoons (30 ml) oil
1½ teaspoons (7 ml) chopped ginger
1½ teaspoons (7 ml) chopped garlic
1 tablespoon (15 ml) yellow bean paste

1 tablespoon (15 ml) chopped green onion
4 teaspoons (20 ml) soy sauce
½ teaspoon (2 ml) brown sugar
2 teaspoons (10 ml) wine
1 teaspoon (5 ml) sesame oil
½ teaspoon (2 ml) cornstarch solution

1. Cut bean curd into ¾" cubes. Set in a colander to drain.
2. Blanch eggplant in boiling water for 3 minutes. Drain.
3. Heat oil in wok over medium-high heat. Add ginger and garlic, stirring for 10 seconds. Stir in bean paste and cook for another 10-15 seconds.
4. Add bean curd and remaining ingredients. Cook, stirring continuously until thickened. Serve hot.

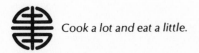

Cook a lot and eat a little.

Steamed Eggs with Bean Curd

This dish is dedicated to you who are dedicated dieters. "Different, delicious and delectable" are the words to describe this dish, guaranteed to decrease the calories of any dieter's diet.

2 squares (1 pound or 450 g) bean
    curd
3 eggs, beaten
1 teaspoon (5 ml) salt
⅓ cup (80 ml) soup stock
3 dried black mushrooms, soaked and
    chopped
2 tablespoons (30 ml) finely chopped
    pickled cucumber

2 tablespoons (30 ml) chopped ham
    (optional)
2 tablespoons (30 ml) frozen green
    peas
2 teaspoons (10 ml) oil
1 teaspoon (5 ml) sesame oil
1 tablespoon (15 ml) cornstarch

1. In a large bowl, mash bean curd with a fork. Add beaten eggs, salt and soup stock. Blend well with a whisk or in a blender.
2. Add remaining ingredients and mix well.
3. Transfer bean curd mixture to an oven-proof pie pan and steam over high heat for 5-7 minutes.

Remarks

- You can substitute dill pickles if pickled cucumber is not available.
- Ham can be omitted if you prefer no meat.

Sweet and Sour Bean Curd

You may have tried many sweet and sour dishes but probably not this particular one. It is light, refreshing and delicious. Great for the busy summer months.

Bean Curd Custard Mixture:
2 squares (1 pound or 450 g) bean curd, mashed
¼ cup (60 ml) finely chopped waterchestnuts
2 tablespoons (30 ml) soaked and finely chopped dried black mushrooms
2 tablespoons (30 ml) finely chopped green onion
2 tablespoons (30 ml) finely chopped carrot
2 egg whites, lightly beaten
1½ tablespoons (22 ml) cornstarch
¾ teaspoon (3 ml) salt
¾ teaspoon (3 ml) sugar
dash of white pepper
¾ teaspoon (3 ml) sesame oil

Sweet and Sour Dip:
1 teaspoon (5 ml) oil
½ teaspoon (2 ml) chopped garlic
2 tablespoons (30 ml) vinegar
2 tablespoons (30 ml) sugar
¼ cup (60 ml) water
2½ tablespoons (37 ml) catsup
1 teaspoon (5 ml) cornstarch
a few drops Tabasco sauce

2 tablespoons (30 ml) cornstarch for dry coating
4 cups oil

1. Combine all bean curd custard ingredients in a large bowl. Use hands to knead and squeeze mixture until well blended.
2. Pat into a small oiled pie pan (mixture should be ¾" or 2 cm thick).
3. Steam over high heat for 8-10 minutes.
4. Remove and cool. Cut into 2" squares. Coat well with cornstarch and let set for about 5 minutes.
5. Shake off excess cornstarch and deep-fry squares in hot oil over medium-high heat for about 1 minute or until golden brown. Drain and keep warm.
6. Combine sweet and sour dip ingredients in sauce pan. Bring to a boil and cook until thickened. Keep warm.
7. Pour sauce over squares or serve as a dip.

Remarks

- If you don't want to drive yourself crazy chopping let your food processor do the work.
- After coating with cornstarch be sure to let bean curd custard set so that the cornstarch can be absorbed.

Tender Chicken Foo Yung

A traditional but unique dish; succulent chicken combined with green onions gives this foo yung a snap! One of my favorites!

½ pound (225 g) chicken breast,
   minced
4-5 egg whites, beaten
1 tablespoon (15 ml) chopped green
   onion
2 tablespoons (30 ml) oil

Chicken Marinade:
½ teaspoon (2 ml) salt
¼ teaspoon (1 ml) sugar
⅛ teaspoon (0.75 ml) sesame oil
dash white pepper
2 tablespoons (30 ml) soup stock
½ teaspoon (2 ml) oil

Sauce:
1 tablespoon (15 ml) oyster-flavored
   sauce
½ teaspoon (2 ml) soy sauce
½ teaspoon (2 ml) sugar
6 tablesoons (90 ml) soup stock
½ teaspoon (2 ml) cornstarch
dash white pepper

1. Marinate chicken for ½ hour.
2. Combine chicken, egg white and onion in a bowl. Mix well.
3. Heat a non-stick pan with 1½ teaspoons oil over medium-high heat. Put in ⅓ of the chicken mixture and spread out evenly in a thin layer. Swirl the pan continuously and cook each side for 1½-2 minutes. Occasionally press with a spatula. Cook over medium-high heat until golden brown.
4. Make 2 more foo yungs with remaining chicken mixture.
5. Combine ingredients for sauce in a small pan and cook over medium-high heat until thickened. Keep warm.
6. To serve, pour sauce over eggs.

Remarks

- To save time, mince chicken using 2 cleavers or place chicken in a food processor.

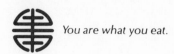

You are what you eat.

The Sunshine Up

If you enjoy eggs for breakfast and can take more cholesterol, this is for you—another delectable way to serve eggs. Try it some morning and add some sunshine to your day!

5 eggs
3 tablespoons (45 ml) oil

Dressing:
2 teaspoons (10 ml) oil
2 dried black mushrooms, soaked and chopped
3 tablespoons (45 ml) chopped green onion
⅓ cup (80 ml) cooked shrimp
¼ cup (60 ml) sliced water chestnuts, slightly chopped
½ tablespoon (7 ml) wine
½ teaspoon (2 ml) sugar
½ teaspoon (2 ml) salt
½ cup (125 ml) soup stock
1 teaspoon (5 ml) cornstarch solution

1. Pan-fry eggs in 3 tablespoons oil, sunny-side-up. Set aside and keep warm.
2. To make dressing, heat oil in skillet over medium-high heat. Add green onion, mushroom and shrimp and stir-fry 1-2 minutes. Add remaining ingredients and cook until slightly thickened.
3. To serve, pour dressing over eggs and "put the whole sun into your mouth."

Tomato Bean Curd Stew

Garden-grown succulent tomatoes with fresh nutritious bean curd is a summertime treat; a great combo for any occasion. Colorful and appetizing.

2½ tablespoons (37 ml) oil
1 teaspoon (2.5 ml) chopped garlic
2 stalks green onion, cut into 2" (5 cm) strips
2 tablespoons (30 ml) dried shrimp, soaked (optional)
2 tomatoes, peeled and cut into bite-size pieces
2 tablespoons (30 ml) frozen peas

2 squares (1 pound or 450 g) bean curd, cut into ¾" (2 cm) cubes
¾ teaspoon (3 ml) salt
3 tablespoons (45 ml) hot catsup
¼ cup (60 ml) soup stock
1 teaspoon (5 ml) sugar
dash of pepper to taste
1 teaspoon (5 ml) cornstarch solution

1. Heat 2 tablespoons oil in pan over medium-high heat. Add garlic, green onion and dried shrimp. Stir-fry for 1 minute.
2. Stir in tomato, peas, bean curd, salt, catsup, soup stock and sugar. Reduce heat to low. Simmer for 4-5 minutes.
3. Stir in cornstarch solution and cook until thickened. Sprinkle ½ tablespoon oil over mixture while swirling pan. Serve hot.

 Those who complain most are most to be complained of.

Zesty Bean Curd

This combination of dill pickles with bean curd is a perfect example of Ying and Yang. The zest of dill pickles and the mild taste of bean curd is great. This is also a good choice for dieters since it is low-calorie, refreshing and quick.

2 squares (1 pound or 450 g) bean curd, cut into ¾" (2 cm) cubes
1½ tablespoons (22 ml) chopped ham (Virginia ham preferred)
½ medium dill pickle, finely chopped

Seasoning Sauce:
1½ tablespoons (22 ml) soy sauce
½ teaspoon (2 ml) sugar
1 teaspoon (5 ml) sesame oil
dash of Tabasco sauce

1. Drain bean curd well, then place in a serving bowl.
2. Mix seasoning sauce ingredients in another bowl and set aside.
3. To serve, pour sauce over bean curd. Garnish with chopped ham and pickles. Serve hot or cold.

Remarks

- If you prefer a hot dish, slightly blanch bean curd in water for 1 minute and heat sauce. Mix and serve.
- Drain bean curd in a colander for about 15-20 minutes to avoid excessive water in the dish.

蔬菜類

Harvest from the Garden
—Vegetables

The Chinese consume large quantities of fresh vegetables, not only for reasons of economy, but also for nutrition and health. They believe that most vegetables are superior foods from a health viewpoint. Most everyday Chinese meals include at least one vegetable dish.

Through the years, the Chinese have developed the art of vegetable cookery to perfection. Chinese cooking is particularly well-suited to the nature of vegetables. They are mostly prepared by quick stir-frying. The application of high temperature and short-time cooking yield a fresh crispness and vivid color that is absolutely extraordinary. The maximum nutritional value is retained as well. Whether leafy or tuberous, vegetables require only a few minutes to cook. They should never be overcooked.

Plain vegetable dishes are rarely served at formal banquets since they are considered to be too common. Many vegetable dishes contain meat or seafood. The Confucian precept is that one-fourth of the dish should consist of meat, and the other three-fourths should consist of vegetables. Soybean curd and wheat gluten are meat substitutes for the strictly vegetarian monks.

One reminder—most frozen vegetables are not recommended. They are excessively high in water content, and when reheated, they will result in a disappointingly mushy mess instead of the rejoicing crispness.

Here you will find simple and delicious vegetable dishes that you can eat as much as you want and still stay slim!

Bean Sprouts and Green Onions

Talk about "down to earth" and simple—there is nothing more basic and quick than this light dish. Both vegetables are abundant in local super-markets. You may even be sprouting sprouts and growing green onions in your own garden!

⅔ pound (300 ml) fresh bean sprouts   ½ teaspoon (2 ml) salt
4 stalks green onions   ½ teaspoon (2 ml) sugar
1½ tablespoons (22 ml) oil   ¼ teaspoon (1 ml) sesame oil
2 slices ginger, shredded   pinch of white pepper

1. Wash sprouts and snap off roots.
2. Split green onions in half lengthwise and cut into 2½" (6.5 cm) strips.
3. Heat oil in wok over high heat. Add ginger, stirring 10-15 seconds; put in onion and stir for 15-20 seconds.
4. Add bean sprouts and stir 1 minute. Add remaining ingredients, stir 15 seconds and serve immediately.

Remarks

- This simple dish can be used as a basis for a meat dish. Choose any meat of your choice. Cook and slice the meat and stir to heat before adding the bean sprouts.
- Snapping off the roots is optional. It could take weeks to remove them all.

Braised Bamboo Shoots and Winter Melon

Braised bamboo shoots are available in Chinese grocery stores. They are a commonly canned vegetable, served as a dish by themselves, or combined with other ingredients. In this recipe, we use the plain, parboiled canned bamboo shoots.

⅔ **pound (300 g) winter melon**
½ **pound (225 g) bamboo shoots**
2 cups (500 ml) oil
2 ginger slices, shredded
3 stalks green onion, white part only,
cut into 1" (2.5 cm) lengths

1 tablespoon (15 ml) dark soy sauce
2 teaspoons (10 ml) oyster-flavored
sauce
¼ **teaspoon (1 ml) salt**
¾ **teaspoon (3 ml) sugar**
¼ **cup (60 ml) soup stock**
¼ **teaspoon (1 ml) cornstarch solution**
dash of white pepper

1. Skin winter melon and remove seeds. Wash and cut into 1" x 1½" (2.5 cm x 4 cm) chunks.
2. Cut bamboo shoots into 1" x 1½" (2.5 cm x 4 cm) chunks. Heat oil in wok over medium-high heat. Deep-fry bamboo shoots until golden brown. Drain well.
3. Remove oil, reserving 1½ tablespoons in wok. Heat oil in wok over high heat. Add ginger, stirring for 10-15 seconds. Add fried bamboo shoots, stirring for 30 seconds.
5. Stir in winter melon and remaining ingredients, except cornstarch solution and white pepper. Reduce heat to medium-low. Cover and simmer for 10-12 minutes. Thicken with cornstarch solution and serve. Sprinkle with white pepper.

Remarks

- For added flavor, toss in a few soaked dried mushrooms or leftover dried mushroom stalks before simmering.

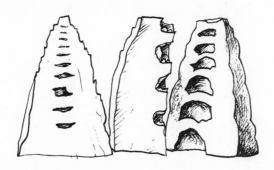

Buddhist Vegetarian Delight

If you are concerned with the size of your belly, this dish is just the answer. Liven up your menu with an exotic and exciting vegetarian dish that will help you build nutritious, low calorie food habits. If you want to be creative, choose the fresh vegetables you like the best.

2½ tablespoons (37 ml) oil
4 dried Chinese black mushrooms,
   soaked and sliced
¼ cup (60 ml) tiger lily buds, soaked
   (optional)
1 tablespoon (15 ml) hair-like seaweed, soaked (optional)
2 ounces (56 g) cellophane noodles,
   soaked
½ cup (125 ml) sliced carrots
½ pound (225 g) Chinese bok choy,
   chopped (if available)
2 ounces (56 g) cabbage, cut into bite-
   size pieces
8 snow pea pods, snap off ends
   (optional)
¼ cup (60 ml) sliced water chestnuts
¼ cup (60 ml) sliced bamboo shoots
1 dried bean curd sheet (optional)

Seasoning Sauce:
2 tablespoons (30 ml) soy sauce
½ teaspoon (2 ml) salt
1½ teaspoons (7 ml) sugar
1¼ teaspoons (6 ml) sesame oil
¾ cup (200 ml) soup stock

1. Drain seaweed and noodles.
2. Heat wok with oil over high heat and stir-fry the mushrooms, tiger lily buds, seaweed and noodles for 1-1½ minutes. Add the remaining vegetables, and stir-fry for 1-1½ minutes. Add seasoning sauce ingredients. Reduce heat to medium and cook for approximately 3 minutes.

Remarks

• Seaweed is dry, dark and resembles hair. It is mainly used in vegetarian dishes and sold in small plastic bags in Chinese stores. It keeps indefinitely in a covered container. Delicious with other dishes or by itself.

Imagination is more important than knowledge.

Cabbage Rolls

A gourmet assortment of vegetables and mushrooms that delights the taste buds and gives an Oriental twist to a typically Western dish. Who knows, this may be the start of a new tradition.

10 cabbage leaves, blanched

Vegetable Filling:
1½ tablespoons (22 ml) oil
1 slice ginger, shredded
1 clove garlic, chopped
1 cup (250 ml) bean sprouts, blanched
½ cup (125 ml) thinly sliced water chestnuts
4-6 dried black mushrooms, soaked and thinly sliced
½ cup (125 ml) thinly sliced straw mushrooms
½ cup (125 ml) shredded bamboo shoots
2-3 wood ears, soaked and shredded (optional)
½ cup (125 ml) shredded carrots
¼ teaspoon (1 ml) salt
¾ teaspoon (3 ml) sugar
½ teaspoon (2 ml) sesame oil
⅔ cup (160 ml) soup stock
¾ teaspoon (3 ml) cornstarch solution

Sauce:
1½ teaspoons (7 ml) sugar
1½ teaspoons (7 ml) dark soy sauce
2 tablespoons (30 ml) oyster-flavored sauce
2 teaspoons (10 ml) wine
1 cup (250 ml) soup stock
dash of white pepper
4½ teaspoons (22 ml) cornstarch solution

1. For filling: Heat wok over high heat with 1½ tablespoons oil. Add ginger and garlic, stirring for 10-15 seconds. Add vegetables and continue to stir for 2 minutes. Add remaining ingredients except cornstarch; mix well. Thicken with cornstarch. Set aside to cool.
2. Divide vegetable filling into 10 equal portions (about 2½ tablespoons each). Place 1 portion in center of each blanched cabbage leaf. Roll leaf around cabbage as you would fold an envelope. Seal with thick flour paste. Arrange rolls on a Pyrex pie pan. Steam over high heat for 4-5 minutes.
3. While steaming, combine sauce mixture in a saucepan. Bring to a boil and cook until thickened. Set aside.
4. To serve, carefully transfer steamed cabbage rolls to a platter; cover with sauce and serve hot.

Remarks

- Make sure all vegetables for filling are shredded into fine strips.
- The flour paste is made by adding ½ tablespoon of water to 1 table-spoon of flour and mixed until wet and sticky; do not overmix.

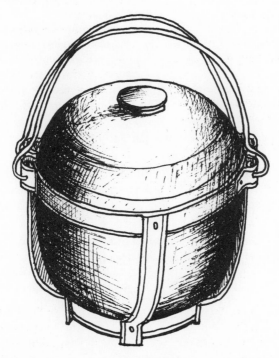

Chinese clay pot for steaming and slow-cooking food.

Chinese Cabbage with Ham

This is a simple preparation. If properly garnished, however, it can be a fancy dish for a dinner party. Also, a perfect, nutritious entree for a hungry family!

2 tablespoons (30 ml) oil
½ head Chinese cabbage (about ¾ pound or 340 g), cut into 2" x 5" (5 cm x 12.5 cm) pieces
¾ teaspoon (3 ml) salt

½ cup (125 ml) soup stock
½ teaspoon (2 ml) sugar
¼ cup (60 ml) milk or half and half
1½ teaspoons (7 ml) cornstarch solution
3 tablespoons (45 ml) minced cooked ham (Virginia or Smithfield ham preferred)

1. Heat oil in wok over medium-high heat. Add cabbage and salt, stirring for 30 seconds. Pour in soup stock. Reduce heat to medium low, cover and cook for 5-7 minutes.
2. Increase heat to high. Stir in sugar and milk; mix well. Thicken with cornstarch solution.
3. Arrange cabbage on a platter, top with cooked ham and garnish with parsley if desired.

Remarks

• Another version uses the following braising sauce in place of milk:

1 tablespoon (15 ml) oyster-flavored sauce
1 teaspoon (5 ml) dark soy sauce

1 teaspoon (5 ml) wine
2 tablespoons (30 ml) soup stock
pinch of white pepper and sesame oil to taste

• Crisp, crumbled bacon can be substituted for the ham.

 Feed moderately on wholesome food; garden herbs surpass rich viands.

Coconut-Flavored Vegetarian Casserole

Be creative, prepare a vegetable dish that would impress the Royal family of China. This colorful combination of vegetables in a rich golden sauce, gives a hint of Hawaii, and will become a family favorite.

2 tablespoons (30 ml) oil
1 clove garlic, chopped
2 slices ginger, shredded
1 cup (250 ml) ¾" cubes (2 cm) carrot
1 cup (250 ml) medium-sized fresh
    whole mushrooms
½ cup (125 ml) ¾" cubes (2 cm)
    zucchini
1 cup (250 ml) cauliflower flowerets
½ cup (125 ml) sliced bamboo shoots
½ cup (125 ml) sliced water chestnuts

Coconut Sauce:
½ cup (125 ml) coconut milk
⅔ cup (160 ml) evaporated milk
2 teaspoons (10 ml) wine
¼ cup (60 ml) soup stock
¾ teaspoon (3 ml) sugar
1 tablespoon (15 ml) tumeric
½ teaspoon (2 ml) salt
pinch of white pepper
2 tablespoons (30 ml) cornstarch solu-
    tion

1. Heat oil in wok over high heat; add garlic and ginger and stir for 15 seconds. Add carrot. Cover and cook for 1 minute. Add remaining vegetables and continue stirring for another 1½ minutes. Transfer vegetables to a casserole dish.
2. In a separate saucepan combine all coconut sauce ingredients except cornstarch, and bring mixture to a boil. Thicken with the cornstarch solution and pour over vegetables.
3. Bake in a preheated oven at 450°F (230°C) for 12-15 minutes. Serve immediately.

Remarks

• Cut all vegetables to about the same size.

Colorful Jewels

This dish is as colorful as jewels in a jewelry box. The sparkling combination of carrots, mushrooms, broccoli, bamboo shoots, water chestnuts and corn will make you feel as though you have found a teasure. A richer person you will be after trying it!

1½ tablespoons (22 ml) oil
2 slices ginger, minced
1 clove garlic, minced
½ cup (125 ml) sliced carrot
3-4 dried black mushrooms, soaked
½ cup (125 ml) medium-sized fresh
   mushrooms
1 cup (250 ml) broccoli flowerets

⅔ cup (160 ml) soup stock
½ cup (125 ml) sliced bamboo shoots
½ cup (125 ml) water chestnuts
½ cup (125 ml) baby corn, cut into
   1½" (4 cm) lengths
1¼ teaspoons (6 ml) salt
¾ teaspoon (3 ml) sugar
1½ teaspoons (7 ml) cornstarch
   solution

1. Heat oil over high heat and stir in ginger and garlic for 10-15 seconds.
2. Add carrots, mushrooms and broccoli. Pour in 4 tablespoons stock, cover and cook 2½ minutes.
3. Stir in remaining ingredients and cook until slightly thickened. Serve immediately.

Remarks

- If you wish to make the dish look nicer, roll-cut the bamboo shoots and carrots.

One man's food is another man's poison; one man's junk is another man's treasure.

Deep-Fried Golden Soybeans

Let's go back to the basis of all fermented, dried or fresh bean curd dishes—the soybean. Deep-fried soybeans are commonly served as a snack or along with soup, soybean milk, or congee (Chinese rice soup). They can be served with a martini on the rocks or a can of cold beer. Serious drinkers may not be able to survive solely on beer, but they can surely survive on beer and soybeans. This recipe is good news for booze lovers.

1½ cups (370 ml) dried soybeans
2 tablespoons (3 ml) sugar or honey
3 cups (750 ml) water
2 cups (500 ml) oil
¾ teaspoon (3 ml) salt

1. Wash soybeans discarding split beans and skin. Dissolve sugar in warm water and soak beans for 3-4 hours to hydrate.
2. Drain beans. Pat dry and spread on paper towels to dry completely. Discard any remaining skins and broken beans.
3. Heat oil in wok over medium-high heat. Deep-fry ½ cup soybeans at a time until golden brown and floating freely on top of oil. Drain well and cool.
4. Roast for 15-20 minutes at 325°F (160°C), stirring soybeans occasionally until beans are crunchy and golden brown.
5. Sprinkle with salt and toss well. Serve hot or cold as a snack.

Remarks

- Soybeans are available in health food stores and most supermarkets. They are inexpensive and nutritious.
- For a different flavor, substitute herb salt for regular salt.

Eggplant Sandwich

A delectable delight for my vegetarian friends and for my friends who are hamburger lovers—one great alternative to the mundane hamburger. Terrific during the summer when eggplant is abundant and fresh.

1 small or medium-sized eggplant
2 tablespoons (30 ml) cornstarch
3 tablespoons (45 ml) oil

Filling Mixture:
3-4 tablespoons (45-60 ml) oil
¼ cup (60 ml) chopped water
    chestnuts
2 tablespoons (30 ml) chopped Chinese preserved turnip
2½ tablespoons (37 ml) soaked and chopped dried black mushrooms
2 tablespoons (30 ml) green onion,
    chopped
¼ teaspoon (1 ml) salt
½ teaspoon (2 ml) sugar
1 teaspoon (5 ml) wine
dash of white pepper
¼ teaspoon cornstarch solution

Braising Sauce:
2 teaspoons (10 ml) chopped garlic
1 tablespoon (15 ml) salted black
    beans, soaked and mashed
2 teaspoons (10 ml) wine
½ teaspoon (2 ml) sugar
⅔ cup (160 ml) soup stock
¾ teaspoon (3 ml) cornstarch

1. Cut eggplant in half, lengthwise, then cut crosswise into ½" (1.5 cm) thick slices. Cut a slit through the center of each slice to make a pocket. Lightly coat each slice with cornstarch. Set aside.
2. To make filling mixture: Heat 1 tablespoon oil in hot skillet and add all the chopped vegetables, stirring for 30 seconds. Stir in remaining ingredients and cook until thickened. Cool.
3. Stuff 1½ teaspoons filling mixture into pocket of each eggplant, slice. Set aside.
4. Heat wok over medium heat; brush eggplant sandwiches with small amount of oil. Brown 4-5 eggplant sandwiches at a time, 1 minute on each side. Reduce heat to medium-low. Return all cooked sandwiches in a skillet over medium-low.
5. Combine ingredients for braising sauce mixture and pour over sandwiches.
6. Cover and simmer for 2 minutes. Arrange sandwiches on platter.

Remarks
• The sponge-like texture of eggplant absorbs a great deal of oil, therefore the oil is lightly brushed over to ensure uniformity.

Eight Treasures Vegetable Plate

Discover a treasure chest full of seven different vegetables and nutritious bean curd. Rich in vitamins and minerals! Sure to make your body wealthy with nutrients.

Cooking Sauce:
1 teaspoon (5 ml) dark soy sauce
1 tablespoon (15 ml) oyster-flavored
    sauce
1 teaspoon (5 ml) wine
½ teaspoon (2 ml) sugar
½ teaspoon (2 ml) sesame oil
pinch of white pepper
½ cup (125 ml) soup stock

1½ tablespoons (22 ml) oil
2 cloves garlic, chopped
¼ cup (60 ml) sliced carrots
6-7 dried black mushrooms, soaked
4-5 baby corn
¼ cup (60 ml) straw mushrooms
5-6 water chestnuts
10 small fresh mushrooms
½ medium zucchini, cut into ¾" (2
    cm) cubes
1 square (8 ounces or 225 g) bean
    curd, cut into 1" (2.5 cm) cubes
1½ teaspoons (7 ml) cornstarch
    solution

1. Combine sauce ingredients and reserve.
2. Heat oil in wok over medium-high heat. Add garlic, stirring for 10-15 seconds. Stir in carrot and black mushrooms and fry for 1 minute.
3. Add remaining vegetables and stir for 1 minute.
4. Add bean curd. Pour cooking sauce over vegetables. Reduce heat to medium-low, cover and cook for 2-2½ minutes. Thicken with cornstarch solution.
5. Spoon onto a platter and separate each kind of vegetable so that you have 8 stacks of scrumptious goodies.

 There are no feasts on earth that do not break up.

Fermented Bean Curd with Green Beans

Fermented bean curd has the texture of soft cheese, with a pungent, distinctive flavor. In southern China it is used to season vegetable and meat dishes but can also be served alone as a side dish. Fermented bean curd changes ordinary green beans into a splendid vegetable dish.

¾ pound (340 g) green beans
1½ tablespoons (22 ml) oil
1 slice ginger, shredded
2 cubes fermented bean curd, mashed

¼ teaspoon (1 ml) salt
½ teaspoon (2 ml) sugar
1 teaspoon (5 ml) wine
½ cup (125 ml) soup stock
½ teaspoon (2 ml) cornstarch solution

1. Wash beans, snap off ends and cut diagonally into 2" (5 cm) strips.
2. Heat oil in wok over high heat. Add ginger and stir for 10-15 seconds. Add green beans and stir for 30 seconds.
3. Stir in remaining ingredients except cornstarch solution. Reduce heat to medium-low, cover and simmer for about 3½ minutes. Thicken with cornstarch solution. Serve immediately.

Remarks

- The distinctive combination of fermented bean curd and sweet green beans will go well with heavy, hearty dishes.
- If Chinese Yard Long beans are available, substitute for green beans.

Golden Fried Eggplant

Watch your tempura! Here's another exceptional dish for eggplant that's remarkably like Japanese tempura—if you like it you'll like this!

½ medium eggplant, about 8-10
    ounces (225-280 g)
1 tablespoon (15 ml) cornstarch
4 cups (1 L) oil

Batter:
¾ cup (200 ml) flour
¼ cup (60 ml) cornstarch
¾ cup (200 ml) flat beer (or water)
1 teaspoon (5 ml) baking powder (or
    1½ teaspoons if using water)
¾ teaspoon (3 ml) oil
½ teaspoon (2 ml) sugar

Dipping Sauce:
2 tablespoons (30 ml) hoisin sauce
1½ tablespoons (22 ml) catsup
1 teaspoon (5 ml) sugar
1½ teaspoons (7 ml) sesame oil

1. Cut eggplant into ¼" x 2" x 2" (0.75 cm x 5 cm x 5 cm) pieces. Lightly dust with cornstarch and set aside.
2. Combine ingredients for batter in mixing bowl. Blend to a smooth consistency.
3. Heat oil in a hot wok over medium-high heat. Shake excess cornstarch off eggplant. Deep-fry 4-5 slices at a time until golden brown. Drain and set aside.
4. Combine ingredients for dipping sauce in a small dish. Immediately dip fried eggplant in sauce and bite!

Remarks

- You can also serve this with soy sauce or mustard instead of the dipping sauce.

 You will have to wait until the time comes for the blossom of roses.

Golden Vegetable Balls

There are many kinds of meat balls in different ethnic cuisines. This recipe is unique, economical and quick. The light-colored round shapes resemble ping pong balls, but don't use them on the ping pong table!

Vegetarian Ball Mixture:
12 ounces (340 g) cooked potatoes,
 mashed
4-5 water chestnuts, finely chopped
3½ tablespoons (52 ml) grated carrot
1½ tablespoons (22 ml) preserved
 mustard green (optional)
3 dried black mushrooms, soaked and
 chopped
2 slices ginger, finely chopped
1 clove garlic, finely chopped
2 tablespoons (30 ml) flour
¾ teaspoon (3 ml) salt
1 teaspoon (5 ml) sugar
½ teaspoon (2 ml) sesame oil
pinch of white pepper
1-1½ egg yolks, lightly beaten

¼ cup (60 ml) cornstarch (for coating)
4 cups (1 L) oil

Dipping Sauce A:
⅔ cup (160 ml) soup stock
1 teaspoon (5 ml) wine
2 teaspoons (10 ml) soy sauce
1¾ teaspoons (8 ml) cornstarch
 solution

Dipping Sauce B:
3 tablespoons (45 ml) vinegar
3 tablespoons (45 ml) catsup
3 tablespoons (45 ml) sugar
1¾ teaspoons (8 ml) cornstarch
 solution

1. Combine vegetarian ball mixture in a large bowl. Shape into 24 one-inch diameter balls, coating each ball with a little cornstarch.
2. Heat oil in wok over high heat. Deep-fry balls until golden brown, 8-10 at a time. Drain and set aside.
3. In a saucepan, combine ingredients for dipping sauce A and bring to a boil; cook until thickened. Combine ingredients for dipping sauce B in a separate saucepan. Boil and cook until thickened. Keep sauces warm.
4. To serve, arrange a few lettuce leaves on a platter. Place vegetable balls on top. Serve with dipping sauces on side.

The peony, though large and beautiful, is useless; the date blossom, though small, yields fruit.

Savory Cabbage

Prepared with or without meat, this dish is just sensational! It's a terrific way to use cabbage, and a basis for being creative, going wild and developing your own famous Chinese dishes!

1 pound (450 ml) cabbage (or Napa
 cabbage)
2½ tablespoons (37 ml) oil
2 slices ginger, shredded
1 tablespoon (15 ml) dried shrimp,
 soaked (optional)
¼ cup (60 ml) shredded carrot
¼ cup (60 ml) shredded bamboo
 shoots
2 tablespoons (30 ml) green peas
1 teaspoon (5 ml) cornstarch solution

Braising Sauce:
1 teaspoon (5 ml) soy sauce
1 tablespoon (15 ml) dark soy sauce
½ teaspoon (2 ml) sugar
¼ teaspoon (1 ml) salt
1 tablespoon (15 ml) wine
½ cup (125 ml) soup stock

1. Cut cabbage into 1" x 2½" (2.5 cm x 6.5 cm) pieces.
2. Heat wok with oil over high heat. Add ginger and shrimp. Stir for 1 minute. Add cabbage and continue to stir for 1 minute. Stir in carrot, bamboo shoots and peas.
3. Combine braising sauce ingredients and add to vegetables. Cover and cook over low heat for 3-3½ minutes.
4. Thicken with cornstarch solution and serve hot.

Silky Smooth Squash

There are thousands of different kinds of squash all over the world. In North America the most abundant and commonly available ones are the butternut and banana squash. The butternut gives this dish a bit of sweetness, while the black beans and ginger marvelously perfume the sauce with their aromatics.

1 pound (450 g) buttercup squash, peeled and seeded	½ teaspoon (2 ml) salt
1½ tablespoons (22 ml) oil	1 teaspoon (5 ml) soy sauce
1 slice ginger, shredded	1 teaspoon (5 ml) sugar
2 teaspoons (10 ml) black bean paste	½ cup (125 ml) soup stock
	¾ teaspoon (3 ml) cornstarch solution

1. Cut squash into ½" x 1½" x 1½" (1.5 cm x 4 cm x 4 cm) pieces.
2. Heat oil over medium-high heat in wok. Put in ginger stirring for 10-15 seconds. Put in black bean paste stirring another 10-15 seconds.
3. Add squash and stir-fry for 30 seconds.
4. Add remaining ingredients except cornstarch solution to wok and mix well. Cover and reduce heat to medium-low and simmer for 10-12 minutes until squash is tender. Thicken with cornstarch solution and serve.

Remarks

- Refer to "Saucy Dips" for instructions on making black bean paste.

 Let there be plenty of food and clothing, and propriety and righteousness will flourish.

Sizzling Rice with Colorful Vegetables

This is a fun dish to create. The crunchy crust and fresh vegetables create a pleasant eating experience. Be sure to top the rice crusts with the vegetables at the table so that your guests can delight in the sizzling sound of the rice.

2 tablespoons (30 ml) oil
2 slices ginger, shredded
1 clove garlic, chopped
2 ounces (¼ cup or 56 g) shredded bamboo shoots
3-4 dried black mushrooms, soaked and shredded
2 ounces (¼ cup or 56 g) shredded carrots
2 tablespoons (30 ml) green peas
¼ cup (60 ml) sliced straw mushrooms (optional)

2 tablespoons (30 ml) soaked and shredded woodear (optional)
2½ teaspoons (12 ml) soy sauce
½ teaspoon (2 ml) brown sugar
1½ teaspoons (7 ml) wine
1 teaspoon (5 ml) sesame oil
1½ teaspoons (7 ml) oyster-flavored sauce
⅔ cup (160 ml) soup stock
2½ teaspoons (12 ml) cornstarch solution
2 cups (500 ml) rice crust
4 cups (1 L) oil

1. Heat oil in wok over high heat. Add ginger and garlic, stirring for 10 seconds.
2. Add all vegetables and stir-fry for 1 minute. Add remaining seasoning except cornstarch. Cover and cook over medium heat for 2½ minutes. Thicken with cornstarch solution and set aside.
3. While stir-frying vegetables, heat oil in wok over high heat. Deep-fry rice crusts half at a time over high heat just until puffed. Do not allow crusts to brown. Remove from oil and place directly on serving platter.
4. Immediately top rice crusts with vegetable mixture.

Remarks

• Be sure to cook rice crusts at the last minute so they sizzle when you add the vegetables.

Spicy Green (String) Beans

Fresh green beans are available in just about all local supermarkets. It is a shame to miss this vegetable when it is in season. This recipe, which adds the hot chili pepper to green beans, brings new dimension to an everyday vegetable.

¾ pound (340 g) fresh string beans
1-2 small red chili pepper, fresh or
  dried
2 tablespoons (30 ml) oil
½ onion, sliced
2 cloves garlic chopped

2 teaspoons (10 ml) wine
2 teaspoons (10 ml) soy sauce
¼ teaspoon (1 ml) salt
¼ teaspoon (1 ml) sugar
½ cup (125 ml) soup stock
1 teaspoon (5 ml) cornstarch solution

1. Trim ends of beans and remove strings. Cut beans into 2" (5 cm) strips.
2. Slice chili pepper into thin strips. Set aside.
3. Heat wok with oil over high heat. Add garlic, onion, and chili pepper and stir-fry for 30 seconds.
4. Add beans and stir-fry for 1 minute.
5. Add the remaining ingredients, except cornstarch solution. Cover and cook over medium-high heat for 4 minutes, or until liquid is slightly reduced.
6. Add cornstarch solution and cook until thickened. Serve.

Remarks

- This dish can be prepared a day ahead and reheated to serve.
- For those who love hot and spicy food, use at least 2 chili peppers.

Sprouting (Your Beans) in Style

Sprouting your own seeds is an easy, delicious and nutritious way to beat ever-mounting food costs. Its extraordinary food value provides a tasty, healthy alternative to expensive meats. They are a most inexpensive addition to your diet. Bean (mung bean) sprouts have exceptional nutritional value and very few calories (approximately 150-160 per pound). These sprouts are very low in carbohydrates (about 30 grams per pound). One pound of mung bean sprouts contains as much protein as 4-4.5%— much higher than most other vegetables. Its vitamin content rivals that of many fruits, with vitamins A and C and large amounts of thiamine (B1), B2 (riboflavin) and niacin. You will also find all kinds of minerals, including calcium, phosphorus, potassium and lots of iron.

Aside from the practical value, growing bean sprouts is also an exciting hobby for all ages, particularly when you first notice the delicate beans cropping up after a very short while. The average harvest costs only 5 cents per pound and takes only 4-5 days. It is under your complete control—you can grow it when you want and grow as much as you want.

The germination of seed requires water, light and the right temperature. For many types of bean sprouting, a room temperature of 68-75° F (20-22°C) is ideal. Oddly enough, no light is required to yield white and tender sprouts. Therefore, it should be grown in a covered pot or placed in a dark corner. Try your bedroom closet, if no other place is available. Just remove your whole wardrobe and use the entire closet for your bean sprouting!

How to Grow Mung or Soybeans

A. Wash ½ cup of the tiny green mung beans (usually available in Chinese stores or any health food store and sold by the pound in plastic bags) to get rid of broken beans and any foreign matter. Soak overnight with 4 times as much water as beans. Beans will hydrate and swell.

B. Pick a large clay pot (12" x 10"). Place a stainless screen or cheesecloth on top of drainage hold. Put soaked mung beans into pot and sprinkle water over beans. Place the pot in a dark area (yes, your closet!!).

C. Water beans 3-4 times a day. If you can't sleep some night, give your beans a couple of extra waterings! The idea is to ensure the moisture content of the beans and to keep the temperature low. Germination gives out heat—it is an exothermic process. Too high a temperature will promote the rotting of seeds and will yield uneven growth.

D. Continue the same procedure for 4-5 days without disturbing the seeds. You will see wonders towards the fifth day.

E. Harvest when the white stems reach about 1½". Don't wait until they grow to become a tree!

F. To harvest, pick them all from the pot and wash them in the sink with lots of water. Wash off the green husks and pick out the nice, white, tender bean sprouts. Store them in a plastic bag with holes and refrigerate for freshness. Serve raw in salads or use them in stir-fried dishes, soups or in anything you can dream of.

 Only eat fresh fish and ripened rice.

Succulent Mushrooms and Cabbage

Different vegetables are often combined in a single dish. If properly selected and prepared, such a dish can be ranked in taste and quality with the other great, popular dishes in Chinese cuisine. This one uses mushrooms and cabbage.

1 tablespoon (15 ml) oil
2 slices ginger, shredded
1 pound (450 g) cabbage, cut into 1½"
   (4 cm) square pieces
4-6 dried black mushrooms, soaked
1 cup (250 ml) fresh mushrooms
1¼ teaspoons (6 ml) sugar

½ teaspoon (2 ml) sesame oil
1 tablespoon (15 ml) oyster-flavored
   sauce
1 tablespoon (15 ml) dark soy sauce
½ cup (125 ml) soup stock
white pepper to taste
2½ teaspoons (12 ml) cornstarch
   solution

1. Heat wok with oil and ginger over high heat. Add cabbage and black mushrooms and stir for 2 minutes.
2. Stir in remaining ingredients except cornstarch solution. Reduce heat to medium-low, cover and braise for 5-7 minutes.
3. Thicken with cornstarch solution and serve hot.

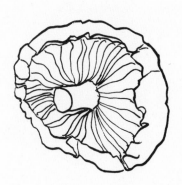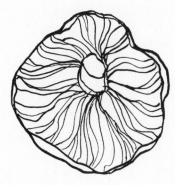

Sweet and Sour Cabbage

I honestly don't know where this dish came from—who cares anyway! If it is good, it is good! I think you might like it; it's a simple, economical dish to serve in the hot, muggy summer, as a salad or as a vegetable dish.

1½ pounds (675 g) cabbage, cut into
    2" (5 cm) squares
2½ tablespoons (37 ml) oil
½ teaspoon (2 ml) salt
3 tablespoons (45 ml) soup stock

Dressing Mix:
2½ tablespoons (37 ml) vinegar
2 tablespoons (30 ml) sugar
3½ tablespoons (52 ml) water
1 teaspoon (5 ml) soy sauce
2 tablespoons (30 ml) catsup
1 teaspoon (5 ml) wine
1 teaspoon (5 ml) sesame oil
1½ teaspoons (7 ml) lemon juice
½ teaspoon (2 ml) Tabasco sauce
pinch of black pepper
1 teaspoon (5 ml) cornstarch solution

1. Heat oil in hot wok over high heat; put in cabbage, stirring for about 30 seconds. Add salt and soup stock. Cover and cook for 2 minutes; cabbage should not be overcooked. Remove and place cabbage on a platter or in a salad bowl to let cool.
2. Combine dressing mix except cornstarch; bring to a slow boil then add cornstarch solution to thicken. Set aside and let cool.
3. To serve, pour dressing over cabbage; serve hot or cold.

Swiss Chard with Black Bean Sauce

Swiss chard is easy to grow in your own garden and is one of my favorite vegetables. When I was a child, we grew Swiss chard everywhere. My mom used to fix it for lunch and dinner seven days a week for seven months. Boy, did I learn to love it! After tasting this savory recipe you may want chard every day too!

2 tablespoon (30 ml) oil	¼ cup (60 ml) soup stock
1 clove garlic, chopped	¼ teaspoon (1 ml) salt
4 teaspoons (20 ml) black bean paste	½ teaspoon (2 ml) sugar
1 pound (450 g) Swiss chard, cut into 2" (5 cm) squares	¾ teaspoon (3 ml) cornstarch solution

1. Heat oil in wok over high heat. Add garlic, stirring for 10 seconds. Add black bean paste and stir for another 15-20 seconds. Stir in Swiss chard and continue to cook for 1 minute.
2. Add soup stock, salt and sugar. Cover and reduce heat to medium low and cook for 2-3 minutes.
3. Thicken with cornstarch solution and serve hot.

Remarks

- Swiss chard goes well with lamb dishes. It seems to enhance the flavor of lamb.

With a friend in the kitchen you will get rice; with a friend at court you can obtain office.

Tri-Colored Vegetable Balls

An artist can create something great from simple things. Here is an example that you can try. Three kinds of colorful vegetables, shaped into balls and cooked in a scrumptious sauce. Wow! It's great for weight watchers—and everybody!

1½ cups (370 ml) carrot balls, 1" (2.5 cm) diameter
1½ cups (370 ml) zucchini or winter melon balls, 1" (2.5 cm) diameter
1½ cups (370 ml) straw mushrooms
2 tablespoons (30 ml) oil
2 slices ginger, finely chopped
1 large clove garlic, finely chopped

½ teaspoon (2 ml) salt
2 teaspoons (10 ml) oyster-flavored sauce
1 teaspoon (5 ml) dark soy sauce
¾ teaspoon (3 ml) sugar
pinch of white pepper
½ cup (125 ml) soup stock
1¾ teaspoons (8 ml) cornstarch solution
lettuce leaves

1. Peel and shape carrot and zucchini (or winter melon) into small 1" (2.5 cm) balls. To shape hard textured vegetables, cut into 1" cubes, then cut off corners.
2. Blanch carrots and melon or zucchini in boiling water for about 2 minutes. Drain and set aside.
3. Heat oil in wok over high heat. Add ginger and garlic, stirring 10-15 seconds. Add blanched vegetables and stir for 30 seconds. Add remaining ingredients except cornstarch. Reduce heat to medium-low, cover and simmer for 2-3 minutes.
4. Thicken with cornstarch solution and serve over lettuce leaves.

Remarks

- If you are retired and looking for something to do, shape vegetables into perfectly round balls. If your time is limited, shape them into cubes.

 Medicine may heal imagined sickness, but wine can never dispel real sorrow.

Vegetable Broth

How to Prepare Broth for Vegetarian Dishes
"Those who are happy do not observe how time goes by." Here's a delightful broth that will make you happy not only because it is so easy, but also because it is very quick to prepare. A light classic taste.

For Instant Broth
Dissolve 1 vegetable stock cube to 2 cups (500 ml) water.

For Homemade Broth
In a large pot, bring 6 Cups (1½ L) water to a boil. Add 2 stalks green onions, 2 slices ginger, ¼ pound (112 g) mushrooms (optional), ½ pound (225 g) carrots (cubed), ½ pound (225 g) onions (cubed), 1 tomato (cut into wedges), 1 cup (250 ml) dried mushroom stalks, 1 tablespoon (15 ml) wine, 2 teaspoons (10 ml) salt and 1 tablespoon (15 ml) soy sauce.

Remarks
• Remember to save dried mushroom stalks to use for broth.
• Vegetable soup broth is available in health food stores or most supermarkets which have a health food section.

Vegetable Surprise

Now you see it, now you don't—a mixture of delectable, wholesome vegetables covered by a golden omelet. Nutritious and low in calories, it is great for dedicated dieters!

Sauce:
1 teaspoon (5 ml) soy sauce
½ teaspoon (1 ml) Tabasco Sauce
1½ tablespoons (22 ml) vinegar
2½ teaspoons (12 ml) sugar
1½ tablespoons (22 ml) catsup
¼ cup (60 ml) soup stock
¾ teaspoon (3 ml) cornstarch solution

2 tablespoons (30 ml) oil
2 cloves garlic, chopped
½ cup (125 ml) shredded carrots
½ cup (125 ml) shredded bamboo
   shoots
½ cup (125 ml) shredded mushrooms
½ cup (125 ml) shredded celery

½ cup (125 ml) shredded zucchini
½ cup (125 ml) bean sprouts
2 stalks green onion, shredded
1 teaspoon (5 ml) sugar
1½ teaspoons (7 ml) sesame oil
1 teaspoon (5 ml) salt
½ cup (125 ml) soup stock
1 teaspoon (5 ml) cornstarch solution
1 teaspoon (5 ml) oil

Omelet:
2 small eggs, lightly beaten
¼ teaspoon (1 ml) salt
dash of white pepper

1. Combine sauce ingredients and bring to a boil. Cook until thickened. Keep warm.
2. Heat wok with 1½ tablespoons oil over high heat. Add garlic and stir for 10 seconds. Add carrot, bamboo shoot and mushrooms; stir for one minute. Add remaining vegetables and continue stirring for another minute.
3. Add sugar, sesame oil, salt and soup stock to vegetables. Cover and cook for 1 minute. Thicken with cornstarch. Mound on a round platter.
4. Combine eggs, salt and pepper. Heat a large non-sticking fry pan with oil and make a thin omelet; set aside.
5. To serve, lay omelet over vegetables and cover with sauce. Cut into serving wedges, like a pie.

Wine does not intoxicate a man; he intoxicates himself. Men are not enticed by vice; they entice themselves.

Vegetarian Bean Curd Roll

For you who are vegetarian gourmets, this is a dish that is rarely found in restaurants. It's similar to the cabbage rolls in this chapter, but instead of steamed vegetables, you use deep-fried or smoked.

5 sheets dried bean curd sheets, whole
2 tablespoons (30 ml) oil
3 slices ginger, shredded
4-5 dried mushrooms, soaked and shredded
½ cup (125 ml) finely shredded carrots
½ cup (125 ml) shredded green onions
¾ cup (200 ml) shredded bamboo shoots
1 cup (250 ml) finely shredded cabbage

2 teaspoons (10 ml) soy sauce
2½ teaspoons (12 ml) oyster-flavored sauce
½ teaspoon (2 ml) sugar
1 teaspoon (5 ml) wine
½ cup (125 ml) soup stock
pinch of white pepper
1½ teaspoons (7 ml) cornstarch solution
4 cups (1 L) oil
flour paste: 2 tablespoons (30 ml) water/ 2 tablespoons (30 ml) flour

1. Soak 4 sheets of dried bean curd sheets in lukewarm water for 5-10 minutes. Drain and set aside. Break the remaining sheet into small pieces and soak for 5-10 minutes also. Drain and set aside.
2. Heat 2 tablespoons oil in hot wok over high heat; add ginger and stir for 10-15 seconds. Stir in mushrooms, carrots, onions, bamboo shoots and broken bean curd pieces and cook for 1 minute. Add the remaining ingredients except cornstarch solution. Reduce heat to medium, cover and cook for 2½ minutes. Thicken with cornstarch solution. Let cool.
3. Cut large bean curd sheets into 8 six-inch (15 cm) squares. Place about 2½ tablespoons (37 ml) vegetable mixture on one side of sheet. Wrap it very tightly, as you would make an envelope to enclose filling, like a spring roll. Seal edges with flour paste.
4. Heat oil in wok over medium high heat. Deep-fry bean curd rolls until golden brown. Drain well. Cut each roll into 3 pieces.

Remarks

- For those who love smoked foods, you can smoke this dish in place of deep-frying. Put a mixture of ½ cup black tea leaves and ½ cup brown sugar in a sauce pan which you are about to throw away. Heat pan over medium heat until smoke point and place rolls on a greased rack. Put rack in sauce pan and cover. Turn on fan exhaust full blast and smoke for 10-12 minutes.

Vegetarian Chicken Celery

Some like it light and delicious—this is one of the most popular dishes in Cantonese restaurants. It's a vegetarian dish that combines tofu and celery in such a way that you'll swear there's chicken in it!

Cooking Sauce:
1½ teaspoons (7 ml) oyster-flavored sauce
1 teaspoon (5 ml) wine
¼ teaspoon (1 ml) ginger juice
¼ teaspoon (1 ml) salt
¼ teaspoon (1 ml) sugar
¼ teaspoon (1 ml) sesame oil
¼ cup (60 ml) soup stock

1 square bean curd, cut into ½" x ½" x 2" (1.5 cm x 1.5 cm x 5 cm) pieces
3 cups (750 ml) oil
1 small carrot, peeled and cut into ½" x ½" x 2" (1.5 cm x 1.5 cm x 5 cm) pieces
2-3 dried black mushrooms, soaked and sliced
2 stalks celery, cut into ½" x 2" (1.5 cm x 5 cm) pieces
2-3 stalks green onion, white part only, cut into 2" (5 cm) lengths
¾ teaspoon (3 ml) cornstarch solution

1. Combine ingredients for cooking sauce. Set aside.
2. Drain bean curd well. Heat oil in wok over medium-high heat. Deep-fry bean curd until golden brown. Drain and set aside.
3. Heat 1½ tablespoons (22 ml) oil in wok over high heat. Add carrot and soaked mushrooms, stirring for 1 minute. Sprinkle soup stock if it becomes dry. Stir in celery and green onion.
4. Stir in cooking sauce. Reduce heat to medium-low, cover and cook for 2 minutes. Stir in bean curd and thicken with cornstarch solution. Serve.

Remarks

- This dish goes well with nuts (either in the dish or around the table).

 Receive all guests that come, making no difference between relatives and strangers.

Nobody "kneads" dough more than Yan.

Vegetarian Toast

If you tried shrimp toast and loved it, you'll find that this is even better. And you can eat more without gaining weight! It makes a really tasty appetizer for a cocktail party. Try it with a glass of wine or a bottle of cold, imported beer.

Spread Mixture:
1 peeled potato (about ½ pound or 225 g), boiled and mashed
2 tablespoons (30 ml) grated carrot
1 tablespoon (15 ml) finely chopped Chinese parsley
3 tablespoons (45 ml) soaked and finely chopped dried black mushroom
3 tablespoons (45 ml) finely chopped water chestnuts
1 egg, lightly beaten
¾ teaspoon (3 ml) salt
1½ tablespoons (22 ml) cornstarch
1 teaspoon (5 ml) wine
½ teaspoon (2 ml) sugar
dash of white pepper

6 slices extra-thin white bread, crusts removed
few sprigs of Chinese parsley
4 cups (1 L) oil
1 large bell pepper
¼ cup (60 ml) catsup
3 tablespoons (45 ml) hot mustard

1. In a mixing bowl, combine ingredients for spread mixture. Blend well and set aside.
2. Cut each slice of bread diagonally into 4 triangles. Spoon 1-1½ tablespoons spread mixture evenly on each triangle. Top each with Chinese parsley.
3. Deep-fry 5-6 toasts in hot oil over medium heat spread side down, for about 1½ minutes. Turn over and continue to fry for 1½ minutes or until golden brown. Repeat with remaining toasts.
4. To serve, cut bell pepper in half, place catsup in one pepper half and mustard in the other. Dip toast in either sauce and bite!

Watercress Salad Plate

Watercress is one of the most common and widely used vegetables in southern China. It's great in soups, salads and stir-fried dishes. This unique watercress salad is perfect for a spring day or a fall day or any day! Unique—and sensational!

1 pound (450 g) watercress

Dressing Sauce:
4 teaspoons (20 ml) soy sauce
2 teaspoons (10 ml) Worcestershire sauce
1½ teaspoons (7 ml) sugar
½ teaspoon (2 ml) Tabasco sauce
1½ tablespoons (22 ml) sesame oil
pinch of white pepper

1. Wash watercress well and blanch in boiling water for 5 seconds. Remove, plunge into cold water and drain. Cut watercress coarsely into 2" (5 cm) lengths.
2. Combine dressing sauce mixture in bowl and blend well.
3. To serve, toss watercress with dressing sauce and refrigerate until serving time.

 Diligence and economy secure plenty to eat and drink; whilst idleness and sloth bring hunger and starvation.

麵食類

Oodles of Noodles
and Lots of Nice Rice

Rice and noodles are the daily staples in China. Rice is mainly available in southern China. Northern China is more suitable for growing wheat; thus wheat becomes the daily staple there in the form of noodles, pancakes, dumplings, and buns. Both rice and noodles are excellent complements to a great many dishes.

It is customary to greet people with the expression "Have you had your rice yet?" as an equivalent to saying "How are you today?" In the Peking dialect, to have a job and good fortune is to have "the grains to chew" and to have lost a job is to have "broken the rice bowl." Many Westerners complain that they are hungry again just a few hours after a Chinese meal. The reason is probably that they eat more of the entrees than the rice—the bread and potatoes of the Chinese!

Long grain rice is the most commonly used for daily meals. When cooked properly, long grain rice is fluffy and separates easily, and is not mushy or sticky. Glutinous rice, also called pearl rice or sweet rice, has a shorter grain and a very sticky consistency when cooked. Glutinous rice is used for stuffing and for a festive dish resembling the tamale. Rice is mostly boiled or steamed and served with other dishes. Leftover rice is either stir-fried or made into congee (rice soup).

Noodles ("mein" in Chinese), symbolic of longevity and the everlasting, are frequently served as the last main course at birthday and wedding parties. They are available in a variety of shapes and sizes: fresh, dry or deep-fried; from plain wheat flour noodles to egg noodles; from rice noodles to beanstarch or cellophane noodles. No matter how they are made, noodles are always long. Most Chinese prefer fresh noodles. Traditionally, fresh noodles are hand-made, and it is quite a demanding task; therefore, few bother to make them at home. With the marketable small-noodle machine, an average homemaker can produce fantastic quality noodles in his or her very own kitchen. Fresh noodles can be frozen until ready to serve.

Whether they be fresh or dried, noodles must be parboiled in boiling water for 2½ to 3½ minutes, then rinsed under cold running water to remove loose starch. Drain the noodles well, and if they are not used immediately, sprinkle them with one teaspoonful of cooking oil and toss well. Set aside for later use.

Have you had your rice yet? Eat more noodles and live a long life. Here are a few recipes to prolong your years in this earthly, polluted world.

Cantonese BBQ Pork Buns

The last time you were in a Chinese restaurant you might have noticed a small cart filled with special delicacies. If you have never tried Chinese "Dim Sum," then you will be amazed at the great variety of delicious morsels passing you by in that little cart. Steamed or baked barbecued pork buns are among the most popular (it is *my* favorite, anyway!). Two or three will fill you up!

Filling:

1½ tablespoons (22 ml) shortening or lard
8 ounces (225 g) barbecued pork, cut in ¼" (0.75 cm) cubes
2 tablespoons (30 ml) finely chopped green onion
1 teaspoon (5 ml) chopped garlic
2 tablespoons (30 ml) oyster-flavored sauce
1½ tablespoons (22 ml) sugar
2 tablespoons (30 ml) soy sauce
2 teaspoons (10 ml) flour
1½ teaspoons (7 ml) cornstarch
⅓ cup (80 ml) water
1 teaspoon (5 ml) sesame oil

1 recipe of Typical Chinese Yeast Dough, page 258.

1. Heat shortening or lard in hot wok over medium-high heat. Add garlic, stirring for 10 seconds. Put in barbecued pork and green onion, stirring for 15-20 seconds. Combine other ingredients and mix well. Slowly pour this mixture over the barbecued pork and cook for 1 extra minute. Place in the refrigerator and chill thoroughly.
2. Turn risen dough onto a lightly-floured board and knead for a few seconds. Shape the dough into a sausage-shaped roll about 18-20" (45-50 cm) long. Cut it into 20 equal pieces and roll into balls.

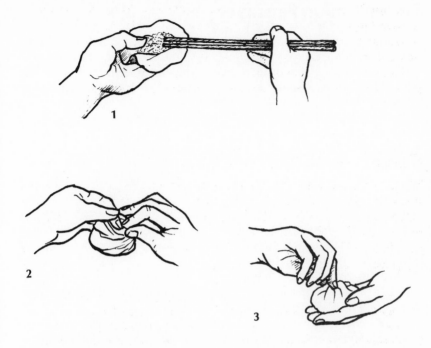

3. Flatten balls with palm into a biscuit shape, then roll the edges out with a rolling pin to make a circle of about 3½" (9 cm) in diameter (roll them out so that the corner of each biscuit is thicker than the edges).
4. Put one rounded tablespoon of barbecued pork in the center of each biscuit. Then gather up the edges to form a pouch by pleating (fluting) with your thumb and forefinger, then pressing to seal the top. Cover with a clean, dry cloth and let rise for 20-30 minutes.
5. Cut out 20 pieces of waxed paper 2" (5 cm) square, then bring water to a boil in a covered wok.
6. Place each bun on a piece of waxed paper and arrange the buns 1½-2" (4-5 cm) apart inside a bamboo steamer. Steam over high heat for 15 minutes, serve hot.

Remarks

• Steamed buns can be made ahead, frozen and re-steamed to serve.

Green Onion Pancakes

In northern China, this is as popular as Cantonese fried rice and chow mein. Local people will prepare many pancakes and then reheat them when ready to serve. Serve as a great nutritious snack or as part of a meal.

3 cups (750 ml) flour
1 cup (250 ml) boiling water
⅓ cup (80 ml) cold water
¼ cup (60 ml) shortening or lard

¼ cup (60 ml) finely chopped green onion
1¼ teaspoons (6 ml) salt
½ cup (125 ml) oil

1. Place flour in a mixing bowl and make a well in the center; pour boiling water into well, stirring rapidly with chopsticks until well-blended. Let cool for 3-5 minutes. Mix in cold water. Turn the dough out onto a lightly floured surface and knead until smooth. Cover and let stand 30 minutes to one hour.
2. Turn dough out onto a lightly floured surface and knead briefly. Roll into a sausage shape about 2" (5 cm) in diameter. Divide dough into 8 pieces. Roll each piece into a ball.
3. Lightly coat your hand with sesame oil. Flatten each ball and roll into a 6" (15 cm) round pancake. Into each pancake rub 1 teaspoon shortening and sprinkle with ⅛ teaspoon (0.5 ml) salt and 1½ teaspoons (7 ml) finely chopped green onion.
4. Roll up each pancake tightly and press ends to seal. Coil into a snail-shape, tucking the outer end into the center of the dough. Flatten coil and roll into a ½" (0.5 cm) thick pancake.
5. Brush a hot skillet with ½ teaspoon (2 ml) oil, place in pan and cover immediately. Fry 3 minutes until golden brown and puffy. Brush pancake again with oil, turn, cover skillet and fry 3 minutes more.
6. Repeat with remaining pancakes and oil. To serve, cut each pancake into wedges.

 Better be hungry and pure than well-fed and corrupt.

Ham and Chicken Noodle Soup

You may have tried chicken noodle soup before, but just wait until you try this recipe. You'll just love it! Don't be too chicken to try it!

Chicken Marinade:
1 tablespoon (15 ml) wine
dash of white pepper
½ teaspoon (2 ml) salt

8 ounces (225 g) boneless chicken
  meat
½ pound (225 g) fresh Chinese
  noodles
1½ teaspoons (7 ml) salt
2 teaspoons (10 ml) sesame oil
6 cups (1½ L) soup stock

2 slices cooked ham, cut into 2" (5 cm)
  strips
8-10 fresh snow peas, cooked and
  shredded
2 stalks green onion, chopped
1 tablespoon (15 ml) soy sauce
2 teaspoons (10 ml) oil

1. Marinate chicken for ½ hour. Steam over high heat for 12-15 minutes. Let cool, thinly shred and keep warm.
2. Parboil fresh noodles in 1 quart of water with ½ teaspoon salt for 1½ minutes. Remove and drain. Toss with 2 teaspoons sesame oil and place noodles in a tureen.
3. Bring the 6 cups broth to a boil. Add the remaining salt and the other ingredients and cook over medium heat for 2 minutes.
4. To serve, pour broth over noodles and top with shredded cooked chicken.

Remarks

• If it is easier, you can serve smaller portions in individual soup bowls.

Mandarin Boiled Pork Dumplings (Jao-Tze)

This tantalizing juicy dumpling can be served as a meal in itself. Similar to pot stickers, it is served for lunch or as a snack in many parts of northern China.

1 cup (250 ml) flour
5-6 tablespoons (75 ml) water

Filling Mixture:
3-4 Chinese cabbage leaves, chopped
4 ounces (112 g) ground pork

2 teaspoons (10 ml) dark soy sauce
1 teaspoon (5 ml) sesame oil
1 tablespoon (15 ml) soup stock
1 tablespoon (15 ml) finely chopped
   green onion
½ teaspoon (2 ml) sugar
½ teaspoon (2 ml) salt

1. Combine flour and water in a mixing bowl. Blend well and knead to a smooth dough. Cover with a damp cloth and let set for 30 minutes.
2. Put all ingredients for filling mixture in a bowl; mix well and set aside.
3. Knead the dough on a lightly floured surface until smooth and elastic. Roll into a sausage shape of about ¼" (0.5 cm) diameter. Cut into 14-16 fairly equal pieces; shape each into a ball. Cover with a damp cloth to keep dough from drying out.
4. Flatten each ball into approximately a 3" (7.5 cm) diameter circle with a rolling pin. Place one round teaspoon of filling in the center of each circle.
5. Fold each circle in half to enclose filling and press edges firmly to seal. If desired, make small pleats around the edge of each dumpling; cover dumplings with a damp cloth.
6. Bring 8 cups (2 L) of water to a vigorous boil; add one dumpling at a time and let boil again uncovered.
7. Pour in ½ cup (125 ml) cold water and wait until water boils again. Continue to cook in boiling water for 1-1½ minutes or until dumplings float on top. Remove dumplings with a strainer and serve hot.

Remarks

- This dumpling can be served with the same sauce that is used for pot stickers.
- If you wish, you can add boiled dumplings to soup stock and serve as a soup.
- Cabbage can be chopped in a food processor to save time.

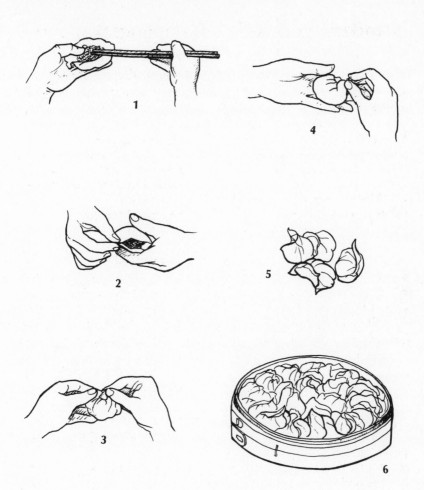

Mandarin Pancakes

All cultures seem to have this old stand-by and the Chinese culture is no exception. This dish is from northern China and is traditionally served with Peking duck and mushi pork. For your convenience these pancakes can be frozen and used as you get the craving! They keep for months.

2 cups (500 ml) flour, unsifted
¾ cup (200 ml) boiling water
1 tablespoon (15 ml) sesame oil

1. Place flour in a mixing bowl and make a well in the center; pour boiling water into well, stirring rapidly with chopsticks until well-blended. Let cool for 3-5 minutes. Turn dough onto a lightly floured board and knead until smooth. Cover and let rest for 30 minutes.
2. Turn dough out onto a lightly floured board and knead briefly. Roll into 1½" diameter roll. Divide dough into 14-16 pieces. Roll each piece into a ball.
3. Slightly flatten all balls with palm. Brush tops of ½ of the balls with ⅛ teaspoon sesame oil. Top each oiled ball with another ball and gently press together. Roll each pair of balls with a rolling pin to ⅛" thick circles.
4. Heat skillet or non-stick pan over medium-high heat. Lightly oil the pan with ½ teaspoon sesame oil. Brown each pancake 30-45 seconds on each side, moving pan constantly.
5. Immediately separate cooked pancakes by throwing firmly onto a clean counter and peeling the layers apart. Keep warm.
6. Continue to cook remaining pancakes in sesame oil until all are cooked. Seal in aluminum foil and steam over high heat for 20-25 minutes.

Remarks

- Prepared pancakes can be kept frozen. To use, defrost and steam in foil over boiling water for 18-20 minutes.

When you put on your clothes, remember the weaver's labor; when you serve food, remember the farmer's hard work.

244

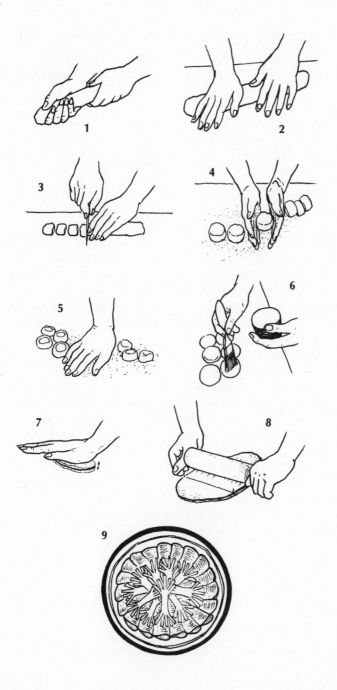

Mandarin Sesame Seed Cake

This traditional Peking sesame seed cake might be a little different from the sesame seed bun you find in local stores. If you are tired of potato, bread or rice, this is for you. Simple to prepare, freeze them and serve as a snack any day, any time, with soup, milk or even a drink.

½ teaspoon (2 ml) active dry yeast
½ cup (125 ml) lukewarm water
¾ teaspoon (4 ml) sugar
1½ cups (375 ml) flour
½ teaspoon (2 ml) salt

2 teaspoons (10 ml) pancake syrup
1 tablespoon (15 ml) hot water
3 tablespoons (45 ml) sesame seeds
1 tablespoon (15 ml) oil
1 teaspoon (5 ml) sesame oil

1. Put yeast in warm water to dissolve for 2-3 minutes. Add sugar and mix well. Let stand for another 2-3 minutes.
2. Put flour in a mixing bowl. Slowly pour in yeast solution and blend well. Knead to a soft dough. Cover with a damp cloth and let stand in a warm area for 30-45 minutes.
3. Punch risen dough and turn over to a lightly floured board. Add salt and knead for 3-4 minutes to get a smooth dough. Sprinkle a little flour on the board while kneading.
4. Roll dough into a 1½" diameter sausage shape. Cut into 6-7 equal portions. Shape each into a ball. Then flatten dough with your palm to a 3½" diameter, ½" thick biscuit.
5. Brush the top of each biscuit with mixture of 2 teaspoons (10 ml) syrup and 1 tablespoon (15 ml) hot water. Immediately dip this side into sesame seeds. Lightly press biscuit with rolling pin to press in sesame seeds. Let stand for 15-20 minutes.
6. Combine 1 tablespoon oil and 1 teaspoon sesame oil and blend well. Heat 2 teaspoons of oil mixture in a skillet or non-sticking pan over medium heat for 1-2 minutes. Put in 2-3 biscuits (sesame seed facing up). Reduce to low and cover to brown for 8-10 minutes. Turn to the sesame side and brown over low heat for 8-10 more minutes until lightly browned. Keep warm and cook the rest. Serve hot.

Remarks

- These mandarin sesame seed cakes can be prepared days ahead of time. Keep frozen. To serve, defrost and reheat in oven at 350°-375°F for 12-15 minutes.
- You can make your own syrup by heating brown sugar in a sauce pan over medium-low heat, adding enough water to achieve desired consistency and sweetness.

Plain Cooked Rice

Rice is the main staple in China where having a meal without rice is like not eating at all. Still, a good pot of rice is tricky to make. This recipe guarantees perfect results!

2 cups (500 ml) long grain rice
3 cups (750 ml) water

1. Rinse rice 2-3 times with cold running water. Then drain well.
2. Combine rice and 3 cups of water in a saucepan. Bring to a boil over high heat, uncovered.
3. Reduce heat to low, and simmer until almost all water has evaporated and crater-like holes appear in the rice. Cover saucepan and simmer for about 20 minutes to achieve total gelatinization.
4. Remove from heat and let stand 8-10 minutes to complete final cooking. Fluff the rice and serve hot.

Remarks

- The purpose of washing the rice is to get rid of excess starch powder and broken rice kernels which make the cooked rice mushy and sticky.
- Cooking time and rice texture are affected by the amount of water used and by storage time. Old rice requires more cooking and more water. Only experience will give the best results.
- Even though the Chinese never use ingredients other than water when cooking rice, you may use soup stock or add salt and butter.
- Cooked rice can be stored in the refrigerator and reheated with a little bit of water to serve.

Pork and Vegetable Lo Mein

"Mein" in Chinese means "noodles," and "Lo" literally translates to "tossed and mixed well." Lo Mein is a generalized term refering to cooked noodles mixed with any choice of meat and vegetables. In this recipe, the noodles are mixed with pork and vegetables. Great for lunch and snacks any time.

Pork Marinade:
2 teaspoons (10 ml) oyster-flavored sauce
1 teaspoon (5 ml) sesame oil
pinch of white pepper
1 teaspoon (5 ml) wine

4 ounces (112 g) boneless lean pork, cut into 2" (5 cm) long strips
10 ounces (306 g) fresh Chinese Noodles
1 teaspoon (5 ml) sesame oil
3-4 tablespoons (45 ml) oil
1 cup (250 ml) shredded cabbage
½ cup (125 ml) shredded bamboo shoots
4 dried black mushrooms, soaked and shredded
1 teaspoon (5 ml) dark soy sauce
4 teaspoons (20 ml) light soy sauce
1 teaspoon (5 ml) sugar
⅓ cup (80 ml) soup stock
2 cups (500 ml) bean sprouts, rinsed

1. Marinade pork for 30 minutes.
2. Parboil noodle in ample boiling water in a large pot for 3 minutes until tender. Rinse well under cold tap water, drain and sprinkle 1 teaspoon sesame oil over noodles, toss and set aside.
3. Heat oil in hot wok over high heat. Add marinated pork, stirring for 1½ minutes. Put in cabbage, bamboo shoots and mushrooms stirring for another minute. Add the remaining ingredients, except bean sprouts, stirring well. Cover and cook for 1-2 minutes.
4. Add cooked noodles and bean sprouts into wok. Stir-fry for another 1-2 minutes until well blended.
5. Serve hot.

Remarks

• You may substitute chicken or beef for pork and other vegetables for cabbage and bamboo shoots. Be creative and use lefovers. Like all other noodles, Lo Mein marries well with hundreds of flavors and textures.

"Is that fellow in the purple shirt the one who complained about my stuffed chicken feet?"

Pot Stickers

These are the best-known dumplings of northern Chinese cookery. They can be steamed, boiled or fried, and are generally served as an appetizer or snack. Dumplings are delicious served with a mixture of soy sauce, vinegar and chili oil. Don't be surprised if you become addicted!

1 cup (250 ml) flour
5-6 tablespoons (75-90 ml) water
2 tablespoons (30 ml) oil
½ cup (125 ml) soup stock or water

Filling Mixture:
¼ pound (112 g) ground pork
3 tablespoons (45 ml) finely chopped
    bamboo shoots
2 tablspoons (30 ml) chopped green
    onion
4 dried black mushrooms, soaked and
    chopped
½ teaspoon (2 ml) sugar
2 teaspoons (10 ml) wine
2½ teaspoons (12 ml) soy sauce
1½ teaspoons (7 ml) cornstarch
1 egg yolk

1. Combine flour and water in a mixing bowl. Blend well and knead to a smooth dough. Cover with a damp cloth and let stand for 20-30 minutes.
2. Put all ingredients for the filling in a mixing bowl. Mix well and stir-fry in wok over high heat 30-40 seconds, just to blend flavors, and set aside.
3. Knead the dough on a lightly floured surface until smooth and elastic. Roll it into a cylinder and divide it into 14-16 equal portions. Shape each into a ball and cover with a damp cloth to keep from drying out.
4. Flatten each ball into a 3" (7.5 cm) diameter circle with your hands or rolling pin. Place one rounded teaspoon of filling in the center of each circle.
5. Fold each circle in half to enclose filling and press edges firmly to seal. If desired, make small pleats around the edge of each pot sticker. While the pot stickers are being made, cover the formed pot stickers with a damp cloth to prevent drying.
6. Heat oil in a 10-11" skillet or non-stick pan over high heat. Add all dumplings and brown for 2-2½ minutes or until bottoms are golden. Swirl the pan occasionally while cooking to ensure even heating. Pour in the soup stock or water, cover and cook for about 5-6 minutes until the water evaporates. Continue swirling the pan occasionally.
7. To serve, transfer pot stickers to a platter and serve with soy sauce, mustard, vinegar and chili sauce, or whatever you like!

Remarks

- A common pot sticker, steamed or boiled dumpling sauce:

  3 tablespoons (45 ml) dark soy sauce
  3 tablespoons (45 ml) vinegar
  2 teaspoons (10 ml) sesame oil
  2 teaspoons (10 ml) grated ginger
  1½ teaspoons (7 ml) minced garlic
  ½ teaspoon (2 ml) sugar
  2 teaspoons (10 ml) hot chili oil

  Combine all ingredients and blend well. You may keep the sauce in jars for future use.

This is Chinese Hundred Spice Stew, give or take ninety-nine.

Spicy Chilled Chinese Noodles

A wholesome meal, these noodles are just right for lunch or a snack. And they're convenient and easy to prepare—a zippy tasting treat for any time or any occasion.

½ teaspoon (2 ml) salt
1 pound (450 g) fresh or dried Chinese noodles
1½ tablespoons (22 ml) sesame oil
8 ounces (225 ml) boneless chicken, cooked and thinly shredded
1 medium cucumber, seeds removed and thinly shredded
4 ounces (112 g) cooked ham, shredded
1½ tablespoons (22 ml) toasted sesame seeds

Spicy sauce
3 tablespoons (45 ml) soy sauce
1½ tablespoons (22 ml) vinegar
1 teaspoon (5 ml) sugar
¾ teaspoon (3 ml) Tabasco Sauce
3 tablespoons (45 ml) chopped green onion
1½ tablespoons (22 ml) sesame seed paste or oil
½ cup (125 ml) soup stock

1. Bring 1½ quarts of water to a boil with ½ teaspoon salt. Add noodles and boil for 1-1½ minutes, stirring occasionally. Remove noodles to colander and rinse with tap water until cooled. Drain well and sprinkle with 1½ tablespoons sesame oil.
2. Mix spicy sauce ingredients in a bowl and set aside.
3. To serve, place cooked noodles on a large serving plate. Garnish with chicken, cucumber and ham. Top with sauce and sprinkle with toasted sesame seeds.

Remarks

• Noodles and sauce can be prepared ahead of time and refrigerated Serve cold or at room temperature. Sensational!
• To keep noodles from sticking together, cooking oil can be substituted for sesame oil if it is first heated and then cooled.

 Friends while dinners and wine last; husband and wife while fuel and food remain.

Treasures over Rice Noodles

The fanciful name of this dish is a perfect description! It is another tasty yet economical dish of colorful vegetables over rice noodles. Kids will love the crunchy peanuts hidden among the "spaghetti."

8 ounces (225 g) rice noodles, broken to separate
2 ounces (56 g) boneless pork or chicken, cut into ½" (1.5 cm) cubes
2½ tablespoons (37 ml) oil
2 tablespoons (30 ml) diced Chinese pickled mustard (optional)
1 small carrot, cut into ½" (1.5 cm) pieces
4 dried black mushrooms, soaked and quartered
½ bell pepper, cut into ½" (1.5 cm) pieces
4 stalks green onion, white part only, cut into ½" (1.5 cm) lengths
¼ cup (60 ml) roasted peanuts
1 teaspoon (5 ml) cornstarch solution
2 cup (500 ml) soup stock

Meat Marinade:
½ teaspoon (2 ml) wine
½ teaspoon (2 ml) soy sauce
¼ teaspoon (1 ml) cornstarch

Cooking Sauce:
¾ teaspoon (3 ml) salt
1 teaspoon (5 ml) soy sauce
1½ teaspoons (7 ml) oyster-flavored sauce
¾ teaspoon (3 ml) sugar
pinch of white pepper
1½ teaspoons (7 ml) sesame oil

1. Combine ingredients for cooking sauce. Set aside.
2. Plunge rice noodles in boiling water for 10 seconds to blanch. Remove to colander, rinse in cold water and drain. Set aside.
3. Marinate meat for 10-15 minutes.
4. Heat oil in hot wok over high heat. Add marinated meat, stirring for 1 minute. Remove and set aside.
5. Add carrot and dried mushrooms to wok, stirring for 1 minute. Stir in remaining vegetables and cooking sauce. Return cooked meat to wok and stir fry for 1 minute. Thicken with cornstarch solution. Set aside.
6. Bring 2 cups soup stock to a boil. Add blanched rice noodles to stock and immediately pour into a soup tureen. Top noodles with meat and vegetable treasures. Serve in individual bowls.

Remarks

• Blanch noodles in 2 batches for even cooking.

Two-Sided Browned Noodles

The name tells it all; the noodles are browned on both sides, then topped with a lively mixture of delicious meat and vegetables. It is a whole meal in itself, a very traditional northern style noodle dish.

½ pound (225 g) flank steak
½ pound (225 g) prawns, shelled and deveined
8 ounces (225 g) fresh Chinese noodles
⅓ cup (80 ml) oil
6 dried black mushrooms, soaked and shredded
1 cup (250 ml) shredded bamboo shoots
½ cup (125 ml) shredded green onions
1 cup (250 ml) shredded cabbage
1 teaspoon (5 ml) salt
2 teaspoons (10 ml) soy sauce
½ teaspoon (2 ml) sugar
½ cup (125 ml) soup stock
1 teaspoon (5 ml) cornstarch solution

Beef Marinade:
2 teaspoons (10 ml) soy sauce
1 teaspoon (5 ml) wine
½ teaspoon (2 ml) sesame oil
1 teaspoon (5 ml) cornstarch

Prawn Marinade:
½ teaspoon (2 ml) salt
2 teaspoons (10 ml) cornstarch

1. Slice flank steak across grain into ¾" x 2" (2 cm x 5 cm) thin slices, marinate for 2 hours.
2. Slit prawns in half from back and marinate for 10-15 minutes.
3. Parboil fresh noodle in ample amount of boiling water for 3 minutes. Rinse under running cold tap water. Drain well and set aside.
4. Heat 1 tablespoon (15 ml) oil in a hot skillet or non-sticking pan over medium-high heat until oil begins to smoke. Carefully place noodles into pan and spread out into a cake, about 8" (20 cm) in diameter. Let brown for 5-8 minutes or longer until golden brown, turn cake over and pour in 1 tablespoon oil. Brown for another 5 minutes. Move and rock skillet frequently to get uniform browning. Pour in 1 tablespoon extra oil if needed.
5. Transfer browned noodle cake onto a large platter and keep warm.
6. Heat 1½ tablespoons (22 ml) oil in a hot wok over medium-high heat. Add prawns, stir until they turn pink, remove and set aside.
7. Heat 1 tablespoon oil in same wok over medium-high heat. Add marinated beef stirring for 1½ minutes. Remove and set aside.
8. Heat same oil with remaining oil over high heat. Add all vegetables stirring for 1 minute. Put in remaining ingredients except cornstarch and cover to cook for 2-3 extra minutes.

9. Return cooked beef and prawns to wok, stirring well and serve on top of browned noodle cake. Serve immediately.

Remarks

- Since the noodles are browned to golden crispness, this dish should be served right away (and completely "consumed!").

Can he, or can't he?

Twin-Flavored Fried Rice

These twins aren't identical twins!—but dramatically as different as night and day. The diversified flavors will delight your palate. Intriguingly scrumptious!!

4 cups (1 L) cooked rice
2½ tablespoons (37 ml) oil
½ teaspoon (2 ml) salt
1 clove garlic, chopped
broth (if necessary)

Flavor A	Flavor B
1 tablespoon (15 ml) oil	2 tablespoons (30 ml) oil
2 ounces (56 g) flank steak, cut into 2" x ½" (5 cm x 1.5 cm) slices	2 ounces (56 g) shrimp, cooked
1 tomato, peeled and diced	3 tablespoons (45 ml) green peas
2 tablespoons (30 ml) catsup	¼ teaspoon (1 ml) salt
¼ teaspoon (1 ml) vinegar	dash of sesame oil
½ teaspoon (2 ml) sugar	dash of pepper
¼ teaspoon (1 ml) salt	1 teaspoon (5 ml) cornstarch in 6 tablespoons (90 ml) broth
½ teaspoon (2 ml) cornstarch in 2 tablespoons (30 ml) broth	2 egg whites, lightly beaten (add last)
	2½ tablespoons (37 ml) half and half

1. Stir cooked rice over medium-high heat with oil, salt and garlic for 2-4 minutes. Remove and keep warm. Add 2-4 tablespoons of broth if dry.
2. Flavor A: Heat oil in wok over high heat. Add flank steak and stir-fry for 1½-2 minutes. Stir in remaining ingredients. Cook until slightly thickened. Set aside.
3. Flavor B: Heat oil in wok over high heat. Add shrimp and green peas and stir-fry for 1 minute. Season with salt, sesame oil and pepper. Add cornstarch solution and cook until thickened. Pour in egg white and cream; mix well. Remove immediately from heat.
4. To serve, place hot rice on a serving platter. Top with flavor A on one side and flavor B on the other.

Remarks

• When preparing flavor B, be sure to add egg whites and cream at the very last minute so as not to overcook them.

Typical Chinese Congee (Chicken)

Congee, also known as jook or rice soup, is one of the most popular dishes for breakfast, an in-between meal filler or a midnight snack. But rice soup is simply a base; you can toss in any ingredients you wish, the most common being fish balls, seafood or assorted meats. Congee goes well with toast, potato chips, corn chips or deep-fried wonton skins.

12 ounces (340 g) rice, washed and drained	1 tablespoon (15 ml) salt
8 cups (2 L) soup stock	1¼ teaspoons (6 ml) sesame oil
3 slices ginger, shredded	pinch of white pepper
4 ounces (112 g) boneless chicken breast, cut into 2" (5 cm) strips	2 stalks gren onion, chopped

1. Put rice and soup stock in a large pot; bring to a boil. Reduce heat to low, then partically cover and simmer for 1½-2 hours until rice becomes a soft pulp.
2. Put in chicken strips and shredded ginger, simmering for 10-15 minutes.
3. Add remaining ingredients except green onions and continue to simmer for 2-3 minutes.
4. Pour congee in a soup tureen, garnish with green onion, and serve in individual bowls.

Remarks

- You can add any leftover meats to the plain rice soup.

 A single kind word keeps one warm for three winters.

Typical Chinese Yeast Dough

This is similar to the common yeast bread dough. Savory sweet Chinese steamed buns are made from this basic dough. The most popular is steamed roast pork bun or red bean paste bun.

3½ cups (875 ml) all-purpose flour
4 teaspoons (20 ml) lard
1 teaspoon (5 ml) active dry yeast

1 cup (250 ml) lukewarm water
3¼ tablespoons (48 ml) sugar
½ teaspoon (2 ml) baking power
(optional)

1. Combine 3 cups flour and lard in a large mixing bowl. Mix well with clean hands.
2. In a separate bowl, combine yeast, sugar, ½ cup lukewarm waster and remaining flour. Mix well.
3. Add yeast mixture to the flour-lard mixture. Blend well and slowly add the remaining ½ cup water. Knead for a few minutes until smooth.
4. Cover bowl with a damp towel and let rise in a warm area (78-82°F or 26-28°C) for 1¾-2 hours or until double in bulk.
5. Punch center of the risen dough; transfer to floured surface and sprinkle with baking powder. Knead for a few minutes until smooth. If necessary, sprinkle extra flour while kneading.
6. Use dough in steamed bun recipes.

Yang Chow Fried Rice

Fried rice is a fascinating wonder in Chinese cooking. Varying the ingredients will give you a new rice dish. This recipe is special. You will never see so many goodies used to make fried rice!

2½ tablespoons (37 ml) oil
2 slices ginger, chopped
1 clove garlic, finely chopped
¾ teaspoon (3 ml) salt
2 stalks green onion, chopped
¼ onion, chopped
2 dried black mushrooms, soaked and shredded (optional)
½ Chinese sausage, thinly sliced (optional)
3 tablespoons (45 ml) frozen peas and carrots

2 ounces (56 g) fresh or cooked shrimp, diced (optional)
1 slice cooked ham, diced
¼ cup (60 ml) diced barbecued pork
¼ cup (60 ml) bean sprouts
2 eggs, lightly beaten and made into thin omelet (cook until firm) then shredded
1 tablespoon (15 ml) dark soy sauce
2 tablespoons (30 ml) light soy sauce
1½ teaspoons (7 ml) sesame oil
dash of white pepper (optional)
¼ cup (60 ml) stock (if needed)
6 cups (1½ L) cooked rice

1. Heat wok with oil, ginger, garlic and salt over high heat for 10 seconds.
2. Add onion, green onion, black mushrooms, Chinese sausage, peas and carrots, and shrimp; stir for 2½ minutes. Add a bit of stock if dry.
3. Reduce heat to medium-low. Add remaining ingredients and stir for 2-2½ minutes or until well mixed. Serve hot.

Remarks

- When refrigerated rice is used, add ¼ cup soup stock in step two to soften rice and cook it a bit longer.
- When fresh rice is used, it may be a bit too sticky. Spread out and let dry awhile before using for the dish.
- After rice is added, use only medium or medium-low heat to stir-fry to avoid burning and sticking of rice; stir the rice continuously.
- Any of the above meats and vegetables can be substituted or simply omitted.
- This dish can be prepared ahead of time and reheated when desired.
- Six cups of rice is a lot. You may end up eating fried rice all week!

 Philosophize to those who understand, and give food to those who are hungry.

食色性也

EDWARD LIM

Special Delectables —Gourmet Dishes

There are some truly exquisite dishes in Chinese cuisine that arouse a gourmet's delight! But don't let the word "gourmet" scare you—these dishes are not necessarily more tricky or expensive to prepare. There is a whole array of ingredients that you can choose from and make into delectable everyday dishes. The combination is indefinite and can be exciting.

There are a number of recipes in this book that are so unique, a separate category is warranted for them. Let your creative culinary imagination go and venture into this world of the gourmet's delights!

BBQ Chicken and Pork Union

Barbecue sauce gives this mouth-watering dish a rich flavor and colorful appearance. The unique combination of chicken and pork will be asked for time and time again!

BBQ Braising Sauce:
3 tablespoons (45 ml) hoisin sauce
2 tablespoons (30 ml) catsup
½ teaspoon (2 ml) five-spice powder
2 tablespoons (30 ml) soy sauce
1 teaspoon (5 ml) salt
1½ teaspoons (7 ml) sugar
1 teaspoon (5 ml) sesame oil
2 teaspoons (10 ml) Worcestershire
    Sauce
dash of ginger juice
dash of garlic juice
¼ cup (60 ml) oil

¾ pound (340 g) chicken, cut into 3" x
    3" x ½" (7.5 cm x 7.5 cm x 1.5 cm)
    slices
¾ pound (340 g) pork tenderloin, cut
    into 2" x 2" x ¼" (5 cm x 5 cm x
    0.75 cm) slices
2 stalks green onion, cut into 1" (2.5
    cm) strips
bamboo skewers

1. Marinate chicken and pork separately with half of barbecue sauce for 30 minutes. Reserve remaining sauce for basting.
2. Alternate chicken, pork and green onion pieces on bamboo skewers.
3. Preheat oven to broil. Broil skewers for 1 minute on each side. Dip them into the barbecue sauce and coat well. Broil for an additional 1½ minutes on each side.

Remarks

- You can bring any leftover barbecue sauce to a boil with 3 tablespoons (45 ml) stock. Pour over entire dish before serving.

 Pride invites calamity; humility reaps its harvest.

Chinese Pizza

Chinese pizza? Why not? If the Italian can learn how to wok, the Chinese can learn how to make pizza! This pizza has an Oriental flavor and is delightfully fun to make and eat.

Crust:
1 package active dry yeast
2 teaspoons (10 ml) sugar
1¼ cups (310 ml) warm water
2 tablespoons (30 ml) salad oil
1 teaspoon (5 ml) salt
4 cups (1 L) flour

Sauce for Crust:
3 tablespoons (45 ml) hoisin sauce
3 tablespoons (45 ml) catsup
1 teaspoon (5 ml) sesame oil

2 tablespoons (30 ml) oil
2 cloves garlic, finely minced
2-3 slices ginger, grated
1 cup (250 ml) thinly sliced Chinese
   sausages
½ cup (125 ml) shredded water
   chestnuts
½ cup (125 ml) bamboo shoots,
   shredded
4-5 dried black mushrooms, shredded
1-2 stalks green onion, shredded
¾ onion, sliced
1 bell pepper, shredded
1 tablespoon (15 ml) soy sauce
2 tablespoons (30 ml) hoisin sauce
2 tablespoons (30 ml) catsup
2 teaspoons (10 ml) sesame oil to
   brush on top of pizza

1. To make crust: Dissolve yeast and sugar in warm water. Let set for 10 minutes. Stir in oil and salt; add flour gradually. Knead dough for 10-15 minutes or until smooth and elastic. Place in greased bowl, cover and let rise in a warm place free from drafts until double in bulk (1½-2 hours). Punch down dough and roll into thin crust. Make 2 pizzas of 12" (30 cm) diameter, ¼" (0.75 cm) thickness. Place crust on baking sheet.
2. Combine ingrdients for sauce and set aside.
3. Heat oil over high heat; put in garlic and ginger, stir for 5 seconds. Add remaining ingredients except hoisin sauce, catsup and sesame oil; reduce heat to medium-high. Stir-fry for 1-2 minutes. Add hoisin sauce and catsup and stir-fry for another minute.
4. Spread sauce on dough, then top with stir-fried vegetables and meat; brush sesame oil on top.
5. Bake pizza at 375°F (190°C) for 15 minutes or until golden brown. Serve and enjoy.

Remarks
- One cup (250 ml) of sausage is equal to 3 sausages.
- For a classier pizza, add ½ cup (125 ml) sliced prawns.
- For added hotness, put ½ teaspoon (2 ml) hot chili oil into the sauce.

Handful of Gold Coins

This dish is dedicated to those who have prejudices, who refuse to explore new horizons and are determined not to try Chinese food. The image of a handful of gold coins bears a symbolic meaning in Chinese; the dish consists of braised mushrooms with duck webs, and the recipe is included here for ambitious cooks who dare to try it at home. If you want to try this exciting dish in a Chinese restaurant, you may have to order it ahead of time.

20 duck webs
1 tablespoon (15 ml) dark soy sauce
3 cups (750 ml) oil
2 cloves garlic, slightly flattened
2 slices ginger, shredded
1-2 whole star anise
2 stalks green onion, white part only, shredded

¼ teaspoon (1 ml) salt
¾ teaspoon (3 ml) sugar
1½ teaspoons (7 ml) wine
1 tablespoon (5 ml) oyster-flavored sauce
1½ cups (370 ml) soup stock
4 dried black mushrooms, soaked
½ teaspoon (2 ml) cornstarch solution
½ head (2 ml) of lettuce

1. Clean duck webs and cook in boiling water for 2-2½ minutes. Dry and rub with dark soy sauce.
2. Deep-fry duck webs in hot oil over medium-high heat until golden brown, about 2 minutes. Remove and set aside.
3. Remove oil, reserving 1½ tablespoons (22 ml) in wok. Heat wok and oil over medium heat. Add garlic and ginger, stirring for 10-15 seconds. Add fried duck web and the remaining ingredients except mushroom, lettuce and cornstarch solution. Reduce heat to medium low and simmer for 1 hour.
4. Add mushrooms and continue to cook for 15 minutes. Thicken with cornstarch solution.
5. Cook lettuce in boiling water for 1 minute. Remove and drain. Line platter with lettuce.
6. To serve, place mushrooms in center with duck webs around mushrooms. Here is the final product. I hope that your guests have the courage to try it—they won't be disappointed!

In everyday life, you should be economical; in entertaining your guests, you must be lavish in hospitality.

Honey of a Ham

In this recipe, ham is coated with a tempting nectar-like glaze. Although this dish is simple to prepare, your friends or family will think you have been in the kitchen for hours!

¾ pound (340 g) cooked Smithfield or
    Virginia ham
6 tablespoons (90 ml) honey
1¼ cups (310 ml) water

½ cup (125 ml) canned or dried lotus
    seeds (optional)
¾ teaspoon (3 ml) cornstarch solution

1. Slice ham into ¼" x 1" x 2" (0.75 cm x 2.5 cm x 5 cm) pieces. Arrange in a shallow bowl or a pie pan. Pour 4 tablespoons (60 ml) honey and ¼ cup (60 ml) water evenly on top of the ham and steam for 25-30 minutes.
2. To use canned lotus seeds, bring 1 cup (250 ml) water to a boil. Add lotus seeds and 2 tablespoons (30 ml) honey and cook over low heat until soft, about 15-20 minutes. Set aside.
3. Arrange ham on a platter and sprinkle with lotus seeds. Thicken ½ cup of the excess juice left from steaming with cornstarch solution and pour on top of the ham. Garnish with lotus seeds and serve hot.

Remarks

- Six tablespoons crushed rock sugar can be substituted for the honey.
- To use dry lotus seeds, soak 2-3 hours. Put seeds in 1 cup of boiling water. Reduce heat to simmer and cook 20-25 minutes, until soft.

In Celebration of a Newborn Baby

According to Cantonese custom, when a lady gives birth to a child, her family will prepare this chicken dish in celebration. It is cooked in an extraordinary amount of wine and served to relatives and friends.

Wine Sauce:
2½ cups (625 ml) rice wine
1½ cups (370 ml) sherry wine
1½ teaspoons (7 ml) salt
1½ teaspoons (7 ml) sugar

2¼ pounds (1012 g) whole chicken
2 tablespoons (30 ml) oil
2 green onions, cut into ½" (1.5 cm) strips
1 cup (250 ml) raw peanuts
½ cup (125 ml) sliced ginger
6 ounces (168 g) lean pork, cut into 1½" (4 cm) chunks
1 ounce (28 g) wood ear, soaked and sliced

1. Combine ingredients for wine sauce in a small bowl. Put aside.
2. Cut whole chicken into 2" (5 cm) square chunks. Heat oil in wok over high-heat; add green onion, peanuts and ginger, stirring for 1 minute. Add chicken and pork stirring for 1½-2 minutes.
3. Mix in wood ear and wine sauce. Bring to a boil. Reduce heat to low, cover and simmer for 17-20 minutes.
4. Serve warm or cold.

Remarks

- Wood ear has a unique medicinal function. A group of medical researchers from the University of Minnesota recently reported that wood ear inhibits blood clots.
- Wood ear is available only in Chinese stores and can be kept for a long period of time.
- This dish calls for a lot of wine so make sure you serve everyone an ample amount with their chicken!

 If the family lives in harmony, all affairs will prosper.

Always start with the freshest ingredients!

Lover's Nest

Two succulent meats prepared in delicate sauces and served in colorful nests are a treat to look at and taste in this special recipe. In Chinese, this presentation of food in a nest means "sweet and cozy."

Female Lover:
2 ounces (56 g) bean thread noodles
1½ tablespoons (22 ml) oil
**4 ounces (112 g) fresh scallops, sliced
  lengthwise**
½ small carrot, sliced
8 small mushrooms
**1 green onion, cut into 1" (2.5 cm)
  strips**
¼ teaspoon (1 ml) salt
¼ teaspoon (1 ml) sugar
¼ teaspoon (1 ml) sesame oil
dash of white pepper
½ teaspoon (2 ml) wine
2 tablespoons (30 ml) soup stock
½ teaspoon (2 ml) cornstarch solution

Male Lover:
4 ounces (112 g) fresh egg noodles
1½ tablespoons (22 ml) oil
1 slice ginger, shredded
**4 ounces (112 g) chicken breast, cut
  into ¾" x 2" (2 cm x 5 cm) thin
  slices**
4 baby corn, sliced in half
¼ cup (60 ml) sliced zucchini
**4-5 Chinese black mushrooms, soaked
  and halved**
1 teaspoon (5 ml) soy sauce
¼ teaspoon (1 ml) sugar
**1 teaspoon (5 ml) oyster-flavored
  sauce**
¼ cup (60 ml) soup stock
½ teaspoon (2 ml) cornstarch solution

5 cups (1¼ L) oil

1. *To make Female Lover's Nest:* cut bean thread noodles into 1½"-2" (4 cm- 5 cm) long pieces; spread noodles evenly inside a strainer (6"-7" diameter) (15 cm-17 cm) and fit another strainer (same size) inside of the first to hold noodle nest. Deep-fry until noodles puff up and remove immediately. Do not allow noodles to brown.
2. *To make Male Lover's Nest:* Bring fresh noodles to a boil in a large pot of water and cook for 1½ minutes; drain well. Spread noodles evenly into an oiled strainer (use same size strainer as above). Fit another oiled strainer into first strainer to hold noodles in nest shape. Deep-fry in hot oil over medium-high heat until golden brown and crisp. If nest sticks, tap handle of strainer lightly against edge of counter to loosen.
3. When both nests are made, place them at opposite ends of a platter, garnish with shredded lettuce, parsley or whatever you fancy. Use garnishes to support the nests in upright position.
4. *To make Female Lover:* Heat ½ tablespoon (7 ml) oil in wok over high heat. Add scallops and stir for 1½ minutes. Remove and set aside. Add sliced carrot, mushroom and green onion; stir for 30 seconds. Add remaining ingredients except cornstarch. Cook for 1½-2 minutes. Add

more soup stock if mixture is dry. Return scallops to wok and thicken with cornstarch. Keep warm.

5. *To make Male Lover:* Heat 1½ tablespoons (22 ml) oil in wok over high heat. Stir in ginger and cook for 10 seconds. Add chicken slices and stir-fry for about 1½ minutes. Add remaining ingredients except cornstarch, and cook for another 1½ minutes. Thicken with cornstarch.

6. To serve, transfer chicken mixture to male lover's nest and spoon scallop mixture into female lover's nest.

Remarks

- This is one of the longest recipes in this humble book, but the actual preparation is simple. Nests can be prepared ahead of time. Add the scallops and chicken mixture to the nests just before serving or they will become soggy. If you finish this dish feeling good, you are OK and should be awarded a medal of courage for undertaking a seemingly complex task!

A popular Chinese wine.

Rainbow Rolls

This may take extra time and effort, but the result is an attractive and delicious showpiece. It will even impress someone who could not stand your cooking in the past.

4 large cabbage leaves
cornstarch for dry-coating
3 eggs, beaten
4 sheets of dried seaweed
flour paste: 2 tablespoons (30 ml) flour
    in 1½ tablespoons (22 ml) water
1½ teaspoons (7 ml) soy sauce
1 teaspoon (5 ml) cornstarch

Filling Mixture:
12 ounces (340 g) lean ground pork
8 ounces (225 g) fresh frozen shrimp,
    thawed and minced
¾ teaspoon (3 ml) salt
½ teaspoon (2 ml) ginger juice
½ teaspoon (2 ml) sugar
1 teaspoon (5 ml) wine
dash of white pepper

1. Blanch cabbage leaves in boiling water for 1-1½ minutes. Drain and dust one side of each leaf with cornstarch. Set aside.
2. In a small frying pan, make 4 thin omelets with eggs. Dust one side of each omelet with cornstarch; set aside.
3. Combine filling mixture in bowl. Mix well and spread thinly and evenly on only the side of cabbage leaves with the cornstarch. Layer omelet (cornstarch side down) and seaweed in the same way. Roll up each piece into a cylinder and seal with flour paste.
4. Set bars in a pie pan and steam for about 20 minutes over medium-high heat. Reserve juice from steaming.
5. Arrange cabbage and omelet on opposite sides of an oval-shaped platter and place seaweed rolls at each end.
6. Stir soy sauce and cornstarch into reserved juice and cook until thickened.
7. To serve, cut each cylinder into ½" (1.5 cm) slices and cover with sauce.

Remarks

- Pound shrimp flat before mincing for a smooth texture.

Spectrum of Flavored Meats

It is not general practice in China to present three kinds of meat in a single dish. When the Chinese do prepare such dishes, they are most commonly served in clay pots. This is an unusually delicious and attractive dish.

4 ounces (112 g) lean pork, cut into 2" (5 cm) thin strips
4 ounces (112 g) boneless chicken breast, cut into 2" (5 cm) thin strips
4 ounces (112 g) flank steak, cut into 2" (5 cm) thin strips
5½ (82 ml) tablespoons oil
3-4 tablespoons (45-60 ml) soup stock
1½ (7 ml) teaspoons cornstarch solution
½ cup (125 ml) shredded bamboo shoot
½ cup (125 ml) shredded onion

Chicken Marinade:
¼ teaspoon (1 ml) salt
½ teaspoon (2 ml) sugar
dash of white pepper
½ egg white
1 teaspoon (5 ml) wine
¼ teaspoon (1 ml) cornstarch

Beef Marinade:
1 teaspoon (5 ml) dark soy sauce
½ teaspoon (2 ml) ginger juice
¼ teaspoon (1 ml) sugar
1½ teaspoons (7 ml) wine
½ teaspoon (2 ml) cornstarch

Pork Marinade:
1 teaspoon (5 ml) soy sauce
½ teaspoon (2 ml) sugar
1 teaspoon (5 ml) wine
½ teaspoon (2 ml) cornstarch
¼ teaspoon (1 ml) five-spice powder

1. Marinate pork, chicken and beef in their marinades for 30 minutes.
2. Heat 1½ tablespoons (22 ml) oil in wok over high heat. Add pork strips and stir-fry for 2 minutes. Sprinkle with 1 tablespoon (15 ml) stock and thicken with ½ teaspoon cornstarch solution. Set aside; keep warm.
3. Clean wok. Heat 1½ tablespoons oil in wok over high heat. Add chicken and stir-fry for 1½-2 minutes. Sprinkle with 1 tablespoon stock and thicken with ½ teaspoon cornstarch solution. Set aside; keep warm.
4. Clean wok. Heat 1½ tablespoons oil in wok over high heat. Add beef and stir-fry for 1-1½ minutes. Add 1 tablespoon soup stock and thicken with ½ teaspoon cornstarch solution. Remove and set aside.
5. Heat 1 tablespoon oil in wok over high heat. Add bamboo shoot and onion. Stir for 1 minute; sprinkle with extra soup stock if mixture becomes dry. Return cooked meats and mix well. Serve hot.

Remarks

- To retain original character and flavor of the meats, they are stir-fried separately and mixed before serving.

Spicy Sauce Mix

Wake up your taste buds with this one—it will keep them awake for a long time! A popular and traditional northern-style sauce, which can be served anytime over rice, noodles or along with other dishes, it includes crunchy peanuts which are a delightful contrast with the fried bean curd.

2 tablespoons (30 ml) oil
1 slice ginger, minced
½ green pepper, cut into ½" (1.5 cm) cubes
½ cup (125 ml) ½" (1.5 cm) cube bamboo shoots
4 fresh mushrooms, quartered
3 dried black mushrooms, soaked and quartered

¼ cup (60 ml) soup stock
1 cup (250 ml) diced deep-fried bean curd (optional)
¼ cup (60 ml) unsalted peanuts
¼ cup (60 ml) brown bean paste
¼ cup (60 ml) garlic-flavored hot bean sauce
½ cup (125 ml) hoisin sauce
2 teaspoons (10 ml) sugar

1. Heat 1 tablespoon oil in wok over high heat. Add ginger, pepper, bamboo shoots and mushrooms; stir for one minute. Sprinkle with 2 tablespoons broth.
2. Add 1 tablespoon oil, bean curd and peanuts and stir 30 seconds. Add remaining ingredients and reduce heat to low. If too thick add remaining broth. Simmer for 10-12 minutes, stirring frequently.
3. Serve sauce hot or cold.

Remarks

- For a more spicy sauce, increase the amount of hot bean sauce.
- Sauce keeps well in the refrigerator. Make it ahead of time and use as desired.

Steamed Egg with Meat and Seafood

This is a working man's (or working woman's) choice—light, nutritious and easy to prepare. My mother told me from the time I was born that I should learn to like this dish. My tender, uneducated tongue tasted this delicacy before I left home—four times a week! Boy, am I glad that now I only have to taste it when I feel like it!!

4 eggs, lightly beaten
1¼ cups (310 ml) cold soup stock
¾ teaspoon (3 ml) salt
½ teaspoon (2 ml) wine

pinch of white pepper
4 ounces (112 g) ground beef, ground
    pork or small shrimp
2-4 sprigs Chinese parsley, chopped
    (optional)

1. Combine eggs, soup stock, salt, wine and white pepper in a bowl. Blend well with a whisk. Stir in meat or shrimp and coriander.
2. Transfer mixture to a Pyrex pie pan and steam over high heat for 2 minutes. Reduce to medium-low and continue to steam for 18-20 minutes or until set. Serve in pie pan.

Remarks

• This is a popular family dish in southern China. Because you can use either pork, beef or shrimp, I have placed it in the gourmet section of this book.
• The aromatic fragrance of coriander adds zest to the dish.

Even though you have ten thousand acres, you can eat but one measure of rice a day; even though your dwelling contains a thousand rooms, you can use but ten feet of space a night.

Treasure Box

Sweet potato is a very popular vegetable in southern China. In America, it is abundant and cheap, yet very few recipes include it. Let's do something about that! This unique recipe should be treasured, kept secret and served only to your most-honored neighbors and in-laws.

The Box:
2 pounds (900 g) sweet potatoes, peeled, cooked and mashed
3 tablespoons (45 ml) cornstarch
1 teaspoon (5 ml) salt
2 egg yolks, lightly beaten
1 teaspoon (5 ml) sesame oil
2½ teaspoons (12 ml) oil

The Treasure:
1½ tablespoons (22 ml) oil
½ teaspoon (2 ml) chopped garlic
1 teaspoon (5 ml) finely chopped ginger
6 ounces (168 g) lean ground beef or pork
2 tablespoons (30 ml) chopped water chestnuts
1½ tablespoons (22 ml) finely chopped green onion
1½ teaspoons (7 ml) soy sauce
pinch of white pepper
1½ teaspoons (7 ml) cornstarch solution

4 cups (1 L) oil

1. Combine "Box" ingredients together in a large bowl and blend well.
2. To make the "Treasure": Heat 1½ tablespoons oil in hot wok over high heat. Add garlic and ginger, stirring for 10-15 seconds. Add ground meat and stir for about 2 minutes. Stir in remaining ingredients except cornstarch solution and cook for one minute. Thicken with cornstarch solution and set aside to cool.
3. Divide box mixture into 12-14 two-inch (5 cm) diameter balls. Oil hands carefully, flatten balls with palm and place 1½ teaspoons (7 ml) of meat mixture in each center. Close and roll balls to seal well. Slightly flatten with palm.
4. Heat oil in wok over medium-high heat. Deep fry sweet potato balls a few at a time until golden brown, about 3-3½ minutes. Serve hot.

Remarks

- Because sweet potato is starch, do not allow the treasure boxes to touch the bottom of the wok. Keep the "Treasure Boxes" elevated with a spoon or strainer for the first few seconds.
- For easy handling, oil spoon and platter; this will help when transferring the "Treasure Boxes" to the frying pan.
- If you can't find sweet potatoes, use yams or plain potatoes.

Water Chestnut Burgers

This dish is often served around Chinese New Year's and symbolizes "triumph and exultation." It is a very common family dish in southern China where pork and water chestnuts abound. Watch out, McDonald's!!

¾ pound (340 g) lean ground beef or pork
2 dried black mushrooms, soaked and chopped
1 stalk green onion, chopped
1 slice ginger, finely chopped
½ teaspoon (2 ml) salt
½ teaspoon (2 ml) sesame oil
1 teaspoon (5 ml) wine
2 teaspoons (10 ml) cornstarch
2 teaspoons (10 ml) oil
½ cup (125 ml) chopped water chestnuts

Dressing Mixture:
½ cup (125 ml) soup stock
2 teaspoons (10 ml) soy sauce
½ teaspoon (2 ml) sugar
1 teaspoon (5 ml) oyster-flavored sauce
1½ teaspoons (7 ml) cornstarch solution
1 tablespoon (15 ml) wine

3-4 tablespoons (45-60 ml) cornstarch for coating
2-3 tablespoons (30-45 ml) oil
¾ pound (340 g) spinach, blanched and kept warm

1. In a bowl, combine ingredients for burgers; mix well and let stand for 10-15 minutes. Make 8 four-inch (20 cm) diameter "burgers." Set aside.
2. Combine dressing mix in sauce pan, bring to a boil, and cook until thickened. Put aside and keep warm.
3. Heat 1½ teaspoons (7 ml) oil in a non-stick pan or skillet over medium-high heat. Dredge surface of burgers with cornstarch. Add 2-3 meat patties to a skillet, fry for 1½-2 minutes per side, until browned. Remove and keep warm. Repeat with remaining patties and oil.
4. To serve, place meat patties in center of a platter and surround with blanched spinach. Pour dressing over patties.

甜
點

EDWARD LIM

Sweet and Happy Endings
—Desserts

Generally speaking, there is no dessert course in most everyday Chinese meals. Sweet dishes are looked upon only as interludes or as snacks eaten between meals. Among the great variety of dishes in Chinese cooking, there are relatively few sweet ones.

Still, Chinese do serve sweet pastries, although rarely as part of a meal. Without an oven, most pastries are either steamed or deep-fried and are always served with tea. You may be amazed to learn that there is quite a repertoire of exotic sweet dishes or desserts which are prepared for formal dinners. Many of these are "sweet soups," consisting entirely or partially of warm liquids. Other common desserts are fresh or dried fruits, nuts, preserved vegetables, rice and wheat flour pastries. The sweetened paste of black and red beans and lotus seeds are among the most popular and traditional fillings for most cakes, puddings, steamed buns and a great variety of other pastries.

Dessert, to the Chinese, is not the essential part of a meal. Thus, there is no way the Chinese desserts measure-up to the Western desserts in glamor, variety and ingenuity. With fewer sweets served, it is no wonder that few Chinese are overweight.

Although it is not a Chinese tradition to serve dessert there is no reason why sweet dishes cannot be included in a Chinese menu. In my opinion, one of the most beautiful ways to conclude a meal is to present a plateful of fresh, succulent fruits. But if you wish to gain extra weight and indulge a sweet tooth, by all means consume as many sweets as you can handle.

Almond Cookies

The almond cookies in China are four times as big as the ones offered in Chinese restaurants here. One cannot qualify to eat them without a "big mouth." I can swallow two at a time!

¾ cup (200 ml) lard
¾ cup (200 ml) sugar
2 large eggs
1¾-2 teaspoons (8-10 ml) almond
   extract

1½ cups (370 ml) flour
1 teaspoon (5 ml) baking powder
15-16 skinless whole blanched
   almonds, cut in half.

1. Combine lard, sugar, 1 egg and almond extract. Beat well.
2. Slowly add baking powder and flour to lard mixture and blend well.
3. Divide dough into 30-32 small balls. Slightly flatten each ball with palm and place almond half in center.
4. Lightly beat the remaining egg and brush over the tops of all cookies to glaze. Transfer cookies to an ungreased cookie sheet, allowing enough space for each cookie to spread in baking.
5. Bake in a preheated oven at 350°F (180°C) for 15-18 minutes or until golden.

Remarks

• Almond cookies can be kept for several weeks and served any time you yearn for a sweet!

Riches and fame are but dreams among men; merit and renown are but gulls floating on the water.

Candied Sweet Potatoes

Here is a magnificent dessert prepared from inexpensive sweet potatoes. Sweet potatoes and yams are popular "tubers" used in the preparation of many Chinese snacks or desserts. Sure to delight those who have a sweet tooth!

1 pound (450 g) sweet potatoes or yams
2 teaspoons (10 ml) salt
2½ tablespoons (37 ml) honey
4¼ cups (1060 ml) water

5 tablespoons (75 ml) Chinese rock sugar or brown sugar
1½ teaspoons (7 ml) vinegar
1 teaspoon (5 ml) cornstarch solution

1. Peel the potatoes and cut lengthwise in ½" x 4" (1.5 cm x 10 cm) wedges. Combine salt, honey, and 2½ cups of water.
2. Add the sweet potato wedges and soak for 15-20 minutes. Remove and drain.
3. Bring 1¾ cups water, sugar, and vinegar to a boil over medium-high heat. Add the sweet potato wedges. Cover and cook over medium heat for 20-25 minutes. Uncover and cook for another 5-10 minutes until the liquid is reduced to about ⅔ cups. Transfer the sweet potatoes to a platter. Thicken the remaining sauce with the cornstarch solution and pour over the sweet potatoes. Serve hot or cold.

Cream of Peanut Soup

This is one of the most traditional and popular desserts in Cantonese banquets and in special dessert restaurants in China or Hong Kong. To perfect this recipe for my first book, I started testing during late 1979 and sent a personal letter to Mr. Jimmy Carter of Plains, Georgia, requesting 50 bags of free Georgian peanuts. Since my request never got a response, I was unable to put this recipe in my first book. Too bad. I could have given Jimmy's peanuts a few good words!

1¼ cups (310 ml) unsalted roasted peanuts

3 tablespoons (45 ml) toasted sesame seeds

6 cups (1½ L) water

¾ cup (200 ml) brown sugar or rock sugar

3 tablespoons (45 ml) cornstarch solution

⅓ cup (80 ml) half and half or evaporated milk

1. Combine roasted peanuts, sesame seeds and 1¼ cups of water in the blender. Blend at high speed until smooth.
2. Bring 4¾ cups water to a boil. Add sugar and stir until dissolved. Stir in blended peanut mixture. Bring to a slow boil.
3. Thicken with cornstarch solution and pour in milk. Blend well and serve hot.

Fortune Cookies

I didn't know fortune cookies existed until I got a job as a busboy in a small Chinese restaurant. I picked up a fortune which had fallen from a customer and opened it. It said, "Work hard, man!" I had a good impression of fortune cookies after that. One interesting thing is that no one gives me fortune cookies when I eat in Chinese restaurants. That's probably why I am still a poor cook!

The only reason that I include this recipe is that I have had over 103 requests for fortune cookies in the three years of my television show. If I were you, I would simply go to a Chinese grocery store, buy a box of 500 cookies and have myself a fortune party!

1 cup (250 ml) flour
1 egg, lightly beaten
¼ cup (60 ml) sugar

¾ teaspoon (3 ml) vanilla extract
(optional)
1 cup (250 ml) lukewarm water

1. Combine all ingredients and let stand for 15 minutes.
2. Heat a Chinese or Scandinavian Krumkake iron over the range to medium-high. Pour 1 tablespoon (15 ml) of flour mixture in center of the iron. Cook 3-3½ minutes on each side, or until mixture is golden brown.
3. Immediately remove flattened cookie, insert a fortune, and fold in half to form a half-circle. Slowly fold over to form a fortune cookie.

Remarks

- Don't forget the fortunes! Keep them at hand to insert immediately into cookies while they are hot and pliable.

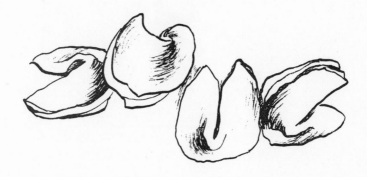

Fried Golden Egg Balls

This recipe is my version of Chinese doughnuts. It's an experience to prepare and well worth it—the result is a sweet and delicate pastry that is crispy on the outside but moist and custardy on the inside.

1¼ cups (310 ml) water
2 tablespoons (30 ml) lard or
    shortening
¾ teaspoon (3 ml) baking powder
¾ cup (200 ml) sifted flour

5 eggs, lightly beaten
5 cups (1¼ L) oil
1 cup (250 ml) granulated or
    powdered sugar

1. Bring water to a boil; melt lard in water. Turn off heat and slowly stir in baking powder and flour. Mix until smooth.
2. Slowly add beaten eggs. Blend well.
3. Heat oil in wok over medium-high heat (about 330-340°F or 165-170°C). Using a small ladle, drop 1-1½ tablespoons (15-22 ml) of batter into oil. Deep-fry over medium-low heat until balls triple in size. Keep turning to allow uniform cooking.
4. Roll fried egg balls in sugar.

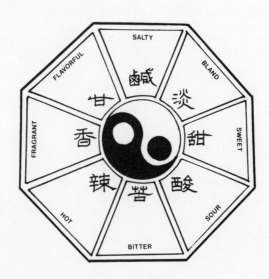

Ginger-Flavored Fruit Cocktail

Fruit cocktail is a favorite dessert, especially among the diet-conscious. The hot ginger and the fresh lychee and pineapple are a perfect combination.

6-8 slices fresh ginger
4 tablespoons (60 ml) chopped candied ginger
12 Chinese pickled ginger pieces, thinly sliced
¼ cup (60 ml) lychee juice
4 teaspoons (20 ml) sugar
1 cup (250 ml) lychee

1 cup (250 ml) 1" (2.5 cm) chunks fresh or canned pineapple
½ cup (125 ml) sliced fresh or canned peaches
½ cup (125 ml) slivered almonds, toasted in oven
8 red cherries

1. Combine fresh ginger, candied ginger, pickled ginger, lychee juice and sugar in a sauce pan. Bring to a boil and cook for 2 minutes. Discard all ginger slices except candied ginger. Cool and set aside.
2. Drain pineapple, peaches and lychee; place in a serving bowl. Pour in cooled ginger-flavored lychee juice. Toss fruits in juice. Chill in refrigerator, stirring occasionally to blend flavors.
3. Garnish with almonds and cherries to serve.

Remarks

• Sweetened, shredded coconut may also be used as a garnish.

 When you paint a tiger, you paint his skin; it is difficult to paint the bones. When you know a man, you know his face but not his heart.

Golden Fried Egg Custard

This is one of the most popular northern Chinese desserts. It would be a marvelous choice for a gourmet dinner party. Prepare it ahead of time and fry just before serving. The golden crispy crust contrasts nicely with the smooth custard inside.

¼ cup (60 ml) sesame seeds
⅓ cup (80 ml) sugar
2½ cups (625 ml) water
⅓ cup (80 ml) cornstarch for coating
3 cups (750 ml) oil

Egg Custard Mixture:
1 cup (250 ml) flour
3 tablespoons (45 ml) cornstarch
1⅓ cups (330 ml) water
2 large eggs, lightly beaten
4 teaspoons (20 ml) sugar

1. Toast sesame seeds in a skillet over medium-low heat until golden brown and fragrant. Swirl pan to keep seeds from burning. Spread seeds on waxed paper and crush with a rolling pin until reduced to a powder. Combine powder with sugar. Set aside.
2. To make egg custard mixture, combine flour, cornstarch and water in a mixing bowl. Blend well with a wire whisk. Slowly pour in beaten egg and whisk until smooth.
3. Bring 2½ cups water to a boil, remove from heat and slowly pour in the custard mixture, stirring continuously with a whisk. Cook over medium-low heat, stirring continuously until mixture becomes elastic. Pour into a small square pan. Refrigerate until set, 4-6 hours.
4. Cut custard into ¾″ x 1″ x 2″ (2 cm x 2.5 cm x 5 cm) pieces. Coat pieces with cornstarch and return to refrigerator for 5 minutes. Keep coated custard in refrigerator until just before frying. Shake off loose starch before frying.
5. Heat 3 cups oil in wok over high heat. Deep fry coated custard pieces a few at a time until golden brown. Remove and drain well.
6. Roll custard pieces in sesame and sugar mixture to serve. Bite in!

Hot Walnut Soup

Can you imagine doing something totally new with walnuts? Walnuts are available everywhere so why not use them? Here's a dessert to start with!

¾ cup (200 ml) walnuts, skinless
  preferred
¼ cup (60 ml) rice flour (long grain)
6½ tablespoons (97 ml) rock sugar or
  brown sugar, crushed

4 cups (1 L) water
¼ cup (60 ml) evaporated milk

1. Roast walnut in 325°F (160°C) oven 10-15 minutes or until fragrant and lightly browned. Grind walnuts to powder in blender.
2. Combine walnut powder, rice flour, sugar and water in a large sauce pan and slowly bring to a boil. Reduce heat to low and simmer, stirring continuously for 15-17 minutes.
3. Stir in milk and bring to a second boil. Serve hot.

Remarks

- If you can't find rice flour, soak 4 tablespoons long grain rice for 3-5 hours. Drain and blend for 2-3 minutes in a blender.
- If rice flour or long grain rice are not available, use cornstarch as a substitute.
- Place rock sugar in a paper bag and hit with the flat side of a cleaver to crush.

A man cannot be known by his looks, nor can the sea be measured with a bushel basket.

Lychee Jello

Most of us love "jello." And when it's combined with the sweet, juicy and succulent lychee fruit it will definitely become a family favorite. Serve as a happy, refreshing ending to an elaborate meal.

2 packages unflavored gelatin
½ cup (125 ml) cold water
1½ cups (370 ml) boiling water
3 tablespoons (45 ml) sugar
½ cup (125 ml) milk
2 cans lychee fruit (15 ounce (425 g) can)
1 whole maraschino cherry per cup-size mold

Syrup:
1 cup (250 ml) lychee syrup
½ cup (125 ml) sugar

1. Soften gelatin in cold water for 5 minutes in a bowl.
2. Pour in boiling water and dissolve gelatin completely.
3. Stir in sugar until dissolved. Add milk, mixing well.
4. Drain lychee fruits, reserving syrup. Arrange lychees and cherries in a 4-cup mold. Slowly pour gelatin mixture over fruits. Refrigerate mold to set.
5. To make syrup, combine sugar and lychee syrup. Bring to a boil and cook until syrup is reduced to one half. Cool and refrigerate until set.
6. Unmold gelatin into serving plate. Pour syrup over mold. Garnish with peach slices or some other colorful fruit if desired.

Magnificent Coral and Pearls

This elegant and enlightening dessert deserves to be on a party menu. Very simple and intriguing.

lots of icy water
1 cup (250 ml) sugar
¼ cup (60 ml) peach or apricot brandy

16-18 ripe strawberries, washed and dried
10-12 canned water chestnuts
18-20 canned lychees

1. Prepare a large pan of ice water.
2. Combine ½ cup sugar and 2 tablespoons brandy in a non-stick pan. Cook over medium-high heat stirring constantly until melted.
3. Dip strawberries in glaze, then immediately submerge in ice water to harden. Drain and set aside.
4. Repeat the same process with water chestnuts, making another glaze with the remaining sugar and brandy.
5. To serve, place glazed water chestnuts in center of the plate and surround with the glazed strawberries and lychees. Serve immediately.

Remarks

- If not served right away, allow glazed strawberries and water chestnuts to harden on a wire rack instead of immersing them in ice water.

Refreshing Hot Orange Soup

This is not orange juice from Florida or California. It is a hot orange drink from China. Try it! Orange drinks are not just for breakfast anymore.

2 cups (500 ml) water
½ cup (125 ml) sugar or rock sugar
2 cups (500 ml) fresh orange juice
2 tablespoons (30 ml) cornstarch
    solution

4 very thin slices of orange
4 very thin slices of lime
4 red cherries
4 mint leaves

1. Bring water and sugar to a boil. Add orange juice, stirring well.
2. Thicken with cornstarch. Transfer soup to a tureen.
3. Ladle soup into bowls. Float an orange slice in each bowl. Top each orange slice with a lemon slice and a cherry. Garnish with mint leaves. Serve hot.

Remarks

- Add fresh grated orange peel for tanginess, if desired.

 Rivers and mountains may easily change, but human nature is changed with difficulty.

Steamed Sweet Pears

Even though I left home hundreds of years ago, I still miss my mother's steamed pears. I used to beg her to make them on cool winter nights. Pears are one of the most popular fruits in China and are believed to soothe coughs and sore throats. They are also thought to slow down aging and to keep the complexion young-looking. I eat half a dozen a day. It hasn't helped me—yet!

4 medium-ripe pears, peeled
¼ cup (60 ml) wild honey
¼ teaspoon (1 ml) cinnamon (optional)

1. Slice 1" (2.5 cm) from the top of each fruit. Save tops as "lids."
2. Carefully core each fruit, being careful not to go through the bottom of the pear (as shown in the figure).
3. Put 1 tablespoon (15 ml) honey into each core. Cover pears with the "lids."
4. Place fruits upright in a pie pan and steam over medium-high heat for 30-35 minutes.
5. To serve, place pears in individual serving bowls. Sprinkle with cinnamon if desired.

Sweet Walnut Balls

A unique and original recipe, but get someone with strong hands to help you or it will drive you nuts! Great for snacks. But watch out, calories can add up very quickly!

1 pound (450 g) blanched walnuts	**½ cup (125 ml) wild honey**
½ cup (125 ml) unsalted peanuts	**¼ cup (60 ml) powdered sugar**

1. Toast walnuts and peanuts in a 325°F (160°C) oven in separate pans until fragrant and lightly browned.
2. Finely chop walnuts and peanuts, keeping both nuts separate.
3. In a bowl, mix walnuts with honey. Shape into 1" (2.5 cm) diameter balls. Squeeze them hard to make firm balls (make about 40 balls).
4. Combine peanuts and powdered sugar and spread on a plate. Roll walnut balls in peanut-sugar mixture to coat well. Refrigerate until ready to serve.

Walnut Candies

You will be extraordinarily lucky if you can find "naked walnuts (walnuts without the skin) outside of China! This unique candy makes a delicious snack as well as a tempting dessert.

6-7 ounces (170-200 g) walnuts or pecans, shelled
¼ cup (60 ml) sugar
3 cups (750 ml) oil

1. Cook nuts in boiling water for 4-5 minutes. Drain well and immediately mix with sugar in a bowl.
2. Spread nuts on wax paper to dry.
3. Heat oil in wok over medium heat. Deep-fry dried nuts ½ cup (125 ml) at a time until lightly caramelized, about 1½-2 minutes, stirring nuts continuously. Nuts will float on top when they are ready. Remove and drain well.

Remarks

- Nuts can be stored for several weeks in an air-tight container.
- In my first book, *The Joy of Wokking,* there is a similar recipe which calls for cashew nuts instead of walnuts.

Wonderful Dessert

Wonton wrappers are a very versatile ingredient, used for deep-fried wontons, steamed dumplings and other things. This dessert is traditionally fixed for the Chinese New Year and other festive occasions. So celebrate life—with the first bite!

20 wonton wrappers
1 egg white, beaten
4 cups (1 L) oil

Filling:
2 tablespoons (30 ml) shredded sweet-ened coconut
3 tablespoons (45 ml) crushed peanuts
2 tablespoons (30 ml) toasted sesame seeds
1½ tablespoons (22 ml) sugar

1. Defrost wonton wrappers inside package. Combine filling ingredients in a bowl.
2. Put 1½ teaspoons (7 ml) of the filling mixture in the center of each wrapper. Moisten outer edges of wrappers with egg white. Bring one corner up and lift over filling to opposite corner to form a triangle. Press edges to seal.
3. Heat oil in wok to medium-high. Deep-fry wonton until golden brown. Gently turn wontons with tongs or chopsticks while frying for even browning.

Remarks

- Store in air-tight container to keep wontons for several days.
- Make sure the edges are securely sealed; otherwise you will have wonton dessert with nothing inside.

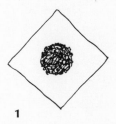

1

2

3

Blessed are the food lovers.

Loose Ends

Cups of Joy
—Tea and Wine

Tea Drinking

There are countless stories about the origins of tea drinking, but most historians and experts agree that tea drinking probably originated in China. In the early days, tea drinking was for medicinal purposes as a cure for all sorts of illnesses. Around the sixth century A.D., the Chinese began to regard tea as a refreshing social beverage. Poets and philosophers wrote about tea drinking. Soon after, tea was introduced to Ceylon, India, Japan and eventually the European countries. Today tea is one of the world's three great beverages, along with coffee and soft drinks.

Tea is grown in many parts of the world. The quality of tea is influenced by water, soil, altitude and climate. Different types of tea can be derived from the same plants through different preparation processes. Most great teas come from warm, humid mountain slopes. There are over 200 types of tea in China. In general, they are classified into four major groups.

The unfermented green tea, with natural bouquet and a light color, is usually roasted immediately after picking. "Dragon Well," grown in Chekiang province near a spring called Dragon Well, is famous for its smooth, soothing quality.

Fermented black tea is much darker in color, with a strong, pungent aroma. "Iron Goddess of Mercy" from Fukien province is the best known example.

Semi-fermented oolong tea is a happy medium between the rich aroma of the black tea and the delicate fragrance of the green tea. Oolong tea from southeastern China is the best known.

Scented tea is prepared from green and black teas chosen for their quality and scented with fresh and fragrant flowers. Because of the aroma, scented tea is also called "Fragrant Tea" or "Tea of Flower Fragrance." It is a specialty among the tea spices. Of the more than 30 major tea-producing countries, only one or two countries in Southeast Asia are

294

now producing this kind of tea. It's production began in the Tang Dynasty in China, so it is a traditional item which must be produced in bulk to meet the needs of Chinese at home and abroad.

There are many different kinds of scented teas. Among those prepared from flowers are Magnolia Tea, and Jasmine Tea which is considered to be the best tea because of its pleasant aftertaste and fragrance. Among the teas blended with leaves are the Hua Lung Chine and Hua Pi Lo.

Drinking tea makes one feel refreshed in mind and body. It can also be used for some medicinal purposes. According to *Outlines of Medical Herbs* written by the noted Chinese doctor Li Shih-chen during the Ming Dynasty, tea can check dehydration and stop coughing and phlegm. According to chemical analysis, tea contains a great deal of tannin which can produce anti-bacterial and astringent effects. It also contains caffeine which is used as a stimulant, cardiotonic and diuretic. Take aspirin for instance; it contains caffeine for curing influenza and headaches.

In ancient times, tea was used for curing some diseases in China. It was mostly used for curing dysentery and gastroenteritis. It also helps digestion and acts as a diuretic. However, since it has stimulative effects and can cause vessel expansion, it is not advisable for patients suffering from high blood pressure to drink too much tea. And no one should drink too much before going to bed.

In the Chinese household, it is customary to serve guests tea any time of the day, without cream or sugar. Knowing how to brew a pot of good tea can be an exciting experience. Tea connoisseurs relish tea for its color, bouquet and taste. To prepare a pot of fine tea, a clean tea pot is first rinsed in hot water to warm it up. Bring fresh water to a rolling boil. For

 The full teapot makes no sound; the half empty teapot is very noisy.

each cup of tea, put in one teaspoonful of tea leaves, then pour in the boiling water and let it brew for approximately 5 minutes. By making tea this way, the fine aroma, the color and taste of tea is at its best. Never boil tea. Try it—it is satisfying and refreshing.

Wine Drinking

Don't talk to me about drinking—my tolerance to alcohol is so low that if I even take a small amount it will give me a sensational hangover. Because of my lack of experience in this area, I do not consider myself qualified enough to discuss all aspects of drinking, but I can tell you how the Chinese drink, what they drink, when they drink, and for what occasions they celebrate when they do drink!

Drinking in China is a social affair and it always accompanies food. Because it is a social affair, Chinese rarely drink wine or any other alcoholic beverage before or after a meal, but always with a meal. And this usually happens at large gatherings of family and friends for special occasions. If you were an honored guest at a banquet, the host would toast you by saying "Kan Pei!" or in other words, "Bottoms up!"

In the Chinese language, there is only one word for spirits, "chiew," whether referring to a drink of low alcoholic content or a hard spirit wine. (They are called spirits because you usually feel like one after consuming them!!) Most of the labeled wines are 80 proof or higher—enough to give you a high on a sip. I hate to think what a whole glass would do.

Chinese wines differ from the Western and European wines by the simple fact that instead of fermenting grape juice, the Chinese distilled wine from rice or other grains. The variety of Chinese wines is incredible—they range from very mild wines to a wine which is as strong as brandy and could probably knock your socks off!! The two most

 If you don't drink, the price of wine is of no value.

296

common Chinese wines are the yellow Shaoshing and the white Kaoling. Shaoshing is made from rice and is similar to sherry, while Koaling is made from millet and is similar to gin or vodka. Of course, there are some very high alcoholic content wines in China, notably the Mao-Tai and Green Bamboo. Almost all wines are up to 150 proof and the Chinese drink them straight—no ice, no mix! And talk about intoxicating! Handle these with care!!

If you know where the closest Chinese store is in your neighborhood, you'll be able to find these wines. But because few Chinese wines are readily available in North America, substitutions may have to be made. For cooking, medium-dry or pale sherry, white wines such as sauterne, German Liebfraumilch, brandy, cognac, gin or Japanese sake can be used.

It may be interesting to point out that in recent years, it is whisky or brandy that is served at Chinese banquets and not the Mao Tai. If you want to serve wine at your next Chinese dinner party, and you're not adventurous enough to try the exotic Chinese wines, many wines are suitable. To name just a few, try premium white wine from sunny California, dry French Graves or Chablis, Italian Soave Bolla, Rhine wine or German Liebfraumilch. If you prefer red wines, try serving them with the heavier dishes such as duck or beef. If you prefer a variety of wines to be served at your dinner party, start with the lighter, white wine and progress to the full-bodied red wines.

Beer also goes well with Chinese food and is widely consumed in China.

> Three cups are the gateway to bliss;
> A jar, and the world is all yours.
> The rapture of drinking, and wine's dizzy joy,
> No man who is sober deserves.
>
> LI PO

 Let those who desire to quit drinking, when sober, look at a drunk.

Grab Your Chopsticks
and Let's Eat Out!

Eating out is a way of life for the Chinese. Most of their celebrating and entertaining is done in restaurants. Almost any occasion calls for a banquet: birthdays, weddings, anniversaries, reunions, and even funerals. No wonder Confucius said: "Food and beauty are human nature." As a result, the Chinese take great pride in their restaurants.

There are commonly three main regional cuisines found in North American Chinese restaurants: Cantonese, Northern (or Mandarin), and Szechwan-Hunan. Most restaurant menus include dishes that are common to all parts of China. A restaurant may be named after one region, but the menu will probably include dishes from other regions. Don't let the facade or decor of the restaurant deter you. Chinese chefs believe that the food will determine the fame of the eating establishment, not the candlelight, the service, or the beautiful, sexy waitresses!

The Chinese have no "main course" per se. A normal Chinese meal consists of several courses which are equally important, with the understanding that a combination of these dishes is to be shared by everybody. When ordering, please keep in mind that chow mein, chop suey or egg rolls are not the only things on the menu. Don't limit your gastronomic experience to "Dinner Number 2" or "Dinner Number 3." Be adventurous and don't be too afraid to experiment. One humble suggestion: order one dish from each food category. Remember to combine a wide variety of flavors, textures, colors and cooking methods to get the maximum enjoyment from the meal. A good example for a dinner for four: winter melon soup, chicken mushroom, sweet and sour pork, beef and greens, and rice. Generally speaking, order one dish less than the number of people. For six people, order five dishes, aside from soup and rice.

If you are not too sure of the menu, consult the waiter or those beautiful waitresses. In most cases, they will be more than willing to assist you. That way, you won't have yourself to blame if you don't like a particular dish.

In banquets, each dish is served separately to savor the individual

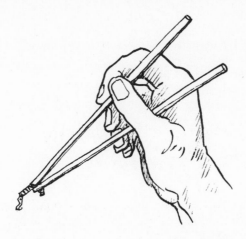

goodness. If the waiter tries to rush you by serving three or four dishes at one time, tell him to "cool it" until you are ready to eat more. Rice or noodles are served at the end of the meal as fillers only. In everyday meals, all dishes are eaten simultaneously. Take portions of each dish and put them in the bowl of rice to eat; rice is always eaten in the bowls, not on plates. Please do not drown the rice or any dish with soy sauce before you even taste it. Most good foods should have been flavored well during preparation and there is no need to add extra seasoning during serving.

Dining out should always be a new and exciting experience. Most Chinese restaurants will provide you with innumerable gastronomic adventures, so do not stick to the same restaurant simply because your great grandpa has been going there for one hundred years! Try new places, new dishes, and meet new waitresses!

It is time to grab your chopsticks and eat out tonight!

And please allow this humble cook to suggest the following menus for your next meal at a Chinese restaurant. The following dishes may or may not be included in this volume. Please select your favorite dishes and do not be afraid to explore new ones.

 There is little difference between dining and eating. Dining is an art. When you eat to please the palate, as well as to satiate the appetite, that, my friend, is dining.

For a Party of 4

A. Mushroom and Abalone Soup
    Stir-Fried Beef and Peppers
    Roast Pork with Chinese Cabbage
    Steamed Chicken and Chinese Sausage
    Rice

B. Mushroom Soup
    Steamed Beef with Preserved Mustard
    Deep-Fried Squab
    Stir-Fried Prawns with Almonds
    Rice

C. Egg Drop Soup
    Stir-Fried Spinach with Crabmeat
    Pork and Lotus Root
    Curried Chicken Balls
    Rice

D. Chicken and Fuzzy Melon Soup
    Stir-Fried Chinese Cabbage
    Tomato Beef
    Scrambled Eggs with Crabmeat
    Rice

For a Party of 6

A. White Simmered Duck Soup
    Steamed Spareribs with Black Bean Sauce
    Diced Chicken with Walnuts
    Braised Pork Balls and Lily Buds
    Stir-Fried Beef and String Beans
    Crabmeat and Cucumbers
    Rice

B. Winter Melon Soup
    Deep-Fried Spiced Duck
    Braised Whole Fish with Shredded Pork
    Stir-Fried Beef and Asparagus
    Simmered Stuffed Green Peppers
    Stir-Fried Prawns with Wine Sauce
    Rice

C. Chicken Velvet Soup
    Drunken Duck
    Shrimp Balls with Chinese Cabbage
    Stir-Fried Pork Kidney and Snow Peas
    Red-Cooked Chicken
    Braised Stuffed Mushrooms
    Fried Rice

If you wish to entertain in a Chinese restaurant, make sure that you have at least ten people present. The following menus are selected from four culinary regions.

A Cantonese Formal Dinner

Glorious Phoenix Cold Meat Platter
Stir-Fried Egg White with Crabmeat
Stuffed Crab Claws
Shark's Fin Soup
Crystal Prawns with Cashews
Cantonese Golden Fried Chicken
Twin Mushroom with Crabmeat Sauce
Braised Duck with Lo-Han Vegetables
Abalone in Oyster-Flavored Sauce
Steamed Garoupa with Ham
Yang Chow Fried Rice
Cream of Peanut Soup

A Szechwan Formal Dinner

Seasoned Jelly-Fish Salad
Tangerine Peel Flavored Chicken
Gold Coin Shrimp Cake
Sliced Pork With Garlic Sauce
Braised Baby Eel with Hot Sauce
Assorted Vegetable Chenu-Tu Style
Family Style Bean Curd
Golden Fried Spicy Duck
Crispy River Carp
Hot and Sour Soup
Szechwan Stir-Fried Noodles
Sweet Walnut and Green Pea Pudding

A Peking Formal Dinner

Jellied Lamb Loaf
Braised Sea Cucumbers with Shrimp Eggs
Stir-Fried Beef with Green Onion
Peking Duck
Fish Fillet in Wine Sauce
Fried Prawns Peking Style
Sweet and Sour Fish with Pine Nuts
Deep-Fried Rice Balls
Peking Duck Soup
Golden-Fried Meat Dumplings
Noodles with Ground Beef and Shredded Celery
Candied Apple or Banana

A Shanghai Formal Dinner

Wino Chicken Wings
Spiced Jellied Pork
Stir-Fried Pork Kidneys
Braised Shark's Fin with Crabmeat
Deep-Fried Spiced Pigeon
Stewed Whole Chicken Casserole
Sauteed Mushroom with Soy Sauce
Braised Bean Curd with Mushroom
Sauteed Tri-Color Prawns
Shanghai Fried Noodles
Special Steamed Dumplings
Chopped Sweet Date Cake

Here is a typical restaurant menu for a formal dinner.

JADE GARDEN
RESTAURANT

Assorted Cold Plate Topped With Crispy Suckling Pig

Stuffed Crab Claw

Scallop With Seasonal Vegetables

Chicken & Shark's Fin Soup

Crispy Chicken Jade Garden Style

Steamed Lobster

Braised Vegetable With Duckling

Steamed Fish

Fried Rice Yang Chow Style

Shrimp Dumpling Soup

Wedding Cookies

Sweet Red Bean Soup

JADE GARDEN
RESTAURANT

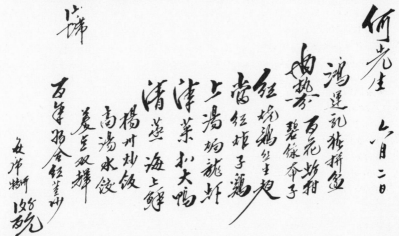

A Feast to Fascinate
Family and Friends

You may have tried many local Chinese restaurants and may have acquired a taste for more than chop suey and egg rolls. When planning a menu at home, there are a few things you should observe. The everyday family menu should be nutritionally adequate, with a good balance of texture, color and flavor; most important, it should be simple and quick to prepare. In fact, you may even choose one recipe each day that can be prepared ahead of time; then you can save all your energy and imagination for weekend entertaining. As a rule of thumb, entertaining at a formal dinner is just like eating at a restaurant. Plan your menu and organize your time. Go for contrast as well as harmony, although it may sound contradictory. Select a menu with a definite contrast in flavor, color, texture and cooking methods, yet at the same time, choose dishes that work in harmony and compliment each other. If one dish is salty, another should be sweet; if one is spicy, another should be bland; if you have an all-meat dish, have an all-vegetarian dish too. The most important point is to avoid repetition. Be honest with your skill and experience. Don't push yourself too hard. Cooking is meant to be enjoyed, not to be endured.

Here are a few ideas and suggestions from this local cook; I have outlined a menu for each day of the week. Sunday is your day off from Chinese food and it is reserved for your "Big Mac." I hope you find these suggestions useful.

 A man whose heart is not content is like a snake which tries to swallow an elephant.

Monday:
Pork and Bean Sprout Soup
Almond Gai Ding
Beef with Fresh Asparagus
Bean Curd Nuts
Rice
Tea

Tuesday:
Hot and Sour Mandarin Soup
Succulent Mushrooms and Cabbage
Tomato Beef with Bean Curd
Drunk Pork Plate
Rice
Tea

Wednesday:
Bean Thread Soup with Curd
Chinese Cabbage with Ham
Sesame Fish Fillet
Garlic-Flavored Chicken
Rice
Tea

Thursday:
High-Protein Cream of Corn Chowder
Watercress Salad Plate
Kuei-Fei Chicken
Steamed Spareribs with Plum Sauce
Rice
Tea

Friday
Sprouting Spring Soup
Fruity Flavored Chicken
Hunan-Style Lamb
Buddhist Vegetarian Delight
Rice
Tea

 With good friends, a thousand cups of wine are few; when opinions disagree, half a sentence is too much.

Saturday: *For Entertaining (dinner for ten—double ingredients in all recipes):*
Hearty Fish Chowder*
Delicious Chicken Drumsticks*
Crispy Walnut Meatballs*
Luscious Lemon Chicken
Five-Spice Crispy Duck*
Cantonese Beef Steak
Sweet and Sour Pork Rolls*
Garlic-Flavored Prawns*
Sesame Fish Fillet
Buddhist Vegetarian Delight
Rainbow Rolls*
Yang Chow Fried Rice
Lychee Jello*

*These dishes may be prepared ahead of time.

 If a man does not receive guests at home, he will meet very few hosts abroad.

Added Attractions
—Garnishes

Like the delicate lines of a Chinese brush painting, a garnish should be simple and complement the main dish. Excessive garnishing detracts from the food. Being creative is fun, but don't get carried away. Your garnish could be mistaken for a main dish! And, it is not necessary to garnish every dish. Even without a garnish, your guests will still want to eat all the food!

Garnishing can add beauty and texture to a dish. Contrasting textures and colors will make the dish more striking and tempting, so you will have fewer leftovers for breakfast! Use your imagination. The garnishes below will be an expression of your personality. They are special, unique and beautiful. Practice makes perfect—so be creative and dress up! Try some of these ideas at home:

Cucumber Folds

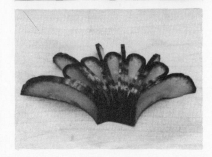

Tomato Slices

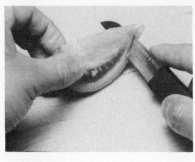 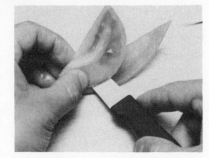

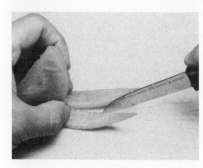 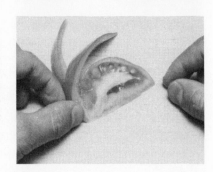

Tomato Rose

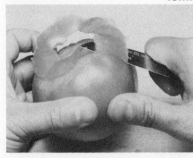 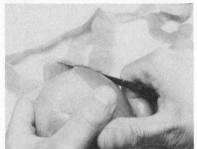

Tomato Flower

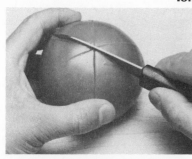 

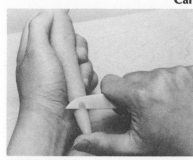 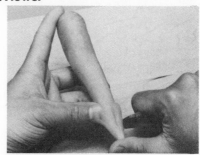

Carrot Flower

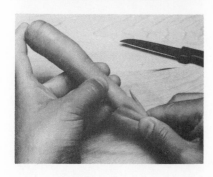 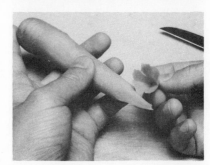

Onion Flower

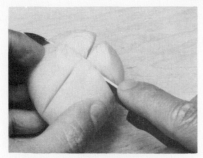 

Green Onion Flower

 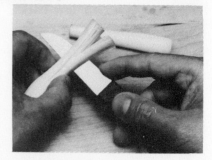

Apple Peaks

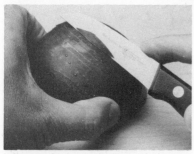 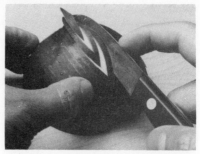

A Wok Through History
—Chop Suey and Chow Mein

Many people ask this question: "Is chop suey really a Chinese dish?" The answer is "more or less." The story of the origin of chop suey has as many versions as Chinese cuisine has ingredients! Most people attribute its origin to the early Chinese immigrants who came to North America to work on the railroads. In the absence of their familiar Chinese delicacies, they used what was available, and created many simple and practical dishes.

In the Cantonese dialect, "chop suey" means "miscellaneous odds and ends." Over the years, chop suey has established its status as the synonym for Chinese food, and a number of chop suey dishes have won honored places on Chinese restaurant menus. Today it generally consists of quick-fried bean sprouts, vegetables and shredded meats served with plenty of sauce and sometimes a few prawns or shrimps.

Chow mein, the sister of chop suey, has a slightly different story. The word "chow mein" means pan-fried noodles—a genuine Chinese dish. At birthday celebrations, the Chinese serve mein (noodles) which symbolize longevity.

Different regions of China have their own styles of frying noodles, but in general they combine parboiled noodles (previously drained dry and chilled) with meat and vegetables. First the noodles are soft-fried in oil and removed from the pan. Next, various meats and vegetables are stir-fried until tender-crisp. The soft-fried noodles are then returned to the pan at the last minute to reheat and blend flavors. Chow mein is a very casual sort of dish and can incorporate any combination of ingredients with good cheer. The type of chow mein served in most North American restaurants—with crispy-fried noodles—is not Chinese. But does it matter if you like it?

Chinese Spices and Life's Ingredients, Too

Most of the items listed in this book can be purchased at your local supermarket, but a few may require a visit to the Chinese specialty store. What most Chinese consider to be the basic ingredients of cooking can be very foreign to most Westerners. There are many traditional and exotic items which a lot of you would not likely see in your whole lifetime! Many others are processed items which can be kept quite a while if properly stored.

Seasonings and Condiments

Black Bean, Salted

A salted, fermented black bean with a strong, pungent aroma and flavor, used along with garlic to make into a paste as seasoning in many Cantonese dishes. It goes well with beef and seafoods. Sold in cans or plastic bags in Chinese stores. Keep in the refrigerator in a covered container or in a cool, dry area.

Brown Bean Sauce

A very thick brownish sauce made from fermented soy beans, flour and salt. This is quite a popular item used as a seasoning sauce in many everyday dishes, such as steamed fish. Sold in bottles or tin cans only in Chinese stores. Keep in the refrigerator.

Chili Oil

This is available at most Oriental groceries in various sized bottles; however, you can also prepare chili oil at home. Heat 1 cup (250 ml) of oil in a saucepan until it begins to smoke. Turn off heat and wait for 15-20 seconds. Put in 4 tablespoons (60 ml) crushed or powdered red pepper, stirring well. Let stand until cool and transfer to a bottle.

Cooking Wine

In gourmet Chinese cooking, different types of wines are selected for different recipes. Wine induces a desirable aroma and allows the different flavors to penetrate into the foods. In some cases it also reduces certain undesirable flavors and aromas in foods and its slight acidity helps to tenderize meat and fish. For stir-frying, wine is always introduced at the last minute, just before thickening, to retain the food's aroma. In stewing, simmering or casserole dishes, wine can be used during the cooking process. In marination of meat, excessive amounts of wine should not be used since it will mask the natural flavor of meat. If Chinese wine is not available, the common dry sherry can be substituted. Use liberally for any dish if you wish to have an "instant hangover!"

Five-Spice Powder

This blend of five different powdered spices—cloves, fennel, cinnamon, anise seeds, and Szechwan peppercorns—is usually sold in small bottles or plastic bags in Chinese stores. Though some brands consist of more than five spices, it is basically an all-purpose seasoning commonly used in barbecue dishes. To make your own five-spice powder: In a blender combine 50-60 Szechwan peppercorns, 4 whole star aniseeds, 2½ teaspoons (12 ml) of fennel seeds, 3-4 one-inch (2.5 cm) pieces of cinnamon bark and 12-14 whole cloves, and mix to get a fine powder. It will yield approximately 5 teaspoons (25 ml) of powder. Keep tightly sealed in a cool, dry area and it will keep forever.

Garlic

One of the most important ingredients in the flavoring of almost all Chinese dishes is garlic. It is usually sauteed in the wok in hot oil, along with ginger slices before adding other ingredients. Garlic has many acclaimed medicinal functions, but you should use a great deal of it only if you want to get rid of your social life! Whether you leave it in the wok or serve it with the dish is entirely up to your individual discretion and taste.

Ginger

This is one of the most frequently used spicy ingredients in Chinese cooking. Ginger helps to impart a delightful flavor and aroma to all foods, and of course, it helps to mask or eliminate undesirable odors as well. Hot and nippy, only a few thin slices are needed to achieve the desired purpose. Peel the ginger and finely chop it before placing in the wok, unless you wish to have hot lips—then use gigantic slices. If you wish, use a garlic press to make ginger juice. To store ginger root, make sure there is no mold, then place in a plastic bag and store in the refrigerator. It will keep for several weeks. Available in most local supermarkets. Dry ginger and ginger powder are not satisfactory substitutes.

Green Onion

The strong flavor and color of green onions will brighten all your dishes. To use, cut into varying lengths, then chop or mince depending on the particular dish.

Hoisin Sauce

This is a dark brown thick sauce with a delightful sweet and spicy flavor made from fermented soy beans, flour, sugar, garlic and spices. Along with plum sauce, it is mostly used for seasoning barbecued dishes and also used as a dip. Sold in bottles or tin cans. Keep in the refrigerator.

Hot Bean Paste

This is a special seasoning sauce frequently used in the dishes from Szechwan. It is made from regular bean paste and crushed chili peppers. Its spiciness gives any dish a muted hotness. If kept in the refrigerator, it can be stored for a long time.

Hot Chili Peppers, Fresh or Dried

Extraordinarily hot peppers! Fresh ones are available in most Oriental, Italian and Spanish stores all year round. They will keep in the refrigerator for several weeks. Crushed, dried peppers are available in most super-market spice sections.

MSG (Monosodium Glutamate)

This crystalline white powder $C_5H_8O_4NaN$, extracted mostly from soybean or other high-protein cereal grains, is basically a flavor enhancer. In Chinese it is called "weiching" which literally translated means "essence of taste." It is commonly sold under the trade names Ajino-Moto (Japanese) or Accent. A good Chinese cook does not use MSG in every dish. With high-quality, fresh ingredients, the right seasonings and proper cooking, a recipe should not require the use of MSG. However, some people may use it on certain dishes with very bland tastes, such as bean curd or frozen vegetables.

"Chinese restaurant syndrome" refers to a group of symptoms including headache, dizziness, skin rashes, feeling of pressure on the temples, pressure on muscles around the neck, extraordinary desire to drink 5 gallons of water, experienced by some people who are allergic to this "chemical." (It is interesting to know that MSG is present in most processed foods, particularly meats and soups.) There is nothing to worry about! Just don't use MSG in your recipe if you are worried that your neck might get stuck. Personally, I prefer homemade soup stock or even bouillon cubes to MSG. The amount of MSG used varies from chef to chef since most Chinese restaurants usually employ several cooks. For those who may experience such a reaction to MSG, may I suggest that you tell the waiter to skip MSG in your dishes when you order in any Chinese restaurant. It is not uncommon for some of their Chinese clientele to request the same.

Mustard, Chinese

This hot and pungent mustard is used mostly in condiments. It is not the same as French mustard. If the Chinese ones are not available, mix 2 tablespoons (30 ml) of English mustard and 3-3½ tablespoons (45-52 ml) cold water, stirring to form a paste. Let it sit for 30 minutes to an hour to mellow the harsh, bitter taste. It can be kept for several weeks.

Oyster-Flavored Sauce

This is a dark brown sauce made from oyster extract, salt and modified starch. It is a very strong flavored and tasty sauce with varying consistencies. Thickness is not the measure of quality. There are many brands with a great range of prices. Try them out, and see which one you prefer. As a seasoning or as a dip, it goes well with practically any meat and vegetable. Keep in the refrigerator.

Parsley, Chinese

A delightful aromatic herb used mostly as a garnish to give a touch of color and flavor in soup and many cold dishes. It is an excellent addition for those who enjoy its distinctive flavor and is mostly sold in Oriental, Mexican or Italian specialty stores. Will keep in a plastic bag in the refrigerator for 4-5 days.

Peppercorn Salt, Roasted
This is one of the few seasonings that is used in several different regions of China. It adds a distinctive touch of spiciness to deep-fried meats. To make your own, combine 1 teaspoon (5 ml) of Szechwan peppercorns with 3 tablespoons (45 ml) table salt in a frying pan. Brown mixture over low heat, shaking the pan continuously. Stir occasionally with spatula until the salt browns slightly. Turn off heat and crush the mixture with a rolling pin or the handle of a cleaver or mortar. Put the mixture in a tightly sealed jar and store it in a cool, dry area.

Plum Sauce
A yellowish brown sauce with a sweet, pungent flavor made from salted plums, vinegar, sugar, sweet potato, hot chili pepper and spices. Commonly used as a seasoning sauce and a dipping sauce, it is also a great accompaniment to hot or cold meats and is served with egg rolls in some Chinese restaurants. Sold in cans or glass jars in Chinese stores. Keep in the refrigerator.

Rock Sugar
This crystallized sugar, also known as rock candy, is pale brown in color and less refined than the common white rock sugar. Its sweetness and rich color give a dish a unique flavor and glossy appearance. Crush it before measuring.

Sesame Oil
This is not the kind of oil you may find in health food stores, where you'll find a lighter colored oil to be used for cooking and frying. Instead, this is a concentrated, strong nutty-flavored oil made from toasted sesame seeds. It is used widely all over China in marinades, soups and in last-minute touches. A few drops will give a dish excellent flavor. To prolong storage, keep in the refrigerator. A small bottle will last you a couple of generations.

Sesame Paste
This paste is commonly used in meat marinades and dressing sauces for cold dishes because of its strong aroma and rich flavor. The Middle Eastern "taheeni" or "tahini" is less flavorful but an acceptable substitute if the Chinese paste is not available. Before using, dilute one part paste with an equal part of water or oil.

Soy Sauce

No Chinese kitchen is complete without soy sauce. It gives Chinese dishes their characteristic flavor. Various regions in China produce their own types of soy sauce differing in color, aroma and flavor, yet the fermentation processes are basically the same. It is made from fermented soybeans, wheat flour, salt and water. In Cantonese cooking, there are two common types: light soy (thin soy)—lighter in color, saltier and used mostly for marinating and seasoning in stir-fried dishes; and dark soy (black soy)—much darker in color, sweeter and used mostly for stewing and sauteeing dishes to add color. It should be pointed out that *not every* Chinese dish calls for soy sauce because soy sauce, light or dark, darkens food. When the natural colors of the food are to be retained, salt is used instead of soy sauce.

Star Anise

Used whole with an eight-point star shape, or powdered, it has a licorice flavor and serves as a seasoning spice in many stewed or barbecue dishes.

Starch

For thickening: In most cases, tapioca, corn or arrow-root starch can be used for thickening purposes at the end of cooking. Simply mix 1 part of starch with 1-2 parts of water or broth and slowly add to the boiling liquid, stirring continuously. Starch solution tends to settle to the bottom, so be sure to stir well before adding to the wok. Most starches, particularly tapioca starch, when used in thickening a dish or making lots of sauce, will give a clear, shiny sauce.

For coating and holding in meat marinades: Cornstarch gives the meat a light coating, which helps to seal in the natural juices, making the final product more tender and juicy. It also helps to hold onto the surface moisture, making the meat smoother and avoiding spatters during deep-frying.

For coating meat in deep-fried dishes: Chinese chefs not only use starch to eliminate excess liquid in the meat, they also mix it with wheat flour, baking powder and water to give a batter of different thickness for coating deep-fried foods.

Water chestnut powder: In gourmet Chinese cooking, water chestnut powder is frequently used in thickening because of its sweetness and its ability to give a more adhesive consistency.

Sugar

As with many great cuisines around the world, a small amount of sugar is often used in Chinese cooking to give a contrast of flavor. Brown sugar is most often used.

Szechwan Chili Paste
Widely used as a basic seasoning for hot Szechwan and Hunan dishes, this paste is made from hot peppers, salt and garlic.

Szechwan Peppercorn
Seeds from berries of Zanthoxylum plants, these have a strong aromatic flavor and are used frequently in specially prepared spicy dishes. When used, they are first browned in a frying pan, then crushed and used as a seasoning. They will keep forever in a sealed container.

Tangerine Peel, Dried
The sundried tangerine skin is commonly used in soups or stewed dishes to add special fragrance and flavor. Wash before use.

Vinegar
There are white, red and black vinegars available in Chinese stores. The white one is used in preparing sweet and sour dishes; the red one is used mostly as a dip for crab and fried dishes; the black one is used in braising dishes and as a table condiment.

White Pepper
Both white and black pepper are produced by the same plant. Pepper is the berry of a perennial vine and white pepper has had the black hull removed to expose the cream-colored core. White pepper, having a more delicate aroma, is less pungent than black. It is often used in meat marinades or to add zest to soups and various dishes. White pepper is available in the spice section of supermarkets.

Dried and Other Preserved Ingredients

Agar-Agar
This is processed seaweed and it is used frequently in cold dishes with meats and vegetables. It can also be used in place of gelatin in jellied dishes—when dissolved in hot water it melts into a gelatinous substance. Agar-agar is sold in three forms: powder, solid rectangular sections, and fine strips. The powdered and solid forms are generally used for desserts, while the fine strips are used in salads.

Bean Curd
Cut into custard-like squares of about 3½" x 3½" x 1" (9 cm x 9 cm x 2.5 cm) in size, bean curd is made from high-protein soybeans. It has long been a favorite in the Orient. Inexpensive, nutritious, low in calories and with no cholestrol, soybean curd blends well with many foods and many flavors.

It is sold fresh daily and should be kept in water and refrigerated. The water should be changed every two days to keep the curd from turning sour. It can be served cold alone, or combined and cooked with countless meat and vegetable dishes. Also known as tofu, many places sell it in plastic sealed containers which indicate the last day of freshness. Bean curd should be left in the container until ready to use.

Bird's Nest
A semi-translucent gelatinous substance from the nests of tiny swallows of the South China Sea. For reasons of scarcity, labor and the difficulty involved in preparing Bird's Nest as a marketable product, it is an expensive delicacy. Mostly served in soup and also prepared as a dessert in formal banquets, it is sold in boxes and available only in Chinese stores. Many Chinese believe bird's nest prolongs life and is a good source of energy. Most of all it is good for the complexion.

Lily Buds
Dried buds from the tiger-lily flowers, yellowish-gold in color and about 3½" (9 cm) long, these are often called "golden needles" by the Chinese and are used as a symbolic food in dishes at ceremonial and festive occasions. It is exciting to serve a plate full of gold needles while the price of gold is sky-rocketing. Soaked before use, they go well with other ingredients in many dishes. Sold in plastic bags only in Chinese stores, lily buds can be kept for a long time.

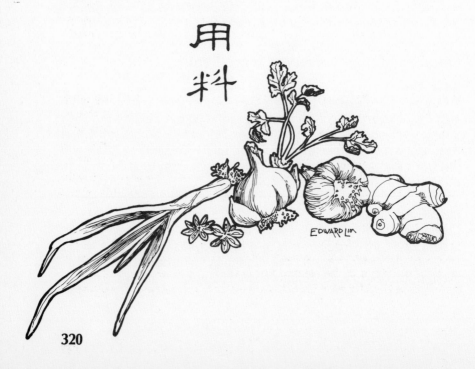

Lychee

The lychee is a snow white, succulent, sweet, juicy fruit from southern China. For many years this fruit was available in North America only in cans, but today fresh lychees are shipped by air to several large China-towns. Even though these fresh lychees are priced at $7 a pound (the canned ones are much cheaper) they are an excellent addition to any sweet and sour dish. They are also terrific served cold or with ice cream. And of course, their juice makes an excellent drink at any cocktail party.

Mushrooms, Dried or Fresh

Here I refer to the Oriental black mushrooms (Shii-ta-ke), long known as "The Emperor's Food" in both China and Japan, and recognized by gourmets worldwide as a precious delicacy. They are richer in flavor than most ordinary mushrooms and can be used along with virtually any ingredients in any dish. For centuries in the Orient these mushrooms have been regarded as the "elixir of life" that will enhance human sexuality, slow down aging and keep man vigorous. These oriental mush-rooms consist of a large amount of calcium, phosphorus and iron. They are also an excellent source of vitamin B and D_2.

Dried black mushrooms are commonly available in Chinese or Japanese stores. They come in various sizes and prices. Before use, they should be soaked in warm water for 30 minutes to soften. They are excellent in combination with most meats and vegetables. Keep in an air-tight con-tainer in a dry, cool area. Fresh ones with milder flavor and a much more superior texture are only available in a few areas, such as Vancouver, Toronto and Los Angeles. For more information on growing or purchasing large quantities of fresh black mushrooms, contact the Royal Mushroom Company Ltd., in Mississauga, Ontario, Canada.

Salted Egg

These are duck eggs, soaked in brine for 1-2 months, or with a salt and mud mixture coating the shell. Due to a chemical reaction, the egg proteins change their appearance and the white becomes watery and very salty, while the yolk firms up and reddens. When served, they are cooked either by hard-boiling or with other ingredients in a dish. Sold in Chinese stores only, hard-boiled salted eggs are very common in family meals, served along with rice, in congee (rice soup) or in vegetable soups.

Sausage Chinese

Chinese sausages are solid, flavorful little links, 5½"-6" (14-15 cm) long, made from pork, pork fat, or duck liver. They are sold individually or by the pound. They may be steamed or boiled before serving, or cut into thin slices and stir-fried with other meats and vegetables. The Chinese often cook several links along with their rice and then serve the sausages as a side dish. They can be kept in the refrigerator for several months and forever in the freezer.

Seaweed
Purple in color with a delicate flavor (from the iodine), seaweed combines well with many meats and vegetables. It is a common ingredient in soups. Rinse with water in a bowl before using.

Shark's Fin
This is the cartilage of the shark's fin and it is one of the most expensive Chinese delicacies. The time, labor and difficulty involved in the cleaning and preparation make it costly, and thus it is used mostly for formal parties. Shark's fin is available only in Chinese stores in dried form or in cans, and is mostly prepared as soup.

Shrimp, Chinese Dried
These shrimp are sold in 4 or 8 ounce packages in Chinese groceries. They have a strong flavor which enhances many vegetable dishes and soups. Soak them in warm water for 30 minutes before using.

Shrimp Chips
These are thin slices of dried dough made from dried shrimp powder, tapioca starch and food coloring. They are mostly used as garnish in deep-fried poultry dishes. To prepare, simply deep-fry in hot oil until they puff up. They are also great to serve as hors d'oeuvres at cocktail parties. With these sensational chips, everyone will drink twice as much and get drunk three times as fast! They can be deep-fried ahead of time and stored in a plastic bag in a cool, dry place for several days.

Soybean Sheets, Dried
When soybean milk is boiled, the thin film on top is removed and dried. These sheets are very brittle and should be handled with care. They are sold by the pound and are available in different shapes and sizes. Use them within one or two months before they turn rancid. Soybean sheets are used in soups, vegetarian dishes and desserts. They may also serve as an edible wrapping in steamed and deep-fried dishes. Soak soybean sheets for about 30 minutes before using.

Thousand-Year-Old Eggs
With a strong, pungent ammonia odor, these eggs are preserved in a coating of salt, lime and ashes and cured for about three months. The ammonium compound derived from the mixture denatures the egg

protein and turns the egg white into a dark amber color and the yolk into a darkish green and cheese-like texture by the capillary action—through the shell. It is a delicacy to the Chinese and is often served along with pickled ginger as hors d'oeuvres. Sold only in Chinese stores. Try it. You might hate it.

Wood Ears (Cloud Ears)
These are actually a tree fungus. Most of them come from the Szechwan province and are widely used throughout China. You will find them in hot and sour soup and many vegetarian dishes. They have little taste, but the notable, crunchy texture combines well with most ingredients. They are sold only in Chinese stores, in small packages of 4 to 8 ounces. Soak in warm water for 15-20 minutes before using. They will expand into resilient clusters of dark petals. The hard "eye" in the center of the petals should be removed and discarded. Rinse the wood ears to remove sand and slice them according to recipe instructions. Recent medical research suggests that wood ears slow down blood clots and should be incorporated in the diets of people with heart problems.

Fresh and Preserved Vegetables

Baby Corn
These little corn cobs are a special variety that only grows 3"-3½" in size. They are canned in water or pickled and are found in Chinese stores, gourmet food shops and many supermarkets. Water-packed corn cobs are used to add color and flavor to Chinese dishes. Baby corn is so sweet and tender that you can eat the whole cob.

Bamboo Shoots
Several varieties of bamboo shoots are grown in different parts of China with usually three crops of shoots annually—the spring bamboo, the summer bamboo and the winter bamboo. Bamboo shoots have a mild taste and a desirable crispy texture that goes well with practically any ingredient and flavor. Sold in 15-ounce or 11-ounce cans, whole or in slices. After opening, keep in water in a covered container and store in the refrigerator, changing water daily. It will keep for 5-6 days.

Bean Sprouts, Fresh
Fresh mung bean sprouts can be purchased by the pound in most local supermarkets. They should be thoroughly washed, and bruised and discolored sprouts should be discarded before using. Only the firm and whitish sprouts should be used. Like other fresh vegetables, bean sprouts should be bought fresh and prepared the same day. Even though they are

an extremely perishable vegetable, they do keep well for 3-4 days if kept in a bag inside the cooler. For information on how to sprout your own and tips on preparing them, refer to the vegetable chapter. Canned bean sprouts are an extremely undesirable substitute, because they are mushy, discolored and taste funny.

Bitter Melon
Bitter melon, also known as Foo Gwa, is actually not a melon. It is more squash-like and used as a vegetable marrow. This green vegetable with bumpy, shiny skin, resembles a "fat cucumber." The young, light green bitter melon darkens and the interior turns red as it matures. Quinine gives the melon its cool, bitter taste. The flavor is tangy, but likeable. Don't peel it, but scoop out the seeds and pulp prior to use. It can be parboiled 2-3 minutes in salt water to reduce the bitterness, if desired, and it is used in stir-fry dishes or cut into rings crosswise and stuffed with minced fish or pork. Look for it either fresh or canned in Chinese grocery stores. It will grow well in your backyard in hot, moist soil. Planting: March-June. Harvesting: June-September.

Bok Choy
Bok Choy is a popular Chinese green which belongs to the loose-leaf cabbage family. Inner leaves and hearts are tender and savory with a gentle hint of mustard flavor. Contains vitamins B and C. Grows best in cool, moist soil. With big, white stalks and large, dark green leaves, it can be used in many meat and vegetable dishes, and in soups. Stalks are crispy if not overcooked. You can try to grow it in your own garden quite easily. Sold in most supermarkets. Planting: March-May. Harvesting: April-June.

Buttercup Squash
This dark green squash has a knob on top and looks like a green brioche. It is available in the fall and has a starchy, sweet taste similar to Chinese pumpkin. Cook it in soups and stews or stir-fry it with black bean sauce. Buttercup squash goes especially well with beef. Banana squash is a good substitute.

Cabbage, Chinese
Chinese cabbage (Siew Choy) is a sweet and succulent member of the cabbage family and is also known as Napa cabbage. It has no strong cabbage odor when cooking, and contains vitamin C. It grows best in cool, rich, moist soil, and its crinkly, light green leaves, which grow close together in a cylinder shape, have a light sweet taste. It can be used in salads, casseroles and soups, or stir-fried with other ingredients. Planting: March-April; Aug.-Oct. Harvesting: May-June; Oct.-Dec.

Leeks

Sold fresh by the bunch in most supermarkets, this perennial plant has large green leaves. Leeks look like giant green onions but they have a milder flavor and a more fibrous texture. They are popular in northern China as a vegetable and as a seasoning. Use them with beef, lamb and liver, in soups or in stir-fried dishes. Cut leeks in half lengthwise, and wash carefully to remove sand and dirt before cutting.

Lotus Root

This tuber, stem of the water lily, has 2-3 sections 2½"-3" in diameter and about 6"-8" long, linked together like sausages. Five to seven tunnels run through the vegetable forming interesting patterns when sliced. The potato-like, crisp texture adds variety when thinly sliced for stir-frying or soups. It is available fresh, canned or dried only in Chinese groceries. Fresh ones are available between July and February. The dried ones must be soaked for at least 20 minutes before cooking. Lotus root can be served as a vegetable in most dishes or as a dessert in light syrup.

Mustard Greens, Chinese

A member of the cabbage family, leafy with dark green stems, mustard greens have a bittersweet taste. They are available fresh or pickled all year round in Chinese groceries, and can be prepared fresh or cooked in pickled form. The crunchy texture and slightly bittersweet taste goes well in most stir-fry dishes and soups. The Cantonese pickle them by parboiling the whole vegetable and then pickling it in brine to ferment until sour. Rinsed sauerkraut may be substituted for pickled mustard greens.

Pickled Vegetables

Pickled vegetables, with sweet and sour tastes, are a delight all over China. Several kinds of vegetables, but mostly cucumber, carrot and turnip, are pickled at various stages of growth, but most commonly at maturity. These pickled vegetables, packed in 8 ounce or 15 ounce cans, can be found in all Chinese groceries. After opening, transfer into a tightly sealed glass jar or plastic container and store in the refrigerator.

Snow Peas

The snow pea is an edible pea pod. The pods are crispy and sugary with tiny, delicate peas. Pick the pods when peas become visible, and snap off the ends to remove the stem and any string along each side. Best grown in a cool climate with moist, non-acid soil and good drainage, these tender and sweet green pea pods are a great choice for practically any dish. They are available in many supermarkets, but be sure to pick the ones which are dark green and flat; the ones which are plump, yellowish and big tend to be overly-matured and too fibrous. Stir-fry or blanch them over high heat for 2-3 minutes or so. Planting: Mar.-May; Aug.-Oct. Harvesting: April-June; Oct.-Dec.

Straw Mushrooms

These dark brown little mushrooms with pointed caps have a texture and flavor completely different from other mushrooms. They go well with meat and vegetable dishes. Straw mushrooms come fresh, canned or dried and are found only in Chinese stores. After opening, canned mushrooms should be stored in water in a glass or plastic container and refrigerated. When the water is changed every couple of days, canned mushrooms will keep for up to a week. The fresh straw mushrooms are very perishable and only keep for a few days.

Szechwan Preserved Vegetable
This hot and spicy canned pickled vegetable is widely used in many northern-style dishes and soups. Wipe off some of the red chili powder if you cannot take it too hot, then slice it thin to use in various dishes. After opening, it will keep for many months in a covered jar in the refrigerator.

Water Chestnut, Canned
Fresh water chestnuts, with a dark brown scaly skin and white pulp, are crunchy and sweet, but hard to find except in Chinese stores around large cities. Mostly sold in cans of 8 or 15 ounces, sliced or whole, these are like bamboo shoots—they go well with all kinds of dishes and soup. After opening, transfer to a covered container with water and store in the refrigerator. They will keep for several days.

White Turnip, Chinese
Also known as lobak or daikon (in Japanese), this is a crisp textured white radish about 7"-10" in length. It looks very much like an overgrown horse radish and has a subtle flavor, but a strong "odor." White turnip goes well with beef in soup and stir-fried dishes. Available only in Chinese groceries and occasionally in some supermarkets.

Winter Melon
This is more or less like a large squash, with frosty but dark green skin and a white core with lots of seeds. It is the size of a large watermelon with a very mild succulent taste. It belongs to the muskmelon family and is sold by the pound in most Chinese stores and prepared in stir-fried dishes and soup. If kept in the refrigerator it will last up to a week. Whole melons can be stored up to several months. For banquets and formal dinners, soup is prepared inside the scooped-out melon with lots of delicious goodies. The Chinese also make the melons into candies.

Rice and Noodles

Cellophane Noodles

These translucent, thread-like noodles made from mung bean starch resemble stiff nylon fishing line. Used in meat or vegetable dishes and soups they are deep-fried when used as a garnish. When used in stir-fried dishes or soup, soak them first in warm water for several minutes and be sure to add enough liquid during cooking since they soak up a large amount of water. When deep-fried, break them up inside a plastic bag, otherwise you might end up having noodles on the floor, in your bedroom and of course in your backyard because they fly all over the place. Sold in 4- or 8-ounce plastic bags in Chinese stores.

Chinese Egg Noodles, Fresh or Dried

If fresh noodles are available, blanch them in boiling water for approximately 1½-2 minutes. Cool under cold tap water, drain well and set aside to use in soup or stir-fried dishes. If dried ones are available, do the same thing. Fresh noodles are sold in 1-pound plastic bags and can be kept in the refrigerator for 3-5 days or can be frozen.

Rice, Long Grain

A daily staple in many parts of the Orient, long grain rice becomes a dry, separated and fluffy rice after cooking. This is the type of rice used to make Chinese fried rice, and it is also ground into rice flour to make different types of pastries and rice cakes in southern China. Sold in 2- and 4-pound bags. For more information, refer to the recipe for plain cooked rice in this book.

Rice, Medium Grain

Mostly grown in California, medium grain rice has a great flavor and aroma when cooked. A good choice to serve as table rice.

Rice, Short Grain

A short grain, pearly, slightly transparent white rice which yields a soft, moist and sticky final product when cooked. It is mainly used in preparing pastries, stuffings and desserts when ground to rice powder.

Rice Flour, Long Grain or Glutinous

Whiter than wheat flour, these fine powders are made either from long grain or glutinous rice. Rice flour is mainly used in pastries and dumplings as well as in wrappings for sweet or salty fillings. Glutinous rice flour is moister and stickier than long grain rice flour.

Rice Noodles, Fresh or Dried

Made from long grain rice flour, these noodles are used exclusively in Cantonese dishes. Similar to bean thread noodles, these dried rice sticks are more brittle but easier to handle. Soak them in hot water for about 10-15 minutes before using in soups or stir-fry dishes. They can also be deep-fried in hot oil (when dried), and they pop up in just a few seconds, like a white nest, when prepared this way. Fresh noodles can be kept in the refrigerator for 3-5 days and kept in the freezer for months. Stir-fried fresh rice noodles with beef is one of the most popular lunch dishes in Cantonese restaurants.

Spring Roll Wrappers

White, pliable and paper-thin, these wrappers are made from soft flour and water, formed into 3" rounds or squares. (They are often confused with those yellowish egg roll wrappers available in supermarkets. In China, there are no egg roll wrappers.) They are sold fresh or frozen only in Chinese stores. When deep-fried over high heat, they give a crispier texture than the common egg roll wrappers. These wrappers dry out extremely fast, so avoid prolonged exposure to the air. Take out a few at a time to work on and keep the rest covered with a damp cloth. When stored in the refrigerator, they will last 7-10 days. If frozen, they will stay fresh for several months, and should be defrosted inside the package before use.

Won Ton Wrappers

These thin pieces of dough, about 3½" square, are made from high-gluten flour, water and eggs. They are usually packed in air-tight plastic bags or waxed paper in 1-pound packages, and are available fresh or frozen in any Chinese store and in most supermarkets. You can fill them with a variety of fillings from sweet to salty. They can be deep-fried, steamed or cooked in soups. During preparation, take out a few at a time and cover the rest with a damp cloth to prevent them from drying out. Store them wrapped in several sheets of plastic wrap in the refrigerator for 7-10 days or in the freezer for up to three months. If frozen, defrost inside the package before using.

The Chinese Connection
—Mail Order

Many of you may not have access to Chinese ingredients so here are the addresses of some mail order sources in major North American cities. If you live hundreds of miles away from a major city, a trip to a Chinese food supplier in a big city once a year can provide you with many ingredients that will last twelve to eighteen months.

Arizona
Phoenix Produce Company
202 South Third Street
Phoenix, 85004

California
Chong Kee Jan Company
838 Grant Avenue
San Francisco, 94108

Kwong On Lung Importers
680 North Spring Street
Los Angeles, 90012

Mow Lee Sing Kee Company
774 Commercial Street
San Francisco, 94108

Wing Chong Lung Company
922 South San Pedro Street
Los Angeles 90015

Florida
South Eastern Food Supply
6732 N.E. Fourth Avenue
Miami, 33138

Georgia
Asia Trading Company
2581 Piedmont
Atlanta, 30324

Hawaii
Tai Yen Company
1023 Maunakea Street
Honolulu, 96817

Illinois
Dong Kee Company
2252 South Wentworth Avenue
Chicago, 60616

Shiroma
1058 West Argyle Street
Chicago, 60640

Indiana
A.B. Oriental Grocery
3709 Suit Shadeland Avenue
Indianapolis, 46226

Maryland
Asia House Grocery
2433 Saint Paul Street
Baltimore, 21218

Massachusetts
Legal Sea Foods Market
237 Hampshire Street
Cambridge, 02139

Wing Wing Imported Groceries
79 Harrison Avenue
Boston, 02111

Michigan
China Merchandise Corporation
31642 John Road
Madison Heights, 48071

Chinese Asia Trading Company
734 S. Washington Road
Royal Oak, 48067

Lun Yick
1339 Third Avenue
Detroit, 48226

Seoul Oriental Market
23031 Beach Road
Southfield, 48075

Missouri
King's Trading
3736 Broadway
Kansas City, 64111

Lun Sing Company
10 South Eigth Street
St. Louis, 63102

New York
Katagiri and Company
224 East 59th Street
New York, 10022

Lee's Oriental Gifts and Food
3053 Main Street
Buffalo, 14214

Wing Fat Company
33-35 Mott Street
New York, 10013

Ohio
Crestview Foodtown
200 East Crestview Road
Columbus, 43202

Friendship Enterprises
3415 Payne Avenue
Cleveland, 44114

Soya Food Products
2356 Wyoming Avenue
Cincinnati, 45214

Oregon
Fong Chong Company
301 N.W. Fourth Avenue
Portland

Pennsylvania
Harmony Oriental
247 Atwood Street
Pittsburgh, 15213

Hon Kee Company
935 Race Street
Philadelphia, 19107

Texas
Oriental Import-Export Company
2009 Polk Street
Houston, 77002

Washington
Wak Yong Company
416 Eighth Avenue, South
Seattle, 98104

Washington, D.C.
Mee Wah Lung Company
608 H Street, N.W.
Washington, D.C., 20001

Canada

Ontario
Wing Tong Trading Company
137 Dundas Street, W.
Toronto, Ontario
Canada M5G 1Z3

Quebec
Leong Jung Company
999 Clark Street
Montreal, Quebec

Wing Noodles Ltd.
1009, rue Côté
Montreal, P.Q.
Canada H2Z 1L1

A Metric Wok?!

Rumor has it that we are on the verge of the "metric age." Personally, I have never used this unique system, because my mentality is not that complex! Throughout my 57-year career as a lousy cook, I have used the conventional system of weights and measures, and it is ingrained in my "sweet and sour" blood. One is instructed not to panic about the inevitable conversion, and if composure is maintained, the change can be made with ease. I am wondering what is going to happen to my career when I have to take the metric plunge! For those who insist on the metric system, I have included metric equivalents and conversion tables in this humble volume. For best results, don't switch back and forth from one system to the other—you might end up being a confused cook! Enjoy yourself and take a metric wok!

Approx. volume measure rounded to nearest 10	
Conventional	Metric
1 teaspoon	5 ml
1 tablespoon	15 ml
¼ cup	60 ml
⅓ cup	80 ml
½ cup	125 ml
¾ cup	200 ml
1 cup	250 ml
1¼ cup	310 ml
1½ cup	370 ml
1¾ cup	430 ml
2 cups	500 ml
4 cups	1 L
6 cups	1½ L

Approx. mass measurements	
Conventional	Metric
½ oz	14 g
1 oz	28 g
2 oz	56 g
4 oz (¼ lb)	112 g
6 oz	168 g
8 oz (½ lb)	225 g
10 oz	280 g
12 oz (¾ lb)	340 g
16 oz (1 lb)	450 g

Other measurements

Ingredients	Conventional	Metric
rice	1 cup	220 g
flour	1 cup	220 g
sugar	1 cup	220 g
chopped veg.	1 cup	220 g
cornstarch	1 teaspoon	5 g (5 ml)
cornstarch	1 tablespoon	15 g (15 ml)
sugar	1 teaspoon	5 g (5 ml)
sugar	1 tablespoon	10 g (15 ml)
salt	1 teaspoon	(5 ml)
salt	1 tablespoon	(15 ml)

The hand-made noodles should be approximately this long.

The Ten Most-Asked Questions

1. *How do I choose a wok?*
The most common wok is a spun (rolled) steel one; this is the type used by most Chinese. The steel wok is practical and available in most cookware stores. The price of steel woks ranges from $6-$14; for a small family, the 12" wok should do just fine. For a larger family, try the 14" size. The steel wok has to be treated or seasoned; take good care of it and it will be yours for life. Refer to "Tools to Wok With" in this book for more detailed information on the wok.

2. *What is the difference between light and dark soy sauce?*
Light soy sauce is also known as thin soy sauce; it is lighter in color and saltier in taste than dark soy sauce. Light soy sauce is commonly used for marinating or seasoning dishes; it is also used as a dip. Aside from being darker in color and less salty than light soy sauce, dark soy sauce tastes sweeter and is thicker in consistency. Dark soy sauce is also referred to as black soy sauce and is used in sauteeing and stewing to give an extra touch of sweetness and color. Not every dish calls for soy sauce; on some occasions, salt is used instead.

3. *How do I cook a Chinese meal and entertain at the same time?*
Plan your menu and organize your time. Have as few stir-fried dishes as possible; instead, include some dishes that can be made ahead of time and be reheated just before serving. Plan ahead and get things ready in advance. If you need a helping hand, don't be afraid to yell for help. This way, you can cook up a storm and be able to enjoy your "creations" with your guests.

4. *Is it true that a Chinese meal takes forever to prepare?*
Yes and no! If you organize yourself, know what you are doing, and learn a few basic techniques, you can whip up a nutritious and delicious meal in 45 minutes. If you are totally lost, take one step at a time and learn a few basics such as slicing, shredding and stir-frying. It

is essential to master the basic preparation and cooking skills to avoid being stuck in the kitchen for 20 years and producing the most memorable charcoal-burnt dishes.

5. *Can I use a wok on an electric stove?*
   Definitely, you can. The electric stove offers the same amount of heat as the gas stove. The only difference is that gas stoves give you an instant heat, thus better control of heat and cooling time. The electric stove takes a couple of extra minutes to bring the wok to the desired temperature, and it also takes a couple of extra minutes to cool down. Therefore, if you have an electric stove, pre-heat your skillet or wok before you start cooking any Chinese dish because most Chinese dishes require fairly accurate cooking times and temperatures. With a little bit of patience and effort you should be able to cook up just as good a dish on an electric stove as on a gas stove. A wok ring (stand) may be required if you have a very sharply curved wok. In the past 50 years, all of the places where I have lived have had only an electric stove, so I know that electric wokking can be done. (In fact, all the recipes in this book were tested on the electric stove in my humble kitchen.)

6. *Most of the Chinese dishes in restaurants seem to be fairly oily. Is Chinese cooking fattening?*
   Absolutely not! In the first place, a good Chinese dish should not be oily. Perhaps the reason why some restaurant dishes are so oily is that their stoves give off a tremendous amount of heat while the dish is being cooked; extra oil is used to prevent food from sticking and burning. A great proportion of the ingredients in Chinese dishes are vegetables which are low in calories. In addition, the traditional Chinese menu does not call for too many deep-fried dishes.

7. *Why am I hungry shortly after I finish a big Chinese meal?*
   Mainly because most of the ingredients are of a vegetable nature and much less meat is used than in the Western diet. Therefore it is much easier for your digestive system to quickly digest the food. To compensate for this, the Chinese use rice as a staple. Rice is the Chinese version of bread and potatoes. It also acts as a "palate cleanser" between courses. So order more rice and you won't go away hungry!

8. *What type of oil is used in Chinese cooking?*
   Peanut oil has been used by the Chinese for hundreds of years because of its high oil content and because it can be extracted easily by a primitive process. In recent years, other vegetable oils have

become increasingly popular in Chinese kitchens. Polyunsaturated vegetable oils, such as corn, soybean, cotton seed and sunflower oil, are being used.

9. *Are chop suey, chow mein, egg rolls, and fortune cookies really authentically Chinese?*
No, they are not. The preparation methods of chow mein, chop suey and egg rolls in North American restaurants are far beyond the dreams of any native Chinese cook. Unfortunately, chop suey and chow mein are often mistaken as synonymous with Chinese food. The crispy fried noodles in chow mein and the batter in egg rolls were created in America by the early immigrants from China. Chow mein, traditionally, is simply stir-fried noodles. Fortune cookies are unheard of in traditional menus. An interesting fact is that fortune cookies are not served to Chinese clientele eating in Chinese restaurants.

10. *Are you really as good as you look on TV?*
Absolutely not! It is just an act—you know how TV cameras can play tricks! I was trained as a dishwasher and later promoted to humble cook. I don't really know how to cook—I only learn the dishes as I go along, taping the show!

Why does a tea kettle whistle?
Because it never learned how to sing.

Why are fish so smart?
Because they always go around in schools.

What did people call "Egg Foo" when he was a kid?
Egg Foo Young.

Do you know what will stay "hot" the longest in the refrigerator?
Red chili pepper.

What is the current standing in the race between a head of cabbage, a water hose and a bottle of tomato catsup?
The cabbage is a head, the hose is still running, and the bottle is trying to catch up.

Many Thanks

No book can be written without a great deal of help, every step of the way, from colleagues, friends and family. The many hours of research, testing and tasting required for this book were met with dedication, enthusiasm and healthy appetites (they had to eat a lot!) from all of my associates. Fortunately, they were very healthy during the testing. To all of them I gratefully and most sincerely offer my thanks for such invaluable contributions to the completion of this book.

Sue, who was my total support; Professor Pangborn, who introduces this humble book; Janet Turnbull and Rick Archbold, my editors, who loved the idea of this book from the beginning and squeezed an advance from their boss so I could buy the food (thank you also Janet, the most charming editor, for spending 25 hours a day, 8 days a week, editing this discombobulated manuscript!); to Dorothy Louie who sweat through many hot woks with me, for her talent, support and inspiration; Gerald Levitch, a very good friend who put in a "better word" here and there; Janet Huddle, who contributed so many creative ideas and great suggestions; the whole Yan Can Cooking Team (a bunch of winners!), for the hours spent slaving over a hot wok, sweating, testing and improving the recipes; C. K. Cheung and Edward Lim, for the beautiful illustrations; C. K. Cheung and Howard Eng, for the clever cartoons that add just the right touch of humor; Rody Lo, whose skill and patience produced the splendid cover photographs; Lean Gill and Karen Loeblich, for all the hours pounding a typewriter and pouring over endless pages of research materials; all my friends and former students who gave so much of their time and energy and helped test and perfect the recipes; and all the "Yan Can" fans and good friends who were my unwitting inspiration—without you, this book would just be a dream. Last, but not least, I must humbly thank myself for working harder (approximately 27 hours a day) on this project than I have ever worked in my entire life.

The "Yan Can Clan" Writes

"Your show is simply fabulous. Your wonderful sense of humor sure cheers one up. I am an addict to Yan Can for life..."

Mrs. Norma Concepciost, Winnipeg, Manitoba

"Congratulations for an excellent show. It is educational, refreshing, and most of all fun to watch...since I started watching the show, I've become an expert in Chinese cuisine..."

Mrs. Campbell, Calgary, Alberta

"Yan Can is about the best thing daytime TV has to offer. It is such a pleasure to watch. Congratulations on a tremendous production."

Mr. A. R. Clarke, Toronto, Ontario

"You are the most energetic and able chef that has come along...so refreshing, neat and "wok" so well...we all love you."

Mrs. A. E. Anderson Snyder, New York

"I've had a great deal of success and lots of fun in trying many of your recipes...I told all of my friends, 'buy a copy of his book'..."

Mrs. L. J. Devine, Euclin, Ohio

"Of all the related shows on TV, yours is by far the best. The ease with which one can learn...good humor at the right time...and the delicious dishes that can be produced at minimal cost...hope that you will continue for a long time...thank you for bringing this extra joy of living into our lives..."

Robert Stewart, Winnipeg, Manitoba

"I am 15...Yan Can make me laugh, Yan Can make me hungry..."
Eileen Lynch, Toronto, Ontario

"Watch your show regularly and enjoy every recipe I've tried, simply terrific..."
Karen Robinson, Edmonton, Alberta

"His ease, personality, professional skill all add up to a special cooking show which out-does every other..."
S. E. Falkner, Meadville, Pennsylvania

"I watch every Yan Can show...when it is on I drop everything to watch. It is most enjoyable and informative..."
T. W. Fisher, Buffalo, New York

"One of the impressive virtues of Yan Can is the personality and attitude of the host, who never strains for laughs or pushes for punch. It makes one sitting at home feel comfortable..."
Mr. Jackson, Cleveland, Ohio

"Warmly presented and beautifully done..."
H. Hale, Kitchener, Ontario

"Everyday I look forward to your show. Your humor and personality are such a joy to watch. I sit there and laugh my heart out..."
Mrs. N. Carter, Edmonton, Alberta

"Yan Can is the only hit show for the whole family..."
Mrs. W. S. Gray, Winnipeg, Manitoba

"I was about to take a Chinese cooking course, but after watching Yan Can, I am not about to waste my money. I have tried many of your great dishes...fantastic!"
F. C. Manning, Vancouver, British Columbia

"You take the mysteries out of Chinese cooking and make it look so easy and fun. Yan Can has got to be one of the best programs for the afternoon..."
Mrs. E. Sherman, Orwell, Ohio

"Congratulations for a great cooking show. Since I started to tune you in last fall...I had all my relatives and friends watch you too..."
J. F. Thomas, Toronto, Ontario

"All my friends and I watch you everyday, not only do we learn a great deal, but we also do most of it laughing. We love your smile, personality and most of all your unique recipes…it is simple and refreshing…"

Mrs. N. Kane. Calgary, Alberta

"Yan Can is low key and refreshing. You've given us so many new ideas and tips. You have the best recipes, your show has education, humor, excitement, and culture…we all love you…"

M. MacPherson, Winnipeg, Manitoba

"Mr. Can, I am only 12 and I watch you every chance I get. You are the best. I will watch you forever…"

Lisa Duncan, Niagara Falls, Ontario

"Yan Can is definitely one of the best cooking shows on TV. Mr. Yan's recipes are simple and easy to follow. He has skill and he is so clear….The show is fun and educational, we wouldn't miss it for anything…"

Mrs. J. M. Shapiro, Vancouver, British Columbia

"Yan Can is just great. It is fascinating and we will keep watching…"

Mrs. Tony Ilnichi, Camrose, Alberta

"I think you are the cutest thing that has come along in a long time….For being so young, we can't understand how you are so adept and so good at the cooking business…"

Mrs. Carolyn White, Jamestown, New York

"I think Martin is just the greatest cooking host. He has a sense of humor and has a wonderful ability to relate his skills and knowledge to the audience. I have prepared many of his recipes with great success…"

B. Gardner, London, Ontario

"My 85-year-old mother and I wouldn't miss your show for anything. As soon as the show is on, she 'demands' that everything you say be put in writing…"

Mrs. L. M. Lewis, Wainwright, Alberta

"Your cooking show is about the best thing on daytime TV…Mr. Yan is a great joy to watch. I especially appreciate his wit and humor…"

M. Taylor, Painesville, Ohio

"None of the cooking shows I watch can compare with Yan Can, it has great recipes, unpredictability and fun…"

Mrs. I. J. Barton, Lackawanna, New York

342

"My name is Samantha. I am 10...I like you and your food very much..."

Samantha Bailey, Medicine Hat, Alberta

"You are such a gem and joy to watch. We are especially fond of the flair and humor that you combine in the kitchen. Your recipes are great and the beautiful final product makes everyone very hungry..."

Mrs. Brown, Guelph, Ontario

"My wife was fortunate to obtain an autographed copy of your book, *The Joy of Wokking*. Ever since, we've been eating like kings and queens—thanks to you..."

Mr. E. Newman, Niagara Falls, New York

All My Dishes
—Index of Recipes

Fowl Plays

Holy Cows and Little Lambs

Bean Curd, Eggs and Other Protein-Rich Foods

Harvest from the Garden—Vegetables

Oodles of Noodles and Lots of Nice Rice

Special Delectables—Gourmet Dishes

Sweet and Happy Endings

All My Other Dishes—Recipes
From *The Joy of Wokking*

Appetizers
BBQ Spareribs
Bronzed Eggs
Cantonese Pickled Cucumber
Chinese Chicken Salad
Chinese Pickle Relish
Golden Shrimp Toast
Imperial Shrimp Balls
Sesame Toast
Special Gifts
Spring Rolls
Stuffed Banana Crisp
Water Chestnuts Take a Wrap
Wonton Delight

Soups
Creamy Chicken Corn Soup
Creative Alternatives for Clear Broth
Cucumber Soup
Egg-Flower Drop Soup
Fish and Spinach Soup
Homemade Soup Stock
Pork Ribs with Soy Bean Sprouts Soup
Seafood and Bean Curd Soup
Singing Rice Soup
Winter Melon Soup
Wonton Soup

Poultry
Almond Chicken Crisp
BBQ Duck
Black Bean Wings
Braised Chicken (or Duck) with a
  Surprise

Braised Lychee Chicken
Braised Plum-Flavored Drumsticks
Chicken and Cucumber in Wine Sauce
Chicken Little
Chicken Rolls with Sweet and Sour
  Sauce
Chicken Stuffed Pineapple
Chilled Chicken (or Duck)
Citrus Pineapple Chicken
Curry Chicken
Delectable Liver
Drunk Chicken
Fried Five-Spice Chicken
Golden Crisp Chicken Cantonese
Heavenly Honeydew Chicken
Hot and Spicy Chicken
Hot Pot Lemon Chicken
Jeweled Chicken
Moo Goo Gai Pan
Peking Duck
Pon-Pon Chicken
Pretty Poached Poultry
Sassy Sauced Chicken
Sea and Sky
Spicy Szechwan Chicken
Stuffed Chicken Breast
Succulent Steamed Chicken
Sweet and Sour Drummettes
Tender Chicken in a Nest
Three Cups Chicken

Beef
A Measure of Beans
Ants Climbing Up The Tree

BBQ Beef and Pork Union
Bean Sprouts and Pepper Beef
Beef and Brocolli with Oyster Sauce
Beef and Leek
Beef and Lobok
Beef Liver in Wine Sauce
Broiled Beef Shish Kebobs
Cantonese Beef Casserole
Cellophane Noodles with Peppered
    Beef
Crispy Beef and Beans
Green Pepper Beef
Mongolian Beef
Oyster-Flavored Beef and Egg-plant
Sautéed Beef with Snow Peas
Spicy Ginger Beef
Spicy Shredded Vegetables and Beef
Spicy Szechwan Beef
Stuffed Lettuce Leaves
Tomato Beef

Pork
Chinese BBQ Pork
Garlic-Flavored Pork
Happy Family with Golden Crown
Hoisin-Flavored Spareribs
Honey Garlic Ribs
Imperial Pork Chops
Oriental Pearls
Pork Cashew Nut Surprise
Pork Steak Cantonese
Ribs to Remember
Royal Lions Head
Spiced Minced Pork with Bean Curd
Steamed Ground Pork Patty
Stuffed Mushrooms
Steamed Spareribs with Black Bean
    Sauce
Stuffed Pork Rolls and Broccoli
Stuffed Sunrise Tomatoes
Sweet and Sour Pork
Twice Cooked Pork

Seafood
Authentic West Lake Fish
Batter Fried Fresh Oysters
Braised Oysters

Braised Whole Fish
Broiled Jumbo Prawns
Crab with Black Bean Sauce
Five-Spice Prawns
Fresh Crab with Ginger and Scallion
Fresh Gingered Fish
Golden Batter Prawns
Happy Family Reunion
Lover's Prawns
Mushroom Abalone in Oyster Sauce
Poached Fish with Curried Cream
    Sauce
Pork and Prawn-Stuffed Fish
Scallops in Wine Sauce
Seafood Combination Hot Pot
Singing Shrimp Surprise
Smoky Fish
Stir-Fried Prawns
Stir-Fried Winter Melon with Prawns
Stuffed Fish Rolls with Velvet Corn
    Sauce
Sweet and Sour Fish Rolls

Eggs and Bean Curd
Braised Stuffed Bean Curd
Braised Szechwan Bean Curd Sand-
    wiches
Colorful Steamed Eggs
Red Cooked Bean Curd
Special Egg Foo Yung
Szechwan-Style Spicy Omelet
Upside-Down Bean Curd Cake

Vegetables
Broccoli with Crab Meat Sauce
Cabbage with Chinese Sausage
Cauliflower and Broccoli in Sweet
    Cream Sauce
Eggplant with Black Beans
Garden Vegetable Platter
Green Beans with Preserved Bean Curd
Mushroom in Two Sauces
Potato Curry and Onion
Preserved Pork with Chinese
    Broccoli
Refreshing Celery Salad
Shoot Some Nuts
Tomato Soy Beans
Twin Color Vegetable Plate

352

Rice and Noodles

Beef with Fresh Rice Noodles
Curry Fried Rice with Beef
Mandarin Style Noodles
Pan-Fried Noodles with Shrimp
Plain Cooked Rice
Singapore Rice Noodles
Spicy Peanut Noodles
Steamed Pork Dumpling (Siu Mai)
Yang Chow Fried Rice

Exotic Delights

Aromatic Fish
Beef and Cabbage in Coconut
  Sauce
Bird's Nest Soup
Coconut Rice Cake
Malay Chicken
Mongolian Fire Pot
Nabuk Kim Chi (Radish Pickles)
Pork Adobo with Coconut Milk

Shark's Fin Soup
Spiced Fish Fillets
Spiced Seafood
Sukiyaki
Tempura
Teriyaki Chicken
Udon

Desserts

Almond Float
Butterflies Are Free
Candy Apple Fritters
Eight Treasures Rice Pudding
Ginger-Ale Melon Balls
Golden Crispy Cashews
Iced Lychees
Open Mouth To Laugh
Sweet Almond Soup
Sweet Sesame Soup
Sweet Sheet Soup

Woks of Thanks!

Are you still there? I'm nearly through. Thank you for getting this far. And I also want to thank those who watch "Yan Can" every single day. You are terrific! And most especially, thanks to everyone who spent their hard-earned cash to buy this little book. This poor Chinese cook is honored. And to everyone, I wish you good food, good health, and most of all, good wokking through many years of happiness.

Praise for Louise Penny

New York Times Bestseller *The Brutal Telling*
Winner of the 2009 Agatha Award for Best Novel

"Louise Penny's mysteries have evolved into world-class novels."
—Linda Ellerbee

"Penny has been compared to Agatha Christie, but that sells her short."
—*Booklist* (starred review)

"Having won numerous mystery prizes, including the prestigious Arthur Ellis and Anthony awards for her debut, *Still Life*, the Canadian author has only gotten better with each succeeding novel. Her fifth in the series is the finest of all. . . . This superb novel will appeal to readers who enjoy sophisticated literary mysteries."
—*Library Journal* (starred review)

"It is Ms. Penny's imaginative prose and her talent for conjuring up the presence of evil amid beauty that make her books remarkably memorable as mysteries."
—*The Washington Times*

"Fans who have followed this seductive series—and if you aren't yet a fan you should be—will be in for more than the usual share of surprises in *The Brutal Telling*."
—*The Plain Dealer* (Cleveland)

"In his acceptance speech for the Nobel Prize in literature, William Faulkner said the best literature is about 'the human heart in conflict with itself.' Penny's fifth novel with Chief Inspector Gamache of the Sûreté du Québec is written with psychological depth and populated with men and women in conflict with their own deceits and desires."
—*Milwaukee Journal Sentinel*

"A treat for the mind and a lesson for the soul, this is a novel full of surprises."
—*Richmond Times-Dispatch*

THE BRUTAL TELLING

ALSO BY LOUISE PENNY

A Rule Against Murder
The Cruelest Month
A Fatal Grace
Still Life

Louise Penny

~

THE
BRUTAL
TELLING

MINOTAUR BOOKS NEW YORK

THE BRUTAL TELLING. Copyright © 2009 by Louise Penny. All rights reserved. Printed in the United States of America. For information, address St. Martin's Press, 175 Fifth Avenue, New York, N.Y. 10010.

www.minotaurbooks.com

Grateful acknowledgment is given for permission to reprint the following:

"The Bells of Heaven" by Ralph Hodgson is used by kind permission of Bryn Mawr College.

Excerpts from "Cressida to Troilius: A Gift" and "Sekhmet, the Lion-Headed Goddess of War" from *Morning in the Burning House: New Poems* by Margaret Atwood. Copyright © 1995 by Margaret Atwood. Reprinted by permission of Houghton Mifflin Harcourt Publishing Company. All rights reserved.

Excerpt from "Gravity Zero" from *Bones* by Mike Freeman. Copyright © 2007 by Mike Freeman. Reproduced with kind permission of the author.

The Library of Congress has cataloged the hardcover edition as follows:

Penny, Louise.
    The brutal telling / Louise Penny.—1st ed.
        p.   cm.
    ISBN 978-0-312-37703-8
    1. Gamache, Armand (Fictitious character)—Fiction.   2. Police—Québec (Province)—Fiction.   3. Villages—Québec (Province)—Fiction.   4. Murder—Investigation—Fiction.   5. Québec (Province)—Fiction.   I. Title.
    PR9199.4.P464B78   2009
    813'.6—dc22

                                                                    2009028462

ISBN 978-0-312-66168-7 (trade paperback)

First published in Great Britain by Headline Publishing Group

10   9   8   7

For the SPCA Monteregie, and all the people
who would "ring the bells of Heaven."

And, for Maggie,
who finally gave all her heart away.

ACKNOWLEDGMENTS

Once again, this book is the result of a whole lot of help from a whole lot of people. I want and need to thank Michael, my husband, for reading and rereading the manuscript, and always telling me it was brilliant. Thank you to Lise Page, my assistant, for her tireless and cheery work and great ideas. To Sherise Hobbs and Hope Dellon for their patience and editorial notes.

I want to thank, as always, the very best literary agent in the world, Teresa Chris. She sent me a silver heart when my last book made the *New York Times* bestseller list (I also thought I'd just mention that!). Teresa is way more than an agent. She's also a lovely, thoughtful person.

I'd also like to thank my good friends Susan McKenzie and Lili de Grandpré, for their help and support.

And finally I want to say a word about the poetry I use in this book, and the others. As much as I'd love not to say anything and hope you believe I wrote it, I actually need to thank the wonderful poets who've allowed me to use their works and words. I adore poetry, as you can tell. Indeed, it inspires me—with words and emotions. I tell aspiring writers to read poetry, which I think for them is often the literary equivalent of being told to eat Brussels sprouts. They're none too enthusiastic. But what a shame if a writer doesn't at least try to find poems that speak to him or her. Poets manage to get into a couplet what I struggle to achieve in an entire book.

I thought it was time I acknowledged that.

In this book I use, as always, works from Margaret Atwood's slim volume *Morning in the Burned House*. Not a very cheerful title, but brilliant poems. I've also quoted from a lovely old work called *The Bells of*

Heaven by Ralph Hodgson. And a wonderful poem called "Gravity Zero" from an emerging Canadian poet named Mike Freeman, from his book *Bones*.

I wanted you to know that. And I hope these poems speak to you, as they speak to me.

ONE

—

 "All of them? Even the children?" The fireplace sputtered and crackled and swallowed his gasp. "Slaughtered?"

"Worse."

There was silence then. And in that hush lived all the things that could be worse than slaughter.

"Are they close?" His back tingled as he imagined something dreadful creeping through the woods. Toward them. He looked around, almost expecting to see red eyes staring through the dark windows. Or from the corners, or under the bed.

"All around. Have you seen the light in the night sky?"

"I thought those were the Northern Lights." The pink and green and white shifting, flowing against the stars. Like something alive, glowing, and growing. And approaching.

Olivier Brulé lowered his gaze, no longer able to look into the troubled, lunatic eyes across from him. He'd lived with this story for so long, and kept telling himself it wasn't real. It was a myth, a story told and repeated and embellished over and over and over. Around fires just like theirs.

It was a story, nothing more. No harm in it.

But in this simple log cabin, buried in the Quebec wilderness, it seemed like more than that. Even Olivier felt himself believing it. Perhaps because the Hermit so clearly did.

The old man sat in his easy chair on one side of the stone hearth with Olivier on the other. Olivier looked into a fire that had been alive for more than a decade. An old flame not allowed to die, it mumbled and popped in the grate, throwing soft light into the log cabin. He gave the

1

embers a shove with the simple iron poker, sending sparks up the chimney. Candlelight twinkled off shiny objects like eyes in the darkness, found by the flame.

"It won't be long now."

The Hermit's eyes were gleaming like metal reaching its melting point. He was leaning forward as he often did when this tale was told.

Olivier scanned the single room. The dark was punctuated by flickering candles throwing fantastic, grotesque shadows. Night seemed to have seeped through the cracks in the logs and settled into the cabin, curled in corners and under the bed. Many native tribes believed evil lived in corners, which was why their traditional homes were rounded. Unlike the square homes the government had given them.

Olivier didn't believe evil lived in corners. Not really. Not in the daylight, anyway. But he did believe there were things waiting in the dark corners of this cabin that only the Hermit knew about. Things that set Olivier's heart pounding.

"Go on," he said, trying to keep his voice steady.

It was late and Olivier still had the twenty-minute walk through the forest back to Three Pines. It was a trip he made every fortnight and he knew it well, even in the dark.

Only in the dark. Theirs was a relationship that existed only after nightfall.

They sipped Orange Pekoe tea. A treat, Olivier knew, reserved for the Hermit's honored guest. His only guest.

But now it was story time. They leaned closer to the fire. It was early September and a chill had crept in with the night.

"Where was I? Oh, yes. I remember now."

Olivier's hands gripped the warm mug even tighter.

"The terrible force has destroyed everything in its way. The Old World and the New. All gone. Except . . ."

"Except?"

"One tiny village remains. Hidden in a valley, so the grim army hasn't seen it yet. But it will. And when it does their great leader will stand at the head of his army. He's immense, bigger than any tree, and clad in armor made from rocks and spiny shells and bone."

"Chaos."

The word was whispered and disappeared into the darkness, where it curled into a corner. And waited.

"Chaos. And the Furies. Disease, Famine, Despair. All are swarming. Searching. And they'll never stop. Not ever. Not until they find it."

"The thing that was stolen."

The Hermit nodded, his face grim. He seemed to see the slaughter, the destruction. See the men and women, the children, fleeing before the merciless, soulless force.

"But what was it? What could be so important they had to destroy everything to get it back?"

Olivier willed his eyes not to dart from the craggy face and into the darkness. To the corner, and the thing they both knew was sitting there in its mean little canvas sack. But the Hermit seemed to read his mind and Olivier saw a malevolent grin settle onto the old man's face. And then it was gone.

"It's not the army that wants it back."

They both saw then the thing looming behind the terrible army. The thing even Chaos feared. That drove Despair, Disease, Famine before it. With one goal. To find what was taken from their Master.

"It's worse than slaughter."

Their voices were low, barely scraping the ground. Like conspirators in a cause already lost.

"When the army finally finds what it's searching for it will stop. And step aside. And then the worst thing imaginable will arrive."

There was silence again. And in that silence lived the worst thing imaginable.

Outside a pack of coyotes set up a howl. They had something cornered.

Myth, that's all this is, Olivier reassured himself. Just a story. Once more he looked into the embers, so he wouldn't see the terror in the Hermit's face. Then he checked his watch, tilting the crystal toward the fireplace until its face glowed orange and told him the time. Two thirty in the morning.

"Chaos is coming, old son, and there's no stopping it. It's taken a long time, but it's finally here."

The Hermit nodded, his eyes rheumy and runny, perhaps from the wood smoke, perhaps from something else. Olivier leaned back, surprised to feel his thirty-eight-year-old body suddenly aching, and realized he'd sat tense through the whole awful telling.

"I'm sorry. It's getting late and Gabri will be worried. I have to go."

"Already?"

Olivier got up and pumping cold, fresh water into the enamel sink he cleaned his cup. Then he turned back to the room.

"I'll be back soon," he smiled.

"Let me give you something," said the Hermit, looking around the log cabin. Olivier's gaze darted to the corner where the small canvas sack sat. Unopened. A bit of twine keeping it closed.

A chuckle came from the Hermit. "One day, perhaps, Olivier. But not today."

He went over to the hand-hewn mantelpiece, picked up a tiny item and held it out to the attractive blond man.

"For the groceries." He pointed to the tins and cheese and milk, tea and coffee and bread on the counter.

"No, I couldn't. It's my pleasure," said Olivier, but they both knew the pantomime and knew he'd take the small offering. "*Merci*," Olivier said at the door.

In the woods there was a furious scrambling, as a doomed creature raced to escape its fate, and coyotes raced to seal it.

"Be careful," said the old man, quickly scanning the night sky. Then, before closing the door, he whispered the single word that was quickly devoured by the woods. Olivier wondered if the Hermit crossed himself and mumbled prayers, leaning against the door, which was thick but perhaps not quite thick enough.

And he wondered if the old man believed the stories of the great and grim army with Chaos looming and leading the Furies. Inexorable, unstoppable. Close.

And behind them something else. Something unspeakable.

And he wondered if the Hermit believed the prayers.

Olivier flicked on his flashlight, scanning the darkness. Gray tree trunks crowded round. He shone the light here and there, trying to find the narrow path through the late summer forest. Once on the trail he hurried. And the more he hurried the more frightened he became, and the more fearful he grew the faster he ran until he was stumbling, chased by dark words through the dark woods.

He finally broke through the trees and staggered to a stop, hands on his bent knees, heaving for breath. Then, slowly straightening, he looked down on the village in the valley.

Three Pines was asleep, as it always seemed to be. At peace with itself and the world. Oblivious of what happened around it. Or perhaps aware of everything, but choosing peace anyway. Soft light glowed at some of the windows. Curtains were drawn in bashful old homes. The sweet scent of the first autumn fires wafted to him.

And in the very center of the little Quebec village there stood three great pines, like watchmen.

Olivier was safe. Then he felt his pocket.

The gift. The tiny payment. He'd left it behind.

Cursing, Olivier turned to look into the forest that had closed behind him. And he thought again of the small canvas bag in the corner of the cabin. The thing the Hermit had teased him with, promised him, dangled before him. The thing a hiding man hid.

Olivier was tired, and fed up and angry at himself for forgetting the trinket. And angry at the Hermit for not giving him the other thing. The thing he'd earned by now.

He hesitated, then turning he plunged back into the forest, feeling his fear growing and feeding the rage. And as he walked, then ran, a voice followed, beating behind him. Driving him on.

"Chaos is here, old son."

TWO

⁓

"You get it."

Gabri pulled up the covers and lay still. But the phone continued to ring and beside him Olivier was dead to the world. Out the window Gabri could see drizzle against the pane and he could feel the damp Sunday morning settling into their bedroom. But beneath the duvet it was snug and warm, and he had no intention of moving.

He poked Olivier. "Wake up."

Nothing, just a snort.

"Fire!"

Still nothing.

"Ethel Merman!"

Nothing. Dear Lord, was he dead?

He leaned in to his partner, seeing the precious thinning hair lying across the pillow and across the face. The eyes closed, peaceful. Gabri smelled Olivier, musky, slightly sweaty. Soon they'd have a shower and they'd both smell like Ivory soap.

The phone rang again.

"It's your mother," Gabri whispered in Olivier's ear.

"What?"

"Get the phone. It's your mother."

Olivier sat up, fighting to get his eyes open and looking bleary, as though emerging from a long tunnel. "My mother? But she's been dead for years."

"If anyone could come back from the dead to screw you up, it'd be her."

"You're the one screwing me up."

"You wish. Now get the phone."

Olivier reached across the mountain that was his partner and took the call.

"*Oui, allô?*"

Gabri snuggled back into the warm bed, then registered the time on the glowing clock. Six forty-three. On Sunday morning. Of the Labor Day long weekend.

Who in the world would be calling at this hour?

He sat up and looked at his partner's face, studying it as a passenger might study the face of a flight attendant during takeoff. Were they worried? Frightened?

He saw Olivier's expression change from mildly concerned to puzzled, and then, in an instant, Olivier's blond brows dropped and the blood rushed from his face.

Dear God, thought Gabri. We're going down.

"What is it?" he mouthed.

Olivier was silent, listening. But his handsome face was eloquent. Something was terribly wrong.

"What's happened?" Gabri hissed.

They rushed across the village green, their raincoats flapping in the wind. Myrna Landers, fighting with her huge umbrella, came across to meet them and together they hurried to the bistro. It was dawn and the world was gray and wet. In the few paces it took to get to the bistro their hair was plastered to their heads and their clothes were sodden. But for once neither Olivier nor Gabri cared. They skidded to a stop beside Myrna outside the brick building.

"I called the police. They should be here soon," she said.

"Are you sure about this?" Olivier stared at his friend and neighbor. She was big and round and wet and wearing bright yellow rubber boots under a lime green raincoat and gripping her red umbrella. She looked as though a beachball had exploded. But she also had never looked more serious. Of course she was sure.

"I went inside and checked," she said.

"Oh, God," whispered Gabri. "Who is it?"

"I don't know."

"How can you not know?" Olivier asked. Then he looked through the mullioned glass of his bistro window, bringing his slim hands up beside his face to block out the weak morning light. Myrna held her brilliant red umbrella over him.

Olivier's breath fogged the window but not before he'd seen what Myrna had also seen. There was someone inside the bistro. Lying on the old pine floor. Face up.

"What is it?" asked Gabri, straining and craning to see around his partner.

But Olivier's face told him all he needed to know. Gabri focused on the large black woman next to him.

"Is he dead?"

"Worse."

What could be worse than death? he wondered.

Myrna was as close as their village came to a doctor. She'd been a psychologist in Montreal before too many sad stories and too much good sense got the better of her, and she'd quit. She'd loaded up her car intending to take a few months to drive around before settling down, somewhere. Any place that took her fancy.

She got an hour outside Montreal, stumbled on Three Pines, stopped for *café au lait* and a croissant at Olivier's Bistro, and never left. She unpacked her car, rented the shop next door and the apartment above and opened a used bookstore.

People wandered in for books and conversation. They brought their stories to her, some bound, and some known by heart. She recognized some of the stories as real, and some as fiction. But she honored them all, though she didn't buy every one.

"We should go in," said Olivier. "To make sure no one disturbs the body. Are you all right?"

Gabri had closed his eyes, but now he opened them again and seemed more composed. "I'm fine. Just a shock. He didn't look familiar."

And Myrna saw on his face the same relief she'd felt when she'd first rushed in. The sad fact was, a dead stranger was way better than a dead friend.

They filed into the bistro, sticking close as though the dead man might reach out and take one of them with him. Inching toward him they stared down, rain dripping off their heads and noses onto his worn clothes and puddling on the wide-plank floor. Then Myrna gently pulled them back from the edge.

And that's how both men felt. They'd woken on this holiday weekend in their comfortable bed, in their comfortable home, in their comfortable life, to find themselves suddenly dangled over a cliff.

All three turned away, speechless. Staring wide-eyed at each other.

There was a dead man in the bistro.

And not just dead, but worse.

As they waited for the police Gabri made a pot of coffee, and Myrna took off her raincoat and sat by the window, looking into the misty September day. Olivier laid and lit fires in the two stone hearths at either end of the beamed room. He poked one fire vigorously and felt its warmth against his damp clothing. He felt numb, and not just from the creeping cold.

When they'd stood over the dead man Gabri had murmured, "Poor one."

Myrna and Olivier had nodded. What they saw was an elderly man in shabby clothing, staring up at them. His face was white, his eyes surprised, his mouth slightly open.

Myrna had pointed to the back of his head. The puddled water was turning pink. Gabri leaned tentatively closer, but Olivier didn't move. What held him spellbound and stunned wasn't the shattered back of the dead man's head, but the front. His face.

"*Mon Dieu*, Olivier, the man's been murdered. Oh, my God."

Olivier continued to stare, into the eyes.

"But who is he?" Gabri whispered.

It was the Hermit. Dead. Murdered. In the bistro.

"I don't know," said Olivier.

Chief Inspector Armand Gamache got the call just as he and Reine-Marie finished clearing up after Sunday brunch. In the dining room of their apartment in Montreal's Outremont *quartier* he could hear his second in command, Jean Guy Beauvoir, and his daughter Annie. They weren't talking. They never talked. They argued. Especially when Jean Guy's wife, Enid, wasn't there as a buffer. But Enid had to plan school courses and had begged off brunch. Jean Guy, on the other hand, never turned down an invitation for a free meal. Even if it came at a price. And the price was always Annie.

It had started over the fresh-squeezed orange juice, coursed through the scrambled eggs and Brie, and progressed across the fresh fruit, croissants and *confitures*.

"But how can you defend the use of stun guns?" came Annie's voice from the dining room.

"Another great brunch, *merci*, Reine-Marie," said David, placing dishes from the dining room in front of the sink and kissing his mother-in-law on the cheek. He was of medium build with short, thinning dark hair. At thirty he was a few years older than his wife, Annie, though he often appeared younger. His main feature, Gamache often felt, was his animation. Not hyper, but full of life. The Chief Inspector had liked him from the moment, five years earlier, his daughter had introduced them. Unlike other young men Annie had brought home, mostly lawyers like herself, this one hadn't tried to out-macho the Chief. That wasn't a game that interested Gamache. Nor did it impress him. What did impress him was David's reaction when he'd met Armand and Reine-Marie Gamache. He'd smiled broadly, a smile that seemed to fill the room, and simply said, "*Bonjour.*"

He was unlike any other man Annie had ever been interested in. David wasn't a scholar, wasn't an athlete, wasn't staggeringly handsome. Wasn't destined to become the next Premier of Quebec, or even the boss of his legal firm.

No, David was simply open and kind.

She'd married him, and Armand Gamache had been delighted to walk with her down the aisle, with Reine-Marie on the other side of their only daughter. And to see this nice man wed his daughter.

For Armand Gamache knew what not-nice was. He knew what cruelty, despair, horror were. And he knew what a forgotten, and precious, quality "nice" was.

"Would you rather we just shoot suspects?" In the dining room Beauvoir's voice had risen in volume and tone.

"Thank you, David," said Reine-Marie, taking the dishes. Gamache handed his son-in-law a fresh dish towel and they dried as Reine-Marie washed up.

"So," David turned to the Chief Inspector, "do you think the Habs have a chance at the cup this year?"

"No," yelled Annie. "I expect you to learn how to apprehend someone without having to maim or kill them. I expect you to genuinely see suspects as just that. Suspects. Not sub-human criminals you can beat up, electrocute or shoot."

"I think they do," said Gamache, handing David a plate to dry and taking one himself. "I like their new goalie and I think their forward line has matured. This is definitely their year."

"But their weakness is still defense, don't you think?" Reine-Marie asked. "The Canadiens always concentrate too much on offense."

"You try arresting an armed murderer. I'd love to see you try. You, you . . ." Beauvoir was sputtering. The conversation in the kitchen stopped as they listened to what he might say next. This was an argument played out every brunch, every Christmas, Thanksgiving, birthday. The words changed slightly. If not tasers they were arguing about daycare or education or the environment. If Annie said blue, Beauvoir said orange. It had been this way since Inspector Beauvoir had joined the Sûreté du Québec's homicide division, under Gamache, a dozen years earlier. He'd become a member of the team, and of the family.

"You what?" demanded Annie.

"You pathetic piece of legal crap."

Reine-Marie gestured toward the back door of the kitchen that gave onto a small metal balcony and fire escape. "Shall we?"

"Escape?" Gamache whispered, hoping she was serious, but suspecting she wasn't.

"Maybe you could just try shooting them, Armand?" David asked.

"I'm afraid Jean Guy is a faster draw," said the Chief Inspector. "He'd get me first."

"Still," said his wife, "it's worth a try."

"Legal crap?" said Annie, her voice dripping disdain. "Brilliant. Fascist moron."

"I suppose I could use a taser," said Gamache.

"Fascist? Fascist?" Jean Guy Beauvoir almost squealed. In the kitchen Gamache's German shepherd, Henri, sat up in his bed and cocked his head. He had huge oversized ears which made Gamache think he wasn't purebred but a cross between a shepherd and a satellite dish.

"Uh-oh," said David. Henri curled into a ball in his bed and it was clear David would join him if he could.

All three looked wistfully out the door at the rainy, cool early September day. Labor Day weekend in Montreal. Annie said something unintelligible. But Beauvoir's response was perfectly clear.

"Screw you."

"Well, I think this debate's just about over," said Reine-Marie. "More coffee?" She pointed to their espresso maker.

"*Non, pas pour moi, merci,*" said David, with a smile. "And please, no more for Annie."

"Stupid woman," muttered Jean Guy as he entered the kitchen. He grabbed a dish towel from the rack and began furiously drying a plate. Gamache figured that was the last they'd see of the India Tree design. "Tell me she's adopted."

"No, homemade." Reine-Marie handed the next plate to her husband.

"Screw you." Annie's dark head shot into the kitchen then disappeared.

"Bless her heart," said Reine-Marie.

Of their two children, Daniel was the more like his father. Large, thoughtful, academic. He was kind and gentle and strong. When Annie had been born Reine-Marie thought, perhaps naturally, this would be the child most like her. Warm, intelligent, bright. With a love of books so strong Reine-Marie Gamache had become a librarian, finally taking over a department at the *Bibliothèque nationale* in Montreal.

But Annie had surprised them both. She was smart, competitive, funny. She was fierce, in everything she did and felt.

They should have had an inkling about this. As a newborn Armand would take her for endless rides in the car, trying to soothe her as she howled. He'd sing, in his deep baritone, Beatles songs, and Jacques Brel songs. "*La Complainte du phoque en Alaska*" by Beau Dommage. That was Daniel's favorite. It was a soulful lament. But it did nothing for Annie.

One day, as he'd strapped the shrieking child into the car seat and turned on the ignition, an old Weavers tape had been in.

As they sang, in falsetto, she'd settled.

At first it had seemed a miracle. But after the hundredth trip around the block listening to the laughing child and the Weavers singing "*Wimoweh, a-wimoweh,*" Gamache yearned for the old days and felt like shrieking himself. But as they sang the little lion slept.

Annie Gamache became their cub. And grew into a lioness. But sometimes, on quiet walks together, she'd tell her father about her fears and her disappointments and the everyday sorrows of her young life. And Chief Inspector Gamache would be seized with a desire to hold her to him, so that she needn't pretend to be so brave all the time.

She was fierce because she was afraid. Of everything.

The rest of the world saw a strong, noble lioness. He looked at his daughter and saw Bert Lahr, though he'd never tell her that. Or her husband.

"Can we talk?" Annie asked her father, ignoring Beauvoir. Gamache nodded and handed the dish towel to David. They walked down the hall and into the warm living room where books were ranged on shelves in orderly rows, and stacked under tables and beside the sofa in not-so-orderly piles. *Le Devoir* and the *New York Times* were on the coffee table and a gentle fire burned in the grate. Not the roaring flames of a bitter winter fire, but a soft almost liquid flame of early autumn.

They talked for a few minutes about Daniel, living in Paris with his wife and daughter, and another daughter due before the end of the month. They talked about her husband David and his hockey team, about to start up for another winter season.

Mostly Gamache listened. He wasn't sure if Annie had something specific to say, or just wanted to talk. Henri jogged into the room and plunked his head on Annie's lap. She kneaded his ears, to his grunts and moans. Eventually he lay down by the fire.

Just then the phone rang. Gamache ignored it.

"It's the one in your office, I think," said Annie. She could see it on the old wooden desk with the computer and the notebook, in the room that was filled with books, and smelled of sandalwood and rosewater and had three chairs.

She and Daniel would sit in their wooden swivel chairs and spin each other around until they were almost sick, while their father sat in his armchair, steady. And read. Or sometimes just stared.

"I think so too."

The phone rang again. It was a sound they knew well. Somehow different from other phones. It was the ringing that announced a death.

Annie looked uncomfortable.

"It'll wait," he said quietly. "Was there something you wanted to tell me?"

"Should I get that?" Jean Guy looked in. He smiled at Annie but his eyes went swiftly to the Chief Inspector.

"Please. I'll be there in a moment."

He turned back to his daughter, but by then David had joined them and Annie had once again put on her public face. It wasn't so different from her private one. Just, perhaps, a bit less vulnerable. And her father wondered briefly, as David sat down and took her hand, why she needed her public face in front of her husband.

"There's been a murder, sir," whispered Inspector Beauvoir. He stood just inside the room.

"*Oui*," said Gamache, watching his daughter.

"Go on, Papa." She waved her hand at him, not to dismiss him, but to free him of the need to stay with her.

"I will, eventually. Would you like to go for a walk?"

"It's pelting down outside," said David with a laugh. Gamache genuinely loved his son-in-law, but sometimes he could be oblivious. Annie also laughed.

"Really, Papa, not even Henri would go out in this."

Henri leaped up and ran to get his ball. The fatal words, "Henri" and "out," had been combined unleashing an undeniable force.

"Well," said Gamache as the German shepherd bounded back into the room. "I have to go to work."

He gave Annie and David a significant look, then glanced over at Henri. His meaning even David couldn't miss.

"Christ," whispered David good-humoredly, and getting off the comfortable sofa he and Annie went to find Henri's leash.

By the time Chief Inspector Gamache and Inspector Beauvoir arrived in Three Pines the local force had cordoned off the bistro, and villagers milled about under umbrellas and stared at the old brick building. The scene of so many meals and drinks and celebrations. Now a crime scene.

As Beauvoir drove down the slight slope into the village Gamache asked him to pull over.

"What is it?" the Inspector asked.

"I just want to look."

The two men sat in the warm car, watching the village through the lazy arc of the wipers. In front of them was the village green with its pond and bench, its beds of roses and hydrangea, late flowering phlox and hollyhocks. And at the end of the common, anchoring it and the village, stood the three tall pines.

Gamache's gaze wandered to the buildings that hugged the village green. There were weathered white clapboard cottages, with wide porches and wicker chairs. There were tiny fieldstone houses built centuries ago by the first settlers, who'd cleared the land and yanked the stones from the earth. But most of the homes around the village green were made of rose-hued brick, built by United Empire Loyalists fleeing the American Revolution. Three Pines sat just kilometers from the Vermont border and while relations now with the States were friendly and affectionate, they weren't back then. The people who created the village had been desperate for sanctuary, hiding from a war they didn't believe in.

The Chief Inspector's eyes drifted up du Moulin, and there, on the side of the hill leading out of the village, was the small white chapel. St. Thomas's Anglican.

Gamache brought his eyes back to the small crowd standing under umbrellas chatting, pointing, staring. Olivier's bistro was smack-dab in the center of the semicircle of shops. Each shop ran into the next. Monsieur Béliveau's general store, then Sarah's Boulangerie, then Olivier's Bistro and finally Myrna's new and used bookstore.

"Let's go," Gamache nodded.

Beauvoir had been waiting for the word and now the car moved slowly forward. Toward the huddled suspects, toward the killer.

But one of the first lessons the Chief had taught Beauvoir when he'd joined the famed homicide department of the Sûreté du Québec was that to catch a killer they didn't move forward. They moved back. Into the past. That was where the crime began, where the killer began. Some event, perhaps long forgotten by everyone else, had lodged inside the murderer. And he'd begun to fester.

What kills can't be seen, the Chief had warned Beauvoir. That's what makes it so dangerous. It's not a gun or a knife or a fist. It's not anything you can see coming. It's an emotion. Rancid, spoiled. And waiting for a chance to strike.

The car slowly moved toward the bistro, toward the body.

"*Merci,*" said Gamache a minute later as a local Sûreté officer opened the bistro door for them. The young man was just about to challenge the stranger, but hesitated.

Beauvoir loved this. The reaction of local cops as it dawned on them that this large man in his early fifties wasn't just a curious citizen. To the young cops Gamache looked like their fathers. There was an air of courtliness about him. He always wore a suit, or the jacket and tie and gray flannels he had on that day.

They'd notice the mustache, trimmed and graying. His dark hair was also graying around the ears, where it curled up slightly. On a rainy day like this the Chief wore a cap, which he took off indoors, and when he did the young officers saw the balding head. And if that wasn't enough they'd notice this man's eyes. Everyone did. They were deep brown, thoughtful, intelligent and something else. Something that distinguished the famous head of homicide for the Sûreté du Québec from every other senior officer.

His eyes were kind.

It was both his strength, Beauvoir knew, and his weakness.

Gamache smiled at the astonished officer who found himself face to face with the most celebrated cop in Quebec. Gamache offered his hand and the young agent stared at it for a moment before putting out his own. "*Patron,*" he said.

"Oh, I was hoping it would be you." Gabri hurried across the room, past the Sûreté officers bending over the victim. "We asked if the Sûreté could send you but apparently it's not normal for suspects to order up a specific officer." He hugged the Chief Inspector then turned to the roomful of agents. "See, I do know him." Then he whispered to Gamache, "I think it would be best if we didn't kiss."

"Very wise."

Gabri looked tired and stressed, but composed. He was disheveled, though that wasn't unusual. Behind him, quieter, almost eclipsed, stood Olivier. He was also disheveled. That was very unusual. He also looked exhausted, with dark rings under his eyes.

"Coroner's just arriving now, Chief." Agent Isabelle Lacoste walked across the room to greet him. She wore a simple skirt and light sweater and managed to make both look stylish. Like most Québécoises, she was petite and confident. "It's Dr. Harris, I see."

They all looked out the window and the crowd parted to let a woman with a medical bag through. Unlike Agent Lacoste, Dr. Harris managed to make her simple skirt and sweater look slightly frumpy. But comfortable. And on a miserable day like this "comfortable" was very attractive.

"Good," said the Chief, turning back to Agent Lacoste. "What do we know?"

Lacoste led Gamache and Inspector Beauvoir to the body. They knelt, an act and ritual they'd performed hundreds of times. It was surprisingly intimate. They didn't touch him, but leaned very close, closer than they'd ever get to anyone in life, except a loved one.

"The victim was struck from behind by a blunt object. Something clean and hard, and narrow."

"A fireplace poker?" Beauvoir asked, looking over at the fires Olivier had set. Gamache also looked. It was a damp morning, but not all that cool. A fire wasn't necessary. Still, it was probably made to comfort more than to heat.

"If it was a poker it would be clean. The coroner will take a closer look, of course, but there's no obvious sign of dirt, ash, wood, anything, in the wound."

Gamache was staring at the gaping hole in the man's head. Listening to his agent.

"No weapon, then?" asked Beauvoir.

"Not yet. We're searching, of course."

"Who was he?"

"We don't know."

Gamache took his eyes off the wound and looked at the woman, but said nothing.

"We have no ID," Agent Lacoste continued. "We've been through his pockets and nothing. Not even a Kleenex. And no one seems to know him. He's a white male, mid-seventies I'd say. Lean but not malnourished. Five seven, maybe five eight."

Years ago, when she'd first joined homicide, it had seemed bizarre to Agent Lacoste to catalog these things the Chief could see perfectly well for himself. But he'd taught them all to do it, and so she did. It was only years later, when she was training someone else, that she recognized the value of the exercise.

It made sure they both saw the same things. Police were as fallible and subjective as anyone else. They missed things, and misinterpreted things. This catalog made it less likely. Either that or they'd reinforce the same mistakes.

"Nothing in his hands and it looks like nothing under his fingernails. No bruising. Doesn't appear to have been a struggle."

They stood up.

"The condition of the room verifies that."

They looked around.

Nothing out of place. Nothing tipped over. Everything clean and orderly.

It was a restful room. The fires at either end of the beamed bistro took the gloom out of the day. Their light gleamed off the polished wood floors, darkened by years of smoke and farmers' feet.

Sofas and large inviting armchairs sat in front of each fireplace, their fabric faded. Old chairs were grouped around dark wooden dining tables. In front of the mullioned bay windows three or four wing chairs waited for villagers nursing steaming *café au lait* and croissants, or Scotches, or burgundy wine. Gamache suspected the people milling outside in the rain could do with a good stiff drink. He thought Olivier and Gabri certainly could.

Chief Inspector Gamache and his team had been in the bistro many times, enjoying meals in front of the roaring fire in winter or a quiet cool drink on the *terrasse* in summer. Almost always discussing murder. But never with an actual body right there.

Sharon Harris joined them, taking off her wet raincoat then smiling at Agent Lacoste and shaking hands solemnly with the Chief Inspector.

"Dr. Harris," he said, bowing slightly. "I'm sorry about disturbing your long weekend."

She'd been sitting at home, flipping through the television channels, trying to find someone who wasn't preaching at her, when the phone had rung. It had seemed a godsend. But looking now at the body, she knew that this had very little to do with God.

"I'll leave you to it," said Gamache. Through the windows he saw the villagers, still there, waiting for news. A tall, handsome man with gray hair bent down to listen as a short woman with wild hair spoke. Peter and Clara Morrow. Villagers and artists. Standing like a ramrod beside them and staring unblinking at the bistro was Ruth Zardo. And her duck, looking quite imperious. Ruth wore a sou'wester that glistened in the rain. Clara spoke to her, but was ignored. Ruth Zardo, Gamache knew, was a drunken, embittered old piece of work. Who also happened to be his favorite poet in the world. Clara spoke again and this time Ruth did respond. Even through the glass Gamache knew what she'd said.

"Fuck off."

Gamache smiled. While a body in the bistro was certainly different, some things never changed.

"Chief Inspector."

The familiar, deep, singsong voice greeted him. He turned and saw Myrna Landers walking across the room, her electric yellow boots clumping on the floor. She wore a pink tracksuit tucked into her boots.

She was a woman of color, in every sense.

"Myrna," he smiled and kissed her on both cheeks. This drew a surprised look from some of the local Sûreté officers, who didn't expect the Chief Inspector to kiss suspects. "What're you doing in here when everyone else is out there?" He waved toward the window.

"I found him," she said, and his face grew grave.

"Did you? I'm sorry. That must've been a shock." He guided her to a chair by the fire. "I imagine you've given someone your statement?"

She nodded. "Agent Lacoste took it. Not much to tell, I'm afraid."

"Would you like a coffee, or a nice cup of tea?"

Myrna smiled. It was something she'd offered him often enough. Something she offered everyone, from the kettle that bubbled away on her woodstove. And now it was being offered to her. And she saw how comforting it actually was.

"Tea, please."

While she sat warming herself by the fire Chief Inspector Gamache went to ask Gabri for a pot of tea, then returned. He sat in the armchair and leaned forward.

"What happened?"

"I go out every morning for a long walk."

"Is this something new? I've never known you to do that before."

"Well, yes. Since the spring anyway. I decided since I turned fifty I needed to get into shape." She smiled fully then. "Or at least, into a different shape. I'm aiming for pear rather than apple." She patted her stomach. "Though I suspect my nature is to be the whole orchard."

"What could be better than an orchard?" he smiled, then looked at his own girth. "I'm not exactly a sapling myself. What time do you get up?"

"Set my alarm for six thirty and I'm out the door by quarter to seven. This morning I'd just left when I noticed Olivier's door was open a little, so I looked in and called. I know Olivier doesn't normally open until later on a Sunday so I was surprised."

"But not alarmed."

"No." She seemed surprised by the question. "I was about to leave when I spotted him."

Myrna's back was to the room, and Gamache didn't glance over to the body. Instead he held her gaze and encouraged her with a nod, saying nothing.

Their tea arrived and while it was clear Gabri wanted to join them he, unlike Gamache's son-in-law David, was intuitive enough to pick up the unspoken signals. He put the teapot, two bone china cups and saucers, milk, sugar and a plate of ginger cookies on the table. Then left.

"At first I thought it was a pile of linen left by the waiters the night before," Myrna said when Gabri was out of earshot. "Most of them're quite young and you never know. But then I looked closer and saw it was a body."

"A body?"

It was the way someone describes a dead man, not a living one.

"I knew he was dead right away. I've seen some, you know."

Gamache did know.

"He was exactly as you see him now." Myrna watched as Gamache poured their tea. She indicated milk and sugar then accepted her cup, with a biscuit. "I got up close but didn't touch him. I didn't think he'd been killed. Not at first."

"What did you think?" Gamache held the cup in his large hands. The tea was strong and fragrant.

"I thought he'd had a stroke or maybe a heart attack. Something sudden, by the look on his face. He seemed surprised, but not afraid or in pain."

That was, thought Gamache, a good way of putting it. Death had surprised this man. But it did most people, even the old and infirm. Almost no one really expected to die.

"Then I saw his head."

Gamache nodded. It was hard to miss. Not the head, but what was missing from it.

"Do you know him?"

"Never seen him before. And I suspect he'd be memorable."

Gamache had to agree. He looked like a vagrant. And while easily ignored they were hard to forget. Armand Gamache put his delicate cup on its delicate saucer. His mind kept going to the question that had struck him as soon as he'd taken the call and heard about the murder. In the bistro in Three Pines.

Why here?

He looked quickly over to Olivier who was talking to Inspector Beauvoir and Agent Lacoste. He was calm and contained. But he couldn't be oblivious of how this appeared.

"What did you do then?"

"I called 911 then Olivier, then went outside and waited for them."

She described what happened, up to the moment the police arrived.

"*Merci*," said Gamache and rose. Myrna took her tea and joined Olivier and Gabri across the room. They stood together in front of the hearth.

Everyone in the room knew who the three main suspects were. Everyone, that was, except the three main suspects.

THREE

Dr. Sharon Harris stood, brushed her skirt clean and smiled thinly at the Chief Inspector.

"Not much finesse," she said.

Gamache stared down at the dead man.

"He looks like a tramp," said Beauvoir, bending down and examining the man's clothing. It was mismatched and worn.

"He must be living rough," said Lacoste.

Gamache knelt down and looked closely at the old man's face again. It was weathered and withered. An almanac face, of sun and wind and cold. A seasoned face. Gamache gently rubbed his thumb across the dead man's cheek, feeling stubble. He was clean shaven, but what might have grown in would've been white. The dead man's hair was white and cut without enthusiasm. A snip here, a snip there.

Gamache picked up one of the victim's hands, as though comforting him. He held it for an instant, then turned it over, palm up. Then he slowly rubbed his own palm over the dead man's.

"Whoever he was he did hard work. These are calluses. Most tramps don't work."

Gamache shook his head slowly. So who are you? And why are you here? In the bistro, and in this village. A village few people on earth even knew existed. And even fewer found.

But you did, thought Gamache, still holding the man's cold hand. You found the village and you found death.

"He's been dead between six and ten hours," the doctor said. "Sometime after midnight but before four or five this morning."

Gamache stared at the back of the man's head and the wound that killed him.

It was catastrophic. It looked like a single blow by something extremely hard. And by someone extremely angry. Only anger accounted for this sort of power. The power to pulverize a skull. And what it protected.

Everything that made this man who he was was kept in this head. Someone bashed that in. With one brutal, decisive blow.

"Not much blood." Gamache got up and watched the Scene of Crime team fanning out and collecting evidence around the large room. A room now violated. First by murder and now by them. The unwanted guests.

Olivier was standing, warming himself by the fire.

"That's a problem," said Dr. Harris. "Head wounds bleed a lot. There should be more blood, lots more."

"It might've been cleaned up," said Beauvoir.

Sharon Harris bent over the wound again then straightened up. "With the force of the blow the bleeding might have been massive and internal. And death almost instantaneous."

It was the best news Gamache ever heard at a murder scene. Death he could handle. Even murder. It was suffering that disturbed him. He'd seen a lot of it. Terrible murders. It was a great relief to find one swift and decisive. Almost humane.

He'd once heard a judge say the most humane way to execute a prisoner was to tell him he was free. Then kill him.

Gamache had struggled against that, argued against it, railed against it. Then finally, exhausted, had come to believe it.

Looking at this man's face he knew he hadn't suffered. The blow to the back of the head meant he probably hadn't even seen it coming.

Almost like dying in your sleep.

But not quite.

They placed him in a bag and took the body away. Outside men and women stood somberly aside to let it pass. Men swept off their damp caps and women watched, tight-lipped and sad.

Gamache turned away from the window and joined Beauvoir, who was sitting with Olivier, Gabri and Myrna. The Scene of Crime team had moved into the back rooms of the bistro, the private dining room, the staff room, the kitchen. The main room now seemed almost normal. Except for the questions hanging in the air.

"I'm sorry this has happened," Gamache said to Olivier. "How're you doing?"

Olivier exhaled deeply. He looked drained. "I think I'm still stunned. Who was he? Do you know?"

"No," said Beauvoir. "Did anyone report a stranger in the area?"

"Report?" said Olivier. "To whom?"

All three turned perplexed eyes on Beauvoir. The Inspector had forgotten that Three Pines had no police force, no traffic lights, no sidewalks, no mayor. The volunteer fire department was run by that demented old poet Ruth Zardo, and most would rather perish in the flames than call her.

The place didn't even have crime. Except murder. The only criminal thing that ever happened in this village was the worst possible crime.

And here they were with yet another body. At least the rest had had names. This one seemed to have dropped from the sky, and fallen on his head.

"It's a little harder in the summer, you know," said Myrna, taking a seat on the sofa. "We get more visitors. Families come back for vacation, kids come home from school. This is the last big weekend. Everyone goes home after this."

"The weekend of the Brume County Fair," said Gabri. "It ends tomorrow."

"Right," said Beauvoir, who couldn't care less about the fair. "So Three Pines empties out after this weekend. But the visitors you describe are friends and family?"

"For the most part," said Myrna, turning to Gabri. "Some strangers come to your B and B, don't they?"

He nodded. "I'm really an overflow if people run out of space in their homes."

"What I'm getting at," said an exasperated Beauvoir, "is that the people who visit Three Pines aren't really strangers. I just want to get this straight."

"Straight we don't specialize in. Sorry," said Gabri. This brought a smile to even Olivier's tired face.

"I heard something about a stranger," said Myrna, "but I didn't really pay any attention."

"Who said it?"

"Roar Parra," she said, reluctantly. It felt a bit like informing, and no one had much stomach for that. "I heard him talking to Old Mundin and The Wife about seeing someone in the woods."

Beauvoir wrote this down. It wasn't the first time he'd heard about the Parras. They were a prominent Czech family. But Old Mundin and The Wife? That must be a joke. Beauvoir's lips narrowed and he looked at Myrna without amusement. She looked back, also without amusement.

"Yes," Myrna said, reading his mind. It wasn't hard. The teapot could read it. "Those are their names."

"Old and The Wife?" he repeated. No longer angry, but mystified. Myrna nodded. "What're their real names?"

"That's it," said Olivier. "Old and The Wife."

"Okay, I'll give you Old. It's just possible, but no one looks at a newborn and decides to call her The Wife. At least I hope not."

Myrna smiled. "You're right. I'm just so used to it I never thought. I have no idea what her real name is."

Beauvoir wondered just how pathetic a woman had to be to allow herself to be called The Wife. It actually sounded slightly biblical, Old Testament.

Gabri put some beers, Cokes and a couple of bowls of mixed nuts on the table. Outside the villagers had finally gone home. It looked wet and bleak, but inside they were snug and warm. It was almost possible to forget this wasn't a social occasion. The Scene of Crime agents seemed to have dissolved into the woodwork, only evident when a slight scratching or mumbling could be heard. Like rodents, or ghosts. Or homicide detectives.

"Tell us about last night," said Chief Inspector Gamache.

"It was a madhouse," said Gabri. "Last big weekend of the summer so everyone came by. Most had been to the fair during the day so they were tired. Didn't want to cook. It's always like that on Labor Day weekend. We were prepared."

"What does that mean?" asked Agent Lacoste, who'd joined them.

"I brought in extra staff," said Olivier. "But it went smoothly. People were pretty relaxed and we closed on time. At about one in the morning."

"What happened then?" asked Lacoste.

Most murder investigations appeared complex but were really quite simple. It was just a matter of asking "And then what happened?" over and over and over. And listening to the answers helped too.

"I usually do the cash and leave the night staff to clean up, but Saturdays are different," said Olivier. "Old Mundin comes after closing and delivers the things he's repaired during the week and picks up any furniture that's been broken in the meantime. Doesn't take long, and he does it while the waiters and kitchen staff are cleaning up."

"Wait a minute," said Beauvoir. "Mundin does this at midnight on Saturdays? Why not Sunday morning, or any other reasonable time? Why late at night?"

It sounded furtive to Beauvoir, who had a nose for things secretive and sly.

Olivier shrugged. "Habit, I guess. When he first started doing the work he wasn't married to The Wife so he'd hang around here Saturday nights. When we closed he'd just take the broken furniture then. We've seen no reason to change."

In a village where almost nothing changed this made sense.

"So Mundin took the furniture. What happened then?" asked Beauvoir.

"I left."

"Were you the last in the place?"

Olivier hesitated. "Not quite. Because it was so busy there were a few extra things to do. They're a good bunch of kids, you know. Responsible."

Gamache had been listening to this. He preferred it that way. His agents asked the questions and it freed him up to observe, and to hear what was said, how it was said, and what was left out. And now he heard a defensiveness creep into Olivier's calm and helpful voice. Was he defensive about his own behavior, or was he trying to protect his staff, afraid they'd fall under suspicion?

"Who was the last to leave?" Agent Lacoste asked.

"Young Parra," said Olivier.

"Young Parra?" asked Beauvoir. "Like Old Mundin?"

Gabri made a face. "Of course not. His name isn't 'Young.' That'd be weird. His name's Havoc."

Beauvoir's eyes narrowed and he glared at Gabri. He didn't like being mocked and he suspected this large, soft man was doing just that. He then looked over at Myrna, who wasn't laughing. She nodded.

"That's his name. Roar named his son Havoc."

Jean Guy Beauvoir wrote it down, but without pleasure or conviction.

"Would he have locked up?" asked Lacoste.

It was, Gamache and Beauvoir both knew, a crucial question, but its significance seemed lost on Olivier.

"Absolutely."

Gamache and Beauvoir exchanged glances. Now they were getting somewhere. The murderer had to have had a key. A world full of suspects had narrowed dramatically.

"May I see your keys?" asked Beauvoir.

Olivier and Gabri fished theirs out and handed them to the Inspector. But a third set was also offered. He turned and saw Myrna's large hand dangling a set of keys.

"I have them in case I get locked out of my place or if there's an emergency."

"*Merci,*" said Beauvoir, with slightly less confidence than he'd been feeling. "Have you lent them to anyone recently?" he asked Olivier and Gabri.

"No."

Beauvoir smiled. This was good.

"Except Old Mundin, of course. He'd lost his and needed to make another copy."

"And Billy Williams," Gabri reminded Olivier. "Remember? He normally uses the one under the planter at the front but he didn't want to have to bend down while he carried the wood. He was going to take it to get more copies made."

Beauvoir's face twisted into utter disbelief. "Why even bother to lock up?" he finally asked.

"Insurance," said Olivier.

Well, someone's premiums are going up, thought Beauvoir. He looked at Gamache and shook his head. Really, they all deserved to be murdered in their sleep. But, of course, as irony would have it, it was the ones who locked and alarmed who were killed. In Beauvoir's experience Darwin was way wrong. The fittest didn't survive. They were killed by the idiocy of their neighbors, who continued to bumble along oblivious.

FOUR

⁓

"You didn't recognize him?" asked Clara as she sliced some fresh bread from Sarah's Boulangerie.

There was only one "him" Myrna's friend could be talking about. Myrna shook her head and sliced tomatoes into the salad, then turned to the shallots, all freshly picked from Peter and Clara's vegetable garden.

"And Olivier and Gabri didn't know him?" asked Peter. He was carving a barbecued chicken.

"Strange, isn't it?" Myrna paused and looked at her friends. Peter—tall, graying, elegant and precise. And beside him his wife Clara. Short, plump, hair dark and wild, bread crust scattered into it like sparkles. Her eyes were blue and usually filled with humor. But not today.

Clara was shaking her head, perplexed. A couple of crumbs fell to the counter. She picked them up absently, and ate them. Now that the initial shock of discovery was receding, Myrna was pretty sure they were all thinking the same thing.

This was murder. The dead man was a stranger. But was the killer?

And they probably all came to the same conclusion. Unlikely.

She'd tried not to think about it, but it kept creeping into her head. She picked up a slice of baguette and chewed on it. The bread was warm, soft and fragrant. The outer crust was crispy.

"For God's sake," said Clara, waving the knife at the half-eaten bread in Myrna's hand.

"Want some?" Myrna offered her a piece.

The two women stood at the counter eating fresh warm bread. They'd normally be at the bistro for Sunday lunch but that didn't seem likely today, what with the body and all. So Clara, Peter and Myrna had gone next door to Myrna's loft apartment. Downstairs the door to her shop was armed with an alarm, should anyone enter. It wasn't really so much an alarm as a small bell that tinkled when the door opened. Sometimes Myrna went down, sometimes not. Almost all her customers were local, and they all knew how much to leave by the cash register. Besides, thought Myrna, if anyone needed a used book so badly they had to steal it then they were welcome to it.

Myrna felt a chill. She looked across the room to see if a window was open and cool, damp air pouring in. She saw the exposed brick walls, the sturdy beams and the series of large industrial windows. She walked over to check, but all of them were closed, except for one open a sliver to let in some fresh air.

Walking back across the wide pine floors, she paused by the black pot-bellied woodstove in the center of the large room. It was crackling away. She lifted a round lid and slipped another piece of wood in.

"It must have been horrible for you," said Clara, going to stand by Myrna.

"It was. That poor man, just lying there. I didn't see the wound at first."

Clara sat with Myrna on the sofa facing the woodstove. Peter brought over two Scotches then quietly retired to the kitchen area. From there he could see them, could hear their conversation, but wouldn't be in the way.

He watched as the two women leaned close, sipping their drinks, talking softly. Intimately. He envied them that. Peter turned away and stirred the Cheddar and apple soup.

"What does Gamache think?" asked Clara.

"He seems as puzzled as the rest of us. I mean really," Myrna turned to face Clara, "why was a strange man in the bistro? Dead?"

"Murdered," said Clara and the two thought about that for a moment.

Clara finally spoke. "Did Olivier say anything?"

"Nothing. He seemed just stunned."

Clara nodded. She knew the feeling.

The police were at the door. Soon they'd be in their homes, in their kitchens and bedrooms. In their heads.

"Can't imagine what Gamache thinks of us," said Myrna. "Every time he shows up there's a body."

"Every Quebec village has a vocation," said Clara. "Some make cheese, some wine, some pots. We produce bodies."

"Monasteries have vocations, not villages," said Peter with a laugh. He placed bowls of rich-scented soup on Myrna's long refectory table. "And we don't make bodies."

But he wasn't really so sure.

"Gamache is the head of homicide for the Sûreté," said Myrna. "It must happen to him all the time. In fact, he'd probably be quite surprised if there wasn't a body."

Myrna and Clara joined Peter at the table and as the women talked Peter thought of the man in charge of the investigation. He was dangerous, Peter knew. Dangerous to whoever had killed that man next door. He wondered whether the murderer knew what sort of man was after him. But Peter was afraid the murderer knew all too well.

Inspector Jean Guy Beauvoir looked around their new Incident Room and inhaled. He realized, with some surprise, how familiar and even thrilling the scent was.

It smelled of excitement, it smelled of the hunt. It smelled of long hours over hot computers, piecing together a puzzle. It smelled of teamwork.

It actually smelled of diesel fuel and wood smoke, of polish and concrete. He was again in the old railway station of Three Pines, abandoned by the Canadian Pacific Railway decades ago and left to rot. But the Three Pines Volunteer Fire Department had taken it over, sneaking in and hoping no one noticed. Which, of course, they didn't, the CPR having long forgotten the village existed. So now the small station was home to their fire trucks, their bulky outfits, their equipment. The walls retained the tongue-in-groove wood paneling, and were papered with posters for scenic trips through the Rockies and life-saving techniques. Fire safety tips, volunteer rotation and old railway timetables competed for space, along with a huge poster announcing the winner of the Governor General's Prize for Poetry. There, staring out at them in perpetuity, was a madwoman.

She was also staring at him, madly, in person.

"What the fuck are you doing here?" Beside her a duck stared at him too.

Ruth Zardo. Probably the most prominent and respected poet in the country. And her duck Rosa. He knew that when Chief Inspector Gamache looked at her he saw a gifted poet. But Beauvoir just saw indigestion.

"There's been a murder," he said, his voice he hoped full of dignity and authority.

"I know there's been a murder. I'm not an idiot."

Beside her the duck shook its head and flapped its wings. Beauvoir had grown so used to seeing her with the bird it was no longer surprising. In fact, though he'd never admit it, he was relieved Rosa was still alive. Most things, he suspected, didn't last long around this crazy old fart.

"We need to use this building again," he said and turned away from them.

Ruth Zardo, despite her extreme age, her limp, and her diabolical temperament, had been elected head of the volunteer fire department. In hopes, Beauvoir suspected, that she'd perish in the flames one day. But he also suspected she wouldn't burn.

"No." She whacked her cane on the concrete floor. Rosa didn't jump but Beauvoir did. "You can't have it."

"I'm sorry, Madame Zardo, but we need it and we plan to take it."

His voice was no longer as gracious as it had been. The three stared at each other, only Rosa blinking. Beauvoir knew the only way this nutcase could triumph was if she started reciting her dreary, unintelligible verse. Nothing rhymed. Nothing even made sense. She'd break him in an instant. But he also knew that of all the people in the village, she was the least likely to quote it. She seemed embarrassed, even ashamed, by what she created.

"How's your poetry?" he asked and saw her waver. Her short, shorn hair was white and thin and lay close to her head, as though her bleached skull was exposed. Her neck was scrawny and ropy and her tall body, once sturdy he suspected, was feeble. But nothing else about her was.

"I saw somewhere that you'll soon have another book out."

Ruth Zardo backed up slightly.

"The Chief Inspector is here too, as you probably know." His voice was kind now, reasonable, warm. The old woman looked as though she was seeing Satan. "I know how much he's looking forward to talking to you about it. He'll be here soon. He's been memorizing your verses."

Ruth Zardo turned and left.

He'd done it. He'd banished her. The witch was dead, or at least gone. He got to work setting up their headquarters. He ordered desks and communications equipment, computers and printers, scanners and faxes. Corkboards and fragrant Magic Markers. He'd stick a corkboard right on top of that poster of the sneering, mad old poet. And over her face he'd write about murder.

The bistro was quiet.

The Scene of Crime officers had left. Agent Isabelle Lacoste was kneeling on the floor where the body had been found, thorough as ever. Making absolutely sure no clues were missed. From what Chief Inspector Gamache could see Olivier and Gabri hadn't stirred: they still sat on the faded old sofa facing the large fireplace, each in his own world, staring at the fire, mesmerized by the flames. He wondered what they were thinking.

"What are you thinking?" Gamache went over and sat in the large armchair beside them.

"I was thinking about the dead man," said Olivier. "Wondering who he was. Wondering what he was doing here, and about his family. Wondering if anyone was missing him."

"I was thinking about lunch," said Gabri. "Anyone else hungry?"

From across the room Agent Lacoste looked up. "I am."

"So am I, *patron*," said Gamache.

When they could hear Gabri clanking pots and pans in the kitchen, Gamache leaned forward. It was just him and Olivier. Olivier looked at him blankly. But the Chief Inspector had seen that look before. It was, in fact, almost impossible to look blank. Unless the person wanted to. A blank face to the Chief Inspector meant a frantic mind.

From the kitchen came the unmistakable aroma of garlic and they could hear Gabri singing, "What shall we do with a drunken sailor?"

"Gabri thought the man was a tramp. What do you think?"

Olivier remembered the eyes, glassy, staring. And he remembered the last time he'd been in the cabin.

Chaos is coming, old son. It's taken a long time, but it's finally here.

"What else could he've been?"

"Why do you think he was killed here, in your bistro?"

"I don't know." And Olivier seemed to sag. "I've been racking my brains trying to figure it out. Why would someone kill a man here? It makes no sense."

"It does make sense."

"Really?" Olivier sat forward. "How?"

"I don't know. But I will."

Olivier stared at the formidable, quiet man who suddenly seemed to fill the entire room without raising his voice.

"Did you know him?"

"You've asked me that before," snapped Olivier, then gathered himself. "I'm sorry, but you have, you know, and it gets annoying. I didn't know him."

Gamache stared. Olivier's face was red now, blushing. But from anger, from the heat of the fire, or did he just tell a lie?

"Someone knew him," said Gamache at last, leaning back, giving Olivier the impression of pressure lifted. Of breathing room.

"But not me and not Gabri." His brow pulled together and Gamache thought Olivier was genuinely upset. "What was he doing here?"

"'Here' meaning Three Pines, or 'here' meaning the bistro?"

"Both."

But Gamache knew Olivier had just lied. He meant the bistro, that was obvious. People lied all the time in murder investigations. If the first victim of war was the truth, some of the first victims of a murder investigation were people's lies. The lies they told themselves, the lies they told each other. The little lies that allowed them to get out of bed on cold, dark mornings. Gamache and his team hunted the lies down and exposed them. Until all the small tales told to ease everyday lives disappeared. And people were left naked. The trick was distinguishing the important fibs from the rest. This one appeared tiny. In which case, why bother lying at all?

Gabri approached carrying a tray with four steaming plates. Within minutes they were sitting around the fireplace eating fettuccine with shrimp and scallops sautéed in garlic and olive oil. Fresh bread was produced and glasses of dry white wine poured.

As they ate they talked about the Labor Day long weekend, about the chestnut trees and conkers. About kids returning to school and the nights drawing in.

The bistro was empty, except for them. But it seemed crowded to the Chief Inspector. With the lies they'd been told, and the lies being manufactured and waiting.

FIVE

⁓

After lunch, while Agent Lacoste made arrangements for them to stay overnight at Gabri's B and B, Armand Gamache walked slowly in the opposite direction. The drizzle had stopped for the moment but a mist clung to the forests and hills surrounding the village. People were coming out of their homes to do errands or work in their gardens. He walked along the muddy road and turning left made his way over the arched stone bridge that spanned the Rivière Bella Bella.

"Hungry?" Gamache opened the door to the old train station and held out the brown paper bag.

"Starving, *merci*." Beauvoir almost ran over, and taking the bag he pulled out a thick sandwich of chicken, Brie and pesto. There was also a Coke and *pâtisserie*.

"What about you?" asked Beauvoir, his hand hesitating over the precious sandwich.

"Oh, I've eaten," the Chief said, deciding it would really do no good describing his meal to Beauvoir.

The men drew a couple of chairs up to the warm pot-bellied stove and as the Inspector ate they compared notes.

"So far," said Gamache, "we have no idea who the victim was, who killed him, why he was in the bistro and what the murder weapon was."

"No sign of a weapon yet?"

"No. Dr. Harris thinks it was a metal rod or something like that. It was smooth and hard."

"A fireplace poker?"

"Perhaps. We've taken Olivier's in for tests." The Chief paused.

"What is it?" Beauvoir asked.

"It just strikes me as slightly odd that Olivier would light fires in both grates. It's rainy but not that cold. And for that to be just about the first thing he'd do after finding a body . . ."

"You're thinking the weapon might be one of those fireplace pokers? And that Olivier lit the fires so that he could use them? Burn away evidence on them?"

"I think it's possible," said the Chief, his voice neutral.

"We'll have them checked," said Beauvoir. "But if one turns out to be the weapon it doesn't mean Olivier used it. Anyone could've picked it up and smashed the guy."

"True. But only Olivier lit the fires this morning, and used the poker."

It was clear as Chief Inspector he had to consider everyone a suspect. But it was also clear he wasn't happy about it.

Beauvoir waved to some large men at the door to come in. The Incident Room equipment had arrived. Lacoste showed up and joined them by the stove.

"I've booked us into the B and B. By the way, I ran into Clara Morrow. We're invited to dinner tonight."

Gamache nodded. This was good. They could find out more at a social event than they ever could in an interrogation.

"Olivier gave me the names of the people who worked in the bistro last night. I'm off to interview them," she reported. "And there are teams searching the village and the surrounding area for the murder weapon, with a special interest in fireplace pokers or anything like that."

Inspector Beauvoir finished his lunch and went to direct the setup of the Incident Room. Agent Lacoste left to conduct interviews. A part of Gamache always hated to see his team members go off. He warned them time and again not to forget what they were doing, and who they were looking for. A killer.

The Chief Inspector had lost one agent, years ago, to a murderer. He was damned if he was going to lose another. But he couldn't protect them all, all the time. Like Annie, he finally had to let them go.

It was the last interview of the day. So far Agent Lacoste had spoken to five people who'd worked at the bistro the night before, and gotten the same answers. No, nothing unusual happened. The place was full all evening, it being both a Saturday night and the long Labor Day weekend. School was back on Tuesday and anybody down for the summer would be heading back to Montreal on Monday. Tomorrow.

Four of the waiters were returning to university after the summer break the next day. They really weren't much help since all they seemed to have noticed was a table of attractive girls.

The fifth waiter was more helpful, since she hadn't simply seen a roomful of breasts. But it was, by all accounts, a normal though hectic evening. No dead body that anyone mentioned, and Lacoste thought even the breast boys would have noticed that.

She drove up to the home of the final waiter, the young man nominally in charge once Olivier had left. The one who'd done the final check of the place and locked up.

The house was set back from the main road down a long dirt driveway. Maples lined the drive and while they hadn't yet turned their brilliant autumn colors, a few were just beginning to show oranges and reds. In a few weeks this approach, Lacoste knew, would be spectacular.

Lacoste got out of the car and stared, amazed. Facing her was a block of concrete and glass. It seemed so out of place, like finding a tent pitched on Fifth Avenue. It didn't belong. As she walked toward it she realized something else. The house intimidated her and she wondered why. Her own tastes ran to traditional but not stuffy. She loved exposed brick and beams, but hated clutter, though she'd given up all semblance of being house-proud after the kids came. These days it was a triumph if she walked across a room and didn't step on something that squeaked.

This place was certainly a triumph. But was it a home?

The door was opened by a robust middle-aged woman who spoke very good, though perhaps slightly precise, French. Lacoste was surprised and realized she'd been expecting angular people to live in this angular house.

"Madame Parra?" Agent Lacoste held up her identification. The woman nodded, smiled warmly and stepped back for them to enter.

"*Entrez.* It's about what happened at Olivier's," said Hanna Parra.

"*Oui.*" Lacoste bent to take off her muddy boots. It always seemed so awkward and undignified. The world famous homicide team of the Sûreté du Québec interviewing suspects in their stockinged feet.

Madame Parra didn't tell her not to. But she did give her slippers from a wooden box by the door, jumbled full of old footwear. Again, this surprised Lacoste, who'd expected everything to be neat and tidy. And rigid.

"We're here to speak to your son."

"Havoc."

Havoc. The name had amused Inspector Beauvoir, but Agent Lacoste found nothing funny about it. And, strangely, it seemed to fit with this cold, brittle place. What else could contain Havoc?

Before driving out she'd done some research on the Parras. Just a thumbnail sketch, but it helped. The woman leading her out of the mudroom was a councillor for the township of Saint-Rémy, and her husband, Roar, was a caretaker, working on the large properties in the area. They'd escaped Czechoslovakia in the mid-80s, come to Quebec and settled just outside Three Pines. There was, in fact, a large and influential Czech community in the area, composed of escapees, people running until they found what they were looking for. Freedom and safety. Hanna and Roar Parra had stopped when they found Three Pines.

And once there, they'd created Havoc.

"Havoc!" his mother cried, letting the dogs slip out as she called into the woods.

After a few more yells a short, stocky young man appeared. His face was flushed from hard work and his curly dark hair was tousled. He smiled and Lacoste knew the other waiters at the bistro hadn't stood a chance with the girls. This boy would take them all. He also stole a sliver of her heart, and she quickly did the figures. She was twenty-eight, he was twenty-one. In twenty-five years that wouldn't matter so much, although her husband and children might disagree.

"What can I do for you?" He bent and took off his green Wellington boots. "Of course, it is that man they found in the bistro this morning. I'm sorry. I should have known."

As he talked they walked into a quite splendid kitchen, unlike any Lacoste had seen in real life. Instead of the classic, and mandatory as far as Lacoste knew, triangle of fitments, the entire kitchen was ranged along one wall at the back of the bright room. There was one very long concrete counter, stainless steel appliances, open floating shelves with pure white dishes in a regimented line. The lower cabinets were dark laminate. It felt at once very retro and very modern.

There was no kitchen island but instead a frosted glass dining table, and what looked like vintage teak chairs stood in front of the counter. As Lacoste sat in one, and found it surprisingly comfortable, she wondered if these were antiques brought from Prague. Then she wondered if people really slipped across borders with teak chairs.

At the other end of the room was a wall of windows, floor to ceiling, that wrapped around the sides giving a spectacular view of fields and forest and a mountain beyond. She could just see a white church spire and a plume of smoke in the distance. The village of Three Pines.

In the living area by the huge windows two sofas lined up perfectly to face each other, with a low coffee table between them.

"Tea?" Hanna asked and Lacoste nodded.

These two Parras seemed at odds in the almost sterile environment and as they waited for the tea to brew Lacoste found herself wondering about the missing Parra. The father, Roar. Perhaps it was his angular, hard stamp on this house. Was he the one who yearned for cool certainty, straight lines, near empty rooms, and uncluttered shelves?

"Do you know who the dead man was?" asked Hanna as she placed a cup of tea in front of Agent Lacoste. A white plate piled with cookies was also put on the spotless table.

Lacoste thanked her and took one. It was soft and warm and tasted of raisin and oatmeal, with a hint of brown sugar and cinnamon. It tasted of home. She noticed the teacup had a smiling and waving snowman in a red suit. Bonhomme Carnaval. A character from the annual Quebec City winter carnival. She took a sip. It was strong and sweet.

Like Hanna herself, Lacoste suspected.

"No, we don't know who he was yet," she said.

"We've heard," Hanna hesitated, "that it wasn't natural. Is that right?"

Lacoste remembered the man's skull. "No, it wasn't natural. He was murdered."

"Dear God," said Hanna. "How awful. And you have no idea who did it?"

"We will, soon. For now I want to hear about last night." She turned to the young man sitting across from her.

Just then a voice called from the back door in a language Lacoste couldn't understand, but took to be Czech. A man, short and square, walked into the kitchen, whacking his knit hat against his coat.

"Roar, can't you do that in the mudroom?" Hanna spoke in French, and despite the slight reprimand she was clearly pleased to see him. "The police are here. About the body."

"What body?" Roar also switched to French, lightly accented. He sounded concerned. "Where? Here?"

"Not here, Dad. They found a body in the bistro this morning. He was killed."

"You mean murdered? Someone was murdered in the bistro last night?"

His disbelief was clear. Like his son he was stocky and muscular. His hair was curly and dark, but unlike his son's it was graying. He'd be in his late forties, Lacoste reckoned.

She introduced herself.

"I know you," he said, his gaze keen and penetrating. His eyes were disconcertingly blue and hard. "You've been in Three Pines before."

He had a good memory for faces, Lacoste realized. Most people remembered Chief Inspector Gamache. Maybe Inspector Beauvoir. But few remembered her, or the other agents.

This man did.

He poured himself tea then sat down. He also seemed slightly out of place in this pristine modern room. And yet he was completely comfortable. He looked a man who'd be comfortable most places.

"You didn't know about the body?"

Roar Parra took a bite of his cookie and shook his head. "I've been working all day in the woods."

"In the rain?"

He snorted. "What? A little rain won't kill you."

"But a blow to the head would."

"Is that how he died?" When Lacoste nodded Parra went on. "Who was he?"

"No one knows," said Hanna.

"But perhaps you do," said Lacoste. She brought a photograph out of her pocket and placed it face down on the hard, cold table.

"Me?" said Roar with a snort. "I didn't even know there was a dead man."

"But I hear you saw a stranger hanging around the village this summer."

"Who told you that?"

"Doesn't matter. You were heard talking about it. Was it a secret?"

Parra hesitated. "Not really. It was just the once. Maybe twice. Not important. It was stupid, just some guy I thought I saw."

"Stupid?"

He gave a smile suddenly, the first one she'd seen from him, and it transformed his stern face. It was as though a crust had broken. Lines creased his cheeks and his eyes lit momentarily.

"Trust me, this is stupid. And I know stupid, having raised a teenage son. I'll tell you, but it can't mean anything. There're new owners at the old Hadley house. A couple bought it a few months ago. They're doing renovations and hired me to build a barn and clear some trails. They also wanted the garden cleaned up. Big job."

The old Hadley house, she knew, was a rambling old Victorian wreck on the hill overlooking Three Pines.

"I think I saw someone in the woods. A man. I'd felt someone looking at me when I worked there, but I thought I was imagining things. It's easy with that place. Sometimes I'd look around fast, to see if someone really was there, but there never was anyone. Except once."

"What happened?"

"He disappeared. I called out and even ran into the woods a little way after him, but he'd gone." Parra paused. "Maybe he was never there at all."

"But you don't believe that, do you? You believe there really was someone there."

Parra looked at her and nodded.

"Would you recognize him?" Lacoste asked.

"I might."

"I have a photograph of the dead man, taken this morning. It might be upsetting," she warned. Parra nodded and she turned the photograph face up. All three looked at it, staring intently, then shook their heads. She left it on the table, beside the cookies.

"Everything was normal last night? Nothing unusual?" she asked Havoc.

What followed was the same description as the other waiters had provided. Busy, lots of tips, no time to think.

Strangers?

Havoc thought about it and shook his head. No. Some summer people, and weekenders, but he knew everyone.

"And what did you do after Olivier and Old Mundin left?"

"Put away the dishes, did a quick look round, turned off the lights and locked up."

"Are you sure you locked up? The door was found unlocked this morning."

"I'm sure. I always lock up."

A note of fear had crept into the handsome young man's voice. But Lacoste knew that was normal. Most people, even innocent ones, grew fearful when examined by homicide detectives. But she'd noticed something else.

His father had looked at him, then quickly looked away. And Lacoste wondered who Roar Parra really was. He worked in the woods now. He cut grass and planted gardens. But what had he done before that? Many men were drawn to the tranquility of a garden only after they'd known the brutality of life.

Had Roar Parra known horrors? Had he created some?

SIX

"Chief Inspector? It's Sharon Harris."

"*Oui*, Dr. Harris," said Gamache into the receiver.

"I haven't done the complete autopsy but I have a couple of pieces of information from my preliminary work."

"Go on." Gamache leaned on the desk and brought his notebook closer.

"There were no identifying marks on the body, no tattoos, no operation scars. I've sent his dental work out."

"What shape were his teeth in?"

"Now that's an interesting point. They weren't as bad as I expected. I bet he didn't go to the dentist very often, and he'd lost a couple of molars to some gum disease, but overall, not bad."

"Did he brush?"

There was a small laugh. "Unbelievably, he did. He also flossed. There's some receding, some plaque and disease, but he took care of his teeth. There's even evidence he once had quite a bit of work done. Cavities filled, root canal."

"Expensive stuff."

"Exactly. This man had money at one time."

He wasn't born a tramp, thought Gamache. But then no one was.

"Can you tell how long ago the work was done?"

"I'd say twenty years at least, judging by the wear and the materials used, but I've sent a sample along to the forensic dentist. Should hear by tomorrow."

"Twenty years ago," mused Gamache, doing the math, jotting figures in his notebook. "The man was in his seventies. That would mean he had the work done sometime in his fifties. Then something happened. He lost his job, drank, had a breakdown; something happened that pushed him over the edge."

"Something happened," agreed Dr. Harris, "but not in his fifties. Something happened in his late thirties or early forties."

"That long ago?" Gamache looked down at his notes. He'd written *20 ans* and circled it. He was confused.

"That's what I wanted to tell you, Chief," the coroner continued. "There's something wrong about this body."

Gamache sat up straighter and took his half-moon reading glasses off. Across the room Beauvoir saw this and walked over to the Chief's desk.

"Go on," said Gamache, nodding to Beauvoir to sit. Then he punched a button on the phone. "I've put you on the speaker. Inspector Beauvoir's here."

"Good. Well, it struck me as strange that this man who seemed a derelict should brush his teeth and even floss. But homeless people can do odd things. They're often mentally unwell, as you know, and can be obsessive about certain things."

"Though not often hygiene," said Gamache.

"True. It was strange. Then when I undressed him I found he was clean. He'd had a bath or a shower recently. And his hair, while wild, was also clean."

"There're halfway homes," said Gamache. "Maybe he was in one of those. Though an agent called all the local social services and he's not known to them."

"How d'you know?" The coroner rarely questioned Chief Inspector Gamache, but she was curious. "We don't know his name and surely his description would sound like any number of homeless men."

"That's true," admitted Gamache. "She described him as a slim, older man in his seventies with white hair, blue eyes and weathered skin. None of the men who match that description and use shelters in this area is missing. But we're having someone take his photo around."

There was a pause on the line.

"What is it?"

"Your description is wrong."

"What do you mean?" Surely Gamache had seen him as clearly as everyone else.

"He wasn't an elderly man. That's what I called to tell you. His teeth were a clue; then I went looking. His arteries and blood vessels have very little plaque, and almost no atherosclerosis. His prostate isn't particularly enlarged and there's no sign of arthritis. I'd say he was in his mid-fifties."

My age, thought Gamache. Was it possible that wreck on the floor was the same age?

"And I don't think he was homeless."

"Why not?"

"Too clean for one thing. He took care of himself. Not *GQ* material, it's true, but not all of us can look like Inspector Beauvoir."

Beauvoir preened slightly.

"On the outside he looked seventy but on the inside he was in good physical condition. Then I looked at his clothes. They were clean too. And mended. They were old and worn, but *propres*."

She used the Québécois word that was rarely used anymore, except by elderly parents. But it seemed to fit here. *Propre*. Nothing fancy. Nothing fashionable. But sturdy and clean and presentable. There was a worn dignity about the word.

"I have to do more work, but that's my preliminary finding. I'll e-mail all this to you."

"*Bon.* Can you guess what sort of work he did? How'd he keep himself in shape?"

"Which gym did he belong to, you mean?" He could hear the smile in her voice.

"That's right," said Gamache. "Did he jog or lift weights? Was he in a spinning class or maybe Pilates?"

Now the coroner laughed. "At a guess I'd say it wasn't much walking, but a lot of lifting. His upper body is slightly more toned than his lower. But I'll keep that question in mind as I go."

"*Merci, docteur*," said Gamache.

"One more thing," said Beauvoir. "The murder weapon. Any further clues? Any ideas?"

"I'm just about to do that part of the autopsy, but I've taken a quick look and my assessment stays the same. Blunt instrument."

"A fireplace poker?" asked Beauvoir.

"Possibly. I did notice something white in the wound. Might be ash."

"We'll have the lab results from the pokers by tomorrow morning," said Gamache.

"I'll let you know when I have more to tell you."

Dr. Harris rung off just as Agent Lacoste arrived back. "Clearing up outside. It's going to be a nice sunset."

Beauvoir looked at her, incredulous. She was supposed to be scouring Three Pines for clues, trying to find the murder weapon and the murderer, interviewing suspects, and the first thing out of her mouth was about the nice sunset?

He noticed the Chief drift over to a window, sipping his coffee. He turned round and smiled. "Beautiful."

A conference table had been set up in the center of their Incident Room with desks and chairs placed in a semicircle at one end. On each desk was a computer and phone. It looked a little like Three Pines, with the conference table as the village green and their desks as the shops. It was an ancient and tested design.

A young Sûreté agent from the local detachment hovered, looking as if he wanted to say something.

"Can I help you?" Chief Inspector Gamache asked.

The other agents from the local detachment stopped and stared. Some exchanged knowing smiles.

The young man squared his shoulders.

"I'd like to help with your investigation."

There was dead silence. Even the technicians stopped what they were doing, as people do when witnessing a terrible calamity.

"I'm sorry?" said Inspector Beauvoir, stepping forward. "What did you just say?"

"I'd like to help." By now the young agent could see the truck hurtling toward him and could feel his vehicle spin out of control. Too late, he realized his mistake.

He saw all this, and stood firm, from either terror or courage. It was hard to tell. Behind him four or five large agents crossed their arms and did nothing to help.

"Aren't you supposed to be setting up desks and telephone lines?" asked Beauvoir, stepping closer to the agent.

"I have. That's all done." He voice was smaller, weaker, but still there.

"And what makes you think you can help?"

Behind Beauvoir stood the Chief Inspector, quietly watching. The young agent looked at Inspector Beauvoir when answering his questions, but then his eyes returned to Gamache.

"I know the area. I know the people."

"So do they." Beauvoir waved at the wall of police behind the agent. "If we needed help why would we choose you?"

This seemed to throw him and he stood silent. Beauvoir waved his hand to dismiss the agent and walked away.

"Because," the agent said to the Chief Inspector, "I asked."

Beauvoir stopped and turned round, looking incredulous. *"Pardon? Pardon?* This is homicide, not a game of Mother May I. Are you even in the Sûreté?"

It wasn't a bad question. The agent looked about sixteen and his uniform hung loosely on him, though an effort had obviously been made to make it fit. With him in the foreground and his *confrères* behind it looked like an evolutionary scale, with the young agent on the extinction track.

"If you have no more work to do, please leave."

The young agent nodded, turned to get back to work, met the wall of other officers, and stopped. Then he walked around them, watched by Gamache and his homicide team. Their last view of the young officer before they turned away was of his back, and a furiously blushing neck.

"Join me please," Gamache said to Beauvoir and Lacoste, who took their seats at the conference table.

"What do you think?" Gamache asked quietly.

"About the body?"

"About the boy."

"Not again," said Beauvoir, exasperated. "There are perfectly good officers already in homicide if we need someone. If they're busy with cases there's always the wait-list. Agents from other divisions are dying to get into homicide. Why choose an untested kid from the boonies? If we need another investigator let's call one down from headquarters."

It was their classic argument.

The homicide division of the Sûreté du Québec was the most prestigious posting in the province. Perhaps in Canada. They worked on the worst of all crimes in the worst of all conditions. And they worked with the best, the most respected and famous, of all investigators. Chief Inspector Gamache.

So why pick the dregs?

"We could, certainly," admitted the Chief.

But Beauvoir knew he wouldn't. Gamache had found Isabelle Lacoste sitting outside her Superintendent's office, about to be fired from traffic division. Gamache had asked her to join him, to the astonishment of everyone.

He'd found Beauvoir himself reduced to guarding evidence at the Sûreté outpost of Trois Rivières. Every day Beauvoir, Agent Beauvoir then, had suffered the ignominy of putting on his Sûreté uniform then stepping into the evidence cage. And staying there. Like an animal. He'd so pissed off his colleagues and bosses this was the only place left to put him. Alone. With inanimate objects. Silence all day, except when other agents came to put something in or take something out. They wouldn't even meet his eye. He'd become untouchable. Unmentionable. Invisible.

But Chief Inspector Gamache saw. He'd come one day on a case, had himself gone to the cage with evidence, and there he'd found Jean Guy Beauvoir.

The agent, the man no one wanted, was now the second in command in homicide.

But Beauvoir couldn't shake the certainty that Gamache had simply gotten lucky so far, with a few notable exceptions. The reality was, untested agents were dangerous. They made mistakes. And mistakes in homicide led to death.

He turned and looked at the slight young agent with loathing. Was this the one who'd finally make that blunder? The magnificent mistake that would lead to another death? It could be me who gets it, thought Beauvoir. Or worse. He glanced at Gamache beside him.

"Why him?" Beauvoir whispered.

"He seems nice," said Lacoste.

"Like the sunset," Beauvoir sneered.

"Like the sunset," she repeated. "He was standing all alone."

There was silence.

"That's it?" asked Beauvoir.

"He doesn't fit in. Look at him."

"You'd choose the runt of the litter? For homicide detail? For God's sake, sir," he appealed to Gamache. "This isn't the Humane Society."

"You think not?" said Gamache with a small smile.

"We need the best for this team, for this case. We don't have time to train people. And frankly, he looks as though he needs help tying his shoes."

It was true, Gamache had to admit, the young agent was awkward. But he was something else as well.

"We'll take him," said the Chief to Beauvoir. "I know you don't approve, and I understand your reasons."

"Then why take him, sir?"

"Because he asked," said Gamache, rising up. "And no one else did."

"But they'd join us in a second," Beauvoir argued, getting up as well. "Anyone would."

"What do you look for in a member of our team?" asked Gamache.

Beauvoir thought. "I want someone smart and strong."

Gamache tipped his head toward the young man. "And how much strength do you think that took? How much strength do you think it takes him to go to work every day? Almost as much as it took you, in Trois Rivières, or you," he turned to Lacoste, "in traffic division. The others might want to join us, but they either didn't have the brains or lacked the courage to ask. Our young man had both."

Our, thought Beauvoir. Our young man. He looked at him across the room. Alone. Coiling wires carefully and placing them in a box.

"I value your judgment, you know that, Jean Guy. But I feel strongly about this."

"I understand, sir." And he did. "I know this is important to you. But you're not always right."

Gamache stared at his Inspector and Beauvoir recoiled, afraid he'd gone too far. Presumed too much on their personal relationship. But then the Chief smiled.

"Happily, I have you to tell me when I make a mistake."

"I think you're making one now."

"Noted. Thank you. Will you please invite the young man to join us."

Beauvoir walked purposefully across the room and stopped at the young agent.

"Come with me," he said.

The agent straightened up. He looked concerned. "Yes, sir."

Behind them an officer snickered. Beauvoir stopped and turned back to the young officer following him.

"What's your name?"

"Paul Morin. I'm with the Cowansville detachment of the Sûreté, sir."

"Agent Morin, will you please take a seat at the table. We'd like your thoughts on this murder investigation."

Morin looked astonished. But not quite as astonished as the burly men behind him. Beauvoir turned back and walked slowly toward the conference table. It felt good.

"Reports, please," said Gamache and glanced at his watch. It was five thirty.

"Results are beginning to come in on some of the evidence we collected this morning in the bistro," said Beauvoir. "The victim's blood was found on the floor and between some of the floorboards, though there wasn't much."

"Dr. Harris will have a fuller report soon," said Gamache. "She thinks the lack of blood is explained by internal bleeding."

Beauvoir nodded. "We do have a report on his clothing. Still nothing to identify him. His clothes were old but clean and of good quality once. Merino wool sweater, cotton shirt, corduroy pants."

"I wonder if he'd put on his best clothes," said Agent Lacoste.

"Go on," said Gamache, leaning forward and taking off his glasses.

"Well." She picked her way through her thoughts. "Suppose he was going to meet someone important. He'd have a shower, shave, clip his nails even."

"And he might pick up clean clothes," said Beauvoir, following her thoughts. "Maybe at a used clothing store, or a Goodwill depot."

"There's one in Cowansville," said Agent Morin. "And another in Granby. I can check them."

"Good," said the Chief Inspector.

Agent Morin looked over at Inspector Beauvoir, who nodded his approval.

"Dr. Harris doesn't think this man was a vagrant, not in the classic sense of the word," said Chief Inspector Gamache. "He appeared in his seventies, but she's convinced he was closer to fifty."

"You're kidding," said Agent Lacoste. "What happened to him?"

That was the question, of course, thought Gamache. What happened to him? In life, to age him two decades. And in death.

Beauvoir stood up and walked to the fresh, clean sheets of paper pinned to the wall. He picked out a new felt pen, took off the cap and instinctively wafted it under his nose. "Let's go through the events of last night."

Isabelle Lacoste consulted her notes and told them about her interviews with the bistro staff.

They were beginning to see what had happened the night before. As he listened Armand Gamache could see the cheerful bistro, filled with villagers having a meal or drinks on Labor Day weekend. Talking about the Brume County Fair, the horse trials, the judging of livestock, the crafts tent. Celebrating the end of summer and saying good-bye to family and friends. He could see the stragglers leaving and the young waiters clearing up, banking the fires, washing the dishes. Then the door opening and Old Mundin stepping in. Gamache had no idea what Old Mundin looked like, so he placed in his mind a character from a painting by Bruegel the Elder. A stooped and cheery peasant. Walking through the bistro door, a young waiter perhaps helping to bring in the repaired chairs. Mundin and Olivier would have conferred. Money would have changed hands and Mundin would have left with new items needing fixing.

Then what?

According to Lacoste's interviews the waiters had left shortly before Olivier and Mundin. Leaving just one person in the bistro.

"What did you think of Havoc Parra?" Gamache asked.

"He seemed surprised by what had happened," said Lacoste. "It might've been an act, of course. Hard to tell. His father told me something interesting, though. He confirmed what we heard earlier. He saw someone in the woods."

"When?"

"Earlier in the summer. He's working at the old Hadley house for the new owners and thinks he saw someone up there."

"Thinks? Or did?" asked Beauvoir.

"Thinks. He chased him, but the guy disappeared."

They were silent for a moment, then Gamache spoke. "Havoc Parra says he locked up and left by one in the morning. Six hours later the man's body was found by Myrna Landers, who was out for a walk. Why would a stranger be murdered in Three Pines, and in the bistro?"

"If Havoc really did lock up, then the murderer had to be someone who knew where to find a key," said Lacoste.

"Or already had one," said Beauvoir. "Do you know what I wonder? I wonder why the murderer left him there."

"What do you mean?" asked Lacoste.

"Well, no one was there. It was dark. Why not pick up the body and take it into the forest? You wouldn't have to take him far, just a few hundred feet. The animals would do the rest and chances are he'd never be found. We'd never know a murder had been committed."

"Why do you think the body was left?" asked Gamache.

Beauvoir thought for a minute. "I think someone wanted him to be found."

"In the bistro?" asked Gamache.

"In the bistro."

SEVEN

 Olivier and Gabri strolled across the village green. It was seven in the evening and lights were beginning to glow in windows, except at the bistro, which was dark and empty.

"Christ," came a growl through the dusk. "The fairies are out."

"*Merde*," said Gabri. "The village idiot's escaped from her attic."

Ruth Zardo limped toward them followed by Rosa.

"I hear you finally killed someone with your rapier wit," said Ruth to Gabri, falling into step.

"Actually, I hear he read one of your poems and his head exploded," said Gabri.

"Would that that were true," said Ruth, slipping her bony arms into each of theirs, so that they walked across to Peter and Clara's arm in arm. "How are you?" she asked quietly.

"Okay," said Olivier, not glancing at the darkened bistro as they passed.

The bistro had been his baby, his creation. All that was good about him, he put in there. All his best antiques, his finest recipes, great wines. Some evenings he'd stand behind the bar, pretending to polish glasses, but really just listening to the laughter and looking at the people, who'd come to his bistro. And were happy to be there. They belonged, and so did he.

Until this.

Who'd want to come to a place where there'd been a murder?

And what if people found out he actually knew the Hermit? What if they found out what he'd done? No. Best to say nothing and see what happened. It was bad enough as it was.

They paused on the walk just outside Peter and Clara's house. Inside they saw Myrna putting her effusive flower arrangement on the kitchen table, already set for supper. Clara was exclaiming at its beauty and artistry. They couldn't hear the words, but her delight was obvious. In the living room Peter tossed another log on the fire.

Ruth turned from the comforting domestic scene to the man beside her. The old poet leaned in to whisper in his ear, so that not even Gabri could hear. "Give it time. It'll be all right, you know that, don't you?"

She turned to glance again through the glow at Clara hugging Myrna and Peter walking into the kitchen and exclaiming over the flowers as well. Olivier bent and kissed the old, cold cheek and thanked her. But he knew she was wrong. She didn't know what he knew.

Chaos had found Three Pines. It was bearing down upon them and all that was safe and warm and kind was about to be taken away.

Peter had poured them all drinks, except Ruth who'd helped herself and was now sipping from a vase filled with Scotch and sitting in the middle of the sofa facing the fire. Rosa was waddling around the room, barely noticed by anyone anymore. Even Lucy, Peter and Clara's golden retriever, barely looked at Rosa. The first time the poet had shown up with Rosa they'd insisted she stay outside, but Rosa set up such a quacking they were forced to let her in, just to shut the duck up.

"*Bonjour.*"

A deep, familiar voice was heard from the mudroom.

"God, you didn't invite Clouseau, did you?" asked Ruth, to the empty room. Empty except for Rosa, who raced to stand beside her.

"It's lovely," said Isabelle Lacoste as they walked from the mudroom into the airy kitchen. The long wooden table was set for dinner with baskets of sliced baguette, butter, jugs of water and bottles of wine. It smelled of garlic and rosemary and basil, all fresh from the garden.

And in the center of the table was a stunning arrangement of hollyhocks and climbing white roses, clematis and sweet pea and fragrant pink phlox.

More drinks were poured and the guests wandered into the living room and milled around nibbling soft runny Brie or orange and pistachio caribou pâté on baguette.

Across the room Ruth was interrogating the Chief Inspector.

"Don't suppose you know who the dead man was."

"Afraid not," said Gamache evenly. "Not yet."

"And do you know what killed him?"

"*Non.*"

"Any idea who did it?"

Gamache shook his head.

"Any idea why it happened in the bistro?"

"None," admitted Gamache.

Ruth glared at him. "Just wanted to make sure you're as incompetent as ever. Good to know some things can be relied upon."

"I'm glad you approve," said Gamache, bowing slightly before wandering off toward the fireplace. He picked up the poker, and examined it.

"It's a fireplace poker," said Clara, appearing at his elbow. "You use it to poke the fire."

She was smiling and watching him. He realized he must have looked a little odd, holding the long piece of metal to his face as though he'd never seen one before. He put it down. No blood on it. He was relieved.

"I hear your solo show is coming up in a few months." He turned to her, smiling. "It must be thrilling."

"If putting a dentist's drill up your nose is thrilling. Yes."

"That bad?"

"Oh, well, you know. It's only torture."

"Have you finished all the paintings?"

"They're all done, at least. They're crap, of course, but at least they're finished. Denis Fortin is coming down himself to discuss how they'll be hung. I have a specific order in mind. And if he disagrees I have a plan. I'll cry."

Gamache laughed. "That's how I got to be Chief Inspector."

"I told you so," Ruth hissed at Rosa.

"Your art is brilliant, Clara. You know that," said Gamache, leading her away from the crowd.

"How'd you know? You've only seen one piece. Maybe the others suck. I wonder if I made a mistake going with the paint by numbers."

Gamache made a face.

"Would you like to see them?" Clara asked.

"Love to."

"Great. How about after dinner? That gives you about an hour to practice saying, 'My God, Clara, they're the best works of art ever produced by anyone, anywhere.'"

"Sucking up?" smiled Gamache. "That's how I made Inspector."

"You're a Renaissance Man."

"I see you're good at it too."

"*Merci*. Speaking of your job, do you have any idea who that dead man is?" She'd lowered her voice. "You told Ruth you didn't, but is that true?"

"You think I'd lie?" he asked. But why not, he thought. Everyone else does. "You mean, how close are we to solving the crime?"

Clara nodded.

"Hard to say. We have some leads, some ideas. It makes it harder to know why the man was killed not knowing who he was."

"Suppose you never find out?"

Gamache looked down at Clara. Was there something in her voice? An imperfectly hidden desire that they never find out who the dead man was?

"It makes our job harder," he conceded, "but not impossible."

His voice, while relaxed, became momentarily stern. He wanted her to know they'd solve this case, one way or another. "Were you at the bistro last night?"

"No. We'd gone to the fair with Myrna. Had a disgusting dinner of fries, burgers and cotton candy. Went on a few rides, watched the local talent show, then came back here. I think Myrna might've gone in, but we were tired."

"We know the dead man wasn't a villager. He seems to have been a stranger. Have you seen any strangers around?"

"People come through backpacking or bicycling," said Clara, sipping her red wine and thinking. "But most of them are younger. I understand this was quite an old man."

Gamache didn't tell her what the coroner had said that afternoon.

"Roar Parra told Agent Lacoste he'd seen someone lurking in the woods this summer. Does that sound familiar?" He watched her closely.

"Lurking? Isn't that a bit melodramatic? No, I haven't seen anyone and neither has Peter. He'd have told me. And we spend a lot of time outside in the garden. If there was someone there we'd have seen him."

She waved toward their backyard, in darkness now, but Gamache knew it was large and sloped gently toward the Rivière Bella Bella.

"Mr. Parra didn't see him there," said Gamache. "He saw him there."

He pointed to the old Hadley house, on the hill above them. The two of them took their drinks and walked out the door to the front veranda. Gamache was wearing his gray flannels, shirt, tie and jacket. Clara had a sweater, and needed it. In early September the nights grew longer and cooler. All around the village lights shone in homes, and even in the house on the hill.

The two looked at the house in silence for a few moments.

"I hear it's sold," said Gamache, finally.

Clara nodded. They could hear the murmur of conversation from the living room, and light spilled out so that Gamache could see Clara's face in profile.

"Few months ago," she said. "What are we now? Labor Day? I'd say they bought it back in July and have been doing renovations ever since. Young couple. Or at least, my age, which seems young to me."

Clara laughed.

It was hard for Gamache to see the old Hadley house as just another place in Three Pines. For one thing, it never seemed to belong to the village. It seemed the accusation, the voyeur on the hill, that looked down on them. Judged them. Preyed on them. And sometimes took one of the villagers, and killed them.

Horrible things had happened in that place.

Earlier in the year he and his wife Reine-Marie had come down and helped the villagers repaint and repair the place. In the belief that everything deserved a second chance. Even houses. And the hopes someone would buy it.

And now someone had.

"I know they hired Roar to work on the grounds," said Clara. "Clean up the gardens. He's even built a barn and started reopening the trails. There must have been fifty kilometers of bridle paths in those woods in Timmer Hadley's time. Grown over, of course. Lots of work for Roar to do."

"He said he saw the stranger in the woods while he worked. Said he'd felt himself being watched for a while but only caught sight of someone once. He'd tried to run after him but the guy disappeared."

Gamache's gaze shifted from the old Hadley house down to Three Pines. Kids were playing touch football on the village green, eking out every last moment of their summer vacation. Snippets of voices drifted to them from villagers sitting on other porches, enjoying the early evening. The main topic of conversation, though, wouldn't be the ripening tomatoes, the cooler nights, or getting in the winter wood.

Into the gentle village something rotten had crawled. Words like "murder," "blood," "body," floated in the night air, as did something else. The soft scent of rosewater and sandalwood from the large, quiet man beside Clara.

Back inside Isabelle Lacoste was pouring herself another watered-down Scotch from the drinks tray on the piano. She looked around the room. A bookcase covered an entire wall, crammed with books, broken only by a window and the door to the veranda through which she could see the Chief and Clara.

Across the living room Myrna was chatting with Olivier and Gabri while Peter worked in the kitchen and Ruth drank in front of the fireplace. Lacoste had been in the Morrow home before, but only to conduct interviews. Never as a guest.

It was as comfortable as she'd imagined. She saw herself going back to her husband in Montreal and convincing him they could sell their home, take the kids out of school, chuck their jobs and move here. Find a cottage just off the village green and get jobs at the bistro or Myrna's bookshop.

She subsided into an armchair and watched as Beauvoir came in from the kitchen, a pâté-smeared piece of bread in one hand and a beer in the other, and started toward the sofa. He halted suddenly, as though repelled, changed course, and went outside.

Ruth rose and limped to the drinks tray, a malevolent sneer on her face. Scotch replenished she returned to the sofa, like a sea monster slipping beneath the surface once again, still waiting for a victim.

"Any idea when we can reopen the bistro?" Gabri asked as he, Olivier and Myrna joined Agent Lacoste.

"Gabri," said Olivier, annoyed.

"What? I'm just asking."

"We've done what we need to," she told Olivier. "You can open up whenever you'd like."

"You can't stay closed long, you know," said Myrna. "We'd all starve to death."

Peter put his head in and announced, "Dinner!"

"Though perhaps not immediately," said Myrna, as they headed for the kitchen.

Ruth hauled herself out of the sofa and went to the veranda door.

"Are you deaf?" she shouted at Gamache, Beauvoir and Clara. "Dinner's getting cold. Get inside."

Beauvoir felt his rectum spasm as he hurried past her. Clara followed Beauvoir to the dinner table, but Gamache lingered.

It took him a moment to realize he wasn't alone. Ruth was standing beside him, tall, rigid, leaning on her cane, her face all reflected light and deep crevices.

"A strange thing to give to Olivier, wouldn't you say?"

The old voice, sharp and jagged, cut through the laughter from the village green.

"I beg your pardon?" Gamache turned to her.

"The dead man. Even you can't be that dense. Someone did this to Olivier. The man's greedy and shiftless and probably quite weak, but he didn't kill anyone. So why would someone choose his bistro for murder?"

Gamache raised his eyebrows. "You think someone chose the bistro on purpose?"

"Well, it didn't happen by accident. The murderer chose to kill at Olivier's Bistro. He gave the body to Olivier."

"To kill both a man and a business?" asked Gamache. "Like giving white bread to a goldfish?"

"Fuck you," said Ruth.

"*Nothing I ever gave was good for you,*" quoted Gamache. "*It was like white bread to a goldfish.*"

Beside him Ruth Zardo stiffened, then in a low growl she finished her own poem.

> "*They cram and cram, and it kills them,*
> *and they drift in the pool, belly up,*
> *making stunned faces*
> *and playing on our guilt*
> *as if their own toxic gluttony*
> *was not their fault.*"

Gamache listened to the poem, one of his favorites. He looked across at the bistro, dark and empty on a night when it should have been alive with villagers.

Was Ruth right? Had someone chosen the bistro on purpose? But that meant Olivier was somehow implicated. Had he brought this on himself? Who in the village hated the tramp enough to kill him, and Olivier enough to do it there? Or was the tramp merely a convenient tool? A poor man in the wrong place? Used as a weapon against Olivier?

"Who do you think would want to do this to Olivier?" he asked Ruth.

She shrugged, then turned to leave. He watched her take her place among her friends, all of them moving in ways familiar to each other, and now to him.

And to the killer?

EIGHT

 The meal was winding down. They'd dined on corn on the cob and sweet butter, fresh vegetables from Peter and Clara's garden and a whole salmon barbecued over charcoal. The guests chatted amicably as warm bread was passed and salad served.

Myrna's exuberant arrangement of hollyhock, sweet pea and phlox sat in the center, so that it felt as though they were eating in a garden. Gamache could hear Lacoste asking her dinner companions about the Parras, and then segueing into Old Mundin. The Chief Inspector wondered if they realized they were being interrogated.

Beauvoir was chatting to his neighbors about the Brume County Fair, and visitors. Across the table from Beauvoir sat Ruth, glaring at him. Gamache wondered why, though with Ruth that was pretty much her only form of expression.

Gamache turned to Peter, who was serving arugula, frizzy lettuce and fresh ripe tomatoes.

"I hear the old Hadley house has been sold. Have you met the new owners?"

Peter passed him the salad bowl of deep-burled wood.

"We have. The Gilberts. Marc and Dominique. His mother lives with them too. Came from Quebec City. I think she was a nurse or something. Long retired. Dominique was in advertising in Montreal and Marc was an investment dealer. Made a fortune then retired early before the market went sour."

"Lucky man."

"Smart man," said Peter.

Gamache helped himself to the salad. He could smell the delicate dressing of garlic, olive oil and fresh tarragon. Peter poured them another glass of red wine and handed the bottle down the long table. Gamache watched to see if Peter's comment held a sting, a subtext. By "smart" did Peter mean "shrewd," "cunning," "sly"? But no, Gamache felt Peter meant what he said. It was a compliment. While Peter Morrow rarely insulted anyone, he rarely complimented them either. But he seemed impressed by this Marc Gilbert.

"Do you know them well?"

"Had them around for dinner a few times. Nice couple." For Peter that was an almost effusive comment.

"Interesting that with all that money they'd buy the old Hadley house," said Gamache. "It's been abandoned for a year or more. Presumably they could've bought just about any place around here."

"We were a little surprised as well, but they said they wanted a clean canvas, some place they could make their own. Practically gutted the house, you know. It also has loads of land and Dominique wants horses."

"Roar Parra's been clearing the trails, I hear."

"Slow job."

As he was talking Peter's voice had dropped to a whisper, so that the two men were leaning toward each other like co-conspirators. Gamache wondered what they were conspiring about.

"It's a lot of house for three people. Do they have children?"

"Well, no."

Peter's eyes shifted down the table, then back to Gamache. Whom had he just looked at? Clara? Gabri? It was impossible to say.

"Have they made friends in the community?" Gamache leaned back and spoke in a normal tone, taking a forkful of salad.

Peter looked down the table again and lowered his voice even more. "Not exactly."

Before Gamache could pursue it Peter got up and began clearing the table. At the sink he looked back at his friends, chatting. They were close. So close they could reach out and touch each other, which they occasionally did.

And Peter couldn't. He stood apart, and watched. He missed Ben, who'd once lived in the old Hadley house. Peter had played there as a child. He knew its nooks and crannies. All the scary places where ghosts and spiders lived. But now someone else lived there and had turned it into something else.

Thinking of the Gilberts, Peter could feel his own heart lift a little.

"What're you thinking about?"

Peter started as he realized Armand Gamache was right beside him. "Nothing much."

Gamache took the mixer from Peter's hand and poured whipping cream and a drop of vanilla into the chilled bowl. He turned it on and leaned toward Peter, his voice drowned out by the whirring machine, lost to all but his companion.

"Tell me about the old Hadley house, and the people there."

Peter hesitated but knew Gamache wasn't going to let it go. And this was as discreet as it was going to get. Peter talked, his words whipped and mixed and unintelligible to anyone more than six inches away.

"Marc and Dominique plan to open a luxury inn and spa."

"At the old Hadley house?"

Gamache's astonishment was so complete it almost made Peter laugh. "It's not the same place you remember. You should see it now. It's fantastic."

The Chief Inspector wondered whether a coat of paint and new appliances could exorcise demons, and whether the Catholic Church knew about that.

"But not everyone's happy about it," Peter continued. "They've interviewed a few of Olivier's workers and offered them jobs at higher wages. Olivier's managed to keep most of his staff, but he's had to pay more. The two barely speak."

"Marc and Olivier?" Gamache asked.

"Won't be in the same room."

"That must be awkward, in a small village."

"Not really."

"Then why are we whispering?" Gamache shut the mixer off and spoke in a normal tone. Peter, flustered, looked over at the table again.

"Look, I know Olivier'll get over it, but for now it's just easier not to bring it up."

Peter handed Gamache a shortcake, which he cut in half, and Peter piled sliced ripe strawberries in their own brilliant red juice on top of it.

Gamache noticed Clara getting up and Myrna going with her. Olivier came over and put the coffee on to perk.

"Can I help?" asked Gabri.

"Here, put cream on. The cake, Gabri," said Peter as Gabri approached Olivier with a spoonful of whipped cream. Soon a small conga line of men assembling strawberry shortcakes was formed. When they'd finished they turned around to take the desserts to the table but stopped dead.

There, lit only by candles, was Clara's art. Or at least three large canvases, propped on easels. Gamache felt suddenly light-headed, as though he'd traveled back to the time of Rembrandt, da Vinci, Titian. Where art was viewed either by daylight or candlelight. Was this how the *Mona Lisa* was first seen? The Sistine Chapel? By firelight? Like cave drawings.

He wiped his hands on a dish towel and walked closer to the three easels. He noticed the other guests did the same thing, drawn to the paintings. Around them the candles flickered and threw more light than Gamache had expected, though it was possible Clara's paintings produced their own light.

"I have others, of course, but these'll be the centerpieces of the exhibition at the Galerie Fortin."

But no one was really listening. Instead they were staring at the easels. Some at one, some at another. Gamache stood back for a moment, taking in the scene.

Three portraits, three elderly women, stared back at him.

One was clearly Ruth. The one that had first caught Denis Fortin's eye. The one that had led him to his extraordinary offer of a solo show. The one that had the art world, from Montreal to Toronto, to New York and London, buzzing. About the new talent, the treasure, found buried in Quebec's Eastern Townships.

And there it was, in front of them.

Clara Morrow had painted Ruth as the elderly, forgotten Virgin Mary. Angry, demented, the Ruth in the portrait was full of despair, of bitterness. Of a life left behind, of opportunities squandered, of loss and betrayals real and imagined and created and caused. She clutched at a rough blue shawl with emaciated hands. The shawl had slipped off one bony shoulder and the skin was sagging, like something nailed up and empty.

And yet the portrait was radiant, filling the room from one tiny point of light. In her eyes. Embittered, mad Ruth stared into the distance, at something very far off, approaching. More imagined than real.

Hope.

Clara had captured the moment despair turned to hope. The moment life began. She'd somehow captured Grace.

It took Gamache's breath away and he could feel a burning in his eyes. He blinked and turned from it, as though from something so brilliant it blinded. He saw everyone else in the room also staring, their faces soft in the candlelight.

The next portrait was clearly Peter's mother. Gamache had met her, and once met, never forgotten. Clara had painted her staring straight at the viewer. Not into the distance, like Ruth, but at something very close. Too close. Her white hair in a loose bun, her face a web of soft lines, as though a window had just shattered but not yet fallen. She was white and pink and healthy and lovely. She had a quiet, gentle smile that reached her tender blue eyes. Gamache could almost smell the talcum powder and cinnamon. And yet the portrait made him deeply uneasy. And then he saw it. The subtle turn of her hand, outward. The way her fingers seemed to reach beyond the canvas. At him. He had the impression this gentle, lovely elderly woman was going to touch him. And if she did, he'd know sorrow like never before. He'd know that empty place where nothing existed, not even pain.

She was repulsive. And yet he couldn't help being drawn to her, like a person afraid of heights drawn to the edge.

And the third elderly woman he couldn't place. He'd never seen her before and he wondered if she was Clara's mother. There was something vaguely familiar about her.

He looked at it closely. Clara painted people's souls, and he wanted to know what this soul held.

She looked happy. Smiling over her shoulder at something of great interest. Something she cared about deeply. She too had a shawl, this of old, rough, deep red wool. She seemed someone who was used to riches but suddenly poor. And yet it didn't seem to matter to her.

Interesting, thought Gamache. She was heading in one direction but looking in the other. Behind her. From her he had an overwhelming feeling of yearning. He realized all he wanted to do was draw an armchair up to that portrait, pour a cup of coffee and stare at it for the rest of the evening. For the rest of his life. It was seductive. And dangerous.

With an effort he pulled his eyes away and found Clara standing in the darkness, watching her friends as they looked at her creations.

Peter was also watching. With a look of unmarred pride.

"*Bon Dieu*," said Gabri. "*C'est extraordinaire.*"

"*Félicitations*, Clara," said Olivier. "My God, they're brilliant. Do you have more?"

"Do you mean, have I done you?" she asked with a laugh. "*Non, mon beau.* Only Ruth and Peter's mother."

"Who's this one?" Lacoste pointed to the painting Gamache had been staring at.

Clara smiled. "I'm not telling. You have to guess."

"Is it me?" asked Gabri.

"Yes, Gabri, it's you," said Clara.

"Really?" Too late he saw her smiling.

The funny thing was, thought Gamache, it almost could have been Gabri. He looked again at the portrait in the soft candlelight. Not physically, but emotionally. There was happiness there. But there was also something else. Something that didn't quite fit with Gabri.

"So which one's me?" asked Ruth, limping closer to the paintings.

"You old drunk," said Gabri. "It's this one."

Ruth peered at her exact double. "I don't see it. Looks more like you."

"Hag," muttered Gabri.

"Fag," she mumbled back.

"Clara's painted you as the Virgin Mary," Olivier explained.

Ruth leaned closer and shook her head.

"Virgin?" Gabri whispered to Myrna. "Obviously the mind fucks don't count."

"Speaking of which," Ruth looked over at Beauvoir, "Peter, do you have a piece of paper? I feel a poem coming on. Now, do you think it's too much to put the words 'asshole' and 'shithead' in the same sentence?"

Beauvoir winced.

"Just close your eyes and think of England," Ruth advised Beauvoir, who had actually been thinking of her English.

Gamache walked over to Peter, who continued to stare at his wife's works.

"How are you?"

"You mean, do I want to take a razor to those and slash them to bits, then burn them?"

"Something like that."

It was a conversation they'd had before, as it became clear that Peter might soon have to cede his place as the best artist in the family, in the village, in the province, to his wife. Peter had struggled with it, not always successfully.

"I couldn't hold her back even if I tried," said Peter. "And I don't want to try."

"There's a difference between holding back and actively supporting."

"These are so good even I can't deny it anymore," admitted Peter. "She amazes me."

Both men looked over at the plump little woman looking anxiously at her friends, apparently unaware of the masterpieces she'd created.

"Are you working on something?" Gamache nodded toward the closed door to Peter's studio.

"Always am. It's a log."

"A log?" It was hard to make that sound brilliant. Peter Morrow was one of the most successful artists in the country and he'd gotten there by taking mundane, everyday objects and painting them in excruciating detail. So that they were no longer even recognizable as the object they were. He zoomed in close, then magnified a section, and painted that.

His works looked abstract. It gave Peter huge satisfaction to know they weren't. They were reality in the extreme. So real no one recognized them. And now it was the log's turn. He'd picked it up off the pile beside their fireplace and it was waiting for him in his studio.

The desserts were served, coffee and cognac poured; people wandered about, Gabri played the piano, Gamache kept being drawn to the paintings. Particularly the one of the unknown woman. Looking back. Clara joined him.

"My God, Clara, they're the best works of art ever produced by anyone, anywhere."

"Do you mean it?" she asked in mock earnestness.

He smiled. "They are brilliant, you know. You have nothing to be afraid of."

"If that was true I'd have no art."

Gamache nodded toward the painting he'd been staring at. "Who is she?"

"Oh, just someone I know."

Gamache waited, but Clara was uncharacteristically closed, and he decided it really didn't matter. She wandered off and Gamache continued to stare. And as he did so the portrait changed. Or perhaps, he thought, it was a trick of the uncertain light. But the more he stared the more he got the sense Clara had put something else in the painting. Where Ruth's was of an embittered woman finding hope, this portrait also held the unexpected.

A happy woman seeing in the near and middle distance things that pleased and comforted her. But her eyes seemed to just be focusing on, registering, something else. Something far off. But heading her way.

Gamache sipped his cognac and watched. And gradually it came to him what she was just beginning to feel.

Fear.

NINE

The three Sûreté officers said their good-byes and walked across the village green. It was eleven o'clock and pitch-black. Lacoste and Gamache paused to stare at the night sky. Beauvoir, a few paces ahead as always, eventually realized he was alone and stopped as well. Reluctantly he looked up and was quite surprised to see so many stars. Ruth's parting words came back to him.

"'Jean Guy' and 'bite me' actually rhyme, don't they?"

He was in trouble.

Just then a light went on above Myrna's bookstore, in her loft. They could see her moving about, making herself tea, putting cookies on a plate. Then the light went out. "We just saw her pour a drink and put cookies on a plate," said Beauvoir.

The others wondered why he'd just told them the obvious.

"It's dark. To do anything inside you need light," said Beauvoir.

Gamache thought about this string of obvious statements, but it was Lacoste who got there first.

"The bistro, last night. Wouldn't the murderer need to put on the lights? And if he did, wouldn't someone have seen?"

Gamache smiled. They were right. A light at the bistro must have been noticed.

He looked around to see which houses were the most likely to have seen anything. But the homes fanned out from the bistro like wings. None would have a perfect view, except the place directly opposite. He turned to look. The three majestic pines on the village green were there. They'd have seen a man take another man's life. But there was something else directly opposite the bistro. Opposite and above.

The old Hadley house. It was a distance away, but at night, with a light on in the bistro, it was just possible the new owners could have witnessed a murder.

"There's another possibility," said Lacoste. "That the murderer didn't put the lights on. He'd know he could be seen."

"He'd use a flashlight, you mean?" asked Beauvoir, imagining the murderer in there the night before, waiting for his victim, turning a flashlight on to make his way around.

Lacoste shook her head. "That could also be seen from outside. He wouldn't want to risk even that, I think."

"So he'd leave the lights off," said Gamache, knowing where this was leading. "Because he wouldn't need lights. He'd know his way around in the dark."

The next morning dawned bright and fresh. There was some warmth in the sun again and Gamache soon took off his sweater as he walked around the village green before breakfast. A few children, up before parents and grandparents, did some last-minute frog hunting in the pond. They ignored him and he was happy to watch them from a distance then continue his solitary and peaceful stroll. He waved at Myrna, cresting the hill on her own solitary walk.

This was the last day of summer vacation, and while it had been decades since he'd gone to school, he still felt the tug. The mix of sadness at the end of summer, and excitement to see his chums again. The new clothes, bought after a summer's growth. The new pencils, sharpened over and over, and the smell of the shavings. And the new notebooks. Always strangely thrilling. Unmarred. No mistakes yet. All they held was promise and potential.

A new murder investigation felt much the same. Had they marred their books yet? Made any mistakes?

As he slowly circled the village green, his hands clasped behind his back and his gaze far off, he thought about that. After a few leisurely circuits he went inside to breakfast.

Beauvoir and Lacoste were already down, with frothy *café au lait* in front of them. They stood up as he entered the room, and he motioned them down. The aroma of maple-cured back bacon and eggs and coffee came from the kitchen. He'd barely sat down when Gabri

swept out of the kitchen with plates of eggs Benedict, fruit and muffins.

"Olivier's just left for the bistro. He's not sure if he'll open today,"
said the large man, who looked and sounded a great deal like Julia Child
that morning. "I told him he should, but we'll see. I pointed out he'd lose
money if he didn't. That usually does the trick. Muffin?"

"*S'il vous plaît*," said Isabelle Lacoste, taking one. They looked like
nuclear explosions. Isabelle Lacoste missed her children and her husband. But it amazed her how this small village seemed able to heal even
that hole. Of course, if you stuff in enough muffins even the largest hole
is healed, for a while. She was willing to try.

Gabri brought Gamache his *café au lait* and when he left Beauvoir
leaned forward.

"What's the plan for today, Chief?"

"We need background checks. I want to know all about Olivier, and I
want to know who might have a grudge against him."

"*D'accord*," said Lacoste.

"And the Parras. Make inquiries, here and in the Czech Republic."

"Will do," said Beauvoir. "And you?"

"I have an appointment with an old friend."

Armand Gamache climbed the hill leading out of Three Pines. He carried his tweed jacket over his arm and kicked a chestnut ahead of him.
The air smelled of apples, sweet and warm on the trees. Everything was
ripe, lush, but in a few weeks there'd be a killing frost. And it would all
be gone.

As he walked the old Hadley house grew larger and larger. He steeled
himself against it. Prepared for the waves of sorrow that rolled from it,
flowing over and into anyone foolish enough to get close.

But either his defenses were better than he'd expected, or something
had changed.

Gamache stopped in a spot of sunshine and faced the house. It was a
rambling Victorian trophy home, turreted, shingles like scales, wide
swooping verandas and black wrought-iron rails. Its fresh paint gleamed
in the sun and the front door was a cheery glossy red. Not like blood,
but like Christmas. And cherries. And crisp autumn apples. The path
had been cleared of brambles and solid flagstones laid. He noticed the

hedges had been clipped and the trees trimmed, the deadwood removed. Roar Parra's work.

And Gamache realized, to his surprise, that he was standing outside the old Hadley house with a smile. And was actually looking forward to going inside.

The door was opened by a woman in her mid-seventies.

"*Oui?*"

Her hair was steel gray and nicely cut. She wore almost no makeup, just a little around the eyes, which looked at him now with curiosity, then recognition. She smiled and opened the door wider.

Gamache offered her his identification. "I'm sorry to bother you, madame, but my name is Armand Gamache. I'm with the Sûreté du Québec."

"I recognize you, monsieur. Please, come in. I'm Carole Gilbert."

Her manner was friendly and gracious as she showed him into the vestibule. He'd been there before. Many times. But it was almost unrecognizable. Like a skeleton that had been given new muscles and sinew and skin. The structure was there, but all else had changed.

"You know the place?" she asked, watching him.

"I knew it," he said, swinging his eyes to hers. She met his look steadily, but without challenge. As a chatelaine would, confident in her place and without need to prove it. She was friendly and warm, and very, very observant, Gamache guessed. What had Peter said? She'd been a nurse once? A very good one, he presumed. The best ones were observant. Nothing got past them.

"It's changed a great deal," he said and she nodded, drawing him farther into the house. He wiped his feet on the area rug protecting the gleaming wooden floor and followed her. The vestibule opened into a large hall with crisp new black and white tiles on the floor. A sweeping staircase faced them and archways led through to various rooms. When he'd last been here it had been a ruin, fallen into disrepair. It had seemed as though the house, disgusted, had turned on itself. Pieces were thrown off, wallpaper hung loose, floorboards heaved, ceilings warped. But now a huge cheerful bouquet sat on a polished table in the center of the hall, filling it with fragrance. The walls were painted a sophisticated tawny color, between beige and gray. It was bright and warm and elegant. Like the woman in front of him.

"We're still working on the house," she said, leading him through the archway to their right, down a couple of steps and into the large living room. "I say 'we' but it's really my son and daughter-in-law. And the workers, of course."

She said it with a small self-deprecating laugh. "I was foolish enough to ask if I could do anything the other day and they gave me a hammer and told me to put up some drywall. I hit a water pipe and an electrical cord."

Her laugh was so unguarded and infectious Gamache found himself laughing too.

"Now I make tea. They call me the tea lady. Tea?"

"*Merci, madame*, that would be very nice."

"I'll tell Marc and Dominique you're here. It's about that poor man in the bistro, I presume?"

"It is."

She seemed sympathetic, but not concerned. As though it had nothing to do with her. And Gamache found himself hoping it didn't.

As he waited he looked around the room and drifted toward the floor-to-ceiling windows, where sun streamed in. The room was comfortably furnished with sofas and chairs that looked inviting. They were upholstered in expensive fabrics giving them a modern feel. A couple of Eames chairs framed the fireplace. It was an easy marriage of contemporary and old world. Whoever had decorated this room had an eye for it.

The windows were flanked by tailored silk curtains that touched the hardwood floor. Gamache suspected the curtains were almost never closed. Why shut out that view?

It was spectacular. From its position on the hill the house looked over the valley. He could see the Rivière Bella Bella wind its way through the village and out around the next mountain toward the neighboring valley. The trees at the top of the mountain were changing color. It was autumn up there already. Soon the reds and auburns and pumpkin oranges would march down the slopes until the entire forest was ablaze. And what a vantage point to see it all. And more.

Standing at the window he could see Ruth and Rosa walking around the village green, the old poet tossing either stale buns or rocks at the other birds. He could see Myrna working in Clara's vegetable garden and Agent Lacoste walking over the stone bridge toward their makeshift Incident Room in the old railway station. He watched as she stopped on the bridge and looked into the gently flowing water. He wondered what she was thinking. Then she moved on. Other villagers were out doing their morning errands, or working in their gardens, or sitting on their porches reading the paper and drinking coffee.

From there he could see everything. Including the bistro.

Agent Paul Morin had arrived before Lacoste and was standing outside the railway station, making notes.

"I was thinking about the case last night," he said, watching her unlock the door then following her into the chilly, dark room. She flipped on the lights and walked over to her desk. "I think the murderer must've turned on the lights of the bistro, don't you? I tried walking around my house at two o'clock this morning, and I couldn't see anything. It was pitch-black. In the city you might get streetlights through the window, but not out here. How'd he know who he was killing?"

"I suppose if he'd invited the victim there, then it was pretty clear. He'd kill the only other person in the bistro."

"I realize that," said Morin, drawing his chair up to her desk. "But murder's a serious business. You don't want to get it wrong. It was a massive hit to the head, right?"

Lacoste typed her password into her computer. Her husband's name. Morin was so busy consulting his notes and talking she was sure he hadn't noticed.

"I don't think that's as easy as it looks," he continued, earnestly. "I tried it last night too. Hit a cantaloupe with a hammer."

Now he had her full attention. Not only because she wanted to know what had happened, but because anyone who'd get up at two in the morning to smack a melon in the dark deserved attention. Perhaps even medical attention.

"And?"

"The first time I just grazed it. Had to hit it a few times before I got it just right. Pretty messy."

Morin wondered, briefly, what his girlfriend would think when she got up and noticed the fruit with holes smashed in it. He'd left a note, but wasn't sure that helped.

I did this, he'd written. *Experimenting.*

He perhaps should have been more explicit.

But the significance wasn't lost on Agent Lacoste. She leaned back in her chair and thought. Morin had the brains to be quiet.

"So what do you think?" she finally asked.

"I think he must have turned the lights on. But it'd be risky." Morin seemed dissatisfied. "It doesn't make sense to me. Why kill him in the bistro when you have thick forests just feet away? You could slaughter tons of people in there and no one would notice. Why do it where the body would be found and you could be seen?"

"You're right," said Lacoste. "It doesn't make sense. The Chief thinks it might have something to do with Olivier. Maybe the murderer chose the bistro on purpose."

"To implicate him?"

"Or to ruin his business."

"Maybe it was Olivier himself," said Morin. "Why not? He'd be just about the only one who could find his way around without lights. He had a key to the place—"

"Everyone had a key to the place. Seems there were sets floating all over the township, and Olivier kept one under the urn at the front door," said Lacoste.

Morin nodded and didn't seem surprised. It was still the country way, at least in the smaller villages.

"He's certainly a main suspect," said Lacoste. "But why would he kill someone in his own bistro?"

"Maybe he surprised the guy. Maybe the tramp broke in and Olivier found him and killed him in a fight," said Morin.

Lacoste was silent, waiting to see if he'd work it all the way through. Morin steepled his hands and leaned his face into them, staring into space. "But it was the middle of the night. If he saw someone in the bistro wouldn't he have called the cops, or at least woken his partner? Olivier Brulé doesn't strike me as the kind of guy who'd grab a baseball bat and rush off alone."

Lacoste exhaled and looked at Agent Morin. If the light was just right, catching this slight young man's face just so, he looked like an idiot. But he clearly wasn't.

"I know Olivier," said Lacoste, "and I'd swear he was stunned by what he'd found. He was in shock. Hard to fake and I'm pretty sure he wasn't faking it. No. When Olivier Brulé woke up yesterday morning he didn't expect to find a body in his bistro. But that doesn't mean he isn't involved somehow. Even unwittingly. The Chief wants us to find out more about Olivier. Where he was born, his background, his family, his schools, what he did before coming here. Anyone who might have a grudge against him. Someone he pissed off."

"This is more than being pissed off."

"How do you know?" asked Lacoste.

"Well, I get pissed off, and I don't kill people."

"No, you don't. But I presume you're fairly well balanced, except for that melon incident." She smiled and he reddened. "Look, it's a huge mistake to judge others by ourselves. One of the first things you learn with Chief Inspector Gamache is that other people's reactions aren't ours. And a murderer's are even more foreign. This case didn't begin with the blow to the head. It started years ago, with another sort of blow. Something happened to our murderer, something we might consider insignificant, trivial even, but was devastating to him. An event, a snub, an argument that most people would shrug off. Murderers don't. They ruminate; they gather and guard resentments. And those resentments grow. Murders are about emotions. Emotions gone bad and gone wild. Remember that. And don't ever think you know what someone else is thinking, never mind feeling."

It was the first lesson she'd been taught by Chief Inspector Gamache, and the first one she'd now passed on to her own protégé. To find a murderer you followed clues, yes. But you also followed emotions. The ones that stank, the foul and putrid ones. You followed the slime. And there, cornered, you'd find your quarry.

There were other lessons, lots of others. And she'd teach him them as well.

That's what she'd been thinking on the bridge. Thinking and worrying about. Hoping she'd be able to pass to this young man enough wisdom, enough of the tools necessary to catch a killer.

"Nathaniel," said Morin, getting up and going over to his own computer. "Your husband's name or your son's?"

"Husband," said Lacoste, a little nonplussed. He'd seen after all.

The phone rang. It was the coroner. She had to speak to Chief Inspector Gamache urgently.

TEN

 At the Chief Inspector's request Marc and Dominique Gilbert were giving him a tour of their home, and now they stood in front of a room Gamache knew well. It had been the master bedroom of the old Hadley house, Timmer Hadley's room.

Two murders had happened there.

Now he looked at the closed door, with its fresh coat of gleaming white paint, and wondered what lay beyond. Dominique swung the door open and sunlight poured out. Gamache couldn't hide his surprise.

"Quite a change," said Marc Gilbert, clearly pleased with his reaction.

The room was, quite simply, stunning. They'd removed all the fretwork and googahs added over the generations. The ornate moldings, the dark mantel, the velvet drapes that kept the light at bay with their weight of dust and dread and Victorian reproach. All gone. The heavy, foreboding four-poster bed was gone.

They'd taken the room back to its basic structure, clean lines that showed off its gracious proportions. The curtains had wide stripes of of sage and gray and let the light stream through. Along the top of each of the large windows was a lintel of stained glass. Original. More than a century old. It spilled playful colors into the room. The floors, newly stained, glowed. The king-size bed had an upholstered headboard and simple, fresh, white bed linen. A fire was laid in the hearth, ready for the first guest.

"Let me show you the en suite," said Dominique.

She was tall and willowy. Mid-forties, Gamache thought, she wore jeans, a simple white shirt and her blonde hair loose. She had an air of quiet confidence and well-being. Her hands were flecked with white paint and her nails cut short.

Beside her Marc Gilbert smiled, happy to be showing off their creation. And Gamache, of all people, knew this resurrection of the old Hadley house was an act of creation.

Marc was also tall, over six feet. Slightly taller than Gamache, and about twenty pounds lighter. His hair was short, almost shaved, and it looked as though if he grew it in he'd be balding. His eyes were a piercing, buoyant blue and his manner welcoming and energetic. But while his wife was relaxed there was something edgy about Marc Gilbert. Not nervous so much as needy.

He wants my approval, thought Gamache. Not unusual really when showing off a project this important to them. Dominique pointed out the features of the bathroom, with its aqua mosaic-glass tiles, spa bath and separate walk-in shower. She was proud of their work, but she didn't seem to need him to exclaim over it.

Marc did.

It was easy to give him what he wanted. Gamache was genuinely impressed.

"And we just put this door in last week," said Marc. Opening a door from the bathroom they stepped onto a balcony. It looked out over the back of the house, across the gardens and a field beyond.

Four chairs were drawn around a table.

"I thought you could use these," a voice said from behind them and Marc hurried to take the tray from his mother. On it were four glasses of iced tea and some scones.

"Shall we?" Dominique indicated the table and Gamache held a chair for Carole.

"*Merci*," the older woman said, and sat.

"To second chances," said the Chief Inspector. He lifted his iced tea and as they toasted he watched them. The three people who'd been drawn to this sad, violated, derelict house. Who'd given it new life.

And the house had returned the favor.

"Well, there's more to do," said Marc. "But we're getting there."

"We're hoping to have our first guests by Thanksgiving," said Dominique. "If Carole would just get off her *derrière* and do some work. But so far she's refused to dig the fence posts or pour concrete."

"Perhaps this afternoon," said Carole Gilbert with a laugh.

"I noticed some antiques. Did you bring them from your home?" Gamache asked her.

Carole nodded. "We combined our belongings, but there was still a lot to buy."

"From Olivier?"

"Some." It was the most curt answer he'd received so far. He waited for more.

"We got a lovely rug from him," said Dominique. "The one in the front hall, I think."

"No, it's in the basement," said Marc, his voice sharp. He tried to soften it with a smile, but it didn't quite work.

"And a few chairs, I think," said Carole, quickly.

That would account for about one one-hundredth of the furnishings in the rambling old place. Gamache sipped his tea, looking at the three of them.

"We picked up the rest in Montreal," said Marc. "On rue Notre Dame. Do you know it?"

Gamache nodded and then listened as Marc described their treks up and down the famed street, which was packed with antique shops. Some were not much more than junk shops but some contained real finds, near priceless antiques.

"Old Mundin's repairing a few items we picked up in garage sales. Don't tell the guests," said Dominique with a laugh.

"Why didn't you get more from Olivier?"

The women concentrated on their scones and Marc poked at the ice in his drink.

"We found his prices a little high, Chief Inspector," said Dominique at last. "We'd have preferred to buy from him, but . . ."

It was left hanging, and still Gamache waited. Eventually Marc spoke.

"We were going to buy tables and beds from him. Made all the arrangements, then discovered he'd charged us almost double what he'd originally asked for them."

"Now, Marc, we don't know that for sure," said his mother.

"Near enough. Anyway, we canceled the order. You can imagine how that went down."

Dominique had been silent for most of this exchange. Now she spoke.

"I still think we should have paid it, or spoken to him quietly about it. He is our neighbor, after all."

"I don't like being screwed," said Marc.

"No one does," said Dominique, "but there are ways of handling it. Maybe we should have just paid. Now look what's happened."

"What's happened?" asked Gamache.

"Well, Olivier's one of the forces in Three Pines," said Dominique. "Piss him off and you pay a price. We don't really feel comfortable going into the village, and we sure don't feel welcome in the bistro."

"I hear you approached some of Olivier's staff," said Gamache.

Marc colored. "Who told you that? Did Olivier?" he snapped.

"Is it true?"

"What if it is? He pays them practically slave wages."

"Did any agree to come?"

Marc hesitated then admitted they hadn't. "But only because he increased their pay. We at least did that for them."

Dominique had been watching this, uncomfortable, and now she took her husband's hand. "I'm sure they were also loyal to Olivier. They seem to like him."

Marc snorted and clamped down on his anger. A man, Gamache realized, ill-equipped for not getting his own way. His wife, at least, appreciated how all this might look and had tried to appear reasonable.

"Now he's bad-mouthed us to the whole village," said Marc, not letting it go.

"They'll come around," said Carole, looking at her son with concern. "That artist couple have been nice."

"Peter and Clara Morrow," said Dominique. "Yes. I like them. She says she'd like to ride, once the horses arrive."

"And when will that be?" asked Gamache.

"Later today."

"*Vraiment?* That must be fun for you. How many?"

"Four," said Marc. "Thoroughbreds."

"Actually, I believe you've changed that slightly, haven't you?" Carole turned to her daughter-in-law.

"Really? I thought you wanted thoroughbreds," said Marc to Dominique.

"I did, but then I saw some hunters and thought since we lived in the country that seemed appropriate." She looked at Gamache once again. "Not that I plan to hunt. It's a breed of horse."

"Used for jumping," he said.

"You ride?"

"Not at that level, but I enjoyed it. Haven't been on a horse in years now."

"You'll have to come," said Carole, though they all knew he almost certainly wasn't going to squeeze himself into a pair of jodhpurs and climb onto a hunter. But he did smile as he imagined what Gabri would make of that invitation.

"What're their names?" asked Marc.

Dominique hesitated and her mother-in-law jumped in. "It's so hard to remember, isn't it? But wasn't one called Thunder?"

"Yes, that's right. Thunder, Trooper, Trojan and what was the other one?" She turned back to Carole.

"Lightning."

"Really? Thunder and Lightning?" asked Marc.

"Brothers," said Dominique.

Their iced teas finished and the scones only crumbs they got to their feet and walked back into the house.

"Why did you move here?" Gamache asked, as they walked down to the main floor.

"*Pardon?*" asked Dominique.

"Why did you move to the country and to Three Pines in particular? It's not exactly easy to find."

"We like that."

"You don't want to be found?" asked Gamache. His voice held humor, but his eyes were sharp.

"We wanted peace and quiet," said Carole.

"We wanted a challenge," said her son.

"We wanted a change. Remember?" Dominique turned to her husband then back to Gamache. "We both had fairly high-powered jobs in Montreal, but were tired. Burned out."

"That's not really true," protested Marc.

"Well, pretty close. We couldn't go on. Didn't want to go on."

She left it at that. She could understand Marc's not wanting to admit what'd happened. The insomnia, the panic attacks. Having to pull the car over on the Ville Marie Expressway to catch his breath. Having to pry his hands off the steering wheel. He was losing his grip.

Day after day he'd gone into work like that. Weeks, months. A year. Until he'd finally admitted to Dominique how he felt. They'd gone away for a weekend, their first in years, and talked.

While she wasn't having panic attacks, she was feeling something else. A growing emptiness. A sense of futility. Each morning she woke up and had to convince herself that what she did mattered. Advertising.

It was a harder and harder sell.

Then Dominique had remembered something long buried and forgotten. A dream since childhood. To live in the country and have horses.

She'd wanted to run an inn. To welcome people, to mother them. They had no children of their own, and she had a powerful need to nurture. So they'd left Montreal, left the demands of jobs too stressful, of lives too callow. They'd come to Three Pines, with their bags of money, to heal first themselves. Then others.

They'd certainly healed this wound of a house.

"We saw an ad for this place in the *Gazette* one Saturday, drove down and bought it," said Dominique.

"You make it sound simple," said Gamache.

"It was, really, once we decided what we wanted."

And looking at her, Gamache could believe it. She knew something powerful, something most people never learned. That people made their own fortune.

It made her formidable.

"And you, madame?" Gamache turned to Carole Gilbert.

"Oh, I've been retired for a while."

"In Quebec City, I understand."

"That's correct. I quit work and moved there after my husband died."

"*Désolé.*"

"No need to be. It was many years ago. But when Marc and Dominique invited me here I thought it sounded like fun."

"You were a nurse? That will come in handy in a spa."

"I hope not," she laughed. "Not planning on hurting people, are you?" she asked Dominique. "God help anyone who asks for my help."

They strolled once more into the living room and the Chief Inspector stopped by the floor-to-ceiling windows, then turned into the room.

"Thank you for the tour. And the tea. But I do have some questions for you."

"About the murder in the bistro," said Marc, and stepped slightly closer to his wife. "It seems so out of character for this village, to have a murder."

"You'd think so, wouldn't you?" said Gamache, and wondered if anyone had told them the history of their own home. Probably wasn't in the real estate agent's description.

"Well, to begin with, have you seen any strangers around?"

"Everyone's a stranger," said Carole. "We know most of the villagers by now, at least to nod to, but this weekend the place is filled with people we've never seen."

"This man would be hard to miss; he'd have looked like a tramp, a vagrant."

"No, I haven't seen anyone like that," said Marc. "Mama, have you?"

"Nobody."

"Where were you all on Saturday night and early Sunday morning?"

"Marc, I think you went to bed first. He usually does. Dominique and I watched the *Téléjournal on Radio-Canada* then went up."

"About eleven, wouldn't you think?" Dominique asked.

"Did any of you get up in the night?"

"I did," said Carole. "Briefly. To use the washroom."

"Why're you asking us this?" Dominique asked. "The murder happened down in the bistro. It has nothing to do with us."

Gamache turned around and pointed out the window. "That's why I'm asking."

They looked. Down in the village a few cars were being packed up. People were hugging, reluctant children were being called off the village green. A young woman was walking briskly up rue du Moulin, in their direction.

"You're the only place in Three Pines with a view over the whole village, and the only place with a direct view into the bistro. If the murderer turned on the lights, you'd have seen."

"Our bedrooms are at the back," Dominique pointed out. Gamache had already noted this in the tour.

"True. But I was hoping one of you might suffer from insomnia."

"Sorry, Chief Inspector. We sleep like the dead here."

Gamache didn't mention that the dead in the old Hadley house had never rested well.

The doorbell rang just then and the Gilberts started slightly, not expecting anyone. But Gamache was. He'd noted Agent Lacoste's progress round the village green and up rue du Moulin.

Something had happened.

"May I see you in private?" Isabelle Lacoste asked the Chief after she'd been introduced. The Gilberts took the cue. After watching them disappear Agent Lacoste turned to Gamache.

"The coroner called. The victim wasn't killed in the bistro."

ELEVEN

Myrna knocked softly on the bistro door, then opened it.

"You okay?" she asked softly into the dim light. It was the first time since she'd lived in Three Pines she'd seen the bistro dark during the day. Even at Christmas Olivier opened.

Olivier was sitting in an armchair, staring. He looked over at her and smiled.

"I'm fine."

"Ruth's FINE? Fucked up, Insecure, Neurotic and Egotistical?"

"That's about right."

Myrna sat across from him and offered a mug of tea she'd brought from her bookshop. Strong, hot, with milk and sugar. Red Rose. Nothing fancy.

"Like to talk?"

She sat quietly, watching her friend. She knew his face, had seen the tiny changes over the years. The crow's-feet appear at his eyes, the fine blond hair thin. What hadn't changed, from what she could tell, was what was invisible, but even more obvious. His kind heart, his thoughtfulness. He was the first to bring soup to anyone ill. To visit in the hospital. To read out loud to someone too weak and tired and near the end to do it for themselves. Gabri, Myrna, Clara, they all organized villagers to help, and when they arrived they'd find Olivier already there.

And now it was their turn to help him.

"I don't know if I want to open again."

Myrna sipped her tea and nodded. "That's understandable. You've been hurt. It must've been a terrible shock to see him here. I know it was for me, and it's not my place."

You have no idea, thought Olivier. He didn't say anything, but stared out the window. He saw Chief Inspector Gamache and Agent Lacoste walking down rue du Moulin from the old Hadley house. He prayed they kept going. Didn't come in here. With their keen eyes and sharp questions.

"I wonder if I should just sell. Move on."

This surprised Myrna, but she didn't show it. "Why?" she asked, softly.

He shook his head and dropped his eyes to his hands, resting in his lap.

"Everything's changing. Everything's changed. Why can't it be like it always was? They took my fireplace pokers, you know. I think Gamache thinks I did it."

"I'm sure he doesn't. Olivier, look at me." She spoke forcefully to him. "It doesn't matter what he thinks. We know the truth about you. And you need to know something about us. We love you. Do you think we come here every day for the food?"

He nodded and smiled slightly. "You mean it wasn't for the croissants? The red wine? Not even the chocolate torte?"

"Well, yes, okay. Maybe the torte. Listen, we come here because of you. You're the attraction. We love you, Olivier."

Olivier raised his eyes to hers. He hadn't realized, until that moment, that he'd always been afraid their affection was conditional. He was the owner of the bistro, the only one in town. They liked him for the atmosphere and welcome. The food and drink. That was the boundary of their feelings for him. They liked him for what he gave to them. Sold to them.

Without the bistro, he was nothing to them.

How'd Myrna know something he hadn't even admitted to himself? As he looked at her she smiled. She was wearing her usual flamboyant caftan. For her birthday coming up Gabri had made her a winter caftan, out of flannel. Olivier imagined her in it in her store. A big, warm ball of flannel.

The world, which had been closing in on him for days, released a bit of its grip.

"We're going to the Brume County Fair. Last day. What do you say? Can we interest you in cotton candy, cream soda, and a bison burger? I hear Wayne's showing his litter of suckling pigs this afternoon. I know how you love a good piglet."

Once, just once, at the annual county fair he'd hurried them over to the pig stalls to look at the babies. And now he was the piglet guy. Still, he quite liked being thought of as that. And it was true, he loved pigs. He had a lot in common with them, he suspected. But he shook his head.

"Not up to it, I'm afraid. But you go along. Bring me back a stuffed animal."

"Would you like company here? I can stay."

And he knew she meant it. But he needed to be alone.

"Thanks, but I really am Fucked up, Insecure, Neurotic and Egotistical."

"Well, as long as you're fine," said Myrna, getting up. After years as a psychologist she knew how to listen to people. And how to leave them alone.

He watched through the window as Myrna, Peter, Clara, Ruth and the duck Rosa got in the Morrows' car. They waved at him and he waved merrily back. Myrna didn't wave. She just nodded. He dropped his hand, caught her eye, and nodded.

He believed her when she'd said they loved him. But he also knew they loved a man who didn't exist. He was a fiction. If they knew the real Olivier they'd kick him out, of their lives and probably the village.

As their car chugged up the hill toward the Brume County Fair he heard the words again. From the cabin hidden in the woods. He could smell the wood smoke, the dried herbs. And he could see the Hermit. Whole. Alive. Afraid.

And he heard again the story. That wasn't, Olivier knew, just a story.

Once upon a time a Mountain King watched over a treasure. He buried it deep and it kept him company for millennia. The other gods were jealous and angry, and warned him if he didn't share his treasure with them they'd do something terrible.

But the Mountain King was the mightiest of the gods, so he simply laughed knowing there was nothing they could do to him. No attack he couldn't repulse, and redouble onto them. He was invincible. He prepared for their attack. Waited for it. But it never came.

Nothing came. Ever.

Not a missile, not a spear, not a war horse, or rider, or dog, or bird. Not a seed in the wind. Not even the wind.

Nothing. Ever. Again.

It was the silence that got to him first, and then the touch. Nothing touched him. No breeze brushed his rocky surface. No ant crawled over him, no bird touched down. No worm tunneled.

He felt nothing.

Until one day a young man came.

Olivier brought himself back to the bistro, his body tense, his muscles strained. His fingernails biting into his palms.

Why, he asked himself for the millionth time. Why had he done it?

Before leaving to see the coroner, the Chief Inspector walked over to the large piece of paper tacked to the wall of their Incident Room. In bold red letters Inspector Beauvoir had written:

WHO WAS THE VICTIM?

WHY WAS HE KILLED?

WHO KILLED HIM?

WHAT WAS THE MURDER WEAPON?

With a sigh the Chief Inspector added two more lines.

WHERE WAS HE MURDERED?

WHY WAS HE MOVED?

So far in their investigation they'd found more questions than clues. But that's where answers came from. Questions. Gamache was perplexed, but not dissatisfid.

Jean Guy Beauvoir was already waiting for him when he arrived at the Cowansville hospital, and they went in together, down the stairs and into the basement, where files and dead people were kept.

"I called as soon as I realized what I was seeing," said Dr. Harris after greeting them. She led them into the sterile room, brightly lit by fluorescents. The dead man was naked on a steel gurney. Gamache wished they'd put a blanket over him. He seemed cold. And, indeed, he was.

"There was some internal bleeding but not enough. This wound," she indicated the collaped back of the victim's head, "would have bled onto whatever surface he fell on."

"There was almost no blood on the floor of the bistro," said Beauvoir.

"He was killed somewhere else," said the coroner, with certainty.

"Where?" asked Gamache.

"Would you like an address?"

"If you wouldn't mind," said the Chief Inspector, with a smile.

Dr. Harris smiled back. "Clearly I don't know, but I've found some things that might be suggestive."

She walked over to her lab table where a few vials sat, labeled. She handed one to the Chief Inspector.

"Remember that bit of white I said was in the wound? I thought it might be ash. Or bone, or perhaps even dandruff. Well, it wasn't any of those things."

Gamache needed his glasses to see the tiny white flake inside the vial, then he read the label.

Paraffin, found in the wound.

"Paraffin? Like wax?"

"Yes, it's commonly called paraffin wax. It's an old-fashioned material, as you probably know. Used to be used for candles, then it was replaced by other sorts of more stable wax."

"My mother uses it for pickling," said Beauvoir. "She melts it on the top of the jar to create a seal, right?"

"That's right," said Dr. Harris.

Gamache turned to Beauvoir. "And where was your mother on Saturday night?"

Beauvoir laughed. "The only one she ever threatens to brain is me. She's no threat to society at large."

Gamache handed the vial back to the coroner. "Do you have any theories?"

"It was buried deep enough in the wound to have been either on the man's head before he was killed or on the murder weapon."

"A jar of pickles?" asked Beauvoir.

"Stranger things have been used," said Gamache, though he couldn't quite think of any.

Beauvoir shook his head. Had to be an Anglo. Who else could turn a dill pickle into a weapon?

"So it wasn't a fireplace poker?" asked Gamache.

"Unless it was a very clean one. There was no evidence of ash. Just that." She nodded to the vial. "There's something else." Dr. Harris pulled a lab chair up to the bench. "On the back of his clothes we found this. Very faint, but there."

She handed Gamache the lab report and pointed to a line. Gamache read.

"Acrylic polyurethane and aluminum oxide. What is that?"

"Varathane," said Beauvoir. "We've just redone our floors. It's used to seal them after they've been sanded."

"Not just floors," said Dr. Harris, taking back the vial. "It's used in a lot of woodworking. It's a finish. Other than the wound to the head the dead man was in good condition. Could've expected to live for twenty-five or thirty years."

"I see he had a meal a few hours before he was killed," said Gamache, reading the autopsy report

"Vegetarian. Organic I think. I'm having it tested," said the coroner. "A healthy vegetarian meal. Not your usual vagrant dinner."

"Someone might've had him in for dinner then killed him," said Beauvoir.

Dr. Harris hesitated. "I considered that, and it's a possibility."

"But?" said Gamache.

"But he looks like a man who ate like that all the time. Not just the once."

"So either he cooked for himself and chose a healthy diet," said Gamache, "or he had someone cook for him and they were vegetarian."

"That's about it," said the coroner.

"I see no alcohol or drugs," said Beauvoir, scanning the report.

Dr. Harris nodded. "I don't think he was homeless. I'm not sure if anyone cared for this man, but I do know he cared for himself."

What a wonderful epitaph, thought Gamache. He cared for himself.

"Maybe he was a survivalist," said Beauvoir. "You know, one of those kooks who take off from the city and hide in the woods thinking the world's coming to an end."

Gamache turned to look at Beauvoir. That was an interesting thought.

"I'm frankly puzzled," said the coroner. "You can see he was hit with a single, catastrophic blow to the back of his head. That in itself is un-usual. To find just one blow . . ." Dr. Harris's voice trailed off and she shook her head. "Normally when someone gets up the nerve to blud-geon someone to death they're in the grip of great emotion. It's like a brainstorm. They're hysterical and can't stop. You get multiple blows. A single one like this . . ."

"What does it tell you?" Gamache asked, as he stared at the collapsed skull.

"This wasn't just a crime of passion." She turned to him. "There was passion, yes, but there was also planning. Whoever did this was in a rage. But he was in command of that rage."

Gamache lifted his brows. That was rare, extremely rare. And dis-concerting. It would be like trying to master a herd of wild stallions, thundering and rearing, nostrils flared and hooves churning.

Who could control that?

Their murderer could.

Beauvoir looked at the Chief and the Chief looked at Beauvoir. This wasn't good.

Gamache turned back to the cold body on the cold gurney. If he was a survivalist, it hadn't worked. If this man had feared the end of the world he hadn't run far enough, hadn't buried himself deep enough in the Canadian wilderness.

The end of the world had found him.

TWELVE

 Dominique Gilbert stood beside her mother-in-law and looked down the dirt road. Every now and then they had to step aside as a carful of people headed out of Three Pines, to the last day of the fair or into the city early to beat the rush.

It wasn't toward Three Pines they gazed, but away from it. Toward the road that led to Cowansville. And the horses.

It still surprised Dominique that she should have so completely forgotten her childhood dream. Perhaps, though, it wasn't surprising since she'd also dreamed of marrying Keith from the Partridge Family and being discovered as one of the little lost Romanov girls. Her fantasy of having horses disappeared along with all the other unlikely dreams, replaced by board meetings and clients, by gym memberships and increasingly expensive clothing. Until finally her cup, overflowing, had upended and all the lovely promotions and vacations and spa treatments became insubstantial. But at the bottom of that cup filled with goals, objectives, targets, one last drop remained.

Her dream. A horse of her own.

As a girl she'd ridden. With the wind in her hair and the leather reins light in her hands she'd felt free. And safe. The staggering worries of an earnest little girl forgotten.

Years later, when dissatisfaction had turned to despair, when her spirit had grown weary, when she could barely get out of bed in the morning, the dream had reappeared. Like the cavalry, like the Royal Canadian Mounted Police, riding to her rescue.

Horses would save her. Those magnificent creatures who so loved their riders they charged into battle with them, through explosions, through terror, through shrieking men and shrieking weapons. If their rider urged them forward, they went.

Who could not love that?

Dominique had awoken one morning knowing what had to be done. For their sanity. For their souls. They had to quit their jobs, buy a home in the country. And have horses.

As soon as they'd bought the old Hadley house and Roar was working on the barn Dominique had gone to find her horses. She'd spent months researching the perfect breed, the perfect temperaments. The height, weight, color even. Palomino, dapple? All the words from childhood came back. All the pictures torn from calendars and taped to her wall next to Keith Partridge. The black horse with the white socks, the mighty, rearing gray stallion, the Arabian, noble, dignified, strong.

Finally Dominique settled on four magnificent hunters. Tall, shining, two chestnut, a black and one that was all white.

"I hear a truck," said Carole, taking her daughter-in-law's hand and holding it lightly. Like reins.

A truck hove into view. Dominique waved. The truck slowed, then followed her directions into the yard and stopped next to the brand new barn.

Four horses were led from the van, their hooves clunking on the wooden ramp. When they were all standing in the yard the driver walked over to the women, tossing a cigarette onto the dirt and grinding it underfoot.

"You need to sign, madame." He held the clipboard out between them. Dominique reached for it and barely taking her eyes off the horses she signed her name then gave the driver a tip.

He took it then looked from the two bewildered women to the horses.

"You sure you want to keep 'em?"

"I'm sure, thank you," said Dominique with more confidence than she felt. Now that they were actually there, and the dream was a reality, she realized she had no real idea what to do with a horse. Never mind four of them. The driver seemed to sympathize.

"Want me to put them in their stalls?"

"No, that's fine. We can do it. *Merci.*" She wanted him to leave, quickly. To not witness her uncertainty, her bumbling, her ineptness. Dominique Gilbert wasn't used to blundering, but she suspected she was about to become very familiar with it.

The driver reversed the empty van and drove away. Carole turned to Dominique and said, "Well, *ma belle*, I suspect we can't do any worse than their last owners."

As the van headed back to Cowansville they caught a glimpse of the word stenciled on the back door. In bold, black letters, so there could be no doubt. *Abattoir*. Then the two women turned back to the four sorry animals in front of them. Matted, walleyed, swaybacked. Hooves overgrown and coats covered in mud and sores.

"*'Twould ring the bells of Heaven*," whispered Carole.

Dominique didn't know about the bells of Heaven, but her head was ringing. What had she done? She moved forward with a carrot and offered it to the first horse. A broken-down old mare named Buttercup. The horse hesitated, not used to kindness. Then she took a step toward Dominique and with large, eloquent lips she picked the sweet carrot from the hand.

Dominique had canceled her purchase of the magnificent hunters and had decided to buy horses destined for slaughter. If she was expecting them to save her, the very least she could do was save them first.

An hour and a half later Dominique, Carole and the four horses were still standing in front of the barn. But now they'd been joined by a vet.

"Once they're bathed you'll need to rub this into their sores." He handed Dominique a bucket of ointment. "Twice a day, in the morning and at night."

"Can they be ridden?" Carole asked, holding the halter of the largest horse. Privately she suspected it wasn't a horse at all, but a moose. Its name was Macaroni.

"*Mais, oui*. I'd encourage it." He was walking round them again, his large, sure hands going over the sorry beasts. "*Pauvre cheval*," he whispered into the ear of the old mare, Buttercup, her mane almost all fallen out, her tail wispy and her coat bedraggled. "They need exercise, they need good food and water. But mostly they need attention."

The vet was shaking his head as he finished his examinations.

"The good news is there's nothing terminally wrong with them. Left to rot in muddy fields and bitter cold barns. Never groomed. Neglected. But this one." He approached the tall, walleyed dark horse, who shied away. The vet waited and approached again quietly, making soothing sounds until the horse settled. "This one was abused. You can see it." He pointed to the scars on the horse's flanks. "He's afraid. What's his name?"

Dominique consulted the bill from the abattoir, then looked at Carole.

"What is it?" the older woman asked, walking over to read the bill as well. "Oh," she said, then looked at the vet. "Can a horse's name be changed?"

"Normally I'd say yes, but not this one. He needs some continuity. They get used to their names. Why?"

"His name's Marc."

"I've heard worse," said the vet, packing up.

The two women exchanged glances. So far Marc, her husband, not the horse, had no idea Dominique had canceled the hunters in favor of these misfits. He almost certainly wouldn't be happy. She'd been hoping he wouldn't notice, and if she gave them mighty, masculine names like Thunder and Trooper he might not care. But he'd certainly notice a half-blind, scarred and scared old wreck named Marc.

"Ride them as soon as you can," said the vet from his car. "Just walk at first until they get their strength back." He gave the two women a warm smile. "You'll be fine. Don't worry. These are four lucky horses."

And he drove off.

"*Oui*," said Carole, "until we saddle the wrong end."

"I think the saddle goes in the middle," said Dominique.

"*Merde*," said Carole.

The Sûreté was out for blood. If the victim hadn't been murdered in the bistro he was killed somewhere else, and they needed to find the crime scene. Blood, and quite a bit of it, had been spilled. And while the murderer had had two days to clean up, blood stained. Blood stuck. It would be almost impossible to completely erase the evidence of this brutal murder. Every home, every business, every shed, every barn, garage, kennel in and around Three Pines was scoured. Jean Guy Beauvoir coordinated it, sending teams of Sûreté officers throughout the village and into the countryside. He stayed in the Incident Room and received their reports, guiding them, occasionally chastising them, his patience eroding as the negative reports flowed in.

Nothing.

No sign of a murder scene or a murder weapon. Not even at the old Hadley house, whose new floors proved bloodless. The lab tests had come back on Olivier's pokers, confirming neither was the weapon. It was still out there, somewhere.

They did find Guylaine's missing boots, and a root cellar under Monsieur Béliveau's house, long overgrown and abandoned, but still housing pickled beets and cider. There was a squirrel's nest in Ruth's attic, not perhaps surprisingly, and suspicious seeds in Myrna's mudroom that turned out to be hollyhock.

Nothing.

"I'll widen the search area," said Beauvoir to the Chief, over the phone.

"Probably a good idea." But Gamache didn't sound convinced.

Through the receiver Beauvoir could hear bells and music and laughter.

Armand Gamache was at the fair.

The Brume County Fair was more than a century old, bringing people in from all over the townships. Like most fairs it had started as a meeting place for farmers, to show their livestock, to sell their autumn produce, to make deals and see friends. There was judging in one barn and displays of handicraft in another. Baking was for sale in the long aisles of open sheds and children lined up for licorice and maple syrup candy, popcorn and freshly made doughnuts.

It was the last celebration of summer, the bridge into autumn.

Armand Gamache walked past the rides and hawkers, then consulted his watch. It was time. He made for a field to the side of the barns, where a crowd had gathered. For the Wellington Boot Toss.

Standing on the edge of the field he watched as kids and adults lined up. The young man in charge settled them down, gave them each an old rubber boot, and standing well back he raised his arm. And held it there.

The tension was almost unbearable.

Then like an ax he dropped it.

The line of people raised their arms in unison and shot them forward, and to whoops of encouragement from onlookers a storm of Wellington boots was released.

Gamache knew in that instant why he'd gotten such an unexpectedly good spot at the side of the field. At least three boots shot his way.

He turned and hunched his back, instinctively bringing his arm up to protect his head. With a series of thuds the boots landed around him, but not on him.

The young man in charge ran over.

"You okay?"

He had curly brown hair that shone auburn in the sun. His face was tanned and his eyes a deep blue. He was stunningly handsome, and pissed off.

"You shouldn't be standing there. I thought for sure you'd move."

Gamache was treated to the look of someone recognizing they were in the presence of immeasurable stupidity.

"*C'était ma faute*," admitted Gamache. "Sorry. I'm looking for Old Mundin."

"That's me."

Gamache stared at the flushed and handsome young man.

"And you're Chief Inspector Gamache." He stuck out his hand, large and calloused. "I've seen you around Three Pines. Didn't your wife take part in the clog dancing on Canada Day?"

Gamache could barely look away from this young man, so full of vigor and light. He nodded.

"Thought so. I was one of the fiddlers. You're looking for me?"

Behind Old Mundin more people were forming up and looking in his direction. He glanced at them, but seemed relaxed.

"I'd like to talk, when you have a moment."

"Sure. We have a couple more heats, then I can leave. Want to try?"

He offered Gamache one of the boots that had almost brained him.

"What do I do?" asked Gamache as he took the boot and followed Mundin to the line.

"It's a Wellington Boot Toss," said Old Mundin, with a laugh. "I think you can figure it out."

Gamache smiled. This perhaps wasn't his brightest day. He took his place beside Clara and noticed Old Mundin jog down the line to a beautiful young woman and a child who'd be about six. He knelt down and handed the boy a small boot.

"Charles," said Clara. "His son."

Gamache looked again. Charles Mundin was also beautiful. He laughed and turned the wrong way, and with patience his parents got him sorted out. Old Mundin kissed his son and jogged back to the line.

Charles Mundin, Gamache saw, had Down's syndrome.

"Ready?" called Mundin, raising his arm. "Set."

Gamache gripped his boot and glanced down the line at Peter and Clara, staring intently ahead of them.

"Toss!"

Gamache swung up his arm and felt his boot whack his back. Then he sliced forward, losing his grip on the muddy boot. It headed sideways to land about two feet ahead of him and to the side.

Clara's grip, while stronger, didn't last much longer, and her boot went almost straight up into the air.

"Fore!" everyone yelled and as one they reeled back, straining to see as it plunged toward them out of the blinding sun.

It hit Peter. Fortunately it was a tiny, pink child's boot and bounced off him without effect. Behind Gamache, Gabri and Myrna were taking bets how long it would take Clara to come up with an excuse and what it would be.

"Ten dollars on 'The boot was wet,'" said Myrna.

"Nah, she used that last year. How about 'Peter walked into it'?"

"You're on."

Clara and Peter joined them. "Can you believe they gave me a wet boot again?"

Gabri and Myrna hooted with laughter and Clara, smiling broadly, caught Gamache's eye. Money changed hands. She leaned into Gamache and whispered, "Next year I'm saying Peter leaned into it. Put some money down."

"Suppose you don't hit him?"

"But I always do," she said earnestly. "He leans into it, you know."

"I had heard."

Myrna waved across the field to Ruth, limping along with Rosa beside her. Ruth gave her the finger. Charles Mundin, seeing this, waved, giving everyone the finger.

"Ruth doesn't do the Wellington Boot Toss?" asked Gamache.

"Too much like fun," said Peter. "She came to find children's clothing in the craft barn."

"Why?"

"Who knows why Ruth does anything," said Myrna. "Any headway with the investigation?"

"Well, there was one important finding," said Gamache, and everyone crowded even closer around him. Even Ruth limped over. "The coroner says the dead man wasn't killed in the bistro. He was killed somewhere else and taken there."

He could hear the midway clearly now, and hawkers promising huge stuffed toys if you shot a tin duck. Bells jingled to call attention to games and the ring announcer warned people the horse show was about to start. But from his audience there was silence. Until finally Clara spoke.

"That's great news for Olivier, isn't it?"

"You mean it makes him less of a suspect?" said Gamache. "I suppose. But it raises a lot more questions."

"Like how'd the body get into the bistro," said Myrna.

"And where he was killed," said Peter.

"We're searching the village. House by house."

"You're what?" asked Peter. "Without our permission?"

"We have warrants," said Gamache, surprised by Peter's vehement reaction.

"It's still a violation of our privacy. You knew we'd be back, you could've waited."

"I could have, but chose not to. These weren't social calls, and frankly your feelings are secondary."

"Apparently our rights are too."

"That's not accurate." The Chief Inspector spoke firmly. The more heated Peter became the calmer Gamache grew. "We have warrants. Your right to privacy I'm afraid ended when someone took a life in your village. We're not the ones who've violated your rights, the murderer is. Don't forget that. You need to help us, and that means stepping aside and letting us do our work."

"Letting you search our homes," said Peter. "How would you feel?"

"I wouldn't feel good about it either," admitted Gamache. "Who would? But I hope I'd understand. This has just begun, you know. It's going to get worse. And before it's over we'll know where everything is hidden."

He looked sternly at Peter.

Peter saw the closed door into his studio. He imagined Sûreté officers opening it. Flicking on the light switch. Going into his most private space. The place he kept his art. The place he kept his heart. His latest work was in there, under a sheet. Hiding. Away from critical eyes.

But now strangers would have opened that door, lifted that veil and seen it. What would they think?

"So far we haven't found anything, except, I understand, Guylaine's missing boots."

"So you found them," said Ruth. "The old bitch accused me of stealing them."

"They were found in the hedge between her place and yours," said Gamache.

"Imagine that," said Ruth.

Gamache noticed the Mundins standing on the edge of the field, waiting for him. "Excuse me."

He walked briskly to the young couple and their son and joined them as they walked to the stall Old Mundin had set up. It was full of furniture, hand made. A person's choices were always revealing, Gamache found. Mundin chose to make furniture, fine furniture. Gamache's educated eye skimmed the tables, cabinets and chairs. This was painstaking, meticulous work. All the joints dovetailed together without nails; the details were beautifully inlaid, the finishes smooth. Faultless. Work like this took time and patience. And the young carpenter could never, ever be paid what these tables, chairs, dressers were worth.

And yet Old Mundin chose to do it anyway. Unusual for a young man these days.

"How can we help?" The Wife asked, smiling warmly. She had very dark hair, cut short to her head, and large, thoughtful, eyes. Her clothing was layered and looked both comfortable and bohemian. An earth mother, thought Gamache, married to a carpenter.

"I have a few questions, but tell me about your furniture. It's beautiful."

"*Merci*," said Mundin. "I spend most of the year making pieces to sell at the fair."

Gamache ran his large hand over the smooth surface of a chest of drawers. "Lovely polish. Paraffin?"

"Not unless we want them to burst into flames," laughed Old. "Paraffin's highly flammable."

"Varathane?"

Old Mundin's beautiful face crinkled in a smile. "You are perhaps mistaking us for Ikea. Easy to do," he joked. "No, we use beeswax."

We, thought Gamache. He'd watched this young couple for just a few minutes but it seemed clear they were a team.

"Do you sell much at the fair?" he asked.

"This's all we have left," The Wife said, indicating the few exquisite pieces around them.

"They'll be gone by the end of the fair tonight," said Old Mundin. "Then I need to get going again. Fall's a great time of year to get into the forests and find wood. I do most of my woodwork through the winter."

"I'd like to see your workshop."

"Any time."

"How about now?"

Old Mundin stared at his visitor and Gamache stared back.

"Now?"

"Is that a problem?"

"Well . . ."

"It's okay, Old," said The Wife. "I'll watch the booth. You go."

"Is it okay if we take Charles?" Old asked Gamache. "It's hard for The Wife to watch him and look after customers."

"I insist he comes along," said Gamache, holding out his hand to the boy, who took it without hesitation. A small shard stabbed Gamache's heart as he realized how precious this boy was, and would always be. A child who lived in a perpetual state of trust.

And how hard it would be for his parents to protect him.

"He'll be fine," Gamache assured The Wife.

"Oh, I know he'll be. It's you I worry about," she said.

"I'm sorry," said Gamache, reaching out to shake her hand. "I don't know your name."

"My actual name is Michelle, but everyone calls me The Wife."

Her hand was rough and calloused, like her husband's, but her voice was cultured, full of warmth. It reminded him a little of Reine-Marie's.

"Why?" he asked.

"It started out as a joke between us and then it took. Old and The Wife. It somehow fits."

And Gamache agreed. It did fit this couple, who seemed to live in their own world, with their own beautiful creations.

"Bye." Charles gave his mother the new one-fingered wave.

"Old," she scolded.

"Wasn't me," he protested. But he didn't rat on Ruth, Gamache noticed.

Old strapped his son into the van and they drove out of the fair parking lot.

"Is 'Old' your real name?"

"I've been called 'Old' all my life, but my real name is Patrick."

"How long have you lived here?"

"In Three Pines? A few years." He thought for a moment. "My God, it's been eleven years. Can hardly believe it. Olivier was the first person I met."

"How do people feel about him?"

"Don't know about 'people,' but I know how I feel. I like Olivier. He's always fair with me."

"But not with everyone?" Gamache had noticed the inflection.

"Some people don't know the value of what they've got." Old Mundin was concentrating on the road, driving carefully. "And lots of people just want to stir up trouble. They don't like being told their antique chest is really just old. Not valuable at all. Pisses them off. But Olivier knows what he's doing. Lots of people set up antique businesses here, but not many really know what they're doing. Olivier does."

After a moment or two of silence as both men watched the countryside go by, Gamache spoke. "I've always wondered where dealers find their antiques."

"Most have pickers. People who specialize in going to auctions or getting to know people in the area. Mostly elderly people who might be interested in selling. Around here if someone knocks on your door on a Sunday morning it's more likely to be an antique picker than a Jehovah's Witness."

"Does Olivier have a picker?"

"No, he does it himself. He works hard for what he gets. And he knows what's worth money and what isn't. He's good. And fair, for the most part."

"For the most part?"

"Well, he has to make a profit, and lots of the stuff needs work. He gives the old furniture to me to restore. That can be a lot of work."

"I bet you don't charge what it's worth."

"Now, worth is a relative concept." Old shot Gamache a glance as they bumped along the road. "I love what I do and if I charged a reasonable amount per hour nobody'd be able to buy my pieces, and Olivier wouldn't hire me to repair the great things he finds. So it's worth it to me to charge less. I have a good life. No complaints here."

"Has anyone been really angry at Olivier?"

Old drove in silence and Gamache wasn't sure he'd heard. But finally he spoke.

"Once, about a year ago. Old Madame Poirier, up the Mountain road, had decided to move into a nursing home in Saint-Rémy. Olivier'd been buzzing around her for a few years. When the time came she sold most of her stuff to him. He found some amazing pieces there."

"Did he pay a fair price?"

"Depends who you talk to. She was happy. Olivier was happy."

"So who was angry?"

Old Mundin said nothing. Gamache waited.

"Her kids. They said Olivier'd insinuated himself, taken advantage of a lonely old woman."

Old Mundin pulled into a small farmhouse. Hollyhocks leaned against the wall and the garden was full of black-eyed Susans and old-fashioned roses. A vegetable garden, well tended and orderly, was planted at the side of the house.

The van rolled to a halt and Mundin pointed to a barn. "That's my workshop."

Gamache unbuckled Charles from the child seat. The boy was asleep and Gamache carried him as the two men walked to the barn.

"You said Olivier made an unexpected find at Madame Poirier's place?"

"He paid her a flat fee for all the stuff she no longer needed. She chose what she wanted to keep and he bought the rest."

Old Mundin stopped at the barn door, turning to Gamache.

"There was a set of six Chippendale chairs. Worth about ten thousand each. I know, because I worked on them, but I don't think he told anyone else."

"Did you?"

"No. You'd be surprised how discreet I need to be in my work."

"Do you know if Olivier gave Madame Poirier any extra money?"

"I don't."

"But her kids were angry."

Mundin nodded curtly and opened the barn door. They stepped into a different world. All the complex aromas of the late summer farm had disappeared. Gone was the slight scent of manure, of cut grass, of hay, of herbs in the sun.

Here there was only one note—wood. Fresh sawn wood. Old barn wood. Wood of every description. Gamache looked at the walls, lined with wood waiting to be turned into furniture. Old Mundin smoothed one fine hand over a rough board.

"You wouldn't know it, but there's burled wood under there. You have to know what to look for. The tiny imperfections. Funny how imperfections on the outside mean something splendid beneath."

He looked into Gamache's eyes. Charles stirred slightly and the Chief Inspector brought a large hand up to the boy's back, to reassure him.

"I'm afraid I don't know much about wood but you seem to have different sorts. Why's that?"

"Different needs. I use maple and cherry and pine for inside work. Cedar for outside. This here's red cedar. My favorite. Doesn't look like much now, but carved and polished . . ." Mundin made an eloquent gesture.

Gamache noticed two chairs on a platform. One was upside down. "From the bistro?" He walked over to them. Sure enough one had a loose arm and the leg of the other was wobbly.

"I picked those up Saturday night."

"Is it all right to talk about what happened at the bistro in front of Charles?"

"I'm sure it is. He'll understand, or not. Either way, it's okay. He knows it's not about him."

Gamache wished more people could make that distinction. "You were there the night of the murder."

"True. I go every Saturday to pick up the damaged furniture and drop off the stuff I've restored. It was the same as always. I got there just after midnight. The last of the customers was leaving and the kids were beginning to clean up."

Kids, thought Gamache. And yet they weren't really that much younger than this man. But somehow Old seemed very, well, old.

"But I didn't see a body."

"Too bad, that would've helped. Did anything strike you as unusual at all?"

Old Mundin thought. Charles woke up and squirmed. Gamache lowered him to the barn floor where he picked up a piece of wood and turned it around and around.

"I'm sorry. I wish I could help, but it seemed like any other Saturday night."

Gamache also picked up a chunk of wood and smoothed the sawdust off it.

"How'd you start repairing Olivier's furniture?"

"Oh, that was years ago. Gave me a chair to work on. It'd been kept in a barn for years and he'd just moved it into the bistro. Now, you must understand . . ."

What followed was a passionate monologue on old Quebec pine furniture. Milk paint, the horrors of stripping, the dangers of ruining a fine piece by restoring it. That difficult line between making a piece usable and making it valueless.

Gamache listened, fascinated. He had a passion for Quebec history, and by extension Quebec antiques, the remarkable furniture made by pioneers in the long winter months hundreds of years ago. They'd made the pine furniture both practical and beautiful, pouring themselves into it. Each time Gamache touched an old table or armoire he imagined the *habitant* shaping and smoothing the wood, going over it and over it with hardened hands. And making something lovely.

Lovely and lasting, thanks to people like Old Mundin.

"What brought you to Three Pines? Why not a larger city? There'd be more work, surely, in Montreal or even Sherbrooke."

"I was born in Quebec City, and you'd think there'd be lots of work there for an antique restorer, but it's hard for a young guy starting out. I moved to Montreal, to an antique shop on Notre Dame, but I'm afraid I wasn't cut out for the big city. So I decided to go to Sherbrooke. Got in the car, headed south, and got lost. I drove into Three Pines to ask directions at the bistro, ordered *café au lait*, sat down and the chair collapsed." He laughed, as did Gamache. "I offered to repair it and that was that."

"You said you'd been here for eleven years. You must've been young when you left Quebec City."

"Sixteen. I left after my father died. Spent three years in Montreal, then down here. Met The Wife, had Charles. Started a small business."

This young man had done a lot with his eleven years, thought Gamache. "How did Olivier seem on Saturday night?"

"As usual. Labor Day's always busy but he seemed relaxed. As relaxed as he ever gets, I suppose." Mundin smiled. It was clear there was affection there. "Did I hear you say the man wasn't murdered at the bistro after all?"

Gamache nodded. "We're trying to find out where he was killed. In fact, while you were at the fair I had my people searching the whole area, including your place."

"Really?" They were at the barn door and Mundin turned to stare into the gloom. "They're either very good, or they didn't actually do anything. You can't tell."

"That's the point." But the Chief noticed that, unlike Peter, Old Mundin didn't seem at all concerned.

"Now, why would you kill someone one place, then move them to another?" asked Mundin, almost to himself. "I can see wanting to get rid of a body, especially if you killed him in your own home, but why take him to Olivier's? Seems a strange thing to do, but I guess the bistro's a fairly central location. Maybe it was just convenient."

Gamache let that statement be. They both knew it wasn't true. Indeed, the bistro was a very inconvenient place to drop a body. And it worried Gamache. The murder wasn't an accident, and the placement of the body wasn't either.

There was someone very dangerous walking among them. Someone who looked happy, thoughtful, gentle even. But it was a deceit. A mask. Gamache knew that when he found the murderer and ripped the mask off, the skin would come too. The mask had become the man. The deceit was total.

THIRTEEN

 "We had a great time at the fair. I got you this." Gabri shut the door and turned on the lights in the bistro. He offered the stuffed lion to Olivier, who took it and held it softly in his lap.

"*Merci.*"

"And did you hear the news? Gamache says the dead man wasn't killed here. And we'll be getting our pokers back. I'd like to get my poker back, wouldn't you?" he asked, archly. But Olivier didn't even respond.

Gabri moved through the gloomy room, turning on lamps, then lit a fire in one of the stone hearths. Olivier continued to sit in the armchair, staring out the window. Gabri sighed, poured them each a beer and joined him. Together they sipped, ate cashews and looked out at the village, quiet now in the last of the day, and the end of the summer.

"What do you see?" asked Gabri at last.

"What d'you mean? I see what you see."

"Can't be. What I see makes me happy. And you're not happy."

Gabri was used to his partner's moods. Olivier was the quiet one, the contained one. Gabri might appear the more sensitive, but they both knew Olivier was. He felt things deeply, and kept them there. Gabri was covered in the flesh wounds of life, but Olivier's wounds were in the marrow, deep and hidden and perhaps even mortal.

But he was also the kindest man Gabri had met, and he'd met, it must be said, quite a few. Before Olivier. That had all changed as soon as he'd clapped eyes on the slim, blond, shy man.

Gabri had lost his quite considerable heart.

"What is it?" Gabri leaned forward and took Olivier's slender hands. "Tell me."

"It's just no fun anymore," said Olivier at last. "I mean, why even bother? No one's going to want to come back here. Who wants to eat in a restaurant where there's been a body?"

"As Ruth says, we're all just bodies anyway."

"Great. I'll put that in the ads."

"Well, at least you don't discriminate. Dead, predead. They're all welcome here. That might be a better slogan."

Gabri saw a quiver at the ends of Olivier's lips.

"*Voyons*, it was great news that the police say the man wasn't killed here. That makes a difference."

"You think?" Olivier looked at him hopefully.

"Do you know what I really think?" Now Gabri was dead serious. "I think it wouldn't matter. Peter, Clara, Myrna? Do you think they'd stop coming even if that poor man had been murdered here? The Parras? Monsieur Béliveau? They'd all come if a mountain of bodies was found here. Do you know why?"

"Because they like it?"

"Because they like you. They love you. Listen, Olivier, you have the best bistro, the finest food, the most comfortable place. It's brilliant. You're brilliant. Everyone loves you. And you know what?"

"What?" asked Olivier, grumpily.

"You're the kindest, most handsome man in the world."

"You're just saying that." Olivier felt like a little boy again. While other kids ran around collecting frogs and sticks and grasshoppers, he'd sought reassurance. Affection. He'd gather up the words and actions, even from strangers, and he'd stuff them into the hole that was growing.

It had worked. For a while. Then he'd needed more than just words.

"Did Myrna tell you to say that?"

"Right. It's not true at all, just a big lie cooked up by Myrna and me. What's wrong with you anyway?"

"You wouldn't understand."

Gabri followed Olivier's stare out the window. And up the hill. He sighed. They'd been through this before.

"There's nothing we can do about them. Maybe we should just—"

"Just what?" Olivier snapped.

"Are you looking for an excuse to be miserable? Is that it?"

Even by Olivier's standards that had been an unreasonable reaction.

He'd been reassured about the body, he'd been reassured that everyone still loved him. He'd been reassured that Gabri wasn't running away. So what was the problem?

"Listen, maybe we should give them a chance. Who knows? Their inn and spa might even help us."

This was not what Olivier wanted to hear. He stood abruptly, almost knocking the chair to the floor. He could feel that bloom of anger in his chest. It was like a superpower. It made him invincible. Strong. Courageous. Brutal.

"If you want to be friends with them, fine. Why don't you just fuck off?"

"I didn't mean that. I meant we can't do anything about them so we might as well be friends."

"You make this sound like kindergarten. They're out to ruin us. Do you understand? When they first came I was nice, but then they decided to steal our customers, even our staff. Do you think anyone's going to come to your tacky little B and B when they can stay there?"

Olivier's face was red and blotchy. Gabri could see it spread even under his scalp, through the thinning and struggling blond hair.

"What're you talking about? I don't care if people come, you know that. We don't need the money. I just do it for fun."

Olivier struggled to control himself now. To not take that one step too far. The two men glared so that the space between them throbbed.

"Why?" Olivier finally said.

"Why what?"

"If the dead man wasn't killed here, why was he put here?"

Gabri felt his anger lift, evaporated by the question.

"I heard from the police today," said Olivier, his voice almost monotone. "They're going to speak to my father tomorrow."

Poor Olivier, thought Gabri, he did have something to worry about after all.

Jean Guy Beauvoir got out of the car and stared across the road at the Poirier home.

It was ramshackle and in need of way more than just a coat of paint. The porch was sloping, the steps looked unsound, pieces of boarding were missing from the side of the house.

Beauvoir had been in dozens of places like this in rural Quebec. Lived in by a generation born there too. Clotilde Poirier probably drank coffee from a chipped mug her mother had used. Slept on a mattress she'd been conceived on. The walls would be covered with dried flowers and spoons sent by relatives who'd escaped to exotic places like Rimouski or Chicoutimi or Gaspé. And there'd be a chair, a rocking chair, by the window, near the woodstove. It would have a slightly soiled afghan on it and crumbs. And after clearing up the breakfast dishes Clotilde Poirier would sit there, and watch.

What would she be watching for? A friend? A familiar car? Another spoon?

Was she watching him now?

Armand Gamache's Volvo appeared over the hill and came to a stop behind Beauvoir. The two men stood and stared for a moment at the house.

"I found out about the Varathane," said Beauvoir, thinking this place could use a hundred gallons or so of the stuff. "The Gilberts didn't use it when they did the renovations. I spoke to Dominique Gilbert. She said they want to be as green as possible. After they had the floors sanded they used tung oil."

"So the Varathane on the dead man's clothing didn't come from the old Hadley house," said the Chief, disappointed. It had seemed a promising lead.

"Why're we here?" Beauvoir asked as they turned back to survey the gently subsiding home and the rusting pickup truck in the yard. He'd received a call from the Chief to meet him here, but he didn't know why.

Gamache explained what Old Mundin had said about Olivier, Madame Poirier and her furniture. Specifically the Chippendale chairs.

"So her kids think Olivier screwed her? And by extension, them?" asked Beauvoir.

"Seems so." He knocked on the door. After a moment a querulous voice called through it.

"Who is it?"

"Chief Inspector Gamache, madame. Of the Sûreté du Québec."

"I ain't done nothing wrong."

Gamache and Beauvoir exchanged glances.

"We need to speak to you, Madame Poirier. It's about the body found in the bistro in Three Pines."

"So?"

It was very difficult conducting an interview through an inch of chipping wood.

"May we come in? We'd like to talk to you about Olivier Brulé."

An elderly woman, small and slender, opened the door. She glared at them then turned and walked rapidly back into the house. Gamache and Beauvoir followed.

It was decorated as Beauvoir had imagined. Or, really, not decorated. Things were put up on the walls as they'd arrived, over the generations, so that the walls were a horizontal archaeological dig. The farther into the house they went, the more recent the items. Framed flowers, plasticized place mats, crucifixes, paintings of Jesus and the Virgin Mary, and yes, spoons, all marched across the faded floral wallpaper.

But the place was clean, spotless and smelled of cookies. Photos of grandchildren, perhaps even great-grandchildren, sat on shelves and tabletops. A faded striped tablecloth, clean and ironed, was on the kitchen table. And in the center of that table was a vase containing late summer flowers.

"Tea?" She lifted a pot from the stove. Beauvoir declined but Gamache accepted. She returned with cups of tea for them all. "Well, go on."

"We understand Olivier bought some furniture from you," said Beauvoir.

"Not just some. He bought the lot. Thank God. Gave me more than anyone else would, despite what my kids mighta told you."

"We haven't spoken to them yet," said Beauvoir.

"Neither have I. Not since selling the stuff." But she didn't seem upset. "Greedy, all of them. Waiting for me to die so they can inherit."

"How did you meet Olivier?" Beauvoir asked.

"He knocked on the door one day. Introduced himself. Asked if I had anything I'd like to sell. Sent him running the first few times." She smiled at the memory. "But there was something about him. He kept coming back. So I eventually invited him in, just for tea. He'd come about once a month, have tea, then leave."

"When did you decide to sell to him?" Beauvoir asked.

"I'm coming to that," she snapped, and Beauvoir began to appreciate how hard Olivier must have worked for that furniture.

"One winter was particularly long. Lots of snow. And cold. So I decided to hell with this, I'd sell up and move into Saint-Rémy, to that new seniors' home. So I told Olivier and we walked through the house. I showed him all that crap my parents left me. Old armoires and dressers. Big pine things. And painted all sorts of dull colors. Blues and greens. Tried to scrape it off some of them, but it was no good."

Beside him Beauvoir heard the Chief inhale, but that was the only sign of pain. Having spent years with Gamache he knew his passion for antiques, and knew that you never, ever strip old paint. It was like skinning something alive.

"So you showed it all to Olivier? What did he say?"

"Said he'd take the lot, including what was in the barn and attic without even seeing it. Tables and chairs been there since before my grandparents. Was going to send it to the dump, but my lazy sons never showed up to do it. So serves them right. I sold the lot to Olivier."

"Can you remember how much you got?"

"I remember exactly. It was three thousand two hundred dollars. Enough to pay for all of this. Sears."

Gamache looked at the legs of the table. Prefabricated wood. There was an upholstered rocker facing the new television, and a dark wood-veneer cabinet, with decorative plates.

Madame Poirier was also looking at the contents of the room, with pride.

"He came by a few weeks later and you know what he'd brought? A new bed. Plastic still on the mattress. Set it up for me too. He still comes by sometimes. He's a nice man."

Beauvoir nodded. A nice man who'd paid this elderly woman a fraction of what that furniture was worth.

"But you're not in the seniors' home? Why not?"

"After I got the new furniture the place felt different. More mine. I kinda liked it again."

She showed them to the door and Beauvoir noticed the welcome mat. Worn, but still there. They said good-bye and headed for her eldest son's place a mile down the road. A large man with a gut and stubble opened the door.

"Cops," he called into the house. It, and he, smelled of beer and sweat and tobacco.

"Claude Poirier?" Beauvoir asked. It was a formality. Who else would this man be? He was nearing sixty, and looked every moment of it. Beauvoir had taken the time before leaving the Incident Room to look up the Poirier family. To see what they were walking into.

Petty crimes. Drunk and disorderly. Shoplifting. Benefit fraud.

They were the type who took advantage, found fault, pointed fingers. Still, it didn't mean that sometimes they weren't right. Like about Olivier. He'd screwed them.

After the introductions Poirier launched into his long, sad litany. It was all Beauvoir could do to keep him focused on Olivier, so long was this man's list of people who'd done him wrong. Including his own mother.

Finally the two investigators lurched from the stale house, taking deep breaths of fresh late afternoon air.

"Do you think he did it?" asked Gamache

"He's certainly angry enough," said Beauvoir, "but unless he could transport a body to the bistro using the buttons on his remote, I think he's off the suspect list. Can't see him getting off that stinking sofa long enough."

They walked back to their cars. The Chief paused.

"What're you thinking?" Beauvoir asked.

"I was remembering what Madame Poirier said. She was about to take all those antiques to the dump. Can you imagine?"

Beauvoir could see that the thought gave Gamache actual pain.

"But Olivier saved them," said the Chief. "Strange how that works. He might not have given Madame enough money, but he gave her affection and company. What price do you put on that?"

"So, can I buy your car? I'll give you twenty hours of my company."

"Don't be cynical. One day you might be elderly and alone and you'll see."

As he followed the Chief's car back to Three Pines Beauvoir thought about that, and agreed that Olivier had saved the precious antiques, and spent time with the crabby old woman. But he could have done it and still given the old woman a fair price.

But he hadn't.

Marc Gilbert looked at Marc the horse. Marc the horse looked at Marc Gilbert. Neither seemed pleased.

"Dominique!" Marc called from the door of the barn.

"Yes?" she said, cheerily, walking across the yard from the house. She'd hoped it would take Marc a few days to find the horses. Actually, she'd hoped he never would. But that was in the same league as the Mrs. Keith Partridge dream. Unlikely at best.

And now she found him cross-armed in the dim barn.

"What are these?"

"They're horses," she said. Though, it must be said, she suspected Macaroni might be a moose.

"I can see that, but what kind? These aren't hunters, are they?"

Dominique hesitated. For an instant she wondered what would happen if she said yes. But she guessed that Marc, while not a horse expert, wouldn't buy that.

"No, they're better."

"How better?"

His sentences were getting shorter, never a good sign.

"Well, they're cheaper."

She could see that actually had a slight mollifying effect. Might as well tell him the full story. "I bought them from the slaughterhouse. They were going to be killed today."

Marc hesitated. She could see him struggling with his anger. Not trying to let it go, but trying to hold on to it. "Maybe there was a reason they were going to be . . . you know."

"Killed. No, the vet's been to see them and he says they're fine, or will be."

The barn smelled of disinfectant, soap and medication.

"Maybe physically, but you can't tell me he's okay." Marc waved at Marc the horse, who flared his nostrils and snorted. "He isn't even clean. Why not?"

Why did her husband have to be so observant? "Well, no one could get close to him." Then she had an idea. "The vet says he needs a very special touch. He'll only let someone quite exceptional near him."

"Is that right?" Marc looked at the horse again, and walked toward him. Marc, the horse, backed up. Her husband reached out his hand. The horse put his ears back, and Dominique grabbed her husband away just as Marc the horse snapped.

"It's been a long day and he's disoriented."

"Hmm," said her husband, walking with her out of the barn. "What's his name?"

"Thunder."

"Thunder," said Marc, trying the name out. "Thunder," he repeated as though riding the steed and urging him on.

Carole greeted them at the kitchen door. "So," she said to her son. "How're the horses? How's Marc?"

"I'm fine, thank you." He looked at her quizzically and took the drink she offered. "And how's Carole?"

Behind him Dominique gestured frantically at her mother-in-law who was laughing and just about to say something when she saw her daughter-in-law's motions and stopped. "Just fine. Do you like the horses?"

"Like is a strong word, as is 'horses,' I suspect."

"It'll take a while for us all to get used to each other," said Dominique. She accepted the Scotch from Carole and took a gulp. Then they walked out the French doors and into the garden.

As the two women talked, more friends than mother and daughter-in-law, Marc looked at the flowers, the mature trees, the freshly painted white fences and the rolling fields beyond. Soon the horses, or whatever they were, would be out there. Grazing.

Once again he had that hollow feeling, that slight rip as the chasm widened.

Leaving Montreal had been a wrench for Dominique, and leaving Quebec City had been difficult for his mother. They left behind friends. But while Marc had pretended to be sorry, had gone to the going-away parties, had claimed he would miss everyone, the truth was, he didn't.

They had to be part of his life for him to miss them, and they weren't. He remembered that Kipling poem his father loved, and taught him. And that one line. *If all men count with you, but none too much.*

And they hadn't. Over forty-five years not a single man had counted too much.

He had loads of colleagues, acquaintances, buddies. He was an emotional communist. Everyone counted equally, but none too much.

You'll be a man, my son. That was how the poem ended.

But Marc Gilbert, listening to the quiet conversation and looking over the rich, endless fields, was beginning to wonder if that was enough. Or even true.

The officers gathered round the conference table and Beauvoir un-capped his red Magic Marker. Agent Morin was beginning to appreciate that the small "pop" was like a starter's gun. In the short time he'd been with homicide he'd developed a fondness for the smell of marker, and that distinctive sound.

He settled into his chair, a little nervous as always, in case he should say something particularly stupid. Agent Lacoste had helped. As they'd gathered up their papers for the meeting she'd seen his trembling hands and whispered that maybe he should just listen this time.

He'd looked at her, surprised.

"Won't they think I'm an idiot? That I have nothing to say?"

"Believe me, there's no way you're going to listen yourself out of this job. Or any job. Just relax, let me do the talking today, and we'll see about tomorrow. Okay?"

He'd looked at her then, trying to figure out what her motives might be. Everyone had them, he knew. Some were driven by kindness, some not. And he'd been at the Sûreté long enough to know that most in the famous police force weren't guided by a desire to be nice.

It was brutally competitive, and nowhere more so than the scramble to get into homicide. The most prestigious posting. And the chance to work with Chief Inspector Gamache.

He was barely in, and barely hanging on. One wrong move and he'd slide right out the door, and be forgotten in an instant. He wasn't going to let that happen. And he knew, instinctively, this was a pivotal moment. Was Agent Lacoste sincere?

"All right, what've we got?"

Beauvoir was standing by the paper tacked to the wall next to a map of the village.

"We know the victim wasn't murdered at the bistro," said Lacoste. "But we still don't know where he was killed or who he was."

"Or why he was moved," said Beauvoir. He reported on their visit to the Poiriers, *mère et fils*. Then Lacoste told them what she and Morin had learned about Olivier Brulé.

"He's thirty-eight. Only child. Born and raised in Montreal. Father an executive at the railway, mother a homemaker, now dead. An affluent upbringing. Went to Notre Dame de Sion school."

Gamache raised his brows. It was a leading Catholic private school. Annie had gone there too, years after Olivier, to be taught by the rigorous nuns. His son Daniel had refused, preferring the less rigorous public schools. Annie had learned logic, Latin, problem solving. Daniel had learned to roll a spliff. Both grew into decent, happy adults.

"Olivier got an MBA from the Université de Montréal and took a job at the Banque Laurentienne," Agent Lacoste continued, reading from her notes. "He handled high-end corporate clients. Apparently very successfully too. Then he quit."

"Why?" asked Beauvoir.

"Not sure. I have a meeting at the bank tomorrow, and I've also set up an appointment with Olivier's father."

"What about his personal life?" Gamache asked.

"I talked to Gabri. They started living together fourteen years ago. Gabri's a year younger. Thirty-seven. He was a fitness instructor at the local YMCA."

"Gabri?" asked Beauvoir, remembering the large, soft man.

"Happens to the best of us," said Gamache.

"After Olivier quit the bank they gave up their apartment in Old Montreal and moved down here, took over the bistro and lived above it, but it wasn't a bistro then. It'd been a hardware store."

"Really?" asked Beauvoir. He couldn't imagine the bistro as anything else. He tried to see snow shovels and batteries and lightbulbs hanging from the exposed beams or set up in front of the two stone fireplaces. And failed.

"But listen to this." Lacoste leaned forward. "I got this by digging into the land registry records. Ten years ago Olivier bought not just his bistro, but the B and B. But he didn't stop there. He bought it all. The general store, the bakery, his bistro and Myrna's bookstore."

"Everything?" asked Beauvoir. "He owns the village?"

"Just about. I don't think anyone else knows. I spoke to Sarah at her boulangerie and to Monsieur Béliveau at the general store. They said they rented from some guy in Montreal. Long-term leases, reasonable rates. They send their checks to a numbered company."

"Olivier's a numbered company?" asked Beauvoir.

Gamache was taking all this in, listening closely.

"How much did he pay?" asked Beauvoir.

"Seven hundred and twenty thousand dollars for the lot."

"Good God," said Beauvoir. "That's a lot of bread. Where'd he get the money? A mortgage?"

"No. Paid cash."

"You say his mother's dead, maybe it was his inheritance."

"Doubt it," said Lacoste. "She only died five years ago, but I'll look into it when I'm in Montreal."

"Follow the money," said Beauvoir. It was a truism in crime investigations, particularly murder. And there was suddenly a great deal of money to follow. Beauvoir finished scribbling on his sheets on the wall, then told them about the coroner's findings.

Morin listened, fascinated. So this was how murderers were found. Not by DNA tests and petrie dishes, ultraviolet scans or anything else a lab could produce. They helped, certainly, but this was their real lab. He looked across the table to the other person who was just listening, saying nothing.

Chief Inspector Gamache took his deep brown eyes off Inspector Beauvoir for a moment and looked at the young agent. And smiled.

Agent Lacoste headed for Montreal shortly after the meeting broke up. Agent Morin left for home and Beauvoir and Gamache walked slowly back over the stone bridge and into the village. They strolled past the darkened bistro and met Olivier and Gabri on the wide veranda of the B and B.

"I left a note for you," said Gabri. "Since the bistro's closed we're all going out for dinner and you're invited."

"Peter and Clara's again?" asked Gamache.

"No. Ruth," said Gabri and was rewarded with their stunned looks. He'd have thought someone had drawn a gun on the two large Sûreté officers. Chief Inspector Gamache looked surprised but Beauvoir looked afraid.

"You might want to put on your athletic protector," Gabri whispered to Beauvoir, as they passed on the veranda steps.

"Well, I'm sure as hell not going. You?" asked Beauvoir when they went inside.

"Are you kidding? Pass up a chance to see Ruth in her natural habitat? Wouldn't miss it."

Twenty minutes later the Chief Inspector had showered, called Reine-Marie and changed into slacks, blue shirt and tie and a camel-hair cardigan. He found Beauvoir in the living room with a beer and potato chips.

"Sure you won't change your mind, *patron*?"

It was tempting, Gamache had to admit. But he shook his head.

"I'll keep a candle in the window," said Beauvoir, watching the Chief leave.

Ruth's clapboard home was a couple of houses away and faced the green. It was tiny, with a porch in front and two gables on the second floor. Gamache had been in it before, but always with his notebook out, asking questions. Never as a guest. As he entered all eyes turned and as one they made for him, Myrna reaching him first.

"For pity's sake, did you bring your gun?"

"I don't have one."

"What d'you mean, you don't have one?"

"They're dangerous. Why do you want it?"

"So you can shoot her. She's trying to kill us." Myrna grabbed Gamache's sleeve and pointed to Ruth who was circulating among her guests wearing a frilly apron and carrying a bright orange plastic tray.

"Actually," said Gabri, "she's trying to kidnap us and take us back to 1950."

"Probably the last time she entertained," said Myrna.

"Hors d'oeuvre, old fruit?" Ruth spotted her new guest and bore down upon him.

Gabri and Olivier turned to each other. "She means you."

Incredibly, she actually meant Gamache.

"Lord love a duck," said Ruth, in a very bad British accent. Behind Ruth waddled Rosa.

"She started speaking like that as soon as we arrived," said Myrna, backing away from the tray and knocking over a stack of *Times Literary Supplement*s. Gamache could see saltine crackers sliding around on the orange tray, smeared with brown stuff he hoped was peanut butter. "I remember reading something about this," Myrna continued. "People speaking in accents after a brain injury."

"Is being possessed by the devil considered a brain injury?" asked Gabri. "She's speaking in tongues."

"Cor blimey," said Ruth.

But the most striking feature of the room wasn't the hoop lamps, the teak furniture, genteel British Ruth with her dubious offering, nor was it the sofas covered in books and newspapers and magazines, as was the green shag carpet. It was the duck.

Rosa was wearing a dress.

"Duck and cover," said Gabri. "Literally."

"Our Rosa." Ruth had put down the peanut-buttered crackers and was now offering celery sticks stuffed with Velveeta.

Gamache watched and wondered if he'd have to make a couple of calls. One to the Humane Society, the other to the psych ward. But neither Rosa nor Ruth seemed upset. Unlike their guests.

"Would you like one?" Clara offered him a ball covered with what looked like seeds.

"What is it?" he asked.

"We think it's suet, for the birds," said Peter.

"And you're offering it to me?" Gamache asked.

"Well, someone should eat it so it doesn't hurt her feelings." Clara nodded to Ruth, just disappearing into the kitchen. "And we're too afraid."

"*Non, merci,*" he smiled and went in search of Olivier. As he passed the kitchen he looked in and saw Ruth opening a can. Rosa was standing on the table watching her.

"Now, we'll just open this," she mumbled. "Maybe we should smell it? What do you think?"

The duck didn't seem to be thinking anything. Ruth smelled the open can anyway. "Good enough."

The old poet wiped her hands on a towel then reached out and lifted the edge of Rosa's dress to replace a ruffled feather, smoothing it down.

"May I help?" Gamache asked from the door.

"Well, aren't you a love."

Gamache winced, expecting her to throw a cleaver after that. But she just smiled and handed him a plate of olives, each stuffed with a section of canned mandarin orange. He took it and returned to the party. Not surprisingly he was greeted as though he'd joined the dark side. He was very grateful Beauvoir wasn't there to see Ruth, nuttier and more Anglo than usual, Rosa wearing a dress and himself offering food that would almost certainly kill or cripple anyone foolish enough to eat it.

"Olive?" he asked Olivier.

The two men looked down at the plate.

"Does that make me the mandarin?" asked Gabri.

"You need to get your head out of your own asshole," said Olivier.

Gabri opened his mouth, but the warning looks on everyone's faces made him shut it again.

Peter, standing a little way off from the conversation and nursing the glass of water Ruth had offered him, smiled. It was much the same thing Clara had said when he'd told her he'd felt violated by the police search.

"Why?" she'd asked.

"Didn't you? I mean, all those strangers looking at your art."

"Isn't that what we call a show? There were more people looking this afternoon than I've had most of my career. Bring on more cops. Hope they brought their checkbooks." She laughed, and clearly didn't care. But she could see he did. "What's the matter?"

"The picture isn't ready to be seen."

"Look, Peter, you make it sound as though this is something to do with your art."

"Well, it is."

"They're trying to find a murderer, not an artist."

And there it had sat, like most uncomfortable truths. Between them.

Gamache and Olivier had wandered away from the group, into a quiet corner.

"I understand you bought your building a few years ago."

Olivier colored slightly, surprised by the question. He instinctively and furtively scanned the room, making sure they weren't overheard.

"I thought it was a good investment. I'd saved some money from my job, and business here was good."

"Must have been. You paid almost three-quarters of a million dollars."

"I bet it's worth a million today."

"Could be. But you paid cash. Was business all that good?"

Olivier shot a look around but no one could hear them. Still he lowered his voice.

"The bistro and B and B are doing very well, for now anyway, but it's the antiques end that's been the surprise."

"How so?"

"Lots of interest in Quebec pine, and lots of great finds."

Gamache nodded. "We spoke to the Poiriers this afternoon."

Olivier's face hardened. "Look, what they say just isn't true. I didn't screw their mother. She wanted to sell. Was desperate to sell."

"I know. We spoke to her too. And the Mundins. The furniture must have been in very bad shape."

Olivier relaxed a little.

"It was. Years sitting in damp, freezing barns and the attic. Had to chase the mice out. Some were warped almost beyond repair. Enough to make you weep."

"Madame Poirier says you came by her home later with a new bed. That was kind."

Olivier dropped his eyes. "Yeah, well, I wanted to thank her."

Conscience, thought Gamache. This man had a huge and terrible conscience riding herd on a huge and terrible greed.

"You said the bistro and B and B were doing well, for now. What did you mean?"

Olivier looked out the window for a moment, then back at Gamache.

"Hi ho, dinner everyone," sang Ruth.

"What should we do?" Clara whispered to Myrna. "Can we run for it?"

"Too late. Either Ruth or the duck would get us for sure. The only thing to do is hunker down and pray for daylight. If the worst happens, play dead."

Gamache and Olivier rose, the last in for dinner.

"I suppose you know what they're doing up at the old Hadley house?" When Gamache didn't answer Olivier continued. "They've almost completely gutted the place and are turning it into an inn and spa. Ten massage rooms, meditation and yoga classes. They'll do a day spa and corporate retreats. People'll be crawling all over the place, and us. It'll ruin Three Pines."

"Three Pines?"

"All right," snapped Olivier. "The bistro and the B and B."

They joined the others in the kitchen and sat at Ruth's white plastic garden table.

"Incoming," warned Gabri as Ruth put a bowl in front of each of them.

Gamache looked at the contents of his bowl. He could make out canned peaches, bacon, cheese and Gummi Bears.

"They're all the things I love," said Ruth, smiling. Rosa was sitting next to her on a nest of towels, her beak thrust under the sleeve of her dress.

"Scotch?" Ruth asked.

"Please." Six glasses were thrust forward and Ruth poured each a Scotch, into their dinners.

About three centuries and many lifetimes later they left, staggering into the quiet, cool night.

"Toodle-oo," waved Ruth. But Gamache was heartened to hear, just as the door closed: "Fuckers."

FOURTEEN

 They arrived back at the B and B to find Beauvoir waiting up for them. Sort of. He was fast asleep in his chair. Beside him was a plate with crumbs and a glass of chocolate milk. The fireplace glowed with dying embers.

"Should we wake him?" asked Olivier. "He looks so peaceful."

Beauvoir's face was turned to the side and there was a slight glisten of drool. His breathing was heavy and regular. On his chest lay the small stuffed lion Gabri had won for Olivier at the fair, his hand resting on it.

"Like a little baby cop," said Gabri.

"That reminds me. Ruth asked me to give him this." Olivier handed Gamache a slip of paper. The Chief took it and when he declined their offer of help watched as the two men trudged wearily up the stairs. It was nine o'clock.

"Jean Guy," Gamache whispered. "Wake up."

He knelt and touched the younger man's shoulder. Beauvoir started awake with a snort, the lion slipping off his chest onto the floor.

"What is it?"

"Time for bed."

He watched Beauvoir sit up. "How was it?"

"No one died."

"That's a bit of an achievement in Three Pines."

"Olivier said Ruth wanted you to have this." Gamache handed him the slip of paper. Beauvoir rubbed his eyes, unfolded the paper and read it. Then, shaking his head, he handed it to the Chief.

*Maybe there's something in all of this
I missed.*

"What does it mean? Is it a threat?"

Gamache frowned. "Haven't a clue. Why would she be writing to you?"

"Jealous? Maybe she's just nuts." But they both knew the "maybe" was being generous. "Speaking of nut, your daughter called."

"Annie?" Gamache was suddenly worried, instinctively reaching for his cell phone, which he knew didn't work in the village in the valley.

"Everything's fine. She wanted to talk to you about some upset at work. Nothing major. She just wanted to quit."

"Damn, that was probably what she wanted to talk about yesterday when we got called down here."

"Well don't worry about it. I handled it."

"I don't think telling her to fuck off can be considered 'handling it.'"

Beauvoir laughed and bending down he picked up the stuffed lion. "There's certainly good reason she's known as 'the lion' in your family. Vicious."

"She's known as the lion because she's loving and passionate."

"And a man-eater?"

"All the qualities you hate in her you admire in men," said Gamache. "She's smart, she stands up for what she believes in. She speaks her mind and won't back down to bullies. Why do you goad her? Every time you come for a meal and she's there it ends in an argument. I for one am growing tired of it."

"All right, I'll try harder. But she's very annoying."

"So are you. You have a lot in common. What was the problem at work?" Gamache took the seat next to Jean Guy.

"Oh, a case she'd wanted was assigned to another lawyer, someone more junior. I talked to her for a while. I'm almost certain she won't kill everyone at work after all."

"That's my girl."

"And she's decided not to quit. I told her she'd regret any hasty decision."

"Oh, you did, did you?" asked Gamache with a smile. This from the king of impulse.

"Well, someone had to give her good advice," laughed Beauvoir. "Her parents are quite mad, you know."

"I'd heard. Thank you."

It was good advice. And he could tell Beauvoir knew it. He seemed pleased. Gamache looked at his watch. Nine thirty. He reached for Gabri's phone.

As Gamache spoke to his daughter Beauvoir absently stroked the lion in his hand.

*Maybe there's something in all of this
I missed.*

That was the fear in a murder investigation. Missing something. Chief Inspector Gamache had assembled a brilliant department. Almost two hundred of them in all, hand picked, investigating crime all over the province.

But this team, Beauvoir knew, was the best.

He was the bloodhound. The one way out in front, leading.

Agent Lacoste was the hunter. Determined, methodical.

And the Chief Inspector? Armand Gamache was their explorer. The one who went where others refused to go, or couldn't go. Or were too afraid to go. Into the wilderness. Gamache found the chasms, the caves, and the beasts that hid in them.

Beauvoir had long thought Gamache did it because he was afraid of nothing. But he'd come to realize the Chief Inspector had many fears. That was his strength. He recognized it in others. Fear more than anything was the thrust behind the knife, the fist. The blow to the head.

And young Agent Morin? What did he bring to the team? Beauvoir had to admit he'd quite warmed to the young man. But that hadn't blinded him to his inexperience. So far Beauvoir the bloodhound could smell fear quite clearly in this case.

But it came from Morin.

Beauvoir left the Chief in the living room speaking to his daughter and walked upstairs. As he climbed he hummed an old Weavers tune and hoped Gamache didn't notice the stuffed animal clutched in his hand.

When Monsieur Béliveau arrived to open his general store the next morning he had a customer already waiting. Agent Paul Morin stood up from the bench on the veranda and introduced himself to the elderly grocer.

"How can I help you?" Monsieur Béliveau asked as he unlocked the door. It wasn't often people in Three Pines were so pressed for his produce they were actually waiting for him. But then, this young man wasn't a villager.

"Do you have any paraffin?"

Monsieur Béliveau's stern face broke into a smile. "I have everything."

Paul Morin had never been in the store before and now he looked around. The dark wooden shelves were neatly stacked with tins. Sacks of dog food and birdseed leaned against the counter. Above the shelves were old boxes with backgammon games. Checkers, Snakes and Ladders, Monopoly. Paint by numbers and jigsaw puzzles were stacked in neat, orderly rows. Dried goods were displayed along one wall, paint, boots, birdfeeders were down another.

"Over there, by the Mason jars. Are you planning on doing some pickling?" he chuckled.

"Do you sell much?" Morin asked.

"At this time of year? It's all I can do to keep it in stock."

"And how about this?" He held up a tin. "Sell many of these?"

"A few. But most people go into the Canadian Tire in Cowansville for that sort of thing, or the building supply shops. I just keep some around in case."

"When was the last time you sold some?" the young agent asked as he paid for his goods. He didn't expect an answer really, but he felt he had to ask.

"July."

"Really?" Morin suspected he'd have to work on his "interrogation" face. "How'd you remember that?"

"It's what I do. You get to know the habits of people. And when they buy something unusual, like this," he held up the tin just before placing it in the paper bag, "I notice. Actually, two people bought some. Regular run on the market."

Agent Paul Morin left Monsieur Béliveau's shop with his goods, and a whole lot of unexpected information.

Agent Isabelle Lacoste started her day with the more straightforward of the interviews. She pressed the button and the elevator swished shut and took her to the top of the Banque Laurentienne tower in Montreal. As she waited she looked out at the harbor in one direction and Mont Royal with its huge cross in the other. Splendid glass buildings clustered all around downtown, reflecting the sun, reflecting the aspirations and achievements of this remarkable French city.

Isabelle Lacoste was always surprised by the amount of pride she felt when looking at downtown Montreal. The architects had managed to make it both impressive and charming. Montrealers never turned their back on the past. The Québécois were like that, for better or worse.

"*Je vous en prie*," the receptionist smiled and indicated a now-opened door.

"*Merci.*" Agent Lacoste walked into a quite grand office where a slender, athletic-looking middle-aged man was standing at his desk. He came round, extending his hand, and introduced himself as Yves Charpentier.

"I have some of the information you asked for," he said in cultured French. It delighted Lacoste when she could speak her own language to top executives. Her generation could. But she'd heard her parents and grandparents talk, and knew enough recent history to know had it been thirty years earlier she'd probably be speaking to a unilingual Englishman. Her English was perfect, but that wasn't the point.

She accepted the offer of coffee.

"This is rather delicate," said Monsieur Charpentier, when his secretary had left and the door was closed. "I don't want you to think Olivier Brulé was a criminal, and there was never any question of laying charges."

"But?"

"We were very happy with him for the first few years. I'm afraid we tend to be impressed by profit and he delivered on that. He moved up quickly. People liked him, especially his clients. A lot of people in this business can be glib, but Olivier was genuine. Quiet, respectful. It was a relief to deal with him."

"But?" Lacoste repeated, with a slight smile she hoped took the edge off her insistence. Monsieur Charpentier smiled back.

"Some company money went missing. A couple of million." He watched for her response but she simply listened. "A very discreet investigation was launched. In the meantime more money disappeared. Eventually we tracked it down to two people. One of them was Olivier. I didn't believe it, but after a couple of interviews he admitted it."

"Could he have been covering for the other employee?"

"Doubtful. Frankly, the other employee, while bright, wasn't smart enough to do this."

"Surely it doesn't take brains to embezzle. I'd have thought you'd have to be quite stupid."

Monsieur Charpentier laughed. "I agree, but I haven't made myself clear. The money was gone from the company account, but not stolen. Olivier showed us what he'd done. The trail. Seems he'd been following some activity in Malaysia, saw what he thought were some fantastic investment opportunities and took them to his boss, who didn't agree. So Olivier did it on his own, without authorization. It was all there. He'd documented it, intending to put it back, with the profits. And he'd been right. Those three million dollars turned into twenty."

Now Lacoste reacted, not verbally, but her expression made Charpentier nod.

"Exactly. The kid had a nose for money. Where is he now?"

"You fired him?" asked Lacoste, ignoring the question.

"He quit. We were trying to decide what to do with him. The executives were torn. His boss was apoplectic and wanted him dangled from the top of the building. We explained we don't do that. Anymore."

Lacoste laughed. "Some of you wanted to keep him on?"

"He was just so good at what he did."

"Which was making money. Are you convinced he was going to give it back?"

"Now, you've hit on the problem. Half of us believed him, half didn't. Olivier finally resigned, realizing he'd lost our trust. When you lose that, well . . ."

Well, thought Agent Lacoste. Well, well.

And now Olivier was in Three Pines. But like everyone who moved, he took himself with him.

Well, well.

The three Sûreté officers gathered round the table in the Incident Room.

"So where are we?" asked Beauvoir, standing once again by the sheets of paper tacked to the walls. Instead of answers to the questions he'd written there, two more had been added.

WHERE WAS HE MURDERED?
WHY WAS HE MOVED?

He shook his head. They seemed to be moving in the wrong direction. Even the few things that seemed possible in this case, like the fire irons being the weapons, turned out to be nothing.

They had nothing.

"We actually know a great deal," said Gamache. "We know the man wasn't killed in the bistro."

"That leaves the rest of the world to eliminate," said Beauvoir.

"We know paraffin and Varathane are involved. And we know that somehow Olivier's involved."

"But we don't even know who the victim was." Beauvoir underlined that question on his sheet in frustration. Gamache let that sit for a moment, then spoke.

"No. But we will. We'll know it all, eventually. It's a puzzle, and eventually the whole picture will be clear. We just need to be patient. And persistent. We need more background information on other possible suspects. The Parras for instance."

"I have that information you asked for," said Agent Morin, squaring his slight shoulders. "Hanna and Roar Parra came here in the mid-80s. Refugees. Applied for status and got it. They're now Canadian citizens."

"All legal?" asked Beauvoir, with regret.

"All legal. One child. Havoc. Twenty-one years old. The family's very involved in the Czech community here. Sponsored a few people."

"Right, right," waved Beauvoir. "Anything interesting?"

Morin looked down at his copious notes. What would the Inspector consider interesting?

"Did you find anything from before they came here?" asked Gamache.

"No, sir. I have calls in to Prague but their record keeping from that time isn't good."

"Okay." Beauvoir snapped the top back on the Magic Marker. "Anything else?"

Agent Morin placed a paper bag on the conference table.

"I dropped by the general store this morning, and bought these."

Out of the bag he brought a brick of paraffin wax. "Monsieur Béliveau says everyone's been buying paraffin, especially at this time of year."

"Not much help," said Beauvoir, taking his seat again.

"No, but this might be." And from the bag he pulled a tin. On it was written *Varathane*. "He sold two tins like this to two different people in July. One to Gabri and the other to Marc Gilbert."

"Oh, really?" Beauvoir uncapped the marker.

Agent Lacoste, like every Montrealer, knew about Habitat, the strange and exotic apartment building created for Expo 67, the great World's Fair. The buildings had been considered avant garde then, and still were. They sat on Île des Soeurs, in the St. Lawrence River, a tribute to creativity and vision. Once seen Habitat was never forgotten. Instead of a square or rectangular building to house people the architect had made each room a separate block, an elongated cube. It looked like a jumble of children's building blocks, piled on top of each other. One interconnected with another, some above, some below, some off to the side, so that daylight shone through the building and the rooms were all bathed in sun. And the views from each room were spectacular, either of the grand river or of the magnificent city.

Lacoste had never been in a Habitat condo, but she was about to. Jacques Brulé, Olivier's father, lived there.

"Come in," he said, unsmiling, as he opened the door. "You said this was about my son?"

Monsieur Brulé was very unlike his son. He had a full head of dark hair and was robust. Behind him she could see the gleaming wood floors, the slate fireplace and the huge windows looking onto the river. The condo was tasteful and expensive.

"I wonder if we could sit down?"

"I wonder if you could come to the point?"

He stood at the door, blocking her way. Not allowing her farther into his home.

"As I mentioned on the phone, I'm with homicide. We're investigating a murder in Three Pines."

The man looked blank.

"Where your son lives." He nodded, once. Lacoste continued. "A body was found in the bistro there."

She'd intentionally not identified the bistro. Olivier's father waited, showing absolutely no recognition, no alarm, no concern at all.

"Olivier's Bistro," she finally said.

"And what do you want from me?"

It was far from unusual in a murder case to find fractured families, but she hadn't expected to find one here.

"I'd like to know about Olivier, his upbringing, his background, his interests."

"You've come to the wrong parent. You'd need to ask his mother."

"I'm sorry, but I thought she'd died."

"She has."

"You told me on the phone he went to Notre Dame de Sion. Quite a good school, I hear. But it only goes to grade six. How about after that?"

"I think he went to Loyola. Or was it Brébeuf? I can't remember."

"*Pardon?* Were you and his mother separated?"

"No, I'd never divorce." This was the most animated he'd been. Much more upset by the suggestion of divorce than death and certainly than murder. Lacoste waited. And waited. Eventually Jacques Brulé spoke.

"I was away a lot, building a career."

But Agent Lacoste, who hunted killers and still knew what schools her children attended, knew that wasn't much of an explanation, or excuse.

"Was he ever in trouble? Did he get into fights? Any problems?"

"With Olivier? None at all. He was a regular boy, mind you. He'd get into scrapes, but nothing serious."

It was like interviewing a marshmallow, or a salesman about a dining room set. Monsieur Brulé seemed on the verge of calling his son "it" throughout the conversation.

"When was the last time you spoke to him?" She wasn't sure that was exactly on topic, but she wanted to know.

"I don't know."

She should have guessed. As she left he called after her, "Tell him I said hello."

Lacoste stopped at the elevator, pressed the button, and looked back at the large man standing in the door frame, shutting out all the light that she knew was streaming into his apartment.

"Maybe you can tell him yourself. Visit even. Have you met Gabri?"

"Gabri?"

"Gabriel. His partner."

"Gabrielle? He hasn't told me about her."

The elevator came and she stepped in, wondering if Monsieur Brulé would ever find Three Pines. She also wondered about this man who kept so much hidden.

But then, clearly, so did his son.

It was late morning and Olivier was in his bistro, at the front door. Trying to decide if he should unlock it. Let people in. Maybe the crowd would drown out the voice in his head. The Hermit's voice. And that terrible story that bound them together. Even unto death.

The young man appeared at the base of the now barren mountain. Like everyone else in the region he'd heard the stories. Of bad children brought here as a sacrifice to the dreadful Mountain King.

He looked for tiny bones on the dusty soil, but there was nothing. No life. Not even death.

As he was about to leave he heard a small sigh. A breeze had blown up where nothing had stirred before. He felt it on the back of his neck, and he felt his skin grow cool and the hairs stand up. He looked down at the lush, green valley, the thick forests and the thatched roofs, and he wondered how he could have been so stupid as to have come up here. Alone.

"Don't," he heard on the wind. "Don't."

The young man turned round. "Go," he heard.

"Don't go," said the sigh.

FIFTEEN

⎯⌣

The three investigators left the Incident Room together, but parted ways at the village green. Beauvoir left the Chief and Agent Morin to interview Olivier and Gabri once again, while he headed to the old Hadley house.

The Inspector was feeling pretty cocky. They'd caught the Gilberts in a lie. Dominique had told him yesterday they never used Varathane. Was quite pleased to tell him how "green" they were. But now there was proof they'd at least bought a *demi-liter* of the stuff.

But the extra spring in his step was because he was curious, anxious even, to see what the Gilberts had done to the old Hadley house.

Gamache tried the door to the bistro and was surprised to find it open. Earlier that morning, over breakfast of *pain doré*, sliced strawberries and bananas, maple syrup and back bacon, Gabri had admitted he didn't know when Olivier might reopen the bistro.

"Maybe never," he said, "then where would we be? I'd have to start taking in paying guests."

"Good thing then that you're a B and B," said Gamache.

"You'd think that would be an advantage, wouldn't you? But I'm handicapped by extreme laziness."

And yet, when Gamache and Agent Morin walked into the bistro there was Gabri behind the bar, polishing it. And from the kitchen came the aroma of fine cooking.

"Olivier," Gabri called, coming around from behind the bar. "Our first customers since the murder are here," he sang out.

"Oh, for God's sake, Gabri," they heard from the kitchen and a pot clanked down. A moment later Olivier punched through the swinging door. "Oh, it's you."

"Just us, I'm afraid. We have a few questions. Do you have a moment?"

Olivier looked as though he was about to say no, but changed his mind and indicated a seat by the hearth. Once again a fire was burning there. And the pokers had been returned.

Gamache looked at Agent Morin. Morin's eyes widened. Surely the Chief Inspector wasn't expecting him to conduct the interview? But the moments dragged by and no one else said anything. Morin searched his mind. *Don't be too forceful*, though he didn't think that would be a problem. *Get the suspect to drop his guard.* Gabri was smiling at him, wiping his hands on an apron and waiting. *So far so good*, thought Morin. *Seems the idiot agent act is working. Now if only it wasn't an act.*

He smiled back at the two men and racked his brain. Up until now the only questioning he'd done was of speeders along Autoroute 10. It didn't seem necessary to ask Gabri whether he had a driver's license.

"Is it about the murder?" asked Gabri, trying to be helpful.

"Yes, it is," said Morin, finding his voice. "Not really so much about the murder as a small issue that's come up."

"Please," said Olivier, indicating a chair, "have a seat."

"This is really nothing," said Morin, sitting along with everyone else. "Just a loose end. We were wondering why you bought Varathane from Monsieur Béliveau in July."

"Did we?" Olivier looked over at Gabri.

"Well, I did. We needed to redo the bar, remember?"

"Will you stop with that? I like the bar the way it is," said Olivier. "Distressed."

"I'm distressed, it's a disgrace. Remember when we bought it? It was all gleaming?"

They looked over at the long wooden bar with the till and jars of all-sorts, jelly beans and licorice pipes. Behind were liquor bottles on shelves.

"It's about atmosphere," said Olivier. "Everything in here should either be old or look old. Don't say it." He held up his hand to ward off Gabri's response to that, then turned to the officers. "We always disagree about this. When we moved here this place was a hardware store. All the original features had been ripped out or covered over."

"The beams were hidden under that sound insulation stuff for ceilings," said Gabri. "Even the fireplaces were ripped out and turned into storage. We had to find a stone mason to rebuild them."

"Really?" said Gamache, impressed. The fireplace looked original. "But what about the Varathane?"

"Yes, Gabri. What about the Varathane?" Olivier demanded.

"Well, I was going to strip the bar and resand and coat it, but . . ."

"But?"

"I was hoping maybe Old Mundin could do it instead. He knows how. He'd love to do it."

"Forget it. No one's going to touch that bar."

"Where's the tin you bought from Monsieur Béliveau?" Agent Morin asked.

"It's in our basement at home."

"Can I see it?"

"If you'd like." Gabri looked at Morin as though he was mad.

Jean Guy Beauvoir couldn't quite believe his eyes. But more than that he couldn't believe something less tangible. He was enjoying this tour of the old Hadley house. So far Marc and Dominique Gilbert had shown him all the magnificent bedrooms, with fireplaces and flat-screen TVs, with spa baths and steam showers. The gleaming mosaic-glass tiles. The espresso maker in each room.

Waiting for the first guests.

And now they were in the spa area, the lower floor, with its muted lighting and soothing colors and calming aromas, even now. Products were being unpacked and waiting to be displayed on shelves not yet built. This area, while clearly as spectacular as the rest of the place, was less finished.

"A month more, we figure," Marc was saying. "We're hoping to have our first guests on the Thanksgiving long weekend. We're just discussing putting an ad in the papers."

"I think it's too soon, but Marc thinks we can get it done. We've hired most of the staff. Four massage therapists, a yoga instructor, a personal trainer and a receptionist. And that's just for the spa."

The two prattled on excitedly. Enid would love it here, Beauvoir thought.

"How much would you charge for a couple?"

"A night at the inn and one healing spa treatment each would start at three hundred and twenty-five dollars," said Marc. "That's for a standard room midweek, but includes breakfast and dinner."

None of the rooms seemed standard to Beauvoir. But neither did the price. How much could creams really cost? Still, for their anniversary, maybe. Olivier and Gabri would kill him, but maybe they didn't need to know. He and Enid could just stay here. At the inn. Not go into Three Pines. Who'd really want to leave?

"That would be each," said Marc, as he turned off the lights and they walked back up the stairs.

"I'm sorry?"

"Three hundred and twenty-five dollars per person. Before tax," said Marc.

Beauvoir was glad he was behind them and no one saw his face. Seemed only the wealthy got healed.

So far, though, he hadn't seen any signs of Varathane. He'd looked at floors, counters, doors, exclaiming over the craftsmanship, to the Gilberts' delight. But he'd also been looking for the telltale gleam. The unnatural shine.

Nothing.

At the front door he debated asking them outright, but he didn't want to show his hand just yet. He wandered around the yard, noticing the now groomed lawns, the newly planted gardens, the trees staked and sturdy.

It all appealed to his sense of order. This was what the country should be. Civilized.

Roar Parra appeared round the corner of the house pushing a wheelbarrow. He stopped when he saw Beauvoir.

"Can I help you?"

Beauvoir introduced himself and looked at the horse manure in the barrow. "More work for you, I suppose." He fell into step with Parra.

"I like horses. Nice to see them back. Old Mrs. Hadley used to keep them. Barns fallen down now and the trails have grown over."

"I hear the new owners have you cutting them again."

Parra grunted. "Big job. Still, my son helps when he can, and I like it. Quiet in the woods."

"Except for the strangers wandering around." Beauvoir saw the wary look on Parra's face.

"What d'you mean?"

"Well, you told Agent Lacoste you'd seen a stranger disappearing into the woods. But it wasn't the dead man. Who do you think it was?"

"I musta been wrong."

"Now, why would you say that? You don't really believe it, do you?"

For once Beauvoir really looked at the man. He was covered in sweat and dirt, and manure. He was stocky and muscled. But none of that made him stupid. In fact, Beauvoir thought this man was very bright. So why had he just lied?

"I'm tired of people looking at me like I just said I'd been kidnapped by aliens. The guy was there one moment, gone the next. I looked for him, but nothing. And no, I haven't seen him since."

"Maybe he's gone."

"Maybe."

They walked in silence. The air was filled with the musky scents of fresh harvested hay and manure.

"I heard the new owners here are very environmentally aware." Beauvoir managed to make it sound a reproach, something slightly silly. Some new-fangled city-folk nonsense. "Bet they won't let you use pesticides or fertilizers."

"I won't use them. Told them so. Had to teach them to compost and even recycle. Not sure they'd ever heard of it. And they still used plastic bags for their groceries, can you believe it?"

Beauvoir, who did too, shook his head. Parra dumped the manure onto a steaming pile and turned back to Beauvoir, chuckling.

"What?" asked Beauvoir.

"They're now greener than green. Nothing wrong with that, of course. Wish everyone was."

"So that means with all those renovations they didn't use any toxic stuff, like Varathane."

Again the stocky man laughed. "Wanted to, but I stopped them. Told them about tung oil."

Beauvoir felt his optimism fade. Leaving Roar Parra to turn over the compost heap he went back to the house and rang the doorbell. It was time to ask them directly. The door was answered by Madame Gilbert, Marc's mother.

"I'd like to speak to your son again, if you don't mind."

"Of course, Inspector. Would you like to come in?"

She was genteel and gracious. Unlike her son. Beneath his cheerful and friendly manner there peeked every now and then a condescension, an awareness that he had a lot and others had less. And somehow that made them less.

"I'll just wait. It's a small point."

After she'd disappeared Beauvoir stood in the entrance admiring the fresh white paint, the polished furniture, the flowers in the hall beyond. The sense of order and calm and welcome. In the old Hadley house. He could hardly believe it. For all Marc Gilbert's flaws, he'd been able to do all this. Light flooded through the window in the foyer and gleamed off the wooden floors.

Gleamed.

SIXTEEN

—

 By the time Madame Gilbert and Marc returned Inspector Beauvoir had the area rug up and was examining the floor of the small entrance hall.

"What is it?" she asked.

Beauvoir looked up from where he was kneeling and gestured to them to stay where they were. Then he bent back down.

The floor had been Varathaned. It was smooth and hard and clear and glossy. Except for one small smudge. He stood up and brushed off his knees.

"Do you have a cordless phone?"

"I'll get it," said Marc.

"Perhaps your mother wouldn't mind." Beauvoir looked at Carole Gilbert who nodded and left.

"What is it?" Marc asked, leaning in and staring at the floor.

"You know what it is, Monsieur Gilbert. Yesterday your wife said you never used Varathane, that you were trying to be as eco-friendly as possible. But that wasn't true."

Marc laughed. "You're right. We did use Varathane here. But that was before we knew there was something better to use. So we stopped."

Beauvoir stared at Marc Gilbert. He could hear Carole returning with the phone, her heels clicking on the wooden floors.

"I use Varathane," said the Inspector. "I'm not as environmentally aware as you, I guess. I know it takes about a day to set. But it really isn't completely hard for a week or so. This Varathane isn't months old. You didn't start with it, did you? This was just done within the last week."

Gilbert finally looked flustered. "Look, I Varathaned it one night when everyone else was asleep. It was last Friday. That's good wood and it's going to get more wear than any other place in the inn, so I decided to use Varathane. But just there. Nowhere else. I don't think Dominique or Mama even know."

"Don't you use this door all the time? It is the main entrance, after all."

"We park around the side and use the kitchen door. We never use the front. But our guests will."

"Here's the phone." Carole Gilbert had reappeared. Beauvoir thanked her and called the bistro.

"Is Chief Inspector Gamache there, *s'il vous plaît*?" he asked Olivier.

"*Oui?*" He heard the Chief's deep voice.

"I've found something. I think you need to come up. And bring a Scene of Crime kit, please."

"Scene of Crime? What's that supposed to mean?" asked Marc, getting irritated now.

But Beauvoir had stopped answering questions.

Within minutes Gamache and Morin arrived and Beauvoir showed them the polished floor. And the little scuff mark marring the perfect shine.

Morin took photographs, then, gloves on and tweezers ready, he took samples.

"I'll get these to the lab in Sherbrooke right away."

Morin left and Gamache and Beauvoir turned back to the Gilberts. Dominique had arrived home with groceries and had joined them.

"What is it?" she asked.

They were standing in the large hall now, away from the entrance, with its yellow police tape and rolled-up carpet.

Gamache was stern, all semblance of the affable man gone. "Who was the dead man?"

Three stunned people stared back.

"We've told you," said Carole. "We don't know."

Gamache nodded slowly. "You did say that. And you also said you'd never seen anyone fitting his description, but you had. Or at least one of you had. And one of you knows exactly what that lab report will tell us."

They stared at each other now.

"The dead man was here, lying in your entrance, on Varathane not quite hardened. He had it stuck to his sweater. And your floor has part of his sweater stuck to it."

"But this is ridiculous," said Carole, looking from Gamache to Beauvoir. She too could shape-shift, and now the gracious chatelaine became a formidable woman, her eyes angry and hard. "Leave our home immediately."

Gamache bowed slightly and to Beauvoir's amazement he turned to go, catching Beauvoir's eye.

They walked down the dirt road into Three Pines.

"Well done, Jean Guy. Twice we searched that house and twice we missed it."

"So why are we leaving? We should be up there, interviewing them."

"Perhaps. But time is on our side. One of them knows we'll have proof, probably before the day's out. Let him stew. Believe me, it's no favor I've done them."

And Beauvoir, thinking about it, knew that to be true.

Just before lunch Marc Gilbert arrived at the Incident Room.

"May I speak to you?" he asked Gamache.

"You can speak to all of us. There're no secrets anymore, are there, Monsieur Gilbert?"

Marc bristled but sat in the chair indicated. Beauvoir nodded to Morin to join them with his notebook.

"I've come voluntarily, you can see that," said Marc.

"I can," said Gamache.

Marc Gilbert had walked down to the old railway station, slowly. Going over and over what he'd tell them. It had sounded good when he'd talked to the trees and stones and the ducks flying south. Now he wasn't so sure.

"Look, I know this sounds ridiculous." He started with the one thing he'd promised himself not to say. He tried to concentrate on the Chief Inspector, not that ferret of an assistant, or the idiot boy taking notes. "But I found the body just lying there. I couldn't sleep so I got up. I was heading to the kitchen to make myself a sandwich when I saw him. Lying there by the front door."

He stared at Gamache who was watching him with calm, interested brown eyes. Not accusing, not even disbelieving. Just listening.

"It was dark, of course, so I turned on a light and went closer. I thought it might be a drunk who'd staggered up the hill from the bistro, saw our place and just made himself comfortable."

He was right, it did sound ridiculous. Still the Chief said nothing.

"I was going to call for help but I didn't want to upset Dominique or my mother, so I crept closer to the guy. Then I saw his head."

"And you knew he'd been murdered," said Beauvoir, not believing a word of this.

"That's it." Marc turned grateful eyes to the Inspector, until he saw the sneer, then he turned back to Gamache. "I couldn't believe it."

"So a murdered man shows up in your house in the middle of the night. Didn't you lock the door?" asked Beauvoir.

"We do, but we're getting a lot of deliveries and since we never use that door ourselves I guess we forgot."

"What did you do, Monsieur Gilbert?" Gamache asked, his voice soothing, reasonable.

Marc opened his mouth, shut it and looked down at his hands. He'd promised himself when it got to this part he wouldn't look away, or down. Wouldn't flinch. But now he did all three.

"I thought about it for a while, then I picked the guy up and carried him down into the village. To the bistro."

There it was.

"Why?" Gamache asked.

"I was going to call the police, actually had the phone in my hand," he held out his empty hand to them as though that was proof, "but then I got to thinking. About all the work we'd put into the place. And we're so close, so close. We're going to open in just over a month, you know. And I realized it would be all over the papers. Who'd want to relax in an inn and spa where someone had just been killed?"

Beauvoir hated to say it, but he had to agree. Especially at those prices.

"So you dumped him in the bistro?" he asked. "Why?"

Now Gilbert turned to him. "Because I didn't want to put him into someone else's home to be found. And I knew Olivier kept the key under a planter by the front door." He could see their skepticism, but plowed ahead anyway. "I took the dead guy down, left him on the floor of the bistro and came home. I moved a rug up from the spa area to cover where the guy had been. I knew no one would miss it downstairs. Too much else going on."

"This is a dangerous time," said Gamache, staring at Marc. "We could charge you with obstruction, with indignities to a body, with hampering the investigation."

"With murder," said Beauvoir.

"We need the full truth. Why did you take the body to the bistro? You could have left him in the woods."

Marc sighed. He didn't think they'd press this point. "I thought about it, but there were lots of kids in Three Pines for the long weekend and I didn't want any of them finding him."

"Noble," said Gamache, with equilibrium. "But that wasn't likely to happen, was it? How often do kids play in the woods around your place?"

"It happens. Would you run that risk?"

"I would call the police."

The Chief let that sentence do its job. It stripped Marc Gilbert of any pretension to higher ground. And left him exposed before them. For a man who, at best, did something unconscionable. At worst he murdered a man.

"The truth," said Gamache, almost in a whisper.

"I took the body to the bistro so that people would think he'd been killed there. Olivier's treated us like shit since we arrived."

"So you paid him back by putting a body there?" asked Beauvoir. He could think of a few people he'd like to dump bodies on. But never would. This man did. That spoke of his hatred of Olivier. A rare, and surprising, degree of hatred. And his resolve.

Marc Gilbert looked at his hands, looked out the window, moved his gaze around the walls of the old railway station. And finally he rested on the large man across from him.

"That's what I did. I shouldn't have done it, I know." He shook his head in wonderment at his own stupidity. Then he looked up suddenly as the silence grew. His eyes were sharp and bright. "Wait a minute. You don't think I killed the man, do you?"

They said nothing.

Gilbert looked from one to the other. He even looked at the idiot agent with the poised pen.

"Why would I do that? I don't even know who he is."

Still they said nothing.

"Really. I'd never seen him before."

Finally Beauvoir broke the silence. "And yet there he was in your house. Dead. Why would a strange body be in your house?"

"You see?" Gilbert thrust his hand toward Beauvoir. "You see? That's why I didn't call the cops. Because I knew that's what you'd think." He put his head into his hands as though trying to contain his scrambling thoughts. "Dominique's going to kill me. Oh, Jesus. Oh, God." His shoulders sagged and his head hung, heavy from the weight of what he'd done and what was still to come.

Just then the phone rang. Agent Morin reached for it. "Sûreté du Québec."

The voice on the other end spoke hurriedly and was muffled.

"*Désolé*," said Morin, feeling bad because he knew he was interrupting the interrogation. "I don't understand." Everyone was looking at him. He colored and tried to listen closely, but he still couldn't make out what was being said. Then he heard and the color in his face changed. "*Un instant.*"

He covered the mouthpiece. "It's Madame Gilbert. There's a man on their land. She saw him in the woods at the back." Morin listened again at the phone. "She says he's approaching the house. What should she do?"

All three men stood up.

"Oh my God, he must have seen me leave and knows they're alone," said Marc.

Gamache took the phone. "Madame Gilbert, is the back door locked? Can you get to it now?" He waited. "Good. Where is he now?" He listened, then began striding to the door, Inspector Beauvoir and Marc Gilbert running beside him. "We'll be there in two minutes. Take your mother-in-law and lock yourselves in an upstairs bathroom. That one you took me to. Yes, with the balcony. Lock the doors, close the curtains. Stay there until we come to get you."

Beauvoir had started the car and Gamache slammed the door and handed the phone back to Morin. "Stay here. You too."

"I'm coming," said Gilbert, reaching for the passenger door.

"You'll stay here and talk to your wife. Keep her calm. You're delaying us, monsieur."

Gamache's voice was intense, angry.

Gilbert grabbed the phone from Morin as Beauvoir gunned the car and they took off over the stone bridge, around the common and up du Moulin, to stop short of the old Hadley house. They were there in less than a minute. They got quickly and quietly out of the car.

"Do you have a gun?" Beauvoir whispered as they ran, crouched, to the corner of the house. Gamache shook his head. Really, thought Beauvoir. There were times he just felt like shooting the Chief himself.

"They're dangerous," said Gamache.

"Which is why he," Beauvoir jerked his head toward the back of the property, "probably has one."

Gamache brought his hand up and Beauvoir was silent. The Chief motioned in one direction, then disappeared around the side of the house. Beauvoir ran past the front door and around the far side. Both making for the back, where Dominique had seen the man.

Hugging the wall and staying low Gamache edged along. There was a need for speed. The stranger had been here for at least five minutes, uninterrupted. He could be in the house by now. A lot can happen in a minute, never mind five.

He edged around a bush and got to the far end of the large old house. There he saw movement. A man. Large. In a hat and gloves and field coat. He was close to the house, close to the back door. If he got inside their job would be far more difficult. So many places to hide. So much closer to the women.

As the Chief Inspector watched the man looked around then made for the French doors into the kitchen.

Gamache stepped out from the wall.

"Hold it," he commanded. "Sûreté du Québec."

The man stopped. His back was to Gamache and he couldn't see whether Gamache had a gun. But neither could Gamache see if he had one.

"I want to see your hands," said Gamache.

There was no movement. That wasn't good, Gamache knew. He prepared to dive sideways if the man swung around and shot. But both stood their ground. Then the man turned quickly.

Gamache, trained and experienced, felt time slow down and the world collapse, so that all that existed was the turning man in front of him. His body, his arms. His hands. And as the man's body swung Gamache saw something gripped in his right hand.

Gamache ducked.

Then the man was on the ground, and Beauvoir was on top of him. Gamache raced forward, pinning the man's hand to the ground.

"He had something in his hand, do you see it?" demanded Gamache.

"Got it," said Beauvoir and Gamache hauled the man to his feet.

Both of them looked at him. The hat had fallen off and the iron-gray hair was disheveled. He was tall and lanky.

"What the hell are you doing?" the man demanded.

"You're trespassing," said Beauvoir, handing what the man had held to Gamache, who looked at it. It was a bag. Of granola. And on the front was a stamp.

Manoir Bellechasse.

Gamache looked more closely at the man. He looked familiar. The man glared back, angry, imperious.

"How dare you. Do you know who I am?"

"As a matter of fact," said Gamache, "I do."

After a call to Morin, Marc Gilbert was released and showed up at his home minutes later, out of breath from running. He'd been told his wife and mother were safe but was relieved to see it for himself. He kissed and hugged them both then turned to Gamache.

"Where is he? I want to see him."

Clearly "see" was a euphemism.

"Inspector Beauvoir's with him in the barn."

"Good," said Marc and headed toward the door.

"Marc, wait." His mother ran after him. "Maybe we should just leave this to the police." Carole Gilbert looked frightened still. And with good reason, thought Gamache as he thought of the man in the barn.

"Are you kidding? This man's been spying on us, maybe more."

"What do you mean, 'maybe more'?"

Gilbert hesitated.

"What aren't you telling us?" his wife asked.

He shot a look at Gamache. "I think he might have killed that man and left his body in our house. As a threat. Or maybe he meant to kill one of us. Thought the stranger was one of us. I don't know. But first the body shows up, then this guy tries to break in. Someone's trying to hurt us. And I want to find out why."

"Wait. Wait a minute." Dominique had her hands up to stop her husband. "What are you saying? That body really was here?" She looked toward the vestibule. "In our home?" She looked at Gamache. "It's true?" She looked back at her husband. "Marc?"

He opened and shut his mouth. Then took a deep breath. "He was here. The police were right. I found him when I got up in the middle of the night. I got scared and did something stupid."

"You took the body to the bistro?" Dominique looked as though she'd been slapped by someone she loved, so great was her shock. His mother was staring at him as though he'd peed in the Château Frontenac dining room. He knew that look from when he was a boy and peed in the Château Frontenac dining room.

Gilbert's lightning mind zipped all over the place, searching dark corners for someone else to blame. Surely it wasn't his fault. Surely there were factors his wife didn't appreciate. Surely this couldn't be the act of complete idiocy her face accused him of.

But he knew it was.

Dominique turned to Gamache. "You have my permission to shoot him."

"*Merci, madame*, but I'd need more than that to shoot him. A gun for instance."

"Pity," she said, and looked at her husband. "What were you thinking?"

He told them, as he had the cops, the reasoning that had appeared so obvious, so dazzling, at three in the morning.

"You did it for the business?" said Dominique when he'd finished. "Something's very wrong when dumping bodies is part of our business plan."

"Well, it wasn't exactly planned," he tried to defend himself. "And yes, I made a terrible mistake, but isn't there a bigger question?" He'd finally found something curled up in one of those dark corners. Something that would take the heat off him. "Yes, I moved the body. But who put it here in the first place?"

They'd obviously been so stunned by his admission they hadn't even thought of that. But Gamache had. Because he'd noticed something else about the Varathaned floor. The shine, the mar. And the complete lack of blood. So had Beauvoir. Even if Marc Gilbert had scrubbed and scrubbed he'd never have gotten all the blood up. There'd be traces.

But there was nothing. Just some fluff from the dead man's cardigan.

No, Gilbert might have killed the man, but he didn't do it at his own front door. The man had already been dead when he'd been placed there.

Gilbert stood up. "That's one of the reasons I want to see the man who tried to break in. I think he had something to do with it."

His mother stood up and touched her son's arm. "I really think you should leave this to the police. The man's probably unwell."

She looked to Gamache, but the Chief Inspector had no intention of stopping Marc Gilbert from confronting the intruder. Just the opposite. He wanted to see what happened.

"Come with me," he said to Marc, then turned to the women. "You're welcome to join us, if you like."

"Well, I'm going," said Dominique. "Maybe you should stay here," she said to her mother-in-law.

"I'm coming too."

As they approached the barn the horses looked up from the field. Beauvoir, who hadn't seen them before, almost stopped in his tracks. He hadn't seen that many horses in real life. On film, yes. And these didn't look like any film horses. But then, most men didn't look like Sean Connery and most women didn't look like Julia Roberts. But even allowing for natural selection, these horses seemed, well, odd. One didn't even look like a horse. They began to mosey over, one walking sideways.

Paul Morin, who had seen a lot of horses, said, "Nice cows."

Dominique Gilbert ignored him. But she felt drawn to the horses. As their own lives so suddenly unraveled the horses' calm attracted her. As did, she thought, their suffering. No, not their suffering, but their forbearance. If they could endure a lifetime of abuse and pain she could take whatever blow that barn had in store. As the others moved past her Dominique stopped and walked back to the paddock, where she stood on a bucket and leaned over the fence. The other horses, still shy, held back. But Buttercup, big, awkward, ugly and scarred, came forward. Buttercup's broad, flat forehead pushed softly into Dominique's chest, as though it fit there. As though it was the key. And as she walked away to join the others and confront whatever that shadow was they could see standing in the barn, she smelled horse on her hands. And felt the reassuring pressure between her breasts.

It took a moment or two for their eyes to adjust as they stepped into the dim barn. Then the shadow became solid, firm. Human. Before them appeared a tall, slender, graceful older man.

"You've kept me waiting," the darkness said.

Marc, whose vision wasn't quite as good as he pretended, could only just see the outline of the man. But the words, the voice, told him more than enough. He felt light-headed and reached out. His mother, standing next to him, took his hand and held him steady.

"Mother?" he whispered.

"It's all right, Marc," the man said.

But Marc knew it wasn't all right. He'd heard the rumors about the old Hadley house, the ghouls that lived there. He'd loved the stories because it meant no one else had wanted the house, and they could get it dirt cheap.

Dirt to dirt. Something filthy had indeed risen. The old Hadley house had produced one more ghost.

"Dad?"

SEVENTEEN

"Dad?"

Marc stared from the shadow, darker than the shade, to his mother. The voice was unmistakable, indelible. The deep, calm voice that carried censure with a slight smile, so that the child, the boy, the man, had never really known where he stood. But he'd suspected.

"Hello, Marc."

The voice held a hint of humor, as though this was in any way close to funny. As though Marc's staggering shock was reason for mirth.

Dr. Vincent Gilbert walked out of the shed and out of the dead, into the light.

"Mom?" Marc turned to the woman beside him.

"I'm sorry, Marc. Come with me." She tugged her only child out into the sun and sat him on a bale of hay. He felt it pricking into his bottom, uncomfortable.

"Can you get him something to drink?" Carole asked her daughter-in-law, but Dominique, hand to her face, seemed almost as stunned as her husband.

"Marc?" Dominique said.

Beauvoir looked at Gamache. This was going to be a long day if all they said was each other's names.

Dominique recovered and walked quickly, breaking into a run, back to the house.

"I'm sorry, have I surprised you?"

"Of course you surprised him, Vincent," snapped Carole. "How did you think he'd feel?"

"I thought he'd be happier than this."

"You never think."

Marc stared at his father, then he turned to his mother. "You told me he was dead."

"I might have exaggerated."

"Dead? You told him I was dead?"

She turned on her husband again. "We agreed that's what I'd say. Are you senile?"

"Me? Me? Do you have any idea what I've done with my life while you played bridge?"

"Yes, you abandoned your family—"

"Enough," said Gamache, and raised a hand. With an effort the two broke off and looked at him. "Let me be absolutely clear about this," said Gamache. "Is he your father?"

Marc finally took a long hard look at the man standing beside his mother. He was older, thinner. It'd been almost twenty years, after all. Since he'd gone missing in India. Or at least that's what his mother had told him. A few years later she said she'd had him declared dead, and did Marc think they should hold a memorial for him?

Marc had given it absolutely no thought. No. He had better things to do than help plan a memorial for a man missing all his life.

And so that had ended that. The Great Man, for that was what Marc's father was, was forgotten. Marc never spoke of him, never thought of him. When he'd met Dominique and she'd asked if his father had been "that" Vincent Gilbert he'd agreed that, yes, he had. But he was dead. Fallen into some dark hole in Calcutta or Bombay or Madras.

"Isn't he a saint?" Dominique had asked.

"That's right. St. Vincent. Who raised the dead and buried the living."

She hadn't asked any more.

"Here." Dominique had returned with a tray of glasses and bottles, not sure what the occasion called for. Never, in all the board meetings she'd chaired, all the client dinners she'd hosted, all the arbitrations she'd attended, had anything quite like this arisen. A father. Risen. But obviously not revered.

She put the drinks tray on a log and brought her hands to her face, softly inhaling the musky scent of horse, and felt herself relax. She dropped her hands, though not her guard. She had an instinct for trouble, and this was it.

"Yes, he's my father," said Marc, then turned to his mother again. "He isn't dead?"

It was, thought Gamache, an interesting question. Not, *He's alive?* but rather, *He isn't dead?* There seemed a difference.

"I'm afraid not."

"I'm standing right here, you know," said Dr. Gilbert. "I can hear."

But he didn't seem put off by any of this, just amused. Gamache knew Dr. Vincent Gilbert would be a formidable opponent. And he hoped this Great Man, for that was what Gamache knew him to be, wasn't also a wicked man.

Carole handed Marc a glass of water and took one herself, sitting on the hay beside him. "Your father and I agreed our marriage was over a long time ago. He went off to India as you know."

"Why did you say he was dead?" Marc asked. If he hadn't Beauvoir would have. He'd always thought his own family more than a little odd. Never a whisper, never a calm conversation. Everything was charged, kinetic. Voices raised, shouting, yelling. Always in each other's faces, in each other's lives. It was a mess. He'd yearned for calm, for peace, and had found it in Enid. Their lives were relaxed, soothing, never going too far, or getting too close.

He really should call her.

But odd as his family might be, they were nothing compared to this. In fact, that was one of the great comforts of his job. At least his family compared well to people who actually killed each other, rather than just thought about it.

"It seemed easier," Carole said. "I was happier being a widow than a divorcee."

"But what about me?" Marc asked.

"I thought it would be easier for you too. Easier to think your father had died."

"How could you think that?"

"I'm sorry. I was wrong," said his mother. "But you were twenty-five, and never close to your father. I really thought you wouldn't care."

"So you killed him?"

Vincent Gilbert, silent until now, laughed. "Well put."

"Fuck off," said Marc. "I'll get to you in a minute." He shifted on the prickly hay bale. His father really was a pain in the ass.

"He agreed, no matter how he's rewritten it now. I couldn't have done it without his cooperation. In exchange for his freedom he agreed to be dead."

Marc turned to his father. "Is that right?"

Now Vincent Gilbert looked less regal, less certain. "I wasn't myself. I wasn't well. I'd gone to India to find myself and felt the best way to do that was to shed the old life completely. Become a new man."

"So I just didn't exist anymore?" Marc asked. "What a fucking great family. Where have you been?"

"The Manoir Bellechasse."

"For twenty years? You've been at a luxury inn for twenty years?"

"Oh, well, no. I've been there off and on all summer. I brought you that." He gestured to the package sitting on a shelf in the shed. "It's for you," he said to Dominique. She picked it up.

"Granola," she said. "From the Bellechasse. Thank you."

"Granola?" asked Marc. "You come back from the dead and bring breakfast cereal?"

"I didn't know what you needed," said his father. "I'd heard from your mother that you'd bought a place down here so I came and watched every now and then."

"You're the one Roar Parra spotted in the woods," said Dominique.

"Roar Parra? Roar? Are you kidding? Is he the troll? The dark, stocky man?"

"The nice man helping your son turn this place around, you mean?" asked Carole.

"I say what I mean."

"Will you two please stop it." Dominique glared at Marc's parents. "Behave yourselves."

"Why're you here?" Marc finally asked.

Vincent Gilbert hesitated than sat on a nearby hay bale. "I'd kept in touch with your mother. She told me about your marriage. Your job. You seemed to be happy. But then she said you'd quit your job and moved to the middle of nowhere. I wanted to make sure you were all right. I'm not a complete fool, you know," said Vincent Gilbert, his handsome, aristocratic face somber. "I know what a shock this is. I'm sorry. I should never have let your mother do it."

"*Pardon?*" said Carole.

"Still, I wouldn't have contacted you, but then that body was found and the police showed up and I thought you might need my help."

"Yes, what about that body?" Marc asked his father, who just stared. "Well?"

"Well what? Wait a minute." Vincent Gilbert looked from his son to Gamache, watching with interest, then back again. He laughed. "You're kidding? You think I had something to do with it?"

"Did you?" demanded Marc.

"Do you really expect me to answer that?" The genial man in front of them didn't just bristle, he radiated. It happened so quickly even Gamache was taken aback by the transformation. The cultured, urbane, slightly amused man suddenly overflowed with a rage so great it engulfed him then spilled off him and swallowed everyone. Marc had poked the monster, either forgetting he was in there or wanting to see if he still existed. And he had his answer. Marc stood stock still, his only reaction being a slight, telltale widening of his eyes.

And what a tale those eyes told Gamache. In them he saw the infant, the boy, the young man, afraid. Never certain what he would find in his father. Would he be loving and kind and warm today? Or would he sizzle the skin off his son? With a look, a word. Leaving the boy naked and ashamed. Knowing himself to be weak and needy, stupid and selfish. So that the boy grew an outer hull to withstand assault. But while those skins saved tender young souls, Gamache knew, they soon stopped protecting and became the problem. Because while the hard outer shell kept the hurt at bay, it also kept out the light. And inside the frightened little soul became something else entirely, nurtured only in darkness.

Gamache looked at Marc with interest. He'd poked the monster in front of him, and sure enough, it came awake and lashed out. But had he also awakened a monster inside himself? Or had that happened earlier?

Someone had left a body on their doorstep. Was it father? Or son? Or someone else?

"I expect you to answer, monsieur," said Gamache, turning back to Vincent Gilbert and holding his hard eyes.

"Doctor," Gilbert said, his voice cold. "I will not be diminished by you or anyone else." He looked again at his son, then back to the Chief Inspector.

"*Désolé*," said Gamache and bowed slightly, never taking his deep brown eyes off the angry man. The apology seemed to further enrage Gilbert, who realized one of them was strong enough to withstand insult and one of them wasn't.

"Tell us about the body," Gamache repeated, as though he and Gilbert were having a pleasant conversation. Gilbert looked at him with loathing. Out of the corner of his eye Gamache noticed Marc the horse approaching from the fields. He looked like something a demon might ride, bony, covered with muck and sores. One eye mad, the other eye blind. Attracted, Gamache supposed, by something finally familiar. Rage.

The two men stared at each other. Finally Gilbert snorted derision and waved, dismissing Gamache and his question as trivial. The monster retreated into his cave.

But the horse came closer and closer.

"I know nothing about it. But I thought it looked bad for Marc so I wanted to be here in case he needed me."

"Needed you to do what?" demanded Marc. "Scare everyone half to death? Couldn't you just ring the doorbell or write a letter?"

"I didn't realize you'd be so sensitive." The lash, the tiny wound, the monster smiled and retreated. But Marc had had enough. He reached over the fence and bit Vincent Gilbert on the shoulder. Marc the horse, that is.

"What the hell?" Gilbert yelped and jumped out of the way, his hand on his slimy shoulder.

"Are you going to arrest him?" Marc asked Gamache.

"Are you going to press charges?"

Marc stared at his father, then at the wreck of a creature behind him. Black, wretched, probably half mad. And Marc the man smiled.

"No. Go back to being dead, Dad. Mom was right. It is easier."

He turned and strode back to his home.

What a family," said Beauvoir. They were strolling into the village. Agent Morin had gone ahead to the Incident Room, and they'd left the Gilberts to devour each other. "Still, there does seem a sort of equilibrium about this case."

"What do you mean?" asked Gamache. Off to their left he noticed Ruth Zardo leaving her home followed by Rosa wearing a sweater. Gamache had written a thank-you note for the dinner the night before and stuck it in her rusty mailbox during his morning stroll. He watched as she collected it, glanced at it, and stuck it into the pocket of her ratty old cardigan.

"Well, one man's dead and another comes alive."

Gamache smiled and wondered if it was a fair exchange. Ruth spotted them just as Beauvoir spotted her.

"Run," he hissed to the Chief. "I'll cover you."

"Too late, old son. The duck's seen us."

And indeed, while Ruth seemed happy to ignore them, Rosa was waddling forward at an alarming pace.

"She appears to like you," said Ruth to Beauvoir, limping behind the duck. "But then she does have a birdbrain."

"Madame Zardo," Gamache greeted her with a smile while Beauvoir glared.

"I hear that Gilbert fellow put the body in Olivier's Bistro. Why haven't you arrested him?"

"You heard that already?" asked Beauvoir. "Who told you?"

"Who hasn't? It's all over the village. Well? Are you going to arrest Marc Gilbert?"

"For what?" asked Beauvoir.

"Murder for one. Are you nuts?"

"Am I nuts? Who's the one with a duck in a sweater?"

"And what would you have me do? Let her freeze to death when winter comes? What kind of man are you?"

"Me? Speaking of nuts, what was with that note you had Olivier give me? I can't even remember what it said, but it sure didn't make sense."

"You think not?" the wizened old poet snarled.

"*Maybe there's something in all of this I missed.*"

Gamache quoted the lines and Ruth turned cold eyes on him. "That was a private message. Not meant for you."

"What does it mean, madame?"

"You figure it out. And this one too." Her hand dived into her other pocket and came out with another slip of paper, neatly folded. She handed it to Beauvoir and walked toward the bistro.

Beauvoir looked at the perfect white square in his palm, then closed his fingers over it.

The two men watched Ruth and Rosa walk across the village green. At the far end they saw people entering the bistro.

"She's crazy, of course," said Beauvoir as they walked to the Incident Room. "But she did ask a good question. Why didn't we arrest anyone?

Between father and son we could've been filling out arrest sheets all afternoon."

"To what end?"

"Justice."

Gamache laughed. "I'd forgotten about that. Good point."

"No, really sir. There was everything from trespassing to murder we could have charged them with."

"We both know the victim wasn't murdered in that foyer."

"But that doesn't mean Marc Gilbert didn't kill him somewhere else."

"And put him in his own house, then picked him up again and took him to the bistro?"

"The father could have done it."

"Why?"

Beauvoir thought about that. He couldn't believe that family wasn't guilty of something. And murder seemed right up their alley. Though it seemed most likely they'd kill each other.

"Maybe he wanted to hurt his son," said Beauvoir. But that didn't seem right. They paused on the stone bridge over the Rivière Bella Bella and the Inspector stared over the side, thinking. The sun bounced off the water and he was momentarily mesmerized by the movement. "Maybe it's just the opposite," he began, feeling his way forward. "Maybe Gilbert wanted back in his son's life but needed an excuse. For anyone else I would think that was ridiculous but he has an ego and it might not have let him just knock and apologize. He needed an excuse. I could see him killing a vagrant, someone he considered so far beneath him. Someone he could use for his purpose."

"And what would that be?" asked Gamache, also staring into the clear waters beneath them.

Beauvoir turned to the Chief, noticing the reflected light playing on the man's face. "To be reunited with his son. But he'd need to be seen as the savior, not just as some deadbeat dad crawling back to the family."

Gamache turned to him, interested. "Go on."

"So he killed a vagrant, a man no one would miss, put him in his son's vestibule and waited for the fireworks, figuring he could sweep in and take command of the family when it needed help."

"But then Marc moved the body and there was no excuse," said Gamache.

"Until now. The timing is interesting. We discover the body was in the old Hadley house and an hour later dad appears."

Gamache nodded, his eyes narrowing, and once again he looked into the flowing waters of the river. Beauvoir knew the Chief well enough to know he was walking slowly now through the case, picking his way along the slippery rocks, trying to make out a path obscured by deceit and time.

Beauvoir unfolded the paper in his hands.

> *I just sit where I'm put, composed*
> *of stone, and wishful thinking:*

"Who's Vincent Gilbert, sir? You seemed to know him."

"He's a saint."

Beauvoir laughed, but seeing Gamache's serious face he stopped. "What do you mean?"

"There're some people who believe that."

"Seemed like an asshole to me."

"The hardest part of the process. Telling them apart."

"Do you believe he's a saint?" Beauvoir was almost afraid to ask.

Gamache smiled suddenly. "I'll leave you here. What do you say to lunch in the bistro in half an hour?"

Beauvoir looked at his watch. Twelve thirty-five. "Perfect."

He watched the Chief walk slowly back across the bridge and into Three Pines. Then he looked down again, at the rest of what Ruth had written.

> *that the deity who kills for pleasure*
> *will also heal,*

Someone else was watching Gamache. Inside the bistro Olivier was looking out the window while listening to the sweet sounds of laughter and the till. The place was packed. The whole village, the whole countryside, had emptied into his place, for lunch, for news, for gossip. To hear about the latest dramatic developments.

The old Hadley house had produced another body and spewed it into the bistro. Or at least, its owner had. Any suspicion of Olivier was lifted, the taint gone.

All round him Olivier heard people talking, speculating, about Marc Gilbert. His mental state, his motives. Was he the murderer? But one thing wasn't debated, wasn't in doubt.

Gilbert was finished.

"Who's gonna wanna stay in that place?" he heard someone say. "Parra says they dumped a fortune into the Hadley place, and now this."

There was general agreement. It was a shame. It was inevitable. The new inn and spa was ruined before it even opened. Olivier watched through the window as Gamache walked slowly toward the bistro. Ruth appeared at Olivier's elbow. "Imagine being chased," she said, watching the Chief Inspector's steadfast approach, "by that."

Clara and Gabri squeezed through the crowd to join them.

"What're you looking at?" Clara asked.

"Nothing," said Olivier.

"Him." Ruth pointed at Gamache, apparently deep in thought, but making progress. Without haste, but also without hesitation.

"He must be pleased," said Gabri. "I hear Marc Gilbert killed that man and put him here, in the bistro. Case closed."

"Then why didn't Gamache arrest him?" Clara asked, sipping her beer.

"Gamache's an idiot," said Ruth.

"I hear Gilbert says he found the body in his house," said Clara. "Already dead."

"Right, like that just happens," said Olivier. His friends decided not to remind Olivier that was exactly what happened to him.

Clara and Gabri fought their way over to the bar to get more drinks.

The waiters were being run ragged. He'd give them a bonus, Olivier decided. Something to make up for two days of lost wages. Faith. Gabri was always telling him he had to have faith, trust that things would work out.

And they had worked out. Beautifully.

Beside him Ruth was tapping her cane rhythmically on the wooden floor. It was more than annoying. It was somehow threatening. So soft, but so unstoppable. Tap, tap, tap, tap.

"Scotch?"

That would get her to stop. But she stood ramrod straight, her cane lifting and dropping. Tap, tap, tap. Then he realized what she was tapping out.

Chief Inspector Gamache was still approaching, slowly, deliberately. And with each footfall came a beat of Ruth's cane.

"I wonder if the murderer knows just how terrible a thing is pursuing him?" asked Ruth. "I feel almost sorry for him. He must feel trapped."

"Gilbert did it. Gamache'll arrest him soon."

But the thumping of Ruth's cane matched the thudding in Olivier's chest. He watched Gamache approach. Then, miraculously, Gamache passed them by. And Olivier heard the little tinkle of Myrna's bell.

So, there was some excitement up at the old Hadley house."

Myrna poured Gamache a coffee and joined him by the bookshelves.

"There was. Who told you?"

"Who didn't? Everyone knows. Marc Gilbert was the one who put the body in the bistro. But what people can't figure out is whether he killed the man."

"What're some of the theories?"

"Well." Myrna took a sip of coffee and watched as Gamache moved along the rows of books. "Some think he must have done it, and dumped the body in the bistro to get back at Olivier. Everyone knows they dislike each other. But the rest think if he was really going to do that he'd kill the man in the bistro. Why kill him somewhere else, then move him?"

"You tell me. You're the psychologist." Gamache gave up his search of the shelves and turned to Myrna.

"Former."

"But you can't retire your knowledge."

"Can't crawl back into Paradise?" Taking their coffee to the armchairs in the bay window they sat and sipped while Myrna thought. Finally she spoke.

"Seems unlikely." She didn't look pleased with her answer.

"You want the murderer to be Marc Gilbert?" he asked.

"God help me, I do. Hadn't thought about it before, really, but now that the possibility's here it would be, well, convenient."

"Because he's an outsider?"

"Beyond the pale," said Myrna.

"I'm sorry?"

"Do you know the expression, Chief Inspector?"

"I've heard it, yes. It means someone's done something unacceptable. That's one way of looking at murder, I suppose."

"I didn't mean that. Do you know where the expression comes from?" When Gamache shook his head she smiled. "It's the sort of arcane knowledge a bookstore owner collects. It's from medieval times. A fortress was built with thick stone walls in a circle. We've all seen them, right?"

Gamache had visited many old castles and fortresses, almost all in ruins now, but it was the brightly colored illustrations from the books he'd pored over as a child he remembered most vividly. The towers with vigilant archers, the crenellated stone, the massive wooden doors. The moat and drawbridge. And inside the circle of the walls was a courtyard. When attacked the villagers would race inside, the drawbridge would be raised, the massive doors closed. Everyone inside was safe. They hoped.

Myrna was holding out her palm, and circling it with a finger. "All around are walls, for protection." Then her finger stopped its movement and rested on the soft center of her palm. "This is the pale."

"So if you're beyond the pale . . ."

"You're an outsider," said Myrna. "A threat." She slowly closed her hand. As a black woman she knew what it meant to be "beyond the pale." She'd been on the outside all her life, until she'd moved here. Now she was on the inside and it was the Gilberts' turn.

But it wasn't as comfortable as she'd always imagined the "inside" to be.

Gamache sipped his coffee and watched her. It was interesting that everyone seemed to know about Marc Gilbert moving the body, but no one seemed to know about the other Gilbert, risen from the dead.

"What were you looking for just now?" she asked.

"A book called *Being*."

"*Being*? That's the one about Brother Albert and the community he built?" She got up and walked toward the bookshelves. "We've talked about this before."

She changed direction and walked to the far end of her bookstore.

"We did, years ago." Gamache followed her.

"I remember now. I gave Old Mundin and The Wife a copy when Charles was born. The book's out of print, I think. Shame. It's brilliant."

They were in her used-books section.

"Ah, here it is. I have one left. A little dog-eared, but the best books are."

She handed Gamache the slim volume. "Can I leave you here? I told Clara I'd meet her in the bistro for lunch."

Armand Gamache settled into his armchair and in the sunshine through the window he read. About an asshole. And a saint. And a miracle.

Jean Guy Beauvoir arrived at the crowded bistro and after ordering a beer from a harried Havoc he squeezed through the crowd. He caught snippets of conversation about the fair, about how horrible the judging was this year, really, the worst so far. About the weather. But mostly he heard about the body.

Roar Parra and Old Mundin were sitting in a corner with a couple of other men. They looked up and nodded at Beauvoir, but didn't move from their precious seats.

Beauvoir scanned the room for Gamache, but knew he wasn't there. Knew as soon as he'd walked in. After a few minutes he managed to snag a table. A minute later he was joined by the Chief Inspector.

"Hard at work, sir?" Beauvoir brushed cookie crumbs from the Chief's shirt.

"Always. You?" Gamache ordered a ginger beer and turned his full attention to his Inspector.

"I Googled Vincent Gilbert."

"And?"

"This is what I found out." Beauvoir flipped open his notebook. "Vincent Gilbert. Born in Quebec City in 1934 into a prominent francophone family. Father a member of the National Assembly, mother from the francophone elite. Degree in philosophy from Laval University then medical degree from McGill. Specializing in genetics. Made a name for himself by creating a test for Down's syndrome, in utero. So that they could be found early enough and possibly treated."

Gamache nodded. "But he stopped his research, went to India, and when he returned instead of going back into the lab immediately and completing his research he joined Brother Albert at LaPorte."

The Chief Inspector put a book on the table and slid it toward Beauvoir.

Beauvoir turned it over. There on the back was a scowling, imperious face. Exactly the same look Beauvoir had seen while kneeling on the man's chest just an hour earlier.

"*Being*," he read, then put it down.

"It's about his time at LaPorte," said Gamache.

"I read about it," said Beauvoir. "For people with Down's syndrome. Gilbert volunteered there, as medical director, when he got back from India. After that he refused to continue his research. I'd have thought working there he'd want to cure it even more."

Gamache tapped the book. "You should read it."

Beauvoir smirked. "You should tell me about it."

Gamache hesitated, gathering his thoughts. "*Being* isn't really about LaPorte. It's not even about Vincent Gilbert. It's about arrogance, humility and what it means to be human. It's a beautiful book, written by a beautiful man."

"How can you say that about the man we just met? He was a shit."

Gamache laughed. "I don't disagree. Most of the saints were. St. Ignatius had a police record, St. Jerome was a horrible, mean-spirited man, St. Augustine slept around. He once prayed, 'Lord, give me chastity, but not just yet.'"

Beauvoir snorted. "Sounds like lots of people. So why's one a saint and someone else just an asshole?"

"Can't tell you that. It's one of the mysteries."

"Bullshit. You don't even go to church. What do you really think?"

Gamache leaned forward. "I think to be holy is to be human, and Vincent Gilbert is certainly that."

"You think more than that, though, don't you? I can see it. You admire him."

Gamache picked up the worn copy of *Being*. He looked over and saw Old Mundin drinking a Coke and eating cheese and pâté on a baguette. Gamache remembered Charles Mundin's tiny hand grasping his finger. Full of trust, full of grace.

And he tried to imagine a world without that. Dr. Vincent Gilbert, the Great Man, would almost certainly have earned a Nobel Prize, had he continued his research. But he'd stopped his research and earned the scorn of his colleagues and much of the world instead.

And yet *Being* wasn't an apology. It wasn't even an explanation. It just was. Like Charles Mundin.

"Ready?" Gabri appeared. They ordered and just as Gabri was about to leave Agent Morin showed up.

"Hope you don't mind."

"Not at all," said Gamache. Gabri took his order, and just as he was about to leave again Agent Lacoste arrived. Gabri ran his hand through his hair.

"Jeez," said Beauvoir. "They'll be coming out of the closet next."

"You'd be surprised," said Gabri, and took Lacoste's order. "Is that it? Are you expecting the Musical Ride?"

"*C'est tout, patron*," Gamache assured him. "*Merci.* I wasn't expecting you," he said to Lacoste when Gabri was out of earshot.

"I didn't expect to come, but I wanted to talk in person. I spoke to both Olivier's boss at the bank and his father."

She lowered her voice and told them what the executive at the Banque Laurentienne had said. When she finished her salad had arrived. Shrimp, mango and cilantro, on baby spinach. But she looked with envy at the steaming plate of Portobello mushrooms, garlic, basil and Parmesan on top of homemade pasta in front of the Chief.

"So it wasn't clear whether Olivier was going to steal the money or give it back," said Beauvoir, eyeing his charcoal steak and biting into his seasoned thin fries.

"The man I talked to believed Olivier was making the money for the bank. Still, he'd probably have been fired, if he hadn't quit."

"Are they sure all the money he made in the Malaysian deal was given to the bank?" Gamache asked.

"They think it was, and so far we can't find any other account for Olivier."

"So we still don't know where the money came from to buy all that property," said Beauvoir. "What did Olivier's father have to say?"

She told them about her visit to Habitat. By the time she finished their plates had been cleared away and dessert menus were placed in front of them.

"Not for me." Lacoste smiled at Havoc Parra. He smiled back, motioned to another waiter to clear and set a nearby table.

"Who'll share a profiterole with me?" asked Beauvoir. They'd have to solve this case soon or he'd need a whole new wardrobe.

"I will," said Lacoste.

The choux pastries filled with ice cream and covered in warm chocolate sauce arrived. Gamache regretted not ordering some himself. He watched, mesmerized, as Beauvoir and Lacoste took spoonfuls of the now melting ice cream mixed with pastry and the warm, dark chocolate.

"So Olivier's father's never been here," said Beauvoir, wiping his face with his napkin. "He has no idea where Olivier lives or what he's doing. He doesn't even know his son's gay?"

"Can't be the only son afraid to tell his father," said Lacoste.

"Secrets," said Beauvoir. "More secrets."

Gamache noticed Morin's face change as he looked out the window. Then the murmur of conversation in the bistro died away. The Chief followed his agent's gaze.

A moose was galumphing down rue du Moulin, into the village. As it got closer Gamache rose. Someone was on its back, clinging to the massive neck.

"You, stay here. Guard the door," he said to Agent Morin. "You come with me," he said to the others. Before anyone else could react Gamache and his team were out the door. By the time anyone else wanted to follow Agent Morin was standing at the door. Short, weedy, but determined. No one was getting by him.

Through the glass panes they watched as the creature bore down, its long legs pumping, awkward and frantic. Gamache walked foward but it didn't slow, its rider no longer in control. The Chief spread his arms to corral him and as it got closer they recognized it as one of the Gilbert animals. A horse, supposedly. Its eyes wild and white, and its hooves spastic and plunging. Beauvoir and Lacoste stood on either side of the Chief, their arms also out.

At his station by the door young Agent Morin couldn't see what was happening outside. All he could see were the faces of the patrons as they watched. He'd been at enough accident scenes to know that at really bad ones people screamed. At the worst, there was silence.

The bistro was silent.

The three officers stood their ground and the horse came straight for them, then veered, shrieking like a creature possessed. The rider fell off onto the grass of the green and Agent Lacoste managed to grab the reins as the horse skidded and twisted. Beside her Gamache also grabbed the reins and between them they fought the horse to a halt.

Inspector Beauvoir was on his knees on the grass, bending over the fallen rider.

"Are you all right? Don't move, just lie still."

But like most people given that advice, the rider sat up and yanked off her riding helmet. It was Dominique Gilbert. Like the horse's, her eyes were wild and wide. Leaving Lacoste to calm the skittish animal Gamache quickly joined Beauvoir, kneeling beside him.

"What's happened?" asked Gamache.

"In the woods," Dominique Gilbert gasped. "A cabin. I looked inside. There was blood. Lots of it."

EIGHTEEN

—

The young man, not much more than a boy, heard the wind. Heard the moan, and heeded it. He stayed. After a day his family, afraid of what they might find, came looking and found him on the side of the terrible mountain. Alive. Alone. They pleaded with him to leave, but, unbelievably, he refused.

"He's been drugged," said his mother.

"He's been cursed," said his sister.

"He's been mesmerized," said his father, backing away.

But they were wrong. He had, in fact, been seduced. By the desolate mountain. And his loneliness. And by the tiny green shoots under his feet.

He'd done this. He'd brought the great mountain alive again. He was needed.

And so the boy stayed, and slowly warmth returned to the mountain. Grass and trees and fragrant flowers returned. Foxes and rabbits and bees came back. Where the boy walked fresh springs appeared and where he sat ponds were created.

The boy was life for the mountain. And the mountain loved him for it. And the boy loved the mountain for it too.

Over the years the terrible mountain became beautiful and word spread. That something dreadful had become something peaceful. And kind. And safe. Slowly the people returned, including the boy's family.

A village sprang up and the Mountain King, so lonely for so long, protected them all. And every night, while the others rested, the boy, now a young man, walked to the very top of the mountain, and lying down on the soft green moss he listened to the voice deep inside.

Then one night while he lay there the young man heard something un-
expected. The Mountain King told him a secret.

Olivier watched the wild horse and the fallen rider along with the rest
of the bistro crowd. His skin crawled and he longed to break out, to
scream and push his way out of the crowd. And to run away. Run, run,
run. Until he dropped.

Because, unlike them, he knew what it meant.

Instead he stood and watched as though he was still one of them. But
Olivier knew now he never would be again.

Armand Gamache walked into the bistro and scanned the faces.

"Is Roar Parra still here?"

"I am," said a voice at the back of the bistro. The bodies parted and
the stocky man appeared.

"Madame Gilbert's found a cabin deep in the forest. Does that sound
familiar?"

Parra, along with everyone else, thought. Then he, and everyone
else, shook their heads. "Never knew there was one there."

Gamache thought for a moment then looked outside where Domin-
ique was just catching her breath. "A glass of water, please," he said, and
Gabri appeared with one. "Come with me," the Chief Inspector said to
Parra.

"How far was the cabin?" he asked Dominique after she'd swallowed
the water. "Can we get there on ATVs?"

Dominique shook her head. "No, the forest's too thick."

"How'd you get there?" asked Beauvoir.

"Macaroni took me." She stroked the sweating horse's neck. "After
what happened this morning I needed time alone, so I saddled up and
decided to try to find the old bridle paths."

"That wasn't very smart," said Parra. "You could've been lost."

"I did get lost. That's how I found the cabin. I was on one of the trails
you cut, then it ended, but I could just make out the old path so I kept
on. And that's when I saw it."

Dominique's mind was filled with images. Of the dark cabin, of the
dark stains on the floor. Of jumping on the horse and trying to find the
path back, and holding down the panic. The warnings every Canadian
hears since childhood. Never, ever go into the woods alone.

"Can you find your way back there?" asked Gamache.

Could she? She thought about it, then nodded. "Yes."

"Good. Would you like to rest?"

"I'd like to get this over with."

Gamache nodded, then turned to Roar Parra. "Come with us, please."

As they walked up the hill, Dominique leading Macaroni with Parra beside her and the Sûreté officers behind, Beauvoir whispered to the Chief.

"If we can't get in with ATVs, how're we going to go?"

"Can you say giddyup?"

"I can say whoa." Beauvoir looked as though Gamache had suggested something obscene.

"Well, I suggest you practice."

Within half an hour Roar had saddled Buttercup and Chester. Marc the horse was nowhere to be seen but Marc the husband emerged from the barn, a riding helmet on his head.

"I'm coming with you."

"I'm afraid not, Monsieur Gilbert," said Gamache. "It's simple math. There are three horses. Your wife needs to be on one, and Inspector Beauvoir and I need to be with her."

Beauvoir eyed Chester, who shuffled from one hoof to another as though listening to a Dixieland band in his head. The Inspector had never ridden a horse before and was pretty certain he wasn't about to now.

They set out, Dominique leading, Gamache behind her with a roll of bright pink ribbon to mark their path and Beauvoir bringing up the rear, though Gamache chose not to describe it as that to him. The Chief had ridden many times before. When he'd started dating Reine-Marie they'd go on the bridle paths on Mont Royal. They'd pack a picnic and take the trails through the forest right in the center of Montreal, stopping at a clearing where they could tie up the horses and look over the city, sipping chilled wine and eating sandwiches. The stables on Mont Royal were now closed, but every now and then he and Reine-Marie would head out on a Sunday afternoon and find a place to go trail riding.

Riding Buttercup, however, was a whole other experience. More like being in a small boat on the high seas. He felt slightly nauseous as Buttercup swayed back and forth. Every ten paces or so he reached out and tied another pink ribbon to a tree. Ahead Dominique was way off the ground on Macaroni, and Gamache didn't dare look behind him, but he knew Beauvoir was still there by the constant stream of swear words.

"*Merde. Tabarnac.* Duck."

Branches snapped back so that it felt as though they were being spanked by nature.

Beauvoir, instructed to keep his heels down and his hands steady, quickly lost both stirrups and clung to the gray mane. Regaining the stirrups he straightened up in time to catch another branch in the face. After that it was an inelegant, inglorious exercise in holding on.

"*Tabarnac, Merde.* Duck."

The path narrowed and the forest darkened, and their pace slowed. Gamache was far from convinced they were still on the path, but there was nothing he could do about it now. Agents Lacoste and Morin were gathering the Crime Scene kit and would join them on ATVs as soon as Parra had opened the path. But that would take a while.

How long would it take Lacoste to realize they were lost? An hour? Three? When would night fall? How lost could they get? The forest grew darker and cooler. It felt as though they'd been riding for hours. Gamache checked his watch but couldn't see the dial in the dimness.

Dominique stopped and the following horses crowded together.

"Whoa," said Beauvoir.

Gamache reached out and took the reins, settling the Inspector's horse.

"There it is," Dominique whispered.

Gamache swayed this way and that, trying to see around the trees. Finally he dismounted and tying his horse to a tree walked in front of Dominique. And still he couldn't see it.

"Where?"

"There," Dominique whispered. "Right beside that patch of sunlight."

One thick column of sun beamed through the trees. Gamache looked beside it, and there it was. A cabin.

"Stay here," he said to her, then motioned to Beauvoir who looked around, trying to figure out how to get off. Eventually he leaned over, hugged a tree and hauled himself sideways. Any other horse might have been upset but Chester had seen worse. He seemed quite fond of Beauvoir by the time the Inspector slid off his back. Not once had Beauvoir

kicked him, whipped him, or punched him. In Chester's lifetime, Beauvoir was by far the gentlest and kindest of riders.

The two men stared at the cabin. It was made of logs. A single rocking chair with a large cushion sat on the front porch. There were windows on either side of the closed door, each with boxes in full bloom. A
stone chimney rose at the side of the cabin, but no smoke came out.

Behind them they could hear the soft rumble of the horses, and the
swish of their tails. They could hear small creatures scurrying for cover.
The forest smelt of moss and sweet pine needles and decaying leaves.

They crept forward. Onto the porch. Gamache scanned the floorboards. A few dry leaves but no blood. He nodded to Beauvoir and indicated one of the windows. Beauvoir quietly positioned himself beside it,
his back against the wall. Gamache took the other window then gave a
small signal. Together they looked in.

They saw a table, chairs, a bed at the far end. No lights, no movement.

"Nothing," said Beauvoir. Gamache nodded agreement. He reached
out for the door handle. The door swung open an inch with a slight
creak. The Chief put his foot forward and pushed it open all the way.
Then looked in.

The cabin was a single room and Gamache saw at once there was no
one there. He walked in. But Beauvoir kept his hand on his gun. In case.
Beauvoir was a cautious man. Being raised in chaos had made him so.

Dust swirled in the little light that struggled through the window.
Beauvoir, by habit, felt for a light switch then realized he wouldn't find
one. But he did find some lamps and lit those. What came to light was a
bed, a dresser, some bookcases, a couple of chairs and a table.

The room was empty. Except for what the dead man had left behind.
His belongings and his blood. There was a large, dark stain on the
wooden floor.

There was no doubt they'd finally found the crime scene.

An hour later Roar Parra had followed the Chief's pink ribbons and
used his chainsaw to widen the path. The ATVs arrived and with them
the Crime Scene investigators. Inspector Beauvoir took photographs
while Agents Lacoste, Morin and the others combed the room for evidence.

Roar Parra and Dominique Gilbert had mounted the horses and gone home, leading Chester behind them. Chester looked back, hoping to catch a peek at the funny man who had forgotten to beat him.

As the clip-clop of the hooves receded the quiet closed in.

With his team inside working, and the space cramped, Gamache decided to explore outside the cabin. Finely carved window boxes bloomed with cheery nasturtiums and greenery. He rubbed his fingers first on one plant then the others. They smelled of cilantro, rosemary, basil and tarragon. He walked over to the column of sunlight breaking through the trees beside the cabin.

A fence, made of twisted branches, formed a large rectangle about twenty feet wide by forty feet long. Vines grew through the fence, and as he got closer Gamache noticed they were heavy with peas. He opened the wooden gate and walked into the garden. Neat rows of vegetables had been planted and tended, intended for a harvest that would not now come. Up and down the long, protected garden the victim had planted tomatoes and potatoes, peas and beans, and broccoli and carrots. Gamache broke off a bean and ate it. A wheelbarrow with some dirt and a shovel stood halfway along the path and at the far end there sat a chair of bent branches, with comfortable and faded cushions. It was inviting and Gamache had an image of the man working in the garden, then resting. Sitting quietly in the chair.

The Chief Inspector looked down and saw the impression of the man in the cushions. He'd sat there. Perhaps for hours. In the column of light.

Alone.

Not many people, Gamache knew, could do that. Even if they wanted to, even if they chose to, most people couldn't take the quiet. They grew fidgety and bored. But not this man, Gamache suspected. He imagined him there, staring at his garden. Thinking.

What did he think about?

"Chief?"

Turning around Gamache saw Beauvoir walking toward him.

"We've done the preliminary search."

"Weapon?"

Beauvoir shook his head. "But we did find Mason jars of preserves and paraffin. Quite a bit of it. I guess we know why." The Inspector looked around the garden, and seemed impressed. Order always impressed him.

Gamache nodded. "Who was he?"

"I don't know."

Now the Chief Inspector turned fully to his second in command. "What do you mean? Did this cabin belong to our victim?"

"We think so. It's almost certainly where he died. But we haven't found any ID. Nothing. No photographs, no birth certificate, passport, driver's license."

"Letters?"

Beauvoir shook his head. "There're clothes in the dressers. Old clothing, worn. But mended and clean. In fact, the whole place is clean and tidy. A lot of books, we're just going through them now. Some have names in them, but all different names. He must have picked them up at used-book stores. We found woodworking tools and sawdust by one of the chairs. And an old violin. Guess we know what he did at night."

Gamache had a vision of the dead man, alive. Healthy even. Coming in after working the garden. Making a simple dinner, sitting by the fire and whittling. Then, as the night drew in, he'd pick up the violin and play. Just for himself.

Who was this man who loved solitude so much?

"The place is pretty primitive," Beauvoir continued. "He had to pump water into the sink in his kitchen. Haven't seen that in years. And there's no toilet or shower."

Gamache and Beauvoir looked around. Down a winding well-worn path they found an outhouse. The thought almost made Beauvoir gag. The Chief opened the door and looked in. He scanned the tiny one-holer, then closed the door. It too was clean, though spider's webs were beginning to form and soon, Gamache knew, more and more creatures and plants would invade until the outhouse disappeared, eaten by the forest.

"How did he wash?" asked Beauvoir as they walked back to the cabin. They knew he had, and regularly, according to the coroner.

"There's a river," said Gamache, pausing. Ahead sat the cabin, a tiny perfect gem in the middle of the forest. "You can hear it. Probably the Bella Bella, as it heads into the village."

Sure enough Beauvoir heard what sounded strangely like traffic. It was comforting. There was also a cistern beside the cabin, designed to catch rainfall.

"We've found fingerprints." Beauvoir held the door open for the

Chief as they entered the cabin. "We think they belong to two different people."

Gamache's brows rose. The place looked and felt as though only one person lived here. But judging by events, someone else had found the cabin, and the man.

Could this be their break? Could the murderer have left his prints?

The cabin was growing dimmer. Morin found a couple more lamps and some candles. Gamache watched the team at work. There was a grace to it, one perhaps only appreciated by another homicide officer. The fluid motions, stepping aside, leaning in and out and down, bowing and lifting and kneeling. It was almost beautiful.

He stood in the middle of the cabin and took it in. The walls were made of large, round logs. Strangely enough there were curtains at the windows. And in the kitchen a panel of amber glass leaned against the window.

A hand pump at the sink was attached to the wooden kitchen counter, and dishes and glasses were neatly placed on the exposed shelves. Gamache noticed food on the kitchen counter. He walked over and looked, without picking anything up. Bread, butter, cheese. Nibbled, and not by anything human. Some Orange Pekoe tea in an open box. A jar of honey. A quart of milk sat opened. He sniffed. Rancid.

He motioned Beauvoir over.

"What do you think?"

"The man did his shopping."

"How? He sure didn't walk into Monsieur Béliveau's general store, and I'm pretty sure he didn't walk to Saint-Rémy. Someone brought this food to him."

"And killed him? Had a cup of tea then bashed his head in?"

"Maybe, maybe," murmured the Chief Inspector as he looked around. The oil lamps threw light very unlike anything an electric bulb produced. This light was gentle. The edges of the world seemed softer.

A woodstove separated the rustic kitchen and the living area. A small table, covered in cloth, seemed to be his dining table. A riverstone fireplace was on the opposite wall with a wing chair on either side. At the far end of the cabin was a large brass bed and a chest of drawers.

The bed was made, the pillows fluffed and ready. Fabric hung on the walls, presumably to keep out the cold drafts, as you'd find in medieval castles. There were rugs scattered about the floor, a floor marred only, but deeply, by a dark stain of blood.

A bookcase lining an entire wall was filled with old volumes. Approaching it Gamache noticed something protruding from between the logs. He picked at it and looked at what he held.

A dollar bill.

It'd been years, decades, since Canada used dollar bills. Examining the wall more closely he noticed other paper protruding. More dollar bills. Some two-dollar bills. In a couple of cases there were twenties.

Was this the man's banking system? Like an old miser, instead of stuffing his mattress had he stuffed his walls? After a tour of the walls Gamache concluded the money was there to keep the cold out. The cabin was made of wood and Canadian currency. It was insulation.

Next he walked over to the riverstone fireplace, pausing at one of the wing chairs. The one with the deepest impressions in the seat and back. He touched the worn fabric. Looking down at the table beside the chair he saw the whittling tools Beauvoir had mentioned, and leaning against the table was a fiddle and bow. A book, closed but with a bookmark, sat beside the tools. Had the man been reading when he was interrupted?

He picked it up and smiled.

"*I had three chairs in my house,*" Gamache read quietly. "*One for solitude, two for friendship, three for society.*"

"*Pardon?*" said Lacoste, from where she was crouching, looking under the table.

"Thoreau. From *Walden*." Gamache held up the book. "He lived in a cabin, you know. Not unlike this, perhaps."

"But he had three chairs," smiled Lacoste. "Our man had only two."

Only two, thought Gamache. But that was enough, and that was significant. *Two for friendship.* Did he have a friend?

"I think he might have been Russian," she said, straightening up. "Why?"

"There're a few icons on the shelf here, by the books." Lacoste waved behind her, and sure enough, in front of the leather-bound volumes were Russian icons.

The Chief frowned and gazed around the small cabin. After a minute he grew very quiet, very still. Except for his eyes, which darted here and there.

Beauvoir approached. "What is it?"

The Chief didn't answer. The room grew hushed. He moved his eyes around the cabin again, not really believing what he saw. So great was his surprise he closed his eyes then opened them again.

"What is it?" Beauvoir repeated.

"Be very careful with that," he said to Agent Morin, who was holding a glass from the kitchen.

"I will," he said, wondering why the Chief would suddenly say that.

"May I have it, please?"

Morin gave it to Gamache who took it to an oil lamp. There, in the soft light, he saw what he expected to see, but never expected to hold in his own hands. Leaded glass, expertly cut. Hand cut. He couldn't make out the mark on the bottom of the glass, and even if he could it would be meaningless to him. He was no expert. But he was knowledgeable enough to know what he held was priceless.

It was an extremely old, even ancient, piece of glass. Made in a method not seen in hundreds of years. Gamache gently put the glass down and looked into the kitchen. On the open rustic shelves there stood at least ten glasses, all different sizes. All equally ancient. As his team watched, Armand Gamache moved along the shelves, picking up plates and cups and cutlery, then over to the walls to examine the hangings. He looked at the rugs, picking up the corners, and finally, like a man almost afraid of what he'd find, he approached the bookcases.

"What is it, *patron*?" asked Beauvoir, joining him.

"This isn't just any cabin, Jean Guy. This is a museum. Each piece is an antiquity, priceless."

"You're kidding," said Morin, putting down the horse figurine jug.

Who was this man? Gamache wondered. Who chose to live this far from other people? *Three for society.*

This man wanted no part of society. What was he afraid of? Only fear could propel a man so far from company. Was he a survivalist, as they'd theorized? Gamache thought not. The contents of the cabin argued against that. No guns, no weapons at all. No how-to magazines, no publications warning of dire plots.

Instead, this man had brought delicate leaded crystal with him into the woods.

Gamache scanned the books, not daring to touch them. "Have these been dusted?"

"They have," said Morin. "And I looked inside for a name, but they're no help. Different names written in most of them. Obviously secondhand."

"Obviously," whispered Gamache to himself. He looked at the one still in his hand. Opening it to the bookmark he read, *I went to the woods because I wished to live deliberately, to front only the essential facts of life, and to see if I could not learn what it had to teach, and not, when I came to die, discover that I had not lived.*

Gamache turned to the front page and inhaled softly.

It was a first edition.

NINETEEN

 "Peter?" Clara knocked lightly on the door to his studio.

He opened it, trying not to look secretive but giving up. Clara knew him too well, and knew he was always secretive about his art.

"How's it going?"

"Not bad," he said, longing to close the door and get back to it. All day he'd been picking up his brush, approaching his painting then lowering the brush again. Surely the painting wasn't finished? It was so embarrassing. What would Clara think? What would his gallery think? The critics? It was unlike anything else he'd ever done. Well, not ever. But certainly since childhood.

He could never let anyone see this.

It was ridiculous.

What it needed, clearly, was more definition, more detail. More depth. The sorts of things his clients and supporters had come to expect. And buy.

He'd picked up and lowered his brush a dozen times that day. This had never happened to him before. He'd watched, mystified, as Clara had been racked by self-doubt, had struggled and had finally produced some marginal piece of work. Her *March of the Happy Ears*, her series inspired by dragonfly wings, and, of course, her masterpiece, the *Warrior Uteruses*.

That's what came of inspiration.

No, Peter was much more clear. More disciplined. He planned each piece, drew and drafted each work, knew months in advance what he'd be working on. He didn't rely on airy-fairy inspiration.

Until now. This time he'd come into the studio with a fireplace log, cut cleanly so that the rings of age were visible. He'd taken his magnifying glass and approached it, with a view to enlarging a tiny part of it beyond recognition. It was, he liked to tell art critics at his many sold-out *vernissages*, an allegory for life. How we blow things out of all proportion, until a simple truth was no longer recognizable.

They ate it up. But this time it hadn't worked. He'd been unable to see the simple truth. Instead, he'd painted this.

When Clara left Peter plopped down in his chair and stared at the bewildering piece of work on his easel and repeated silently to himself, *I'm brilliant, I'm brilliant*. Then he whispered, so quietly he barely heard it himself, "I'm better than Clara."

Olivier stood on the *terrasse* outside the bistro and looked into the dark forest on the hill. In fact, Three Pines was surrounded by forest, something he'd never noticed, until now.

The cabin had been found. He'd prayed this wouldn't happen, but it had. And for the first time since he'd arrived in Three Pines he felt the dark forest closing in.

But if all these things," Beauvoir nodded to the interior of the single room, "are priceless why didn't the murderer take them?"

"I've been wondering that myself," said Gamache from the comfort of the large wing chair by the empty fireplace. "What was the murder about, Jean Guy? Why kill this man who seems to have lived a quiet, secret life in the woods for years, maybe decades?"

"And then once he's dead, why take the body but leave the valuables?" Beauvoir sat in the chair opposite the Chief.

"Unless the body was more valuable than the rest?"

"Then why leave it at the old Hadley house?"

"If the murderer had just left the body here we'd never have found it," reasoned Gamache, perplexed. "Never known there'd been a murder."

"Why kill the man, if not for his treasure?" asked Beauvoir.

"Treasure?"

"What else is it? Priceless stuff in the middle of nowhere? It's buried treasure, only instead of being buried in the ground it's buried in the forest."

But the murderer had left it there. And instead, had taken the only thing he wanted from that cabin. He'd taken a life.

"Did you notice this?" Beauvoir got up and walked to the door. Opening it he pointed upward, with a look of amusement.

There on the lintel above the door was a number.

16

"Now, you can't tell me he got mail," said Beauvoir as Gamache stared, puzzled. The numbers were brass and tarnished green. Almost invisible against the dark wooden door frame. Gamache shook his head then looked at his watch. It was almost six.

After a bit of discussion it was decided Agent Morin would stay at the cabin overnight, to guard the possessions.

"Come with me," Gamache said to Morin. "I'll drive you in while the others finish the job. You can pack an overnight bag and arrange for a satellite phone."

Morin got on the ATV behind the Chief Inspector and searched for something to grip, settling on the bottom of the seat. Gamache started up the machine. His investigations had taken him into tiny fishing outports and remote settlements. He'd driven snowmobiles, power boats, motorcycles and ATVs. While appreciating their convenience, and necessity, he disliked them all. They shattered the calm with their banshee screams, polluting the wilderness with noise and fumes.

If anything could wake the dead, these could.

As they bounced along Morin realized he was in trouble, and letting go of the seat he flung his small arms around the large man in front of him and held on tight, feeling the Chief's wax coat against his cheek and the strong body underneath. And he smelled sandalwood and rosewater.

The young man sat up, one hand on the Mountain, the other to his face. He couldn't quite believe what the Mountain had told him. Then he started to giggle.

Hearing this, the Mountain was puzzled. It wasn't the shriek of terror he normally heard from creatures who came near him.

As he listened the Mountain King realized this was a happy sound. An infectious sound. He too started to rumble and only stopped when the people in the village grew frightened. And he didn't want that. Never again did he want to scare anything away.

He slept well that night.

The boy, however, did not. He tossed and turned and finally left his cabin to stare up at the peak.

Every night from then on the boy was burdened by the Mountain's secret. He grew weary and weak. His parents and friends commented on this. Even the Mountain noticed.

Finally, one night well before the sun rose the boy nudged his parents awake.

"We need to leave."

"What?" his bleary mother asked.

"Why?" his father and sister asked.

"The Mountain King has told me of a wonderful land where people never die, never grow sick or old. It's a place only he knows about. But he says we need to leave now. Tonight. While it's still dark. And we need to go quickly."

They woke up the rest of the village and well before dawn they'd packed up. The boy was the last to leave. He took a few steps into the forest and kneeling down he touched the surface of the sleeping Mountain King.

"Good-bye," he whispered.

Then he tucked the package under his arm, and disappeared into the night.

Jean Guy Beauvoir stood outside the cabin. It was almost dark and he was starving. They'd finished their work and he was just waiting for Agent Lacoste to pack up.

"I have to pee," she said, joining him on the porch. "Any ideas?"

"There's an outhouse over there." He pointed away from the cabin.

"Great," she said and grabbed a flashlight. "Isn't this how horror movies start?"

"Oh no, we're well into the second reel by now," said Beauvoir with a smirk. He watched Lacoste pick her way along the path to the outhouse.

His stomach growled. At least, he hoped it was his stomach. The sooner they got back to civilization, the better. How could anyone live out here? He didn't envy Morin spending the night.

A bobbing flashlight told him Lacoste was returning.

"Have you been into the outhouse?" she asked.

"Are you kidding? The Chief looked in, but I didn't." Even thinking about it made him gag.

"So you didn't see what was in there."

"Don't tell me, the toilet paper was money too."

"Actually it was. One- and two-dollar bills."

"You're joking."

"I'm not. And I found this." She held a book in her hand. "A first edition. Signed by E. B. White. It's *Charlotte's Web*."

Beauvoir stared at it. He had no idea what she was talking about.

"It was my favorite book as a child. Charlotte the spider?" she asked. "Wilbur the pig?"

"If they didn't get blown up I didn't read it."

"Who leaves a signed first edition in an outhouse?"

"Who leaves money there?" Beauvoir suddenly felt an urge to go.

Salut, patron," waved Gabri from the living room. He was folding tiny outfits and putting them into a box. "So, the cabin in the woods. Was it where the guy lived? The dead man?"

"We think so." Gamache joined him. He watched Gabri fold the small sweaters.

"For Rosa. We're collecting them from everyone to give to Ruth. Is this too big for Rosa?" He held up a boy's blazer. "It's Olivier's. He says he made it himself but I can't believe that, though he's very good with his hands." Gamache ignored that.

"It's a little big. And masculine, for Rosa, don't you think?" he said.

"True." Gabri put it in the reject pile. "In a few years it might fit Ruth though."

"Did no one ever mention a cabin before? Not old Mrs. Hadley?"

Gabri shook his head but continued working. "No one." Then he stopped folding and put his hands in his lap. "I wonder how he survived? Did he walk all the way to Cowansville or Saint-Rémy for food?"

One more thing we don't know, thought Gamache as he went up the stairs. He showered and shaved and called his wife. It was getting dark and in the distance he could hear the shriek from the forest. The ATVs returning. To the village and to the cabin.

In the living room of the B and B, Gabri had been replaced by someone else. Sitting in the comfortable chair by the fire was Vincent Gilbert.

"I've been over to the bistro but people kept bothering me, so I came here to bother you. I've been trying to get out of my son's way. Funny how coming back from the dead isn't as popular as it once was."

"Did you expect him to be happy?"

"You know, I actually did. Amazing, isn't it, our capacity for self-deceit."

Gamache looked at him quizzically.

"All right, my capacity for it," snapped Gilbert. He studied Gamache. Tall, powerfully built. Probably ten pounds overweight, maybe more. Go to fat if he's not careful. Die of a heart attack.

He imagined Gamache suddenly clutching his chest, his eyes widening then closing in pain. Staggering against the wall and gasping. And Dr. Vincent Gilbert, the celebrated physician, folding his arms, doing nothing, as this head of homicide slipped to the ground. It comforted him to know he had that power, of life and death.

Gamache looked at this rigid man. In front of him was the face he'd seen staring, glaring, from the back of that lovely book, *Being*. Arrogant, challenging, confident.

But Gamache had read the book, and knew what lay behind that face.

"Are you staying here?" They'd told Gilbert not to leave the area and the B and B was the only guesthouse.

"Actually, no. I'm the first guest at Marc's inn and spa. Don't think I'll ask for a treatment, though." He had the grace to smile. Like most stern people, he looked very different when he smiled.

Gamache's surprise was obvious.

"I know," agreed Gilbert. "It was actually Dominique who invited me to stay, though she did suggest I might want to be . . ."

"Discreet?"

"Invisible. So I came into town."

Gamache sat in an armchair. "Why did you come looking for your son now?"

It had escaped no one that both Gilbert and the body had shown up at the same time. Again Gamache saw the cabin, with its two comfortable chairs by the fire. Had two older men sat there on a summer's night? Talking, discussing? Arguing? Murdering?

Vincent Gilbert looked down at his hands. Hands that had been inside people. Hands that had held hearts. Repaired hearts. Got them beating again, and restored life. They trembled, unsteady. And he felt a pain in his chest.

Was he having a heart attack?

He looked up and saw this large, steady man watching him. And he thought if he was having a heart attack this man would probably help.

How to explain his time at LaPorte, living with men and women with Down's syndrome? At first he'd thought his job was to simply look after their bodies.

Help others.

That's what the guru had told him to do. Years he'd been at the ashram in India and the guru had finally acknowleged his presence. Almost a decade he'd spent there, in exchange for two words.

Help others.

So that's what he did. He returned to Quebec and joined Brother Albert at LaPorte. To help others. It never, ever occurred to him that they'd help him. After all, how could people that damaged have anything to offer the great healer and philosopher?

It had taken years, but he'd woken up one morning in his cottage in the grounds of LaPorte and something had changed. He'd gone down to breakfast and realized he knew everyone's name. And everyone spoke to him, or smiled. Or came up and showed him something they'd found. A snail, a stick, a blade of grass.

Mundane. Nothing. And yet the whole world had changed, as he slept. He'd gone to bed helping others, and woken up healed himself.

That afternoon, in the shade of a maple tree, he'd started writing *Being*.

"I'd kept an eye on Marc. Watched his successes in Montreal. When they sold their home and bought down here I knew the signs."

"Signs of what?" Gamache asked.

"Burnout. I wanted to help."

Help others.

He was just beginning to appreciate the power of those two simple words. And that help came in different forms.

"By doing what?" asked Gamache.

"By making sure he was all right," Gilbert snapped. "Look, they're all upset up there about the body. Marc did a stupid thing moving it, but I know him. He's not a murderer."

"How do you know?"

Gilbert glared at him. His rage back in full force. But Armand Gamache knew what was behind that rage. What was behind all rage.

Fear.

What was Vincent Gilbert so afraid of?

The answer was easy. He was afraid his son would be arrested for murder. Either because he knew his son had done it, or because he knew he hadn't.

A few minutes later a voice cut across the crowded bistro, aimed at the Chief Inspector, who'd arrived seeking a glass of red wine and quiet to read his book.

"You bugger."

More than one person looked up. Myrna sailed across the room and stood next to Gamache's table, glaring down at him. He got up and bowed slightly, indicating a chair.

Myrna sat so suddenly the chair gave a little crack.

"Wine?"

"Why didn't you tell me why you wanted that?" She gestured toward *Being* in his hand. Gamache grinned.

"Secrets."

"And how long did you think it'd remain a secret?"

"Long enough. I hear he was over here having a drink. Did you meet him?"

"Vincent Gilbert? If you can call ogling and sputtering and fawning 'meeting,' then yes. I met him."

"I'm sure he'll have forgotten it was you."

"Because I'm so easily mistaken for someone else? Is he really Marc's father?"

"He is."

"Do you know, he ignored me when I tried to introduce myself? Looked at me like I was a crumb." The wine and a fresh bowl of cashews had arrived. "Thank God I told him I was Clara Morrow."

"So did I," said Gamache. "He might be growing suspicious."

Myrna laughed and felt her annoyance slip away. "Old Mundin says it was Vincent Gilbert in the forest, spying on his own son. Was it?"

Gamache wondered how much to say, but it was clear this was not much of a secret anymore. He nodded.

"Why spy on his own son?"

"They were estranged."

"First good thing I've heard about Marc Gilbert," said Myrna. "Still, it's ironic. The famous Dr. Gilbert helps so many kids, but is estranged from his own."

Gamache thought again about Annie. Was he doing the same thing to her? Was he listening to the troubles of others, but deaf to his own daughter? He'd spoken to her the night before and reassured himself she was fine. But fine and flourishing were two different things. It had clearly gotten bad when she was willing to listen to Beauvoir.

"*Patron*," said Olivier, handing Gamache and Myrna menus.

"I'm not staying," said Myrna.

Olivier hovered. "I hear you found out where the dead man lived. He was in the forest all along?"

Lacoste and Beauvoir arrived just then and ordered drinks. With one last gulp of wine, and taking a large handful of cashews, Myrna got up to leave.

"I'm going to be paying a lot more attention to the books you buy," she said.

"Do you happen to have *Walden*?" Gamache asked.

"Don't tell me you found Thoreau back there too? Anyone else hiding in our woods? Jimmy Hoffa perhaps? Amelia Earhart? Come by after dinner and I'll give you my copy of *Walden*."

She left and Olivier took their orders then brought warm rolls smothered in melting monarda butter and spread with pâté. Beauvoir produced a sheaf of photographs of the cabin from his satchel and handed them to the Chief.

"Printed these out as soon as we got back." Beauvoir took a bite of his warm roll. He was starving. Agent Lacoste took one as well and sipping on her wine she looked out the window. But all she could see was the reflection of the bistro. Villagers eating dinner, some sitting at the bar with beer or whiskey. Some relaxing by the fire. No one paying attention to them. But then she met a pair of eyes in the reflection. More specter than person. She turned just as Olivier disappeared into the kitchen.

A few minutes later a plate of *escargots* bathed in garlic butter was placed in front of Beauvoir with a bowl of minted sweetpea soup for Lacoste and cauliflower and stilton soup with pear and date relish for Gamache.

"Hmm," said Lacoste, taking a spoonful. "Fresh from the garden. Yours too, probably." She nodded to Beauvoir's snails. He smirked but ate them anyway, dipping the crusty bread into the liquid garlic butter.

Gamache was looking at the photographs. Slowly he lowered the pictures. It was like stumbling across King Tut's tomb.

"I have a call in to Superintendent Brunel," he said.

"The head of property crime?" asked Lacoste. "That's a good idea."

Thérèse Brunel was an expert in art theft and a personal friend of Gamache.

"She's going to die when she sees that cabin," Beauvoir laughed. Olivier removed their dishes.

"How could the dead man have collected all these things?" Gamache wondered. "And gotten them in there?"

"And why?" said Beauvoir.

"But there were no personal items," said Lacoste. "Not a single photograph, no letters, bank books. ID. Nothing."

"And no obvious murder weapon," said Beauvoir. "We sent the fireplace poker and a couple of garden tools to be tested, but it doesn't look promising."

"But I did find something after you left." Lacoste put a bag onto the table and opened it. "It was way under the bed, against the wall. I missed it the first time I looked," she explained. "I fingerprinted it and took samples. They're on the way to the lab."

On the table was a carved piece of wood, stained with what looked like blood.

Someone had whittled a word in the wood.

Woe.

TWENTY

———

Agent Morin wandered round inside the cabin, humming. In one hand he gripped the satellite phone, in the other he gripped a piece of firewood. Not for the woodstove, which was lit and throwing good heat. Nor the fireplace, also lit and light. But in case anything came at him out of the shadows, out of the corners.

He'd lit all the oil lamps and all the candles. The dead man seemed to have made them himself, from paraffin left over after the preserves had been sealed.

Morin missed his television. His cell phone. His girlfriend. His mother. He brought the phone up to his mouth again, then lowered it for what felt like the hundredth time.

You can't call the Chief Inspector. What'll you say? You're scared? To be alone in a cabin in the woods? Where a man was murdered?

And he sure couldn't call his mother. She'd find a way to reach the cabin, and the team would find him next morning, with his mother. Ironing his shirts and frying bacon and eggs.

No, he'd rather die.

He wandered around some more, poking things here and there, but being very, very careful. Elmer Fudd–like he crept round, picking up glass and peering at odds and ends. A pane of amber at the kitchen window, an engraved silver candlestick. Eventually he took a sandwich from the brown paper bag and unfolded the waxed paper. Ham and Brie on baguette. Not bad. He took the Coca-Cola, snapped it open, then he sat by the fire. The chair was exceptionally comfortable. As he ate he relaxed and by the time he got to the pastry he was feeling himself again.

He reached for the fiddle by his side, but thought better of it. Instead he took a book at random from the shelves and opened it.

It was by an author he'd never heard of. Some guy named Currer Bell. He started to read about a girl named Jane growing up in England. After a while his eyes, strained from reading by the weak light, grew tired. He thought it was probably time for bed. It must be after midnight.

He looked at his watch. Eight thirty.

Reaching over, he hesitated, then picked up the violin. Its wood was deep and seemed warm to the touch. He smoothed his young hand over it, softly, caressing and turning it round in practiced hands. He put it down quickly. He shouldn't be touching it. He went back to the book, but after a minute or so he found the fiddle in his hands again. Knowing he shouldn't, begging himself not to, he reached for the horse-hair bow. Knowing there was no going back now, he stood up.

Agent Morin tucked the violin under his chin and drew the bow across the strings. The sound was deep and rich and seductive. It was more than the young agent could resist. Soon the comforting strains of "Colm Quigley" filled the cabin. Almost to the corners.

Their main courses had arrived. A fruit-stuffed Rock Cornish game hen, done on the spit, for Gamache; melted Brie, fresh tomato and basil fettuccine for Lacoste; and a lamb and prune tagine for Beauvoir. A platter of freshly harvested grilled vegetables was also brought to the table.

Gamache's chicken was tender and tasty, delicately flavored with Pommery-style mustard and vermouth.

"What does that piece of wood mean?" Gamache asked his team as they ate.

"Well, it was just about the only thing in the cabin that wasn't an antique," said Lacoste. "And what with the whittling tools I'm guessing he made it himself."

Gamache nodded. It was his guess as well. "But why woe?"

"Could that be his name?" Beauvoir asked, but without enthusiasm.

"Monsieur Woe?" asked Lacoste. "That might also explain why he lived alone in a cabin."

"Why would someone carve that for himself?" Gamache put down his knife and fork. "And you found nothing else in the cabin that looked as though it had been whittled?"

"Nothing," said Beauvoir. "We found axes and hammers and saws. All well used. I think he must have made that cabin himself. But he sure didn't whittle it."

Woe, thought Gamache, picking up his knife and fork again. Was the Hermit that sad?

"Did you notice our photographs of the stream, sir?" Lacoste asked.

"I did. At least now we know how the dead man kept his groceries cool."

Agent Lacoste, on investigating the stream, had found a bag anchored there. And in it were jars of perishable foods. Dangling in the cold water.

"But he obviously didn't make his own milk and cheese, and no one remembers seeing him in the local shops," said Beauvoir. "So that leaves us with one conclusion."

"Someone was taking him supplies," said Lacoste.

"Everything all right?" asked Olivier.

"Fine, *patron, merci*," said Gamache with a smile.

"Do you need more mayonnaise or butter?" Olivier smiled back, trying not to look like a maniac. Trying to tell himself that no matter how many condiments or warm buns or glasses of wine he brought it would make no difference. He could never ingratiate himself.

"*Non, merci*," said Lacoste, and reluctantly Olivier left.

"We at least have prints from the cabin. We should find out something tomorrow," said Beauvoir.

"*I think we know why he was killed just now*," said Gamache.

"The paths," said Lacoste. "Roar Parra was cutting riding paths for Dominique. One path was almost at the cabin. Close enough to see it."

"Which Madame Gilbert did," said Beauvoir. "But we have only her word that she didn't find the cabin on an earlier ride."

"Except that they didn't have the horses then," said Lacoste. "They didn't arrive until the day after the murder."

"But she might have walked the old paths," suggested Gamache, "in preparation for the horses, and to tell Roar which ones he should open."

"Roar might have walked them too," said Beauvoir. "Or that son of his. Havoc. Parra said he was going to help him."

The other two thought. Still, there seemed no very good reason why either Parra would walk the old riding paths before clearing them.

"But why kill the recluse?" Lacoste said. "Even supposing one of the Parras or Dominique Gilbert found him. It makes no sense. Killing for the treasure, maybe. But why leave it all there?"

"Maybe it wasn't," said Beauvoir. "We know what we found. But maybe there was more."

It struck Gamache like a ton of bricks. Why hadn't he thought of that? He'd been so overwhelmed by what was there, he'd never even considered what might be missing.

Agent Morin lay in the bed and tried to get comfortable. It felt strange to be sleeping in a bed made by a dead man.

He closed his eyes. Turned over. Turned back. Opening his eyes he stared at the firelight flickering in the hearth. The cabin was less frightening. In fact, it was almost cozy.

He punched the pillow a few times to fluff it up, but something resisted.

Sitting up he took the pillow and scrunched it around. Sure enough, there was something besides feathers inside. He got up and lighting an oil lamp he took the pillow out of its case. A deep pocket had been sewn inside. Carefully, feeling like a vet with a pregnant horse, he slipped his arm in up to the elbow. His hand closed over something hard and knobby.

Withdrawing it he held an object to the oil lamp. It was an intricate carving. Of men and women on a ship. They were all facing the bow. Morin marveled at the workmanship. Whoever carved this had captured the excitement of a journey. The same excitement Morin and his sister had felt as kids when they took family car trips to the Abitibi or the Gaspé.

He recognized the happy anticipation on the shipboard faces. Looking closer he saw most had bags and sacks and there was a variety of ages, from newborns to the very old and infirm. Some were ecstatic, some expectant, some calm and content.

All were happy. It was a ship full of hope.

The sails of the ship were, incredibly, carved of wood shaved thin. He turned it over. Something was scratched into the bottom. He took it right up to the lamp.

OWSVI

Was it Russian? Agent Lacoste thought the dead man might be Russian because of the icons. Was this his name? Written in that strange alphabet they use?

Then he had an idea. He went back to the bed and tried the other pillow, which had been below the first. There was something hard in there too. Pulling it out he held another sculpture, also of wood, equally detailed. This one showed men and women gathered at a body of water, looking out at it. Some seemed perplexed, but most appeared content to just be there. He found letters scratched on the bottom of that one too.

MRKBVYDDO

Righting it again he placed it on the table beside the other one. There was a sense of joy, of hope, about these works. He stared at them with more fascination than he ever got from TV.

But the more he looked the more uneasy he became until it felt as though something was watching him. He looked into the kitchen then quickly scanned the room. Turning back to the carvings he was surprised to find the sense of foreboding was coming from them.

He felt a creeping up and down his back and turned quickly into the dark room, instantly regretting not putting on more lamps. A glittering caught his attention. Up high. In the farthest corner of the cabin. Was it eyes?

Picking up his piece of wood he crept closer, crouching down. As he approached the corner the glitter began to form a pattern. It was a spider's web, just catching the soft glow of the lamp. But there was something different about it. As his eyes adjusted the hair on the back of his neck rose.

A word had been woven into the web.

Woe.

TWENTY-ONE

Everyone was already around the table next morning when Morin arrived, more than a little disheveled. They glanced at him, and Agent Lacoste indicated the seat next to her, where, miraculously for the hungry young agent, there waited a bowl of strong *café au lait* along with a plate of scrambled eggs, bacon and thick-cut toast with jams.

Morin wolfed down the food and listened to the reports, and then it was his turn.

He placed the two carvings on the table and moved them slowly to the center. So lively were the sculptures it looked as though the ship had taken sail and was moving on its own. And it looked as though the people on the shore were eagerly awaiting the arrival of the ship.

"What are those?" asked Gamache, rising from his chair and moving round the table for a closer look.

"I found them last night. They were hidden in the pillows on the bed."

The three officers looked stunned.

"You're kidding," said Lacoste. "In the pillows?"

"Sewn into the pillows on the bed. Well hidden, though I'm not sure whether he was hiding them or protecting them."

"Why didn't you call?" demanded Beauvoir, tearing his eyes from the carvings to look at Morin.

"Should I have?" He looked stricken, his eyes bouncing among the officers. "I just thought there was nothing we could do until now anyway."

He'd longed to call; only a mighty effort had stopped him from dialing the B and B and waking them all up. But he didn't want to give in to his fear. But he could see by their faces he'd made a mistake.

All his life he'd been afraid, and all his life it had marred his judgment. He'd hoped that had stopped, but apparently not.

"Next time," the Chief said, looking at him sternly, "call. We're a team, we need to know everything."

"*Oui, patron.*"

"Have these been dusted?" Beauvoir asked.

Morin nodded and held up an envelope. "The prints."

Beauvoir grabbed it out of his hand and took it to his computer to scan in. But even from there his eyes kept going back to the two carvings.

Gamache was leaning over the table, peering at them through his half-moon glasses

"They're remarkable."

The joy of the little wooden travelers was palpable. Gamache knelt down so that he was at eye level with the carvings, and they were sailing toward him. It seemed the carvings were two halves of a whole. A ship full of people sailing toward a shore. And more happy people waiting.

So why did he feel uneasy? Why did he want to warn the ship to go back?

"There's something written on the bottom of each," Morin offered. He picked one up and showed it to the Chief who looked then handed it to Lacoste. Beauvoir picked up the other and saw a series of letters. It was nonsense, but of course it wasn't really. It meant something. They just had to figure it out.

"Is it Russian?" Morin asked.

"No. The Russian alphabet is Cyrillic. This is the Roman alphabet," said Gamache.

"What does it mean?"

The three more seasoned officers looked at each other.

"I have no idea," admitted the Chief Inspector. "Most artisans mark their works, sign them in some way. Perhaps this is how the carver signed his works."

"Then wouldn't the lettering under each carving be the same?" asked Morin.

"That's true. I'm at a loss. Perhaps Superintendent Brunel can tell us. She'll be here this morning."

"I found something else last night," said Morin. "I took a picture of it. It's still in my camera. You can't see it too well, but . . ."

He turned on his digital camera and handed it to Beauvoir, who looked briefly at the image.

"Too small. I can't make it out. I'll throw it up onto the computer."

They continued to discuss the case while Beauvoir sat at his computer, downloading the image.

"*Tabarnac*," they heard him whisper.

"What is it?" Gamache walked to the desk. Lacoste joined him and they huddled round the flat screen.

There was the web, and the word.

Woe.

"What does it mean?" Beauvoir asked, almost to himself.

Gamache shook his head. How could a spider have woven a word? And why that one? The same word they'd found carved in wood and tossed under the bed.

"Some pig."

They looked at Lacoste.

"*Pardon?*" Gamache asked.

"When I was in the outhouse yesterday I found a signed first edition."

"About a girl named Jane?" Morin asked, then wished he hadn't. They all looked at him as though he'd said "some pig." "I found a book in the cabin," he explained. "By a guy named Currer Bell."

Lacoste looked blank, Gamache looked perplexed, and Morin didn't even want to think what look Beauvoir was giving him.

"Never mind. Go on."

"It was *Charlotte's Web*, by E. B. White," said Agent Lacoste. "One of my favorites as a child."

"My daughter's too," said Gamache. He remembered reading the book over and over to the little girl who pretended she wasn't afraid of the dark. Afraid of the closed closet, afraid of the creaks and groans of the house. He'd read to her every night until finally she'd fall asleep.

The book that gave her the most comfort, and that he'd practically memorized, was *Charlotte's Web*.

"Some pig," he repeated, and gave a low, rumbling laugh. "The book's about a lonely piglet destined for the slaughterhouse. A spider named Charlotte befriends him and tries to save his life."

"By weaving things about him into her web," explained Lacoste.

"Things like 'Some pig' so the farmer would think Wilbur was special. The book in the outhouse is signed by the author."

Gamache shook his head. Incredible.

"Did it work?" asked Morin. "Was the pig saved?"

Beauvoir looked at him with disdain. And yet, he had to admit, he wanted to know as well.

"He was," said Gamache. Then his brows drew together. Obviously in real life spiders don't weave messages into their webs. So who had put it there? And why? And why "woe?"

He was itching to get back up there.

"There's something else."

All eyes once again turned to the simple-looking agent.

"It's about the outhouse." He turned to Lacoste. "Did you notice anything?"

"You mean besides the signed first edition and the stacks of money as toilet paper?"

"Not inside. Outside."

She thought then shook her head.

"It was probably too dark," said Agent Morin. "I used it last night and didn't notice then either. It wasn't until this morning."

"What, for God's sake?" Beauvoir snapped.

"There's a trail. It runs to the outhouse, but doesn't stop there. It goes on. I followed it this morning and it came out here."

"At the Incident Room?" asked Beauvoir.

"Well, not exactly. It wound through the woods and came out up there."

He waved toward the hill overlooking the village.

"I marked the place it comes out. I think I can find it again."

"That was foolish of you," said Gamache. He looked stern and his voice was without warmth. Morin instantly reddened. "Never, ever wander on your own into the woods, do you understand? You might have been lost."

"But you'd find me, wouldn't you?"

They all knew he would. Gamache had found them once, he'd find them again.

"It was an unnecessary risk. Don't ever let your guard down." Gamache's deep brown eyes were intense. "A mistake could cost you your life. Or the life of someone else. Never relax. There are threats all around, from the woods, and from the killer we're hunting. Neither will forgive a mistake."

"Yes sir."

"Right," said Gamache. He got up and the rest jumped to their feet. "You need to show us where the path comes out."

Down in the village, Olivier stood at the window of the bistro, oblivious of the conversation and laughter of breakfasters behind him. He saw Gamache and the others walk along the ridge of the hill. They paused, then walked back and forth a bit. Even from there he could see Beauvoir gesture angrily at the young agent who always looked so clueless.

It'll be fine, he repeated to himself. *It'll be fine. Just smile.*

Their pacing stopped. They stared at the forest, as he stared at them.

And a wave crashed over Olivier, knocking the breath he'd been holding for so long out of him. Knocking the fixed smile off his face.

It was almost a relief. Almost.

There it is," said Morin.

He'd tied his belt around a branch. It had seemed a clever solution when he'd done it, but now searching for a thin brown belt on the edge of a forest didn't seem such a brilliant idea.

But they found it.

Gamache looked at the path. Once you knew it was there it was obvious. It almost screamed. Like those optical illusions deliberately placed in paintings that once found you couldn't stop seeing. The tiger in the crockery, the spaceship in the garden.

"I'll join you at the cabin when I can," said Gamache and watched with Lacoste as Beauvoir and Morin headed into the woods. Like nuns, he felt they were safe if not alone. It was, he supposed, a conceit. But it comforted him. He watched until he couldn't see them anymore. But still he waited, until he could no longer hear them. And only then did he descend into Three Pines.

Peter and Clara Morrow were both in their studios when the doorbell rang. It was an odd, almost startling sound. No one they knew ever rang the bell, they just came in and made themselves at home. How often had Clara and Peter found Ruth in their living room? Feet up on the sofa reading a book and drinking a martini at ten in the morning, Rosa nestled on the worn carpet beside her. They thought they'd have to call a priest to get rid of them.

More than once they'd found Gabri in their bath.

"Anybody home?" sang a man's deep voice.

"I'll get it," Clara called.

Peter didn't bother to answer. He was wandering around his studio, circling the work on the easel, getting close, then heading away. His mind might be on his art, as it always was, but his heart was elsewhere. Since word of Marc Gilbert's treachery had hit the village Peter had thought of little else.

He'd genuinely liked Marc. Was drawn to him in a way he felt drawn to cadmium yellow and marian blue, and Clara. He'd felt excited, almost giddy, at the thought of visiting Marc. Having a quiet drink together. Talking. Going for walks.

Marc Gilbert had ruined that as well. Trying to ruin Olivier was one thing, a terrible thing. But secretly Peter couldn't help but feel this was just as bad. Like taking a rusty nail to something lovely. And rare. At least for Peter.

He hated Marc Gilbert now.

Outside his studio he heard Clara talking, and a familiar voice replying.

Armand Gamache.

Peter decided to join them.

"Coffee?" Clara offered the Chief Inspector, after he and Peter had greeted each other.

"*Non, merci.* I can't stay long. I've come on business."

Clara thought that was a funny way of putting it. Murder business.

"You had a busy day yesterday," said Clara, as the three of them sat at the kitchen table. "It's all Three Pines can talk about. It's hard to know what's the most shocking. That Marc Gilbert was the one who moved the body, that Vincent Gilbert's here or that the dead man seemed to be living in the forest all along. Did he really live there?"

"We think so, but we're just waiting for confirmation. We still don't know who he was."

Gamache watched them closely. They seemed as puzzled as he was.

"I can't believe no one knew he was there," said Clara.

"We think someone knew. Someone was taking him food. We found it on the counter."

They looked at each other in amazement.

"One of us? Who?"

One of us, thought Gamache. Three short words, but potent. They more than anything had launched a thousand ships, a thousand attacks. One of us. A circle drawn. And closed. A boundary marked. Those inside and those not.

Families, clubs, gangs, cities, states, countries. A village.

What had Myrna called it? Beyond the pale.

But it went beyond simple belonging. The reason "belonging" was so potent, so attractive, so much a part of the human yearning, was that it also meant safety, and loyalty. If you were "one of us" you were protected.

Was that what he was up against, Gamache wondered. Not just the struggle to find the killer, but the efforts of those on the inside to protect him? Was the drawbridge up? The pale closed? Was Three Pines protecting a killer? One of them?

"Why would someone take him food then kill him?" asked Clara.

"Doesn't make sense," agreed Peter.

"Unless the murderer didn't show up intending to kill," said Gamache. "Maybe something happened to provoke him."

"Okay, but then if he lashed out and murdered the man, wouldn't he have just run away? Why take the body all the way through the woods to the Gilbert place?" asked Clara.

"Why indeed," asked Gamache. "Any theories?"

"Because he wanted the body found," said Peter. "And the Gilberts' is the nearest place."

The murderer wanted the body found. Why? Most murderers went to huge lengths to hide the crime. Why had this man advertised it?

"Either the body found," Peter continued, "or the cabin."

"We think it would have been found in a few days anyway," Gamache said. "Roar Parra was cutting riding paths in that area."

"We're not being much help," said Clara.

Gamache reached into his satchel. "I actually came by to show you something we found in the cabin. I'd like your opinions."

He brought out two towels and placed them carefully on the table.

They looked like newborns, protected against a chilly world. He slowly unwrapped them.

Clara leaned in.

"Look at their faces." She looked up directly into Gamache's. "So beautiful."

He nodded. They were. Not just their features. It was their joy, their vitality, that made them beautiful.

"May I?" Peter reached out and Gamache nodded. He picked up one of the sculptures and turned it over.

"There's writing, but I can't make it out. A signature?"

"Of sorts, perhaps," said Gamache. "We haven't figured out what the letters mean."

Peter studied the two works, the ship and the shore. "Did the dead man carve them?"

"We think so."

Though, given what else was in the cabin, it wouldn't have surprised Gamache to discover they were carved by Michelangelo. The difference was every other piece was in plain sight, but the dead man had kept these hidden. Somehow these were different.

As he watched he saw first Clara's then Peter's smile fade until they both looked almost unhappy. Certainly uncomfortable. Clara fidgeted in her chair. It had taken the Morrows less time than it took the Sûreté officers that morning to sense something wrong. Not surprising, thought Gamache. The Morrows were artists and presumably more in tune with their feelings.

The carvings emanated delight, joy. But beneath that was something else. A minor key, a dark note.

"What is it?" Gamache asked.

"There's something wrong with them," said Clara. "Something's off."

"Can you tell me what?"

Peter and Clara continued to stare at the pieces, then looked at each other. Finally they looked at Gamache.

"Sorry," said Peter. "Sometimes with art it can be subliminal, unintended by the artist even. A proportion slightly off. A color that jars."

"I can tell you though," said Clara, "they're great works of art."

"How can you tell?" asked Gamache.

"Because they provoke a strong emotion. All great art does."

Clara considered the carvings again. Was there too much joy? Was that the problem? Was too much beauty and delight and hope disquieting?

She thought not, hoped not. No, it was something else about these works.

"That reminds me," said Peter. "Don't you have a meeting with Denis Fortin in a few minutes?"

"Oh, damn, damn, damn," said Clara, springing up from the table.

"I won't keep you," said Gamache, rewrapping the sculptures.

"I have a thought," she said, joining Gamache at the door. "Monsieur Fortin might know more about sculpture than us. Hard to know less, really. Can I show one to him?"

"It's a good idea," said Gamache. "A very good idea. Where're you meeting him?"

"In the bistro in five minutes."

Gamache took one of the towels out of his satchel and handed it to Clara.

"This is great," she said as they walked down the path to the road. "I'll just tell him I made it."

"Would you have liked to?"

Clara remembered the blossoming horror in her chest as she'd looked at the carvings.

"No," she said.

TWENTY-TWO

Gamache arrived back at the Incident Room to find Superintendent Thérèse Brunel sitting at the conference table, surrounded
by photographs. As he entered she rose, smiling.

"Chief Inspector." She advanced, her hand out. "Agent Lacoste has
made me so comfortable I feel I could move right in."

Thérèse Brunel was of retirement age, though no one in the Sûreté
would ever point that out. Not out of fear of the charming woman, or
delicacy. But because she, more than any of them, was irreplaceable.

She'd presented herself at the Sûreté recruitment office two decades
earlier. The young officer on duty thought it was a joke. Here was a sophisticated woman in her mid-forties, dressed in Chanel and wanting
an application form. He'd given it to her, thinking it was almost certainly a threat for a disappointing son or daughter, then watched with
increasing bafflement as she'd sat, legs crossed at the ankles, delicate
perfume just a hint in the air, and filled it out herself.

Thérèse Brunel had been the chief of acquisitions at the world famous Musée des Beaux Arts in Montreal, but had nursed a secret passion for puzzles. Puzzles of all sorts. And once her children had gone off
to college she'd marched right over to the Sûreté and signed up. What
greater puzzle could there be than unravelling a crime? Then, taking
classes at the police college from Chief Inspector Armand Gamache,
she'd discovered another puzzle and passion. The human mind.

She now out-ranked her mentor and was the head of the property
crime division. She was in her mid-sixties and as vibrant as ever.

Gamache shook her hand warmly. "Superintendent Brunel."

Thérèse Brunel and her husband Jérôme had often been to the

Gamaches' for dinner, and had them back to their own apartment on rue Laurier. But at work they were "Chief Inspector" and "Superintendent."

He then walked over to Agent Lacoste, who'd also stood as he entered.

"Anything yet?"

She shook her head. "But I just called and they expect the lab results any moment."

"*Bon. Merci.*" He nodded to Agent Lacoste and she sat once more at her computer. Then he turned his attention to Superintendent Brunel.

"We're expecting fingerprint results. I really am most grateful to you for coming at such short notice."

"*C'est un plaisir.* Besides, what could be more exciting?" She led him back to the conference table and leaning close she whispered, "*Voyons,* Armand, is this for real?"

She pointed to the photographs scattered across the table.

"It is," he whispered back. "And we might need Jérôme's help as well."

Jérôme Brunel, now retired from medicine, had long shared his wife's love of puzzles, but while hers veered toward the human mind, his settled firmly on ciphers. Codes. From his comfortable and disheveled study in their Montreal home he entertained desperate diplomats and security people. Sometimes cracking cryptic codes and sometimes creating them.

He was a jolly and cultured man.

Gamache took the carving from his bag, unwrapped it and placed it on the table. Once again the blissful passengers were sailing across the conference table.

"Very nice," she said, putting on her glasses and leaning closer. "Very nice indeed," she mumbled to herself as she studied the piece, not touching it. "Beautifully made. Whoever the artist is, he knows wood, feels it. And knows art."

She stepped back now and stared. Gamache waited for it, and sure enough her smile faded and she even leaned a little away from the work.

This was the third time he'd seen it that morning. And he had felt it himself. The carvings seemed to burrow to the core, to the part most deeply hidden and the part most commonly shared. They found people's humanity. Then, like a dentist, they began to drill. Until that joy turned to dread.

After a moment her face cleared, and the professional mask descended. The problem-solver replaced the person. She leaned in to the work, moving herself round the table, not touching the carving. Finally, when she'd seen it from all angles, she picked it up, and like everyone else looked underneath.

"OWSVI," she read. "Upper case. Scratched into the wood, not painted." She sounded like a coroner, dissecting and dictating. "It's a heavy wood, a hardwood. Cherry?" She looked closer and even sniffed. "No, the grain isn't right. Cedar? No, the color is off, unless . . ." She took it to the window and placed it in a stream of sunshine. Then lowering it she smiled at Gamache over her glasses. "Cedar. Redwood. From British Columbia almost certainly. It's a good choice of wood, you know. Cedar lasts forever, especially the redwood. It's a very hard wood too. And yet it's surprisingly easy to sculpt. The Haida on the west coast used it for centuries to make totem poles."

"And they're still standing."

"They would be, if most of them hadn't been destroyed in the late 1800s by the government or the church. But you can still see a fine one in the Museum of Civilization in Ottawa."

The irony wasn't lost on either of them.

"So what are you doing here?" she said to the sculpture. "And what are you so afraid of?"

"Why do you say that?"

Over at her desk Agent Lacoste looked up, wanting to know the answer too.

"Surely you felt it too, Armand?" She'd used his first name, a sign that while she appeared composed she was in fact nonplussed. "There's something cold about this work. I hesitate to say evil . . ."

Gamache cocked his head in surprise. Evil wasn't a word he heard often outside a sermon. Brutal, malevolent, cruel, yes. Horror, even; investigators sometimes talked about the horror of a crime.

But never evil. But that was what made Thérèse Brunel a brilliant investigator, a solver of puzzles and crimes. And his friend. She placed conviction above convention.

"Evil?" asked Lacoste from her desk.

Superintendent Brunel looked at Agent Lacoste. "I said I hesitated to call it that."

"And do you still hesitate?" Gamache asked.

Brunel picked up the work once again and bringing it up to eye level she peered at the Lilliputian passengers. All dressed for a long voyage, the babies in blankets, the women with bags of bread and cheese, the men strong and resolute. And all looking ahead, looking forward to something wonderful. The detail was exquisite.

She turned it round then jerked it away from her as though it had bitten her nose.

"What is it?" Gamache asked.

"I've found the worm," she said.

Neither Carole Gilbert nor her son had slept well the night before, and she suspected Dominique hadn't either. To Vincent, sleeping in the small room off the landing, she gave no thought. Or rather every time he emerged into her conscious mind she shoved him back into his little room, and tried to lock the door.

It had been a lovely, soft dawn. She'd shuffled around the kitchen making a pot of strong French Pressé coffee, then putting a mohair throw round her shoulders she'd picked up the tray and taken it outside, installing herself on the quiet patio overlooking the garden and the mist-covered fields.

The day before had felt like one endless emergency, with claxtons sounding in her head for hours on end. They'd pulled together as a family and presented a united front through revelation after revelation.

That Marc's father was still alive.

That Vincent was in fact standing right there.

That the murdered man had been found in their new home.

And that Marc had moved him. To the bistro. In a deliberate attempt to hurt, perhaps even ruin, Olivier.

By the time Chief Inspector Gamache had left they all felt punch-drunk. Too dazed and tired to go at each other. Marc had made his feelings clear, then gone into the spa area to plaster and paint and hammer. Vincent had had the sense to leave, only returning late that night. And Dominique had found the cabin while out riding on the least damaged of the horses.

'Twould ring the bells of Heaven, Carole thought to herself as she stared at the horses, now in the misty field. Grazing. Leery of one another. Even from there she could see their sores.

The wildest peal for years,
If Parson lost his senses
And people came to theirs,
And he and they together
knelt down with fervent prayers
For tamed and shabby tigers,
And dancing dogs and bears.

"Mother."

Carole jumped, lost in her own thoughts and now found by her son. She got to her feet. He looked bleary, but showered and shaved. His voice was cold, distant. They stared at each other. Would they blink, sit down, pour coffee and talk about the weather? The headlines? The horses. Would they try to pretend the storm wasn't all around them? And wasn't of their own making.

Who had done worse? Carole by lying to her son for years, and telling him his father was dead? Or Marc by moving a dead man down to the bistro, and in one gesture ruining their chances of being accepted in the small community.

She'd marred his past, and he'd marred their future.

They were quite a team.

"I'm sorry," said Carole, and opened her arms. Silently Marc moved across the stones and almost fell into them. He was tall and she wasn't, but still she held him and rubbed his back and whispered, "There, there."

Then they sat, the tray with croissants and fresh strawberry jam between them. The world looked very green that morning, very fresh, from the tall maples and oaks to the meadow. Marc poured coffee while Carole pulled the mohair throw round her shoulders and watched as the horses ate grass in the field and occasionally looked up into a day they should not have seen, into a world they should have left two days ago. Even now, standing in the mist, they seemed to straddle the two worlds.

"They almost look like horses," said Marc, "if you squint."

Carole looked over at her son and laughed. He was making a face, trying to morph the creatures in the field into the magnificent hunters he'd been expecting.

"Seriously, is that really a horse?" He pointed to Chester, who in the uncertain light looked like a camel.

Carole was suddenly very sad that they might have to leave this house, cast out by their own actions. The garden had never looked lovelier, and with time it would only get better as it matured and the various plants mingled and grew together.

"I'm worried about that one." Marc pointed to the darkest horse, off on his own. "Thunder."

"Yes, well." Carole shifted uncomfortably to look at him. "About him . . ."

"Suppose he decides to bite one of the guests? Not that I don't appreciate what he did to Dad."

Carole suppressed a smile. Seeing the Great Man with horse slime on his shoulder was the only good thing about a very bad day.

"What do you suggest?" she asked.

"I don't know."

Carole was silent. They both knew what Marc was suggesting. If the horse didn't learn manners in a month, by Thanksgiving he'd have to be put down.

"*For wretched, blind pit ponies,*" she murmured. "*And little hunted hares.*"

"*Pardon?*" asked Marc.

"His, ah, his name isn't really Thunder. It's Marc."

"You're kidding." But neither was laughing. Marc looked out into the field at the malevolent, mad animal keeping his distance from the others. A black blotch in the misty meadow. Like a mistake. A mar.

A Marc.

Later, when Marc headed off with Dominique to get groceries and building supplies, Carole found four carrots in the kitchen and fed them to the horses, who at first were reluctant to trust. But first Buttercup, then Macaroni and finally Chester tiptoed forward and seemed to kiss the carrot off her palm.

But one remained.

She whispered to Marc the horse, cooing at him. Enticing him. Begging him. Standing at the fence she leaned forward, quietly holding the carrot out as far as she could. "Please," she coaxed. "I won't hurt you."

But he didn't believe her.

She went inside, climbed the stairs and knocked on the door to the small bedroom.

Armand Gamache took the carving and stared into the crowd on deck.

It was easy to miss, but still he could have kicked himself. It now appeared so obvious. The small figure at the very back of the boat, crouching just in front of the matronly woman and her large sack.

He felt his skin crawl as he examined the face of the tiny wooden man, barely more than a boy, looking over his shoulder. Past the matronly woman. Looking behind the boat. While everyone else was gazing ahead, he was slumped down and staring back. To where they'd been.

And the look on his face turned Gamache's blood cold. Cold to the bone, cold to the marrow. Cold to the core.

This was what terror looked like. Felt like. The small, wooden face was a transmitter. And its message was horrific. Gamache suddenly had the nearly uncontrollable urge to look behind himself, see what might be lurking there. Instead, he put his glasses on and leaned closer.

In his arms the young man was gripping a package.

Finally Gamache put it down and removed his glasses. "I see what you mean."

Superintendent Brunel sighed. "Evil. There's evil on that voyage."

Gamache didn't disagree. "Does it look familiar? Could the carving be on your active list of stolen art?"

"There're thousands of items on that list," she smiled. "Everything from Rembrands to engraved toothpicks."

"And I bet you have them all memorized."

Her smile broadened and she inclined her head slightly. He knew her well.

"But nothing like this. It would stand out."

"Is it art?"

"If you mean is it valuable, I'd say it's almost priceless. If one of these had come on the market while I was at the Musée des Beaux Arts I'd have jumped at it. And paid a small fortune."

"Why?"

She looked at the large, calm man in front of her. So like an academic. She could see him in cap and gown moving like a ship of state through the halls of an ancient university, eager students in his wake. When she'd first met him, lecturing at the police college, he'd been twenty years younger but still a commanding figure. Now he carried that authority with even greater ease. His wavy dark hair was receding, his temples were graying as was his trim mustache, his body was expanding. As was, she knew, his influence.

He'd taught her many things. But one of the most valuable was not to just see, but to listen. As he listened to her now.

"What makes a work of art unique isn't its color or composition or subject. It has nothing whatsoever to do with what we see. Why are some paintings masterpieces while others, perhaps even more competent, are forgotten? Why are some symphonies still beloved hundreds of years after the composer has died?"

Gamache thought about it. And what came to mind was the painting placed so causally on an easel after dinner a few nights ago. Badly lit, unframed.

And yet he could have stared at it forever.

It was the painting of the elderly woman, her body headed forward, but her face turned back.

He'd known her longing. That same root which spasmed when gazing at the carving had ached when he'd looked at that woman. Clara hadn't simply painted a woman, hadn't even painted a feeling. She'd created a world. In that one image.

That was a masterpiece.

He suddenly felt very badly for Peter, and hoped deeply that Peter was no longer trying to compete with his wife. She was nowhere to be found on that battlefield.

"That," Superintendent Brunel pointed with one manicured finger at the carving, "will be remembered long after you and I are dead. Long after this charming village has fallen to dust."

"There's another one, you know," he said and had the rare pleasure of seeing Thérèse Brunel surprised. "But before we see it I think we should head to the cabin."

He looked at her feet. She wore elegant new shoes.

"I've brought boots with me, Chief Inspector," she said, her voice holding a faint and mocking reproach as she walked briskly ahead of him to the door. "When have you ever taken me anywhere that didn't have mud?"

"I believe they hosed down Place des Arts before the last symphony we were at," he said, smiling over his shoulder at Agent Lacoste as they left.

"Professionally, I meant. Always mud and always a body."

"Well this time there is certainly mud, but no body."

"Sir." Lacoste jogged over to the car, holding a printout. "I thought you'd like to see this."

She handed the paper to him and pointed. It was a lab report. The results were beginning to come in, and would continue all day. And this one brought a satisfied smile to his face. He turned to Thérèse Brunel.

"They found woodchips, sawdust really, beside a chair in the cabin. They also found traces on his clothes. The lab says it was red cedar. From British Columbia."

"I guess we found the artist," she said. "Now if we only knew why he carved so much terror."

Why indeed, thought Gamache as he got into the car and drove up du Moulin. ATVs were waiting for them and they headed deep into the Quebec forest. A professor and an elegant expert on art. Neither was as they appeared, and they were heading for a rustic cabin that certainly wasn't.

Gamache stopped the ATV just before the final turn in the path. He and Superintendent Brunel dismounted and walked the rest of the way. It was another world inside the forest, and he wanted to give her a feeling for where the victim had chosen to live. A world of cool shadows and diffuse light, of rich dark scents of things decaying. Of creatures unseen but heard, scampering and scurrying.

Gamache and Brunel were very aware of being the outsiders here.

And yet it wasn't threatening. Not now. In twelve hours, when the sun was down, it would feel different again.

"I see what you mean." Brunel looked around. "A man could easily live here without being found. It's very peaceful, isn't it?" She sounded almost wistful.

"Could you live here?" Gamache asked.

"I think I could, you know. Does that surprise you?"

Gamache was silent but smiled as he walked.

"I don't need much," she continued. "I used to. When I was younger. Trips to Paris, a nice apartment, good clothes. I have all that now. And I'm happy."

"But not because you have those thing," suggested Gamache.

"As I get older I need less and less. I really believe I could live here. Between us, Armand? Part of me yearns for it. Could you?"

He nodded and saw again the simple little cabin. One room.

"One chair for solitude, two for friendship and three for society," he said.

"*Walden*. And how many chairs would you need?"

Gamache thought about it. "Two. I don't mind society, but I need one other person."

"Reine-Marie," said Thérèse. "And I only need Jérôme."

"There's a first edition of *Walden* in the cabin, you know."

Thérèse sighed. "*Incroyable*. Who was this man, Armand? Do you have any idea?"

"None."

He stopped and beside him she stopped too, following his gaze.

At first it was difficult to see, but then, slowly, she made out the simple log cabin, as though it had materialized just for them. And was inviting them in.

Come in," he said.

Carole Gilbert breathed deeply then stepped forward, past the solid ground she'd cultivated for decades. Past the quiet lunches with lifelong friends, past the bridge nights and volunteer shifts, past the enjoyable rainy afternoons reading by the window watching the container ships move slowly up and down the St. Lawrence river. She plunged past this gentle widow's life within the fortified old walls of Quebec City, constructed to keep anything unpleasant out.

"Hello, Carole."

The tall, slender man stood in the center of the room, contained. Looking as though he'd been expecting her. Her heart pounded and her hands and feet had gone cold, numb. She was a little afraid she'd fall down. Not faint, but lose all ability to stand up for herself.

"Vincent." Her voice was firm.

His body had changed. That body she knew better than most. It had shrunk, shriveled. His hair, once thick and shiny, had thinned and grown almost white. His eyes were still brown, but where they'd been sharp and sure now they were questioning.

He held out one hand. It all seemed to happen excruciatingly slowly.

The hand had spots on it she didn't recognize. How often had she held that hand in the first years, then later longed for it to hold her? How often had she stared at it as it held *Le Devoir* up to his face? Her only contact with the man she'd given her heart to, those long, sensitive fingers holding the daily news that was clearly more important than her news. Those fingers were evidence of another human in the room, but barely. Barely there and barely human.

And then one day he'd lowered the paper, stared at her with laser eyes and said he wasn't happy.

She'd laughed.

It was, she remembered, a genuinely mirthful laugh. Not that she thought it was a joke. It was because he was serious. This brilliant man actually seemed to think if he wasn't happy it was a catastrophe.

It was, in many ways, perfect. Like so many men his age he was having an affair. She'd known it for years. But this affair he was having was with himself. He adored himself. In fact, that was just about the only thing they had in common. They both loved Vincent Gilbert.

But suddenly that wasn't enough. He needed more. And like the great man he knew he was, the answer could never be found close to home. It would have to be hiding in some mountain cave in India.

Because he was so extraordinary, his salvation would have to be too.

They'd spent the rest of the breakfast plotting his death. It appealed to Vincent's sense of drama, and her sense of relief. It was, ironically, the best talk they'd had in years.

Of course, they'd made one very big mistake. They should have told Marc. But who'd have thought he'd care?

Too late she'd realized—was it less than a day ago?—that Marc had been deeply damaged by his father's death. Not the actual death, mind. That he'd accepted easily. No, it was his father's resurrection that had created the scars, as though Vincent, in rising, had clawed his way past Marc's heart.

And now the man stood, shriveled, dotted and maybe even dotty, with one unwavering hand out. Inviting her in.

"We need to talk," she said.

He lowered his hand and nodded. She waited for him to point out her faults and flaws, all the mistakes she'd made, the immeasurable hurt she'd caused him.

"I'm sorry," said Vincent. She nodded.

"I know you are. So am I." She sat on the side of the bed and patted it. He sat next to her. This close she could see worry lines crawling over his face. It struck her as interesting that worry lines only appeared on the head.

"You look well. Are you?" he asked.

"I wish none of this had happened."

"Including my coming back?" He smiled and took her hand.

But instead of setting her heart racing, it turned her heart to stone. And she realized she didn't trust this man, who'd blown in from the past and was suddenly eating their food and sleeping in their bed.

He was like Pinocchio. A man made of wood, mimicking humanity. Shiny and smiling and fake. And if you cut into him you'd see rings. Circles of deceit and scheming and justification. It's what he was made of. That hadn't changed.

Lies within lies within lies lay within this man. And now he was here, inside their home. And suddenly their lives were unravelling.

TWENTY-THREE

"*Bon Dieu.*"

It was all Superintendent Brunel could say, and she said it over and over as she walked round the log cabin. Every now and then she stopped and picked up an object. Her eyes widened as she stared at it, then replaced it. Carefully. And went on to the next.

"*Mais, ce n'est pas possible.* This's from the Amber Room, I'm sure of it." She approached the glowing orange panel leaning against the kitchen window. "*Bon Dieu,* it is," she whispered and all but crossed herself.

The Chief Inspector watched for a while. He knew she hadn't really been prepared for what she'd find. He'd tried to warn her, though he knew the photographs didn't do the place justice. He'd told her about the fine china.

The leaded crystal.

The signed first editions.

The tapestries.

The icons.

"Is that a violin?" She pointed to the instrument by the easy chair, its wood deep and warm.

"It's moved," said Beauvoir, then stared at the young agent. "Did you touch it last night?"

Morin blushed and looked frightened. "A little. I just picked it up. And . . ."

Superintendent Brunel held it now up to the light at the window, tipping it this way and that. "Chief Inspector, can you read this?" She handed him the violin and pointed to a label. As Gamache tried to read she picked up the bow and examined it.

"A Tourte bow," she almost snorted and looked at their blank faces. "Worth a couple of hundred thousand." She batted it in their direction then turned to Gamache. "Does it say Stradivari?"

"I don't think so. It seems to say Anno 1738," he strained, "Carlos something. *Fece in Cremona*." He took off his glasses and looked at Thérèse Brunel. "Mean anything to you?"

She was smiling and still holding the bow. "Carlos Bergonzi. He was a luthier. Stradivari's best pupil."

"So it's not the finest violin?" asked Beauvoir, who'd at least heard of Stradivarius violins, but never this other guy.

"Perhaps not quite as fine as his master, but a Bergonzi is still worth a million."

"A Bergonzi?" said Morin.

"Yes. Do you know about them?"

"Not really, but we found some original sheet music for violin with a note attached. It mentions a Bergonzi." Morin went over to the bookcase and rummaged for a moment, emerging with a sheaf of music and a card. He handed it to the Superintendent who glanced at it and passed it on to Gamache.

"Any idea what language it's in?" she asked. "Not Russian, not Greek."

Gamache read. It seemed addressed to a B, it mentioned a Bergonzi and was signed C. The rest was unintelligible, though it seemed to include terms of endearment. It was dated December 8, 1950.

"Could B be the victim?" Brunel asked.

Gamache shook his head. "The dates don't match. He wouldn't have been born yet. And I presume B couldn't be Bergonzi?"

"No, too late. He was long dead. So who were B and C and why did our man collect the music and the card?" Brunel asked herself. She glanced at the sheet music and smiled. Handing the sheaf to Gamache she pointed to the top line. The music was composed by a BM.

"So," said Gamache, lowering the pages. "This original score was composed by a BM. The note attached was addressed to a B and mentions a Bergonzi violin. Seems logical to assume B played the violin and composed and someone, C, gave him this gift." He nodded to the violin. "So who was BM and why did our victim have his music and his violin?"

"Is it any good?" Brunel asked Morin. Gamache handed him the score. The young agent, mouth slightly open, thick lips glistening, was looking particularly stupid. He stared at the music and hummed. Then looked up.

"Seems okay."

"Play it." Gamache handed him the million-dollar violin. Morin took it, reluctantly. "You played it last night, didn't you?" the Chief asked.

"You what?" demanded Beauvoir.

Morin turned to him. "It'd been dusted and photographed and I didn't think it'd matter."

"Did you also juggle the china or have batting practice with the glasses? You don't mess around with evidence."

"Sorry."

"Play the music, please," said Gamache. Superintendent Brunel gave him the near-priceless bow.

"I didn't play this last night. I only really know fiddle music."

"Just do your best," said the Chief.

Agent Morin hesitated then placed the violin under his chin and curving his body he brought the bow up. And down. Across the gut strings.

The slow, full notes of a tune left the instrument. So rich was the sound the notes were almost visible as they filled the air. The tune they heard was slower than intended by BM, Gamache suspected, since Agent Morin was stuggling to follow the music. But it was still beautiful, complex and accomplished. Obviously BM knew what he was doing. Gamache closed his eyes and imagined the dead man there, alone. On a winter's night. Snow piling up outside. A simple vegetable soup on the stove, the fireplace lit and throwing heat. And the small cabin filled with music. This music.

Why this music and no other?

"Do you know it?" Gamache looked at Superintendent Brunel, who was listening with her eyes closed. She shook her head and opened her eyes.

"*Non*, but it's lovely. I wonder who BM was."

Morin lowered the violin, relieved to stop.

"Was the violin in tune when you played yesterday or did you have to adjust it?" she asked.

"It was in tune. He must have played it recently." He went to put it down but the Chief Inspector stopped him.

"What did you play last night, if not that?" He pointed to the sheet music.

"Just some fiddle music my father taught me. Nothing much. I know I shouldn't have—"

Gamache put up his hand to silence the apologies. "It's all right. Just play for us now what you played last night."

When Morin looked surprised Gamache explained, "What you just did wasn't really a fair test for the violin, was it? You were picking out the tune. I'd like to hear the violin as the victim heard it. As it was meant to be played."

"But, sir, I only play fiddle, not violin."

"What's the difference?" Gamache asked.

Morin hesitated. "No real difference, at least not in the instrument. But the sound of course is different. My dad always said a violin sings and a fiddle dances."

"Dance, then."

Morin, blushing in the most unbecoming way, put the fiddle, né violin, up to his chin once again. Paused. Then drew the bow across the strings.

What came out surprised them all. A Celtic lament left the bow, left the violin, left the agent. It filled the cabin, filled the rafters. Almost into the corners. The simple tune swirled around them like colors and delicious meals and conversation. And it lodged in their chests. Not their ears, not their heads. But their hearts. Slow, dignified, but buoyant. It was played with confidence. With poise.

Agent Morin had changed. His loose-limbed awkward body contorted perfectly for the violin, as though created and designed for this purpose. To play. To produce this music. His eyes were closed and he looked the way Gamache felt. Filled with joy. Rapture even. Such was the power of this music. This instrument.

And watching his agent the Chief Inspector suddenly realized what Morin reminded him of.

A musical note. The large head and the thin body. He was a walking note, awaiting an instrument. And this was it. The violin might be a masterpiece, but Agent Paul Morin certainly was.

After a minute he stopped and the music faded, absorbed by the logs, the books, the tapestries. The people.

"That was beautiful," said Superintendent Brunel.

He handed the violin to her. "It's called 'Colm Quigley.' My favorite."

As soon as the violin left his hand he went back to being the gangly, awkward young man. Though never again totally that for the people who had heard him play.

"*Merci*," said Gamache.

Superintendent Brunel put the violin down.

"Let me know what you find out about these." Gamache handed Morin the note and sheet music.

"Yes sir."

Thérèse Brunel returned to the rest of the room, walking up to the treasures, mumbling "*Bon Dieu*" every now and then. Each seemed more astonishing than the last.

But nothing was more surprising than what awaited Chief Inspector Gamache. In the farthest corner of the cabin, near the rafters. If the search team the day before had seen it they'd have dismissed it as the only normal thing in the whole place. What could be more natural than a spider's web in a cabin?

But it turned out to be the least normal, the least natural.

"*Bon Dieu*," they heard from the Superintendent as she held up a plate with frogs on it. "From the collection of Catherine the Great. Lost hundreds of years ago. Unbelievable."

But if she wanted "unbelievable," thought Gamache, she needed to look over here. Beauvoir had turned on his flashlight.

Until he'd seen it Gamache hadn't quite believed it. But there it was, twinkling almost merrily in the harsh artificial light, as though mocking them.

Woe, said the web.

"Woe," whispered Gamache.

Superintendent Brunel found Armand Gamache an hour later in the bent branch chair in the corner of the vegetable garden.

"I've finished looking round."

Gamache stood and she sat wearily in the chair, exhaling deeply.

"I've never seen anything like it, Armand. We've broken art theft rings and found the most amazing collections. Remember the Charbonneau case last year in Lévis?"

"The van Eycks."

She nodded, then shook her head as though trying to clear it. "Fantastic finds. All sorts of original sketches and even an oil no one knew existed."

"Wasn't there a Titian too?"

"*Oui.*"

"And you're saying this place is even more amazing?"

"I don't mean to lecture, but I'm not sure you or your people appreciate the scope of the find."

"Lecture away," Gamache reassured her. "That's why I invited you."

He smiled and not for the first time she thought the rarest thing she'd ever found was Chief Inspector Gamache.

"You might want to grab a seat," she said. He found a sawn log and turned it on its end and sat on it. "The Charbonneau case was spectacular," Superintendent Brunel went on. "But in many ways mundane. Most art theft rings, and most black market collectors, have one maybe two specialties. Because the market's so specialized and there's so much money involved, the thieves become experts, but only in one or two tiny areas. Italian sculpture from the 1600s. Dutch masters. Greek antiquities. But never all of those fields. They specialize. How else would they know they weren't stealing forgeries, or replicas? That's why with Charbonneau we found some astonishing things, but all in the same 'family.' *Vous comprenez?*"

"*Oui.* They were all Renaissance paintings, mostly by the same artist."

"*C'est ça.* That's how specialized most thieves are. But here," she waved at the cabin, "there're handmade silk tapestries, ancient leaded glass. Under that embroidered tablecloth do you know what we found? Our victim ate off the most exquisite inlaid table I've ever seen. It must be five hundred years old and made by a master. Even the table cloth was a masterpiece. Most museums would keep it under glass. The Victoria and Albert in London would pay a fortune for it."

"Maybe they did."

"You mean it might have been stolen from there? Could be. I have a lot of work to do."

She looked as though she could hardly wait. And yet, she also looked as though she was in no hurry to leave this cabin, this garden.

"I wonder who he was." She reached out and pulled a couple of runner beans from a vine, handing one to her companion. "*Most unhappiness comes from not being able to sit quietly in a room.*"

"Pascal," said Gamache, recognizing the quote, and the appropriateness of it. "This man could. But he surrounded himself with objects that had a lot to say. That had stories."

"That's an interesting way of putting it."

"What's the Amber Room?"

"How do you know about that?" She turned a searching eye on him.

"When you were looking around you mentioned it."

"Did I? You can see it from here. That orange thing in the kitchen window." He looked and sure enough, there it was, glowing warm in what little light it caught. It looked like a large, thick piece of stained glass. She continued to stare, mesmerized, then finally came out of it. "Sorry. I just never expected to be the one to find it."

"What do you mean?"

"The Amber Room was created in the early 1700s in Prussia by Friedrich the First. It was a huge room made of amber and gold. Took artists and artisans years to construct and when it was completed it was one of the wonders of the world." He could tell she was imagining what it looked like, her eyes taking on a faraway look. "He had it made for his wife, Sophia Charlotte. But a few years later it was given to the Russian Emperor and stayed in St. Petersburg until the war."

"Which war?"

She smiled. "Good point. The Second World War. The Soviets apparently dismantled it once they realized the Nazis would take the city, but they didn't manage to hide it. The Germans found it."

She stopped.

"Go on," said Gamache.

"That's it. That's all we know. The Amber Room disappeared. Historians, treasure hunters, antiquarians have been searching for it ever since. We know the Germans, under Albert Speer, took the Amber Room away. Hid it. Presumably for safe keeping. But it was never seen again."

"What're the theories?" the Chief Inspector asked.

"Well, the most accepted is that it was destroyed in the Allied bombing. But there's another theory. Albert Speer was very bright, and many argue he wasn't a true Nazi. He was loyal to Hitler, but not to most of his ideals. Speer was an internationalist, a cultured man whose priority became saving the world's treasures from destruction, by either side."

"Albert Speer may have been cultured," said Gamache, "but he was a Nazi. He knew of the death camps, knew of the slaughter, approved it. He simply looked good while doing it."

The Chief Inspector's voice was cold and his eyes hard.

"I don't disagree with you, Armand. Just the opposite. I'm simply telling you what the theories are. The one involving Speer had him hiding the Amber Room far from both the German and the Allied armies. In the Ore Mountains."

"Where?"

"A mountain range between Germany and what's now the Czech Republic."

They both thought about that, and finally Gamache spoke. "So how did a piece of the Amber Room get here?"

"And where's the rest of it?"

Denis Fortin sat across from Clara Morrow. He was younger than he had any right to be. Early forties probably. A failed artist who'd discovered another, greater, talent. He recognized talent in others.

It was enlightened self-interest. The best kind, as far as Clara could see. No one was the martyr, no one was owed or owing. She was under no illusion that the reason Denis Fortin held a St. Amboise beer in Olivier's Bistro in Three Pines was not because he thought there was something in it for him.

And the only reason Clara was there, besides unbridled ego, was to get something from Fortin. Namely fame and fortune.

At the very least a free beer.

But there was something she needed to do before she got caught up in the unparalleled glory that was Clara Morrow. Reaching into her bag she brought out the balled-up towel. "I was asked to show you this. A man was found dead here a couple of days ago. Murdered."

"Really? That's unusual, isn't it?"

"Not as unusual as you might think. What was unusual is that no one knew him. But the police just found a cabin in the woods, and this was inside it. The head of the investigation asked me to show it to you, in case you could tell us anything about it."

"A clue?" He looked keen and watched closely as she unwrapped the bundle. Soon the little men and women were standing on the shore, looking across the expanse of wood to the micro-brew in front of Fortin.

Clara watched him. His eyes narrowed and he leaned closer to the work, pursing his lips in concentration.

"Very nice. Good technique, I'd say. Detailed, each face quite different, with character. Yes, all in all I'd say a competent piece of carving. Slightly primitive, but what you'd expect from a backwoods whittler."

"Really?" said Clara. "I thought it was very good. Excellent even."

He leaned back and smiled at her. Not patronizing, but as one friend smiles at another, a kinder, friend.

"Perhaps I'm being too harsh, but I've seen so many of these in my career."

"These? Exactly the same?"

"No, but close enough. Carved images of people fishing or smoking a pipe or riding a horse. They're the most valuable. You can always find a buyer for a good horse or dog. Or pig. Pigs are popular."

"Good to know. There's something written underneath." Clara turned it over and handed it to Fortin.

He squinted then putting on his glasses he read, frowned and handed it back. "I wonder what it means."

"Any guesses?" Clara wasn't about to give up. She wanted to take something back to Gamache.

"Almost certainly a signature, or a lot number. Something to identify it. Was this the only one?"

"There're two. How much would this be worth?"

"Hard to say." He picked it up again. "It's quite good, for what it is. It's no pig, though."

"Pity."

"Hmm." Fortin considered for a moment. "I'd say two hundred, maybe two hundred and fifty dollars."

"Is that all?"

"I might be wrong."

Clara could tell he was being polite, but getting bored. She rewrapped the carving and put it in her bag.

"Now." Denis Fortin leaned forward, an eager look on his handsome face. "Let's talk about really great art. How would you like your work to be hung?"

"I've done a few sketches." Clara handed him her notebook and after a few minutes Fortin lifted his head, his eyes intelligent and bright.

"This is wonderful. I like the way you've clustered the paintings then left a space. It's like a breath, isn't it?"

Clara nodded. It was such a relief talking to someone who didn't need everything explained.

"I particularly like that you haven't placed the three old women together. That would be the obvious choice, but you've spread them around, each anchoring her own wall."

"I wanted to surround them with other works," said Clara excitedly.

"Like acolytes, or friends, or critics," said Fortin, excited himself. "It's not clear what their intentions are."

"And how they might change," said Clara, leaning forward. She'd shown Peter her ideas, and he'd been polite and encouraging, but she could tell he really didn't understand what she was getting at. At first glance her design for the exhibition might seem unbalanced. And it was. Intentionally. Clara wanted people to walk in, see the works that appeared quite traditional and slowly appreciate that they weren't.

There was a depth, a meaning, a challenge to them.

For an hour or more Clara and Fortin talked, exchanging ideas about the show, about the direction of contemporary art, about exciting new artists, of which, Fortin was quick to assure Clara, she was in the forefront.

"I wasn't going to tell you because it might not happen, but I sent your portfolio to FitzPatrick at MoMA. He's an old friend and says he'll come to the *vernissage*—"

Clara exclaimed and almost knocked her beer over. Fortin laughed and held up his hand.

"But wait, that wasn't what I wanted to tell you. I suggested he spread the word and it looks as though Allyne from the *New York Times* will be there . . ."

He hesitated because it looked as though Clara was having a stroke. When she closed her mouth he continued. "And, as luck would have it, Destin Browne will be in New York that month setting up a show with MoMA and she's shown interest."

"Destin Browne? Vanessa Destin Browne? The chief curator at the Tate Modern in London?"

Fortin nodded and held tightly to his beer. But now, far from being in danger of knocking anything over, Clara appeared to have ground to a complete halt. She sat in the cheery little bistro, late summer light teeming through the mullioned windows. Beyond Fortin she saw the old homes, warming in the sun. The perennial beds with roses and clematis and hollyhocks. She saw the villagers, whose names she knew and whose habits she was familiar with. And she saw the three tall pines, like beacons. Impossible to miss, even surrounded by forest. If you knew what to look for, and needed a beacon.

Life was about to take her away from here. From the place where she'd become herself. This solid little village that never changed but helped its inhabitants to change. She'd arrived straight from art college full of avant-garde ideas, wearing shades of gray and seeing the world in black and white. So sure of herself. But here, in the middle of nowhere, she'd discovered color. And nuance. She'd learned this from the villagers, who'd been generous enough to lend her their souls to paint. Not as perfect human beings, but as flawed, struggling men and women. Filled with fear and uncertainty and, in at least one case, martinis.

But who remained standing. In the wilderness. Her graces, her stand of pines.

She was suddenly overcome with gratitude to her neighbors, and to whatever inspiration had allowed her to do them justice.

She closed her eyes and tilted her face into the sun.

"You all right?" he asked.

Clara opened her eyes. He seemed bathed in light, his blond hair glowing and a warm, patient smile on his face.

"You know, I probably shouldn't tell you this, but a few years ago no one wanted my works. Everyone just laughed. It was brutal. I almost gave up."

"Most great artists have the same story," he said, gently.

"I almost flunked out of art school, you know. I don't tell many people that."

"Another drink?" asked Gabri, taking Fortin's empty glass.

"Not for me, *merci*," he said, then turned back to Clara. "Between us? Most of the best people did flunk out. How can you test an artist?"

"I was always good at tests," said Gabri, picking up Clara's glass. "No, wait. That was testes."

He gave Clara an arch look and swept away.

"Fucking queers," said Fortin, taking a handful of cashews. "Doesn't it make you want to vomit?"

Clara froze. She looked at Fortin to see if he was kidding. He wasn't. But what he said was true. She suddenly wanted to throw up.

TWENTY-FOUR

Chief Inspector Gamache and Superintendent Brunel walked back to the cabin, each lost in thought.

"I told you what I found," said the Superintendent, once back on the porch. "Now it's your turn. What were you and Inspector Beauvoir whispering about in the corner, like naughty schoolboys?"

Not many people would consider calling Chief Inspector Gamache a naughty schoolboy. He smiled. Then he remembered the thing that had gleamed and mocked and clung to the corner of the cabin.

"Would you like to see?"

"No, I think I'll go back to the garden and pick turnips. Of course I'd like to see," she laughed and he took her over to the corner of the room, her eyes darting here and there, stealing glances at the masterpieces she was passing. Until they stopped in the darkest corner.

"I don't see anything."

Beauvoir joined them and switched on his flashlight. She followed it. Up the wall to the rafters.

"I still don't see."

"But you do," said Gamache. As they waited Beauvoir thought about other words, left up to be found. Tacked to the door of his bedroom at the B and B that morning.

He'd asked Gabri if he knew anything about the piece of paper stuck into the wood with a thumbtack, but Gabri had looked perplexed and shaken his head.

Beauvoir had stuffed it into his pocket and only after the first *café au lait* of the day did he have the guts to read.

226

and the soft body of a woman
and lick you clean of fever,

What upset Beauvoir most wasn't the thought that the mad old poet had invaded the B and B and put that on his door. Nor was it that he didn't understand a word of it. What upset him the most was the comma.

It meant there was more.

"I'm sorry, I really don't see anything." Superintendent Brunel's voice brought Beauvoir back to the cabin.

"Do you see a spider's web?" Gamache asked.

"Yes."

"Then you see it. Look more closely."

It took a moment but finally her face changed. Her eyes widened and her brows lifted. She tilted her head slightly as though she wasn't seeing quite straight.

"But there's a word up there, written in the web. What does it say? Woe? How is that possible? What kind of spider does that?" she asked, clearly not expecting an answer, and not getting one.

Just then the satellite phone rang and after answering it Agent Morin handed it to the Chief Inspector. "Agent Lacoste for you, sir."

"*Oui, allô?*" he said, and listened for a few moments. "Really?" He listened some more, glancing around the room then up again at the web. "*D'accord. Merci.*"

Gamache hung up, thought a moment, then reached for the nearby stepladder.

"Would you like me . . ." Beauvoir gestured to it.

"*Ce n'est pas necessaire.*" Taking a breath Gamache started up the Annapurna ladder. Two steps up he put out an unsteady hand and Beauvoir moved forward until the large trembling fingers found his shoulder. Steadied, Gamache reached up and poked the web with a pen. Slowly, unseen by the people craning their necks below, he moved a single strand of the web.

"*C'est ça,*" he murmured.

Backing down the ladder and onto terra firma he nodded toward the corner. Beauvoir's light shone on the web.

"How did you do that?" asked Beauvoir.

The web had changed its message. It no longer said Woe. Now it said Woo.

"A strand had come loose."

"But how did you know it had?" Beauvoir persisted. They'd all taken a close look at the web. Clearly a spider hadn't spun it. It appeared to be made from thread, perhaps nylon fishing line, made to look like a spider's web. They'd take it down soon and have it properly analyzed. It had a great deal to tell them, though changing the word from Woe to Woo didn't seem a move toward clarity.

"More results are coming into the Incident Room. Fingerprint results, which I'll tell you about in a minute, but remember that piece of wood that was found under the bed?"

"The one that also said Woe?" asked Morin, who had joined them.

Gamache nodded. "It had blood on it. The victim's blood, according to the lab. But when they removed it they discovered something else. The block of wood wasn't carved to say Woe. The smear of blood made a mess of the lettering. When the blood was lifted it said—"

"Woo," said Beauvoir. "So you thought if one said it maybe the other did too."

"Worth a try."

"I think I prefer Woe." Beauvoir looked at the web again. "At least it's a word. What does Woo mean?"

They thought. Had someone been wandering by the cabin and chanced to look in they would have seen a group of adults standing quite still, staring into space and muttering "Woo" every now and then.

"Woo," Brunel said. "Don't people pitch woo?"

"Woohoo? No, that's boo," said Beauvoir. "Boohoo, not woo."

"Isn't it what they call kangaroos?" asked Morin.

"Kangawoos? That's roo," snapped Beauvoir.

"*Chalice*," swore Brunel.

"Woo, woo," said Morin under his breath, begging himself to come up with something that didn't sound like a choo-choo train. But the more he said it the more it sounded like nonsense. "Woo," he whispered.

Only Gamache said nothing. He listened to them but his mind kept going to the other piece of news. His face grew stern as he thought about what else had been revealed when the bloody fingerprints were lifted from the carving.

He can't stay here."

Marc swished his arms under the tap at the kitchen sink.

"I don't want him here either, but at least here we can watch him," his mother said.

All three looked out the kitchen window to the old man sitting cross-legged on the grass, meditating.

"What do you mean, 'watch him'?" asked Dominique. She was fascinated by her father-in-law. He had a sort of broken-down magnetism about him. She could see he once had had a powerful personality, and a powerful hold over people. And he behaved as though that was still true. There was a shabby dignity about him, but also a cunning.

Marc grabbed the bar of soap and rubbed it over his forearms, looking like a surgeon scrubbing up. In fact, he was scrubbing away dust and plaster after dry-walling.

It was hard work, and work he was almost certainly doing for someone else. The next owner of the inn and spa. Which was just as well, since he was doing it very badly.

"I mean that things happen around Vincent," said Carole. "Always have. He's sailed through life, this glorious ship of state. Oblivious of the wreckage in his wake."

It might not have sounded like it, but she was being charitable. For the sake of Marc. The truth was, she wasn't at all convinced Vincent had been oblivious of the damage he caused. She'd come to believe he actually deliberately sailed right over people. Destroyed them. Gone out of his way to do it.

She'd been his nurse, his assistant, his dogsbody. His witness and, finally, his conscience. Which was probably why he'd grown to hate her. And her him.

Once again they looked at the cross-legged man, sitting calmly in their garden.

"I can't cope with him right now," said Marc, drying his hands.

"We have to let him stay," said Dominique. "He's your father."

Marc looked at her with a mixture of amusement and sadness. "He's done it to you, now, hasn't he? Charmed you."

"I'm not some naïve schoolgirl, you know."

And this brought Marc up short. He realized she'd faced down some of the wealthiest, most manipulative bullies in Canadian finance. But Dr. Vincent Gilbert was different. There was something bewitching about him. "I'm sorry. So much is happening."

He'd thought moving to the country would be a breeze compared to the greed and fear and manipulation of the financial district. But so far here he'd found a dead body, moved it, ruined their reputation in the village, and been accused of murder; now he was about to kick a saint out of their home, and had almost certainly messed up the dry-walling.

And the leaves hadn't even changed yet.

But by then they'd be gone. To find another home somewhere else and hope they did better. He longed for the relative ease of the business world, where cut-throats lurked in every cubicle. Here everything looked so pleasant and peaceful, but wasn't.

He looked out the window again. In the foreground was his father, sitting cross-legged in the garden, and behind him in the field two broken-down old horses, what might or might not be a moose, and in the distance a muck-encrusted horse that by all rights should have been dog food by now. This wasn't what he had in mind when he'd moved to the country.

"Marc's right, you know," said Carole to her daughter-in-law. "Vincent either bullies, charms, or guilts his way in. But he always gets what he wants."

"And what does he want?" Dominique asked. It seemed a sensible question. Then why was it so difficult to answer?

The doorbell rang. They looked at each other. They'd come, in the last twenty-four hours, to dread that sound.

"I'll get it," said Dominique and walked briskly out of the kitchen, reappearing a minute later followed by a little boy and Old Mundin.

"I think you know my son," said Old, after greeting everyone with a smile. "Now, Charlie, what did The Mother tell you to say to these nice people?"

They waited while Charlie considered, then he gave them the finger.

"He learned that from Ruth, actually," Old explained.

"Quite a role model. Would he like a Scotch?" asked Carole. Old Mundin's handsome tanned face broke into a smile.

"No, Ruth just gave him a martini and we're trying not to mix drinks." Now the young man looked uncomfortable and putting his hands down on his son's shoulders he hugged Charlie to him. "I've heard he's here. Would you mind?"

Marc, Dominique, and Carole looked confused.

"Mind?" Dominique asked.

"Dr. Gilbert. I'd seen him in the forest, you know. I knew who he was but didn't know he was your father."

"Why didn't you say something?" Dominique asked.

"It wasn't my business. He didn't seem to want to be seen."

And Marc thought maybe it was simpler here after all, and he was the one who complicated things. The business world had somehow made him think everything was his business, when it wasn't.

"I don't want to disturb him," Mundin continued, "but I just wondered if maybe we could see him. Maybe introduce Charlie to him." The dignified young father looked as though this effort was hurting him. "I've read and reread his book, *Being*. Your father's a great man. I envy you."

And Marc envied him. His touching his son, holding him. Protecting him and loving him. Being willing to humble himself, for his son.

"He's in the garden," said Marc.

"Thanks." At the door Old Mundin stopped. "I have tools. Maybe I can come back tomorrow and help. A man can always use help."

You'll be a man, my son. Why hadn't his own father told him a man could always use help?

Marc nodded, not unaware of the significance of what had just happened. Old Mundin was offering to help the Gilberts build their home, not leave it. Because his father was Vincent Gilbert. His fucking father had saved them.

Mundin turned to Dominique. "The Wife says hello, by the way."

"Please say hello back," said Dominique, then hesitated a breath. "To The Wife."

"I will." He and Charlie went into the garden leaving the other three to watch.

Dr. Vincent Gilbert, late of the forest, had somehow become the center of attention.

As the young man and his son approached, Vincent Gilbert opened one eye and through the slit in his long lashes he watched. Not the two walking quietly toward him, but the three in the window.

Help others, he'd been told. And he intended to. But first he had to help himself.

It was quiet in the bistro. A few villagers sat at tables outside in the sunshine, relishing their *café* and Camparis and calm. Inside Olivier stood at the window.

"Good God, man, you'd think you'd never seen the village before," Gabri said from behind the bar where he was polishing the wood and replenishing the candy jars, most of which he'd helped empty.

For the last few days, every time Gabri looked for Olivier he'd find him standing in the same spot, in the bay window, looking out.

"Pipe?" Gabri walked over to his partner and offered him a licorice pipe, but Olivier seemed under a spell. Gabri bit into the licorice himself, eating the candied end first, as per the rules.

"What's bothering you?" Gabri followed the other man's gaze and saw only what he'd expect to see. Certainly nothing riveting. Just the customers on the *terrasse*, then the village green with Ruth and Rosa. The duck was now wearing a knitted sweater.

Olivier's eyes narrowed as he too focused on the duck. Then he turned to Gabri.

"Does that sweater look familiar to you?"

"Which?"

"The duck's, of course." Olivier studied Gabri closely. The large man never could lie. Now he ate the rest of the pipe and put on his most perplexed face.

"I have no idea what you're talking about."

"That's my sweater, isn't it?"

"Come off it, Olivier. Do you really think you and the duck wear the same size?"

"Not now, but when I was a kid. Where're my baby clothes?"

Now Gabri was silent, damning Ruth for parading Rosa in her new wardrobe. Well, maybe not so new.

"I thought it was time to get rid of them," said Gabri. "Ruth needed sweaters and things for Rosa to keep her warm in the fall and winter and I thought of your baby clothes. What were you saving them for anyway? They were just taking up space in the basement."

"How much space could they take up?" Olivier demanded, feeling himself breaking apart inside, his reserve crumbling. "How could you?" he snarled at Gabri, who leaned away, shocked.

"But you'd talked about getting rid of them yourself."

"Me, me. Me getting rid of them. Not you. You had no right."

"I'm sorry, I had no idea they meant that much to you."

"Well they do. Now what am I going to do?"

Olivier watched as Rosa waddled behind Ruth, who muttered away to the duck, saying God knew what. And Olivier felt tears sting his eyes, and a swell of emotion erupt from his throat. He couldn't very well take the clothes back. Not now. They were gone. Gone forever.

"Do you want me to get them back?" asked Gabri, taking Olivier's hand.

Olivier shook his head. Not even sure why he felt so strongly. He had so much else to worry about. And it was true, he'd thought about getting rid of the box of old baby clothes. The only reasons he hadn't were laziness, and not being sure who to give them to.

Why not Rosa? A distant honking was heard in the sky and both Rosa and Ruth lifted their heads. Overhead a formation of ducks headed south.

Sadness washed over Olivier. Gone. It was all gone. Everything.

For weeks and weeks the villagers journeyed through the forests. At first the young man hurried them along looking behind him now and then. He regretted telling his family and friends to leave with him. He could have been much farther away without the old men and women, and the children. But as the weeks went by and peaceful day followed peaceful day, he began to worry less and was even grateful for the company.

He'd almost forgotten to look over his shoulder when the first sign appeared.

It was twilight, only the twilight never died. Night never fell completely. He wasn't sure if any of the others noticed. It was, after all, just a small glow in the distance. At the horizon. The next day the sun rose, but not completely. There was a darkness to the sky. But again, just at the horizon. As though a shadow had spilled over from the other side.

The young man knew then.

He clutched his parcel tighter and hurried everyone along, rushing forward. Driving them onward. They were willing to hurry. After all, immortality, youth, happiness awaited. They were almost giddy with joy. And in that joy he hid.

At night the light grew in the sky. And during the day the shadow stretched toward them.

"Is that it?" his elderly aunt asked eagerly, as they crested a hill. "Are we there?"

In front of them was water. Nothing but water.

And behind them the shadow lengthened.

TWENTY-FIVE

"Olivier?"

The blond head was bowed, studying the receipts of the day so far. It was getting on for lunch and the bistro was filled with the aroma of garlic and herbs and roast chicken.

Olivier had seen them coming, had heard them even. That shriek as though the forest itself was crying out. They'd emerged from the woods on their ATVs and parked at the old Hadley house. Much of the village stopped what it was doing to watch as Chief Inspector Gamache and Inspector Beauvoir walked into the village. They were deep in conversation and no one disturbed them. Olivier had turned away then, walking further into his bistro and behind the bar. Around him the young waiters set tables while Havoc Parra wrote specials on the board.

The door opened and Olivier turned his back. Claiming every last moment.

"Olivier?" said the Chief Inspector. "We need to talk. In private, please."

Olivier turned and smiled, as though if he ingratiated himself enough they might not do this thing. The Chief Inspector smiled back, but it never reached his thoughtful eyes. Leading them into the back room that overlooked the Rivière Bella Bella Olivier indicated the chairs at the dining table and sat himself.

"How can I help?"

His heart thudded in his chest and his hands were cold and numb. He could no longer feel his extremities, and dots danced before his eyes. He struggled for breath and felt light-headed.

"Tell us about the man who lived in the cabin," Chief Inspector

Gamache said, matter-of-factly. "The dead man." He folded his hands, settling in. A good dinner companion who wanted to hear your stories.

There was no escape, Olivier knew. He'd known it from the instant he'd seen the Hermit dead on the bistro floor. He'd seen this avalanche sliding toward him, gaining momentum. Olivier couldn't run. Could never outrun what was coming.

"He was one of my first customers when Gabri and I moved to Three Pines."

The words, kept inside for so long, crawled out. Rotting. Olivier was surprised his breath didn't stink.

Gamache gave him a small nod of encouragement.

"We just had an antique shop then. I hadn't turned this into a bistro, yet. We rented the space above to live in. It was awful. Crammed full of junk, and filthy. Someone had plastered over all the original features. But we worked day and night to restore it. I think we'd only been here a few weeks when he walked in. He wasn't the man you saw on the floor. Not then. This was years ago."

Olivier saw it all again. Gabri was upstairs in their new home, stripping the beams and taking the drywall off, exposing the magnificent original brick walls. Each discovery more exciting than the last. But none could rival the growing awareness that they'd found a home. A place they could finally settle. At first they'd been so intent on unpacking they didn't really take in the details of the village. But slowly, over the first few weeks and months, the village revealed itself.

"I was still setting up the business and didn't have much stuff, just odds and ends collected over the years. I'd always dreamed of opening an antique store, since I was a kid. Then the chance came."

"It didn't just come," said Gamache quietly. "It was helped along."

Olivier sighed. He should have known Gamache would find out.

"I'd quit my job in the city. I'd been quite successful, as you might have heard."

Gamache nodded again.

Olivier smiled, remembering those heady days. Of silk suits and gym memberships, of visiting the Mercedes dealership when the only issue was the color of the car.

And of taking that one step too far.

It'd been humiliating. He'd been so depressed he was afraid of what he might do to himself, so he'd sought help. And there, in the waiting room of the therapist, was Gabri. Large, voluble, vain and full of life.

At first Olivier had been repulsed. Gabri was everything he'd come to despise. Olivier thought of himself and his friends as gay men. Discreet, elegant, cynical.

Gabri was just queer. Common. And fat. There was nothing discreet about him.

But neither was there anything mean. And over time Olivier grew to appreciate how very beautiful kindness was.

And he fell in love with Gabri. Deeply, totally, indiscreetly in love.

Gabri had agreed to leave his job at the Y in Westmount and move out of the city. It didn't matter where. They got in their car and drove south. And there, over a rise in the road, they'd stopped the car. Finally admitting they were lost. Though since they had no destination they couldn't be lost, Gabri happily told Olivier, who was busy in the driver's side wrestling with a Carte Routière du Québec. Eventually he realized Gabri was standing outside and softly tapping on his window. He lowered it and Gabri gestured.

Annoyed, Olivier shoved the map into the backseat and got out.

"What?" he snapped at Gabri, who was looking ahead. Olivier followed his gaze. And found home.

He knew it immediately.

It was the place in all the fairy tales he'd read as a kid, under the bedding, when his father thought, hoped, he was reading about naval battles. Or naked girls. Instead he'd been reading about villages, and cottages, and gardens. And little wisps of smoke, and dry stone walls older than anyone in the village.

He'd forgotten all that, until that very moment. And in that instant he remembered his other childhood dream. Of opening an antique shop. A modest little affair where he could put his finds.

"Shall we, *ma belle*?" Gabri took Olivier's hand and leaving the car where it stood they walked down the dirt road and into Three Pines.

"I was disappointed at first when the Hermit came in—"

"The Hermit?" Gamache asked.

"That's what I called him."

"But didn't you know his name?"

"He never told me and I never asked."

Gamache caught Beauvoir's eye. The Inspector was looking both disappointed and disbelieving.

"Go on," said Gamache.

"His hair was a little long and he looked a bit scruffy. Not the sort to do a lot of buying. But it was quiet and I talked to him. He came back a week later, and then about once a week for a few months. Finally he took me aside and said he had something he wanted to sell. That was pretty disappointing too. I'd been nice to the guy but now he was asking me to buy some piece of junk and it pissed me off. I almost asked him to leave, but by then he had the piece in his hand."

Olivier remembered looking down. They were at the back and the lighting wasn't good, but it didn't gleam or glitter. In fact it looked very dull. Olivier reached out for it but the Hermit drew his hand back. And then it caught the light.

It was a miniature portrait. The two men walked to the window and Olivier got a good view.

It was in a tarnished old frame and must have been painted with a single horse hair, so fine was the detail. It showed a man in profile, powdered wig, blowsy clothing.

Even the memory made Olivier's heart quicken.

"How much do you want?"

"Maybe some food?" the Hermit had asked, and the deal was sealed.

Olivier looked at Gamache, whose thoughtful brown eyes never wavered.

"And that's how it started. I agreed to take the painting in exchange for a few bags of groceries."

"And what was it worth?"

"Not much." Olivier remembered carefully taking the miniature from its frame, and seeing the old lettering on the back. It was some Polish count. With a date. 1745. "I sold it for a few dollars."

He held Gamache's eyes.

"Where?"

"Some antique place along rue Notre Dame in Montreal."

Gamache nodded. "Go on."

"After that the Hermit brought stuff to the shop every now and then and I'd give him food. But he became more and more paranoid. Didn't want to come into the village anymore. So he invited me to his cabin."

"Why did you agree to go? It was quite an inconvenience."

Olivier had been afraid of that question.

"Because the things he was giving me turned out to be quite good. Nothing spectacular, but decent quality and I was curious. When I first visited the cabin it took me a few minutes to realize what he had. It all just looked like it belonged, in a strange sort of way. Then I looked closer. He was eating off plates worth tens of thousands, hundreds of thousands of dollars. Did you see the glasses?" Olivier's eyes were gleaming with excitement. "*Fantastique.*"

"Did he ever explain how he came to have items that were priceless?"

"Never, and I never asked. I was afraid to scare him off."

"Did he know the value of what he had?"

That was an interesting question, and one Olivier had debated himself. The Hermit treated the finest engraved silver the way Gabri treated Ikea flatware. There was no attempt to coddle anything. But neither was the Hermit cavalier. He was a cautious man, that much was certain.

"I'm not sure," said Olivier.

"So you gave him groceries and he gave you near-priceless antiques?"

Gamache's voice was neutral, curious. It held none of the censure Olivier knew it could, and should.

"He didn't give me the best stuff, at least not at first. And I did more than take him groceries. I helped dig his vegetable garden, and brought the seeds to plant."

"How often did you visit?"

"Every two weeks."

Gamache considered, then spoke. "Why was he living in the cabin away from everyone else?"

"Hiding, I guess."

"But from what?"

Olivier shook his head. "Don't know. I tried to ask but he was having none of it."

"What can you tell us?" Gamache's voice wasn't quite as patient as it had been. Beauvoir looked up from his notebook, and Olivier shifted in his seat.

"I know the Hermit built the cabin over several months. Then he carried all the stuff in himself." Olivier was studying Gamache, eager for his approval, eager for the thaw. The large man leaned forward slightly and Olivier rushed on. "He told me all about it. Most of his things weren't big.

Just the armchairs, really, and the bed. The rest anybody could've carried. And he was strong."

Still, Gamache was silent. Olivier squirmed.

"I'm telling the truth. He never explained how he got all those things, and I was afraid to ask, but it's kind of obvious, isn't it? He must have stolen them. Otherwise, why hide?"

"So you thought they were stolen and you didn't say anything?" asked Gamache, his voice still without criticism. "Didn't call the police."

"No. I know I should have, but I didn't."

For once Beauvoir didn't sneer. This he found completely natural and understandable. How many people would, after all? It always amazed Beauvoir when he heard about people finding suitcases full of money, and turning it in. He had to wonder about the sanity of such people.

For his part Gamache was thinking about the other end of the deal. The people who'd owned the things. The fabulous violin, the priceless glassware, the china and silver and inlaid wood. If the Hermit was hiding in the woods someone had chased him there. "Did he say where he was from?" Gamache asked.

"No. I asked once but he didn't answer."

Gamache considered. "What did he sound like?"

"I'm sorry?"

"His voice."

"It was normal. We spoke in French."

"Quebec French, or France French?"

Olivier hesitated. Gamache waited.

"Quebec, but . . ."

Gamache was still, as though he could wait all day. All week. A lifetime.

". . . but he had a slight accent. Czech, I think," said Olivier in a rush.

"Are you sure?"

"Yes. He was Czech," said Olivier in a mumble. "I'm sure."

Gamache saw Beauvoir make a note. It was the first clue to the man's identity.

"Why didn't you tell us you knew the Hermit when the body was found?"

"I should have, but I thought you might not find the cabin."

"And why would you hope that?"

Olivier tried to take a breath, but the oxygen didn't seem to reach his lungs. Or his brain. His compressed lips felt cold and his eyes burned. Hadn't he told them enough? But still Gamache sat across from him, waiting. And Olivier could see it in his eyes. He knew. Gamache knew the answer, and still he demanded Olivier say it himself.

"Because there were things in the cabin I wanted. For myself."

Olivier looked exhausted, as though he'd coughed up his insides. But Gamache knew there was more.

"Tell us about the carvings."

Clara walked along the road from the Incident Room, over the bridge into Three Pines, and stood looking first one way then the other.

What should she do?

She'd just been to the Incident Room to return the carving.

Fucking queers.

Two words.

Surely she could ignore them. Pretend Fortin hadn't said it. Or, better still, maybe she could find someone who'd assure her what she'd done was quite right.

She'd done nothing. Said nothing. She'd simply thanked Denis Fortin for his time, agreed this was exciting, agreed to keep in touch as the show approached. They'd shaken hands and kissed on both cheeks.

And now she stood, lost, looking this way and that. Clara had considered talking to Gamache about it, then dismissed the idea. He was a friend, but he was also a cop, investigating a crime worse than nasty words.

And yet, Clara wondered. Was that where most murders began? Did they start as words? Something said that lodged and festered. That curdled. And killed.

Fucking queers.

And she'd done nothing.

Clara turned right and made for the shops.

What carvings?"

"This carving for one." Gamache placed the sailing ship, with its miserable passenger hiding among the smiles, on the table.

Olivier stared at it.

They camped at the very edge of the world, crowded together, looking out to the ocean. Except the young man, who stared back. To where they'd come from.

It was impossible to miss the lights in the dark sky now. And the sky was almost perpetually dark. There was no longer a distinction between night and day. And yet, such was the villagers' joy and anticipation, they didn't seem to notice, or care.

The light sliced like a saber through the darkness, through the shadow thrown toward them. Almost upon them.

The Mountain King had arisen. Had assembled an army made of Bile and Rage and led by Chaos. Their wrath carved the sky ahead of them, searching for one man, one young man. Barely more than a boy. And the package he held.

They marched on, closer and closer. And the villagers waited on shore, to be taken to the world they'd been promised. Where nothing bad happened, and no one sickened or grew old.

The young man ran here and there, trying to find a hiding place. A cave perhaps, somewhere he could curl up and hide, and be very, very small. And quiet.

"Oh," said Olivier.

"What can you tell me about this?" asked Gamache.

One small hill separated the dreadful army from the villagers. An hour, maybe less.

Olivier heard the voice again, the story filling the cabin, even the dark corners.

"Look," one of the villagers shouted, pointing to the water. The young man turned, wondering what horror was coming from the sea. But instead he saw a ship. In full sail. Hurrying toward them.

"Sent by the gods," said his old aunt as she stepped on board. And he knew that was true. One of the gods had taken pity on them and sent a strong ship and a stronger wind. They hurried aboard and the ship left immediately. Out at sea the young man looked back in time to see, rising behind the final hill, a dark shape. It rose higher and higher and around its

peak flew the Furies, and on its now naked flank there marched Sorrow and Grief and Madness. And at the head of the army was Chaos.

As the Mountain spied the tiny vessel on the ocean it shrieked, and the howl filled the sails of the vessel so that it streaked across the ocean. In the bow the happy villagers searched for land, for their new world. But the young man, huddling among them, looked back. At the Mountain of Bitterness he'd created. And the rage that filled their sails.

"Where did you find that?" Olivier asked.

"In the cabin." Gamache was watching him closely. Olivier seemed stunned by the carving. Almost frightened. "Have you seen it before?"

"Never."

"Or others like it?"

"No."

Gamache handed it to Olivier. "It's a strange subject matter, don't you think?"

"How so?"

"Well, everyone's so happy, joyful even. Except him." Gamache placed his forefinger on the head of the crouching figure. Olivier looked closer and frowned.

"I know nothing about art. You'll have to ask someone else."

"What did the Hermit whittle?"

"Nothing much. Just pieces of wood. Tried to teach me once but I kept cutting myself. Not good with my hands."

"That's not what Gabri says. He tells me you used to make your own clothes."

"As a kid." Olivier reddened. "And they were crap."

Gamache took the carving from Olivier. "We found whittling tools in the cabin. The lab's working on them and we'll know soon enough if they were used to make this. But we both know the answer to that, don't we?"

The two men stared at each other.

"You're right," said Olivier with a laugh. "I'd forgotten. He used to whittle these strange carvings, but he never showed me that one."

"What did he show you?"

"I can't remember."

Gamache rarely showed impatience, but Inspector Beauvoir did. He slammed his notebook shut. It made a not very satisfactory sound. Certainly not nearly enough to convey his frustration at a witness who was behaving like his six-year-old nephew accused of stealing cookies. Denying everything. Lying about everything however trivial, as though he couldn't help himself.

"Try," said Gamache.

Olivier sighed. "I feel badly about this. He loved carving, and he asked me to get him the wood. He was very specific. Red cedar, from British Columbia. I got it from Old Mundin. But when the Hermit started handing me these I was pretty disappointed. Especially since he wasn't giving me as many antiques from his cabin. Just those." He flicked his hand at the carving.

"What did you do with them?"

"I threw them away."

"Where?"

"Into the woods. When I walked home I tossed them into the forest. Didn't want them."

"But he didn't give you this one, or even show it to you?"

Olivier shook his head.

Gamache paused. Why did the Hermit hide this one, and the other? What was different about them? Maybe he suspected Olivier had thrown the others away. Maybe he realized his visitor couldn't be trusted with his creations.

"What does this mean?" The Chief Inspector pointed to the letters carved under the ship.

OWSVI

"I don't know." Olivier seemed perplexed. "The others didn't have that."

"Tell me about woo," said Gamache so quietly Olivier thought he'd misheard.

Clara sat in the deep, comfortable armchair and watched Myrna serve Monsieur Béliveau. The old grocer had come in for something to read, but he wasn't sure what. He and Myrna talked about it and she made some suggestions. Myrna knew everyone's tastes, both the ones they declared and their actual ones.

Finally Monsieur Béliveau left with his biographies of Sartre and

Wayne Gretzky. He bowed slightly to Clara, who bowed back from her chair, never sure what to do when the courtly old man did that.

Myrna handed Clara a cool lemonade and sat in the chair opposite. The afternoon sun poured through the bookshop window. Here and there they saw a dog chase a ball for a villager, or vice versa.

"Didn't you have your meeting this morning with Monsieur Fortin?" Clara nodded.

"How'd it go?"

"Not bad."

"Do you smell smoke?" asked Myrna, sniffing. Clara, alarmed, looked around. "Oh, there it is," Myrna pointed to her companion. "Your pants are on fire."

"Very funny." But that was all the encouragement Clara needed. She tried to keep her voice light as she described the meeting. When Clara listed the people who would almost certainly be at the opening night at Fortin's gallery Myrna exclaimed and hugged her friend.

"Can you believe it?"

"Fucking queer."

"Stupid whore. Is this a new game?" laughed Myrna.

"You're not offended by what I said?"

"Calling me a fucking queer? No."

"Why not?"

"Well, I know you don't mean it. Did you?"

"Suppose I did?"

"Then I'd be worried for you," smiled Myrna. "What's this about?"

"When we were sitting in the bistro Gabri served us and as he left Fortin called him a fucking queer."

Myna took a deep breath. "And what did you say?"

"Nothing."

Myna nodded. Now it was her turn to say nothing.

What?"

"Woo," repeated the Chief Inspector.

"Woo?" Olivier seemed baffled, but he'd feigned that at every turn in this interview. Beauvoir had long stopped believing anything the man said.

"Did the Hermit ever mention it?" Gamache asked.

"Mention woo?" Olivier asked. "I don't even know what you're asking."

"Did you notice a spider's web, in a corner of the cabin?"

"A spider's web? What? No, I never noticed one. But I'll tell you something, I'd be surprised if there was one. The Hermit kept that cabin spotless."

"*Propre*," said Gamache.

"*Propre*," Olivier repeated.

"Woo, Olivier. What does it mean to you?"

"Nothing."

"And yet it was the word on the piece of wood you took from the hand of the Hermit. After he'd been murdered."

It was worse than Olivier had imagined, and he'd imagined pretty bad. It seemed Gamache knew everything. Or at least almost everything.

Pray God he doesn't know it all, thought Olivier.

"I picked it up," Olivier admitted. "But I didn't look at it. It was lying on the floor by his hand. When I saw there was blood on it I dropped it. It said Woo?"

Gamache nodded and leaned forward, his powerful hands lightly holding each other as his elbows rested on his knees.

"Did you kill him?"

TWENTY-SIX

 Finally Myrna spoke. She leaned forward and took Clara's hand.

"What you did was natural."

"Really? Because it feels like shit."

"Well, most of your life is shit," said Myrna, nodding her head sagely. "So it would feel natural."

"Har, har."

"Listen, Fortin is offering you everything you ever dreamed of, everything you ever wanted."

"And he seemed so nice."

"He probably is. Are you sure he wasn't kidding?"

Clara shook her head.

"Maybe he's gay himself," suggested Myrna.

Clara shook her head again. "I thought of that, but he has a wife and a couple of kids and he just doesn't seem gay."

Both Clara and Myrna had a finely honed gay-dar. It was, they both knew, imperfect, but it probably would have picked up the Fortin blip. But nothing. Only the immense, unmistakable object that was Gabri, sailing away.

"What should I do?" Clara asked.

Myrna remained silent.

"I need to speak to Gabri, don't I?"

"It might help."

"Maybe tomorrow."

As she left she thought about what Myrna had said. Fortin was offering her everything she'd ever wanted, the only dream she'd had since childhood. Success, recognition as an artist. All the sweeter after years in the wilderness. Mocked and marginalized.

And all she had to do was say nothing.

She could do that.

No, I didn't kill him."

But even as Olivier said it he realized the disaster of what he'd done. In lying at every turn he'd made the truth unrecognizable.

"He was already dead when I arrived."

God, even to his own ears it sounded like a lie. I didn't take the last cookie, I didn't break the fine bone china cup, I didn't steal the money from your purse. I'm not gay.

All lies. All his life. All the time. Until he'd come to Three Pines. For an instant, for a glorious few days he'd lived a genuine life. With Gabri. In their little rented wreck of an apartment above the shop.

But then the Hermit had arrived. And with him a trail of lies.

"Listen, it's the truth. It was Saturday night and the place was hopping. The Labor Day long weekend's always a madhouse. But by midnight or so there were only a few stragglers. Then Old Mundin arrived with the chairs and a table. By the time he left the place was empty and Havoc was doing the final cleanup. So I decided to visit the Hermit."

"After midnight?" Gamache asked.

"That's normally when I went. So no one could see."

Across from Olivier the Chief Inspector slowly leaned back, distancing himself. The gesture was eloquent. It whispered that Gamache didn't believe him. Olivier stared at this man he'd considered a friend and he felt a tightening, a constriction.

"Weren't you afraid of the dark?"

Gamache asked it so simply, and in that instant Olivier knew the genius of the man. He was able to crawl into other people's skins, and burrow beyond the flesh and blood and bone. And ask questions of deceptive simplicity.

"It's not the dark I'm afraid of," said Olivier. And he remembered the freedom that came only after the sun set. In city parks, in darkened theaters, in bedrooms. The bliss that came with being able to shed the outer shell and be himself. Protected by the night.

It wasn't the dark that scared him, but what might come to light.

"I knew the way and it only took about twenty minutes to walk it."

"What did you see when you arrived?"

"Everything looked normal. There was a light in the window and the lantern on the porch was lit."

"He was expecting company."

"He was expecting me. He always lit the lantern for me. I didn't realize there was anything wrong until I was in the door and saw him there. I knew he was dead, but I thought he'd just fallen, maybe had a stroke or a heart attack and hit his head."

"There was no weapon?"

"No, nothing."

Gamache leaned forward again.

Were they beginning to believe him, Olivier wondered.

"Did you take him food?"

Olivier's mind revved, raced. He nodded.

"What did you take?"

"The usual. Cheese, milk, butter. Some bread. And as a treat I took some honey and tea."

"What did you do with it?"

"The groceries? I don't know. I was in shock. I can't remember."

"We found them in the kitchen. Open."

The two men stared at each other. Then Gamache's eyes narrowed in a look that Olivier found harrowing.

Gamache was angry.

"I was there twice that night," he mumbled into the table.

"Louder, please," said the Chief.

"I returned to the cabin, okay?"

"It's time now, Olivier. Tell me the truth."

Olivier's breath came in short gasps, like something hooked and landed and about to be filleted.

"The first time I was there that night the Hermit was alive. We had a cup of tea and talked."

"What did you talk about?"

Chaos is coming, old son, and there's no stopping it. It's taken a long time, but it's finally here.

"He always asked about people who'd come to the village. He peppered me with questions about the outside world."

"The outside world?"

"You know, out here. He hadn't been more than fifty feet from his cabin in years."

"Go on," said Gamache. "What happened then?"

"It was getting late so I left. He offered to give me something for the groceries. At first I refused, but he insisted. When I got out of the woods I realized I'd left it behind, so I went back." No need to tell them about the thing in the canvas bag. "When I got there he was dead."

"How long were you gone?"

"About half an hour. I didn't dawdle."

He saw again the tree limbs snapping back and felt them slapping him, smelled the pine needles, and heard the crashing through the woods, like an army, running. Racing. He'd thought it was just his own noise, magnified by fear and the night. But maybe not.

"You saw and heard nothing?"

"Nothing."

"What time was that?" Gamache asked.

"About two I guess, maybe two thirty."

Gamache laced his fingers together. "What did you do once you realized what had happened?"

The rest of the story came out quickly, in a rush. Once he'd realized the Hermit was dead, another idea had come to Olivier. A way the Hermit might help. He'd put the body in the wheelbarrow and taken him through the woods to the old Hadley house.

"It took a while, but I finally got him there. I'd planned to leave him on the porch, but when I tried the door it was unlocked, so I laid him in the front hall."

He made it sound gentle, but he knew it wasn't. It was a brutal, ugly, vindictive act. A violation of a body, a violation of a friendship, a violation of the Gilberts. And finally, it was a betrayal of Gabri and their lives in Three Pines.

It was so quiet in the room he could almost believe himself alone. He looked up and there was Gamache, watching him.

"I'm sorry," said Olivier. He scolded himself, desperate not to be the gay guy who cried. But he knew his actions had taken him far beyond cliché, or caricature.

And then Armand Gamache did the most extraordinary thing. He leaned forward so that his large, certain hands were almost touching

Olivier's, as though it was all right to be that close to someone so vile, and he spoke in a calm, deep voice.

"If you didn't kill the man, who else could have? I need your help."

In that one sentence Gamache had placed himself next to Olivier. He might still be on the outer reaches of the world, but at least he wasn't alone.

Gamache believed him.

Clara stood outside Peter's closed studio door. She almost never knocked, almost never disturbed him. Unless it was an emergency. Those were hard to come by in Three Pines and were generally Ruth-shaped and difficult to avoid.

Clara had walked around the garden a few times, then come inside and walked around the living room, and then the kitchen in ever decreasing circles until finally she found herself here. She loved Myrna, she trusted Gamache, she adored Gabri and Olivier and many other friends. But it was Peter she needed.

She knocked. There was a pause, then the door opened.

"I need to talk."

"What is it?" He came out immediately and closed the door behind him. "What's wrong?"

"I met Fortin, as you know, and he said something."

Peter's heart missed a beat. And in that missed beat lived something petty. Something that hoped Fortin would change his mind. Would cancel Clara's solo show. Would say they'd made a mistake and Peter was really the one they wanted.

His heart beat for Clara every hour of every day. But every now and then it stumbled.

He took her hands. "What'd he say?"

"He called Gabri a fucking queer."

Peter waited for the rest. The part about Peter being the better artist. But Clara just stared at him.

"Tell me about it." He led her to a chair and they sat.

"Everything was going so well. He loved my ideas for hanging the show, he said FitzPatrick would be there from MoMA, and so would Allyne from the *Times*. And he thinks even Vanessa Destin Browne, you know, from the Tate Modern. Can you believe it?"

Peter couldn't. "Tell me more."

It was like throwing himself over and over at a wall of spikes.

"And then he called Gabri a fucking queer, behind his back. And said it made him want to vomit."

The spiked wall turned smooth, and soft.

"What did you say?"

"Nothing."

Peter dropped his eyes, then looked up. "I probably wouldn't have either."

"Really?" asked Clara, searching his face.

"Really." He smiled and squeezed her hands. "You weren't expecting it."

"It was a shock," said Clara, eager to explain. "What should I do?"

"What d'you mean?"

"Should I just forget about it, or say something to Fortin?"

And Peter saw the equation immediately. If she confronted the gallery owner she was running the risk of angering him. In fact, it almost certainly would. At the very least it would mar their relationship. He might even cancel her show.

If she said nothing, she'd be safe. Except that he knew her. It would eat away at Clara's conscience. A conscience, once aroused, could be a terrible thing.

Gabri poked his head into the back room.

"*Salut*. Why so serious?"

Olivier, Gamache and Beauvoir all looked at him. None was smiling.

"Wait a minute, are you telling Olivier about your visit to his father?" Gabri sat down beside his partner. "I wanna hear too. What'd he say about me?"

"We weren't talking about Olivier's father," said Gamache. Across from him Olivier's eyes were pleading for a favor Gamache couldn't grant. "We were talking about Olivier's relationship with the dead man."

Gabri looked from Gamache to Olivier, then over to Beauvoir. Then back to Olivier. "What?"

Gamache and Olivier exchanged looks and finally Olivier spoke. He told Gabri about the Hermit, his visits to the cabin, and the body. Gabri listened, silent. It was the first time Beauvoir had ever seen him go more than a minute without talking. And even when Olivier stopped, Gabri didn't start. He sat there as though he might never speak again.

But then, he did. "How could you be so stupid?"

"I'm sorry. It was dumb."

"It was more than dumb. I can't believe you didn't tell me about the cabin."

"I should've told you, I know. But he was so afraid, so secretive. You didn't know him—"

"I guess not."

"—but if he'd known I'd told anyone he'd have stopped seeing me."

"Why did you want to see him anyway? He was a hermit, in a cabin for God's sake. Wait a minute." There was silence while Gabri put it all together. "Why'd you go there?"

Olivier looked at Gamache, who nodded. It would all come out anyway.

"His place was full of treasure, Gabri. You wouldn't believe it. Cash stuffed between the logs for insulation. There was leaded crystal and tapestries. It was fantastic. Everything he had was priceless."

"You're making that up."

"I'm not. We ate off Catherine the Great's china. The toilet paper was dollar bills."

"*Sacré.* It's like your wet dream. Now I know you're kidding."

"No, no. It was unbelievable. And sometimes when I visited he'd give me a little something."

"And you took it?" Gabri's voice rose.

"Of course I took it," Olivier snapped. "I didn't steal it, and those things are no use to him."

"But he was probably nuts. It's the same as stealing."

"That's a horrible thing to say. You think I'd steal stuff from an old man?"

"Why not? You dumped his body at the old Hadley house. Who knows what you're capable of."

"Really? And you're innocent in all this?" Olivier's voice had grown cold and cruel. "How do you think we could afford to buy the bistro? Or the B and B? Eh? Didn't you ever wonder how we went from living in that dump of an apartment—"

"I fixed it up. It wasn't a dump anymore."

"—to opening the bistro and a B and B? How did you think we could afford it suddenly?"

"I thought the antique business was going well." There was silence. "You should've told me," said Gabri, finally, and wondered, as did Gamache and Beauvoir, what else Olivier wasn't saying.

It was late afternoon and Armand Gamache walked through the woods. Beauvoir had volunteered to go with him, but he preferred to be alone with his thoughts.

After they left Olivier and Gabri they'd returned to the Incident Room where Agent Morin had been waiting.

"I know who BM is," he said, eagerly following them, barely allowing them to take off their coats. "Look."

He took them over to his computer. Gamache sat and Beauvoir leaned over his shoulder. There was a black-and-white, formal, photo of a man smoking a cigarette.

"His name is Bohuslav Martinů," said Morin. "He wrote that violin piece we found. His birthday was December the eighth, so the violin must have been a birthday present from his wife. C. Charlotte was her name."

Gamache, while listening, was staring at one line in the biography his agent had found. Martinů had been born December 8, 1890. In Bohemia. What was now the Czech Republic.

"Did they have any children?" Beauvoir asked. He too had noticed the reference.

"None."

"Are you sure?" Gamache twisted in his chair to look at Morin, but the agent shook his head.

"I double- and triple-checked. It's almost midnight there but I have a call in to the Martinů Conservatory in Prague to get more information and I'll ask them, but it doesn't seem so."

"Ask about the violin, would you?" said Gamache, rising and putting his coat back on. He'd headed to the cabin, walking slowly through the woods, thinking.

A Sûreté officer guarding the cabin greeted him on the porch.

"Come with me, please," said Gamache and led the agent to the wheelbarrow sitting by the vegetable patch. He explained it had been used to carry a body and asked the officer to take samples. While she did that, Gamache went into the cabin.

It would be emptied the next morning, everything taken away for cataloguing, safe keeping. Put away in a dark vault. Away from human hands and eyes.

But before that happened Gamache wanted to see it all one last time.

Closing the door behind him he waited for his eyes to adjust to the dim interior. As always, it was the smell that first impressed him. Wood, and woodsmoke. Then the musky undertone of coffee and finally the sweeter scent of coriander and tarragon, from the window boxes.

The place was peaceful, restful. Cheerful even. While everything in it was a masterpiece, it all seemed at home in the rustic cabin. The Hermit might have known their worth, but he certainly knew their use, and used everything as it was intended. Glasses, dishes, silverware, vases. All put to purpose.

Gamache picked up the Bergonzi violin and cradling it he sat in the Hermit's chair by the fireplace. *One for solitude, two for friendship.*

The dead man had no need, or desire, for society. But he did have company.

They now knew who had sat in that other comfortable chair. Gamache had thought it was Dr. Vincent Gilbert, but he'd been wrong. It was Olivier Brulé. He'd come to keep the Hermit company, to bring him seeds and staples, and companionship. And in return the Hermit had given him what Olivier wanted. Treasure.

It was a fair trade.

But had someone else found him? If not, or if Gamache couldn't prove it, then Olivier Brulé would be arrested for murder. Arrested, tried and probably convicted.

Gamache couldn't shake the thought that it was too convenient that Dr. Vincent Gilbert had arrived just as the Hermit had been killed. Hadn't Olivier said the dead man was worried about strangers? Maybe Gilbert was that stanger.

Gamache tipped his head back and thought some more. Suppose Vincent Gilbert wasn't the one the Hermit was hiding from. Suppose it was another Gilbert. After all, it was Marc who'd bought the old Hadley house. He'd quit a successful job in the city to come here. He and Dominique had plenty of money; they could have bought any place in the

Townships. So why buy a broken-down old wreck? Unless it wasn't the house they wanted, but the forest.

And what about the Parras? Olivier had said the Hermit spoke with a slight accent. A Czech accent. And Roar was clearing the trail. Heading straight here.

Maybe he'd found the cabin. And the treasure.

Maybe they knew he was here somewhere and had been looking. When Gilbert bought the place maybe Roar took the job so that he could explore the woods. Searching for the Hermit.

And Havoc. What was the case against him? He seemed, by all reports, like a regular young man. But a young man who chose to stay here, in this backwater, while most of his friends had moved away. To university. To careers. Waiting table couldn't be considered a career. What was such a personable, bright young man doing here?

Gamache sat forward. Seeing the last night of the Hermit's life. The crowd at the bistro. Old Mundin arriving with the furniture then leaving. Olivier leaving. Havoc locking up. Then noticing his employer do something unexpected. Something bizarre even.

Had Havoc seen Olivier turn toward the woods instead of going home?

Curious, Havoc would have followed Olivier. Straight to the cabin. And the treasures.

It played out before Gamache's eyes. Olivier leaving and Havoc confronting the frightened man. Demanding some of the things. The Hermit refusing. Maybe he shoved Havoc away. Maybe Havoc struck out, picking up a weapon and smashing the Hermit. Frightened, he'd fled. Just before Olivier returned.

But that didn't explain everything.

Gamache put down the violin and looked up at the web in the corner. No, this wasn't a murder that had happened out of the blue. There was cunning here. And cruelty. The Hermit was tortured first, then killed. Tortured by a tiny word.

Woo.

After a few minutes Gamache got up and slowly wandered the room, picking up pieces here and there, touching things he never thought he'd see never mind hold. The panel from the Amber Room that threw pumpkin light into the kitchen. Ancient pottery used by the Hermit for herbs. Stunning enameled spoons and silk tapestries. And first editions. One was on the bedside table. Gamache picked it up idly, and looked at it.

Currer Bell was the author. Agent Morin had mentioned this book. He flipped it open. Another first edition. Then he noticed the title of the book.

Jane Eyre: An Autobiography. Currer Bell. That was the pseudonym used by—

He opened the book again. Charlotte Brontë. He was holding a first edition of *Jane Eyre*.

Armand Gamache stood very quietly in the cabin. But there wasn't complete silence. One word whispered to him, and had from the first moment they'd found the cabin. Repeated over and over. In the children's book found in the outhouse, in the Amber panel, in the violin, and now in the book he held in his hand. One word. A name.

Charlotte.

TWENTY-SEVEN

"We're getting more results from the lab," said Lacoste.

Upon his return the Chief had gathered his team at the conference table and now Agent Lacoste was handing around the printouts. "The web was made of nylon fishing line. Readily available. No prints, of course, and no trace of DNA. Whoever made it probably used surgical gloves. All they found was a little dust and a cobweb." She smiled.

"Dust?" asked Gamache. "Do they have any idea how long it was up?"

"No more than a few days, they guess. Either that or the Hermit dusted it daily, which seems unlikely."

Gamache nodded.

"So who put it there?" asked Beauvoir. "The victim? The murderer?"

"There's something else," said Lacoste. "The lab's been looking at the wooden Woo. They say it was carved years ago."

"Was it made by the Hermit?" Gamache asked.

"They're working on it."

"Any progress on what woo might mean?"

"There's a film director named John Woo. He's from China. Did *Mission Impossible II*," said Morin seriously, as though giving them vital information.

"Woo can stand for World of Outlaws. It's a car-racing organization." Lacoste looked at the Chief, who stared back blankly. She looked down hurriedly at her notes for something more helpful to say. "Or there's a video game called Woo."

"Oh, no. I can't believe I forgot that," said Morin, turning to Gamache.

"Woo isn't the name of the game, it's the name of a character in a game. The game is called King of the Monsters."

"King of the Monsters?" Gamache thought it unlikely the Hermit or his tormentor had a video game in mind. "Anything else?"

"Well, there's the woo cocktail," suggested Lacoste. "Made from peach schnapps and vodka."

"Then there's woo-woo," said Beauvoir. "It's English slang."

"*Vraiment?*" said Gamache. "What does it mean?"

"It means crazy." Beauvoir smiled.

"And there's wooing a person. Seducing them," said Lacoste, then shook her head. They weren't any closer.

Gamache dismissed the meeting, then walking back to his computer he typed in a word.

Charlotte.

Gabri chopped the tomatoes and peppers and onions. He chopped and he chopped and he chopped. He'd already chopped the golden plums and strawberries, the beets and pickles. He'd sharpened his knife and chopped some more.

All afternoon and into the evening.

"Can we talk now?" asked Olivier, standing in the doorway to the kitchen. It smelled so comforting, but felt so foreign.

Gabri, his back to the door, didn't pause. He reached for a cauliflower and chopped that.

"Mustard pickles," said Olivier, venturing into the kitchen. "My favorite."

Clunk, clunk, clunk, and the cauliflower was tossed into the boiling pot to blanch.

"I'm sorry," said Olivier.

At the sink Gabri scrubbed lemons, then cutting them into quarters he shoved them into a jar and sprinkled coarse salt on top. Finally he squeezed the leftover lemons and poured the juice over the salt.

"Can I help?" asked Olivier, reaching for the top of a jar. But Gabri put his body between Olivier and the jars and silently sealed them.

Every surface of the kitchen was packed with colorful jars filled with jams and jellies, pickles and chutneys. And it looked as though

Gabri would keep this up forever. Silently preserving everything he could.

Clara chopped the ends off the fresh carrots and watched Peter toss the tiny new potatoes into boiling water. They'd have a simple dinner tonight of vegetables from the garden with herbs and sweet butter. It was one of their favorite meals in late summer.

"I don't know who to feel worse for, Olivier or Gabri," she said.

"I do," said Peter, shelling some peas. "Gabri didn't do anything. Can you believe Olivier's been visiting that guy in the woods for years and didn't tell anyone? I mean, what else isn't he telling us?"

"Did you know he's gay?"

"He's probably straight and isn't telling us."

Clara smirked. "Now that would really piss Gabri off, though I know a couple of women who'd be happy." She paused, knife in mid-air. "I think Olivier feels pretty horrible."

"Come on. He'd still be doing it if the old man hadn't been murdered."

"He didn't do anything wrong, you know," said Clara. "The Hermit gave him everything."

"So he says."

"What do you mean?"

"Well, the Hermit's dead. Isn't that convenient?"

Clara stopped chopping. "What're you saying?"

"Nothing. I'm just angry."

"Why? Because he didn't tell us?"

"Aren't you pissed off?"

"A little. But I think I'm more amazed. Listen, we all know Olivier likes the finer things."

"You mean he's greedy and tight."

"What amazes me is what Olivier did with the body. I just can't imagine him lugging it through the woods and dumping it in the old Hadley house," said Clara. "I didn't think he had the strength."

"I didn't think he had the anger," said Peter.

Clara nodded. Neither did she. And she also wondered what else their friend hadn't told them. All this, though, had also meant that

Clara couldn't possibly ask Gabri about being called a "fucking queer." Over dinner she explained this to Peter.

"So," she concluded, her plate almost untouched, "I don't know what to do about Fortin. Should I go into Montreal and speak to him directly about this, or just let it go?"

Peter took another slice of baguette, soft on the inside with a crispy crust. He smeared the butter to the edges, covering every millimeter, evenly. Methodically.

Watching him Clara felt she'd surely scream or explode, or at the very least grab the fucking baguette and toss it until it was a grease stain on the wall.

Still Peter smoothed the knife over the bread. Making sure the butter was perfect.

What should he tell her? To forget it? That what Fortin said wasn't that bad? Certainly not worth risking her career. Just let it go. Besides, saying something almost certainly wouldn't change Fortin's mind about gays, and might just turn him against Clara. And this wasn't some tiny show Fortin was giving her. This was everything Clara had dreamed of. Every artist dreamed of. Everyone from the art world would be there. Clara's career would be made.

Should he tell her to let it go, or tell Clara she had to speak to Fortin? For Gabri and Olivier and all their gay friends. But mostly for herself.

But if she did that Fortin might get angry, might very well cancel her show.

Peter dug the tip of the knife into a hole in the bread to get the butter out.

He knew what he wanted to say, but he didn't know if he'd be saying it for his sake, or for Clara's.

"Well?" she asked, and heard the impatience in her voice. "Well?" she asked more softly. "What do you think?"

"What do you think?"

Clara searched his face. "I think I should just let it go. If he says it again maybe then I'll say something. It's a stressful time for all of us."

"I'm sure you're right."

Clara looked down at her uneaten plate. She'd heard the hesitation in Peter's voice. Still, he wasn't the one risking everything.

Rosa quacked a little in her sleep. Ruth eased the little flannel night-shirt off the duck and Rosa fluttered her wings then went back to sleep, tucking her beak under her wing.

Olivier had come to visit, flushed and upset. She'd cleared old *New Yorkers* off a chair and he'd sat in her front room like a fugitive. Ruth had brought him a glass of cooking sherry and a celery stick smeared with Velveeta and sat with him. For almost an hour they sat, not speaking, until Rosa entered the room. She waddled in wearing a gray flannel blazer. Ruth saw Olivier's lips press together and his chin pucker. Not a sound escaped. But what did escape were tears, wearing warm lines down his handsome face.

And then he told her what had happened. About Gamache, about the cabin, about the Hermit and his belongings. About moving the body and owning the bistro, and the boulangerie and almost everything else in Three Pines.

Ruth didn't care. All she could think of was what she'd give in exchange for words. To say something. The right thing. To tell Olivier that she loved him. That Gabri loved him and would never, ever leave. That love could never leave.

She imagined herself getting up and sitting beside him, and taking his trembling hand and saying, "There, there."

There, there. And softly rubbing his heaving back until he caught his breath.

Instead she'd poured herself more cooking sherry and glared.

Now, with the sun set and Olivier gone, Ruth sat in her kitchen in the white plastic garden chair at the plastic table she'd found at the dump. Sufficiently drunk, she pulled the notebook close and with Rosa quietly quacking in the background, a small knit blanket over her, Ruth wrote:

> *She rose up into the air and the jilted earth let out a sigh.*
> *She rose up past telephone poles and rooftops of houses where the*
> *   earthbound hid.*
> *She rose up but remembered to politely wave good-bye . . .*

And then kissing Rosa on the head she limped up the stairs to bed.

TWENTY-EIGHT

 When Clara came down the next morning she was surprised to find Peter in the garden, staring into space. He'd put on the coffee, and now she poured a couple of cups and joined him.

"Sleep well?" she asked, handing him a mug.

"Not really. You?"

"Not bad. Why didn't you?"

It was an overcast morning with a chill in the air. The first morning that really felt as though summer was over, and autumn on the way. She loved the fall. The brilliant leaves, the lit fireplaces, the smell of woodsmoke through the village. She loved huddling at a table outside the bistro, wrapped in sweaters and sipping *café au lait*.

Peter pursed his lips and looked down at his feet, in rubber boots to protect against the heavy dew.

"I was thinking about your question. What to do about Fortin."

Clara grew still. "Go on."

Peter had thought about it most of the night. Had got up and gone downstairs, pacing around the kitchen and finally ending up in his studio. His refuge. It smelled of him. Of body odor, and oil paint and canvas. It smelled faintly of lemon meringue pie, which he couldn't explain. It smelled like no other place on earth.

And it comforted him.

He'd gone into his studio last night to think, and finally to stop thinking. To clear his mind of the howl that had grown, like something massive approaching. And finally, just before sunrise, he knew what he had to say to Clara.

"I think you should talk to him."

There. He'd said it. Beside him Clara was silent, her hands grasping the warm cup of coffee.

"Really?"

Peter nodded. "I'm sorry. Do you want me to come with you?"

"I'm not even sure I'm going yet," she snapped and walked a couple of paces away.

Peter wanted to run to her, to take it back, to say he was wrong. She should stay there with him, should say nothing. Should just do the show.

What had he been thinking?

"You're right." She turned back to him, miserable. "He won't mind, will he?"

"Fortin? No. You don't have to be angry, just tell him how you feel, that's all. I'm sure he'll understand."

"I can just say that maybe I misheard. And that Gabri is one of our best friends."

"That's it. Fortin probably doesn't even remember saying it."

"I'm sure he won't mind." Clara walked slowly inside to call Fortin.

"Denis? It's Clara Morrow. Yes, that was fun. Really, is that a good price? Sure, I'll tell the Chief Inspector. Listen, I'm going to be in Montreal today and thought maybe we could get together again. I have . . . well, a few thoughts." She paused. "Uh-huh. Uh-huh. That sounds great. Twelve thirty at the Santropole on Duluth. Perfect."

What have I done? Peter asked himself.

Breakfast at the B and B was a somber affair of burned toast, rubber eggs and black bacon. The coffee was weak and the milk seemed curdled, as did Gabri. By mutual, unspoken consent they didn't discuss the case, but waited until they were back at the Incident Room.

"Oh, thank God," said Agent Lacoste, as she fell on the Tim Hortons double double coffees Agent Morin had brought. And the chocolate-glazed doughnuts. "I never thought I'd prefer this to Gabri's breakfasts." She took a huge bite of soft, sweet doughnut. "If this keeps up we might have to solve the case and leave."

"There's a thought," said Gamache, putting on his half-moon reading glasses.

Beauvoir went over to his computer to check messages. There, taped to the monitor, was a scrap of paper with familiar writing. He ripped it off, scrunched it up and tossed it to the floor.

Chief Inspector Gamache also looked at his screen. The results of his Google search of "Charlotte."

Sipping his coffee he read about Good Charlotte, the band, and Charlotte Brontë, and Charlotte Church and *Charlotte's Web*, the city of Charlotte in North Carolina and Charlottetown on Prince Edward Island and the Queen Charlotte Islands on the other side of the continent, off British Columbia. Most of the places were named after Queen Charlotte, he discovered.

"Does the name Charlotte mean anything to you?" he asked his team.

After thinking for a moment, they shook their heads.

"How about Queen Charlotte? She was married to King George."

"George the Third? The crazy one?" Morin asked. The others looked at him in amazement. Agent Morin smiled. "I was good at history in school."

It helped, thought Gamache, that school for him wasn't all that long ago. The phone rang and Agent Morin took it. It was the Martinù Conservatory, in Prague. Gamache listened to Morin's side of the conversation until his own phone rang.

It was Superintendent Brunel.

"I arrived to find my office looking like Hannibal's tent. I can barely move for your Hermit's items, Armand." She didn't sound displeased. "But I'm not calling about that. I have an invitation. Would you like to join Jérôme and me for lunch at our apartment? He has something he'd like to show you. And I have news as well."

It was confirmed he'd meet them at one o'clock at the Brunel apartment on rue Laurier. As he hung up the phone rang again.

"Clara Morrow for you, sir," said Agent Morin.

"*Bonjour*, Clara."

"*Bonjour.* I just wanted to let you know I spoke to Denis Fortin this morning. In fact, we're having lunch today. He told me he'd found a buyer for the carvings."

"Is that right? Who?"

"I didn't ask, but he says they're willing to pay a thousand dollars for the two. He seemed to think that was a good price."

"That is interesting. Would you like a lift into town? I'm meeting someone myself."

"Sure, thank you."

"I'll be by in about half an hour."

When he hung up Agent Morin was off his call.

"They said Martinů had no children. They were aware of the violin, but it disappeared after his death in," Morin consulted his notes, "1959. I told them we'd found the violin and an original copy of the score. They were very excited and said it would be worth a lot of money. In fact, it would be considered a Czech national treasure."

There was that word again. Treasure.

"Did you ask about his wife, Charlotte?"

"I did. They were together a long time, but only actually married on his deathbed. She died a few years ago. No family."

Gamache nodded, thinking. Then he spoke to Agent Morin again. "I need you to look into the Czech community here, especially the Parras. And find out about their lives in the Czech Republic. How they got out, who they knew there, their family. Everything."

He went over to Beauvoir. "I'm heading into Montreal for the day to talk to Superintendent Brunel and follow some leads."

"*D'accord.* As soon as Morin gets the information on the Parras I'll go up there."

"Don't go alone."

"I won't."

Gamache stooped and picked up the scrap of paper on the floor by Beauvoir's desk. He opened it and read, *In the midst of your nightmare,*

"*In the midst of your nightmare,*" he repeated, handing it to Beauvoir. "What do you think it means?"

Beauvoir shrugged and opened the drawer to his desk. A nest of balled-up words lay there. "I find them everywhere. In my coat pocket, pinned to my door in the morning. This one was taped to my computer."

Gamache reached into the desk and chose a scrap at random.

>   *that the deity who kills for pleasure*
>   *will also heal,*

"They're all like this?"

Beauvoir nodded. "Each crazier than the last. What'm I supposed to do with them? She's just pissed off because we took over her fire hall. Do you think I can get a restraining order?"

"Against an eighty-year-old winner of the Governor General's award, to stop her sending you verse?"

When put that way it didn't sound likely.

Gamache looked again at the balls of paper, like hail. "Well, I'm off."

"Thanks for your help," Beauvoir called after him.

"*De rien*," waved Gamache and was gone.

In the hour or so drive into Montreal Gamache and Clara talked about the people of Three Pines, about the summer visitors, about the Gilberts, who Clara thought might stay now.

"Old Mundin and Charles were in the village the other day. Old is very taken with Vincent Gilbert. He apparently knew it was him in the woods, but didn't want to say anything."

"How would he have recognized him?"

"*Being*," said Clara.

"Of course," said Gamache, merging onto the autoroute into Montreal. "Charles has Down's syndrome."

"After he was born Myrna gave them a copy of *Being*. Reading it changed their lives. Changed lots of lives. Myrna says Dr. Gilbert's a great man."

"I'm sure he wouldn't disagree."

Clara laughed. "Still, I don't think I'd like to be raised by a saint."

Gamache had to agree. Most saints were martyrs. And they took a lot of people down with them. In companionable silence they drove past signs for Saint-Hilaire, Saint-Jean and a village named Ange Gardien.

"If I said 'woo,' what would you think?" Gamache asked.

"Beyond the obvious?" She gave him a mock-worried look.

"Does the word mean anything to you?"

The fact he'd come back to it alerted Clara. "Woo," she repeated. "There's pitching woo, an old-fashioned way of saying courting."

"Old-fashioned for courting?" He laughed. "But I know what you mean. I don't think that's what I'm looking for."

"Sorry, can't help."

"Oh, it probably doesn't matter." They were over the Champlain Bridge. Gamache drove up Boulevard Saint-Laurent, turned left then left again and dropped her at the Santropole restaurant for lunch.

Climbing the steps she turned and walked back. Leaning into the car window she asked, "If a person insulted someone you cared about, would you say something?"

Gamache thought about that. "I hope I would."

She nodded and left. But she knew Gamache, and knew there was no "hope" about it.

TWENTY-NINE

After a luncheon of herbed cucumber soup, grilled shrimp and fennel salad and peach tarte Gamache and the Brunels settled into the bright living room of the second-floor apartment. It was lined with bookcases. *Objets trouvés* lay here and there. Pieces of aged and broken pottery, chipped mugs. It was a room that was lived in, where people read, and talked and thought and laughed.

"I've been researching the items in the cabin," said Thérèse Brunel.

"And?" Gamache leaned forward on the sofa, holding his *demi-tasse* of espresso.

"So far nothing. Amazing as it sounds, none of the items has been reported stolen, though I haven't finished yet. It'll take weeks to properly trace them."

Gamache slowly leaned back and crossed his long legs. If not stolen, then what? "What's the other option?" he asked.

"Well, that the dead man actually owned the pieces. Or that they were looted from dead people, who couldn't report it. In a war, for instance. Like the Amber Room."

"Or maybe they were given to him," suggested her husband, Jérôme.

"But they're priceless," objected Thérèse. "Why would someone give them to him?"

"Services rendered?" he said.

All three were silent then, imagining what service could exact such a payment.

"*Bon*, Armand, I have something to show you." Jérôme rose to his full height of just five and a half feet. He was an almost perfect square but carried his bulk with ease as though his body was filled with the thoughts overflowing from his head.

He wedged himself onto the sofa beside Gamache. He had in his hands the two carvings.

"First of all, these are remarkable. They almost speak, don't you find? My job, Thérèse told me, was to figure out what they're saying. Or, more specifically, what these mean."

He turned the carvings over to reveal the letters carved there.

MRKBVYDDO was etched under the people on the shore.

OWSVI was under the sailing ship.

"This's a code of some sort," explained Jérôme, putting his glasses on and peering closely at the letters again. "I started with the easiest one. Qwerty. It's the one an amateur's most likely to use. Do you know it?"

"It's a typewriter's keyboard. Also a computer's," said Gamache. "Qwerty is the first few letters on the top line."

"What the person using Qwerty generally does is go to the keyboard and type the letter next to the one you really mean. Very easy to decode. This isn't it, by the way. No." Jérôme hauled himself up and Gamache almost tumbled into the void left by his body. "I went through a whole lot of ciphers and frankly I haven't found anything. I'm sorry."

Gamache had been hopeful this master of codes would be able to crack the Hermit's. But like so much else with this case, it wouldn't reveal itself easily.

"But I think I know what sort of code it is. I think it's a Caesar's Shift."

"Go on."

"*Bon*," said Jérôme, relishing the challenge and the audience. "Julius Caesar was a genius. He's really the cipher fanatic's emperor. Brilliant. He used the Greek alphabet to send secret messages to his troops in France. But later he refined his codes. He switched to the Roman alphabet, the one we use now, but he shifted the letters by three. So if the word you want to send is kill, the code in Caesar's Shift becomes . . ." He grabbed a piece of paper and wrote the alphabet.

A B C D E F G H I J K L M N O P Q R S T U V W X Y Z

Then he circled four letters.

NLOO

"See?"

Gamache and Thérèse leaned over his messy desk.

"So he just shifted the letters," said Gamache. "If the code under the carvings is a Caesar's Shift, can't you just decode it that way? Move the letters back by three?"

He looked at the letters under the sailing ship.

"That would make this . . . L, T, P. Okay, I don't have to go further. It makes no sense."

"No, Caesar was smart and I think this Hermit was too. Or at least, he knew his codes. The brilliance of the Caesar's Shift is that it's almost impossible to break because the shift can be whatever length you want. Or, better still, you can use a key word. One you and your contact aren't likely to forget. You write it at the beginning of the alphabet, then start the cipher. Let's say it's Montreal."

He went back to his alphabet and wrote Montreal under the first eight letters, then filled in the rest of the twenty-six beginning with A.

A B C D E F G H I J K L M N O P Q R S T U V W X Y S
M O N T R E A L A B C D E F G H I J K L M N O P Q R

"So, now if the message we want to send is kill, what's the code?" Jérôme asked Gamache.

The Chief Inspector took the pencil and circled four letters.

CADD

"Exactly," beamed Dr. Brunel. Gamache stared, fascinated. Thérèse, who'd seen all this before, stood back and smiled, proud of her clever husband.

"We need the key word." Gamache straightened up.

"That's all," laughed Jérôme.

"Well, I think I have it."

Jérôme nodded, pulled up a chair and sat down. In a clear hand he wrote the alphabet once again.

A B C D E F G H I J K L M N O P Q R S T U V W X Y Z

His pencil hovered over the next line down.

"Charlotte," said Gamache.

Clara and Denis Fortin lingered over their coffee. The back garden of the Santropole restaurant was almost empty. The rush of the lunch crowd, mostly bohemian young people from the Plateau Mont Royal *quartier*, had disappeared.

The bill had just arrived and Clara knew it was now or never.

"There is one other thing I wanted to talk to you about."

"The carvings? Did you bring them?" Fortin leaned forward.

"No, the Chief Inspector still has them, but I told him about your offer. I think part of the problem is they're evidence in the murder case."

"Of course. There's no rush, though I suspect this buyer might not be interested for long. It really is most extraordinary that anyone would want them."

Clara nodded and thought maybe they could just leave. She could go back to Three Pines, make up a guest list for the *vernissage* and forget about it. Already Fortin's comment about Gabri was fading. Surely it wasn't that serious.

"So, what did you want to talk about? Whether you should buy a home in Provence or Tuscany? How about a yacht?"

Clara wasn't sure if he was kidding, but she did know he wasn't making this easy.

"It's just a tiny thing, really. I must have heard wrong, but it seemed to me when you came down to Three Pines yesterday you said something about Gabri."

Fortin looked interested, concerned, puzzled.

"He was our waiter," Clara explained. "He brought us our drinks."

Fortin was still staring. She could feel her brain evaporate. Suddenly, after practicing most of the morning what she'd say, she couldn't even remember her own name. "Well, I just thought, you know . . ."

Her voice trailed off. She couldn't do it. This must be a sign, she thought, a sign from God that she wasn't supposed to say anything. That she was making something out of nothing.

"Doesn't matter," she smiled. "I just thought I'd tell you his name."

Fortunately she figured Fortin was used to dealing with artists who were drunk, deranged, stoned. Clara appeared to be all three. She must, in his eyes, be a brilliant artist to be so unhinged.

Fortin signed for the bill and left, Clara noticed, a very large tip.

"I remember him." Fortin led her back through the restaurant with its dark wood and scent of tisane. "He was the fag."

VDTK?? MMF/X

They stared at the letters. The more they stared the less sense they made, which was saying something.

"Any other suggestions?" Jérôme looked up from his desk.

Gamache was flabbergasted. He was sure they had it, that "Charlotte" was the key to break the cipher. He thought for a moment, scanning the case.

"Woo," he said. They tried that.

Nothing.

"Walden." But he knew he was grasping. And sure enough, nothing. Nothing, nothing, nothing. What had he missed?

"Well, I'll keep trying," said Jérôme. "It might not be a Caesar's Shift. There're plenty of other codes."

He smiled reassuringly and the Chief Inspector had a sense of what Dr. Brunel's patients must have felt. The news was bad, but they had a man who wouldn't give up.

"What can you tell me about one of your colleagues, Vincent Gilbert?" Gamache asked.

"He was no colleague of mine," said Jérôme, testily. "Not of anyone's from what I remember. He didn't suffer fools easily. Do you notice most people who feel like that consider everyone a fool?"

"That bad?"

"Jérôme's only annoyed because Dr. Gilbert thought himself God," said Thérèse, perching on the arm of her husband's chair.

"Difficult to work with," said Gamache, who'd worked with a few gods himself.

"Oh no, it wasn't that," smiled Thérèse. "It annoyed Jérôme because he knows he's the one true God and Gilbert refused to worship."

They laughed but Jérôme's smile faded first. "Very dangerous man, Vincent Gilbert. I think he really does have a God complex. Megalomaniac. Very clever. That book he wrote . . ."

"*Being*," said Gamache.

"Yes. It was designed, every word calculated for effect. And I've got to hand it to him, it worked. Most people who've read it agree with him. He is at the very least a great man, and perhaps even a saint."

"You don't believe it?"

Dr. Brunel snorted. "The only miracle he's performed is convincing everyone of his saintliness. No mean feat, given what an asshole he is. Do I believe it? No."

"Well, it's time for my news." Thérèse Brunel stood up. "Come with me."

Gamache followed her, leaving Jérôme to fiddle with the cipher. The study was filled with more papers and magazines. Thérèse sat at her computer and after a few quick taps a photograph appeared. It showed a carving of a shipwreck.

Gamache pulled up a chair and stared. "Is it . . ."

"Another carving? *Oui.*" She smiled, like a magician who'd produced a particularly spectacular rabbit.

"The Hermit made this?" Gamache twisted in his chair and looked at her. She nodded. He looked back at the screen. The carving was complex. On one side was the shipwreck, then some forest, and on the other side a tiny village being built. "Even in a photograph it seems alive. I can see the little people. Are they the same ones from the other carvings?"

"I think so. But I can't find the frightened boy."

Gamache searched the village, the ship on the shore, the forest. Nothing. What happened to him? "We need to have the carving," he said.

"This's in a private collection in Zurich. I've contacted a gallery owner I know there. Very influential man. He said he'd help."

Gamache knew enough not to press Superintendent Brunel about her connections.

"It's not just the boy," he said. "We need to know what's written underneath it."

Like the others this one was, on the surface, pastoral, peaceful. But something lurked on the fringes. A disquiet.

And yet, once again, the tiny wooden people seemed happy.

"There's another one. In a collection in Cape Town." The screen flickered and another carving appeared. A boy was lying, either asleep or dead, on the side of a mountain. Gamache put on his glasses and leaned closer, squinting.

"Hard to tell, but I think it's the same young man."

"So do I," said the Superintendent.

"Is he dead?"

"I wondered that myself, but I don't think so. Do you notice something about this carving, Armand?"

Gamache leaned back and took a deep breath, releasing some of the tension he felt. He closed his eyes, then opened them again. But this time not to look at the image on the screen. This time he wanted to sense it.

After a moment he knew Thérèse Brunel was right. This carving was different. It was clearly the same artist, there was no mistaking that, but one significant element had changed.

"There's no fear."

Thérèse nodded. "Only peace. Contentment."

"Even love," said the Chief Inspector. He longed to hold this carving, to own it even, though he knew he never would. And he felt, not for the first time, that soft tug of desire. Of greed. He knew he'd never act on it. But he knew others might. This was a carving worth owning. All of them were, he suspected.

"What do you know about them?" he asked.

"They were sold through a company in Geneva. I know it well. Very discreet, very high end."

"What did he get for them?"

"They sold seven of them. The first was six years ago. It went for fifteen thousand. The prices went up until they reached three hundred thousand for the last one. It sold this past winter. He says he figures he could get at least half a million for the next one."

Gamache exhaled in astonishment. "Whoever sold them must have made hundreds of thousands."

"The auction house in Geneva takes a hefty commission, but I did a quick calculation. The seller would have made about one point five million."

Gamache's mind was racing. And then it ran into a fact. Or rather into a statement.

I threw the carvings away, into the woods, when I walked home.

Olivier had said it. And once again, Olivier had lied.

Foolish, foolish man, thought Gamache. Then he looked back at the computer screen and the boy lying supine on the mountain, almost caressing it. Was it possible, he asked himself.

Could Olivier have actually done it? Killed the Hermit?

A million dollars was a powerful motive. But why kill the man who supplied the art?

No, there was more Olivier wasn't telling, and if Gamache had any hope of finding the real killer it was time for the truth.

Why does Gabri have to be such a fucking queer, thought Clara. And a fag. And why do I have to be such a fucking coward?

"Yes, that's the one," she heard herself say, in an out-of-body moment. The day had warmed up but she pulled her coat closer as they stood on the sidewalk.

"Where can I drive you?" Denis Fortin asked.

Where? Clara didn't know where Gamache would be but she had his cell-phone number. "I'll find my own way, thanks."

They shook hands.

"This show's going to be huge, for both of us. I'm very happy for you," he said, warmly.

"There is one other thing. Gabri. He's a friend of mine."

She felt his hand release hers. But still, he smiled at her.

"I just need to say that he's not queer and he's not a fag."

"He isn't? He sure seems gay."

"Well, yes, he's gay." She could feel herself growing confused.

"What're you saying, Clara?"

"You called him queer, and a fag."

"Yes?"

"It just didn't seem very nice."

Now she felt like a schoolgirl. Words like "nice" weren't used very often in the art world. Unless it was as an insult.

"You're not trying to censor me, are you?"

His voice had become like treacle. Clara could feel his words sticking to her. And his eyes, once thoughtful, were now hard. With warning.

"No, I'm just saying that I was surprised and I didn't like hearing my friend called names."

"But he is queer and a fag. You admitted it yourself."

"I said he's gay." She could feel her cheeks sizzling and knew she must be beet red.

"Oh," he sighed and shook his head. "I understand." He looked at her with sadness now, as one might look at a sick pet. "It's the small-town girl after all. You've been in that tiny village too long, Clara. It's made you small-minded. You censor yourself and now you're trying to stifle my voice. That's very dangerous. Political correctness, Clara. An artist needs to break down boundaries, push, challenge, shock. You're not willing to do that, are you?"

She stood staring, unable to grasp what he was saying.

"No, I didn't think so," he said. "I tell the truth, and I say it in a way that might shock, but is at least real. You'd prefer something just pretty. And nice."

"You insulted a lovely man, behind his back," she said. But she could feel the tears now. Of rage, but she knew how it must look. It must look like weakness.

"I'm going to have to reconsider the show," he said. "I'm very disappointed. I thought you were the real deal, but obviously you were just pretending. Superficial. Trite. I can't risk my gallery's reputation on someone not willing to take artistic risks."

There was a rare break in traffic and Denis Fortin darted across Saint-Urbain. On the other side he looked back and shook his head again. Then he walked briskly to his car.

Inspector Jean Guy Beauvoir and Agent Morin approached the Parra home. Beauvoir had expected something traditional. Something a Czech woodsman might live in. A Swiss chalet perhaps. To Beauvoir there was Québécois and then "other." Foreign. The Chinese were all alike, as were Africans. The South Americans, if he thought of them at all, looked the same, ate the same foods and lived in exactly the same homes. A place somewhat less attractive than his own. The English he knew to be all the same. Nuts.

Swiss, Czech, German, Norwegian, Swedish all blended nicely together. They were tall, blond, good athletes if slightly thick and lived in A-frame homes with lots of paneling and milk.

He slowed the car and it meandered to a stop in front of the Parra place. All he saw was glass, some gleaming in the sun, some reflecting the sky and clouds and birds and woods, the mountains beyond and a small white steeple. The church at Three Pines, in the distance, brought forward by this beautiful house that was a reflection of all life around it.

"You just caught me. I was heading back to work," said Roar, opening the door.

He led Beauvoir and Morin into the house. It was filled with light. The floors were polished concrete. Firm, solid. It made the house feel very secure while allowing it to soar. And soar it did.

"*Merde*," Beauvoir whispered, walking into the great room. The combination kitchen, dining area and living room. With walls of glass on three sides it felt as though there was no division between this world and the next. Between in and out. Between forest and home.

Where else would a Czech woodsman live but in the woods. In a home made of light.

Hanna Parra was at the sink, drying her hands, and Havoc was just putting away the lunch dishes. The place smelled of soup.

"Not working at the bistro?" Beauvoir asked Havoc.

"Split shift today. Olivier asked if I'd mind."

"And do you?"

"Mind?" They walked over to the long dining table and sat. "No. I think he's pretty stressed."

"What's he like to work for?" Beauvoir noticed Morin take out his notebook and a pen. He'd told the young agent to do that when they arrived. It rattled suspects and Beauvoir liked them rattled.

"He's great, but I only have my dad to compare him to."

"And what's that supposed to mean?" asked Roar. Beauvoir studied the small, powerful man for signs of aggression, but it seemed a running joke in the family.

"At least Olivier doesn't make me work with saws and axes and machetes."

"Olivier's chocolate torte and ice cream are far more dangerous. At least you know to be careful with an axe."

Beauvoir realized he'd cut to the quick of the case. What appeared threatening wasn't. And what appeared wonderful, wasn't.

"I'd like to show you a picture of the dead man."

"We've already seen it. Agent Lacoste showed it to us," said Hanna.

"I'd like you to look again."

"What's this about, Inspector?" asked Hanna.

"You're Czech."

"What of it?"

"Been here for a while, I know," Beauvoir continued, ignoring her. "Lots came after the Russian invasion."

"There's a healthy Czech community here," Hanna agreed.

"In fact, it's so big there's even a Czech Association. You meet once a month and have pot-luck dinners."

All this and more he'd learned from Agent Morin's research.

"That's right," said Roar, watching Beauvoir carefully, wondering where this was leading.

"And you've been the president of the association a few times," Beauvoir said to Roar, then turned to Hanna. "You both have."

"That's not much of an honor, Inspector," smiled Hanna. "We take turns. It's on a rotation basis."

"Is it fair to say you know everyone in the local Czech community?"

They looked at each other, guarded now, and nodded.

"So you should know our victim. He was Czech." Beauvoir took the photograph out of his pocket and placed it on the table. But they didn't look. All three were staring at him. Surprised. That he knew? Or that the man was Czech?

Beauvoir had to admit it could have been either.

Then Roar picked up the photo and stared at it. Shaking his head he handed it to his wife. "We've already seen it, and told Agent Lacoste the same thing. We don't know him. If he was Czech he didn't come to any dinners. He made no contact with us at all. You'll have to ask the others, of course."

"We are." Beauvoir tucked the picture into his pocket. "Agents are talking to other members of your community right now."

"Is that profiling?" asked Hanna Parra. She wasn't smiling.

"No, it's investigating. If the victim was Czech it's reasonable to ask around that community, don't you think?"

The phone rang. Hanna went to it and looked down. "It's Eva." She picked it up and spoke in French, saying a Sûreté officer was with her now, and no she didn't recognize the photograph either. And yes, she was also surprised the man had been Czech.

Clever, thought Beauvoir. Hanna put down the receiver and it immediately rang again.

"It's Yanna," she said, this time leaving it. The phone, they realized, would ring all afternoon. As the agents arrived, interviewed and left. And the Czech community called each other.

It seemed vaguely sinister, until Beauvoir reluctantly admitted to himself he'd do the same thing.

"Do you know Bohuslav Martinù?"

"Who?"

Beauvoir repeated it, then showed them the printout.

"Oh, Bohuslav Martinù," Roar said, pronouncing it in a way that was unintelligible to Beauvoir. "He's a Czech composer. Don't tell me you suspect him?"

Roar laughed, but Hanna didn't and neither did Havoc.

"Does anyone here have ties to him?"

"No, no one," said Hanna, with certainty.

Morin's research of the Parras had turned up very little. Their relations in the Czech Republic seemed limited to an aunt and a few cousins. They'd escaped in their early twenties and claimed refugee status in Canada, which had been granted. They were now citizens.

Nothing remarkable. No ties to Martinù. No ties to anyone famous or infamous. No woo, no Charlotte, no treasure. Nothing.

And yet Beauvoir was convinced they knew more than they were telling. More than Morin had managed to find.

As they drove away, their retreating reflection in the glass house, Beauvoir wondered if the Parras were quite as transparent as their home.

I have a question for you," said Gamache as they wandered back into the Brunel living room. Jerome looked up briefly then went back to trying to tease some sense from the cryptic letters.

"Ask away."

"Denis Fortin—"

"Of the Galerie Fortin?" the Superintendent interrupted.

Gamache nodded. "He was visiting Three Pines yesterday and saw one of the carvings. He said it wasn't worth anything."

Thérèse Brunel paused. "I'm not surprised. He's a respected art dealer. Quite remarkable at spotting new talent. But his specialty isn't sculpture, though he handles some very prominent sculptors."

"But even I could see the carvings are remarkable. Why couldn't he?"

"What're you suggesting, Armand? That he lied?"

"Is it possible?"

Thérèse considered. "I suppose. I always find it slightly amusing, and sometimes useful, the general perception of the art world. People on the outside seem to think it's made up of arrogant, crazed artists, numbskull buyers and gallery owners who bring the two together. In fact it's a business, and anyone who doesn't understand that and appreciate it gets buried. In some cases hundreds of millions of dollars are at stake. But even bigger than the piles of cash are the egos. Put immense wealth and even larger egos together and you have a volatile mix. It's a brutal, often ugly, often violent world."

Gamache thought about Clara and wondered if she realized that. Wondered if she knew what was waiting for her, beyond the pale.

"But not everyone's like that, surely," he said.

"No. But at that level," she nodded to the carvings on the table by her husband, "they are. One man's dead. It's possible as we look closer others have been killed."

"Over these carvings?" Gamache picked up the ship.

"Over the money."

Gamache peered at the sculpture. He knew that not everyone was motivated solely by money. There were other currencies. Jealousy, rage, revenge. He looked not at the passengers sailing into a happy future, but at the one looking back. To where they'd been. With terror.

"I do have some good news for you, Armand."

Gamache lowered the ship and looked at the Superintendent.

"I've found your 'woo.'"

THIRTY

"There it is." Thérèse Brunel pointed.

They'd driven into downtown Montreal and now the Superintendent was pointing at a building. Gamache slowed the car and immediately provoked honking. In Quebec it was almost a capital crime to slow down. He didn't speed up, ignored the honking, and tried to see what she was pointing at. It was an art gallery. Heffel's. And outside was a bronze sculpture. But the car had drifted past before he got a good look. He spent the next twenty minutes trying to find a parking spot.

"Can't you just double-park?" asked Superintendent Brunel.

"If we want to be slaughtered, yes."

She harrumphed, but didn't disagree. Finally they parked and walked back along Sherbrooke Street until they were in front of Heffel's Art Gallery, staring at a bronze sculpture Gamache had seen before but never stopped to look at.

His cell phone vibrated. "*Pardon*," he said to the Superintendent, and answered it.

"It's Clara. I'm wondering when you might be ready."

"In just a few minutes. Are you all right?" She'd sounded shaky, upset.

"I'm just fine. Where can I meet you?"

"I'm on Sherbrooke, just outside Heffel's Gallery."

"I know it. I can be there in a few minutes. Is that okay?" She sounded keen, even anxious, to leave.

"Perfect. I'll be here."

He put the phone away and went back to the sculpture. Silently he walked around it while Thérèse Brunel watched, a look of some amusement on her face.

What he saw was an almost life-sized bronze of a frumpy middle-aged woman standing beside a horse, a dog at her side and a monkey on the horse's back. When he arrived back at Superintendent Brunel he stopped.

"This is 'woo'?"

"No, this is Emily Carr. It's by Joe Fafard and is called *Emily and Friends.*"

Gamache smiled then and shook his head. Of course it was. Now he could see it. The woman, matronly, squat, ugly, had been one of Canada's most remarkable artists. Gifted and visionary, she'd painted mostly in the early 1900s and was now long dead. But her art only grew in significance and influence.

He looked more closely at the bronze woman. She was younger here than the images he'd seen of her in grainy old black-and-white photos. They almost always showed a masculine woman, alone. In a forest. And not smiling, not happy.

This woman was happy. Perhaps it was the conceit of the sculptor.

"It's wonderful, isn't it?" Superintendent Brunel said. "Normally Emily Carr looks gruesome. I think it's brilliant to show her happy, as she apparently only was around her animals. It was people she hated."

"You said you'd found 'woo.' Where?"

He was disappointed and far from convinced Superintendent Brunel was right. How could a long dead painter from across the continent have anything to do with the case?

Thérèse Brunel walked up to the sculpture and placed one manicured hand on the monkey.

"This is Woo. Emily Carr's constant companion."

"Woo's a monkey?"

"She adored all animals, but Woo above all."

Gamache crossed his arms over his chest and stared. "It's an interesting theory, but the 'woo' in the Hermit's cabin could mean anything. What makes you think it's Emily Carr's monkey?"

"Because of this."

She opened her handbag and handed him a glossy brochure. It was for a retrospective of the works of Emily Carr, at the Vancouver Art Gallery. Gamache looked at the photographs of Carr's unmistakable paintings of the West Coast wilderness almost a century ago.

Her work was extraordinary. Rich greens and browns swirled together so that the forest seemed both frenzied and tranquil. It was a forest long gone. Logged, clear-cut, ruined. But still alive, thanks to the brush and brilliance of Emily Carr.

But that wasn't what had made her famous.

Gamache flipped through the brochure until he found them. Her signature series. Depicting what haunted any Canadian soul who saw them.

The totem poles.

Sitting on the shores of a remote Haida fishing village in northern British Columbia. She'd painted them where the Haida had put them.

And then a single perfect finger pointed to three small words.

Queen Charlotte Islands.

That's where they were.

Charlotte.

Gamache felt a thrill. Could they really have found Woo?

"The Hermit's sculptures were carved from red cedar," said Thérèse Brunel. "So was the word Woo. Red cedar grows in a few places, but not here. Not Quebec. One of the places it grows is in British Columbia."

"On the Queen Charlotte Islands," whispered Gamache, mesmerized by the paintings of the totem poles. Straight, tall, magnificent. Not yet felled as heathen, not yet yanked down by missionaries and the government.

Emily Carr's paintings were the only images of the totems as the Haida meant them to be. She never painted people, but she painted what they created. Long houses. And towering totem poles.

Gamache stared, losing himself in the wild beauty, and the approaching disaster.

Then he looked again at the inscription. Haida village. Queen Charlottes.

And he knew Thérèse was right. Woo pointed to Emily Carr, and Carr pointed to the Queen Charlotte Islands. This must be why there were so many references to Charlotte in the Hermit's cabin. *Charlotte's Web*, Charlotte Brontë. Charlotte Martinù, who'd given her husband the violin. The Amber Room had been made for a Charlotte. All leading him here. To the Queen Charlotte Islands.

"You can keep that." Superintendent Brunel pointed to the brochure. "It has a lot of biographical information on Emily Carr. It might be helpful."

"*Merci.*" Gamache closed the catalog and stared at the sculpture of Carr, the woman who had captured Canada's shame, not by painting the displaced, broken people, but by painting their glory.

Clara stared at the gray waters of the St. Lawrence as they drove over the Champlain Bridge.

"How was your lunch?" Gamache asked when they were on the autoroute heading to Three Pines.

"Well, it could have been better."

Clara's mood was swinging wildly from fury to guilt to regret. One moment she felt she should have told Denis Fortin more clearly what a piece of *merde* he was, the next she was dying to get home so she could call and apologize.

Clara was a fault-magnet. Criticisms, critiques, blame flew through the air and clung to her. She seemed to attract the negative, perhaps because she was so positive.

Well, she'd had enough. She sat up straighter in her seat. Fuck him. But, then again, maybe she should apologize and stand up for herself after the solo show.

What an idiot she'd been. Why in the world had she thought it was a good idea to piss off the gallery owner who was offering her fame and fortune? Recognition. Approval. Attention.

Damn, what had she done? And was it reversible? Surely she could have waited until the day after the opening, when the reviews were in the *New York Times*, the London *Times*. When his fury couldn't ruin her, as it could now.

As it would now.

She'd heard his words. But more important, she'd seen it in Fortin's face. He would ruin her. Though to ruin implied there was something built up to tear down. No, what he'd do was worse. He'd make sure the world never heard of Clara Morrow. Never saw her paintings.

She looked at the time on Gamache's dashboard.

Ten to four. The heavy traffic out of the city was thinning. They'd be home in an hour. If they got back before five she could call his gallery and prostrate herself.

Or maybe she should call and tell him what an asshole he was.

It was a very long drive back.

"Do you want to talk about it?" Gamache asked after half an hour of silence. They'd turned off the highway and were heading toward Cowansville.

"I'm not really sure what to say. Denis Fortin called Gabri a fucking queer yesterday in the bistro. Gabri didn't hear it, but I did, and I didn't say anything. I talked to Peter and Myrna about it, and they listened, but they pretty much left it up to me. Until this morning when Peter kinda said I should talk to Fortin."

Gamache turned off the main road. The businesses and homes receded and the forest closed in.

"How did Fortin react?" he asked.

"He said he'd cancel the show."

Gamache sighed. "I'm sorry about that, Clara."

He glanced over at her unhappy face staring out the window. She reminded him of his daughter Annie the other night. A weary lion.

"How was your day?" she asked. They were on the dirt road now, bumping along. It was a road not used by many. Mostly just by people who knew where they were going, or had completely lost their way.

"Productive, I think. I have a question for you."

"Ask away." She seemed relieved to have something else to do besides watching the clock click closer to five.

"What do you know about Emily Carr?"

"Now, I'd never have bet that was the question," she smiled, then gathered her thoughts. "We studied her in art school. She was a huge inspiration to lots of Canadian artists, certainly the women. She inspired me."

"How?"

"She went into the wilderness where no one else dared to go, with just her easel."

"And her monkey."

"Is that a euphemism, Chief Inspector?"

Gamache laughed. "No. Go on."

"Well, she was just very independent. And her work evolved. At first it was representational. A tree was a tree, a house a house. It was almost a documentary. She wanted to capture the Haida, you know, in their villages, before they were destroyed."

"Most of her work was on the Queen Charlotte Islands, I understand."

"Many of her most famous works are, yes. At some point she realized that painting exactly what could be seen wasn't enough. So she really let go, dropped all the conventions, and painted not just what she saw, but what she felt. She was ridiculed for it. Ironically those are now her most famous works."

Gamache nodded, remembering the totem poles in front of the swirling, vibrant forest. "Remarkable woman."

"I think it all started with the brutal telling," said Clara.

"The what?"

"The brutal telling. It's become quite well known in artistic circles. She was the youngest of five daughters and very close to her father. It was apparently a wonderful relationship. Nothing to suggest it wasn't simply loving and supportive."

"Nothing sexual, you mean."

"No, just a close father-daughter bond. And then in her late teens something happened and she left home. She never spoke to him or saw him again."

"What happened?" Gamache was slowing the car. Clara noticed this, and watched the clock approaching five to five.

"No one knew. She never told anyone, and her family said nothing. But she went from being a happy, carefree child to an embittered woman. Very solitary, not very likeable apparently. Then, near the end of her life, she wrote to a friend. In the letter she said that her father had said something to her. Something horrible and unforgivable."

"The brutal telling."

"That's how she described it."

They'd arrived. He stopped in front of her home and they sat there quietly for a moment. It was five past five. Too late. She could try, but knew Fortin wouldn't answer.

"Thank you," he said. "You've been very helpful."

"And so have you."

"I wish that was true." He smiled at her. But, remarkably, she seemed to be feeling better. Clara got out of the car, and instead of going inside she paused on the road then slowly started to walk. Around the village green. Round and round she strolled, until the end met the beginning and she was back where she started. And as she walked she thought about Emily Carr. And the ridicule she'd endured at the hands of gallery owners, critics, a public too afraid to go where she wanted to take them.

Deeper. Deeper into the wilderness.

Then Clara went home.

It was late at night in Zurich when an art collector picked up the odd little carving he'd paid so much for. The one he'd been assured was a great work of art, but more important, a great investment.

At first he'd displayed it in his home, until his wife had asked him to move it. Away. So he'd put in into his private gallery. Once a day he'd sit in there with a cognac, and look at the masterpieces. The Picassos, the Rodins and Henry Moores.

But his eyes kept going back to the jolly little carving, of the forest, and the happy people building a village. At first it had given him pleasure, but now he found it spooky. He was considering putting it somewhere else again. A closet perhaps.

When the broker had called earlier in the day and asked if he'd consider sending it back to Canada for a police investigation he'd refused. It was an investment, after all. And there was no way he could be forced. He'd done nothing wrong and they had no jurisdiction.

The broker, though, had passed on two requests from the police. He knew the answer to the first, but still he picked up the carving and looked at its smooth base. No letters, no signature. Nothing. But the other question just sounded ridiculous. Still, he'd tried. He was just about to replace the carving and e-mail that he'd found nothing when his eyes caught something light among the dark pines.

He peered closer. There, deep in the forest, away from the village, he found what the police were looking for.

A tiny wooden figure. A young man, not much more than a boy, hiding in the woods.

THIRTY-ONE

It was getting late. Agent Lacoste had left and Inspector Beauvoir and Agent Morin were reporting on their day.

"We checked into the Parras, the Kmeniks, the Mackus. All the Czech community," said Beauvoir. "Nothing. No one knew the Hermit, no one saw him. They'd all heard of that violinist guy—"

"Martinù," said Morin.

"—because he's some famous Czech composer, but no one actually knew him."

"I spoke to the Martinù Institute and did background checks on the Czech families," said Morin. "They're what they claim to be. Refugees from the communists. Nothing more. In fact, they seem more law-abiding than most. No connection at all with Martinù."

Beauvoir shook his head. If lies annoyed the Inspector the truth seemed to piss him off even more. Especially when it was inconvenient.

"Your impression?" Gamache asked Agent Morin, who glanced at Inspector Beauvoir before answering.

"I think the violin and the music have nothing to do with the people here."

"You may be right," conceded Gamache, who knew they'd have to look into many empty caves before they found their killer. Perhaps this was one. "And the Parras?" he asked, though he knew the answer. If there'd been anything there Beauvoir would have told him already.

"Nothing in their background," Beauvoir confirmed. "But . . ."

Gamache waited.

"They seemed defensive, guarded. They were surprised that the dead man was Czech. Everyone was."

"What do you think?" asked the Chief.

Beauvoir wiped a weary hand across his face. "I can't put it all together, but I think it fits somehow."

"You think there is a connection?" pressed Gamache.

"How can there not be? The dead man was Czech, the sheet music, the priceless violin, and there's a big Czech community here including two people who could have found the cabin. Unless . . ."

"Yes?"

Beauvoir leaned forward, his nervous hands clasped together on the table. "Suppose we've got it wrong. Suppose the dead man wasn't Czech."

"You mean, that Olivier was lying?" said Gamache.

Beauvoir nodded. "He's lied about everything else. Maybe he said it to take us off the trail, so that we'd suspect others."

"But what about the violin and the music?"

"What about it?" Beauvoir was gaining momentum. "There're lots of other things in that cabin. Maybe Morin's right." Though he said it in the same tone he'd use to say maybe a chimp was right. With a mixture of awe at witnessing a miracle, and doubt. "Maybe the music and violin have nothing to do with it. After all, there were plates from Russia, glass from other places. The stuff tells us nothing. He could've been from anywhere. We only have Olivier's word for it. And maybe Olivier wasn't exactly lying. Maybe the guy did speak with an accent, but it wasn't Czech. Maybe it was Russian or Polish or one of those other countries."

Gamache leaned back, thinking, then he nodded and sat forward. "It's possible. But is it likely?"

This was the part of investigating he liked the most, and that most frightened him. Not the cornered and murderous suspect. But the possibility of turning left when he should have gone right. Of dismissing a lead, of giving up on a promising trail. Or not seeing one in his rush to a conclusion.

No, he needed to step carefully now. Like any explorer he knew the danger wasn't in walking off a cliff, but in getting hopelessly lost. Muddled. Disoriented by too much information.

In the end the answer to a murder investigation was always devastatingly simple. It was always right there, obvious. Hiding in facts and evidence and lies, and the misperceptions of the investigators.

"Let's leave if for now," he said, "and keep an open mind. The Hermit might have been Czech, or not. Either way there's no denying the contents of his cabin."

"What did Superintendent Brunel have to say? Any of it stolen?" asked Beauvoir.

"She hasn't found anything, but she's still looking. But Jérôme Brunel's been studying those letters under the carving and he thinks they're a Caesar's Shift. It's a type of code."

He explained how a Caesar's Shift worked.

"So we just need to find the key word?" asked Beauvoir. "Should be simple enough. It's Woo."

"Nope. Tried that one."

Beauvoir went to the sheet of foolscap on the wall and uncapped the magic marker. He wrote the alphabet. Then the marker hovered.

"How about violin?" asked Morin. Beauvoir looked at him again as at an unexpectedly bright chimp. He wrote *violin* on a separate sheet of paper. Then he wrote *Martinù, Bohuslav.*

"Bohemia," suggested Morin.

"Good idea," said Beauvoir. Within a minute they had a dozen possibilities, and within ten minutes they'd tried them all and found nothing.

Beauvoir tapped his Magic Marker with some annoyance and stared at the alphabet, as though it was to blame.

"Well, keep trying," said Gamache. "Superintendent Brunel is trying to track down the rest of the carvings."

"Do you think that's why he was killed?" asked Morin. "For the carvings?"

"Perhaps," said Gamache. "There's not much some people wouldn't do for things that valuable."

"But when we found the cabin it hadn't been searched," said Beauvoir. "If you find the guy, find the cabin, go there and kill him, wouldn't you tear the place apart to find the carvings? And it's not like the murderer had to worry about disturbing the neighbors."

"Maybe he meant to but heard Olivier returning and had to leave," said Gamache.

Beauvoir nodded. He'd forgotten about Olivier coming back. That made sense.

"That reminds me," he said, sitting down. "The lab report came in on the whittling tools and the wood. They say the tools were used to do the sculptures but not to carve Woo. The grooves didn't match, but apparently the technique didn't either. Definitely different people."

It was a relief to have something definite about this case.

"But red cedar was used for all of them?" Gamache wanted to hear the confirmation.

Beauvoir nodded. "And they're able to be more specific than that, at least with the Woo carving. They can tell by looking at water content, insects, growth rings, all sorts of things, where the wood actually came from."

Gamache leaned forward and wrote three words on a sheet of paper. He slid it across the table and Beauvoir read and snorted. "You talked to the lab?"

"I talked to Superintendent Brunel."

He told them then about Woo, and Emily Carr. About the Haida totem poles, carved from red cedar.

Beauvoir looked down at the Chief's note.

Queen Charlotte Islands, he'd written.

And that's what the lab had said. The wood that became Woo had started life as a sapling hundreds of years earlier, on the Queen Charlotte Islands.

Gabri walked, almost marched, up rue du Moulin. He'd made up his mind and wanted to get there before he changed it, as he had every five minutes all afternoon.

He'd barely exchanged five words with Olivier since the Chief Inspector's interrogation had revealed just how much his partner had kept from him. Finally he arrived and looked at the gleaming exterior of what had been the old Hadley house. Now a carved wooden sign hung out front, swinging slightly in the breeze.

Auberge et Spa.

The lettering was tasteful, clear, elegant. It was the sort of sign he'd been meaning to have Old Mundin make for the B and B, but hadn't gotten around to. Above the lettering three pine trees were carved in a row. Iconic, memorable, classic.

He'd thought of doing that for the B and B as well. And at least his place was actually in Three Pines. This place hovered above it. Not really part of the village.

Still, it was too late now. And he wasn't here to find fault. Just the opposite.

He stepped onto the porch and realized Olivier had stood there as well, with the body. He tried to shove the image away. Of his gentle, kind and quiet Olivier. Doing something so hideous.

Gabri rang the bell and waited, noting the shining brass of the handle, the bevelled glass and fresh red paint on the door. Cheerful and welcoming.

"*Bonjour?*" Dominique Gilbert opened the door, her face the image of polite suspicion.

"Madame Gilbert? We met in the village when you first arrived. I'm Gabriel Dubeau."

He put out his large hand and she took it. "I know who you are. You run that marvelous B and B."

Gabri knew when he was being softened up, having specialized in that himself. Still, it was nice to be on the receiving end of a compliment, and Gabri never refused one.

"That's right," he smiled. "But it's nothing compared to what you've done here. It's stunning."

"Would you like to come in?" Dominique stood aside and Gabri found himself in the large foyer. The last time he'd been there it'd been a wreck and so had he. But it was clear the old Hadley house no longer existed. The tragedy, the sigh on the hill, had become a smile. A warm, elegant, gracious *auberge*. A place he himself would book into, for pampering. For an escape.

He thought about his slightly worn B and B. What moments ago had seemed comfortable, charming, welcoming, now seemed just tired. Like a grande dame past her prime. Who would want to visit Auntie's place when you could come to the cool kids' inn and spa?

Olivier had been right. This was the end.

And looking at Dominique, warm, confident, he knew she couldn't fail. She seemed born to success, to succeed.

"We're just in the living room having drinks. Would you like to join us?"

He was about to decline. He'd come to say one thing to the Gilberts and leave, quickly. This wasn't a social call. But she'd already turned, assuming his consent, and was walking through a large archway.

But for all the easy elegance, of the place and the woman, something didn't fit.

He examined his hostess as she walked away. Light silk blouse, Aquascutum slacks, loose scarf. And a certain fragrance. What was it?

Then he had it. He smiled. Instead of wearing Chanel this chatelaine was wearing Cheval. And not just horse, but a haughty undercurrent of horse shit.

Gabri's spirits lifted. At least his place smelled of muffins.

"It's Gabriel Dubeau," Dominique announced to the room. The fire was lit and an older man was standing staring into it. Carole Gilbert sat in an armchair and Marc was by the drinks tray. They all looked up.

Chief Inspector Gamache had never seen the bistro so empty. He sat in an armchair by the fire and Havoc Parra brought him a drink.

"Quiet night?" he asked as the young man put down the Scotch and a plate of Quebec cheese.

"Dead," Havoc said and reddened a little. "But it'll probably pick up."

They both knew that wasn't true. It was six thirty. The height of what should be the cocktail and predinner rush. Two other customers sat in the large room while a small squadron of waiters waited. For a rush that would never come. Not that night. Perhaps not ever again.

Three Pines had forgiven Olivier a lot. The body had been dismissed as bad luck. Even Olivier knowing about the Hermit and the cabin had been shrugged off. Not easily, granted. But Olivier was loved and with love there was leeway. They'd even managed to forgive Olivier's moving the body. It was seen as a kind of *grand mal* on his part.

But that had ended when they'd found out that Olivier had secretly made millions of dollars off a recluse who was probably demented. Over the course of years. And then had quietly bought up most of Three Pines. He was Myrna's, Sarah's and Monsieur Béliveau's landlord.

This was Olivierville, and the natives were restless. The man they had thought they knew was a stranger after all.

"Is Olivier here?"

"In the kitchen. He let the chef off and decided to do the cooking himself tonight. He's a terrific cook, you know."

Gamache did know, having enjoyed his private meals a number of times. But he also knew this decision to cook allowed Olivier to hide. In the kitchen. Where he didn't have to see the accusing, unhappy faces of people who were his friends. Or worse still, see the empty chairs where friends once sat.

"I wonder if you could ask him to join me?"

"I'll do my best."

"Please."

In that one word Chief Inspector Gamache conveyed that while it might sound like a polite request, it wasn't. A couple of minutes later Olivier lowered himself into the chair across from Gamache. They needn't worry about keeping their voices down. The bistro was now empty.

Gamache leaned forward, took a sip of Scotch, and watched Olivier closely.

"What does the name Charlotte mean to you?"

Olivier's brows went up in surprise. "Charlotte?" He thought for a few moments. "I've never known a Charlotte. I knew a girl named Charlie once."

"Did the Hermit ever mention the name?"

"He never mentioned any name."

"What did you talk about?"

Olivier heard again the dead man's voice, not deep but somehow calming. "We talked about vegetable gardens and building and plumbing. He learned from the Romans, the Greeks, the early settlers. It was fascinating."

Not for the first time Gamache wished there'd been a third chair in that cabin, for him. "Did he ever mention Caesar's Shift?"

Once again Olivier looked perplexed, then shook his head.

"How about the Queen Charlotte Islands?" Gamache asked.

"In British Columbia? Why would he talk about them?"

"Is anyone in Three Pines from BC that you know?"

"People're from all over, but I can't remember anyone from British Columbia. Why?"

Gamache brought out the sculptures and placed them on the table so that the ship looked to be running from the cheese, and the cheese, runny, seemed to be chasing it.

"Because these are. Or at least, the wood is. It's red cedar from the

Queen Charlottes. Let's start again," Gamache said quietly. "Tell me what you know about these sculptures."

Olivier's face was impassive. Gamache knew that look. It was the look of a liar, caught. Trying to find the last way out, the back door, the crack. Gamache waited. He sipped his Scotch and smoothed a bit of cheese on the very excellent nut bread. He placed a slice in front of Olivier then prepared one for himself. He ate and waited.

"The Hermit carved them," said Olivier, his voice even, flat.

"You've told us that already. You also told us he gave you some and you threw them into the forest."

Gamache waited, knowing the rest would come out now. He looked through the window and noticed Ruth walking Rosa. The duck, for some reason, was wearing a tiny, red raincoat.

"I didn't throw them away. I kept them," Olivier whispered, and the world beyond the circle of light from the fireplace seemed to disappear. It felt as though the two men were in their own little cabin. "I'd been visiting the Hermit for about a year when he gave me the first."

"Can you remember what it was?"

"A hill, with trees. More like a mountain really. And a boy lying on it."

"This one?" Gamache brought out the photo Thérèse Brunel had given him.

Olivier nodded. "I remember it clearly because I didn't know the Hermit did stuff like this. His cabin was packed with wonderful things, but things other people made."

"What did you do with it?"

"I kept it for a while, but had to hide it so Gabri wouldn't start asking questions. Then I figured it was just easier to sell it. So I put it up on eBay. It went for a thousand dollars. Then a dealer got in touch. Said he had buyers, if there were any more. I thought he was joking, but when the Hermit gave me another one eight months later I remembered the guy and contacted him."

"Was it Denis Fortin?"

"Clara's gallery owner? No. It was someone in Europe. I can give you his coordinates."

"That would be helpful. What did the second carving look like?"

"Plain. Simple. On the surface. I was kind of disappointed. It was a forest, but if you looked closely beneath the canopy of trees you could see people walking in a line."

"Was the boy one of them?"

"Which boy?"

"The one from the mountain."

"Well, no. This was a different piece."

"I realize that," said Gamache, wondering if he was making himself clear. "But it seems possible the Hermit carved the same figures into each of his sculptures."

"The boy?"

"And the people. Anything else?"

Olivier thought. There was something else. The shadow over the trees. Something loomed just behind them. Something was rising up. And Olivier knew what it was.

"No, nothing. Just a forest and the people inside. The dealer was pretty excited."

"What did it sell for?"

"Fifteen thousand." He watched for the shock on Gamache's face.

But Gamache's gaze didn't waver, and Olivier congratulated himself on telling the truth. It was clear the Chief Inspector already knew the answer to that question. Telling the truth was always a crapshoot. As was the telling of lies. It was best, Olivier had found, to mingle the two.

"How many carvings did he make?"

"I thought eight, but now that you've found those, I guess he did ten."

"And you sold all the ones he gave you?"

Olivier nodded.

"You'd told us he started out giving you other things from his cabin, as payment for food. Where did those go?"

"I took them to the antique stores on rue Notre Dame in Montreal. But then once I realized the stuff was valuable I found private dealers."

"Who?"

"I haven't used them in years. I'll have to look it up. People in Toronto and New York." He leaned back and looked around the empty room. "I suppose I should let Havoc and the others off for the night."

Gamache remained quiet.

"Do you think people'll come back?"

The Chief Inspector nodded. "They're hurt by what you did."

"Me? Marc Gilbert's way worse. Be careful with him. He's not what he seems."

"And neither are you, Olivier. You've lied all along. You may be lying now. I'm going to ask you a question and I need you to think carefully about the answer."

Olivier nodded and straightened up.

"Was the Hermit Czech?"

Olivier immediately opened his mouth but Gamache quickly brought up a hand to stop him. "I asked you to think about your answer. Consider it. Could you have been wrong? Maybe there was no accent," Gamache watched his companion closely. "Maybe he spoke with an accent but it wasn't necessarily Czech. Maybe you just assumed. Be careful what you say."

Olivier stared at Gamache's large, steady hand and as it lowered he switched his gaze to the large, steady man.

"There was no mistake. I've heard enough Czech over the years from friends and neighbors. He was Czech."

It was said with more certainty than anything Olivier had said to Gamache since the investigation began. Still, Gamache stared at the slight man across from him. He examined his mouth, his eyes, the lines on his forehead, his coloring. Then the Chief Inspector nodded.

"Chilly night," said Ruth, plopping onto the seat beside Gamache and managing to knock his knee quite hard with her muddy cane. "Sorry," she said, then did it again.

She was completely oblivious of the conversation she was interrupting and the tension between the two men. She looked from Olivier to Gamache.

"Well, enough of this gay banter. Can you believe what Olivier did with that body? His idiocy eclipses even your own. Gives me a sense of the infinite. It's almost a spiritual experience. Cheese?"

She took the last bite of Gamache's Saint-André and reached for his Scotch, but he got there first. Myrna arrived, then Clara and Peter dropped by and told everyone about Denis Fortin. There was general commiserating and all agreed Clara had done the right thing. Then they agreed she should call in the morning and beg his forgiveness. Then they agreed she shouldn't.

"I saw Rosa outside," said Clara, anxious to change the subject. "She's looking very smart in her rain jacket." It had occurred to her to wonder why a duck might need a raincoat, but she supposed Ruth was just training Rosa to get used to wearing coats.

Eventually the conversation came back to Olivier, and the Hermit, dead, and the Hermit alive. Ruth leaned over and took Olivier's hand. "It's all right, dear, we all know you're greedy." Then she looked at Clara. "And we all know you're needy, and Peter's petty and Clouseau here," she turned to Gamache, "is arrogant. And you're . . ." She looked at Myrna, then turned back to Olivier, whispering loudly, "Who is that anyway? She's always hanging around."

"You're a nasty, demented, drunken old fart," said Myrna.

"I'm not drunk, yet."

They finished their drinks and left, but not before Ruth handed Gamache a piece of paper, carefully, precisely folded, the edges sharpened. "Give this to that little fellow who follows you around."

Olivier kept looking out into the village where Rosa was sitting quietly on the village green, waiting for Ruth. There was no sign of the one not there, the one Olivier longed to see.

Gabri was mostly curious to meet the saint. Vincent Gilbert. Myrna was in awe of him, and she wasn't in awe of many people. Old Mundin and The Wife said he'd changed their lives with his book *Being*, and his work at LaPorte. And by extension, he'd changed little Charlie's life.

"*Bonsoir*," said Gabri, nervously. He looked over to Vincent Gilbert. Growing up in the Catholic Church he'd spent endless hours staring at the gleaming windows showing the wretched lives and glorious deaths of the saints. When Gabri had wandered from the Church he'd taken one thing with him. The certainty that saints were good.

"What do you want?" Marc Gilbert asked. He stood with his wife and mother by the sofa. Forming a semicircle. His father a satellite off to the side. Gabri waited for Vincent Gilbert to calm his son, to tell him to greet their guest nicely. To invite Marc to be reasonable.

Gilbert said nothing.

"Well?" said Marc.

"I'm sorry I haven't been up sooner to welcome you."

Marc snorted. "The Welcome Wagon's already left us our package."

"Marc, please," said Dominique. "He's our neighbor."

"Not by choice. If he had his way we'd be long gone."

And Gabri didn't deny it. It was true. Their troubles arrived with the Gilberts. But here they were and something had to be said.

"I came to apologize," he said, standing to his full six foot one. "I'm sorry I haven't made you feel more welcome. And I'm very sorry about the body."

Yes, that definitely sounded as lame as he'd feared. But he hoped it at least sounded genuine.

"Why isn't Olivier here?" Marc demanded. "You didn't do it. It's not up to you to apologize."

"Marc, really," said Dominique. "Can't you see how difficult this is for him?"

"No, I can't. Olivier probably sent him hoping we won't sue. Or won't tell everyone what a psycho he is."

"Olivier's not a psycho," said Gabri, feeling a kind of trill inside as his patience unraveled. "He's a wonderful man. You don't know him."

"You're the one who doesn't know him if you think he's wonderful. Does a wonderful man dump a body at a neighbor's home?"

"You tell me."

The two men advanced on each other.

"I didn't take the body into a private home to scare the occupants half to death. That was a terrible thing to do."

"Olivier was pushed to it. He tried to make friends when you first arrived but then you tried to steal our staff and open this huge hotel and spa."

"Ten guest rooms isn't huge," said Dominique.

"Not in Montreal, but out here it is. This's a small village. We've been here for a long time living quietly. You come here and change all that. Made no effort to fit in."

"By 'fit in' you mean tug our forelocks and be grateful you've allowed us to live here?" Marc demanded.

"No, I mean being respectful of what's here already. What people've worked hard to establish."

"You want to raise the drawbridge, don't you?" said Marc in disgust. "You're in and you want to keep everyone else out."

"That's not true. Most of the people in Three Pines have come from somewhere else."

"But you only accept people who follow your rules. Who do as you say. We came here to live our dream and you won't let us. Why? Because it clashes with yours. You're threatened by us and so you need to run us out of town. You're nothing but bullies, with big smiles."

Marc was almost spitting.

Gabri stared at him, amazed. "But you didn't really expect us to be happy about it, did you? Why would you come here and deliberately upset people who were going to be your neighbors? Didn't you want us as friends? You must've known how Olivier would react."

"What? That he'd put a body in our home?"

"That was wrong. I've already said that. But you provoked him. All of us. We wanted to be your friends but you made it too difficult."

"So, you'll be friends with us as long as what? We're just a modest success? Have a few guests, a couple of treatments a day? Maybe a small dining room, if we're lucky? But nothing to compete with you and Olivier?"

"That's right," said Gabri.

That shut Marc up.

"Listen, why do you think we don't make croissants?" Gabri continued. "Or pies? Or any baking? We could. It's what I love to do. But Sarah's Boulangerie was already here. She'd lived in the village all her life. The bakery belonged to her grandmother. So we opened a bistro instead. All our croissants, and pies, and breads are baked by Sarah. We adjusted our dreams to fit the dreams already here. It'd be cheaper and more fun to bake ourselves but that's not the point."

"What is the point?" asked Vincent Gilbert, speaking for the first time.

"The point isn't to make a fortune," said Gabri, turning to him gratefully. "The point is to know what's enough. To be happy."

There was a pause and Gabri silently thanked the saint for creating that space for reason to return.

"Maybe you should remind your partner of that," said Vincent Gilbert. "You talk a good line but you don't live it. It suits you to blame my son. You dress up your behavior as moral and kindly and loving, but you know what it is?"

Vincent Gilbert was advancing, closing in on Gabri. As he neared he seemed to grow and Gabri felt himself shrink.

"It's selfish," Gilbert hissed. "My son has been patient. He's hired local workers, created jobs. This is a place of healing, and you not only try to ruin it, you try to make him out to be at fault."

Vincent stepped next to his son, having finally found the price of belonging.

There was nothing more to say, so Gabri left.

Lights glowed at windows as he made his way back into the village. Overhead ducks flew south in their V formation, away from the killing cold that was gathering and preparing to descend. Gabri sat on a tree stump by the side of the road and watched the sun set over Three Pines and thought about *les temps perdus* and felt very alone, without even the certainty of saints for comfort.

A beer was placed on the table for Beauvoir and Gamache nursed his Scotch. They settled into their comfortable chairs and examined the dinner menu. The bistro was deserted. Peter, Clara, Myrna and Ruth had all gone and Olivier had retreated to his kitchen. Havoc, the last of the waiters, took their order then left them to talk.

Gamache broke up a small baguette and told his second in command about his conversation with Olivier.

"So, he still says the Hermit was Czech. Do you believe him?"

"I do," said Gamache. "At least, I believe Olivier is convinced of it. Any luck with the Caesar's Shift?"

"None." They'd given up when they started putting their own names in. Both slightly relieved it didn't work.

"What's wrong?" Gamache asked. Beauvoir had leaned back in his seat and tossed his linen napkin onto the table.

"I'm just frustrated. It seems every time we make progress it gets all muddied. We still don't even know who the dead man was."

Gamache smiled. It was their regular predicament. The further into a case they went the more clues they gathered. There came a time when it seemed a howl, as though they had hold of something wild that screamed clues at them. It was, Gamache knew, the shriek of something cornered and frightened. They were entering the last stages of this investigation. Soon the clues, the pieces, would stop fighting, and start betraying the murderer. They were close.

"By the way, I'm going away tomorrow," said the Chief Inspector after Havoc brought their appetizers and left.

"Back to Montreal?" Beauvoir took a forkful of chargrilled calamari while Gamache ate his pear and prosciutto.

"A little further than that. The Queen Charlotte Islands."

"Are you kidding? In British Columbia? Up by Alaska? Because of a monkey named Woo?"

"Well, when you put it like that . . ."

Beauvoir speared a blackened piece of calamari and dipped it in garlic sauce. "*Voyons*, doesn't it strike you as, well, extreme?"

"No, it doesn't. The name Charlotte keeps repeating." Gamache ticked the points off on his fingers. "The Charlotte Brontë first edition, *Charlotte's Web* first edition, the Amber Room panel? Made for a princess named Charlotte. The note the Hermit kept about the violin was written by a Charlotte. I've been trying to figure out what they could all mean, this repetition of the name Charlotte, then this afternoon Superintendent Brunel gave me the answer. The Queen Charlotte Islands. Where Emily Carr painted. Where the wood for the carvings came from. It might be a dead end, but I'd be a fool not to follow this lead."

"But who's doing the leading? You or the murderer? I think they're leading you away. I think the murderer is here, in Three Pines."

"So do I, but I think the murder began on the Queen Charlotte Islands."

Beauvoir huffed, exasperated. "You're taking a bunch of clues and putting them together to suit your purpose."

"What are you suggesting?"

Beauvoir needed to watch himself now. Chief Inspector Gamache was more than his superior. They had a relationship that went deeper than any other Beauvoir had. And he knew Gamache's patience had its limits.

"I think you see what you want to see. You see things that aren't really there."

"You mean just aren't visible."

"No, I mean aren't there. To leap to one conclusion isn't the end of the world, but you're leaping all over the place and where does it take you? The end of the fucking world. Sir."

Beauvoir glanced out the window, trying to cool down. Havoc removed their plates and Beauvoir waited for him to leave before continuing. "I know you love history and literature and art and that the Hermit's cabin must seem like a candy shop, but I think you're seeing a whole lot more in this case than exists. I think you're complicating it. You know I'd follow you anywhere, we all would. You just point, and I'm there. I trust you that much. But even you can make mistakes. You always say that murder is, at its core, very simple. It's about an emotion. That emotion is here, and so's the murderer. We have plenty of clues to follow without thinking about a monkey, a hunk of wood and some godforsaken island to hell and gone across the country."

"Finished?" Gamache asked.

Beauvoir sat upright and took a deep breath. "There may be more."

Gamache smiled. "I agree with you, Jean Guy, the murderer is here. Someone here knew the Hermit, and someone here killed him. You're right. When you strip away all the shiny baubles it's simple. A man ends up with antiquities worth a fortune. Perhaps he stole them. He wants to hide so he comes to this village no one knows about. But even that isn't enough. He takes it a step further and builds a cabin deep in the woods. Is he hiding from the police? Maybe. From something or someone worse? I think so. But he can't do it on his own. If nothing else he needs news. He needs eyes and ears on the outside. So he recruits Olivier."

"Why him?"

"Ruth said it tonight."

"More Scotch, asshole?"

"Well, that too. But she said Olivier was greedy. And he is. So was the Hermit. He probably recognized himself in Olivier. That greed. That need to own. And he knew he could have a hold over Olivier. Promising him more and better antiques. But over the years something happened."

"He went nuts?"

"Maybe. But maybe just the opposite. Maybe he went sane. The place he built to hide became a home, a haven. You felt it. There was something peaceful, comforting even, about the Hermit's life. It was simple. Who doesn't long for that these days?"

Their dinners arrived and Beauvoir's gloom lifted as the fragrant boeuf bourguignon landed in front of him. He looked across at the Chief Inspector smiling down at his lobster Thermidor.

"Yes, the simple life in the country." Beauvoir lifted his red wine in a small toast.

Gamache tipped his glass of white toward his Inspector, then took a succulent forkful. As he ate he thought of those first few minutes in the Hermit's cabin. And that moment when he realized what he was looking at. Treasures. And yet everything was put to purpose. There was a reason for everything in there, whether practical or pleasure, like the books and violin.

But there was one thing. One thing that didn't seem to have a purpose.

Gamache slowly laid his fork down and stared beyond Beauvoir. After a moment the Inspector also put his fork down and looked behind him. There was nothing there. Just the empty room.

"What is it?"

Gamache put up a finger, a subtle and gentle request for quiet. Then he reached into his breast pocket and bringing out a pen and notebook he wrote something down, quickly, as though afraid it would get away. Beauvoir strained to read it. Then, with a thrill, saw what it was.

The alphabet.

Silently he watched his Chief write the line beneath. His face opened in wonder. Wonder that he could have been so stupid. Could have missed what now seemed obvious.

Beneath the alphabet, Chief Inspector Gamache had written: SIX-TEEN.

"The number above the door," whispered Beauvoir, as though he too was afraid he might scare this vital clue away.

"What were the code letters?" asked Gamache, in a hurry now. Anxious to get there.

Beauvoir scrambled in his pocket and brought out his notebook.

"MRKBVYDDO under the people on the shore. And OWSVI under the ship."

He watched as Gamache worked to decode the Hermit's messages.

```
A B C D E F G H I J K L M N O P Q R S T U V W X Y Z
S I X T E E N A B C D E F G H I J K L M N O P Q R S
```

Gamache read the letters out as he found them. "T, Y, R, I, some-thing . . ."

"Tyri," Beauvoir mumbled. "Tyri . . ."

"Something, K, K, V." He looked up at Beauvoir.

"What does it mean? Is it a name? Maybe a Czech name?"

"Maybe it's an anagram," said Gamache. "We have to rearrange the letters."

They tried that for a few minutes, taking bites of their dinner as they worked. Finally Gamache put his pen down and shook his head. "I thought I had it."

"Maybe it's right," said Beauvoir, not ready to let go yet. He jotted more letters, tried the other code. Rearranged letters and finally staggered to the same conclusion.

The key wasn't "sixteen."

"Still," said Beauvoir, dipping a crusty baguette into his gravy, "I wonder why that number's up there."

"Maybe some things don't need a purpose," said Gamache. "Maybe that's their purpose."

But that was too esoteric for Beauvoir. As was the Chief Inspector's reasoning about the Queen Charlotte Islands. In fact, Beauvoir wouldn't call it reasoning at all. At best it was intuition on the Chief's part, at worst it was a wild guess, maybe even manipulated by the murderer.

The only image Beauvoir had of the moody archipelago at the very end of the country was of thick forests and mountains and endless gray water. But mostly it was mist.

And into that mist Armand Gamache was going, alone.

"I almost forgot, Ruth Zardo gave me this." Gamache handed him the slip of paper. Beauvoir unfolded it and read out loud.

"and pick your soul up gently by the nape of the neck
and caress you into darkness and paradise."

There was, at least, a full stop after "paradise." Was this, finally, the end?

THIRTY-TWO

~

Armand Gamache arrived in the late afternoon on the brooding islands after taking increasingly smaller planes until it seemed the last was nothing more than fuselage wrapped round his body and thrust off the end of the Prince Rupert runway.

As the tiny float plane flew over the archipelago off the coast of northern British Columbia Gamache looked down on a landscape of mountains and thick ancient forests. It had been hidden for millennia behind mists almost as impenetrable as the trees. It had remained isolated. But not alone. It was a cauldron of life that had produced both the largest black bears in the world and the smallest owls. It was teeming with life. Indeed, the first men were discovered in a giant clam shell by a raven off the tip of one of the islands. That, according to their creation stories, was how the Haida came to live there. More recently loggers had also been found on the islands. That wasn't part of creation. They'd looked beyond the thick mists and seen money. They'd arrived on the Charlottes a century ago, blind to the crucible they'd stumbled upon and seeing only treasure. The ancient forests of red cedar. Trees prized for their durability, having been tall and straight long before Queen Charlotte was born and married her mad monarch. But now they fell to the saw, to be made into shingles and decks and siding. And ten small carvings.

After landing smoothly on the water the young bush pilot helped extricate the large man from her small plane.

"Welcome to Haida Gwaii," she said.

When Gamache had woken early that morning in Three Pines and found a groggy Gabri in the kitchen making a small picnic for the drive to the Montreal airport, he knew nothing about these islands half a world away. But on the long flights from Montreal to Vancouver, to Prince Rupert and into the village of Queen Charlotte, he'd read about the islands and he knew that phrase.

"Thank you for bringing me to your homeland."

The pilot's deep brown eyes were suspicious, as well they would be, thought Gamache. The arrival of yet another middle-aged white man in a suit was never a good sign. You didn't have to be Haida to know that.

"You must be Chief Inspector Gamache."

A burly man with black hair and skin the color of cedar was walking across the dock, his hand out. They shook.

"I'm Sergeant Minshall, of the RCMP. We've been corresponding."

His voice was deep and had a slight sing-song quality. He was Haida.

"*Ah, oui, merci.* Thank you for meeting the plane."

The Mountie took the overnight bag from the pilot and slung it over his shoulder. Thanking the pilot, who ignored them, the two men walked to the end of the dock, up a ramp and along the road. There was a bite to the air and Gamache had to remember they were closer to Alaska than Vancouver.

"I see you're not staying long."

Gamache looked out into the ocean and knew the mainland had disappeared. No, it was not that it had vanished, but that it didn't exist at all here. This was the mainland.

"I wish I could stay longer, it's beautiful. But I have to get back."

"Right. I've arranged a room for you at the lodge. I think you'll enjoy it. There aren't many people on the Queen Charlottes, as you probably know. Maybe five thousand, with half being Haida and half," he hesitated slightly, "not. We get quite a few tourists, but the season's ending."

The two men had slowed and now they stopped. They'd walked by a hardware store, a coffee shop, a little building with a mermaid out front. But it was the harbor that drew Gamache's attention. He'd never seen such scenery in all his life, and he'd seen some spectacularly beautiful places in Quebec. But none, he had to admit, came close to this.

It was wilderness. As far as he could see there were mountains rising from the water, covered in dark forest. He could see an island and fishing boats. Overhead, eagles soared. The men walked onto the beach, which was covered in pebbles and shells, and stood silent for a few minutes, listening to the birds and the lapping water and smelling the air with that combination of seaweed and fish and forest.

"There're more eagle nests here than anywhere else in Canada, you know. It's a sign of good luck."

It wasn't often an RCMP officer spoke of signs, unless it was traffic signs. Gamache didn't turn to look at the man, he was too taken by the view, but he listened.

"The Haida have two clans. The Eagle and the Raven. I've arranged for you to meet with elders from both clans. They've invited you for dinner."

"Thank you. Will you be there?"

Sergeant Minshall smiled. "No. I thought it'd be more comfortable without me. The Haida are very warm people, you know. They've lived here for thousands of years, undisturbed. Until recently."

It was interesting, Gamache thought, that he referred to the Haida as "they" not "we." Perhaps it was for Gamache's benefit, so he didn't appear biased.

"I'll try not to disturb them tonight."

"It's too late."

Armand Gamache showered, shaved and wiped the vapor from the mirror. It was as though the mist that hung over the ancient forests had crept into his room. Perhaps to watch him. To divine his intentions.

He made a small hole in the moisture and saw a very tired Sûreté officer, far from home.

Changing into a fresh shirt and dark slacks he picked out a tie and sat on the side of the double bed, which was covered in what looked like a hand-stitched quilt.

The room was simple and clean and comfortable. But it could be filled with turnips and it wouldn't matter. All anyone would notice was the view. It looked directly over the bay. The sunset filled the sky with gold and purples and reds, undulating and shifting. Alive. Everything seemed alive here.

He gravitated to the window and stared while his hands tied his green silk tie. There was a knock on the door. He opened it, expecting the landlady or Sergeant Minshall, and was surprised to see the young bush pilot.

"Noni, my great-grandmother, asked me to bring you to dinner."

She still didn't smile. In fact, she seemed singularly unhappy about the fact. He put on a gray jacket and his coat and they walked into the darkening night. Lights were on in the homes that hugged the harbor. The air was cold and damp, but fresh, and it woke him up so that he felt more alert than he had all afternoon. They climbed into an old pickup truck and headed out of town.

"So you're from the Charlottes?"

"I'm from Haida Gwaii," she said.

"Of course, I'm sorry. Are you with the Eagle clan?"

"Raven."

"Ah," said Gamache, and realized he sounded slightly ridiculous, but the young woman beside him didn't seem to care. She seemed more interested in ignoring him completely.

"Your family must be very pleased you're a pilot."

"Why?"

"Well, flying."

"Because I'm a Raven? Everyone here flies, Chief Inspector. I just need more help."

"Have you been a pilot long?"

There was silence then. Evidently his question wasn't worth answering. And he had to agree. Silence was better. His eyes adjusted to the night and he was able to make out the line of mountains across the bay as they drove. After a few minutes they arrived at another village. The young pilot stopped the pickup in front of a nondescript white building that had a sign out front. *Skidegate Community Hall.* She got out and walked to the door, never looking back to see if he was following. She either trusted he was there or, more likely, didn't care.

He left the twilit harbor and followed her through the door into the Community Hall. And into an opera house. Gamache turned round to make sure there was a door there and he hadn't, magically, emerged into another world. They were surrounded by ornate balconies on three sides. Gamache did a slow 360, his feet squeaking a little on the polished wood floor. Only then did he realize his mouth was slightly open. He closed it and looked at the young woman beside him.

"*Mais, c'est extraordinaire.*"

"*Haw'aa.*"

Wide, gracious staircases led up to the balconies and at the far end of the room was a stage. Behind it a mural had been painted on the wall.

"That's a Haida village," she said, nodding toward it.

"*Incroyable*," whispered Gamache. The Chief Inspector was often surprised, astonished, by life. But he was rarely dumbfounded. He was now.

"Do you like it?"

Gamache looked down and realized they'd been joined by another woman, much older than his companion or himself. And unlike his companion this woman smiled. It looked, by the ease of it, as though she found a lot of humor in life.

"Very much." He put out his hand, and she took it.

"This is my noni," said the pilot.

"Esther," she said.

"Armand Gamache," said the Chief, bowing slightly. "It's an honor."

"The honor is mine, Chief Inspector. Please." She motioned into the center of the room where a long table had been set. There was a rich aroma of cooked food, and the room was filled with people talking, greeting, calling to each other. And laughing.

He'd expected the gathering of Haida elders to be in traditional garb. He was embarrassed now by that cliché. Instead the men and women were dressed as they'd come from work, some in T-shirts and heavy sweaters, some in suits. Some worked in the bank, the school, the clinic; some worked on the cold waters. Some were artists. Painters, but mostly carvers.

"This is a matrilineal society, Chief Inspector," Esther explained. "But most of the chiefs are men. Though that doesn't mean women are powerless. Quite the opposite."

She looked at him, her eyes clear. It was a simple statement. Not a boast.

She then introduced him to everyone, one by one. He repeated their names and tried to keep them straight, though he was frankly lost after half a dozen. Finally Esther took him over to the buffet table, where food had been put out.

"This is Skaay," she said, introducing a tiny old man who looked up from his plate. His eyes were milky, blind. "Of the Eagle clan."

"Robert, if you prefer," Skaay said, his voice strong and his grip stronger. He smiled. "The women of both clans have done a traditional Haida feast for you, Chief Inspector." The blind man led Gamache down the long table, naming each dish. "This is *k'aaw*. It's herring roe on kelp. This over here is pepper-smoked salmon, or if you prefer there's wood-smoked salmon over there. Caught this morning by Reg. He spent the day smoking it. For you."

They walked slowly the length of the buffet. Octopus balls, crab cakes, halibut. Potato salad; fresh bread, still warm. Juices and water. No alcohol.

"We have dances here. This is where most people have their wedding parties. And funerals. So many dinners. When the Eagle clan is hosting the Raven clan serves. And vice versa, of course. But tonight we're all hosting. And you're our honored guest."

Gamache, who'd been to state dinners in grand palaces, banquets given for him, awards presentations, had rarely felt so honored.

He took a helping of everything and sat down. To his surprise, the young pilot joined him. Over dinner they all talked, but he noticed the Haida elders asked more questions than they answered. They were interested in his work, his life, his family. They asked about Quebec. They were informed and thoughtful. Kind, and guarded.

Over cake, fresh bumbleberries and Cool Whip, Gamache told them about the murder. The Hermit in the cabin buried deep in the forest. The elders, always attentive, grew even more still as he told them about the man, surrounded by treasure, but alone. A man whose life had been taken, his goods left behind. A man with no name, surrounded by history, but with none himself.

"Was he happy, do you think?" Esther asked. It was almost impossible to figure out if there was a leader of this group, by election or mutual consent. But Gamache guessed if there was one, it would be her.

He hesitated. He hadn't actually asked himself that question.

Was the Hermit happy?

"I think he was content. He led a small, peaceful life. One that appeals to me."

The young pilot turned to look at him. Up until that moment she'd been looking straight ahead.

"He was surrounded by beauty," continued Gamache. "And he had company every now and then. Someone who'd bring him what he couldn't provide for himself. But he was afraid."

"Hard to be both happy and afraid," said Esther. "But fear can lead to courage."

"And courage can lead to peace," said a young man in a suit.

It reminded Gamache of what the fisherman had written on the wall of the diner in Mutton Bay a few years earlier. He'd looked at Gamache across the room and smiled so fully it had taken the Chief Inspector's breath away. Then the fisherman had scribbled something on the wall and left. Gamache had gone to the wall, and read:

> *Where there is love there is courage,*
> *where there is courage there is peace,*
> *where there is peace there is God.*
> *And when you have God, you have everything.*

Gamache spoke the words, and then there was silence in the hall. The Haida were good at silence. And so was Gamache.

"Is that a prayer?" Esther finally asked.

"A fisherman wrote it on a wall in a place called Mutton Bay, a long way off."

"Perhaps not so far," said Esther.

"A fisherman?" asked the man in the suit, with a smile. "Figures. They're all crazy."

An older man beside him, dressed in a thick sweater, gave him a swat and they laughed.

"We're all fishermen," said Esther, and Gamache had the feeling she was including him. She thought for a moment then asked, "What did your Hermit love?"

Gamache thought about that. "I don't know."

"Perhaps when you do, you'll find his killer. How can we help?"

"There were a couple of references to Woo and Charlotte in the Hermit's cabin. They led me to Emily Carr, and she led me here."

"Well, you're far from the first," an elderly man said with a laugh. It wasn't a smug or derisive laugh. "Her paintings have been bringing people to Haida Gwaii for years."

It was hard to tell if that was considered a good thing.

"I think the Hermit was on the Queen Charlotte Islands, maybe fifteen or more years ago. We think he was Czech. He'd have spoken with an accent."

Gamache brought out the photographs, taken at the morgue. He'd warned them what they'd see but he wasn't worried. These were people who lived comfortably with life and death in a place where the line was blurred, and people, animals, and spirits walked together. Where blind men saw and everyone had the gift of flight.

Over strong tea they looked at the dead man. They looked long and hard. Even the young pilot gave the photographs her attention.

And as they looked at the photos, Gamache looked at them. To see a flicker of recognition. A twitch, a change in breathing. He became hyperaware of every one of them. But all he saw were people trying to help.

"We've disappointed you, I'm afraid," said Esther as Gamache put the pictures back in his satchel. "Why didn't you just e-mail them to us?"

"Well, I e-mailed them to Sergeant Minshall and he circulated them among the police, but I wanted to be here myself. And there's something I couldn't e-mail. Something I brought with me."

He put the two balls of towel on the table and carefully unwrapped the first.

Not a spoon clinked against a mug, not a creamer was popped, peeled and opened, not a breath. It was as though something else had joined them then. As though silence had taken a seat.

He gently unwrapped the next one. And it sailed across the table to join its sibling.

"There're others. Eight we think."

If they heard him they gave no indication. Then one man, middle-aged and stocky, reached out. Stopping, he looked at Gamache.

"May I?"

"Please."

He picked it up and in large, worn hands he held the sailing ship. He lifted it to his face so that he was staring into the eyes of the tiny men and women who were looking ahead with such pleasure, such joy.

"That's Haawasti," whispered the bush pilot. "Will Sommes."

"That's Will Sommes?" Gamache asked. He'd read about this man. He was one of Canada's greatest living artists. His Haida carvings were bursting with life and snapped up by private collectors and museums worldwide. He'd assumed Sommes was a recluse, having grown so famous surely he'd be in hiding. But the Chief Inspector was beginning to appreciate that on Haida Gwaii legends came alive, walked among them, and sometimes sipped black tea and ate Cool Whip.

Sommes picked up the other piece and turned it round and round. "Red cedar."

"From here," confirmed Gamache.

Sommes looked under the sailing ship. "Is that a signature?"

"Perhaps you could tell me."

"Just letters. But it must mean something."

"It seems to be in code. We haven't figured it out yet."

"The dead man made these?" Sommes held up the carving.

"He did."

Sommes looked down at what he held in his hand. "I can't tell you who he was, but I can tell you this much. Your Hermit wasn't just afraid, he was terrified."

THIRTY-THREE

Next morning Gamache awoke to a fresh, cold breeze bringing sea air and the shriek of feeding birds through his open window. He turned over in bed and, drawing the warm quilt around him, he stared out the window. The day before had seemed a dream. To wake up in Three Pines and go to sleep in this Haida village beside the ocean.

The sky was brilliant blue and he could see eagles and seagulls gliding. Getting out of bed he quickly put on his warmest clothing and cursed himself for forgetting his long underwear.

Downstairs he found a full breakfast of bacon, eggs, toast and strong coffee.

"Lavina called and said to be at the dock by nine or she was leaving without you."

Gamache looked round to see who the landlady was talking to.

He was alone in the room. "*Moi?*"

"Yes you. Lavina said don't be late."

Gamache looked at his watch. It was half past eight and he had no idea who Lavina was, where the dock was, or why he should go. He had one more cup of coffee, went to his room to use the washroom and get his coat and hat, then came back down to speak to the landlady.

"Did Lavina say which dock?"

"I suppose it's the one she always uses. Can't miss it."

How often had Gamache heard that, just before missing it? Still, he stood on the porch and taking a deep breath of bracing air he surveyed the coastline. There were several docks.

But at only one was there a seaplane. And the young bush pilot look-

ing at her watch. Was her name Lavina? To his embarrassment he realized he'd never asked her.

He walked over and as his feet hit the wooden boards of the dock he
saw she wasn't alone. Will Sommes was with her.

"Thought you'd like to see where those pieces of wood came from,"
the carver said, inviting Gamache into the small pontoon plane. "My
granddaughter's agreed to fly us. The plane you came in on yesterday's
a commercial flight. This is her own."

"I have a granddaughter too," said Gamache, looking he hoped not
too frantically for the seat belt as the plane pushed off from the wharf
and headed into the sound. "And another on the way. My granddaughter
makes me finger paintings."

He almost added that at least a finger painting wasn't likely to kill
you, but he thought that would be ungracious.

The plane gathered speed and began bouncing off the small waves. It
was then Gamache noticed the torn canvas straps inside the plane, the
rusting seats, the ripped cushions. He looked out the window and
wished he hadn't had that full breakfast.

Then they were airborne and banking to the left they climbed into
the sky and headed down the coastline. For forty minutes they flew. It
was too noisy inside the tiny cabin to do anything other than yell at
each other. Every now and then Sommes would lean over and point
something out. He'd gesture down to a small bay and say things like,
"That's where man first appeared, in the clam shell. It's our Garden of
Eden." Or a little later, "Look down. Those are the last virgin red ce-
dars in existence, the last ancient forest."

Gamache had an eagle's-eye view of this world. He looked down on
rivers and inlets and forest and mountains carved by glaciers. Eventually they descended into a bay whose peaks were shrouded in mist even
on this clear day. As they got lower and skimmed over the water toward
the dark shoreline Will Sommes leaned in to Gamache again and
shouted, "Welcome to Gwaii Haanas. The place of wonders."

And it was.

Lavina got them as close as she could then a man appeared on the
shore and shoved a boat out, leaping into it at the last moment. At the
door to the seaplane he held out his hand to help the Chief Inspector
into the tippy boat and introduced himself.

"My name's John. I'm the Watchman."

Gamache noticed he was barefooted, and saw Lavina and her grand-father taking their shoes and socks off and rolling up their cuffs as John rowed. Gamache soon saw why. The boat could only get so close. They'd have to walk the last ten feet. He removed his shoes and socks, rolled up his pants and climbed over the side. Almost. As soon as his big toe touched the water it, and he, recoiled. Ahead of him he saw Lavina and Sommes smile.

"It is cold," admitted the Watchman.

"Oh, come on, princess, suck it up," said Lavina. Gamache wondered if she was channeling Ruth Zardo. Was there one in every pack?

Gamache sucked it up and joined them on the beach, his feet purple from just a minute in the water. He nimbly walked over the stones to a stump and, sitting down, he rubbed the dirt and shards of shell from his soles and put his socks and shoes back on. He couldn't remember the last time he felt such relief. Actually, when the pontoon plane landed was probably the last time.

He'd been so struck by the surroundings, by the Watchman, by the frigid water, he'd failed to see what was actually there. Now he saw. Standing on the very edge of the forest was a solemn semicircle of totem poles.

Gamache felt all his blood rush to his core, his center.

"This is Ninstints," whispered Will Sommes.

Gamache didn't answer. He couldn't. He stared at the tall poles into which was carved the Mythtime, that marriage of animals and spirits. Killer whales, sharks, wolves, bears, eagles and crows were all staring back at him. And something else. Things with long tongues and huge eyes, and teeth. Creatures unknown outside the Mythtime, but very real here.

Gamache had the feeling he was standing at the very edge of memory.

Some totem poles were straight and tall, but most had tumbled over or were lurching sideways.

"We are all fishermen," said Will. "Esther was right. The sea feeds our bodies, but that feeds our souls." He opened his hands in a simple, small gesture toward the forest.

John the Watchman spoke softly as they picked their way among the totem poles.

"This is the largest collection of standing totem poles in the world.

The site's now protected, but it wasn't always. Some poles commemorate a special event, some are mortuary poles. Each tells a story. The images build on each other and are in a specific and intentional order."

"This is where Emily Carr did much of her painting," said Gamache.

"I thought you'd like to see it," said Sommes.

"*Merci*. I'm very grateful to you."

"This settlement was the last to fall. It was the most isolated, and perhaps the most ornery," said John. "But eventually it collapsed too. A tidal wave of disease, alcohol and missionaries finally washed over this place, as it had all the others. The totems were torn down, the longhouses destroyed. That's what's left." He pointed to a bump in the forest, covered by moss. "That was a longhouse."

For an hour Armand Gamache wandered the site. He was allowed to touch the totems and he found himself reaching high and placing his large, certain hand on the magnificent faces, trying to feel whoever had carved such a creature.

Eventually he walked over to John, who'd spent that hour standing in one spot, watching.

"I'm here investigating a murder. May I show you a couple of things?"

John nodded.

"The first is a photograph of the dead man. I think he might have spent time on Haida Gwaii, though I think he'd have called them the Charlottes."

"Then he wasn't Haida."

"No, I don't think he was." Gamache showed John the picture.

He took it and studied it carefully. "I'm sorry, I don't know him."

"It would have been a while ago. Fifteen, maybe twenty years."

"That was a difficult time. There were a lot of people here. It was when the Haida finally stopped the logging companies, by blocking the roads. He might have been a logger."

"He might have been. He certainly seemed comfortable in a forest. And he built himself a log cabin. Who here could teach him that?"

"Are you kidding?"

"No."

"Just about anyone. Most Haida live in villages now, but almost all of us have cabins in the woods. Ones we built ourselves, or our parents built."

"Do you live in a cabin?"

Did John hesitate? "No, I have a room at the Holiday Inn Ninstints," he laughed. "Yes. I built my own cabin a few years ago. Want to see it?"

"If you don't mind."

While Will Sommes and his granddaughter wandered around, John the Watchman took Gamache deeper into the forest. "Some of these trees are more than a thousand years old, you know."

"Worth saving," said Gamache.

"Not all would agree." He stopped and pointed. To a small cabin, in the forest, with a porch, and one rocking chair.

The image of the Hermit's.

"Did you know him, John?" asked Gamache, suddenly very aware he was alone in the woods with a powerful man.

"The dead man?"

Gamache nodded.

John smiled again. "No." But he'd come very close to Gamache.

"Did you teach him to build a log cabin?"

"No."

"Did you teach him to carve?"

"No."

"Would you tell me if you had?"

"I have nothing to fear from you. Nothing to hide."

"Then why are you here, all alone?"

"Why are you?" John's voice was barely a whisper, a hiss.

Gamache unwrapped a carving. John stared at the men and women in the boat and backed away.

"It's made from red cedar. From Haida Gwaii," said Gamache. "Perhaps even from these trees in this forest. The murdered man made it."

"That means nothing to me," said John and with a last glance at the carving he walked away.

Gamache followed him out and found Will Sommes on the beach, smiling.

"Have a nice talk with John?"

"He hadn't much to say."

"He's a Watchman, not a Chatter."

Gamache smiled and started rewrapping the carving, but Sommes touched his hand to stop him and took the carving once again.

"You say it's from here. Is it old growth?"

"We don't know. The scientists can't say. They'd have to destroy the carving to get a big enough sample and I wouldn't let them."

"This is worth more than a man's life?" Sommes held the carving up.

"Few things are worth more than a man's life, monsieur. But that life has already been lost. I'm hoping to find who did it without destroying his creation as well."

This seemed to satisfy Sommes, who handed the carving back, but reluctantly.

"I'd like to have met the man who did that. He was gifted."

"He might have been a logger. Might have helped cut down your forests."

"Many in my family were loggers. It happens. Doesn't make them bad men or lifelong enemies."

"Do you teach other artists?" Gamache asked, casually.

"You think maybe he came here to talk to me?" asked Sommes.

"I think he came here. And he's a carver."

"First he was a logger, now he's a carver. Which is it, Chief Inspector?"

It was said with humor, but the criticism wasn't lost on Gamache. He was fishing, and he knew it. So did Sommes. So did Esther. We're all fishermen, she'd said.

Had he found anything on this visit? Gamache was beginning to doubt it.

"Do you teach carving?" he persisted.

Sommes shook his head. "Only to other Haida."

"The Hermit used wood from here. Does that surprise you?"

"Not at all. Some stands are now protected, but we've agreed on areas that can be logged. And replanted. It's a good industry, if managed properly. And young trees are great for the ecosystem. I advise all wood carvers to use red cedar."

"We should be going. The weather's changing," said Lavina.

As the float plane took off and banked away from the sheltered bay Gamache looked down. It appeared as though one of the totem poles had come alive, and waved. But then he recognized it as John, who guarded the haunting place but had been afraid of the small piece of wood in Gamache's hand. John, who'd placed himself beyond the pale.

"He was involved in the logging dispute, you know," Sommes shouted over the old engine.

"Seems a good person to have on your side."

"And he was. On your side, I mean. John was a Mountie. He was forced to arrest his own grandmother. I can still see him as he led her away."

"John's my uncle," Lavina shouted from the cockpit. It took Gamache a moment to put it all together. The quiet, somber, solitary man he'd met, the man who watched their plane fly away, had arrested Esther.

"And now he's a Watchman, guarding the last of the totem poles," said Gamache.

"We all guard something," said Sommes.

Sergeant Minshall had left a message for him at the guesthouse, and an envelope. Over a lunch of fresh fish and canned corn, he opened it and drew out more photographs, printed from the sergeant's computer. And there was an e-mail.

Armand,

We've tracked down four of the remaining carvings. There are two we still can't find, the one Olivier sold on eBay and one of the ones auctioned in Geneva. None of the collectors has agreed to send us the actual work of art, but they did send photos (see attached). No other carving has printing underneath.

Jérôme continues to work on your code. No luck yet.

What do you make of these pictures? Quite shocking, don't you think?

I've been working on the items from the cabin. So far none has been re-ported stolen and I can't seem to find a connection among them. I thought a gold bracelet might be Czech, but turns out to be Dacian. An astonishing find. Predates the current Romanians.

But it's very odd. The items don't seem to be related. Unless that's the key? Will have to think about it some more. I'm trying to keep the lid on these finds, but already I'm getting calls from around the world. News agencies, museums. Can't imagine how the word spread, but it has. Mostly about the Amber Room. Wait until they find out about the rest.

I hear you're on the Queen Charlotte Islands. Lucky man. If you meet Will Sommes tell him I adore his work. He's a recluse, so I doubt you'll see him.

Thérèse Brunel

He pulled out the photographs and looked at them as he ate. By the time the coconut cream pie arrived he'd been over them all. He'd laid them out on the table in a fan in front of him. And now he stared.

The tone of them had shifted. In one the figures seemed to be loading up carts, packing their homes. They seemed excited. Except the young man, who was gesturing anxiously to them to hurry. But in the next there seemed a growing unease among the people. And the last two were very different. In one the people were no longer walking. They were in huts, homes. But a few figures looked out the windows. Wary. Not afraid. Not yet. That was saved for the very last one Superintendent Brunel sent. It was the largest carving and the figures were standing and staring. Up. At Gamache, it seemed.

It was the oddest perspective. It made the viewer feel like part of the work. And not a pleasant part. He felt as though he was the reason they were so afraid.

Because they were, now. What had Will Sommes said the night before, when he'd spotted the boy huddled inside the ship?

Not just afraid, but terrified.

Something terrible had found the people in his carvings. And something terrible had found their creator.

What was odd was that Gamache couldn't see the boy in the last two carvings. He asked the landlady for a magnifying glass and feeling like Sherlock Holmes he leaned over and minutely examined the photographs. But nothing.

Leaning back in his chair he sipped his tea. The coconut cream pie remained untouched. Whatever terror had taken the happiness from the carvings had also stolen his appetite.

Sergeant Minshall joined him a few minutes later and they walked once more through town, stopping at Greeley's Construction.

"What can I do for you?" An older man, beard and hair and eyes all gray, but his body green and powerful.

"We wanted to talk to you about some of the workers you might've had back in the eighties and early nineties," said Sergeant Minshall.

"You're kidding. You know loggers. They come and go. Especially then."

"Why especially then, monsieur?" asked Gamache.

"This is Chief Inspector Gamache, of the Sûreté du Québec." Minshall introduced the men and they shook hands. Gamache had the definite impression that Greeley wasn't a man to be crossed.

"Long way from home," said Greeley.

"I am. But I'm being made to feel most welcome. What was so special about that time?"

"The late eighties and early nineties? Are you kidding? Ever heard of Lyall Island? The roadblocks, the protests? There're thousands of acres of forest and the Haida suddenly get all upset about the logging. You didn't hear about it?"

"I did, but I wasn't here. Maybe you can tell me what happened."

"It wasn't the Haida's fault. They were wound up by the shit-disturbers. Those über-environmentalists. Terrorists, nothing more. They recruited a bunch of thugs and kids who just wanted attention. It had nothing to do with the forests. Listen, it wasn't like we were killing people, or even killing animals. We were taking down trees. Which grow back. And we were the biggest employer around. But the environmentalists got the Haida all worked up. Fed the kids a bunch of bullshit."

Beside Gamache, Sergeant Minshall shifted his feet. But said nothing.

"And yet the average age of the arrested Haida was seventy-six," said Gamache. "The elders placed themselves between the young protesters and you."

"A stunt. Means nothing," Greeley snapped. "I thought you said you didn't know anything about it."

"I said I wasn't here. I've read the reports, but it's not the same thing."

"Fucking right. Media swallowed it whole. We looked like the bad guys and all we were trying to do was log a few hundred acres that we had a right to."

Greeley's voice was rising. The wound, the rage, wasn't far beneath the surface.

"There was violence?" asked Gamache.

"Some. Bound to be. But we never started it. We just wanted to do our jobs."

"A lot of people came and went at that time? Loggers and protesters, I suppose."

"People crawling all over the place. And you want help finding one?" Greeley snorted. "What was his name?"

"I don't know." Gamache ignored the derisive laugh from Greeley and his people. Instead he showed the photo of the dead man. "He might have spoken with a Czech accent." Greeley looked at it and handed it back.

"Please look more closely," said the Chief Inspector.

The two men stared at each other for a moment.

"Perhaps if you stared at the picture instead of me, monsieur." His voice, while reasonable, was also hard.

Greeley took it back and looked longer. "Don't know him. He might've been here but who can tell? He'd have been a lot younger too, of course. Frankly he doesn't look like a logger or any forester. Too small."

It was the first helpful thing Greeley had said. Gamache glanced again at the dead recluse. Three sorts of visitors were on the Queen Charlottes in that time. Loggers, environmentalists, and artists. It seemed most likely this man was the latter. He thanked Greeley and left.

Once on the street he looked at his watch. If he could get Lavina to fly him to Prince Rupert he could still catch the red-eye to Montreal. But Gamache took a moment to make one more call.

"Monsieur Sommes?"

"Yes, Chief Inspector. Do you suspect your man might have been an eco-terrorist now?"

"*Voyons*, how did you know?"

Will Sommes laughed. "How can I help you?"

"John the Watchman showed me his cabin in the woods. Have you seen it?"

"I have."

"It's exactly the same as our dead man's home, across the country, in the woods of Quebec."

There was a pause on the line. "Monsieur Sommes?" Gamache wasn't sure if he'd lost the connection.

"I'm afraid that can't mean much. My cabin is also the same. All of them are, with very few exceptions. Sorry to disappoint you."

Gamache hung up, anything but disappointed. He knew one thing now without question. The Hermit had been on the Queen Charlotte Islands.

Chief Inspector Gamache only just managed to make the red-eye flight out of Vancouver. He squeezed into his middle seat and as soon as the plane took off the man in front put his seat all the way back until he was almost on Gamache's lap. The two people on either side each claimed an arm rest, and that left the Chief Inspector seven hours to listen to the little boy across the aisle play GI Joe.

He put on his half-moon glasses and read more about Emily Carr, her art, her travels, her "brutal telling." He stared at her paintings of the Queen Charlotte Islands, and appreciated even more the powerful, poetic images. He stared longest at her paintings of Ninstints. She'd captured it just before the fall, when the totems were tall and straight and the longhouses weren't yet covered by moss.

Flying over Winnipeg he pulled out the photographs of the Hermit's sculptures.

He looked at them, letting his mind drift. In the background the boy had developed an entire intricate story of war and attack and heroics. Gamache thought about Beauvoir back in Three Pines, hounded by an onslaught of facts, and Ruth Zardo's words. He closed his eyes and rested his head, thinking of the couplets Ruth kept sending, as though poetry was a weapon, which of course, it was. For her.

> *and pick your soul up gently by the nape of the neck*
> *and caress you into darkness and paradise.*

How beautiful was that, thought Gamache, drifting off to an uneasy sleep as Air Canada flew him home. And just as he nodded off another couplet floated up.

> *that the deity who kills for pleasure*
> *will also heal,*

By the time they were flying over Toronto Gamache knew what the carvings meant, and what he had to do next.

THIRTY-FOUR

 While Gamache had been in the mist of the Queen Charlotte Islands Clara had been in her own sort of fog. She'd spent the day circling the telephone, getting closer and closer then shooting away.

Peter watched all this from his studio. He no longer knew what he hoped would happen. That Clara would call Fortin, or not. He no longer knew what would be best. For her, for himself.

Peter stared at the picture on his easel. Picking up his brush, he dipped it in paint and approached. Determined to give it the detail people expected from his works. The complexity. The layers.

He added a single dot, then stepped back.

"Oh, God," he sighed and stared at the fresh dot on the white canvas.

Clara was once again approaching the telephone, via the refrigerator. Chocolate milk in one hand and Oreo cookies in the other she stared at the phone.

Was she being willful? Obstinate? Or was she standing up for what she believed in? Was she a hero or a bitch? Strange how often it was hard to tell.

She went into the garden and weeded without enthusiasm for a few minutes, then showered, changed, kissed Peter good-bye, got in her car and drove to Montreal. To the Galerie Fortin, to pick up her portfolio.

On the way home she made a last-minute detour, to visit Miss Emily Carr. Clara stared at the sculpture of the frumpy, eccentric woman with the horse and the dog and the monkey. And conviction in the face of a brutal telling.

Inspector Beauvoir met Gamache at Trudeau Airport.

"Any word from Superintendent Brunel?" the Chief Inspector asked as Beauvoir tossed his case into the backseat.

"She found one more carving. Some guy in Moscow has it. Won't let it out of his hands but he sent some pictures." Beauvoir handed an envelope to the Chief Inspector. "You? What did you find out?"

"Did you realize the lines Ruth's given you are all part of a single poem?"

"You found that out on the Queen Charlotte Islands?"

"Indirectly. Have you kept them?"

"The scraps of paper? Of course not. Why? Are they important to the case?"

Gamache sighed. He was weary. He had a distance to go that day and he couldn't afford a stumble. Not now.

"No. I suppose not. But it's a shame to lose them."

"Yeah, you say that. Just wait until she turns her pen on you."

" . . . *and pick your soul up gently by the nape of the neck and caress you into darkness and paradise,*" Gamache whispered.

"Where to?" Beauvoir asked as they bumped along the road toward Three Pines.

"The bistro. We need to speak to Olivier again. You looked into his finances?"

"He's worth about four million. One and a half from the sales of the carvings, a little over a million from the antiques the Hermit gave him and his property's worth about a million. We're not much further along," said Beauvoir, grimly.

But Gamache knew they were very close indeed. And he knew this was when the ground either became solid, or fell out from beneath them.

The car glided to a stop in front of the bistro. The Chief Inspector had been so quiet in the passenger seat Beauvoir thought maybe he was catching a nap. He looked tired, and who wouldn't after the long flight on Air Canada? The carrier that charged for everything. Beauvoir was convinced there'd soon be a credit card slot next to the emergency oxygen.

The Inspector looked over and sure enough Gamache's head was down and his eyes closed. Beauvoir hated to disturb him, he looked so peaceful. Then he noticed the Chief's thumb softly rubbing the picture he held loosely in his hand. Beauvoir looked more closely. The Chief's eyes weren't closed, not altogether.

They were narrow and staring intently at the image in his hand.

On it was the carving of a mountain. Barren, desolate. As though it had been clear-cut. Just a few scraggly pines at its base. There was a sadness about it, Gamache felt, an emptiness. And yet there was something about this work that was very different from the others. There was also a kind of levity. He narrowed his eyes and peering closer he saw it. What he'd mistaken for another pine at the foot of the mountain wasn't.

It was a young man. A boy, stepping hesitantly onto the base of the carving.

And where he stepped, some seedlings sprouted.

It reminded him of Clara's painting of Ruth. Capturing that moment when despair turned to hope. This remarkable carving was forlorn, but also strangely hopeful. And without needing to look any closer Gamache knew this boy was the one in the other works. But the fear was gone. Or had it not yet arrived?

Rosa quacked on the village green. Today she wore a pale pink sweater set. And pearls?

"*Voyons*," said Beauvoir, jerking his head toward the duck as they got out of the car. "Can you imagine listening to that all day long?"

"Wait till you have kids," said Gamache, pausing outside the bistro to watch Rosa and Ruth.

"They quack?"

"No, but they sure make noise. And other things. Are you planning on kids?"

"Maybe one day. Enid isn't keen." He stood next to the Chief and they both stared at the peaceful village. Peaceful except for the quacking. "Any word from Daniel?"

"Madame Gamache spoke to them yesterday. All's well. Baby should be along in a couple of weeks. We'll be going to Paris as soon as it happens."

Beauvoir nodded. "That's two for Daniel. How about Annie? Any plans?"

"None. I think David would like a family but Annie's not good with kids."

"I saw her with Florence," said Beauvoir, remembering when Daniel had visited with the Chief Inspector's granddaughter. He'd watched Annie holding her niece, singing to her. "She adores Florence."

"She claims not to want any. Frankly we don't want to push her."

"Best not to interfere."

"It's not that. We saw what a balls-up she made of every babysitting job she had as a kid. As soon as the child cried Annie called us and we'd have to go over. We made more money babysitting than she did. And Jean Guy." Gamache leaned toward his Inspector and lowered his voice. "Without going into details, whatever happens never let Annie diaper me."

"She asked the same thing of me," Beauvoir said and saw Gamache smile. Then the smile dimmed.

"Shall we?" The Chief gestured to the door to the bistro.

The four men chose to sit away from the windows. In the cool and quiet interior. A small fire muttered in both open fireplaces, at either end of the room. Gamache remembered the first time he'd walked into the bistro years before and seen the mismatched furniture, the armchairs and wing chairs and Windsor chairs. The round and square and rectangular tables. The stone fireplaces and wooden beams. And the price tags hanging from everything.

Everything was for sale. And everyone? Gamache didn't think so, but sometimes he wondered.

"*Bon Dieu*, are you saying you haven't told your father about me?" Gabri asked.

"I did. I told him I was with a Gabriel."

"Your father thinks it's a Gabrielle you're with," said Beauvoir.

"*Quoi*?" said Gabri, glaring at Olivier. "He thinks I'm a woman? That means . . ." Gabri looked at his partner, incredulous. "He doesn't know you're gay?"

"I never told him."

"Maybe not in so many words, but you sure told him," said Gabri, then turned to Beauvoir. "Almost forty, not married, an antiques dealer. Good God, he told me when the other kids would dig for China he dug for Royal Doulton. How gay is that?" He turned back to Olivier. "You had an Easy Bake oven and you sewed your own Halloween costumes."

"I haven't told him and don't plan to," Olivier snapped. "It's none of his business."

"What a family," sighed Gabri. "It's actually a perfect fit. One doesn't want to know and the other doesn't want to tell."

But Gamache knew it was more than simply not wanting to tell. It was about a little boy with secrets. Who became a big boy with secrets. Who became a man. He brought an envelope out of his satchel and placed seven photographs on the table in front of Olivier. Then he unwrapped the carvings and put them on the table too.

"What order do they go in?"

"I can't remember which he gave me when," said Olivier. Gamache stared at him then spoke softly.

"I didn't ask you that. I asked what order they go in. You know, don't you?"

"I don't know what you mean." Olivier looked confused.

Then Armand Gamache did something Beauvoir had rarely seen. He brought his large hand down so hard on the table the little wooden figures jumped. As did the men.

"Enough. I've had enough."

And he looked it. His face was hard, carved and sharp and burnished by lies and secrets. "Do you have any idea what trouble you're in?" His voice was low, strained, forced through a throat that threatened to close. "The lies must stop now. If you have any hope, any hope at all, you must tell us the truth. Now."

Gamache moved his splayed hand over the photographs and shoved them toward Olivier, who stared as though petrified.

"I don't know," he stumbled.

"For God's sake, Olivier, please," Gabri begged.

Gamache radiated anger now. Anger, frustration and fear that the real murderer would slip away, hiding in another man's lies. Olivier and the Chief Inspector stared at each other. One man who spent his life burying secrets and the other who spent his life unearthing them.

Their partners stared, aware of the battle but unable to help.

"The truth, Olivier," Gamache rasped.

"How did you know?"

"The place of wonders. Ninstints on the Queen Charlotte Islands. The totem poles told me."

"They told you?"

"In their way. Each image built on the last. Each told its own story and was a wonder unto itself. But when taken as a whole they told a larger story."

Beauvoir, listening to this, thought about Ruth's couplets. The Chief had told him they did the same thing. If put together, in the right order, they too would tell a story. His hand slipped into his pocket and touched the scrap of paper shoved under his door that morning.

"What story do these tell, Olivier?" Gamache repeated. It had actually come to him on the plane as he'd listened to the little boy and the intricate GI Joe world he created. He'd thought about the case, thought about the Haida, the Watchman. Who, driven by his conscience, had finally found peace. In the wilderness.

The Chief Inspector suspected the same thing had happened to the Hermit. He'd gone into the forest a greedy man, to hide. But he'd been found. Years ago. By himself. And so he used his money as insulation and toilet paper. He used his first editions for knowledge and companionship. He used his antiquities as everyday dishes.

And in that wilderness he found freedom and happiness. And peace.

But something still eluded him. Or, perhaps more to the point, something still clung to him. He'd unburdened himself of the "things" of his life, but one more burden remained. The truth.

And so he decided to tell it to someone. Olivier. But he couldn't go quite that far. Instead, he hid the truth in a fable, an allegory.

"He made me promise never to tell." Olivier had dropped his head and spoke into his lap.

"And you didn't. Not while he was alive. But you need to tell now."

Without another word Olivier reached out and moved the photographs about, hesitating briefly over a couple, switching the order at least once. Until finally, spread in front of them, was the Hermit's story.

And then Olivier told them, placing his hand over each image as he spoke. And as Olivier's soft, almost hypnotic voice filled the space between them Gamache could see the dead man, alive again. In his cabin late at night. His one visitor sitting across the flickering fireplace. Listening, to this tale of hubris, of punishment and love. And betrayal.

Gamache watched as the villagers, happy in their ignorance, left their homes. And the young man raced ahead, clutching his small package, encouraging them to hurry. Toward paradise, they thought. But the boy knew differently. He'd stolen the Mountain's treasure.

And worse.

He'd stolen the Mountain's trust.

Now each figure the Hermit had carved took on a significance. The men and women waiting by the shore, having run out of land. And the boy, cowering, having run out of hope.

Then the ship arrived, sent by gods jealous of the Mountain.

But behind was the ever-present shadow. And the threat of something unseen but very real. The ghastly army, assembled by the Mountain. Made up of Fury and Vengeance, promising catastrophe. Fueled by Rage. And behind them the Mountain itself. That couldn't be stopped and wouldn't be denied.

It would find all the villagers and it would find the young man. And it would find the treasure he'd stolen.

As this army pressed forward it provoked wars and famine, floods and plagues. It laid waste to the world. Chaos led the army and chaos was left behind.

Beauvoir listened to this. His hand in his pocket scrunched Ruth's latest couplet and he could feel it damp with sweat. He looked down at the photos of the carvings and saw the happy, ignorant villagers slowly transformed as they too first sensed something approaching, then knew it.

And he shared their horror.

Finally the wars and famine arrived on the shores of the New World. For years the wars raged around their new home, not quite touching it. But then . . .

They all looked at the final image. Of the villagers bunched together. Emaciated, their clothing in tatters. Looking up. In terror.

At them.

Olivier's voice stopped. The story stopped.

"Go on," whispered Gamache.

"That's it."

"What about the boy?" asked Gabri. "He's not in the carvings anymore. Where'd he go?"

"He buried himself in the forest, knowing the Mountain would find the villagers."

"He betrayed them too? His own family? His friends?" asked Beauvoir.

Olivier nodded. "But there was something else."

"What?"

"Something was behind the Mountain. Something driving it on. Something that terrified even the Mountain."

"Worse than Chaos? Worse than death?" asked Gabri.

"Worse than anything."

"What was it?" Gamache asked.

"I don't know. The Hermit died before we got that far. But I think he carved it."

"What do you mean?" asked Beauvoir.

"There was something in a canvas sack that he never showed me. But he saw me looking at it. I couldn't help myself. He'd laugh and say one day he'd show it to me."

"And when you found the Hermit dead?" asked Gamache.

"It was gone."

"Why didn't you tell us this before?" snapped Beauvoir.

"Because then I'd have to admit everything. That I knew him, that I'd taken the carvings and sold them. It was his way of ensuring I'd come back, you know. Parceling out bits of his treasure."

"A pusher to an addict," said Gabri, with no rancor, but with no surprise either.

"Like Sheherazade."

Everyone turned to Gamache.

"Who?" Gabri asked.

"It's an opera, by Rimsky-Korsakov. It tells the story of the Thousand and One Nights."

They looked blank.

"The king would take a wife at night and kill her in the morning," said the Chief Inspector. "One night he chose Sheherazade. She knew his habits and knew she was in trouble so she came up with a plan."

"Kill the king?" asked Gabri.

"Better. Every night she told him a story, but left it unfinished. If he wanted to know the ending he had to keep her alive."

"Was the Hermit doing it to save his life?" asked Beauvoir, confused.

"In a way, I suppose," said the Chief. "Like the Mountain, he longed for company, and perhaps he knew Olivier well enough to realize the only way to get him to keep coming back was to promise more."

"That's not fair. You make me sound like a whore. I did more than take his things. I helped him garden and brought supplies. He got a lot out of it."

"He did. But so did you." Gamache folded his large hands together and looked at Olivier. "Who was the dead man?"

"He made me promise."

"And secrets are important to you. I understand that. You've been a good friend to the Hermit. But you have to tell us now."

"He was from Czechoslovakia," said Olivier at last. "His name was Jakob. I never knew his last name. He came here just as the Berlin wall was falling. I don't think we understood how chaotic it was. I remember thinking how exciting it must have been for the people. To finally have freedom. But he described something else. Every system they knew collapsed. It was lawless. Nothing worked. The phones, the rail service. Planes fell out of the air. He said it was horrible. But it was also a perfect time to run. To get out."

"He brought everything in that cabin with him?"

Olivier nodded. "For American money, hard currency he called it, you could arrange anything. He had contacts with antiques dealers here so he sold them some of his stuff and used the money to bribe officials in Czechoslovakia. To get his things out. He put them on a container ship and got them to the Port of Montreal. Then he put them all in storage and waited."

"For what?"

"To find a home."

"He first went to the Queen Charlotte Islands, didn't he?" said Gamache. After a pause Olivier nodded. "But he didn't stay there," Gamache continued. "He wanted peace and quiet, but the protests began and people came from all over the world. So he left. Came back here. Close to his treasures. And he decided to find a place in Quebec. In the woods here."

Again Olivier nodded.

"Why Three Pines?" Beauvoir asked.

Olivier shook his head, "I don't know. I asked, but he wouldn't tell me."

"Then what happened?" Gamache asked.

"As I said before, he came down here and started to build his cabin. When it was ready he got the things out of storage and put them there. It took a while, but he had the time."

"The treasures that he got out of Czechoslovakia, were they his?" Gamache asked.

"I never asked, and he never told me, but I don't think they were. He was just too afraid. I know he was hiding from something. Someone. But I don't know who."

"Do you have any idea how much time you've wasted? My God, what were you thinking?" demanded Beauvoir.

"I just kept thinking you'd find who'd killed him and none of this other stuff needed to come out."

"Other stuff?" said Beauvoir. "Is that how you think of it? As though it was all just details? How'd you think we'd find the murderer with you lying and letting us hare off all over the place?"

Gamache raised his hand slightly and with an effort Beauvoir pulled back, taking a deep breath.

"Tell us about Woo," Gamache asked.

Olivier lifted his head, his eyes strained. He was pale and gaunt and had aged twenty years in a week. "I thought you'd said it was that monkey that belonged to Emily Carr."

"I thought so too, but I've been thinking about it. I think it meant something else to the dead man. Something more personal. Frightening. I think it was left in the web, and carved, as a threat. Something maybe only he and his murderer understood."

"Then why ask me?"

"Because Jakob might have told you. Did he, Olivier?"

Gamache's eyes bored into Olivier's, insisting on the truth.

"He told me nothing," said Olivier at last.

Disbelief met this remark.

Gamache stared at him, trying with his considerable might to look beyond the mist of lies. Was Olivier finally telling the truth?

Gamache got up. At the door he turned and looked back at the two men. Olivier drained, empty. Nothing left. At least, Gamache hoped there was nothing left. Each lie was like ripping off a piece of Olivier's skin, until finally he sat in the bistro, torn to pieces.

"What happened to the young man?" asked Gamache. "The one in the story. Did the Mountain find him?"

"It must have. He's dead, isn't he?" said Olivier.

THIRTY-FIVE

At the B and B Gamache showered and shaved and changed his clothing. He glanced briefly at his bed, with its clean, crisp sheets and the duvet turned back. Waiting for him. But he avoided that siren song and before long he and Beauvoir were back across the village green and at the Incident Room, where Agents Lacoste and Morin waited.

They sat round the conference table, mugs of strong coffee and the Hermit's carvings in front of them. Succinctly the Chief Inspector told them about his trip to the Queen Charlottes and their interview with Olivier.

"So the dead man was telling a story all along. With his carvings," said Lacoste.

"Let's walk through this," said Beauvoir, going over to the sheets of paper on the wall. "The Hermit gets out of Czechoslovakia with the treasures just as the Soviet Union's crumbling. It's chaos there so he bribes port officials to get the goods shipped to the Port of Montreal. Once there he puts them into storage."

"If he was a refugee or an immigrant his fingerprints would've shown up on record," said Agent Morin.

Agent Lacoste turned to him. He was young, she knew, and inexperienced. "There're illegal immigrants all over Canada. Some hiding, some with false papers that pass for real. A little money to the right people."

"So he snuck in," said Morin. "But what about the antiques? Were they stolen? Where'd he get them? Like the violin, and that Amber Room thing?"

"Superintendent Brunel says the Amber Room disappeared in the

Second World War," said Gamache. "There're a lot of theories about what happened to it, including that it was hidden by Albert Speer in a mountain range. Between Germany and Czechoslovakia."

"Really?" said Lacoste, her mind working rapidly. "Suppose this Jakob found it?"

"If he found it he'd have the whole thing," said Beauvoir. "Suppose someone else found it, or part of it, and sold it to the Hermit."

"Suppose," said Morin, "he stole it."

"Suppose," said Gamache, "you're all right. Suppose someone found it, maybe decades ago. And split it up. And all that was left to one family was the one pane. Suppose that pane was entrusted to the Hermit, to smuggle out of the country."

"Why?" asked Lacoste, leaning forward.

"So they could start a new life," Beauvoir jumped in. "They wouldn't be the first who smuggled a family treasure out and sold it to start a business or buy a home in Canada."

"So they gave it to the Hermit to get out of the country," said Morin.

"Did it all come from different people?" wondered Lacoste. "A book here, a piece of priceless furniture or glass or silver there? Suppose all his things came from different people, all hoping to start a new life here? And he smuggled it all out."

"It would answer Superintendent Brunel's question about why there's such a range of items," said Gamache. "It's not from one collection, but many."

"No one would trust anyone with things that valuable," said Beauvoir.

"Maybe they had no choice," said the Chief. "They needed to get them out of the country. If he was a stranger they might not have trusted him. But if he was a friend . . ."

"Like the boy in the story," said Beauvoir. "Betraying everyone who trusted him."

They stared ahead. Silent. Morin had never realized murderers were caught in silence. But they were.

What would have happened? Families waited in Prague, in smaller cities and towns and villages. Waiting for word. From their trusted friend. At what stage did hope turn to despair? And finally to rage? And revenge?

Had one of them made it out, come across to the New World, and found the Hermit?

"But why did he come here?" asked Agent Morin.

"Why not?" asked Beauvoir.

"Well, there's a big Czech population here. If he was bringing all sorts of stolen goods, stuff he'd taken from people in Czechoslovakia, wouldn't he stay as far away from them as possible?"

They appealed to Gamache, who was listening, and thinking. Then he sat forward and drew the photographs of the carvings to him. Particularly the one of the happy people building a new village, in their new home. Without the young man.

"Maybe Olivier isn't the only one who lies," he said, getting up. "Maybe the Hermit wasn't alone when he came here. Maybe he had accomplices."

"Who are still in Three Pines," said Beauvoir.

Hanna Parra was clearing up lunch. She'd made a hearty soup and the place smelled of her mother's home in her Czech village. Of broth and parsley and bay leaves, and garden vegetables.

Her own gleaming metal and glass home couldn't be more different from the wooden chalet she'd grown up in. Full of wonderful aromas, and a hint of fear. Fear of attracting attention. Of standing out. Her parents, her aunts, her neighbors, had all lived comfortable lives of conformity. The fear of being found different, though, created a thin film between people.

But here everything really was transparent. She'd felt light as soon as they'd arrived in Canada. Where people minded their own business.

Or so she thought. Her hand hovered over the marble counter as some glint in the sun caught her eye. A car rolling up the drive.

Armand Gamache stared at the glass and metal cube in front of him. He'd read reports of the interviews with the Parras, including descriptions of their home, but still it took him aback.

The house gleamed in the sun. Not blinding, but it seemed to glow as though it lived in a world slightly different from theirs. A world of light.

"It's beautiful," said Gamache, almost under his breath.

"You should see inside."

"I think I should," Gamache nodded and the two men strolled across the yard.

Hanna Parra let them in and took their coats. "Chief Inspector, this is a pleasure."

Her voice was slightly accented but her French was perfect. Someone who'd not just learned the language but loved it. And it showed with every syllable. Gamache knew it was impossible to split language from culture. That without one the other withered. To love the language was to respect the culture.

That was why he'd learned English so well.

"We'd like to speak to your husband and son as well, if possible."

He spoke gently but somehow the very civility of the man lent his words weight.

"Havoc's out in the woods, but Roar's here."

"Where in the woods, madame?" Beauvoir asked.

Hanna seemed slightly flustered. "Out back. Cutting deadwood for the winter."

"Can you get him in, please?" said Beauvoir. His attempts at politeness simply made him seem sinister.

"We don't know where he is."

The voice came from behind them and both men turned to see Roar standing in the doorway to the mudroom. He was four-square, stocky and powerful. His hands were on his hips and his elbows out, like a threatened animal trying to make itself appear larger.

"Then perhaps we can speak to you," said Gamache.

Roar didn't budge.

"Please, come into the kitchen," said Hanna. "It's warmer there."

She led them deeper into the house and shot Roar a warning look as she passed.

The kitchen was filled with natural warmth from the sun that spilled in.

"*Mais, c'est formidable*," Gamache said. Out of the floor-to-ceiling windows he could see field then forest and in the distance St. Thomas's steeple, in Three Pines. It felt as though they were living in nature, that the house was no intrusion at all. It was unexpected, certainly unusual. But it wasn't foreign. Just the opposite. This home belonged here. It was perfect.

"Félicitations." He turned to the Parras. "This is a magnificent achievement. It must've been something you'd dreamed of for a long time."

Roar dropped his arms and indicated a seat at the glass table. Gamache accepted.

"We talked about it for a while. It wasn't my first choice. I wanted something more traditional."

Gamache looked at Hanna, who'd taken the chair at the head of the table. "Must've taken some convincing," he smiled.

"He did," she said, returning his smile. Hers was polite, without warmth or humor. "Took years. There'd been a cabin on the property and we lived there until Havoc was about six, but he was growing and I wanted a place that felt like ours."

"Je comprends, but why this?"

"You don't like it?" She didn't sound defensive, only interested.

"Just the reverse. I think it really is magnificent. It feels as though it belongs here. But you must admit, it's unusual. No one else has a place quite like it."

"We wanted something completely different from where we grew up. We wanted a change."

"We?" asked Gamache.

"I came around," said Roar, his voice hard, his eyes wary. "What's all this about?"

Gamache nodded and sat forward, splaying his large hands on the cool surface of the table. "Why did your son work for Olivier?"

"He needs the money," said Hanna. Gamache nodded.

"I understand. But wouldn't he make more money working in the woods? Or working construction? Surely a waiter is paid very little, even with the tips."

"Why're you asking us?" Hanna asked.

"Well, I would ask him, if he were here."

Roar and Hanna exchanged glances.

"Havoc takes after his mother," said Roar finally. "He looks like me, but has his mother's temperament. He likes people. He enjoys working in the woods but prefers working with people. The bistro suits him perfectly. He's happy there."

Gamache nodded slowly.

"Havoc worked late at the bistro every night," said Beauvoir. "What time did he get home?"

"About one, rarely later."

"But sometimes later?" Beauvoir asked.

"Sometimes, I guess," said Roar. "I didn't wait up."

"I imagine you did." Beauvoir turned to Hanna.

"I did," she admitted. "But I can't remember him ever coming home after one thirty. If customers were late, especially if there was a party, he'd have to clean up, so he'd be a little later than usual, but never much."

"Be careful, madame," said Gamache quietly.

"Careful?"

"We need the truth."

"You're getting the truth, Chief Inspector," said Roar.

"I hope so. Who was the dead man?"

"Why do you people keep asking us that?" asked Hanna. "We didn't know him."

"His name was Jakob," said Beauvoir. "He was Czech."

"I see," said Roar, his face twisting in anger. "And all Czech people know each other? Do you have any idea how insulting that is?"

Armand Gamache leaned toward him. "It's not insulting. It's human nature. If I lived in Prague I'd gravitate to the Québécois there, especially at first. He came here more than a decade ago and built a cabin in the woods. He filled it with treasures. Do you know where they might have come from?"

"How would we know?"

"We think he might have stolen them from people back in Czechoslovakia."

"And because they came from Czechoslovakia we'd know about it?"

"If he'd stolen the things do you really think the first thing he'd do is come to a potluck dinner with the Czech Association?" Hanna demanded. "We don't know this Jakob."

"What did you do before you came here?" Gamache asked them.

"We were both students. We met at Charles University in Prague," said Hanna. "I was studying political science and Roar was studying engineering."

"You're a councilor for the area," said Gamache to Hanna, then turned to Roar. "But you don't seem to have pursued your interests here. Why not?"

Parra paused, then looked down at his large, rough hands, picking at a callus. "I was fed up with people. Wanted nothing to do with them. Why do you think there's a huge Czech community out here, away from cities? It's because we're sickened by what people can do. People goaded by others, emboldened. Infected by cynicism and fear and suspicion. By jealousy and greed. They turn on each other. I want nothing to do with them. Let me work quietly in a garden, in the woods. People are horrible creatures. You must know that, Chief Inspector. You've seen what they can do to each other."

"I have," Gamache admitted. He stopped talking for a moment, and in that moment lived all the terrible things the head of homicide might see. "I know what people are capable of." He smiled then, and spoke quietly. "The bad, but also the good. I've seen sacrifice, and I've seen forgiveness where none seemed possible. Goodness exists, Monsieur Parra. Believe me."

And for a moment it seemed Roar Parra might. He stared wide-eyed at Gamache as though the large, calm man was inviting him into a home he longed to enter. But then he stepped back.

"You're a fool, Chief Inspector," he laughed derisively.

"But a happy one," smiled Gamache. "Now, what were we talking about? Ah, yes. Murder."

"Whose car's in the driveway?" The young voice floated to them from the mudroom and a moment later a door slammed shut.

Beauvoir stood up. Hanna and Roar also rose and stared at each other. Gamache went to the door of the kitchen.

"It's my car, Havoc. Can we have a word?"

"Sure."

The young man walked into the kitchen, taking off his cap. His face was sweaty and dirty and he smiled disarmingly. "Why so serious?" Then his expression changed. "There hasn't been another murder, has there?"

"Why'd you say that?" asked Gamache, watching him.

"Well, you all look so glum. I feel like it's report card day."

"In a way it is, I guess. Time to take stock." Gamache pointed to a chair next to Havoc's father and the young man sat. Gamache also sat.

"You and Olivier were the last people in the bistro last Saturday night?"

"That's right. Olivier left and I locked up."

"And where did Olivier go?"

"Home, I guess." Havoc looked amused by the question.

"We know now that Olivier visited the Hermit late at night. Saturday nights."

"Is that right?"

"That's right." The young man's composure was a little too perfect. A little too practiced, Gamache thought. "But someone else knew about the Hermit. Not just Olivier. There are a couple of ways Jakob could have been found. One was to follow the overgrown horse trails. The other was to follow Olivier. To the cabin."

Havoc's smile faltered. "Are you saying I followed Olivier?" The young man looked from Gamache to his parents, searching their faces, and back again.

"Where were you just now?"

"In the woods."

Gamache nodded slowly. "Doing what?"

"Cutting wood."

"And yet we heard no saw."

"I'd already cut it and was just stacking it." Now the boy's eyes moved more quickly from Gamache to his father and back.

Gamache got up, walked a couple of steps to the door to the kitchen, bent down and picked something up. He sat back down and placed it on the polished table. It was a wood chip. No. A shaving. It curled back on itself.

"How did you afford this house?" Gamache asked Roar.

"What do you mean?" Roar asked.

"It would cost hundreds of thousands of dollars. The materials alone are worth that. Add in designs and specifications for such an unusual house, then labor? You say you built it about fifteen years ago. What happened then that allowed you to do it? Where'd you get the money?"

"What do you think happened?" Roar leaned in to the Chief Inspector. "You Québécois, so insular. What happened all those years ago? Let's see. There was a sovereignty referendum in Quebec, there was a huge forest fire in Abitibi, there was an election in the province. Nothing much else to report."

The shaving on the table trembled as his words brushed past on their way to Gamache.

"I've had it," Roar said. "God, how can you not know what happened back then?"

"Czechoslovakia broke up," said Gamache. "And became Slovakia and the Czech Republic. That actually happened twenty years ago, but the impact can take time. Those walls came down, and these ones," he glanced at the bank of glass, "went up."

"We could see our families again," said Hanna. "So many of the things we left behind we could have again. Family, friends."

"Art, silver, heirlooms," said Beauvoir.

"Do you think those things mattered?" asked Hanna. "We'd lived without them for so long. It was the people we missed, not the things. We barely dared hope it was real. We'd been fooled before. The summer of '68. And certainly the reports we were seeing in the West were different from the stories we heard from people back home. Here we only heard how wonderful it was. We saw people waving flags and singing. But my cousins and aunts told a different story. The old system was horrible. Corrupt, brutal. But it was at least a system. When it went they were left with nothing. A vacuum. Chaos."

Gamache tilted his head slightly at the word. Chaos. Again.

"It was terrifying. People were being beaten, murdered, robbed, and there were no cops, no courts."

"A good time to smuggle things out," said Beauvoir.

"We wanted to sponsor our cousins but they decided to stay," said Roar.

"And my aunt wanted to stay with them, of course."

"Of course," said Gamache. "If not people, what about things?"

After a moment Hanna nodded. "We managed to get some family heirlooms out. My mother and father hid them after the war and told us they were to be kept for barter, for bargaining, if things got bad."

"Things got bad," said Gamache.

"We smuggled them out and sold them. So that we could build the home of our dreams," said Hanna. "We struggled with that decision a long time, but finally I realized both my parents would understand and approve. They were only things. Home is what matters."

"What did you have?" asked Beauvoir.

"Some paintings, some good furniture, some icons. We needed a house more than we needed an icon," said Hanna.

"Who did you sell them to?"

"A dealer in New York. A friend of a friend. I can give you his name. He took a small commission but got a fair price," said Parra.

"Please. I'd like to speak to him. You certainly made good use of the money." The Chief Inspector turned to Roar. "Are you a carpenter too?"

"I do some."

"And you?" Gamache asked Havoc, who shrugged. "I'll need more than that."

"I do some."

Gamache reached out and slowly pushed the wood shaving along the glass table until it sat in front of Havoc. He waited.

"I was in the woods whittling," admitted Havoc. "When I finish my work I like to sit quietly and shave down a piece of wood. It's relaxing. A chance to think. To cool off. I make little toys and things for Charles Mundin. Old gives me chunks of old wood and showed me how. Most of the stuff I make is crap and I just throw it away or burn it. But sometimes it's not too bad, and I give it to Charles. Why do you care if I whittle?"

"A piece of wood was found near the dead man. It was carved into the word Woo. Jakob didn't do it. We think the murderer did."

"You think Havoc—" Roar couldn't finish the sentence.

"I have a search warrant and a team on the way."

"What're you looking for?" asked Hanna, blanching. "Just the whittling tools? We can give them to you."

"It's more than that, madame. Two things are missing from Jakob's cabin. The murder weapon and a small canvas sack. We're looking for them too."

"We've never seen them," said Hanna. "Havoc, get your tools."

Havoc led Beauvoir to the shed while Gamache waited for the search team, who showed up a few minutes later. Beauvoir returned with the tools, and something else.

Chunks of wood. Red cedar. Whittled.

It was agreed that Beauvoir would direct the search while Gamache returned to the Incident Room. At the car the two men talked.

"Which of them did it, do you think?" Beauvoir asked, handing the keys to Gamache. "Havoc could've followed Olivier and found the cabin. But it might've been Roar. He might've found the cabin when he was clearing the trail. Could've been the mother, of course. The murder didn't take a lot of strength. Anger, yes, adrenaline, but not strength. Suppose Jakob stole from the Parra family back in Czechoslovakia then when he came here they recognized him. And he recognized them. So he took off into the woods and hid there."

"Or perhaps Jakob and the Parras were in it together," said Gamache. "Maybe all three convinced friends and neighbors in Czechoslovakia to give them their precious things, then disappeared with them."

"And once here Jakob screwed his partners, taking off into the woods. But Roar found the cabin as he cut the trails."

Gamache watched the search teams start their methodical work. Before long there wouldn't be anything they didn't know about the Parras.

He needed to gather his thoughts. He handed the car keys to Beauvoir. "I'll walk."

"Are you kidding?" asked Beauvoir, for whom walking was a punishment. "It's miles."

"It'll do me good, clear my mind. I'll see you back in Three Pines." He set off down the dirt road, giving Beauvoir a final wave. A few wasps buzzed in the ripe autumn air but were no threat. They were fat and lazy, almost drunk on the nectar from apples and pears and grapes.

It felt a little as though the world was on the verge of rotting.

As Gamache strolled, the familiar scents and sounds receded and he was joined by John the Watchman, and Lavina who could fly, and the little boy across the aisle on Air Canada. Who also flew, and told stories.

This murder seemed to be about treasure. But Gamache knew it wasn't. That was just the outward appearance. It was actually about something unseen. Murder always was.

This murder was about fear. And the lies it produced. But, more subtly, it was about stories. The tales people told the world, and told themselves. The Mythtime and the totems, that uneasy frontier between fable and fact. And the people who fell into the chasm. This murder was about the stories told by Jakob's carvings. Of Chaos and the Furies, of a Mountain of Despair and Rage. Of betrayal. And something else. Something that horrified even the Mountain.

And at its heart there was, Gamache now knew, a brutal telling.

THIRTY-SIX

The search parties had already been over the structure a couple of times, but they looked again. Even more closely this time. Beneath floorboards, beneath eaves, behind paintings. They looked and they looked and they looked.

And finally, they found.

It was behind the bricks in the huge stone fireplace. Behind what seemed a perpetual fire. The fire had had to be extinguished and the smoldering logs removed. But there the Sûreté team found first one, then two, then four loose bricks. Removed, they revealed a small compartment.

Inspector Beauvoir reached a gloved hand in carefully, but not before smearing soot on his arm and shoulder.

"I have something," he said. All eyes were on him. Everyone stared as his arm slowly came out of the cavity. On the table in front of the Chief Inspector he placed a silver candelabra. A menorah. Even Beauvoir, who knew nothing about silver, recognized it as something remarkable. It was simple and refined and old.

This menorah had survived sieges, pogroms, slaughters, the holocaust. People had cherished it, hidden it, guarded it, prayed before it. Until one night in a forest in Quebec, someone had ruined it.

The menorah had killed a man.

"Paraffin?" Inspector Beauvoir pointed to bits of translucent material stuck to it. Mixed with dried blood. "He made his own candles. That's what the paraffin in the cabin was for, not just preserves but candles." The Chief nodded.

Beauvoir returned to the hearth and put his arm back down the black hole. They watched his face and finally saw that slight change, the surprise. As his hand hit something else.

He placed a small burlap bag beside the menorah. No one spoke, until finally Chief Inspector Gamache asked a question of the man sitting opposite him.

"Have you looked inside?"

"No."

"Why not?"

There was another long pause, but Gamache didn't hurry him. There was no rush now.

"I didn't have time. I just grabbed it out of the Hermit's cabin and hid it along with the candlestick, thinking I could take a closer look in the morning. But then the body was discovered and there was too much attention."

"Is that why you lit the fires, Olivier? Before the police arrived?"

Olivier hung his head. It was over. Finally.

"How'd you know where to look?" he asked.

"I didn't, at first. But sitting here watching the search I remembered you'd said the bistro used to be a hardware store. And that the fireplaces had to be rebuilt. They were the only new thing in the room, though they looked old. And I remembered the fires, lit on a damp but not cold morning. The first thing you did when the body was discovered. Why?" He nodded toward the things on the table. "To make sure we wouldn't find those."

Armand Gamache leaned forward, toward Olivier on the other side of the menorah and the burlap bag. Beyond the pale. "Tell us what happened. The truth this time."

Gabri sat beside Olivier, still in shock. He'd been amused at first when the Sûreté search party had shown up, moved from the Parra place back to the bistro. He had made a few feeble jokes. But as the search became more and more invasive Gabri's amusement had faded, replaced by annoyance, then anger. And now shock.

But he'd never left Olivier's side, and he didn't now.

"He was dead when I found him. I admit, I took those." Olivier gestured to the items on the table. "But I didn't kill him."

"Be careful, Olivier. I'm begging you to be careful." Gamache's voice held an edge that chilled even the Sûreté officers.

"It's the truth." Olivier shut his eyes, almost believing if he couldn't see them they weren't there. The silver menorah and squalid little sack wouldn't be sitting on a table in his bistro. The police wouldn't be there. Just he and Gabri. Left in peace.

Finally he opened his eyes, to see the Chief Inspector looking directly at him.

"I didn't do it, I swear to God, I didn't do it."

He turned to Gabri who stared back, then took his hand and turned to the Chief Inspector. "Look, you know Olivier. I know Olivier. He didn't do this."

Olivier's eyes darted from one to the other. Surely there was a way out? Some crack, even the tiniest one, he could squeeze through.

"Tell me what happened," Gamache repeated.

"I already did."

"Again," said Gamache.

Olivier took a deep breath. "I left Havoc to close up and went to the cabin. I stayed for about forty-five minutes, had a cup of tea, and when I left he wanted to give me a little creamer. But I forgot it. When I got back to the village I realized what I'd done and was angry. Pissed off that he kept promising me that," he jabbed his finger at the sack, "but never gave it to me. Only small stuff."

"That creamer was valued at fifty thousand dollars. It belonged to Catherine the Great."

"But it wasn't that." Again Olivier shot a look at the bag. "When I returned the Hermit was dead."

"You told us the sack was gone."

"I lied. It was there."

"Had you seen the menorah before?"

Olivier nodded. "He used it all the time."

"For worship?"

"For light."

"It's also almost certainly priceless. You knew that, I suppose."

"You mean that's why I took it? No, I took it because it had my fingerprints all over it. I'd touched it hundreds of times, lighting candles, putting new ones in."

"Walk us through it," said Gamache, his voice calm and reasonable.

And as Olivier spoke the scene unfolded before them. Of Olivier arriving back at the cabin. Seeing the door partly open, the sliver of light spilling onto the porch. Olivier pushing the door open and seeing the

Hermit there. And blood. Olivier'd approached, stunned, and picked up the object by the Hermit's hand. And seeing the blood, too late, he'd dropped it. It had bounced under the bed to be found by Agent Lacoste. Woo.

Olivier had also seen the menorah, toppled over on the floor. Coated with blood.

He'd backed out of the room, onto the porch, preparing to run. Then he stopped. In front of him was the horrible scene. A man he knew and had come to care about, violently dead. And behind him the dark forest, and the trail running through it.

And caught between the two?

Olivier.

He'd collapsed into the rocking chair on the porch to think. His back to the terrible scene in the cabin behind him. His thoughts stretching forward.

What to do?

The problem, Olivier knew, was the horse trail. He'd known it for weeks. Since the Gilberts unexpectedly bought the old Hadley house, and even more unexpectedly decided to reopen the bridle paths.

"Now I understand why you hated them so much," said Gabri softly. "It seemed such an overreaction. It wasn't just the competition with the bistro and B and B, was it?"

"It was the trails. I was afraid, angry at them for getting Roar to open them. I knew he'd find the cabin and it'd all be over."

"What did you do?" asked Gamache.

And Olivier told them.

He'd sat on the porch for what seemed ages, thinking. Going round and round the situation. And finally he'd arrived at his *coup de grâce*. He decided the Hermit could do him one more favor. He could ruin Marc Gilbert and stop the trails, all at once.

"So I put him in the wheelbarrow and took him to the old Hadley house. I knew if another body was found there it would kill the business. No inn and spa, then no horse trails. Roar would stop work. The Gilberts would leave. The paths would grow over."

"And then what?" asked Gamache, again. Olivier hesitated.

"I could take what I wanted from the cabin. It would all work out."

Three people stared at him. None with admiration.

"Oh, Olivier," said Gabri.

"What else could I do?" he pleaded with his partner. "I couldn't let them find the place." How to explain how reasonable, brilliant even, this all seemed at two thirty in the morning. In the dark. With a body ten feet away.

"Do you know how this looks?" rasped Gabri.

Olivier nodded and hung his head.

Gabri turned to Chief Inspector Gamache. "He'd never have done it if he'd actually killed the man. You wouldn't, would you? You'd want to hide the murder, not advertise it."

"Then what happened?" Gamache asked. Not ignoring Gabri but not wanting to be sidetracked either.

"I took the wheelbarrow back, picked up those two things and left."

They looked at the table. The most damning items. And the most precious. The murder weapon and the sack.

"I brought them back here and hid them in the space behind the fireplace."

"You didn't look in the bag?" Gamache asked again.

"I thought I'd have plenty of time, when all the attention was on the Gilbert place. But then when Myrna found the body here the next morning I almost died. I couldn't very well dig the things out. So I lit the fires, to make sure you wouldn't look in there. For days after there was too much attention on the bistro. And by then I just wanted to pretend they didn't exist. That none of this had happened."

Silence met the story.

Gamache leaned back and watched Olivier for a moment. "Tell me the rest of the story, the one the Hermit told in his carvings."

"I don't know the rest. I won't know until we open that." Olivier's eyes were barely able to look away from the sack.

"I don't think we need to just yet." Gamache sat forward. "Tell me the story."

Olivier looked at Gamache, flabbergasted. "I've told you all I know. He told me up to the part where the army found the villagers."

"And the Horror was approaching, I remember. Now I want to hear the end."

"But I don't know how it ends."

"Olivier?" Gabri looked closely at his partner.

Olivier held Gabri's gaze then looked over at Gamache. "You know?"

"I know," said Gamache.

"What do you know?" asked Gabri, his eyes moving from the Chief Inspector to Olivier. "Tell me."

"The Hermit wasn't the one telling the story," said Gamache.

Gabri stared at Gamache, uncomprehending, then over at Olivier. Who nodded.

"You?" Gabri whispered.

Olivier closed his eyes and the bistro faded. He heard the mumbling of the Hermit's fire. Smelled the wood of the log cabin, the sweet maple wood from the smoke. He felt the warm tea mug in his hands, as he had hundreds of times. Saw the violin, gleaming in the firelight. Across from him sat the shabby man, in clean and mended old clothing surrounded by treasure. The Hermit was leaning forward, his eyes glowing and filled with fear. As he listened. And Olivier spoke.

Olivier opened his eyes and was back in the bistro. "The Hermit was afraid of something, I knew that the first time I met him in this very room. He became more and more reclusive as the years passed until he'd hardly leave his cabin to go into town. He'd ask me for news of the outside world. So I'd tell him about the politics and the wars, and some of the things happening locally. Once I told him about a concert at the church here. You were singing," he looked at Gabri, "and he wanted to go."

There he was, at the point of no return. Once spoken, these words could never be taken back.

"I couldn't let that happen. I didn't want anyone else to meet him, to maybe make friends with him. So I told the Hermit the concert had been canceled. He wanted to know why. I don't know what came over me, but I started making up this story about the Mountain and the villagers and the boy stealing from it, and running away and hiding."

Olivier stared down at the edge of the table, focusing on it. He could see the grain of the wood where it had been worn smooth. By hands touching it, rubbing it, resting on it, for generations. As his did now.

"The Hermit was scared of something, and the stories made him more afraid. He'd become unhinged, impressionable. I knew if I told him about terrible things happening outside the forest he'd believe me."

Gabri leaned away, to get the full picture of his partner. "You did that on purpose? You made him so afraid of the outside world he wouldn't leave? Olivier."

The last word was exhaled, as though it stank.

"But there was more to it than that," said Gamache, quietly. "Your stories not only kept the Hermit prisoner, and his treasure safe from anyone else, but they also inspired the carvings. I wonder what you thought when you saw the first."

"I did almost throw it away, when he gave it to me. But then I convinced myself it was a good thing. The stories were inspiring him. Helping him create."

"Carvings with walking mountains, and monsters and armies marching his way? You must have given the poor man nightmares," said Gabri.

"What did Woo mean?" Gamache asked.

"I don't know, not really. But sometimes when I told the story he'd whisper it. At first I thought it was just an exhale, but then I realized he was saying a word. Woo."

Olivier imitated the Hermit saying the word, under his breath. Woo.

"So you made the spider's web with the word in it, to mimic *Charlotte's Web*, a book he'd asked you to find."

"No. How could I do that? I wouldn't even know how to start."

"And yet Gabri told us you'd made your own clothes as a kid. If you wanted to, you could figure it out."

"No," Olivier insisted.

"And you admitted the Hermit taught you how to whittle, how to carve."

"But I wasn't any good at it," said Olivier, pleading. He could see the disbelief in their faces.

"It wasn't very well made. You carved Woo." Gamache forged forward. "Years ago. You didn't have to know what it meant, only that it meant something to the Hermit. Something horrible. And you kept that word, to be used one day. As countries warehouse the worst of weapons, against the day it might be needed. That word carved in wood was your final weapon. Your Nagasaki. The last bomb to drop on a weary and frightened and demented man.

"You played on his sense of guilt, magnified by isolation. You guessed he'd stolen those things so you made up the story of the boy and the Mountain. And it worked. It kept him there. But it also inspired him to produce those carvings, which ironically turned out to be his greatest treasure."

"I didn't kill him."

"You just kept him prisoner. How could you?" said Gabri.

"I didn't say anything he wasn't willing to believe."

"You don't really think that?" said Gabri.

Gamache glanced at the items on the table. The menorah, used to murder. And the small sack. The reason for murder. He couldn't put it off any longer. It was time for his own brutal telling. He stood.

"Olivier Brulé," said Chief Inspector Gamache, his voice weary and his face grim, "I'm arresting you on a charge of murder."

THIRTY-SEVEN

The frost was thick on the ground when Armand Gamache next appeared in Three Pines. He parked his car by the old Hadley house and took the path deeper and deeper into the woods. The leaves had fallen from the trees and lay crisp and crackling beneath his feet. Picking one up he marveled, not for the first time, at the perfection of nature where leaves were most beautiful at the very end of their lives.

He paused now and then, not to get his bearings because he knew where he was going and how to get there, but to appreciate his surroundings. The quiet. The soft light now allowed through the trees and hitting ground that rarely saw the sun. The woods smelled musky and rich and sweet. He walked slowly, in no rush, and after half an hour came to the cabin. He paused on the porch, noticing again with a smile the brass number above the door.

Then he entered.

He hadn't seen the cabin since all the treasures had been photographed, fingerprinted, catalogued and taken away.

He paused at the deep burgundy stain on the plank floor.

Then he walked round the simple room. He could call this place home, he knew, if it had only one precious thing. Reine-Marie.

Two chairs for friendship.

As he stood quietly, the cabin slowly filled with glittering antiques and antiquities and first editions. And with a haunting Celtic melody. The Chief Inspector again saw young Morin turn the violin into a fiddle, his loose limbs taut, made for this purpose.

Then he saw the Hermit Jakob, alone, whittling by the fire. Thoreau on the inlaid table. The violin leaning against the river rock of the hearth. This man who was his own age, but appeared so much older. Worn down by dread. And something else. The thing that even the Mountain feared.

He remembered the two carvings hidden by the Hermit. Somehow different from the rest. Distinguished by the mysterious code beneath. He'd really thought the key to breaking the Caesar's Shift had been Charlotte. Then he'd been sure the key was sixteen. That would explain those odd numbers over the door.

But the Caesar's Shift remained unbroken. A mystery.

Gamache paused in his thinking. Caesar's Shift. How had Jérôme Brunel explained it? What had Julius Caesar done with his very first code? He hadn't used a key word, but a number. He'd shifted the alphabet over by three letters.

Gamache walked to the mantelpiece and reaching into his breast pocket he withdrew a notebook and pen. Then he wrote. First the alphabet, then beneath it he counted spaces. That was the key. Not the word sixteen but the number. 16.

A B C D E F G H I J K L M N O P Q R S T U V W X Y Z
K L M N O P Q R S T U V W X Y Z A B C D E F G H I J

Carefully, not wanting to make a mistake in haste, he checked the letters. The Hermit had printed MRKBVYDDO under the carving of the people on the shore. C, H, A, R . . . Gamache concentrated even harder, forcing himself to slow down. L, O, T, T, E.

A long sigh escaped, and with it the word. Charlotte.

He then worked on the code written under the hopeful people on the boat. OWSVI.

Within moments he had that too.

Emily.

Smiling he remembered flying over the mountains covered in mist and legend. Spirits and ghosts. He remembered the place forgotten by time, and John the Watchman, who could never forget. And the totems, captured forever by a frumpy painter.

What message was Jakob the Hermit sending? Did he know he was in danger and wanted to pass on this message, this clue? Or was it, as Gamache suspected, something much more personal? Something comforting, even?

This man had kept these two carvings for a reason. He'd written under them for a reason. He'd written Charlotte and Emily. And he'd made them out of red cedar, from the Queen Charlotte Islands, for a reason.

What does a man alone need? He had everything else. Food, water, books, music. His hobbies and art. A lovely garden. But what was missing?

Company. Community. To be within the pale. Two chairs for friendship. These carvings kept him company.

He might never be able to prove it, but Gamache knew without doubt the Hermit had been on the Queen Charlotte Islands, almost certainly when he'd first arrived in Canada. And there he'd learned to carve, and learned to build log cabins. And there he'd found his first taste of peace, before having it disrupted by the protests. Like a first love, the place where peace is first found is never, ever forgotten.

He'd come into these woods to re-create that. He'd built a cabin exactly like the ones he'd seen on the Charlottes. He'd whittled red cedar, to be comforted by the familiar smell and feel. And he'd carved people for company. Happy people.

Except for one.

These creations became his family. His friends. He kept them, protected them. Named them. Slept with them under his head. And they in turn kept him company on the long, cold, dark nights as he listened for the snap of a branch, and the approach of something worse than slaughter.

Then Gamache heard a twig crack and tensed.

"May I join you?"

Standing on the porch was Vincent Gilbert.

"*S'il vous plaît.*"

Gilbert walked in and the two men shook hands.

"I was at Marc's place and saw your car. Hope you don't mind. I followed you."

"Not at all."

"You looked deep in thought just now."

"A great deal to think about," said Gamache, with a small smile, tucking his notebook back into his breast pocket.

"What you did was very difficult. I'm sorry it was necessary."

Gamache said nothing and the two men stood quietly in the cabin.

"I'll leave you alone," said Gilbert eventually, making for the door.

Gamache hesitated then followed. "No need. I'm finished here." He closed the door without a backward glance and joined Vincent Gilbert on the porch.

"I signed this for you." Gilbert handed him a hardcover book. "They've reissued it after all the publicity surrounding the murder and the trial. Seems it's a bestseller."

"*Merci.*" Gamache turned over the gleaming copy of *Being* and looked at the author photo. No more sneer. No more scowl. Instead a handsome, distinguished man looked back. Patient, understanding. "*Félicitations,*" said Gamache.

Gilbert smiled, then unfolded a couple of aluminum garden chairs. "I brought these with me just now. The first of a few things. Marc says I can live in the cabin. Make it my home."

Gamache sat. "I can see you here."

"Away from polite society," smiled Gilbert. "We saints do enjoy our solitude."

"And yet, you brought two chairs."

"Oh, you know that quote too?" said Gilbert. "*I had three chairs in my house: one for solitude, two for friendship, three for society.*"

"My favorite quote from Thoreau is also from *Walden*," said Gamache. "*A man is rich in proportion to the number of things he can afford to let alone.*"

"In your job you can't let many things alone, can you?"

"No, but I can let them go, once they're done."

"Then why are you here?"

Gamache sat quietly for a moment then spoke. "Because some things are harder to let go than others."

Vincent Gilbert nodded but said nothing. While the Chief Inspector stared into space the doctor pulled out a small Thermos from a knapsack and poured them each a cup of coffee.

"How are Marc and Dominique?" Gamache asked, sipping the strong black coffee.

"Very well. The first guests have arrived. They seem to be enjoying it. And Dominique's in her element."

"How's Marc the horse?" He was almost afraid to ask. And the slow shaking of Vincent's head confirmed his fears. "Some horse," murmured Gamache.

"Marc had no choice but to get rid of him."

Gamache saw again the wild, half-blind, half-mad, wounded creature. And he knew the choice had been made years ago.

"Dominique and Marc are settling in, and have you to thank for that," Gilbert continued. "If you hadn't solved the case they'd have been ruined. I take it from the trial that was Olivier's intention in moving the body. He wanted to close the inn and spa."

Gamache didn't say anything.

"But it was more than that, of course," said Gilbert, not letting it go. "He was greedy, I suppose."

And still Gamache said nothing, not wanting to further condemn a man he still considered a friend. Let the lawyers and judges and jury say those things.

"The Hungry Ghost," said Gilbert.

That roused Gamache, who twisted in his garden chair to look at the dignified man next to him.

"Pardon?"

"It's a Buddhist belief. One of the states of man from the Wheel of Life. The more you eat the hungrier you get. It's considered the very worst of the lives. Trying to fill a hole that only gets deeper. Fill it with food or money or power. With the admiration of others. Whatever."

"The Hungry Ghost," said Gamache. "How horrible."

"You have no idea," said Gilbert.

"You do?"

After a moment Gilbert nodded. He no longer looked quite so magnificent. But considerably more human. "I had to give it all up to get what I really wanted."

"And what was that?"

Gilbert considered for a long time. "Company."

"You came to a cabin in the woods to find company?" smiled Gamache.

"To learn to be good company for myself."

They sat quietly until Gilbert finally spoke. "So Olivier killed the Hermit for the treasure?"

Gamache nodded. "He was afraid it'd be found. He knew it was only a matter of time, once your son moved here and Parra started opening the trails."

"Speaking of the Parras, did you consider them?"

Gamache looked at the steaming mug of coffee warming his large hands. He'd never tell this man the full story. It wouldn't do to admit that Havoc Parra in particular had been their main suspect. Havoc worked late. He could have followed Olivier to the cabin after closing the bistro. And while Havoc's whittling tools had tested negative maybe he used others. And wasn't the Hermit Czech?

Or if not Havoc then his father Roar, who cut the trails and was almost certainly heading straight for the cabin. Maybe he found it.

Maybe, maybe, maybe.

A wide trail of "maybe's" led directly to the Parras.

But Gamache also chose not to tell Gilbert that he had also been a suspect, as had his son and daughter-in-law. The cabin was on their land. Why had they bought the ruined old house when they could have had any place? Why had they ordered the trails reopened so quickly? It was almost the first thing they did.

And why had the saintly Dr. Gilbert and the body both appeared at the same time?

Why, why, why.

A wide trail of "why's" led directly to the front door of the old Hadley house.

They all made good suspects. But all the actual evidence pointed to Olivier. The fingerprints, the murder weapon, the canvas sack, the carvings. They'd found no whittling tools in Olivier's possession, but that meant nothing. He would have gotten rid of them years ago. But they had found nylon line in the B and B. The same weight and strength used for the web. Olivier's defense argued it was the standard ply and proved nothing. Gabri testified that he'd used it for gardening, to tie up honeysuckle.

It proved nothing.

"But why put that word up in the web, and carve it in wood?" asked Vincent.

"To frighten the Hermit into giving him the treasure in the sack."

It had been a shockingly simple solution. The trail was getting closer every day. Olivier knew time was running out. He had to convince the Hermit to hand it over, before the cabin was found. Because once that happened the Hermit would realize the truth: Olivier had been lying. There was no Mountain. No army of Dread and Despair. No Chaos. Just a greedy little antique dealer, who could never get enough.

No approaching horror, just another Hungry Ghost.

Olivier's last hope of getting the burlap bag from the Hermit was to convince him the danger was imminent. To save his life Jakob had to get rid of the treasure. So that when the Mountain arrived he'd find the Hermit, but no sack.

But when the story failed to terrify enough, when the trail had come too close, Olivier had brought out his napalm, his mustard gas, his buzz bomb. His *Enola Gay*.

He'd put the web up in the corner. And placed the whittled word somewhere in the cabin, for Jakob to find. Knowing that when the Hermit saw it he would—what? Die? Perhaps. But he would certainly panic. Knowing he'd been found. The thing he'd hidden from, the thing he'd fled from. The thing he most feared. Had found him. And left its calling card.

What had gone wrong? Had the Hermit not seen the web? Had the Hermit's greed exceeded even Olivier's? Whatever happened one thing Gamache knew for certain. Olivier, his patience at an end, his nerves frazzled, his rage in full flood, had reached out, clasped the menorah. And struck.

His lawyer had opted for a jury trial. A good strategy, thought Gamache. A jury could be convinced it was temporary insanity. Gamache himself had argued that Olivier should be tried for manslaughter, not murder, and the prosecution had agreed. The Chief Inspector knew Olivier had done many terrible things to the Hermit, on purpose. But killing him wasn't one. Imprisoning Jakob, yes. Manipulating and taking advantage of him, yes. Unbalancing an already fragile mind, yes. But not murder. That, Gamache believed, had surprised and appalled even Olivier.

Such an appropriate word. Manslaughter.

That's what Olivier had done. He'd slaughtered a man. Not with that one terrible blow, but over time. Wearing him down, so that the Hermit's face was scored with worry lines and his soul cringed with every scrape of a twig.

But it turned into a murder/suicide. Olivier had killed himself in the process. Whittling away what was kind and good about himself, until loathing replaced self-respect. The man he could have been was dead. Consumed by the Hungry Ghost.

What finally damned Olivier wasn't speculation but facts. Evidence.

Only Olivier could be placed at the cabin. His prints were found here, and on the murder weapon. He knew the Hermit. He sold some of his treasures. He sold the carvings. He stole the burlap bag. And finally, the murder weapon was found hidden in the bistro, along with the bag. His lawyer would try to come up with all sorts of arguments, but this case would hold. Gamache had no doubt.

But while facts might be enough for a prosecutor, a judge, a jury, they weren't enough for Gamache. He needed more. He needed motive. That thing that could never be proved because it can't be seen.

What drove a man to slaughter?

And that's what had sealed it for Gamache. As he'd been walking back to Three Pines, having ordered the Parra place searched yet again, he'd thought about the case. The evidence. But also the malevolent spirit behind it.

He realized that all the things that pointed to the Parras' possibly doing it also applied to Olivier. Fear and greed. But what tipped it toward Olivier was that while the Parras had shown little inclination toward greed, Olivier had wallowed in it.

Olivier was afraid of two things, Gamache knew. Being exposed, and being without.

Both were approaching, both threatening.

Gamache sipped his coffee and thought again about those totem poles in Ninstints, rotting, falling, fallen. But they still had a story to tell.

It was there the idea had been planted. That this murder was about tales told. And the Hermit's carvings were the key. They weren't random, individual carvings. They were a community of carvings. Each could stand on its own, but taken together they told an even bigger story. Like the totem poles.

Olivier had told tales to control and imprison the Hermit. The Hermit had used them to create his remarkable carvings. And Olivier had used those carvings to get wealthier even than he had dreamed.

But what Olivier hadn't appreciated was that his stories were actually true. An allegory, yes. But no less real for that. A mountain of misery was approaching. And growing with each new lie, each new tale.

A Hungry Ghost.

The wealthier Olivier grew the more he wanted. And what he wanted more than anything was the one thing denied him. The contents of the little canvas sack.

Jakob had come to Three Pines with his treasures, almost certainly stolen from friends and neighbors in Czechoslovakia. People who had trusted him. Once the Iron Curtain had collapsed and those people could leave, they started asking for their money. Demanding it. Threatening to show up. Perhaps even showing up.

So he'd taken his treasure, their treasures, and hidden it and himself in the woods. Waiting for it to blow over, for the people to give up. To go home. To leave him in peace.

Then he could sell it all. Buy private jets and luxury yachts. A townhouse in Chelsea, a vineyard in Burgundy.

Would he have been happy then? Would it have finally been enough?

Find out what he loved, and maybe then you'll find his murderer, Gamache had been told by Esther, the Haida elder. Had the Hermit loved money?

Perhaps at first.

But then hadn't he used money in the outhouse? As toilet paper. Hadn't they found twenty-dollar bills stuffed into the walls of the log cabin, as insulation?

Had the Hermit loved his treasure? Perhaps at first.

But then he'd given it away. In exchange for milk and cheese and coffee.

And company.

When Olivier had been taken away Gamache had sat back down and stared at the sack. What could be worse than Chaos, Despair, War? What would even the Mountain flee from? Gamache had given it a lot of thought. What haunted people even, perhaps especially, on their deathbed? What chased them, tortured them and brought some to their knees? And Gamache thought he had the answer.

Regret.

Regret for things said, for things done, and not done. Regret for the people they might have been. And failed to be.

Finally, when he was alone, the Chief Inspector had opened the sack and looking inside had realized he'd been wrong. The worst thing of all wasn't regret.

Clara Morrow knocked on Peter's door.

"Ready?"

"Ready," he said, and came out wiping the oil paint from his hand. He'd taken to sprinkling his hands with paint so that Clara would think he'd been hard at work when in fact he'd finished his painting weeks earlier.

He'd finally admitted that to himself. He just hadn't admitted it to anyone else.

"How do I look?"

"Great." Peter took a piece of toast from Clara's hair.

"I was saving that for lunch."

"I'll take you out for lunch," he said, following her out the door. "To celebrate."

They got in the car and headed into Montreal. That terrible day when she'd gone to pick up her portfolio from Fortin, she'd stopped at the sculpture of Emily Carr. Someone else was there eating her lunch and Clara had sat at the far end of the bench and stared at the little bronze woman. And the horse, the dog and the monkey. Woo.

Emily Carr didn't look like one of the greatest visionary artists ever. She looked like someone you'd meet across the aisle on the Number 24 bus. She was short. A little dumpy. A little frumpy.

"She looks a bit like you," came the voice beside Clara.

"You think so?" said Clara, far from convinced it was a compliment.

The woman was in her sixties. Beautifully dressed. Poised and composed. Elegant.

"I'm Thérèse Brunel." The woman reached out her hand. When Clara continued to look perplexed she added, "Superintendent Brunel. Of the Sûreté du Québec."

"Of course. Forgive me. You were in Three Pines with Armand Gamache."

"Is that your work?" She nodded toward the portfolio.

"Photographs of it, yes."

"May I see?"

Clara opened the portfolio and the Sûreté officer looked through, smiling, commenting, drawing in breath occasionally. But she stopped at one picture. It was of a joyous woman facing forward but looking back.

"She's beautiful," said Thérèse. "Someone I'd like to know."

Clara hadn't said anything. Just waited. And after a minute her companion blinked then smiled and looked at Clara.

"It's quite startling. She's full of Grace, but something's just happened, hasn't it?"

Still Clara remained silent, staring at the reproduction of her own work.

Thérèse Brunel went back to looking at it too. Then she inhaled sharply and looked at Clara. "The Fall. My God, you've painted the Fall. That moment. She's not even aware of it, is she? Not really, but she sees something, a hint of the horror to come. The Fall from Grace." Thérèse grew very quiet, looking at this lovely, blissful woman. And that tiny, nearly invisible awareness.

Clara nodded. "Yes."

Thérèse looked at her more closely. "But there's something else. I know what it is. It's you, isn't it? She's you."

Clara nodded.

After a moment Thérèse whispered so that Clara wasn't even sure the words had been spoken aloud. Maybe it was the wind. "What are you afraid of?"

Clara waited a long time to speak, not because she didn't know the answer, but because she'd never said it out loud. "I'm afraid of not recognizing Paradise."

There was a pause. "So am I," said Superintendent Brunel.

She wrote a number and handed it to Clara. "I'm going to make a call when I get back to my office. Here's my number. Call me this afternoon."

Clara had, and to her amazement the elegant woman, the police officer, had arranged for the Chief Curator at the Musée d'art contemporain in Montreal to see the portfolio.

That had been weeks ago. A lot had happened since. Chief Inspector Gamache had arrested Olivier for murder. Everyone knew that had been a mistake. But as the evidence grew so did their doubts. As all of this was happening Clara had taken her work into the MAC. And now they'd asked for a meeting.

"They won't say no," said Peter, speeding along the autoroute. "I've never known a gallery to invite an artist to a meeting to turn him down. It's good news, Clara. Great news. Way better than anything Fortin could have done for you."

And Clara dared to think that was true.

As he drove Peter thought about the painting on his own easel. The one he now knew was finished. As was his career. On the white canvas

Peter had painted a large black circle, almost, but not quite, closed. And where it might have closed he'd put dots.

Three dots. For infinity. For society.

Jean Guy Beauvoir was in the basement of his home looking down at the ragged strips of paper. Upstairs he could hear Enid preparing lunch.

He'd gone to the basement every chance he got in the last few weeks. He'd flip the game on the television then sit with his back to the TV. At his desk. Mesmerized by the scraps of paper. He'd hoped the mad old poet had written the whole thing on a single sheet of paper and simply torn it into strips so he could fit them together like a jigsaw puzzle. But, no, the pieces of paper wouldn't fit together. He had to find the meaning in the words.

Beauvoir had lied to the Chief. He didn't do it often, and he had no idea why he'd done it this time. He'd told the Chief he'd thrown them all out, all the stupid words Ruth had tacked onto his door, shoved into his pocket. Given others to give to him.

He'd wanted to throw them out, but even more than that he'd wanted to know what they meant. It was almost hopeless. Perhaps the Chief could decipher it, but poetry had always been a big fat pile of crap to Beauvoir. Even when presented with it whole. How could he ever assemble a poem?

But he'd tried. For weeks.

He slipped one scrap between two and moved another to the top.

I just sit where I'm put, composed
of stone and wishful thinking:
that the deity who kills for pleasure
will also heal,

He took a swig of beer.

"Jean Guy," his wife sang to him. "Luh-hunch."

"Coming."

that in the midst of your nightmare,
the final one, a kind lion

will come with bandages in her mouth
and the soft body of a woman,

Enid called again and he didn't answer but instead stared at the poem. Then his eyes moved to the furry little feet dangling over the shelf above his desk. At eye level, where he could see it. The stuffed lion he'd quietly taken from the B and B. First to his room, for company. He'd sat it in the chair where he could see it from his bed. And he imagined her there. Maddening, passionate, full of life. Filling the empty, quiet corners of his life. With life.

And when the case was over he'd slipped the lion into his bag and brought it down here. Where Enid never came.

The kind lion. With its soft skin and smile. "Wimoweh, a-wimoweh," he sang under his breath as he read the final stanza.

and lick you clean of fever,
and pick your soul up gently by the nape of the neck
and caress you into darkness and paradise.

An hour later Armand Gamache walked out of the woods and down the slope into Three Pines. On the porch of the bistro he took a deep breath, composed himself, and entered.

It took a moment for his eyes to adjust. When they did he saw Gabri behind the bar, where Olivier had always stood. The large man had diminished, lost weight. He looked careworn. Tired.

"Gabri," said Gamache, and the two old friends stared at each other.

"Monsieur," said Gabri. He shifted a jar of allsorts and another of jelly beans on the polished wood counter, then came around. And offered Gamache a licorice pipe.

Myrna walked in a few minutes later to find Gabri and Gamache sitting quietly by the fire. Talking. Their heads together. Their knees almost touching. An uneaten licorice pipe between them.

They looked up as she entered.

"I'm sorry." She stopped. "I can come back. I just wanted to show you this." She held a piece of paper out to Gabri.

"I got one too," he said. "Ruth's latest poem. What do you think it means?"

"I don't know." She couldn't get used to coming into the bistro and seeing only Gabri. With Olivier in jail it felt as though something vital was missing, as though one of the pines had been cut down.

It was excruciating, what was happening. The village felt torn and ragged. Wanting to support Olivier and Gabri. Appalled at the arrest. Not believing it. And yet knowing that Chief Inspector Gamache would never have done it unless he was certain.

It was also clear how much it had cost Gamache to arrest his friend. It seemed impossible to support one without betraying the other.

Gabri rose, as did Gamache. "We were just catching up. Did you know the Chief Inspector has another granddaughter? Zora."

"Congratulations." Myrna embraced the grandfather.

"I need fresh air," said Gabri, suddenly restless. At the door he turned to Gamache. "Well?"

The Chief Inspector and Myrna joined him and together they walked slowly round the village green. Where all could see. Gamache and Gabri, together. The wound not healed, but neither was it getting deeper.

"Olivier didn't do it, you know," said Gabri, stopping to look at Gamache directly.

"I admire you for standing by him."

"I know there's a lot about him that sucks. Not surprisingly, those are some of my favorite parts." Gamache gave a small guffaw. "But there's one question I need answered."

"*Oui?*"

"If Olivier killed the Hermit, why move the body? Why take it to the Hadley house to be found? Why not leave it in the cabin? Or stick it in the woods?"

Gamache noticed the "he" had become an "it." Gabri couldn't accept that Olivier had killed, and he certainly couldn't accept that Olivier had killed a "he" not an "it."

"That was answered in the trial," said Gamache, patiently. "The cabin was about to be found. Roar was cutting a path straight for it."

Gabri nodded, reluctantly. Myrna watched and willed her friend to be able to accept the now undeniable truth.

"I know," said Gabri. "But why move it to the Hadley house? Why not just take it deeper into the woods and let the animals do the rest?"

"Because Olivier realized the body wasn't the most damning evidence against him. The cabin was. Years of evidence, of fingerprints, of hairs, of food. He couldn't hope to clean it all up, at least not right away. But if our investigation focused on Marc Gilbert and the Hadley house he might stop the progress of the paths. If the Gilberts were ruined there was no need of horse trails."

Gamache's voice was calm. No sign of the impatience Myrna knew it could hold. This was at least the tenth time she'd heard the Chief Inspector explain it to Gabri, and still Gabri didn't believe it. And even now Gabri was shaking his head.

"I'm sorry," said Gamache, and clearly meant it. "There was no other conclusion."

"Olivier isn't a murderer."

"I agree. But he did kill. It was manslaughter. Unintentional. Can you really tell me you believe he's not capable of killing out of rage? He'd worked years to get the Hermit to give him the treasure, and feared he might lose it. Are you sure Olivier wouldn't be driven to violence?"

Gabri hesitated. Neither Gamache nor Myrna dared breathe, for fear of chasing away timid reason fluttering around their friend.

"Olivier didn't do it." Gabri sighed heavily, exasperated. "Why would he move the body?"

The Chief Inspector stared at Gabri. Words failed him. If there was any way to convince this tormented man, he would. He'd tried. He hated the thought that Gabri would carry this unnecessary burden, the horror of believing his partner falsely imprisoned. Better to accept the wretched truth than struggle, twisting, to make a wish a reality.

Gabri turned his back on the Chief Inspector and walked onto the green, to the very center of the village, and sat on the bench.

"What a magnificent man," said Gamache, as he and Myrna resumed their walk.

"He is that. He'll wait forever, you know. For Olivier to come back."

Gamache said nothing and the two strolled in silence. "I ran into Vincent Gilbert," he finally said. "He says Marc and Dominique are settling in."

"Yes. Turns out when he's not moving bodies around the village Marc's quite nice."

"Too bad about Marc the horse."

"Still, he's probably happier."

This surprised Gamache and he turned to look at Myrna. "Dead?"

"Dead? Vincent Gilbert had him sent to LaPorte."

Gamache snorted and shook his head. The asshole saint indeed.

As they passed the bistro he thought about the canvas bag. The thing that had, more than anything else, condemned Olivier when found hidden behind the fireplace.

Ruth's door opened and the old poet, wrapped in her worn cloth coat, hobbled out, followed by Rosa. But today the duck was without clothing. Just feathers.

Gamache had grown so used to seeing Rosa in her outfits it seemed almost unnatural that she should be without one now. The two walked across the road to the green where Ruth opened a small paper bag and tossed bread for Rosa, who waddled after the crumbs, flapping her wings. A quacking could be heard overhead, getting closer. Gamache and Myrna turned to the sound. But Ruth's eyes remained fixed, on Rosa. Overhead, ducks approached in V formation flying south for the winter.

And then, with a cry that sounded almost human Rosa rose up and flew into the air. She circled and for an instant everyone thought she would return. Ruth raised her hand, offering bread crumbs from her palm. Or a wave. Good-bye.

And Rosa was gone.

"Oh, my God," breathed Myrna.

Ruth stared, her back to them, her face and hand to the sky. Bread crumbs tumbling to the grass.

Myrna took out the crumpled paper from her pocket and gave it to Gamache.

She rose up into the air and the jilted earth let out a sigh.
She rose up past telephone poles and rooftops of houses where the
*   earthbound hid.*
She rose up sleeker than the sparrows that swirled around her like a
*   jubilant cyclone*
She rose up, past satellites and every cell phone down on earth
*   rang at once.*

"Rosa," whispered Myrna. "Ruth."

Gamache watched the old poet. He knew what was looming behind the Mountain. What crushed all before it. The thing the Hermit most feared. The Mountain most feared.

Conscience.

Gamache remembered opening the coarse sack, his hand sliding over the smooth wood inside. It was a simple carving. A young man in a chair, listening.

Olivier. He'd turned it over and found three letters etched into the wood. GYY.

He'd decoded them in the cabin just minutes before and had stared at the word.

Woo.

Hidden in the rude rough sack it was far finer, even, than the more detailed carvings. This was simplicity itself. Its message was elegant and horrific. The carving was beautiful and yet the young man seemed utterly empty. His imperfections worn away. The wood hard and smooth so that the world slid right off it. There would be no touch and therefore no feeling.

It was the Mountain King, as a man. Unassailable, but unapproachable. Gamache felt like throwing it deep into the forest. To lie where the Hermit had put himself. Hiding from a monster of his own making.

But there was no hiding from Conscience.

Not in new homes and new cars. In travel. In meditation or frantic activity. In children, in good works. On tiptoes or bended knee. In a big career. Or a small cabin.

It would find you. The past always did.

Which was why, Gamache knew, it was vital to be aware of actions in the present. Because the present became the past, and the past grew. And got up, and followed you.

And found you. As it had the Hermit. As it had Olivier. Gamache stared at the cold, hard, lifeless treasure in his hand.

Who wouldn't be afraid of this?

Ruth limped across the green to the bench and sat. With a veined hand she clutched her blue cloth coat to her throat while Gabri reached out and taking her other hand in his and rubbing it softly and murmured, "there, there."

She rose up but remembered to politely wave good-bye . . .

THE END

Turn the page for an excerpt of Louise Penny's new book

BURY
YOUR DEAD

Available Fall 2010

ONE

⁓

Up the stairs they raced, taking them two at a time, trying to be as quiet as possible. Gamache struggled to keep his breathing steady, as though he was sitting at home, as though he had not a care in the world.

"Sir?" came the young voice over Gamache's headphones.

"You must believe me, son. Nothing bad will happen to you."

He hoped the young agent couldn't hear the strain in his voice, the flattening as the Chief Inspector fought to keep his voice authoritative, certain.

"I believe you."

They reached the landing. Inspector Beauvoir stopped, staring at his Chief. Gamache looked at his watch.

Forty-seven seconds.

Still time.

In his headphones the agent was telling him about the sunshine and how good it felt on his face.

The rest of the team made the landing, tactical vests in place, automatic weapons drawn, eyes sharp. Trained on the Chief. Beside him Inspector Beauvoir was also waiting for a decision. Which way? They were close. Within feet of their quarry.

Gamache stared down one dark, dingy corridor in the abandoned factory, then down the other.

They looked identical. Light scraped through the broken, grubby windows lining the halls and with it came the December day.

Forty-three seconds.

He pointed decisively to the left and they ran, silently, toward the door at the end. As he ran Gamache gripped his rifle and spoke calmly into the headset.

"There's no need to worry."

"There's forty seconds left, sir." Each word was exhaled as though the man on the other end was having difficulty breathing.

"Just listen to me," said Gamache, thrusting his hand toward a door. The team surged ahead.

Thirty-six seconds.

"I won't let anything happen to you," said Gamache, his voice convincing, commanding, daring the young agent to contradict. "You'll be having dinner with your family tonight."

"Yes, sir."

The tactical team surrounded the closed door with its frosted, filthy window. Darkened.

Gamache paused, staring at it, his hand hanging in the air ready to give the signal to break it down. To rescue his agent.

Twenty-nine seconds.

Beside him Beauvoir strained, waiting to be loosed.

Too late, Chief Inspector Gamache realized he'd made a mistake.

Give it time, Armand."

"*Avec le temps?*" Gamache returned the older man's smile and made a fist of his right hand. To stop the trembling. A tremble so slight he was certain the waitress in the Québec City café hadn't noticed. The two students across the way tapping on their laptops wouldn't notice. No one would notice.

Except someone very close to him.

He looked at Emile Comeau, crumbling a flaky croissant with sure hands. He was nearing eighty now, Gamache's mentor and former chief. His hair was white and groomed, his eyes through his glasses a sharp blue. He was slender and energetic, even now. Though with each visit Armand Gamache noticed a slight softening about the face, a slight slowing of the movements.

Avec le temps.

Widowed five years, Emile Comeau knew the power, and length, of time.

Gamache's own wife, Reine-Marie, had left at dawn that morning after spending a week with them at Emile's stone home within the old walled city of Québec. They'd had quiet dinners together in front of the fire, they'd walked the narrow snow-covered streets. Talked. Were silent. Read the papers, discussed events. The three of them. Four, if you counted their German shepherd, Henri.

And most days Gamache had gone off on his own to a local library, to read.

Emile and Reine-Marie had given him that, recognizing that right now he needed society but he also needed solitude.

And then it was time for her to leave. After saying good-bye to Emile she turned to her husband. Tall, solid, a man who preferred good books and long walks to any other activity, he looked more like a distinguished professor in his mid-fifties than the head of the most prestigious homicide unit in Canada. The Sûreté du Québec. He walked her to her car, scraping the morning ice from the windshield.

"You don't have to go, you know," he said, smiling down at her as they stood in the brittle, new day. Henri sat in a snow bank nearby and watched.

"I know. But you and Emile need time together. I could see how you were looking at each other."

"The longing?" laughed the Chief Inspector. "I'd hoped we'd been more discreet."

"A wife always knows." She smiled, looking into his deep brown eyes. He wore a hat, but still she could see his graying hair, and the slight curl where it came out from under the fabric. And his beard. She'd slowly become used to the beard. For years he'd had a moustache, but just lately, since it happened, he'd grown the trim beard.

She paused. Should she say it? It was never far from her mind now, from her mouth. The words, she knew, were useless, if any words could be described as that. Certainly she knew they could not make the thing happen. If they could she would surround him with them, encase him with her words.

"Come home when you can," she said instead, her voice light.

He kissed her. "I will. In a few days, a week at the most. Call me when you get there."

"*D'accord.*" She got into the car.

"*Je t'aime*," he said, putting his gloved hand into the window to touch her shoulder.

Watch out, her mind screamed. *Be safe. Come home with me. Be careful, be careful, be careful.*

She put her own gloved hand over his. "*Je t'aime.*"

And then she was gone, back to Montreal, glancing in the rearview mirror to see him standing on the deserted early morning street, Henri naturally at his side. Both watching her, until she disappeared.

The Chief Inspector continued to stare even after she'd turned the corner. Then he picked up a shovel and slowly cleared the night's fluffy snowfall from the front steps. Resting for a moment, his arms crossed over the handle of the shovel, he marveled at the beauty as the first light hit the new snow. It looked more pale blue than white, and here and there it sparkled like tiny prisms where the flakes had drifted and collected, then caught, remade, and returned the light. Like something alive and giddy.

Life in the old walled city was like that. Both gentle and dynamic, ancient and vibrant.

Picking up a handful of snow, the Chief Inspector mashed it into a ball in his fist. Henri immediately stood, his tail going so hard his entire rear swayed. His eyes burning into the ball.

Gamache tossed it into the air and the dog leapt, his mouth closing over the snowball and chomping down. Landing on all fours Henri was once again surprised that the thing that had been so solid had suddenly disappeared.

Gone, so quickly.

But next time would be different.

Gamache chuckled. He might be right.

Just then Emile stepped out from his doorway, bundled in an immense winter coat against the biting February cold.

"Ready?" The elderly man clamped a toque onto his head, pulling it down so that it covered his ears and forehead, and put on thick mitts, like boxing gloves.

"For what? A siege?"

"For breakfast, *mon vieux*. Come along, before someone gets the last croissant."

He knew how to motivate his former subordinate. Hardly pausing for Gamache to replace the shovel, Emile headed off up the snowy street. Around them the other residents of Quebec City were waking up. Coming out into the tender morning light to shovel, to scrape the snow from their cars, to walk to the boulangerie for their morning baguette and café.

The two men and Henri set out along rue St.-Jean, past the restaurants and tourist shops, to a tiny side street called rue Couillard, and there they found Chez Temporel.

They'd been coming to this café for fifteen years, ever since Superintendent Emile Comeau had retired to old Quebec City and Gamache had come to visit, to spend time with his mentor, and to help with the little chores that piled up. Shoveling, stacking wood for the fireplace, sealing windows against drafts. But this visit was different. Like no other in all the winters Chief Inspector Gamache had been coming to Quebec City.

This time it was Gamache who needed help.

"So." Emile leaned back, cupping his bowl of *café au lait* in slender hands. "How's the research going?"

"I can't yet find any references to Captain Cook actually meeting Bougainville before the Battle of Québec, but it was 250 years ago. Records are scattered and weren't well kept. But I know they're in there," said Gamache. "It's an amazing library, Emile. The volumes go back centuries."

Comeau watched his companion talk about sifting through arcane books in a local library and the tidbits he was unearthing about a battle long ago fought and lost. At least, from his point of view lost. Was there a spark in those beloved eyes at last? Those eyes he'd stared into so often at the scenes of dreadful crimes as they'd hunted murderers. As they'd raced through woods and villages and fields, through clues and evidence and suspicions. *Adown Titanic glooms of chasmed fears,* Emile remembered the quote as he remembered those days. Yes, he thought, that described it. *Chasmed fears.* Both their own, and the murderers'. Across tables across the province he and Gamache had sat. Just like this.

But now it was time to rest from murder. No more killing, no more deaths. Armand had seen too much of that lately. No, better to bury himself in history, in lives long past. An intellectual pursuit, nothing more.

Beside them Henri stirred and Gamache instinctively lowered his hand to stroke the shepherd's head and reassure him. And once again Emile noted the slight tremble. Barely there now. Stronger at times. Sometimes it disappeared completely. It was a tell-tale tremble, and Emile knew the terrible tale it had to tell.

He wished he could take that hand and hold it steady and tell him it would be all right. Because it would, he knew.

With time.

Watching Armand Gamache he noticed again the jagged scar on his left temple and the trim beard he'd grown. So that people would stop staring. So that people would not recognize the most recognizable police officer in Quebec.

But, of course, it didn't matter. It wasn't them Armand Gamache was hiding from.

The waitress at Chez Temporel arrived with more coffee.

"*Merci*, Danielle," the two men said at once and she left, smiling at the two men who looked so different but seemed so similar.

They drank their coffees and ate *pain au chocolat* and *croissants aux amandes* and talked about the Carnaval de Québec, starting that night. Occasionally they'd lapse into silence, watching the men and women hurrying along the icy cold street outside to their jobs. Someone had scratched a three-leaf clover into a slight indent in the center of their wooden table. Emile rubbed it with his finger.

And wondered when Armand would want to talk about what happened.

It was ten thirty and the monthly board meeting of the Literary and Historical Society was about to start. For many years the meetings had been held in the evening, when the library was closed, but then it was noticed that fewer and fewer members were showing up.

So the chairman, Porter Wilson, had changed the time. At least, he thought he'd changed the time. At least, it had been reported in the board minutes that it had been his motion, though he privately seemed to remember arguing against it.

And yet, here they were meeting in the morning, and had been for some years. Still, the other members had adjusted, as had Porter. He had to, since it had apparently been his idea.

The fact the board had adjusted at all was a miracle. The last time they'd been asked to change anything it had been the worn leather on the Lit and His chairs, and that had been sixty-three years ago. Members still remembered fathers and mothers, grandparents, ranged on either side of the upholstered Mason-Dixon Line. Remembered vitriolic comments made behind closed doors, behind backs, but before children. Who didn't forget, sixty-three years later, that devious alteration from old black leather to new black leather.

Pulling out his chair at the head of the table Porter noticed it was looking worn. He sat quickly so that no one, least of all himself, could see it.

Small stacks of paper were neatly arranged in front of his and every other place, marching down the wooden table. Elizabeth MacWhirter's doing. He examined Elizabeth. Plain, tall and slim. At least, she had been that when the world was young. Now she just looked freeze-dried. Like those ancient cadavers pulled from glaciers. Still obviously human, but withered and gray. Her dress was blue and practical and a very good cut and material, he suspected. After all, she was one of those MacWhirters. A venerable and moneyed family. One not given to displays of wealth, or brains. Her brother had sold the shipping empire about a decade too late. But there was still money there. She was a little dull, he thought, but responsible. Not a leader, not a visionary. Not the sort to hold a community in peril together. Like him. And his father before him. And his grandfather.

For the tiny English community within the walls of old Québec City had been in peril for many generations. It was a kind of perpetual peril that sometimes got better and sometimes got worse, but never disappeared completely. Just like the English.

Porter Wilson had never fought a war, being just that much too young, and then too old. Not, anyway, an official war. But he and the other members of his board knew themselves to be in a battle nevertheless. And one, he secretly suspected, they were losing.

At the door Elizabeth MacWhirter greeted the other board members as they arrived and looked over at Porter Wilson already seated at the head of the table, reading over his notes.

He'd accomplished many things in his life, Elizabeth knew. The choir he'd organized, the amateur theater, the wing for the nursing home. All built by force of will and personality. And all less than they might have been had he sought and accepted advice.

The very force of his personality both created and crippled. How much more could he have accomplished had he been kinder? But then, dynamism and kindness often didn't go together, though when they did they were unstoppable.

Porter was stoppable. Indeed, he stopped himself. And now the only board that could stand him was the Lit and His. Elizabeth had known Porter for seventy years, since she'd seen him eating lunch alone, every day, at school and gone to keep him company. Porter decided she was sucking up to one of the great Wilson clan, and treated her with disdain.

Still, she kept him company. Not because she liked him but because she knew even then something it would take Porter Wilson decades to realize. The English of Quebec City were no longer the juggernauts, no longer the steamships, no longer the gracious passenger liners of the society and economy.

They were a life raft. Adrift. And you don't make war on others in the raft.

Elizabeth MacWhirter had figured that out. And when Porter rocked the boat, she righted it.

She looked at Porter Wilson and saw a small, energetic, toupéed man. His hair, where not imported, was dyed a shade of black the chairs would envy. His eyes were brown and darted about nervously.

Mr. Blake arrived first. The oldest board member, he practically lived at the Lit and His. He took off his coat, revealing his uniform of gray flannel suit, laundered white shirt, blue silk tie. He was always perfectly turned out. A gentleman, who managed to make Elizabeth feel young and beautiful. She'd had a crush on him when she'd been an awkward teen and he in his dashing twenties.

He'd been attractive then and sixty years later he was still attractive, though his hair was thin and white and his once fine body had rounded and softened. But his eyes were smart and lively, and his heart was large and strong.

"Elizabeth," Mr. Blake smiled and took her hand, holding it for a moment. Never too long, never too familiar. Just enough, so that she knew she'd been held.

He took his seat. A seat, Elizabeth thought, that should be replaced. But then, honestly, so should Mr. Blake. So should they all.

What would happen when they died out and all that was left of the board of the Literary and Historical Society were worn, empty chairs?

"Right, we need to make this fast. We have a practice in an hour."

Tom Hancock arrived, followed by Ken Haslam. The two were never far apart these days, being unlikely team members in the ridiculous upcoming race.

Tom was Elizabeth's triumph. Her hope. And not simply because he was the minister of St. Andrew's Presbyterian Church next door.

He was young and new to the community, having moved to Quebec City three years earlier. At thirty-three he was about half the age of the next youngest board member. Not yet cynical, not yet burned out. He still believed his church would find new parishioners, the English community would suddenly produce babies with the desire to stay in Quebec City. He believed the Québec government when it promised job equality for Anglophones. And health care in their own language. And education. And nursing homes so that when all hope was lost, they might die with their mother tongue on caregivers' lips.

He'd managed to inspire the board to believe maybe all wasn't lost. And even, maybe, this wasn't really a war. Wasn't some dreadful extension of the Battle of the Plains of Abraham, one which the English lost this time. Elizabeth glanced up at the oddly petite statue of General James Wolfe. The martyred hero of the battle 250 years ago hovered over the library of the Literary and Historical Society, like a wooden accusation. To witness their petty battles and to remind them, in perpetuity, of the great battle he'd fought, for them. Where he'd died, but not before triumphing on that blood-soaked farmers field. Ending the war, and securing Québec for the English. On paper.

And now from his corner of the lovely old library General Wolfe looked down on them. In every way, Elizabeth suspected.

"So, Ken," Tom said, taking his place beside the older man. "You in shape? Ready for the race?"

Elizabeth didn't hear Ken Haslam's response. But then she didn't expect to. Ken's thin lips moved, words were formed, but never actually heard.

They all paused, thinking perhaps this was the day he would produce a word above a whisper. But they were wrong. Still, Tom Hancock continued to talk to Ken, as though they were actually having a conversation.

Elizabeth loved Tom for that as well. For not giving in to the notion that because Ken was quiet he was stupid. Elizabeth knew him to be anything but. In his mid-sixties he was the most successful of all of them, building a business of his own. And now, having achieved that, Ken Haslam had done something else remarkable.

He'd signed up for the treacherous ice canoe race. Signed on to Tom Hancock's team. He would be the oldest member of the team, the oldest member of any team. Perhaps the oldest racer ever.

Watching Ken, quiet and calm, and Tom, young, vital, handsome, Elizabeth wondered if maybe they understood each other very well after all. Perhaps both had things they weren't saying.

Not for the first time Elizabeth wondered about Tom Hancock. Why he'd chosen to minister to them, and why he stayed within the walls of old Québec City. It took a certain personality, Elizabeth knew, to choose to live in what amounted to a fortress.

"Right, let's start," said Porter, sitting up even straighter.

"Winnie isn't here yet," said Elizabeth.

"We can't wait."

"Why not?" Tom asked, his voice relaxed. But still Porter heard a challenge.

"Because it's already past ten thirty and you're the one who wanted to make this quick," Porter said, pleased at having scored a point.

Once again, thought Elizabeth, Porter managed to look at a friend and see a foe.

"Quite right. Still, I'm happy to wait," smiled Tom, unwilling to take to the field.

"Well, I'm not. First order of business?"

They discussed the purchase of new books for a while before Winnie arrived. Small and energetic, she was fierce in her loyalty. To the English community, to the Lit and His, but mostly to her friend.

She marched in, gave Porter a withering look, and sat next to Elizabeth.

"I see you started without me," she said to him. "I told you I'd be late."

"You did, but that doesn't mean we had to wait. We're discussing new books to buy."

"And it didn't occur to you this might be an issue best discussed with the librarian?"

"Well, you're here now."

The rest of the board watched this as though at Wimbledon, though with considerably less interest. It was pretty clear who had the balls, and who would win.

Fifty minutes later they'd almost reached the end of the agenda. There was one oatmeal cookie left, the members staring but too polite to take it. They'd discussed the heating bills, the membership drive, the ratty old volumes left to them in wills, instead of money. The books were generally sermons, or lurid Victorian poetry, or the dreary daily diary of a trip up the Amazon or into Africa to shoot and stuff some poor wild creature.

They discussed having another sale of books, but after the last debacle that was a short discussion.

Elizabeth took notes and had to force herself not to lip-synch to each board member's comments. It was a liturgy. Familiar, soothing in a strange way. The same words repeated over and over every meeting. For ever and ever. Amen.

A sound suddenly interrupted that comforting liturgy, a sound so unique and startling Porter almost jumped out of his chair.

"What was that?" whispered Ken Haslam. For him it was almost a shout.

"It's the doorbell, I think," said Winnie.

"The doorbell?" asked Porter. "I didn't know we had one."

"Put in in 1897 after the Lieutenant Governor visited and couldn't get in," said Mr. Blake, as though he'd been there. "Never heard it myself."

But he heard it again. A long, shrill bell. Elizabeth had locked the front door to the Literary and Historical Society as soon as everyone had arrived. A precaution against being interrupted. Though since hardly anyone ever visited it was more habit than necessity. She'd also hung a sign on the thick wooden door. *Board Meeting in Progress. Library will reopen at noon. Thank you.* Merci.

The bell sounded again. Someone was leaning on it, finger jammed into the button.

Still they stared at each other.

"I'll go," said Elizabeth.

Porter looked down at his papers, the better part of valor.

"No," Winnie stood. "I'll go. You all stay here."

They watched Winnie disappear down the corridor and heard her feet on the wooden stairs. There was silence. Then a minute later her feet on the stairs again.

They listened to the footsteps clicking and clacking closer. She arrived but stopped at the door, her face pale and serious.

"There's someone there. Someone who wants to speak to the board."

"Well," demanded Porter, remembering he was their leader, now that the elderly woman had gone to the door. "Who is it?"

"Augustin Renaud," she said and saw the looks on their faces. Had she said "Dracula" they could not have been more startled. Though, for the English, startled meant raised eyebrows.

Every eyebrow in the room was raised, and if General Wolfe could have managed it, he would have.

"I left him outside," she said into the silence.

As if to underscore that the doorbell shrieked again.

"What should we do?" Winnie asked, but instead of turning to Porter she looked at Elizabeth. They all did.

"We need to take a vote," Elizabeth said at last. "Should we see him?"

"He's not on the agenda," Mr. Blake pointed out.

"That's right," said Porter, trying to wrestle back control. But even he looked at Elizabeth.

"Who's in favor of letting Augustin Renaud speak to the board?" Elizabeth asked.

Not a hand was raised.

Elizabeth lowered her pen, not taking note of the vote. Giving one curt nod she stood. "I'll tell him."

"I'll go with you," said Winnie.

"No, dear, you stay here. I'll be right back. I mean, really?" She paused at the door, taking in the board and General Wolfe above. "How bad could it be?"

But they all knew the answer to that. When Augustin Renaud came calling it was never good.

"An eternally lovely and deeply affecting series...
that transcends the genre and works, as worthy
literature should, on multiple levels.... A treat
for the mind and a lesson for the soul."

—RICHMOND TIMES-DISPATCH

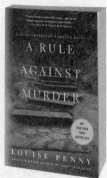

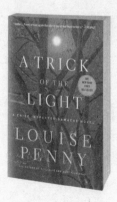

Don't Miss *The Beautiful Mystery* Available September 2012

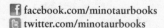